Reading Tests and Teachers:
a practical guide

Robert Schreiner, Editor
University of Minnesota

D1614317

INTERNATIONAL READING ASSOCIATION
800 Barksdale Road • Newark, Delaware 19711

Copyright 1979 by the
International Reading Association, Inc.

Library of Congress Cataloging in Publication Data
Main entry under title:

Reading tests and teachers.

Bibliography: p.
1. Reading—Ability testing. I. Schreiner,
Robert, 1937-   II. International Reading Association.
Evaluation of Tests Committee.
LB1050.46.R4   428'.4'076   79-17271
ISBN 0-87207-726-8
Second printing, October 1980

Contents

Foreword

Gathering information regarding students' reading achievements is an integral part of instruction, and one means of gathering such information is through the use of tests. Testing should, therefore, be a normal and well understood activity; but that is often not the case. Because of the technical vocabulary used in testing, the aura of sophistication of tests, and an increasing reliance on tests (particularly in state minimum competency programs), testing has become a seemingly complex activity.

The International Reading Association's Committee on the Evaluation of Tests has attempted to reduce the complexity and confusion surrounding tests and their uses. In previous years, the committee has published user oriented reviews of tests. Edited by Robert Schreiner, this monograph on *Reading Tests and Teachers: A Practical Guide* expands on previous committee publications and should take some of the mystery out of testing.

The Committee has developed this publication as a guide which first puts testing in proper perspective as one aspect of evaluation. It then leads the test user through a practical discussion of how to select tests and how to develop valid and reliable tests. Once a test has been selected and administered, the results should be used to plan instruction; and the guide includes a very functional approach to using test scores.

Competency testing, criterion referenced measurement, accountability, and a host of other test and test related concepts face reading teachers every day. This practical guide will help test users through the morass of jargon and help them to make tests a tool for planning instruction rather than a device that dictates the curriculum.

Roger Farr, *President*
International Reading Association
1979-1980

v

Acknowledgements

This guide to the construction and use of tests and the interpretation of test results is a project of the International Reading Association Evaluation of Tests Committee.

The committee is deeply indebted to many individuals for this final product. Initially an outline of the contents was prepared following an extensive survey of assessment and evaluation needs of teachers, school administrators, reading consultants, and college and university professors. Authors were contacted and writing tasks agreed upon. Extensive authorial review and rewriting occurred before the first draft was critically reviewed. Rewriting followed the initial review and the final manuscript was edited.

I am particularly indebted to George Canney, Michael Kamil, Kenneth Kavale, and Fred Pyrczak for their perseverance and dedication to this project. Leo M. Schell (Kansas State University), provided extensive editing and review expertise. Clarence Brock (St. Clair County, Michigan, Public Schools), Ronald Carver (University of Missouri at Kansas City), and Roger Farr (Indiana University), aided us with extensive constructive criticism. Finally Walter MacGinitie (Teachers College, Columbia University), Ralph C. Staiger (Executive Director, International Reading Association), and the members of the Evaluation of Tests Committee provided constant professional support for this effort.

Without all these dedicated professionals, this project would not have materialized.

Robert Schreiner, *Editor*

EVALUATION OF TESTS COMMITTEE
1977-1978

Robert Schreiner, *Chairing*
University of Minnesota at Minneapolis

Jean E. Robertson, *Board Liaison*
University of Alberta

George Canney
University of Idaho

Ronald P. Carver
University of Missouri at Kansas City

Warwick Elley
University of South Pacific

Roger Farr
Indiana University

Sherry Gable
University of Northern Iowa

Vincent Greaney
St. Patrick's College
Dublin, Ireland

Martha Rupp Haggard
Northern Illinois University at DeKalb

Karen M. Hanson
Eden Prairie, Minnesota

Michael L. Kamil
Purdue University

Kenneth Kavale
University of California at Riverside

Fred Pyrczak
California State University at Los Angeles

Leo M. Schell
Kansas State University

TABLE OF FIGURES

Chapter One
Testing and Reading: A Plan for Evaluation

Robert Schreiner
University of Minnesota at Minneapolis

The primary purpose of this publication is to assist classroom teachers, reading consultants, and/or school administrators in making decisions about measuring the reading achievement of students.

The use of tests in any total reading program is intimately linked with decision making. School personnel are constantly faced with a variety of decisions about reading instruction: What are the appropriate goals of instruction? What kinds of instructional needs do my students have? What skills should be taught? How might the skills be translated into instructional objectives? Which materials will best aid instruction? What grouping plan is best? Who is making progress? Is more help needed? The questions may be never ending, but the answers must be arrived at rationally.

A variety of published tests is available to assist in making instructional decisions. In addition, many informal testing techniques may be used.

The following flow chart suggests a set of systematic procedures to use in making decisions regarding student performance in reading.

Figure 1.1
Steps for Making Diagnostic and Instructional Decisions
in Assessing Reading Achievement

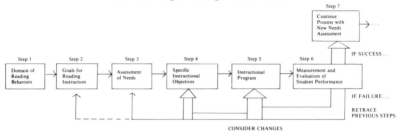

Step 1   *Domain of Reading Behaviors* ➤

Examining the Domain of Reading Behaviors

The domain of reading behavior includes all the perceptual, linguistic and cognitive skills we bring to printed words to pronounce them and understand them, including our recognition and understanding of letters, letter sound relationships, decoding of whole words, phrases and sentences, the grammatical aspects of our language, and how we obtain meaning from print. All the aspects of written language, of course, are not related to the reading act. We are only interested in those behaviors people use and need in the reading act. Behavioral theorists have identified these tasks for us. We only need to think a moment to recall those aspects of visual and auditory perception, cognition, and learning from psychology textbooks that are relevant for reading. These components also include affective behaviors, such as motivation and interest that relate to the act of reading. The domain of reading behaviors can also be referred to as the constructs of the reading act.

➤ *Step 2*   *Goals for Reading Instruction* ➤

Determining the Goals for Reading Instruction

The goals for teaching students how to read reflect how we translate the domain of reading behaviors into instructional

2   Schreiner

practices. This translation normally takes place in school. We teach students *how* to read. That is, reading instruction is both systematic and developmental. For example, at the appropriate time, we provide phonics or decoding lessons based on what we know about symbol/sound correspondence. We instruct students to read whole words, phrases, and sentences with understanding. Comprehension and vocabulary building activities are based on how we think young people learn and use syntactic and semantic information. Instructional strategies are deliberate and planned. These plans are not haphazard and they are based on our knowledge of the constructs involved in reading.

Both the domain of reading behaviors and the development of goals for reading instruction are crucial aspects of assessment and evaluation. If there are serious gaps in our knowledge of cognitive processes or in our translation of that information to sound reading practices, the outcome of assessment may be questioned. Thus, it is important to learn as much as possible about language and thinking and how it relates to the teaching of reading. In other words, our practices must be based on sound theory.

→ *Step 3   Assessment of Needs* →

Assessment begins when we measure or test student performance relative to the established goals for reading instruction. Assessment of needs seeks answers to two complementary questions: How well do students presently read? and What do they need to know to improve their reading performance?

In seeking answers to the above questions, we may wish to use existing background information on students, including information found in the permanent school records. While students should not be classified solely by previous test scores, such information can be used as an indication of instructional needs. The major points of information for us include 1) the reading achievement level estimated from the achievement test records for the previous year and 2) major strengths and weaknesses in reading ability as recorded by previous teachers. For these reasons, testing is a crucial part of a needs assessment. Through tests, we obtain information useful for planning instructional strategies. We gain information regarding a student's progress, placement, and readiness or we may diagnose reading strengths and/or weaknesses.

Through a variety of tests, we can accumulate information about the abilities of a class. We are now in a position to make statements about student performance and needs. We should focus upon answers to the following questions:

1. What is the student's current level of performance in word recognition, vocabulary meaning, and reading comprehension?
2. What additional instruction would aid students to perform at a higher level?
3. What combination of instructional program, materials, and techniques is most suitable for student needs?

When we compile this information for an individual or group of students, assessment of needs is well underway.

➤ *Step 4*   *Specific Instructional Objectives* ➤

Once we know "where they are" we deal with the question of "where are they going?" We can develop instructional goals based on the results of a needs assessment. Barrett (*1*) suggested three categories of interrelated and interdependent goals for reading programs:

Categories of Goals of the Reading Program

Perceptual Goals	Cognitive Goals	Affective Goals
are concerned with the flexibility rate and accuracy of word perception	are concerned with the types and levels of thought generated during reading	are concerned with the feelings children have toward reading

Depending upon the existing needs, each goal will be emphasized to different degrees.

The goals for the reading program should lead to specific instructional objectives. Objectives give direction to the educational process by aiding you in 1) making students aware of the goals to be achieved; 2) planning learning activities designed to achieve various goals; 3) organizing time, space, and materials for carrying out learning activities; and 4) providing a criterion for evaluating performance.

Consider the following three factors regarding goals and objectives when selecting a reading test.

First, the final level to be attained depends on the initial status of the student or students. The goals and objectives may be expressed in terms of growth (a year's growth in reading for a year's instruction) or they may be expressed in terms of expectancy (expected reading performance for various ability levels).

Second, how directly or indirectly do the goals and objectives specify reading skills? A direct goal refers to specific reading skills (locating supporting details, identifying "long" vowel sounds, or differentiating singular from plural forms of words). An indirect goal refers to behavior which is related to reading skills but does not directly involve the skill (enjoyment of reading or reading for pleasure).

Third, how are the goals and objectives differentiated in terms of the content of the curriculum? The following categories of major goals and objectives of reading instruction appear in most college methods of teaching reading textbooks:

Decoding skills (word attack or phonics); vocabulary (pronunciation and meaning); structural analysis skills (syllabication, root words, inflected endings, prefixes, and suffixes); oral reading skills (pronunciation, phrasing, and appropriate voice inflection); silent reading; reading rate; reading comprehension (literal and inferential); reading study skills; critical and evaluative reading abilities; affective components such as motivation and student interest; reading in the content areas; and ability to recognize literary devices such as mood, plot, characterization, and setting.

Decisions regarding the point and degree of emphasis of these objectives need to be made in relation to the reading materials used and the age and abilities of the readers.

This component of instructional decision making refers to the actual way in which teaching is done. It includes the instructional materials, the delivery of the content to the student, and also the setting in which the instruction is provided.

We need to determine which method of instruction is most appropriate. We may need to use various methods until we find the most efficient or useful procedure. For example, if we find that a student has serious deficits in decoding skills, we may wish to begin instruction with a single-letter phonics approach. Thus, our instruction would be directed toward learning symbol/sound relationships and blending these sounds into words. This method would also suggest that instruction take place in a one-to-one or small group setting. Similar plans would be appropriate if we prescribed a whole word or sight word method for teaching word attack skills. In this case, students would learn whole words and then later analyze new words, using previous knowledge or skills. Instruction in whole word recognition skills is frequently provided in a group setting. We may further consider a combination method that utilizes components of both a structured phonics and whole word method for teaching word attack skills.

The instructional program, as you can see, is crucial in the overall sequence for making instructional decisions. We need to learn as much as possible about the various methods and techniques for all the goals of reading listed earlier as well as how these can best be taught.

➤ *Step 6*   *Measurement and Evaluation of Performance* ➤

With the goals and objectives of the reading program established, we then focus upon actual instruction. After a period of time, the final step in the assessment sequence must be considered: Evaluation of student performance with respect to progress towards achieving the stated goals and objectives of the reading program. The essential concern is to identify discrepancies, if any, between "what is" and "what should be." If the desired goals have been attained, we can then formulate new objectives for the students. If the desired goals have *not* been attained, it is suggested that we reexamine the instructional component. We may wish to continue with the same instructional program or we may wish to make changes in it.

Sometimes we may want to reexamine the specific instructional objectives with the intent of making revisions. This should happen less often than the revision of instructional programs. Still less frequent should be the reexamination of needs assessment. A faulty needs assessment, in some instances, can be the cause of irrelevant instruction and consequent failure of students to learn to read.

In summary, the steps for making diagnostic and instructional decisions in assessing reading achievement (Figure 1.1) should be followed systematically to complete the evaluation process. The evaluation process is completed with Step 6 (Measurement and Evaluation of Student Performance). If success is achieved, new instructional objectives are presented and the cycle continues. If failure is encountered, we must retrace the steps to determine what caused the failure. As the flow chart suggests (Figure 1.1) we might return to the steps and ask the following questions:

1. Did we use appropriate instruments and/or evaluative techniques to assess student performance? (Step 6)

2. Was the instructional program sensitive enough to affect student progress? (Step 5)

3. Were the instructional objectives appropriate? (Step 4)

4. How satisfactory (reliable and/or valid) were the instruments upon which the original needs assessment were based? (Step 3)

5. Were the goals for reading instruction well delineated? (Step 2)

As can be seen, any breakdown in this chain of events can cause difficulties in the evaluation process.

The remainder of this publication deals more specifically with the steps for making instructional decisions related to measuring reading progress. In Chapter Two, suggestions are made to aid you in selecting appropriate commercially prepared tests that measure reading progress. Discussion is also directed toward strengths and weaknesses of various kinds of reading tests. Chapter Three provides specific examples of the construction of tests that measure reading progress. Discussion is directed toward the usefulness of both norm and criterion referenced test items. The content of Chapter Four is directed toward classroom uses of the results of measurement and evaluation. Chapter Five presents definitions of the various aspects of the discipline of measurement and evaluation. It also includes a glossary of technical terms used in measurement and evaluation.

Reference

1. Barrett, T.C. "Goals of the Reading Program: The Basis for Evaluation," in T.C. Barrett (Ed.), *The Evaluation of Children's Reading Achievement*. Newark, Delaware: International Reading Association, 1967.

Schreiner

Chapter Two
Selecting and Evaluating Reading Tests

Kenneth Kavale
University of California at Riverside

The major purpose of this chapter is to aid the teacher in answering the question: "Which reading test should I use?" A test should not be used because it is the only one available or because it is the one which has always been used. Old tests sometimes remain in the school long after the curriculum has changed. Such tests may become outdated and no longer serve the original purpose. However, some of the older tests may be among the best available. Consequently, test selection requires time and careful evaluation.

The purposes of testing in reading are quite diverse and no single test can accomplish all these purposes. Different types of tests are implied by each purpose. Therefore, when deciding which test(s) to select, the first consideration should be a detailed examination of the purposes for which the testing is to be done. *If the uses for the test results are not known in advance, the best test to use is none at all.*

Merwin *(15)* has proposed a useful guide for decisions related to test selection. It bases test selection upon a scheme which inquires about the testing of *what, who*, by *whom*, to *what.* Below are some examples of how the guide may be used with respect to reading assessment.

1. Assessing reading achievement of a third grade student by a teacher to aid in selecting reading materials.
2. Assessing reading readiness of a group of kindergarten students by a teacher to aid in forming instructional groups.
3. Assessing word recognition skills of a second grade student by a teacher to decide whether a supplementary phonics program is necessary.
4. Assessing gain in reading achievement of a group of fifth grade students by a curriculum supervisor to determine the effectiveness of a new set of instructional materials.
5. Assessing levels of inferential reading comprehension of a tenth grade student by a teacher to determine understanding.
6. Assessing reading performance of a group of eighth grade students by a reading support teacher to decide who needs supplemental instruction.

These examples reveal a portion of the diverse purposes of testing in reading. Therefore, it is essential for the teacher to realize that the reason for measurement will be the primary factor in determining the methods of measurement, that is, which test to choose.

What tests are available? Once the teacher has identified the aims of testing, the next task for the teacher is to locate suitable tests. Perhaps the best single source is *The Eighth Mental Measurements Yearbook* (5) or its companion, *Reading: Tests and Reviews* (4), with reviews on nearly all published reading tests. Many reading instruction textbooks also list numerous tests and publishers. Basically, the teacher seeks answers to the following questions:
1. Which tests might serve my present purpose?
2. What are the new tests in the field?
3. What is test X like?
4. What do specialists in the field of measurement have to say about test Y?

From among the many tests currently available, several will typically appear to be appropriate for the purpose(s) identified. Choosing from among the identified available tests is the next problem for the teacher.

The decision as to which test is best should be based upon the technical properties of the tests. This is not to suggest that teachers need to be measurement experts but rather that issues such as the content measured by the test, the consistency of the obtained scores, the validity of subtest and total test scores, the adequacy of the normative group (when appropriate), the adequacy of the test manual, and the ease of administration and scoring are important considerations if the best test is to be chosen. (See Chapter Five for more detailed discussion of measurement terms.) A teacher knowledgeable about the strengths and weaknesses of particular tests is far more likely to select the best instrument available for the specified purpose.

Factors in Test Selection

Two major facets of measurement are important for the teacher to consider in test selection: validity and reliability.

Validity

The first and foremost question to be asked with respect to a test instrument is: "Does the test measure what it is intended to measure?" The primary concern for the teacher is whether testing has an effect upon instructional practice and materials. Can the obtained data be used to make significant changes in instruction or by making materials more focused and effective?

Two kinds of validity are important for teachers to consider.

1. *Content validity* which assesses whether the test measures the content being taught. Consider a test prepared to measure reading achievement. How can we tell how well the test does, in fact, measure reading achievement? Three factors are important to consider:

   a. First, there must be some agreement as to the skills, knowledge, and understandings which comprise your definition of reading achievement.
   b. Second, it is necessary to examine the test to determine what skills, knowledge, and understandings are required for it.

c. Finally, it is necessary to determine the match which exists between test content and course content (instructional objectives). To the extent that the course content is represented in the test, the test is considered to possess adequate content validity. An excellent way for teachers to determine content validity is to take the test. Then they may be in a better position to pass judgment about just what the test is really testing and to determine whether what is being tested matches what is being taught in the classroom.

2. *Face validity*, sometimes considered, refers to the fact that the test looks as if it should be valid. It is important for motivational purposes, for students are more likely to cooperate if they sense that the nature of the items logically correspond to the overall purpose of the test. For example, basal reader tests can be considered to have high face validity. However, the presence of face validity does not guarantee that the test is valid in any other sense.

It would be unwise to assume that the name or title of a test reveals what it measures. An examination of various tests of reading comprehension will reveal that certain tests require the student to determine the main idea of a paragraph; others demand only the retrieval of literal meaning; and a few ask the reader to discern the intent and mood of the author. Tests of reading rate vary in time from 60 seconds to much longer periods of reading. Some give credit for speed, even if many questions are not answered correctly; others give no credit for rate unless comprehension occurs. Some vocabulary tests are constructed of items listing a word with several possible synonyms from which to select the correct answer; in others, the examiner reads a sentence and the student is required to select one of several words to complete the sentence. In still a third type, an underlined word in a sentence is presented and the student responds by marking one of several possible synonyms. It is quite possible that some students will perform better on one type of test for comprehension, rate, or vocabulary than on others; yet, all may have identical titles.

Reliability

While validity ranks as an important attribute of any test, reliability is another important facet to be considered in test selection. Reliability refers to how consistently a test measures whatever it does measure.

Test results should not reflect chance scores with a child's obtaining a high score by luck, guessing, or other extraneous factors. Any factor that tends to exert a varying influence on test scores has an adverse effect on the reliability of a test. Such factors as examinee differences, influence of the scorer, testing situation, time influences, and test content can affect scores differentially, which increases the amount of error and, consequently, lowers the reliability. In examining a test, it is usually the case that reliability will be greater for scores which are:

1. from a longer test than from a shorter test,
2. from a test composed of more homogeneous items than from a more heterogeneous test,
3. from a test whose items are of middle difficulty than from a test composed mainly of quite difficult or quite easy items,
4. obtained from a group having a wide range of ability than from a group more homogeneous in ability.

While validity and reliability are somewhat related, they are by no means identical. Validity refers to the degree to which a test actually serves the purpose for which it is intended; reliability refers to the test's capacity to yield consistent information regardless of whether it serves the purpose or purposes for which it is intended and, in doing so, provide consistent information.

Usability

In addition to the psychometric qualities of validity and reliability, another dimension to be considered in test selection is usability. This refers to a variety of practical considerations such as ease of administration, convenience of scoring, economy, and adequacy of the test manual.

Consider two reading tests, A and B. Test A possesses very high reliability and validity. Test B possesses a lower but adequate level of validity and reliability. There seems to be little question that Test A is the preferred instrument. However, what if Test A required 3 hours to administer, was given individually, took an hour to score, cost 50 cents per student, and could only be administered by a person who has received extensive training? On the other hand, Test B could be administered to a group in one hour, has reusable test booklets, has answer sheets which cost 10 cents each, and one test could be scored in 5 minutes. The decision is now reversed and there is little question that Test B would be preferred.

Thus, usability determines whether a test is practical for widespread use. The question arises as to how the teacher can determine the usability of a test. There is no better way to learn about problems in administration, scoring, appropriateness of content, and adequacy of the test manual than to take the test and then give it to a few children. It should be realized, however, that there is no point in testing unless there is some confidence in the results. While practical factors should be considered, they are important only if the test has satisfactory reliability and validity.

Norm Information

A final important consideration in test selection, when test results are to be used for comparisons of individuals (norm referenced measurement), is the adequacy of the normative information supplied. (A discussion of an alternative to norm referenced measurement, criterion referenced measurement, appears in a later section.)

Norms should be evaluated before they are used. The most important criterion for the teacher to consider before using the norms supplied is: Can the students in my class be legitimately considered equivalent to the population represented by the standardized group? If the answer is yes, then the test would appear to be appropriate, other things being equal. But if the answer is no, then it appears questionable whether the test is appropriate for that particular group of students since the comparisons made may be inappropriate and/or unfair.

Kavale

Test Selection: The Final Process

Various factors have been presented which should be considered in test selection. The importance of the task cannot be overemphasized because tests must be selected according to specific criteria to prevent relatively superficial factors from exerting too great an influence upon the selection process. A test should never be chosen on the basis of its reputation nor should its contents be judged from the title alone. An examination of the test itself is the only way for the teacher to determine what and how the test is measuring and, consequently, decide whether it will yield the required information.

To aid in compiling the required information, the following test selection checklist may be used as a guide. The teacher may follow the outline for each test to be considered and when completed, the checklists can be used for comparisons among the tests. The teacher is then in a position to choose the best instrument for the desired purposes.

Test Selection Checklist

    I. What is your purpose for evaluating this test?
       A. Why do I need a test?
       B. What information do I require?
    II. Test Overview
       A. Test information
          1. Name of test—what does name imply about purpose?
          2. Author.
          3. Publisher.
          4. Date of publication and last revision.
       B. Target population
          1. Age level—appropriate for your situation?
          2. Grade level—appropriate for your situation?
          3. Individual or group administration.
          4. Number of available forms—is another form available for future use?
       C. What construct or quality is this test designed to measure?

II. Practical features
  A. Time considerations
    1. Time required to administer total test.
    2. Could the time requirement be handled in your situation?
    3. Time required to score—how involved and time consuming is the scoring procedure?
    4. Who could score the test in your situation? Does scoring involve judgment or simply tallying right and wrong responses?
    5. Is machine scoring available?
  B. Financial considerations
    1. Cost of test booklet.
    2. Cost of answer sheets
    3. Cost of test manuals.
    4. Cost of replacement materials.
    5. Cost of scoring services.
  C. General considerations
    1. Are the directions for administering clear and is the language appropriate for the students in your class?
    2. Are the directions for scoring clear?
    3. Are answer sheets appropriate for age and ability level of students?
    4. What training is required to administer the test?
  D. Format design
    1. Are illustrations current?
    2. Is print size adequate?
IV. Validity
  A. What evidence of validity is given?
  B. Does reported validity appear adequate in relation to intended purposes?
  C. Subtest validity
    1. Does the name adequately describe the subject?
    2. Does the subtest seem logically related to the test as a whole?
V. Reliability
  A. What evidence for reliability is given?
  B. Do the reported reliabilities appear adequate?

C. Subtest reliability
  1. Are reported coefficients adequate?
  2. Are subtests sufficiently long?
VI. Norms (when appropriate)
  A. Are the norms provided adequate and appropriate?
  B. Does the normative sample seem truly representative?
    1. Up-to-date?
    2. Age—does the sample cover age range in your class?
    3. Sex—were appropriate numbers of boys and girls included?
    4. Socioeconomic level—does sample cover SES found in your class?
    5. Range of ability—does the sample include ability levels found in your class?
  C. Are the norms relevant for your class and purposes?
VII. Bias
  A. Is there evidence in the test content of sex stereotyping?
  B. Is there evidence in the test content of racial or ethnic bias?
VIII. General evaluation
  A. What is your general evaluation of the test?
  B. For what purpose and group would you recommend this test?

What Types of Tests are Available?

The final consideration with respect to test selection concerns information about the types of tests available for the teacher. (See Chapter Five for a more detailed discussion of types of tests.) Most reading tests can be classified under four headings: reading achievement and/or survey tests, informal tests, diagnostic tests, and readiness tests. These types differ with respect to what they attempt to measure.

Standardized Norm Referenced Reading Achievement and/or Survey Tests

Reading achievement or reading survey tests are defined as tests which provide an approximate level at which a child is functioning in relation to a specified group. Such tests are usually standardized in terms of administration procedures and normative information. These tests usually measure word recognition, vocabulary, comprehension, and, in some cases, rate of reading. Some may measure more competencies but all usually attempt a general achievement score which reflects overall reading performance.

The diversity of test titles among available reading achievement tests raises two questions which may influence test selection. First, although test titles may differ, do the tests agree on the tasks they require students to perform? Second, do tests which purport to measure similar abilities measure them in the same way?

An examination of standardized achievement and survey tests of reading at the primary level reveals a fair degree of uniformity in the reading dimensions measured; usually word recognition and comprehension are most often measured. However, differences emerge in the labels used to identify the dimensions and the manner in which they are measured.

Tests which measure word recognition, at the primary level, may also be called vocabulary, word knowledge, or word meaning on some tests. In addition, there are a number of different ways word recognition can be measured. For some tests, the task is selecting the word associated with a picture from among four choices. Another type of task requires the reading of brief incomplete sentences prior to selecting a word which completes that sentence. Some other tests require students to select from several printed choices the word which has been pronounced by the teacher. This task is quite different from the matching or selection tasks of the first two examples since both auditory and visual discrimination are required for successful completion. Yet, all three tasks may carry similar labels.

The content of reading comprehension tests, at the primary level, also reflects different types of items. Some tests require students to examine several pictures and mark them in accordance with directions given in a sentence. Another variation is to present a single picture and require the selection of an appropriate sentence from among several which accompany the picture. A third type requires the child to read a short paragraph and demonstrate understanding by recognizing what was read in translated form. Again, each of these tests will probably have a similar title but all use different techniques to assess comprehension. A question arises as to whether the tests are really measuring the same facets of comprehension.

A similar situation exists with respect to standardized achievement and survey tests used in the intermediate grades. While word knowledge and comprehension are again the basic components, there is disagreement concerning the labeling of the subtests; and the measurement tasks are quite different from test to test, even though apparently the same ability is being measured.

Some differences do exist between primary and intermediate grade standardized reading achievement and survey tests. First, intermediate grade tests rarely use pictures; thus, students cannot rely upon picture clues. Second, subtests attempt to measure more specific areas of comprehension (finding main idea, determining cause and effect, predicting outcomes). Third, there is an increased emphasis on requiring inferences which go beyond the literal meanings stated.

Values and uses of standardized reading tests. Basically, these tests can provide data to help teachers answer the following five questions.

1. What is the general reading performance of a student or a group? A student or a group can be compared to the norm sample (using standard scores) or students in a group can be rank ordered, high to low.

2. What are the general areas of strengths and weaknesses for a student or a group? Since most of these tests give at least two subtest scores as well as a total score, subtest scores can occasionally indicate real differences in achievement between major skill areas if certain cautions discussed in Chapter Five ("percentile bands" and "standard error of measurement") are followed. Instruction can then be adjusted to reflect these discrepancies.

3. Which students in the group have the same general

needs? Standard scores can help teachers form groups within a class or help make placements to classes.

4. Is appropriate instructional material available? Students achieving above and below average probably need special instructional material or need the use of the materials adapted to their performance levels. Material may need to be bought, located, created, or adapted.

5. Has a student or a group made measurable progress in general reading performance? Comparing test results on two different occasions can help determine how much progress has been made during instruction. Nearly all good standardized tests provide at least two different forms for such use. [There are some problems in such a procedure. Interested readers should consult a measurement text such as *Measurement and Evaluation in Psychology and Education (23)*.]

Limitation of standardized reading tests. The standardized norm referenced reading achievement and/or survey tests are integral parts of most reading programs. They possess a number of positive values and uses previously described for the reading program. However, it should be realized that these tests have certain limitations as well.

1. The very fact that a test is "standardized" in terms of administration and scoring may make it inappropriate for use with certain individuals or groups. The test may be too difficult or too easy; items may be meaningless or placed at inappropriate levels; directions may be difficult to understand.

2. The test maker's quest for brevity may result in unrealistic time limits and a choice between depth and breadth in sampling. The scores of children who work very slowly but accurately may be suspect; the sampling of behavior may be superficial or constricted.

3. Group administration may work to the disadvantage of certain individuals. The group situation combined with the standardizing conditions may invalidate the test results in some instances.

4. The format of the test may restrict the type of items used. A machine scorable format, for example, virtually

demands some form of multiple-choice items. Certain abilities may not be adequately sampled with multiple-choice items.

5. The quality of the information obtained about an individual student may be less specific than that obtained for groups of students. Therefore, caution should be exercised in making use of the scores when planning for individuals.

Criterion Referenced Testing

There has been much debate on the degree to which norm referenced tests can help teachers make instructional decisions. It has been suggested that norm referenced tests result in little information about what a student can do. For example, what does a raw score of 121 points, a grade score of 4.2, or a percentile of 63 mean with regard to the actual reading tasks a student can do? Scores like these usually are useful for decisions of a comparative nature rather than revealing specifically what a student can and cannot do.

What are criterion referenced tests? If present standardized reading tests do not meet instructional needs, what approaches exist for developing assessment procedures to meet these needs? Criterion referenced measurement has been suggested as a useful alternative. A student's score is interpreted by comparing it to some absolute standard, usually some specified behavioral criterion of performance; the focus is on what the student can do. For example, a criterion referenced phonic analysis test may state that a score above 80 percent is necessary for adequate learning to be assumed. What other students score is not important. The question is whether the student has demonstrated a required level of proficiency in a skill and, thus, has reached a specified goal of instruction.

Criterion referenced tests are tied to the concept of mastery: the purpose of such a test is to measure achievement of a specific behavior in an either/or situation. For example, has June mastered the essential readiness skills to move on to formal instruction? Has Lila mastered the skills necessary for critical reading? Can Phillip read orally with 80 percent word recognition accuracy? In each situation, the criterion is quite definite and the individual student is assessed to determine whether the task can be completed successfully. In other words, the prespecified objectives and levels of achievement either have or have not been attained.

Criterion referenced tests often resemble commercial diagnostic tests and their results are often used for nearly identical purposes. Most diagnostic reading tests are usually administered by a special reading teacher only after other reading tests have been given or after teacher observation raises the possibility of some rather severe reading problems, while many criterion referenced tests are used routinely by classroom teachers as an ongoing part of the total instructional program.

Limitations of criterion referenced tests. Several inter-related assumptions appear to be necessary in the criterion referenced approach. Although there is some debate about these assumptions, they include:

1. Mastery (a student either has or has not achieved the objective(s) satisfactorily) is a reasonable criterion.

2. Each item in a test has inherent worth by design.

3. A hierarchy or sequence of skills and knowledge exists in any skill or content area.

4. There is common consensus regarding the skills selected for testing.

Some limitations of criterion referenced measurement include:

1. Objectives involving hard-to-measure qualities, such as appreciation, attitudes, or inferential reading comprehension, may be included on the test and the resulting scores may be suspect.

2. Objectives involving the retention and transfer of what is learned may become secondary to the one-time demonstration of mastery of stated objectives.

3. Specifying the domain of tasks (determining critical instructional objectives) is of extreme importance. Good tests will do nothing to overcome the problem of poorly developed objectives.

4. Determining proficiency standards can be troublesome.

Kavale

Perfect or near-perfect performance should be required if a) the criterion objective calls for mastery, b) the skill is important for future learning, and c) items are objective type and guessing is likely.

5. Test items frequently represent skills in too isolated a context rather than in an applied and/or functional situation.

Which type of measurement is best? Teachers need not choose between norm referenced and criterion referenced measures. The two types of measures ought to complement each other, with each type chosen according to the purpose for testing. If instruction is individualized so that time is a variable and a student keeps at a task until mastery results, then criterion referenced testing or teacher made tests are appropriate. On the other hand, if instruction is structured so time is constant, then students will be expected to achieve at different levels, and norm referenced measures should be used to discern differential achievement.

The teacher and criterion referenced tests. Reflection on criterion referenced measurement may make teachers wonder whether the idea is new. The answer is "Not really." Teachers have always had instructional objectives and have assessed students to determine whether those objectives have been achieved. The increased emphasis on criterion referenced measurement is in the availability of commercial tests for formal assessment in much the same way that norm referenced tests are now used. Also, many people are encouraging teachers to write criterion referenced tests for use in their own classrooms. This aspect is discussed in Chapter Three.

The teacher of reading should be most concerned with the concept of criterion referenced testing as it is used in the variety of informal tests which are used as part of the reading program. It is in assessing daily or weekly progress that the notion of criterion referenced measurement has the most utility. Here the teacher is concerned with how well a student is doing in terms of the stated instructional objectives. In essence, this is criterion referenced measurement.

Informal Reading Measures

In planning and assessing a reading program, teachers will often find it necessary to seek information that is not available from existing tests or to supplement information from them. When this is the case, it is often necessary to devise informal measuring instruments. Informal measurement can be the heart of diagnostic teaching since it can be done regularly and frequently in the classroom setting and can be used to quickly and effectively emulate a number of classroom reading situations.

What are various types of informal reading measures? Following are examples of some of the most useful informal techniques for assessing reading ability, particularly regarding strengths and weaknesses in specific skill areas.

Teacher observation. This is the most naturalistic informal technique. It is often overlooked but is a viable means by which teachers can diagnose student reading skills in the classroom. An alert, skillful teacher has countless opportunities during the day to gather much information about student progress and needs by observation and, thus, gain real insights into the problems a child may be encountering when faced with a particular reading task.

Observation can be most useful for evaluation of word recognition, comprehension, oral reading fluency, and interest in and attitude toward reading. Through observation, answers to the following questions about a student's progress in learning to recognize and use words can be determined:

1. Does the student retain words previously introduced?
2. Has there been an increase in ability to use phonic and/or structural elements in words?
3. Is there improvement in the ability to understand word meanings?
4. Has the ability to analyze and pronounce words independently increased?
5. Has there been an increase in oral reading ability?
6. Is spelling ability improving?

With respect to comprehension, information can help answer the following questions:

Kavale

1. Can materials be read with greater ease, speed, and comprehension than previously?

2. Has there been improvement in the ability to follow directions for completing class and independent assignments?

3. Has skill in retelling materials read increased?

4. Has the ability to recall specific facts from a reading selection improved?

5. Has there been improvement in the ability to answer thought-type questions based upon reading materials?

Interest in and attitude toward reading can also be assessed through observation. It should be directed by the following questions:

1. Does the student read independently more eagerly than in the past?

2. Has the quantity of independent reading increased?

3. Has the student developed special reading interests?

4. Does the student read a wider variety or higher quality of materials than previously?

Some teachers find observation difficult because they do not know what to look for. The checklist in Chapter Four may serve as a practical means for systematizing observations.

Teacher observations can be further systematized by use of anecdotal records. The simplest form consists of a folder where dated observations, gathered in either a systematic or incidental manner, are kept in chronological order. In addition, samples of a student's work collected along with the anecdotes can be valuable. The primary purpose is to aid the teacher in assessing the developing reading characteristics of the child. Without readily available checkpoints, gradual but steady improvement may be mistaken for no improvement. They may also be superb for communication with parents, other teachers, administrators, and support personnel.

Informal tests. Many basal reading series include non-standardized tests which can be used for quick checks of students' word analysis skills, comprehension abilities, oral reading behavior, or any associated skill. (Teacher made criterion referenced tests, discussed in Chapter Three, are examples of informal tests.) Such tests can also be constructed by the teacher to assess students' understanding of just-presented material or to obtain samples of various kinds of reading behavior.

Bliesmer (*3*) has suggested several "do's and don'ts" for teachers in order that they may make more effective use of informal testing in teaching reading:

DO	*DON'T*
1. do try to test informally in settings where children can share application of skills in realistic and functional situations	1. don't make every testing situation a formal occasion
2. do make sure materials used for informal testing are of appropriate levels of difficulty	2. don't assume materials are too easy just because a child answers all or most questions over the material quickly and correctly
3. do try to find out why children responded as they did	3. don't assume that a child who has marked or written a "wrong answer" has necessarily answered incorrectly
4. do minimize the writing required to answer or respond to test items	4. don't try to make testing an attempt to check on all the various reading skills
5. do use questions which call for exercise and exhibition of various thinking skills and which get at various levels of comprehension	5. don't test mainly for the recall of facts
6. do be sure that materials permit a child to show or practice the skills which are supposedly being checked	6. don't assume that almost any material will be appropriate for checking almost any skill
7. do remember that a number of and the testing of them are basically oral matters	7. don't try to do all testing through silent reading

Informal measures are useful in providing continuous assessment of student performance. Since it more closely parallels the actual reading situations the child encounters in the classroom, an informal test can provide the information necessary for prescribing immediate corrective instruction.

Informal reading inventories. Many teachers use an informal reading inventory (IRI) to measure a student's oral and silent reading. Since standardized tests of reading may not be accurate for placing children in instructional materials, informal reading inventories offer a solution to the problem of which book best fits a child. IRIs can be used to determine a student's functional reading levels.

The three functional reading levels include:

1. Independent level—the level at which the student can read fluently without teacher assistance. The student can read material with no help and virtually perfect performance. The usual criteria for the independent level is 99 percent accuracy in word recognition and 90 percent or better comprehension.

2. Instructional level—the level at which the student can make maximum progress under teacher guidance. It is the level where the student is challenged but not frustrated. To be considered at the instructional level, materials should be read with 95 percent word recognition accuracy and, at least, 75 percent or better accuracy in comprehension.

3. Frustration level—the level at which the student can no longer function effectively. The student is unable to deal with the material and manifests a variety of behavioral characteristics to indicate the difficulty, including refusal to read, lack of expression in oral reading, excessive lip movements during silent reading, word pronunciation difficulties, word-by-word reading, and others. In addition to the behavioral characteristics, the formal criteria are word recognition of below 90 percent and 50 percent or less comprehension.

Johnson and Kress (*12*) provide detailed instructions for constructing an informal reading inventory. In addition, there are prepared graded selections for use in constructing informal reading inventories. However, in addition to informal reading inventories which can be constructed by the teacher, there are "formal" informal reading inventories. They are almost identical to teacher made IRIs and contain graded word lists and graded paragraph selections with questions to test comprehension. The major distinguishing characteristic lies in the fact that formal IRIs are published commercially. Neither type of IRI is free of difficulties. Problems concerning the reliability, the adequacy of the comprehension questions, and others are found in teacher made IRIs, but the content validity of the instrument is usually satisfactory for forming instructional reading groups. Commercially available IRIs usually do not have relevant technical data available, although it can probably be assumed that the instrument was carefully constructed.

Diagnostic Reading Tests

While standardized achievement or survey tests can be used to locate strengths and weaknesses, questions about specific aspects of reading performance are best answered by diagnostic type tests. If students seem to have unusual difficulty with a particular phase of reading or if there seems to be a wide discrepancy in the scores made on different sections of a reading achievement test, then a diagnostic test should be administered. They are usually given only after other tests have been given or teacher observation raises the possibility of some rather severe problems. These tests usually yield more subtest scores than an achievement or survey test. A diagnostic test or battery may include measures of oral reading, comprehension, and word analysis skills including sight vocabulary, visual and auditory discrimination, rate of reading, or reading-study skills. Special teachers rather than classroom teachers will probably select, administer, score, and interpret these tests because of their specialized nature but the classroom teacher may see the results or be asked to adjust instruction in light of the interpretation of these results.

Data from diagnostic tests should answer the following questions:
1. In what specific skills may a student be deficient?
2. Is the student having difficulty with understanding the basic skills, or is the problem mainly that of skills application?
3. Is there a discrepancy between the student's knowledge of phonic rules and facility in using them?
4. In light of the testing, which of the student's weaknesses should receive attention initially?

What do reading diagnostic tests really diagnose? In attempting to answer the question, "What do diagnostic reading tests really diagnose?" Winkley (*25*) studied nine diagnostic reading tests. It was concluded that no common definition of a "diagnostic reading test" was found. Several other problems were identified which suggests that caution should be exercised in using and interpreting diagnostic reading tests. However, these problems should not preclude their use since they do present a more systematic analysis of reading skills requiring assessment than procedures devised by a classroom teacher. The reading diagnostic test can make a more comprehensive analysis of reading abilities which can then be supplemented with referral measures specifically designed for individual students.

Choosing a diagnostic reading test. How does a teacher choose a diagnostic test? The same principles which are utilized in selecting other types of tests are appropriate for diagnostic tests. The factors of validity, reliability, and usability are again most important.

The validity of each subtest should be determined to see whether they represent meaningful areas for providing remedial instruction. If subtests are too global, then they do not provide much more information than what is available from a survey test. Also, while the same label may be used on several different subtests, they may measure entirely different abilities.

Reliability should be primarily assessed with regard to whether it is sufficiently high for individual use. Because a variety of subtests is found in diagnostic tests, the teacher must determine whether the subtest is long enough to be sufficiently reliable since the longer the subtest the more likely it is to be reliable. A high level of reliability is required when interpreting and comparing subtest difference scores of individuals. Teachers should not assume that just any difference between subtest scores is diagnostically meaningful. Standard errors of measurement (see Chapter Five) require that there be considerable differences between subtest scores before teachers conclude that there is a real difference in achievement between the subtest categories. An example is given under "percentile bands" in Chapter Five.

In addition to the above factors, Ramsey (*20*) has suggested other desirable criteria for diagnostic tests:

1. The reality criterion—Does the test assess an ability in much the same manner as the ability is used in real reading?

2. The guessing criterion—Does the test make it impossible for the student to guess the correct answer to an item?

3. The specificity criterion—Does an item measure a specific ability rather than a constellation of abilities?

4. The active criterion—Does the response demand some overt, observable behavior so that the examiner can clearly discern the nature of the student's difficulty?

5. The comprehension criterion—Do items that assess understanding of what is read actually test comprehension and interpretation rather than pure memory of what has been read?

Thus, for those pupils who are experiencing difficulty in reading, an instrument to pinpoint the nature of the problems contributing to poor reading performance is required so remedial instruction can be appropriately planned. The diagnostic reading test is designed to fill this need.

Reading Readiness Tests

Another type of test which many teachers will encounter is the reading readiness test. In a majority of elementary schools, reading readiness tests are administered and considered important components of the beginning reading program.

What is reading readiness? Reading readiness remains a controversial topic because of the issue of whether readiness is an intrinsic state of the student or whether it is the accumulated experience of the individual. Traditionally, individuals attempting to define reading readiness have viewed it as the result of maturation. Recent knowledge, however, has suggested that a student's readiness to learn to read is a product of both maturation and environmental factors. Within this framework, reading readiness is defined as the capacity to profit from systematic reading instruction.

This view of readiness, however, is incomplete since an integral component of the readiness process is a consideration of the types of learning opportunities which will be made available. This suggests that readiness is related to a set of circumstances in the form of methods, materials, and the level at which instruction begins.

What do reading readiness tests measure? The typical reading readiness test is intended to help select students who are ready to begin formal, systematic reading instruction.

Predictive validity of readiness tests. The teacher should seek evidence that the test accurately predicts which students will learn to read best. Do students who score high on a readiness test become good readers? And vice versa? The evidence generally suggests that, on the whole, readiness scores alone have only a fair degree of precision in predicting reading achievement for individual students.

Does this mean that reading readiness tests are not valid predictors? MacGinitie (*13*) called attention to two considerations which suggest that reading readiness tests can be useful. First, the predictive validity of present readiness tests is comparable to other instruments used for the purpose of prognosis in achievement. Second, readiness tests do appear to measure factors which have a relationship with first grade reading achievement. This is especially true if the tasks used to assess readiness closely resemble the criterion, that is, reading behavior. The reasons for the predictive validity of tasks that closely resemble reading are 1) they are more likely to require similar kinds of learnings, 2) they measure the past influence of environmental and motivational factors that are likely to continue to influence in a similar way the further acquisition of reading skills, and 3) what a student already knows cannot fail to be learned. Thus, the more closely factors in readiness tests resemble actual reading behavior, the higher the relationship between the readiness test and subsequent reading achievement.

Teachers should be aware that test scores obtained from preschool children are frequently highly unreliable. This means that test scores are subject to rapid change based on the effectiveness of school learning situations and developmental changes. Therefore, judgments must be tempered accordingly. For example, it is often helpful to have loose rather than rigid grouping of students for reading in primary grades based on kindergarten test results.

Factors in choosing a reading readiness test. The following are some considerations for using readiness tests:

1. Reading programs should be analyzed to determine the skills and abilities most important for success in beginning reading. For example, a teacher utilizing a whole word or look-say approach, would probably consider visual discrimination of letters and words a critical skill. Conversely, a strong phonics emphasis in beginning reading would suggest auditory discrimination as a crucial factor for success.

2. It should be realized that not all the important readiness factors are measurable with standardized tests. Therefore, teachers can enhance predictions by combining readiness tests with observation and evaluation of factors such as oral language facility, experiential background, attitude toward reading, and rate of learning in classroom situations.

Conclusion

The purpose of this chapter has been to provide guidelines and information relevant for test selection. This is vitally important for a successful reading program because the selection of tests is one of the more neglected aspects in the planning of a testing program. Test selection, at first glance, appears to be a routine procedure that any teacher can handle with little preparation. On the contrary, the wise selection of tests to be used is an important phase of a testing program which calls for considerable understanding if reading tests are to be servants of the reading program.

References

1. Barrett, T.C. "Predicting Reading Achievement through Readiness Tests," in J.A. Figurel (Ed.), *Reading and Inquiry*. Newark, Delaware: International Reading Association, 1965, 26-28.
2. Berg, P.C. "Evaluating Reading Abilities," in W.H. MacGinitie (Ed.), *Assessment Problems in Reading*. Newark, Delaware: International Reading Association, 1973, 27-34.
3. Bliesmer, E.P. "Informal Teacher Testing in Reading," *Reading Teacher, 26* (1972), 268-272.
4. Buros, O.K. (Ed.). *Reading: Tests and Reviews*. Highland Park, New Jersey: Gryphon Press, 1968.
5. Buros, O.K. (Ed.). *The Eighth Mental Measurements Yearbook*. Highland Park, New Jersey: Gryphon Press, 1978.

6. Farr, R., and N. Anastasiow. *Tests of Reading Readiness and Achievement: A Review and Evaluation.* Newark, Delaware: International Reading Association, 1969.
7. Farr, R. *Reading: What Can Be Measured?* Newark, Delaware: International Reading Association, 1969.
8. Glock, M. "How the Classroom Teacher Can Use a Knowledge of Tests and Measurements," in R.E. Leibert (Ed.), *Diagnostic Viewpoints in Reading.* Newark, Delaware: International Reading Association, 1971, 31-40.
9. Harmer, W.R. "The Selection and Use of Survey Reading Achievement Tests," in T.C. Barrett (Ed.), *The Evaluation of Children's Reading Achievement.* Newark, Delaware: International Reading Association, 1967, 53-64.
10. Hayward, P. "Evaluating Diagnostic Reading Tests," *Reading Teacher, 21* (1968), 523-529.
11. Hieronymous, A.N. "Evaluation and Reading: Perspective '72," *Reading Teacher, 26* (1972), 264-267.
12. Johnson, M.S., and R.A. Kress. *Informal Reading Inventories.* Newark, Delaware: International Reading Association, 1965.
13. MacGinitie, W.H. "Evaluating Readiness for Learning to Read. A Critical Review and Evaluation of Research," *Reading Research Quarterly, 4* (1969), 396-410.
14. McDonald, A.S. "Using Standardized Tests to Determine Reading Proficiency," *Journal of Reading, 8* (1964), 58-61.
15. Merwin, J.C. "Educational Measurement of What Characteristic, of Whom (or What), by Whom, and Why," *Journal of Educational Measurement, 10* (1973), 1-6.
16. Millman, J. "Criterion Referenced Measurement: An Alternative," *Reading Teacher, 26* (1972), 278-281.
17. Mitchell, A.S. "Values and Limitations of Standardized Reading Tests," in J.A. Figurel (Ed.), *Forging Ahead in Reading.* Newark, Delaware: International Reading Association, 1967, 163-167.
18. Otto, W. "Evaluating Instruments for Assessing Needs and Growth in Reading," in W.H. MacGinitie (Ed.), *Assessment Problems in Reading.* Newark, Delaware: International Reading Association, 1973, 14-20.
19. Prescott, G.A. "Criterion Referenced Test Interpretation in Reading," *Reading Teacher, 24* (1971), 347-354.
20. Ramsey, W. "The Values and Limitations of Diagnostic Reading Tests for Evaluation in the Classroom," in T.C. Barrett (Ed.), *The Evaluation of Children's Reading Achievement.* Newark, Delaware: International Reading Association, 1967, 65-78.
21. Robinson, H.A., and E. Hanson. "Reliability of Measures of Reading Achievement," *Reading Teacher, 21* (1968), 307-313.
22. Sipay, E.R. "A Comparison of Standardized Reading Scores and Functional Reading Levels," *Reading Teacher, 17* (1964), 265-268.
23. Thorndike, R.L., and E. Hagen. *Measurement and Evaluation in Psychology and Education,* Fourth Edition. New York: John Wiley and Sons, 1976.

24. Traxler, A.E., and R.D. North. "The Selection and Use of Tests in a School Testing Program," *The Impact and Improvement of School Testing Programs: The Sixty-Second Yearbook of the National Society for the Study of Education*, Part II. Chicago: University of Chicago Press, 1963.
25. Winkley, C. "What Do Diagnostic Reading Tests Really Diagnose?" in R.E. Leibert (Ed.), *Diagnostic Viewpoints in Reading*. Newark, Delaware: International Reading Association, 1971, 64-80.
26. Womer, F.B. "What Is Criterion Referenced Measurement?" in W.E. Blanton, R. Farr, and J. Tuinman (Eds.), *Measuring Reading Performance*. Newark, Delaware: International Reading Association, 1974, 34-43.

Chapter Three
Construction and Analysis of Reading Tests

Michael L. Kamil
Purdue University

The array of tests in reading seems to force a choice between norm referenced and criterion referenced tests. As an aid in understanding the differences between such tests, this chapter will compare and contrast items from norm referenced tests with items from criterion referenced tests for a group of reading skills. Then some of the ways that published tests can be supplemented by teacher constructed items and tests will be examined. Finally some techniques for writing items and constructing tests will be reviewed.

This chapter will cover five skill areas:
1. Reading readiness
2. Decoding
3. Word analysis
4. Comprehension
5. Vocabulary assessment

Several important areas of reading instruction have, for brevity's sake, been omitted from this chapter: work-study skills, content field reading, rate and flexibility, literary appreciation, and interest in and attitude toward reading. Readers interested in evaluating one or more of these areas should consult a methods textbook on the teaching of reading.

In order to choose or develop a test, needs and objectives must be carefully determined. Tests must always be closely related to objectives, since objectives should determine teaching content. As specific classroom objectives are clearly established, subskills in the broader areas (like those listed above) will be determined. Such specific objectives could then be translated into formal tests which could, in turn, be compared to items on a test. The degree to which the content of the test items matches the content of the objectives will determine the value of the particular tests for that specific application. There are other considerations that determine the value of a test. Among them is the use to which the results are put (discussed in Chapter Two).

We will examine items on published tests that might be appropriate to measure each of these skill areas. This is not intended to be an exhaustive treatment, but rather a sketchy outline of the more complete procedure. It is assumed that the entire range of objectives in each of these areas is available elsewhere.

Reading Readiness Skills

The skills that are necessary for a child to begin formal reading instruction typically include some or all of these: auditory and visual discrimination, following directions, listening comprehension, letter name knowledge, vocabulary, blending sounds together to make words, and reading words.

Figure 3.1 is an example of an item taken from the Metropolitan Readiness Test, a norm referenced test. This item, from the School Language and Listening subtest, requires a child to mark a picture that corresponds to the sentence the examiner reads.

Figure 3.2, from the Cooper-McGuire Diagnostic Word Analysis Test, a criterion referenced test, illustrates another way in which reading readiness is assessed. This item requires the child to be able to discriminate initial sounds. The test's authors feel that a score of 80 percent or better correct on this subtest indicates that the child has adequate auditory discrimination to begin formal reading instruction.

Figure 3.1

TEST 5: SCHOOL LANGUAGE AND LISTENING   P. I

A. Put your finger on the little black BALL. Mark
the picture that shows this: The duck is beside
the flower... The duck is beside the flower.

Reproduced from the Metropolitan Readiness Tests. Copyright ©1974 by
Harcourt Brace Jovanovich, Inc. Reproduced by special permission.

Figure 3.2
Test R3: Auditory Discrimination

Objective R 3: Given four pictures whose names begin with three
different sounds, the learner will be able to mark two pictures beginning with the
same sound as two dictated words with 80 percent accuracy.

Percentages Recorded:

%	7	13	20
27	33	40	47
53	60	67	73
80	87	93	100

Sample Test Item: The pupil is presented with pictures of four common
objects. The teacher identifies the pictures (e.g., "The names of these pictures are
letter, book, fish, light"), and the pupil is asked to mark two pictures that begin
with the same sound as two additional words pronounced by the teacher (e.g.,
leg and *lamp*).

Rationale: The ability to discriminate initial sounds is an important
readiness step that leads directly into the more complex skills of identifying
sounds with appropriate letters, which is presented in Test P1. The 15 sounds
that were chosen for the test are important only insofar as they measure a
general ability to discriminate sounds; therefore, percentages (instead of the
particular sounds) are noted on the Class Record Chart. An 80 percent criterion
level is sufficient for the establishment of this readiness skill. Further instruction
in auditory discrimination is given in meeting Objective P1, and complete (100
percent) mastery is expected at that time.

Cooper-McGuire Diagnostic Word Analysis Test, J. Louis Cooper and Marion
L. McGuire. New London, Connecticut: Croft Educational Services, Inc., 1972.

Construction and Analysis of Tests   37

Teachers can also develop tests of reading readiness if the contents of published tests do not seem appropriate. For example, the uppercase letters of the alphabet could be written on cards and children asked to name the letters. Or auditory discrimination could be tested by asking children to listen to word pairs and then say whether they were the same or different (ran-man, play-plan, than-then).

Decoding Skills

These skills, often broadly called phonics, are related to readers' abilities to translate letter (or spelling) patterns into sound.

The Stanford Diagnostic Reading Test, a norm referenced and criterion referenced test, has items such as those in Figure 3.3. These items tap the ability of students to match a letter with the sound it represents.

In one example in the Wisconsin Design for Reading Skill Improvement, a criterion referenced test, the teacher reads a list of words such as *man* and the student names the vowel letter in each word. Items in this subtest do not seem to tap a reading skill directly. But these items are examples of construct validity (see Chapter Five), they predict which children will most likely have the highest end-of-first-grade reading achievement.

Teacher made items can be based on any letter-to-sound correspondence rule. Children could be given an example of CVCE patterns (as in the word *mate*) and asked to pronounce them. Some reading authorities suggest using nonsense words like *vate* to insure that children don't know the word by sight and must apply the rules. If a teacher is unable to find these items on a published test, this alternative would be useful.

Structural Analysis Skills

These skills are differentiated from decoding skills by the unit of analysis and include inflected endings, prefixes and suffixes, and syllabication skills.

The Stanford Diagnostic Reading Test, a norm referenced and criterion referenced test, uses items to test syllabication

Figure 3.3

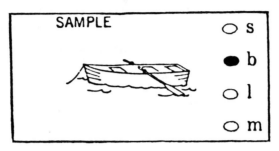

Look at the shaded box at the top of the page where you see a picture of a boat. Think of the beginning sound of the word "boat"... "boat." What is the first sound in "boat"?

Pause for replies.

Yes, it is /b/ ("buh"). "Boat" begins with the /b/ sound. Which letter in the shaded box stands for the /b/ sound?

Pause for replies.

Yes, it is "b" ("bee"); that is why the space next to the "b" has been filled in in your booklet. You will do the same with the other questions on this page. I will tell you what the picture is. Then you will fill in the answer space in front of the letter or group of letters that stands for the beginning sound or sounds of the word I say. Mark only one letter or group of letters for each picture. Does everyone understand what to do?

(Figure 3.4). In this type of item, the student is required to segment the *first* syllable of a printed word and match it with its visual representation.

The same test also requires the child to mark the syllable that is "extra" when two of the choices form a word. This item is from Part B, structural analysis, Stanford Diagnostic Reading Test and is designed to illustrate a student's ability to blend syllables into words (Figure 3.5). Blending of this sort is not precisely a structural analysis skill. The teacher must decide whether this subtest has the desired validity and must be certain that this information will be important for instructional decisions.

Figure 3.4

A   tiptoe   t   ti   tip

Look at line A in the shaded box at the top of the page.
(Demonstrate.) You see the word "tiptoe." "Tiptoe" can be
divided into parts (syllables) that can help you say the word.
Look at the three groups of letters next to "tiptoe." Which
group of letters is the *first* part (syllable) of "tiptoe?"

Figure 3.5

Part B

Samples			
A	my	so	self
B	mon	key	ber
1	air	one	plane
2	con	cor	test

Look at line A in the shaded box at the top of the page.
Here you see three word parts. Two of these parts can be
put together to make a real word. The other part is extra.
The parts that make the word are in the correct order,
from left to right. What word can you make from two of
the three parts in line A?

Pause for replies. Say:

Yes, the word is "myself." What is the extra part? (Pause.)
Yes, the extra part is "so." That is why the space under
"so" has been filled in in your booklet. Now look at line B.
Find the word that can be made from two word parts.
(Pause.) What is the extra part?

Pause for replies. Then say:

Yes, the extra part is "ber." So fill in the space under "ber."
"Mon" and "key" make "monkey," so "ber" is left over.
Are there any questions about what you are to do?

The Cooper-McGuire Diagnostic Word Analysis Test
measures the use of prefixes and suffixes as shown in Figure 3.6.

Figure 3.6
Test S6: Use of Prefixes and Suffixes

Objective S6: Given a list of prefixes and suffixes, the learner will be able to identify the affix to be added to a given root word to make sense in a sentence with 100 percent accuracy.

Sample Test Item: The pupil is presented with a sentence in which one of the words needs the addition of a prefix or a suffix (e.g., "When everything fell out of his suitcase, he had to ____pack it"). The pupil chooses an appropriate affix (one that satisfies the meaning of the sentence) from a list of prefixes and suffixes.

Prefixes

Meaning Units	Visual Units
anti-(against; the opposite of)	a-
circum-(around)	ab-
dis-(opposite of; apart)	ante-
ex-(out of; former)	com-, con-, col-
extra-(outside; beyond)	contra-
im-(not)	de-
in-(in; into)	inter-
in-(not)	per-
intra-, intro-(inside)	peri-
mal-(bad)	post-
mis-(wrong)	super-
non-(not; the reverse)	trans-
out-(more than; beyond)	be-
over-(too much)	en-
pre-(before)	
pro-(in front of)	
re-(again; back)	
self-(see dictionary)	
sub-(under)	
under-(below; not enough)	
un-(not; opposite of)	

Cooper-McGuire Diagnostic Word Analysis Test, J. Louis Cooper and Marion L. McGuire. New London, Connecticut: Croft Educational Services, Inc., 1972.

A specific instructional objective is given for each subtest of this test. This makes comparison with objectives of a particular instructional program quick and easy.

Teacher made items can be used to measure skills that are not found on commercial tests. Thus, a teacher who wants to know about children's knowledge of final syllables could create items analogous to those in Figure 3.4.

Vocabulary Skills

This broad category includes the meanings of words as well as the recognition of individual words.

There are two major types of tests for vocabulary skills, recognition and production. In recognition tests, a stimulus word is to be matched with its synonym from among several responses. Production tests require the student to make a response, not merely select an option.

Meaning vocabulary is measured normatively by recognition procedures on tests like the Gates-McKillop Reading Diagnotic Test (Figure 3.7).

Figure 3.7

Directions. Say to the child: "This is a test to find out how wel you know the meanings of words. I am going to read part of a sentence: 'A head is part of a _____.' Now I'm going to read four choices for finishing the sentence: 'coat, saw, man, box. A head is part of a coat, saw, man, box.' Which of the choices tells you what 'head' means?"

1. A head is part of a   coat   saw   man   box

Gates-McKillop Reading Diagnostic Tests, Forms 1 & 2, Arthur I. Gates and Anne S. McKillop. New York: Teachers College Press, Teachers College, Columbia University, 1962.

The skill involved here is the ability to recognize synonyms or attributes from a list of alternatives.

A production type task would be to ask a child, "In this selection, what does *responded* mean?"

Sight vocabulary tests emphasize recognition and pronunciation instead of word meaning. The Slosson Oral Reading Test gives measures of sight vocabulary in a norm referenced manner (Figure 3.8). This is a production task where the student must read the words in this list.

Figure 3.8

Directions:
1. Allow the child to read from one sheet while you keep score on another. At the start, say the following: "I want to see how many of these words you can read. Please begin here and read each word aloud as carefully as you can." (Indicate at what list to start.) "When you come to a

difficult word, do the best you can and if you can't read it, say 'blank' and go on to the next one."

List P

1. see
2. look
3. mother
4. little
5. here

Slosson Oral Reading Test (SORT), Richard L. Slosson. East Aurora, New York: Slosson Educational Publications, Inc., 1963.

The Johnson Basic Sight Vocabulary Test, a criterion referenced test, measures sight vocabulary (Figure 3.9).

Figure 3.9

Directions for Grade 1

In the row with a *1* in front of it, find the word RED and draw a circle around it, *RED.*

1. reed   red   ready   rod

From Form B of the *Johnson Basic Sight Vocabulary Test* by Dale D. Johnson. © Copyright, 1976, by Ginn and Company (Xerox Corporation). Used with permission.

The two examples of sight vocabulary measures differ in their objectives. One requires the student to produce a spoken response, the other requires the student to match a printed word with a word spoken by the teacher.

If teachers decide that the word samples used on published tests do not adequately match those of the instructional material, they may produce their own items. The results cannot be used indiscriminately, but this will be discussed thoroughly later.

Comprehension Skills

These are skills used by the reader to extract meaning from chunks of text larger than single words. Comprehension is most often measured by a series of questions following a passage. Figure 3.10 is an item taken from the Davis Reading Test, a norm referenced test.

Figure 3.10

Most people consider red salmon better than pink salmon, and it usually sells for more. A canner of pink salmon printed on his labels, "Guaranteed not to turn red in the can."

8. What word is understood after "more"?
   A People
   B Uses
   C Money
   D Stores
   E Customers

An example of a criterion referenced comprehension test is the typical informal reading inventory (IRI) which accompanies many basal readers. If the child can meet the traditional criteria of 95 percent word recognition accuracy and 75 percent comprehension accuracy on a passage drawn from instructional material, it is assumed that the child can adequately handle that level material in a directed reading situation.

If teachers are unable to find sufficient diversity of question types in published tests to suit their needs, they can create their own questions. This is not as simple as it might first seem. Helpful guidelines can be found in *Classroom Questions* by Sanders and in *Teaching Reading Comprehension* by Pearson and Johnson. Additional suggestions are given later in this chapter in the section titled "Constructing Test Items."

More global measures of comprehension may be obtained by using cloze procedures for specific passages. The cloze procedure is a relatively simple test in which a student is required to fill in blanks in a passage of text. The results can be used normatively to rank a group of students or in a criterion referenced manner much as in an IRI in matching a child and instructional material.

The following steps can be used as a guide in producing cloze tests.

1. Select a passage of about 50-200 words, beginning with and ending with a complete sentence. The lower the readability level of the passage, the shorter it should be; for young students, passages should be kept short; for older students, they can be longer.

Kamil

2. Leave the first sentence and last sentence intact and, beginning with the second sentence, retype the passage omitting every fifth word. Make the blanks all the same length.

3. Reproduce the passage and have the student fill in the blanks.

Once the student has filled in the blanks, score the passage by counting the number of *exactly correct* words filled in. Synonyms can be counted, but they won't change the rankings of students much and frequently it is very difficult to determine whether a word is acceptable.

Reading levels can be determined as follows: If a student scores 50 percent or better, the material is at the *independent level*; if he scores between 30-50 percent, the material is at the *instructional level*; below 30 percent, the material is too difficult and may be considered to be at the *frustration level*. (These levels are to be used as guidelines only. A student may score low for a variety of reasons. Also the cloze score is not readily generalizable to other materials.)

The following is a sample of a cloze passage of about second grade difficulty (*6*):

The Twin Rabbits

On the way to Ann's house, they saw two children going to the party. One was dressed as _____ white rabbit. The other _____ wearing a sailor suit.

_____ boy dressed as a _____ was standing at the _____ of Ann's house. He _____ the door for the _____ .

"That is Ann's _____ Tommy," Penny whispered to _____ .

Ann looked hard at the twin rabbits.

Because of the time, effort, and knowledge required to produce valid and reliable reading tests, it is strongly recommended that teachers make efforts to use commercially available tests. If a test meets your needs, use it rather than prepare your own. However, if you feel that published tests do not meet your requirements, prepare one. It would be unprofessional to try to make do with an inappropriate test.

Initial Considerations

Before beginning to construct a test, the following questions should be answered:

1. *What function is the particular test going to serve?* Is is going to be an integral part of a diagnostic teaching program; is it going to be a program evaluation; or will it serve some other function?
2. *Just what are the objectives that the test is designed to measure?* These may be specific instructional objectives or they may be general programmatic objectives.
3. *What types of test exercises will be most suitable?* The general choice is between objective and essay types of questions. Within the objective category, items may be true/false, multiple choice, matching, etc. Essay questions can require short answers or more involved, lengthier answers.

These decision processes are not easy. They require, first, that the teacher be intimately familiar with the educational goals and instructional objectives to be used. Second, the task of determining whether one's needs are met in a test takes time *and* effort. Finally, there is no guarantee a test can be found that will meet teachers' needs. In that case, teachers should use teacher made tests, which can be based directly on their own objectives.

The following are the things that need to be considered in analyzing or beginning to construct a test:

1. The types of instructional decisions you want to make.
2. The specific teaching philosophy and goals.
3. The amount of resources (time, money, personnel) to be used in evaluating or creating test instruments.
4. The amount of time to be spent in testing and/or evaluation.
5. The specific items on a test.

Constructing Objectives and Test Items

The first steps in writing test items are shown in the flow chart (Figure 1.1) in Chapter One. The chart shows that a needs assessment is necessary before specific instructional objectives can be formulated. *After* instruction, a student's performance is measured and evaluated. This section is concerned with the way in which tests and test items can be written by a teacher.

Kamil

Writing Objectives

After a needs assessment has been conducted, general goals should be apparent. That is, some rather broad areas in which students need instruction should be evident. This section will first consider how to write specific objectives that can be used in instruction.

Generally, an objective should have two components: a specific behavior the student should be able to demonstrate and a level of acceptable performance. Thus, an objective like "The student will learn to read" is unacceptable. Neither the behavior nor the level of performance is specified. For a child learning to read, the objective would be improved if it were restated, "By the end of the school year, the child will read orally at the 1.9 grade level with fewer than 5 percent errors." Some readers may believe that this objective is still too general to be useful.

Here are some characteristics of objectives that will make them more useful:

1. *The objective should state a behavior that is observable.* Thus, an objective like "The students will be interested in reading" is poor because it is not really possible to observe "being interested in reading." An improved objective might be, "The students will voluntarily select and read five books of their own choice in x weeks' time."

2. *The objective should be specific and unambiguous.* The words used in the objective should not mean different things to different people. "The student will comprehend reading material at the fifth grade level" is not specific enough because comprehension has many meanings. A better choice might be, "The student will be able to correctly *paraphrase* passages at the fifth grade level of difficulty."

3. *Objectives should be unitary.* It is undesirable to cover more than one behavior in an objective. If two or more behaviors are in the same objective, it is difficult to specify the criteria. For example, this objective is poor, "The students will be able to *decode* and *define* words at

their reading levels." A better procedure is to have two objectives: 1) "The students will be able to decode words at their reading levels with 95 percent accuracy." 2) "The students will be able to define words at their reading levels with 80 percent accuracy."

4. *Objectives should be attainable under normal circumstances.* Given the amount of time allotted for instruction and the amount of resources a teacher can devote to instruction, the objective should be realistically attainable. For students reading two years below their grade placement, the objective, "The students will read at grade level at the end of this year," is probably unattainable.

Objectives should be constructed by first determining the desired student behavior, making sure that the characteristics mentioned above are not violated, even at the level of behavior. Performance should then be specified, preferably using active verbs like *to answer, to define, to say,* or *to locate.* Verbs such as *to feel, to think,* or *to grow* should be avoided. Finally, an outcome should be stated. The outcome should be an observable or measurable performance and should include a statement of the task and a level of mastery or a criterion to be achieved. For example: "The students will be able to categorize known words with the long or short sound of *oo* into two groups with 90 percent accuracy." The behavior is to classify words with *oo* in them. The students must distinguish between the long and short sounds of the letter combination. On a test of this skill, students must obtain a score of 90 percent before attaining that objective.

Notice that each objective specifies, in itself, a test. If a student satisfies the objective, instruction should move to new objectives. If a student does not meet the criterion, revisions in instruction, in the objective itself, or in the needs assessment may be necessary. A complete discussion of this process appears with the flow chart presented in Chapter One.

Writing objectives is probably much easier for certain enabling reading skills like decoding. More global skills like comprehension are fairly difficult to adapt to this purpose. That is, it is simpler to write test items that measure the ability to pronounce the sound of a letter than it is to measure the understanding of even a short passage.

An important point to be derived from the discussion and examples above is that norm referenced and criterion referenced types of tests *can* be different, but they do not *have* to be different. When the comparison is between good instruments, the two types of tests are not very different.

Writing Items

There are some precautions that must be taken when writing tests and test items. Objective type items will be considered first, even though some of these warnings will apply to essay items and tests as well.

1. The most important single principle is that *the reading level and vocabulary difficulty should be within the range of the students who are going to take the test.* An item which reads, "separate the following list of words into two categories representing the same initial phoneme" is clearly beyond the reading abilities of most primary school students. It would be better to write, "Make two groups of words from the following list so that all of the words in each group start with the same sound."

2. *The items should be clear and unambiguous.* If you ask whether the words *bring* and *thing* sound alike, the question is ambiguous. It is better to ask whether the two words rhyme or end with the same sound.

3. *Test items should cover important content.* The more trivial the answer to a test item, the less effective it is in tapping a reading related skill.

4. *Items should be independent.* The answer to a question should not depend on whether the student has been able to answer a previous question correctly. If you are testing comprehension of a story, ask: "True or False, the events in this story occurred before 1863," rather than "True or False, the Civil War occurred before 1863."

5. *Every test item should have a single correct answer.* If

experts in the field can agree on the answer, it is appropriate. If there is some disagreement, the item should be discarded or revised. It is important to remember that an item should be constructed so that a student can get it correct *only* if the corresponding learning objective has been attained.

Test constructors favor the selection of items, for statistical reasons, that are missed by about 50 percent of the norming population. (Although, this is not the *same* 50 percent for each item). Items are also selected to maximize the overall reliability of the test. In addition, the items should be those that best predict the behavior that is being tested. Thus, it is not always readily apparent that an item is related to a particular behavior. Test constructors often are primarily concerned with predicting the presence (or absence) of a skill or behavior.

An example may serve to illustrate this last point. Discrimination is important in reading readiness. Readiness items often deal with colors, pictures, or abstract symbols. For norm referenced tests, these items might have been shown to be valid by correlating performance on them with performance on other, independent measures of reading readiness.

Criterion referenced tests often demand that items be more directly related to actual reading behaviors. That is, the items should involve words or letters rather than other pictures or symbols.

For many criterion referenced tests, a sequence of skill assessment *and* instruction is specified. In general, this is not the case for norm referenced tests. When test items relate directly to instruction, the sequence of assessment should also match directly.

For essay test items, some of the same criteria apply. The test must deal with important content. The task proposed must be specific. Above all, there must be a correct answer.

In general, it is easier to construct essay or short answer items; however, what is gained in construction is often lost in the additional complexity of scoring. Essay items are limited in the amount of content that can be sampled, whereas objective questions can be used to cover more of the content. The units of learning you want to emphasize will also determine the type of test you choose. Essay tests cause students to focus on much larger, integrated chunks of content than do objective tests.

The Finishing Touches

When the objective items have been completed, some care must be taken with the format of the test before it is administered. Above all, it must be easy to read. Items should not be squeezed so close together that they are hard to distinguish. It is a good idea to group items of the same type together. That is, true/false items should not be mixed with multiple choice or matching items. When testing several different types of content in the same test, group together those items which relate to similar content. A test should probably start with the easier items and progress to the more difficult ones. This will allow the test taker to gain some confidence and help sustain motivation. Directions must be clear and specific. The reading level of directions must certainly be within the capabilities of the students taking the test. It is also important to avoid patterns of answers, e.g. alternating true and false answers (T, F, T, F, etc.) or sequencing multiple choice answers (ABCDCBA, etc.).

Before using a teacher made test, construct it and put it away for some time. Then, go back, read it over, and take it yourself. Have a colleague take the test, also. Revise or eliminate any items that fail to meet the criteria discussed, that you have difficulty with, or that seem odd. This may mean that more items will have to be written. Teachers shouldn't be discouraged if their efforts at constructing tests don't yield the results wanted. The procedures followed by commercial test producers are very involved, very expensive, and highly specialized. It is not suggested that teachers can replace all tests with those that they make themselves, but rather that they can supplement commercial tests with teacher made tests for their own specific goals.

References
1. Cooper, J. Louis, and Marion L. McGuire. *Cooper-McGuire Diagnostic Word-Analysis Test.* New London, Connecticut: Croft Educational Services, Test Manual, 1972, 4-5, 18-19.

2. Davis, Frederick B., and Charlotte Croon Davis. *Davis Reading Test,* Form 2A, Series 2. New York: The Psychological Corporation, 1961, 2-3.
3. Gates, Arthur I., and Anne S. McKillop. *Gates-McKillop Reading Diagnostic Tests,* Forms 1 & 2. *Pupil Record Booklet,* 15; *Manual of Direction,* 10-11. New York: Teachers College Press, Teachers College, Columbia University, 1962.
4. Johnson, Dale D. *Johnson Basic Sight Vocabulary Test,* Forms A & B. *Directions Manual,* 8-9; student copy, 4-5. Lexington, Massachusetts: Ginn, 1976.
5. Karlsen, Bjorn, Richard Madden, and Eric F. Gardner. *Stanford Diagnostic Reading Test,* red and green levels. *Manual for Administering and Interpreting,* 20-21 (green level); 25-27 (red level). *Student Booklet,* 7-8 (red level), 7-8 (green level). New York: Harcourt Brace Jovanovich, 1976.
6. McKee, Paul M., et al. *Come Along,* level 2[1]. Hopewell, New Jersey: Houghton Mifflin, 1966, 205.
7. Nurss, Joanne R., and Mary E. McGauvran. *Metropolitan Readiness Tests,* Level 1, Form P. *Teacher's Manual: Directions for Administering,* 26; *Metropolitan Readiness Tests,* 17. New York: Harcourt Brace Jovanovich, 1976.
8. Otto, Wayne. *Wisconsin Design for Reading Skill Development.* Minneapolis, Minnesota: National Computer Systems, 1972, 31.
9. Pearson, P. David, and Dale D. Johnson. *Teaching Reading Comprehension.* New York: Holt, 1978.
10. Sanders, Norris, *Classroom Questions.* New York: Harper and Row, 1966.
11. Slosson, Richard L. *Slosson Oral Reading Test* (SORT). East Aurora, New York: Slosson Educational Publications, 1963.

Kamil

Chapter Four
Organizing and Applying Test Results

George Canney
University of Idaho at Moscow

There is an old saying, "Someone who jumps from a plane without a parachute is likely to jump to a conclusion." Teachers who do not exercise judgment and knowledge of the students they teach run the risk of "jumping to conclusions" that are no more satisfactory or instructionally sound than are those of the ill-fated airplane passenger. Teachers should interpret test data in light of daily observations of students' reading, while always remaining ready to question discrepant pieces of information. If teachers accept test scores as *truth*, whether or not the scores fit with their perceptions of individual students, then they are unlikely to be successful with students who really need help. Test scores are to be viewed as one source of information on student progress; to be meaningful for instructional purposes, teachers will have to examine scores carefully and keep any decisions tentative—always tentative.

How to Use Test Scores

Measuring student reading ability always results in some inaccurate information. However, by following the procedures suggested below, poor decisions based upon incomplete or inaccurate test results can be avoided. These guides are represented by the acronym VERIFI:

*V*alidate the content of the test items,

Keep *E*quilibrium in the assessment program by using different types of testing procedures.

*R*eview student progress frequently in order to check judgments about instructional procedures.

*I*nvestigate discrepancies between test scores and inclass performance.

*F*ormulate an instructional plan with students and share the general results of tests with them.

*I*nterpret all test data in light of what is known about the student and curriculum objectives.

Willingness to VERIFI information from tests, so that student progress is clear both to you and to students, will affect instructional success. Without VERIFIcation, test scores will be of little value and may even decrease the effectiveness of instruction. A more detailed review of these six steps may explain how they relate to effective teaching.

Validate. Examine test items carefully. Be certain that the test items actually reflect the content and skills you want to measure.

Otherwise, scores are meaningless for instructional purposes, and further item examination subsequent to testing is useless because you do not plan to present that content or skill.

You will want to study the items missed by a student. A low score may be the result of a single type of misconception, rather than a general confusion in the areas assessed.

Preparing a chart similar to the one presented in Figure 4.1 can assist in identifying test items that proved easy or difficult in order to make decisions about which skills or materials to present next. In this example, students were given a teacher-constructed test of their ability to identify five prefixes (+ refers to correct responses, - refers to incorrect responses).

From the patterns of correct and incorrect responses on this prefix assessment, it appears that Shawn is probably confused about all of these prefixes while Willie, Tom and Debbie can recognize in- and re- but have difficulty with sub-,

Figure 4.1
An Item-response Chart Showing Correct (+) and Incorrect (-) Responses on a
Test of Prefixes.

Objective	Recognizing common prefixes										
Prefixes	in		re		sub		dis			un		
Items	1	4	6	12	2	9	3	8	10	5	7	11
Willie T.	+	+	+	+	-	-	-	+	-	+	+	-
Susan S.	+	+	+	+	+	+	+	+	-	+	+	-
Daphene J.	+	+	+	+	+	+	+	+	+	+	+	+
Tom B.	+	+	+	+	+	-	-	-	-	-	-	-
Shawn P.	+	-	-	-	-	+	-	-	-	-	+	-
Debbie M.	+	+	+	+	-	+	+	-	-	+	+	-
Ryan M.	+	+	+	+	+	+	+	+	+	+	+	+

dis-, and un-. Susan, Daphene, and Ryan have performed
somewhat better than the other members of the group. But the
entire group seems unsure about the prefixes dis- and un-.
Another possibility is that items 10 and 11 may not be
satisfactory items, since only two students answered them
correctly.

Although time-consuming, procedures like the one just
described are necessary if group administered tests are to be
useful for making instructional decisions. This is especially true
when using commercial tests which may contain items on content
not yet presented, or tests which require students to respond
differently from the way they ordinarily answer test questions.

Equilibrium. Keep a balance in your assessment program. Each
form of measurement, especially observation, can
contribute information useful for instruction.

If you use a standardized achievement test, consider the
following procedures to assist in creating instructional groups.

Arrange the class test booklets in rank order, using
reading comprehension scores. Form three groups of test scores
approximating the top quarter, middle half, and bottom quarter
of the class. On a separate sheet of paper, record the students'

names and reading comprehension scores. Then examine these scores. First, what is the range of scores and does this range represent a typical distribution for the school; is it broader or narrower, or higher or lower than usual? Such information will allow you to compare this class with other groups from your teaching experiences. Next, compare the three groups of test scores. Are they fairly close to each other, or distinctly separate? If they are close, the class may be fairly homogeneous in reading ability and you may want to consider grouping students quite flexibly. If the groups are quite different, and the students within the groups are also different from one another, you will definitely want to consider more than three reading groups.

An examination of other subtest scores, such as vocabulary, word attack skills, or rate, may help to estimate the homogeneity of the reading groups you have proposed. If discrepancies exist between a student's subtest scores (reading comprehension and reading rate or vocabulary), you may want to concentrate your instruction in those areas that appear weak. Students who achieve similar scores on a particular subtest may be grouped temporarily in a special skills group, even though their general reading performance differs widely.

To determine whether score discrepancies are significant, create bands or ranges of scores by adding the standard error of measurement, plus and minus, to the student's percentile rank score. If the score bands created for each subtest overlap a standard error of measurement by half or more, it is unlikely that the student's performance is really stronger in one skill than in the other. Less overlap suggests that the student *may* be stronger in one skill and requires special instruction in the areas deemed weak. Similar comparisons can be made for a group's subtest scores, created by averaging across the students' scores in the group. In this way you can obtain some estimate of group instructional needs in addition to the needs of individual students.

At this point the decision on how much further testing is needed before instruction can begin depends on how low the students scored relative to the expected achievement levels of your school. You will want to learn as much as possible about students having difficulty in reading before placing them in materials that may be too difficult. When starting, it is better to be conservative than to overestimate a student's reading level. Improper grouping may lead to student frustration, loss of motivation, and subsequent instructional or behavioral problems.

You also want to learn more about the reading levels and strengths of the other children in your class; but since you have limited time to conduct needed testing for the low scoring children, you can probably place the more able students in materials and initiate instruction. Even if you place a student in an inappropriate group, your observations and the student's daily performance should lead to rapid adjustments in instruction.

Depending on the number of students you believe need further testing, you may now decide to use either a group diagnostic reading test or an individual one. Administering the individual diagnostic test is usually more time consuming, especially if you are using it with several students; but it will normally provide a more detailed picture of reading performance than a group test. Both types of tests often allow some latitude in using parts of the test battery, but the individual diagnostic test allows you to terminate some subtests if they prove too easy or too difficult for a particular student. The administration of specific subtests may be spread over several days. Your observations of the impact of careful instruction during this period, together with the student's performance on the subtests you administer, should help you adjust instruction to the student's abilities and interests.

If you wish to assess student abilities to read material from the specific texts used in your classroom, you may also employ an informal reading inventory (IRI) or your own test to gather highly specific information on each student's reading skills.

By coupling the use of test instruments with informal observations of student performance in both testing and learning situations, you bring an equilibrium, or balance, to the assessment program in reading.

Review. Review student progress frequently in order to monitor instructional effectiveness.

Once you have formed *tentative* judgments about each student's strengths, weaknesses, and interests, plan to observe individual progress frequently. Otherwise, it is difficult to check the accuracy of initial estimates of each student's reading level or monitor growth over time as a result of teaching and student effort. Quizzes, tests at the end of units, daily performance on assignments, conferences, and regular checks of oral reading performance (ordinarily used for beginning readers) will help you in making estimates of student needs.

Frequently, the most helpful method for monitoring student growth is diagnostic teaching. This is when students are assessed on the same material covered on a systematic daily basis. Oral reading for diagnosis is one assessment procedure that meets this criterion. On a frequent basis, once or twice a week, each student should read aloud from a new story in the reading text. As the student reads, record miscues (significant errors) on a separate copy of the story. Usually two minutes of reading (from 75 words for beginning readers to 200-word passages for better readers) provides an adequate sample to assess oral reading performance. Unless a student is particularly self-conscious about reading aloud in a group, oral reading for diagnosis can be done as a regular part of a group reading activity. Teacher proficiency in using oral reading for diagnosis comes with practice.

By using the marking system shown in Figure 4.2 and tape recording the student's oral reading, a useful record of student strengths and weaknesses in oral reading can be obtained. The tape recording permits rechecking; it also can be kept and replayed later to help students recognize their own progress in reading.

Pikulski (1974) notes in an article on informal reading inventories (IRI) that writers in the field of reading disagree on what oral responses constitute errors or miscues. Some writers do not consider omissions, substitutions, repetitions, or insertions as errors unless they affect comprehension. Others prefer to

Figure 4.2

Code System for Oral Reading for Diagnosis

Example:

The (little) girl was standing near the /st͡op/sign.   While she
was waiting //for the bus, she watched the squirrels playing
in the trees. A big bird hopped from branch to branch.   The
little girl forgot to watch for the bus. While she was looking
at the animals in the tree, the bus went past her. So the little
girl began to cry.

Error Type	Code	Example
Omission	⬯	(little)
Insertion	∧	to near ∧ the
Reversal	∿	spot /st͡op/
Substitution	＼	next near
Repetition	⟵	girl was standing ⟵
Hesitation	//	waiting // for
Teacher Assisted	T	T squirrels
Self-corrected	✓	saw watched
Disregards Punctuation	⌢	sign. While

examine patterns of errors to ascertain the strategies that a
student is using to read, rather than to make a simple tally of
those errors.

   A second way of frequently reviewing progress is by using
multiple response or every pupil response (EPR) techniques (1,
2). Those procedures permit you to assess each student's
performance on word attack skills and vocabulary. They are

designed for use in a group setting, since the students use the EPR devices to respond nonverbally to questions.

There are numerous variations of the EPR idea; two will be described here. Figure 4.3 depicts two EPR devices. In Example One a tongue depressor has been glued to a circle of tagboard 6 inches in diameter. Holes cut large enough for a child to insert a finger are arranged around the perimeter of the tagboard and numbered. The numbers correspond to the lines on a pocket chart (Example Two). The pocket chart, when made small enough (9"x12"), can be an individual student's EPR device. Students point to particular word cards on their pocket charts in response to the teacher's questions.

As an example of how the EPR technique works, suppose that nine previously introduced words, listed below, have been put onto phrase cards and arranged on the teacher's pocket chart as shown in Figure 4.3.

line 1	would	line 6	mountains
line 2	brake	line 7	shake
line 3	pleased	line 8	goats
line 4	cold	line 9	flint
line 5	replace	line 10	_____

After reading through the words once, the students are given a handheld EPR device and instructed to answer each of the questions you ask. They are to respond by inserting one or more fingers through the numbered holes in the EPR device that correspond to the numbered lines on the teacher's pocket chart. If the students are using their EPR pocket charts, each student has a miniature pack of nine words arranged on his pocket chart in the same order as found on the teacher's pocket chart. The students will simply point to the appropriate words on their pocket charts.

With the students arranged facing you so that you can see each one clearly, begin asking prepared questions:

1. Does the word on line seven mean "an old cabin"? (word meaning)
2. Which word has the same sound in the middle as the

Figure 4.3
Every Pupil Response Devices for Maximizing
Practice in Reading

Example One: Hand-held EPR device

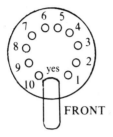

FRONT

BACK

Example Two: EPR Pocket Chart

	would		mountain	
1			6	
	brake		shake	
2			7	
	pleased		goats	
3			8	
	cold		flint	
4			9	
	replace			
5			10	

   word /sit/?
   (auditory analysis) 9
3. Which word means the opposite of hot?
   (word meaning-antonyms) 4
4. Which word has an ending that means more than one?
   (structural analysis-inflected endings) 6,8

More than one correct response to a question is
sometimes possible. This encourages students to be somewhat

more independent in making decisions about the correct answer. It also provides an opportunity for students to explain why their answers may differ.

The EPR procedures are useful for reviewing student progress because they provide a brief, fast-paced means to observe how much each student in a group knows about the various skills and vocabulary being presented. A student who continually selects the wrong answer or who frequently looks at peer choices is often the student who is less sure about the skills than other students in the group. Poor performance may also indicate that the instructional material is too difficult.

Of course, continued observation of student performance on daily assignments such as worksheets, independent projects, and choices of books during free reading periods contributes significantly to the review of each student's progress. However, unless a means is developed to record your observations of student performance, you may not remember each student's strengths and weaknesses in planning future lessons. The teacher's guide could become your record of what students know and have yet to learn.

Commercially developed recording systems are available, usually as part of skills management systems like The Wisconsin Design for Reading Skill Development (1973) or the Science Research Associates Mastery Kit (1974). Many basal reading programs also have management systems available.

One school developed their own progress chart (Figure 4.4). The chart reflects most word attack skills and could be expanded to include other areas of concern in reading. Skills could be added or deleted to better serve the instructional concerns of particular schools and teachers. Printed on a manilla folder sized cardboard, the chart can be used to hold recent assessment information useful for planning weekly assignments and creating special skills groups.

A modified checklist procedure is used to record student strengths. Where appropriate (letter/sound correspondence, etc.), the term *mastery* is used. Elsewhere, the terms *reads* and *spells* are employed. The teacher records the month and year when a particular skill is *introduced* (I); then, when the student can read/spell that pattern well, the teacher checks *reads* (R)/*spells* (S). The chart accompanies the student from year to year, or from classroom teacher to reading specialist, to facilitate communication. Skills checked M (mastery), R (reads), or S (spells) are reviewed in later lessons.

Such charts allow teachers to review the progress of each student on specific skills. A blank cell might indicate the need for additional instruction, a special worksheet, or the creation of a special skills group to consolidate the student's knowledge in this area.

While it does take time to review student progress, there is no other way to match effectively your own teaching expertise and the materials you have at hand to the needs and interests of students.

Investigate. Examine discrepancies between test scores and daily class performance.

As part of the VERIFIcation process, compare student test scores with their inclass performance. Usually, the manuals of standardized tests provide estimates of the degree to which particular scores are unreliable or can change on a random basis from one testing experience to the next. This fluctuation of test scores is termed the standard error of measurement (SEmeas) and is normally provided for each subtest in the examiner's manual. Single scores should always be thought of as a midpoint within a range of possible scores. When interpreting scores, add or subtract 1 SE_{meas} to the single score point to obtain a range or score band. This will provide a more accurate picture of the student's true score (see Chapter Five for a more detailed discussion of Standard Error of Measurement).

Many factors combine to affect how a student performs on a test at any given moment. If you observe that a student's scores are lower than inclass performance would suggest, consider that nonacademic factors, such as fatigue or disinterest, may have contributed toward the lower test score. On the other hand, if the student's scores are higher than inclass performance

Figure 4.4

PUPIL PROGRESS CHART

GRADE: _____ TEACHER: _____
GRADE: _____ TEACHER: _____
GRADE: _____ TEACHER: _____
GRADE: _____ TEACHER: _____
GRADE: _____ TEACHER: _____
GRADE: _____ TEACHER: _____
GRADE: _____ TEACHER: _____

KEY

R - Reads   D - Defines   M - Mastery
S - Spells   I - Introduced   a - adequate
W - Writes

ALPHABET

LETTER	Naming I	Naming M	Visual Discrimination I	Visual Discrimination M	Matching Sound/Letter I	Matching Sound/Letter M	Sound Production I	Sound Production M	Manuscript I	Manuscript M	Cursive Lower I	Cursive Lower M	Cursive Upper I	Cursive Upper M
A														
B														
C														
C (cat)														
D														
F														
G														
G (huge)														
H														
J														
K														
L														
M														
N														
P														
R														
S														
T														
V														
Q(U)														
W														
X														
Y														
Z														
E														
I														
O														
U														

READING READINESS

	adequate
Directionality { Left-to-Right	
Top-to-Bottom	
Visual Discrimination	
Visual Memory	
Auditory Discrimination	
Auditory Memory	
Kinesthetic Readiness	

SIGHT VOCABULARY

GRADE	adequate
1	
2	
3	
4	
5	
6	

Canney

Table rotated to landscape. Header at top: **SPECIAL TEACHER NOTES** — with sub-columns **major series used** and **comments**.

STUDY SKILLS	K	1	2	3	4	5	6
Reference Materials							
1. Dictionary							
locate words							
selects appropriate definition							
pronunciation keys							
guide words							
3. Encyclopedia							
locates subject							
guide words							
cross-references							
4. Card Catalog							
subject							
title							
author							
5. Thesaurus							
6. Atlas							
7. Filmstrips							
8. References by topic							
9. Glossary							
10. Bibliography							
11. Footnotes							
12. Maps							
13. Graphs							
14. Charts							
15. Takes notes from writings							
films							
lectures							
Reporting Skills							
1. Summarizes main idea of sentence							
paragraph							
2. Places events in proper sequence							
3. Identifies topic sentence							
4. Report Formats:							
oral							
composition							
book report							
summary							

SPECIAL TEACHER NOTES section rows labeled K, 1, 2, 3, 4, 5, 6 (major series used / comments).

Figure 4.4 (continued)

PREDICTABLE SPELLING PATTERNS
(SINGLE SYLLABLE WORDS)

CVC closed syllable	I	R	S	CVCe silent E	I	R	S	CV open syllable	I	R	S	CVVC vowel teams	I	R	S
a												ai			
e												ay			
i												ea			
o												ee			
u												ei			
y												ie			
												oa			

SPECIAL SPELLING PATTERNS
(SINGLE SYLLABLE WORDS)

	I	R	S		I	R	S
alk				ost			
all				ough			
ight				ff			
ild				ll			
ind				ss			
old				zz			

SYLLABLE PATTERNS
(WORDS OF MORE THAN ONE SYLLABLE)

	I	R	S
closed syllable (con/fess)			
open syllable (fi/nal)			
double consonant (fun/ny)			
r - controlled (par/ent)			
with (cle) (ca/ble)			

VOWEL CLUSTERS

	I	R	S		I	R	S
au (auto)				aw			
ea (head)				ew (few)			
ie (chief)				ow (show)			
oi (boil)				ow (how)			
oo (look)				oy			
oo (boot)							
ou (stout)							
ue (blue)							
ui (suit)							

L & R CONTROLLED VOWELS

	I	R	S		I	R	S
al				are			
ar				ore			
er				air			
ir				ear (fear)			
or				ear (pear)			
ur				our (sour)			

CONTRACTIONS

	I	R	S
word + are			
word + have			
word + is			
word + not			
word + will/shall			
word + would			

CONSONANT CLUSTERS

	I	R	S		I	R	S		I	R	S
-ck				sc				-nd			
-tch				sk				-nt			
ch				sl				-ct			
sh				sm				-pt			
wh				sn				-sp			
th (this)				sp				-lm			
th (thin)				st				-ng			
-th				sw				-sk			
				bl				-mp			
				cl				-lk			
				fl				-nk			
				gl				-rk			
				pl				-ft			
				br				scr			
				cr				spl			
				dr				spr			
				fr				str			
				gr				squ			
				pr				thr			
				tr				kn			
								gn			
								wr			
								-dge			
								gh.			
								ph /f/			
								-gh /f/			

Canney

SUFFIXES

	I	S	D
ed			
er			
est			
ing			
ance,ence,cy			
ar, er, or			
ent			
ful			
ic, ically			
ity			
less			
ly			
ment			
ness			
sion, tion			

PREFIXES

	I	S	D
anti			
de			
dis			
ex			
extra			
il, im, ir			
inter			
mis			
non			
over			
pre			
re			
semi			
sub			
super			
trans			
un			
under			
with			

ALPHABETIZING

	M	I
by initial letter		
by first two letters		
by whole word		

FIGURES OF SPEECH

	synonyms	antonyms	homonyms
1			
2			
3			
4	d	d	d
5	d	d	d
6	d	d	d

SENTENCE PATTERNS

	I	R	W
noun - verb			
noun - verb - noun			
noun - linking verb - noun			
noun - linking verb - adjective			
noun - linking verb - adverb			
passive			
negative			

PUNCTUATION

	1	2	3	4	5	6
capitalization						
proper nouns						
sentences						
titles						
period						
question mark						
exclamation mark						
possessives						
comma						
colon						
semi-colon						
abbreviations						

PLURALIZATION

	I	R	S
-s			
-ves			
-s/z/			
-ies			
-es			

KNOWLEDGE OF LITERARY FORMATS

	dialect	letters	newspapers	poetry	humorous	mystery	autobiography	science fiction	historical	science	fantasy	biography
initial exposure												
recognizes format												
identifies characteristic elements of												
is able to write in this format												

would have led you to expect, examine the types of activities you are using in your classroom. It is possible that the test is not accurately measuring what has been presented or that the student is inconsistent in the ability to use the skills (or that you may have underestimated the student's reading ability).

Such efforts to *investigate* discrepant pieces of information about student performance will contribute significantly toward your overall teaching effectiveness.

Formulate. Consider instructional plans in light of test scores but include the student in some of the planning.

When test results are considered as an indication of progress and are presented as indicating strengths rather than weaknesses (skills learned rather than items missed), then they can be used positively. Most people tend to persist in something when they experience early and frequent success in it and to lose interest when their efforts repeatedly lead to failure. Since poor readers have usually experienced more than their share of failure, especially on tests, using test results in a positive manner to encourage renewed effort may prove beneficial. In addition to a conference with a student, a visual chart that describes progress may prove helpful in maintaining student interest and suggesting new instructional plans.

Interpret. Use test results to assist in determining the effectiveness of instruction and interpret all test data in light of your knowledge about the students and the instructional objectives.

There is no substitute for sound judgment. Teachers should know the instructional capabilities of their students better than anyone else. This does not mean, however, that teachers can afford to ignore evidence that is inconsistent with their beliefs. For example, Charlie was a student who regularly received Cs and Ds in school. What the teachers thought of his ability was never clear. In taking the Scholastic Aptitude Test in eighth grade, prior to entering high school, Charlie scored 30 points higher on the test than the "best" student in the class. What factors contributed to Charlie's poor performance in class? One dismaying possibility is that his teachers "knew" that Charlie was a C and D student and, consequently, he was seldom expected or encouraged to do better.

The point is that people may slip easily into interpreting information in terms of their expectations. Teachers must always subject their interpretations to independent (outside) verification and to question any discrepancies they observe. In this framework lies the key to the successful use of test scores: your willingness to VERIFI what you think you know about your students.

Using Assessment to Guide Instruction

The information obtained through measures of reading performance, including daily observations, can be used to suggest the need for programatic changes and to guide instruction.

The purpose of assessment continues to be the determination of student progress in learning to read and the acquisition of evidence to guide programatic changes in light of that purpose.

In a single building, where the conventional unit of analysis is the classroom or a grade level, scores on standardized achievement tests or criterion referenced tests in skills management programs may be used by the principal or reading teacher to evaluate the school reading program. If large discrepancies in student performance appear, questions about particular classroom reading programs may require that the principal and teacher(s) confer about reading instruction in that building.

The principal might also be interested in identifying strengths and weaknesses in the reading program, especially across grade levels. For example, the reading program adopted for the primary grades may be developing superior decoding skills in the students so that reading achievement scores are above average. However, the principal may observe a sharp drop in reading test scores in fourth grade, suggesting that the primary reading program may not be balanced sufficiently to produce students who read text with comprehension, not simply decode print. In this setting, combining reading scores by grade level may reveal serious deficiencies (or strengths!) in the school's reading curriculum and prompt the establishment of a special curriculum committee to study the reading program.

If test data are used to assess program effectiveness, these questions may prove helpful:

1. How do students compare in reading growth at the same grade level, ability level, and cultural/economic group? In this type of analysis, national, state, and district norms are especially helpful because they provide an independent standard for comparison.

2. How well have the students attained specific program objectives? While district norms for standardized achievement tests might be used, group diagnostic reading tests, criterion referenced tests, and teacher made tests are also helpful.

3. How well are students progressing this year in light of past achievement in reading? Parents and teachers alike are interested in this comparison. A marked change in reading growth might be a powerful indicator of program strengths and weaknesses, although other nonprogramatic factors could produce similar changes.

4. How effective is this program with students of different ability levels? Perhaps a special reading program is needed for the more able students, the slowest readers, or the culturally different students.

While these questions focus on reading program effectiveness, in the final analysis each student's progress must be of primary concern. No program has ever been found to be 100 percent successful; consequently, to teach diagnostically requires that teachers attend to each student's needs. Questions like these can help individualize instruction:

1. Is there a need to provide further instruction in this area?

2. Is further practice all that is necessary to consolidate the student's knowledge in this area?

3. Is a different instructional approach needed for this student?

4. Is there a need for materials that more appropriately match this student's interests and ability?
5. Is there some indication that the student belongs with another group?

In seeking answers to these questions, an examination of achievement tests, diagnostic tests, quizzes, assignments and general classroom performance should contribute useful information for you to assess student growth in reading. Teachers prepared to VERIFI the observations they make can expect to discover new ways to assist their students toward becoming independent and critical readers.

References

1. Gambrell, Linda, and Robert Wilson. *Focussing on the Strengths of Children.* Belmont, California: Fearon Press, 1972.
2. Manning, John. "Using Every Pupil Response Techniques to Manage Skills Instruction," personal communication, 1973.
3. Otto, Wayne, and Eunice Askov. *The Wisconsin Design for Reading Skill Development.* Minneapolis: National Computer Systems, 1970.

Chapter Five
Definitions of Measurement Terms

Fred Pyrczak
California State University at Los Angeles

These definitions are arranged topically, with topics arranged to maximize understanding for readers who wish to read the chapter in its entirety. The following alphabetical guide to the definitions is designed for those who seek information on specific terms.

Stanine	77
Survey Test	75
Validity	77

Types of Tests

Norm referenced test—a test that is tried out with a sample of examinees called a norm group so that an individual's performance can be described relative to that of the group. Often, the norm group consists of a carefully selected sample drawn from across the nation.

Norm referenced tests permit us to make statements such as this one: "Roger's performance was considerably better than that of the majority in the norm group, which consisted of students at his own grade level." Assuming that there were no special considerations in Roger's case, we probable would conclude that Roger's reading ability is above average. (See "Criterion Referenced Test.")

Criterion referenced test—a test designed to measure the extent to which an examinee can perform a desired behavior. A criterion referenced test usually is used to determine whether a student has reached a desired performance standard, hence the word *criterion*. The standard is determined independently of how a sample of examinees may have performed on the test. Usually, the standard is determined on the basis of the importance of the skill(s) being tested to the next skill in a hierarchy of skills or on the basis of the importance of the skill(s) to crucial, everyday activities.

A criterion referenced test usually measures a cluster of closely related skills. Often, the items in such a test are derived directly from a homogeneous group of instructional objectives. Criterion referenced tests usually have this characteristic since performance standards are easier to establish for tests confined to a limited number of objectives than they are for wide ranging tests.

The characteristics of a criterion referenced test may be understood by considering this example. Suppose we built a test on initial consonant sounds. The content of the test is limited in scope and refers to a clearly identifiable and restricted reading objective. We could establish a performance standard in terms of numbers of items that must be marked correctly before a student is ready to move on to the next instructional objective, which might cover consonant blends. Unfortunately, there is no simple mechanical rule for establishing a performance standard for a test of this type. The test constructor or teacher would have to establish the standard in light of what is known about the importance of the skill tested to the next skill in the instructional sequence; in the absence of objective information on this matter, the standard would have to be established on a more or less subjective basis. Note that the performance of some group of examinees, such as other students in the class, would not be used to establish the standard.

Domain referenced test—a test in which the tasks are based upon a systematic analysis of specific subskills underlying a broad skill area called a domain. To the extent that we can identify all of the subskills and associated processes that underlie the domain of reading, we can build a domain referenced test by systematically sampling subskills to be covered in the test. Note that all good tests are based upon careful planning of skills to be measured. The crucial difference between a domain referenced test and other types of tests is the degree to which the tasks for a test are based upon a systematic sample of subskills and processes thought to underlie the entire domain.

Development of domain referenced tests is a relatively new endeavor. To reduce the scope of the task, some researchers are concentrating on the development of domain referenced tests that cover only one or more portions of the domain of reading.

Diagnostic test—a test that measures reading skills that are thought to be independent and yields a separate score for each skill. Diagnostic tests are based upon the notion that there are discrete reading skills; the portion of a diagnostic test that measures a given skill often is called a subtest. For example, the Diagnostic Reading Scales by Spache yields separate scores for

Word Recognition, Oral Reading, Silent Reading, and eight subtests in Phonics. Analysis of the pattern of scores indicates an examinee's areas of strength and weakness (see "Survey Test").

Survey test—a test that measures a variety of reading skills but yields only one score to represent an examinee's overall performance. In practice, few tests are pure survey tests since most yield two or more scores that may be compared in order to diagnose areas of strength and weakness (see "Diagnostic test"). Tests which measure only a limited number of broadly defined reading skills, however, often are referred to as survey tests. For example, the Davis Reading Test commonly is referred to as a survey test even though it yields separate scores for level-of-comprehension and speed-of-comprehension.

Group test—a test designed to be administered to a group of examinees at one time. Most group tests present examinees with written materials as well as oral directions; examinees are asked to respond by making marks on an answer sheet or in a test booklet (see "Individual test").

Individual test—a test designed to be administered to only one student at a time. Obviously, individual tests are less efficient than group tests because fewer students can be tested in a given amount of time. They are more flexible, however, for three reasons. First, they can be used to test skills (such as oral reading ability) that cannot be tested in a group situation. Second, when test directions permit, we can ask additional questions to be sure that a student understands the tasks being presented. Finally, we can adjust the beginning and ending level of a test according to a student's ability. For example, if the test directions permit and if the items are arranged in order of difficulty, we may stop testing once an examinee has missed a given number of consecutive items (see "Group test").

Types of Scores

Percentile rank—a type of score that indicates the percent of examinees in a norm group that scored below a given point.

Juan's percentile rank of 79, for example, indicates his performance on a test was better than that of 79 percent of the examinees in the norm group. The norm group for a test usually consists of a national sample of examinees at a given grade level. (See "Norm referenced test.")

Percentile band—a range of percentile ranks for an individual that helps us adjust our interpretation in light of random errors. We know that most scores deviate somewhat from what we would obtain if we could measure with complete precision. For example, if Bertha obtained a percentile rank of 89 on a vocabulary subtest and the band for her score ranged from 86 to 92, we would know with a specified degree of confidence that if we could measure with perfect precision, she would probably obtain a score somewhere between 86 and 92. The degree of confidence usually is 68 percent; that is, chances are 68 out of 100 that her true score is between 86 and 92.

When bands are given for two or more subtests, we can use them to interpret subtest score differences. For example, if Bertha also obtained a percentile rank of 81 on a comprehension subtest and had a band that ranged from 75 to 87, we would see that the bands for vocabulary and comprehension overlap. When bands overlap, we may conclude that the difference between the two performances may not be of practical importance in light of the lack of precision associated with the test.

Grade equivalent—a type of score that indicates the grade level (expressed in months of a grade) at which the average examinee in a norm group had a given number right. For example, Sarah's grade-equivalent of 5.7 indicates that the number of items she marked correctly was equal to that of the average norm-group examinee enrolled in the seventh month of the fifth grade.

Grade equivalents do *not* indicate the appropriate grade placement for an examinee. To understand why this is so, suppose that Sarah was enrolled in the third grade and took a test containing second, third, and fourth grade material. Her grade equivalent of 5.7 cannot possibly mean that she can do fifth grade work since she was not tested on fifth grade material. It merely tells us that she can perform second, third, and fourth grade tasks as well as the average students in the seventh month of the fifth grade can perform these below grade level tasks. Even if Sarah's grade equivalent had fallen within the grade level range covered by the material in the test, it would not indicate appropriate grade placement for her since her score would represent some unknown combination of successes and failures on tasks for three different grade levels. Because of possible misinterpretations of grade equivalents, the most recent edition of *Standards for Educational and Psychological Tests and Manuals* calls upon test publishers to abandon or discourage the use of grade equivalents. For comparing a student's performance with that of a norm group, other types of scores such as percentile ranks are preferred.

Stanine—a type of score that places students into one of nine categories based upon the performance of a norm group. A stanine of "1," for example, indicates that the examinee's performance was roughly equivalent to that of the bottom four percent of those in the norm group. The following figure shows the meanings of stanines.

Stanine	1	2	3	4	5	6	7	8	9
Percent of Norm Group	Bottom 4%	7%	12%	17%	Middle 20%	17%	12%	7%	Top 4%

Stanines are useful when coarse groupings of examinees are desired.

Essential Characteristics of Tests

Validity—usefulness of a test for a given purpose. A reading readiness test designed to predict reading achievement, for example, is valid to the extent that it makes good predictions. A reading achievement test designed to measure second grade achievement is valid to the extent that is measures representative reading skills covered in instruction. Since the particular skills taught in two different second grade classrooms may vary, a test may be a valid measure of achievement in one classroom but not the other.

Note that a test may be valid for an illegal or unethical purpose. A test that discriminates against members of a minority group is a valid test for a test user who seeks to discriminate; it is invalid for one who wishes to measure and evaluate without discrimination. Hence, any discussion of validity must deal with the suitability of the purpose for which a test will be used.

Validity is sometimes divided into four major types:

Construct validity—the goodness of a test judged in terms of the extent to which the scores yielded by the test are meaningful in light of our theories and common sense notions. For example, a reading test that consistently failed to show gains for students exposed to systematic, intensive, and long term reading instruction (across different programs and different groups of examinees) would be said to lack construct validity, given that we have reason to believe that reading instruction does affect reading ability.

Content validity—The goodness of a test judged in terms of the appropriateness of the content (and skills) covered by the test.

Careful test planning is the key to insuring a high degree of content validity. Most commercial test publishers go to great pains to draw up outlines of content and skills commonly taught at specified grade levels and use them as a basis for writing test items. Teachers can produce tests with a high degree of content validity by drawing representative samples of objectives used for instruction and writing one or more test items per objective.

Criterion related validity—the goodness of a test judged in terms of the extent to which scores correlate with (put examinees in the same rank order as) some independent measurements of the trait being measured. For example, some reading tests have been validated by correlating the test scores with independent ratings of reading ability made by teachers.

When a test is administered at about the same time as the independent measurements are obtained, we say that we are estimating the test's *concurrent validity*, a type of criterion related validity. If we administered a test at about the same time teachers assigned grades in reading, for example, and correlated the test scores with teachers' grades, we would be estimating concurrent validity. When the test is administered at a time substantially in advance of the collection of independent measurements, we say that we are estimating the test's *predictive validity*, another type of criterion related validity. If we administered the test at the beginning of the first grade, and correlated the scores with teachers' grades assigned at the end of first grade, we would be estimating predictive validity.

The degree of criterion related validity possessed by a test usually is expressed with a correlation coefficient, a statistic with a range from -1.00 to +1.00. When used for expressing criterion related validity, the coefficient usually is known simply as a "validity coefficient." In practice, validity coefficients are positive in value. A coefficient close to "one" indicates high validity; a coefficient close to "zero" indicates low validity. Validity coefficients larger than .75 are rare.

Face validity—the goodness of a test as judged by its appearance. Usually, face validity refers to the goodness of a test from the point of view of people who are not trained in measurement. Face validity is not a scientific concept. It is important for tests to have face validity, however, in order to promote public acceptance of tests and testing.

Because there currently is a great interest in criterion referenced testing, individuals working on the theory for such tests have recently developed new, specialized notions of validity. Most can be classified in terms of the major categories given above. For example, for criterion referenced tests based upon specific instructional objectives, we may examine "congruence validity"—the extent to which independent judges can match test items with objectives when they are given the items in random order. This type of validity may be thought of as a specialized type of "content validity."

Reliability—consistency of scores. The following illustrates one of the meanings of "consistency" when we are talking about norm referenced tests:

> The vocabulary knowledge of two students was measured with a test. James was found to have the most knowledge; Stan was found to have the least. A few days later, vocabulary knowledge was measured again with the same test. Again, James was found to have the most knowledge, and Stan was found to have the least. The two sets of results were consistent; the test was reliable. Note that we have not determined how useful (valid) our measurements are for a given purpose (see "Validity").

Reliability of norm referenced tests is expressed as a "reliability coefficient," a statistic with a range from -1.00 to +1.00. In practice, reliability coefficients are positive in value. A value close to 1.00 indicates high reliability; a value close to 0.00 indicates low reliability. Reliability coefficients of .80 and above are common and desirable for norm referenced tests. There is a variety of ways to estimate the reliability of norm referenced tests, and each has a different name. Hence, test manuals will use terms such as "split-half reliability," "parallel forms reliability," and "Kuder-Richardson reliability."

The reliability of criterion referenced tests is also a matter of concern, but the reliability of such tests is not usually expressed as a reliability *coefficient*. Other types of information should be provided—such as the percentage of examinees who may be misclassified as reaching the performance standard as a result of lack of precision in the test. Unfortunately, such information often is lacking for currently available criterion referenced tests.

Standard error of measurement—(abbreviated S_{meas} or SE $_{meas}$) is a statistic that tells us how many score points we should "allow" for random errors that result from factors such as guessing and the emotional and physical status of examinees. For example, if Chuck obtained a score of 65 on a test with a standard error of measurement of seven points, he would probably obtain a score somewhere within seven points of 65 (58-72) if we could measure without error. Our allowance would be sufficient in about two-thirds of the cases; that is, we have about 68 percent confidence that the allowance is large enough. Therefore, in order not to deceive ourselves as to the accuracy of a score, it is best to think of a score as probably occurring within a band of scores rather than at a specific point.

The standard error of measurement is related to the reliability of a test. Other things being equal, the higher the reliability, the smaller the standard error of measurement will be. The relationship is not perfect, however, since the variance (differences) in test scores must also be taken into account in computing S_{meas}.

Ruling the World?

Constitutionalism, International Law, and Global Governance

Edited by

JEFFREY L. DUNOFF
Temple University Beasley School of Law

JOEL P. TRACHTMAN
Fletcher School of Law and Diplomacy, Tufts University

CAMBRIDGE UNIVERSITY PRESS

CAMBRIDGE UNIVERSITY PRESS
Cambridge, New York, Melbourne, Madrid, Cape Town, Singapore, São Paulo, Delhi

Cambridge University Press
32 Avenue of the Americas, New York, NY 10013-2473, USA

www.cambridge.org
Information on this title: www.cambridge.org/9780521735490

First published 2009

Printed in the United States of America

A catalog record for this publication is available from the British Library.

Library of Congress Cataloging in Publication data
Ruling the world? : constitutionalism, international law,
and global governance / edited by Jeffrey L. Dunoff, Joel P. Trachtman.
p.   cm.
Includes bibliographical references and index.
ISBN 978-0-521-51439-2 (hardback) – ISBN 978-0-521-73549-0 (pbk.)
1. Constitutional law.   2. International law.   3. Globalization.   4. International cooperation.
5. International organization.   I. Dunoff, Jeffrey L., 1960–   II. Trachtman, Joel P.   III. Title.
K3165.R86   2009
342–dc22   2009002760

ISBN   978-0-521-51439-2 hardback
ISBN   978-0-521-73549-0 paperback

Contents

The Puzzle of Democratic Legitimacy

Contributors

Samantha Besson, Professor of Public International Law and European Law, University of Fribourg, Switzerland

Michael W. Doyle, Harold Brown Professor of International Affairs, Law and Political Science, Columbia University

Jeffrey L. Dunoff, Professor of Law and Director, Institute for International Law and Public Policy, Temple University Beasley School of Law

Bardo Fassbender, Professor of International Law, University of the Armed Forces, Munich, Germany

Thomas M. Franck, Murry and Ida Becker Professor of Law Emeritus, New York University School of Law

Stephen Gardbaum, Professor of Law, UCLA School of Law

Daniel Halberstam, Eric Stein Collegiate Professor of Law and Director, European Legal Studies Program, University of Michigan

David Kennedy, University Professor of Law and David and Mariana Fisher University Professor of International Relations, Brown University, and Manley O. Hudson Visiting Professor of Law, Harvard Law School

Mattias Kumm, Professor of Law and Director Program in International and Comparative Law, New York University School of Law

Miguel Poiares Maduro, Advocate General, Court of Justice of the European Communities

Andreas L. Paulus, Chair of Public and International Law, Georg-August-University Göttingen, Germany

Joel P. Trachtman, Professor of International Law, The Fletcher School of Law and Diplomacy, Tufts University

Neil Walker, Professor of Public Law and the Law of Nature and Nations, School of Law, University of Edinburgh

Preface: International Institutions: Why Constitutionalize?

THOMAS M. FRANCK

[I]t can feel like a project of the utmost seriousness and urgency to interpret the world in constitutional terms.

–David Kennedy
"The Mystery of Global Governance"

International institutions, with a few minor and ad hoc exceptions, are firmly grounded in treaties that establish their objectives, conditions of membership, and internal and external operational parameters. These treaties are binding on their party members and, perhaps – in the instance of near-universal organizations – also on nonmembers.

It could be argued that it little matters whether such an institution's foundational instrument is regarded as a constitution. Yet leading thinkers, such as the authors of this volume, seem to think the issue is worth serious examination. They express strongly held views as to why the issue is important and argue that how it is answered can have a significant impact on the role and operation of leading international organizations.

An international organization grounded in a constitution, they believe, has a different gravitas from the many purely ad hoc reciprocal arrangements made for the passing convenience of states.

The authors of these chapters do not merely note the phenomenon of greater gravitas but also explore how constitutionalization affects the practice of an institutionalized system of cooperation. For one thing, it determines how the institution absorbs the need for change. Whereas a constitutionally based system accommodates and adapts to its own practice, lesser consensual arrangements tend to insist on strict literal construction of their terms and resist their transformation through interpretative practice.

In other words, the way the institution created by a constitutional treaty is authorized to operate can be affected by the way it actually discharges its responsibilities in practice. Consistent patterns in institutional practice may affect the ambit of the institution's jurisdiction and its modus operandi. Other more purely functional cooperative arrangements, when based on a treaty, are literally tied to the text that establishes their mandates.

One need but examine the evolving scope of jurisdiction exercised by the UN Security Council to see how the Charter's license, set out in article 2(7), to deal with matters not "essentially within the domestic jurisdiction of any state" has evolved and broadened in practice. Who, in 1945, would have thought that this jurisdictional formula could evolve to authorize collective military intervention in situations such as racism and anarchy occurring solely within a single state? Yet when it came to dealing with apartheid in Southern Rhodesia and South Africa or social anarchy in Somalia, the Charter, in the practice of the principal organs of the United Nations, has been definitely construed to permit intervention. This has been based not on a strict reading of text but rather on a clearly defining, gradually accruing body of institutional practice. Because the UN Charter is widely recognized as constitutional in nature, such adaption in practice is treated as inevitable.

The greater capacity of constitutionalized systems of cooperation to accommodate such operational evolution is the reason why keen observers of global governance insist on the "constitutionalization paradigm." There is, however, another valid reason for such insistence. Constitutions, in contrast to lesser arrangements for ongoing cooperation, contain elements of checks and balances intended to operate autonomously to prevent abuses of power by the institution. This may take the form of resisting the incorporation of new practices that seem to lead in erroneous directions. Precisely because constitution-based systems are understood to be, like a tree, capable of gradual growth, extra care is taken to trim the branches.[1] Constitutionalized systems ensure that the power of organic growth does not go institutionally unchecked and unbalanced.

In practice, this means that constitution-based systems of cooperation are structured to accommodate a form of separation of powers. This hallmark of constitutionalization further distinguishes these foundational instruments from such lesser forms of systematic cooperation as bilateral treaties and memoranda of understanding.

In the instance of the UN Charter, chapters 4, 5, 10, and 14 set out, respectively, the jurisdictional parameters of the General Assembly, Security Council, Economic and Social Council, and International Court of Justice.

---

[1] The expression "living tree" was first applied to describe the constitutional capacity for organic growth in Edwards v. Attorney-General for Canada, [1930] AC 124 (PC), at 136 (Lord Sankey).

Besides these black-letter texts, the constitutionally based institutions regularly refer to institutional practice to legitimate the evolving delineation that separates and coordinates the inevitably overlapping jurisdictions of the respective organs.

An example is the practice that has propelled the Security Council into responsibility for administering territories in transition. This used to be an exclusive prerogative of the Trusteeship Council and the 73(e) Committee of the General Assembly. More recently, however, in response to the challenge of an array of civil wars and failed states (Yugoslavia, Somalia, East Timor) the role of intervenor has increasingly devolved to the Security Council.

Practice and text, in a constitutionally based system, are supplemented by jurisprudence. When an institution is constitutionally based, the jurisdictional boundaries are usually policed and supervised by a tribunal. In the instance of the United Nations, this function is performed by the International Court of Justice, which, for example, has rendered opinions as to the respective (and overlapping) powers of the Security Council and General Assembly,[2] and those of the Security Council vis-à-vis the International Court of Justice itself.[3]

Implicit in such a constitutionalized system is the idea of judicial review, which subordinates assumptions of institutional jurisdiction to review for excès de pouvoir to prevent those powers given to international institutions from incurring the self-aggrandizement that afflicts all concentrations of power. This notion of judicial review acts as a balance to correct practices that, if left unrestrained, would facilitate excessive jurisdictional imperialism. A constitutionally based international organization is marked by an institutional process for determining, through "second opinions," when a part of the system is threatening to spin out of control.

It is the institutional capacity to limit evolutionary development through judicial review that justifies and legitimates the capacity of constitutionally based institutions to evolve in practice. It thus appears, paradoxically, that the constitutionalization of international systems of ongoing cooperation has the effect both of facilitating reform through the accommodation of institutional practice and of containing that impetus within limits impartially deducible from the tenor of the foundational instrument. The UN Charter is dramatic evidence of the capacity to achieve institutional reform through institutional practice, something richly illustrated by the ensuing chapters of

[2] Certain Expenses of the United Nations (art. 17, para. 2, of the Charter), (Advisory Opinion), 1962 I.C.J. Reports 151.
[3] Question of Interpretation and Application of the 1971 Montreal Convention Arising from the Aerial Incident at Lockerbie (Libyan Arab Jamahiriya v. United States), Preliminary Objections, 1998 I.C.J. Reports 115.

this book. But, the same Charter, by institutionalizing judicial review by the International Court of Justice, also creates the opportunity and the means for subjecting practice to scrutiny for conformity to the Charter's foundational parameters.

Of the several indicators of a constitutionalized system of institutionalized cooperation among states, this may be the most functionally significant: that it separates the respective areas of jurisdiction both among the organs of the institution and between the institution and its member states. In making this important move to a separation of powers, the foundational instrument, if it is to operate as a constitution, ensures that the lines separating the various concentrations of jurisdiction among the institution's organs will be patrolled by an independent expert legal body, such as the International Court of Justice. So will be the allocation of powers between the institution and its members. These lines of demarcation are essential to the efficacy of the institution, to its ability to adjust to changing priorities and issues, and to prevent it from growing into a Leviathan.

If a body like the United Nations is to retain its vitality and relevance over many decades of changing agendas, the distribution of functions and powers among its principal organs must be amenable to change through innovative practice and without necessarily invoking the cumbersome process of formal treaty amendment. The system must be capable of spontaneous regeneration through modifications achieved by agreed practice. Yet such regeneration must not go unchecked and unbalanced. To that end, the system must be "constitutional" – capable of organic growth, yet growth controlled by checks and balances deployed by a legitimate institutional umpire. To that end, the UN system is constitutionalized by the inclusion of a legitimate organ authorized to render "second opinions" regarding issues of jurisdiction arising among the principal organs and between the institution and its state members.

Thus, it is apparent that the issue of constitutionalization, which is so thoroughly canvassed in this volume, is far from one purely of theory but rather concerns itself profoundly with institutional efficacy. Is the institution capable of gradual, autochthonous growth, and, paradoxically, is it capable itself of curbing the institutional appetite for unlimited expansion of its powers? If, as in the instance of the United Nations, the answer is "yes," then its architects, almost certainly, have written a constitution. That makes it appropriate, as David Kennedy points out in his chapter, to think of the project of this book "not only as description but also as program." The point of recognizing the UN Charter as a constitution is to unleash the institution's capacity to evolve while subjecting that capacity to independent review for consistency with the institution's stated, essential purposes.

Acknowledgments

This volume reflects the contributions and advice of many colleagues and friends who have shared our interest in constitutional developments at transnational sites of governance. We have been fortunate to work with an extraordinary group of scholars, and to have enjoyed significant support from the institutions with which we are affiliated.

Temple University Beasley School of Law generously sponsored a book workshop in December 2007. The workshop afforded an opportunity for authors to present their papers and receive feedback from one another, as well as an outstanding group of experts, including Robert Ahdieh, Dan Bodansky, Elizabeth Borgwardt, Rebecca Bratspies, Allen Buchanan, Grainne de Burca, Orfeo Fioretos, Carol Gould, Larry Helfer, Duncan Hollis, Vicki Jackson, R. Daniel Kelemen, Harold Koh, Andrew Lang, Peter Lindseth, Burt Neuborne, Gerald Neuman, Ernst-Ulrich Petersmann, Mark Pollack, Russell Powell, Mark Rahdert, Jaya Ramji-Nogales, Steve Ratner, Henry Richardson, Kim Lane Scheppele, Joanne Scott, Peter Spiro, Andy Strauss, Mark Tushnet, and Joseph Weiler. We thank each of these individuals for their thoughtful comments and many constructive suggestions.

We are grateful to Temple Law School, and particularly to Dean Robert Reinstein, for supporting this event. We also thank Debbie Feldman, Dimitri Ferrell, Joel Houkom, and Dorothy Lee for their efforts in ensuring the success of the workshop.

Jeff Dunoff undertook research on this project while at Temple and during appointments as a Visiting Senior Research Scholar in the Program in Law and Public Affairs at the Woodrow Wilson School, Princeton University, and as a Visiting Professor at Harvard Law School. He is grateful for the support received from these institutions.

Joel Trachtman is grateful to The Fletcher School for its support during his work on this project, and to Jeremy Leong for his superb research assistance.

We express thanks to John Berger and the editorial team at Cambridge University Press for their support and guidance through the editorial and publishing processes.

Most of all, we thank our families – Theresa, Elizabeth and Joel, and Lauren, Hannah, Sam, and Aaron for their unflagging support of this project. They graciously tolerated the long hours during which this volume ruled our worlds, and we lovingly dedicate this book to them.

PART I: WHAT IS CONSTITUTIONALIZATION BEYOND THE STATE?

Understanding the Demand for International Constitutionalization

1. A Functional Approach to International Constitutionalization

JEFFREY L. DUNOFF AND JOEL P. TRACHTMAN

The problem of international constitutionalism is the central challenge faced by international philosophers in the twenty-first century.[1]

Introduction

This is a book about constitutional practice – and constitutional discourse – at transnational sites of governance. For some readers, this may seem an odd topic. As a historical matter, constitutional discourse has predominantly – but not exclusively – occurred in the domestic legal setting. However, as described in the essays in this volume, recent years have witnessed an intensification of constitutional discourse in many sites of transnational governance. In response, a rapidly growing body of scholarship explores the existence and implications of international constitutions. Drawing on insights from scholarship in international relations, international law, and global governance, the essays in this volume extend earlier efforts and describe, analyze, and advance international constitutional debates. To do so, these chapters examine the conceptual coherence and normative desirability of constitutional orders beyond the state and explore what is at stake in debates over global constitutionalism.

---

[1] Philip Allot, *The Emerging Universal Legal System*, 3 INT'L L.F. 12, 16 (2001).

We are grateful to Bill Alford, Louis Aucoin, Antonia Chayes, Daniel Drezner, Michael Glennon, Ryan Goodman, Hurst Hannum, Ian Johnstone, David Luban, Gerry Neuman, Jeswald Salacuse, Beth Simmons and Carlos Vazquez for exceptionally detailed reactions to earlier drafts. Versions of this paper were presented at seminars or workshops at the Fletcher School of Law and Diplomacy, Harvard Law School, Kennedy School of Government, Michigan Law School, and the Woodrow Wilson School at Princeton University, and we are grateful to participants at these events for useful comments and criticisms.

This is a particularly auspicious time to undertake such a project. As discussed below, the enhanced salience of debates over constitutional orders beyond the state reflects, in part, larger trajectories in international relations, including the increased density and reach of international norms, the increasing importance of new legal actors in international legal processes, and the rise of new topics of international legal regulation – along with an increasing sense that some of these developments threaten elements of domestic constitutional structures. Furthermore, debates over constitutionalization occur as the international community continues to adjust to the end of the bipolar era and as questions arise over the role and status of international norms in a rapidly changing international order. More broadly, debates over international constitutionalization are part of broader inquiries into global governance that are occurring in the international legal academy and in the policy sciences more generally, including around the concepts of legal pluralism and new governance. Thus, this volume appears at a time of great ferment in the highly diffuse and pluralistic processes of global governance, and at a scholarly moment consisting, as David Kennedy notes in his contribution, "both of great unknowing and of disciplinary reinvention."

In this brief introduction, we do not attempt a comprehensive survey of these diverse and complex trends. Rather, for current purposes it is sufficient to outline briefly some of the most important developments that have led to the current fascination with global constitutionalization. After situating debates over constitutionalization in this larger context, we argue that a functional approach to questions of global constitutionalization can be particularly fruitful at this time. As explained in more detail below, a functional approach can provide a set of conceptual tools and inquiries that scholars can use to identify and evaluate constitutional developments in various international domains.

We posit that the distinguishing feature of international constitutionalization is the extent to which law-making authority is granted (or denied) to a centralized authority. We thus focus on the extent to which international constitutions enable or constrain the production of international law. We also provide an additional goal of international legal constitutionalization: supplementing domestic constitutions that have been reduced in effect due to globalization. Hence our approach is largely taxonomic, rather than normative, and we take no position in this chapter on the general utility or desirability of international constitutionalization.

After outlining this approach to the functions of constitutionalization, we explain how a number of mechanisms associated with constitutionalization – including fundamental rights, direct effect, supremacy, and others – might be understood in terms of these functions. We then provide a constitutional matrix that identifies which constitutional mechanisms are found in various international regimes and that is a tool for comparison and analysis of different constitutional settlements. We conclude this chapter with some brief observations regarding the relationship between constitutionalization and constitutional pluralism, constitutional coordination, and constitutional synthesis.

I. The Demand for International Constitutionalization

A number of contemporary developments contribute to the demand for international constitutionalization. For current purposes, we focus on two of these developments: globalization and the fragmentation of international law. Although the two developments are related, and in some ways mutually reinforcing, for ease of exposition we treat them separately in the paragraphs that follow.

A. *Globalization*
Globalization is the umbrella term used to capture the enormous increase in the flow of people, capital, goods, services, and ideas across national borders. Several influential strands of thought suggest that pressures for international constitutionalization are a product of globalization and the accompanying increase in the reach and density of international legal norms. One goal of this volume is to examine this claim critically: to what extent does globalization drive constitutionalization in international law? In his contribution to this volume, Joel Trachtman analyzes the causes and consequences of constitutionalization at the WTO in terms of constitutional economics, focusing on globalization's role.

Preliminarily, we note as a descriptive matter that globalization has a mutually reinforcing relationship with certain types of international law, including prominently those types that advance market liberalization. The relationship is mutually reinforcing because, on the one hand, the increase in transnational activities associated with globalization induces greater demand for many forms of ordinary international law, including international economic law. On the other hand, international economic law facilitates the international flows of goods, capital, people, and ideas associated with globalization.

Other types of international law, such as human rights law or environmental law, generally do not promote globalization per se. However, these bodies of law may expand to address regulatory concerns that arise only with globalization – such as concerns regarding transnational externalities or regulatory competition – or with the advance of international law aimed at market liberalization. To the extent that international law of economic integration, international environmental law, and at least some types of human rights law address these types of concerns, perhaps they should be understood as subconstitutional or ordinary international law.

Hence, globalization expands the set of possible beneficial cooperative arrangements. At the same time, the increased transnational interactions that globalization enables give rise to the possibility of various forms of market or political failure. Therefore, increased globalization may make it more valuable for actors to enter into denser legal and institutional relationships, including constitutionalized relationships. Indeed, there may be a dialectical relationship between globalization and constitutionalization along the following lines: Technological and social change yields greater possibilities for beneficial international interactions, including prominently international commerce, but also including international environmental stewardship, international cooperation to combat organized crime, and so on. International legal rules become more valuable to realize the increased benefits of these international interactions. Increasing demand for production of international legal rules gives rise to increasing demand for international constitutional norms and processes that facilitate the production of international legal rules.

B. Fragmentation

Another prominent strand of thought understands international constitutionalization as a response to the fragmentation of the international legal order. International law is the product of highly decentralized processes. Specifically, international norms often develop in specialized functional regimes, such as human rights, environment, trade, or international criminal law. Each functionally differentiated area of law has its own treaties, principles, and institutions. However, the values and interests advanced by any particular regime are not necessarily consistent with those advanced by other specialized regimes. In practice, specialized law making, institution building, and dispute resolution in any particular field tend to be relatively insulated from developments in adjoining fields, risking inconsistent judgments, conflicting jurisprudence, and outcomes that fail to take sufficient account of the full range of relevant values.

Recent practice reveals several ways that conflicts can arise. Perhaps most dramatically, different tribunals can provide conflicting interpretations of a particular legal norm. Thus, for example, in considering whether Serbia and Montenegro was responsible for the acts of irregular forces during the conflict in the former Yugoslavia, the International Criminal Tribunal for the Former Yugoslavia (ICTY) considered the International Court of Justice's (ICJ) pronouncements regarding state responsibility in the *Nicaragua* case. The ICTY determined that the ICJ's interpretation was not a correct statement of international law on state responsibility and articulated its own test for determining when states are responsible for acts by irregular militias.[2] Thereafter, the ICJ revisited the question of state responsibility and reaffirmed the *Nicaragua* test. The ICJ found the ICTY's interpretation to be "unsuitable" and its arguments in favor of adopting its test "unpersuasive."[3] Furthermore, domestic and international tribunals can interpret the same international norm differently.[4]

Alternatively, conflicts can arise when an international body declines to follow a general rule of international law on the grounds that a *lex specialis* rule applies. A well-known example of this type of conflict occurred in the *Belilos* case, where the European Court of Human Rights (ECHR) declined to apply the general rules concerning treaty reservations and held (1) that a state's purported reservation to a treaty was invalid and (2) that the state was bound by the treaty.[5] Notably, the ECHR has justified its departure from established rules on treaty reservations by invoking the constitutional character of the European Convention on Human Rights.[6]

Moreover, conflicts can arise when disputes are considered by multiple fora in which potentially inconsistent norms from different international legal regimes are applicable. For example, the Chile–European Community swordfish dispute was submitted to World Trade Organization (WTO) dispute settlement and to a special chamber of the International Tribunal for the Law of the Sea. Notably, this form of conflict is not limited to interstate disputes; the proliferation of human rights and investment tribunals has enabled private parties to pursue identical or related claims in multiple fora, either simultaneously or sequentially. Multiple litigations arising out of the same facts raise serious efficiency and finality concerns as well as, of course, the very real possibility of conflicting judgments.[7]

---

[2] Prosecutor v. Tadic, Case No. IT-94-1-A, Judgment, para. 145 (July 15, 1999).

[3] *See* Case Concerning the Application of the Convention on the Prevention and Punishment of the Crime of Genocide (Bosnia and Herzegovina v. Serbia and Montenegro) 2007 I.C.J. 91 (Feb. 26), at para. 404 ("unpersuasive"); *id.* at para. 406 ("unsuitable").

[4] *See* Sanchez-Llamas v. Oregon, 548 U.S. 331, 356 (2006).

[5] Belilos v. Switzerland, 132 Eur. Ct. H.R. (ser. A) (1988).

[6] *See* Loizidou v. Turkey, 310 Eur. Ct. H.R. (ser. A), at para. 75 (1995) (preliminary objections).

[7] For a particularly notorious example of inconsistent judgments, *compare* Lauder v. Czech Republic, UNCITRAL, Final Award (Sept. 3, 2001) (London arbitral tribunal finds that state action did not constitute expropriation, did not violate obligation to provide fair and equitable treatment, and did not breach duty to provide investor with full protection

Finally, conflicts can arise when bodies "located" in one specialized area of international law are asked to interpret or apply norms generated in other specialized areas. For example, in the *Beef-Hormones* dispute, the European Community asked the WTO's Appellate Body (AB) to apply the precautionary principle in the context of the European Community's ban on beef from cattle treated with certain hormones. The AB suggested that the precautionary principle might be part of international environmental law but not general international law, and in any event was not applicable to the dispute. Similarly, in the *GMO* dispute, a WTO panel declined the invitation to refer to an international environmental treaty, and in the *Soft Drinks* dispute between the United States and Mexico, the AB declined to determine rights and duties under the North American Free Trade Agreement. These disputes suggest that the same case might be resolved differently in different tribunals, depending, inter alia, on the law that they apply.

Many claim that fragmentation raises questions about "[international law's] stability as well as the consistency of international law and its comprehensive nature"[8] – a view that finds expression in this volume in essays by Andreas Paulus and Mattias Kumm. To the extent that fragmentation arises because of the lack of centralized legislative and adjudicative institutions, constitutionalization can respond by providing centralized institutions or by specifying a hierarchy among rules or adjudicators. That is, constitutionalization can be seen as a way of introducing hierarchy and order, or at least a set of coordinating mechanisms, into an otherwise chaotic system marked by proliferating institutions and norms. Hierarchically superior norms and coordinating mechanisms can manage or resolve legal conflicts and thereby produce greater predictability and certainty for actors subject to the rules.

On the other hand, the claim that constitutionalization can bring order to an otherwise highly fragmented legal domain is highly controversial. Some claim that this argument presupposes a broad global agreement around core values that simply does not exist. Others view efforts to understand constitutionalization along these lines as thinly veiled political efforts by one specialized legal order or, more precisely, by specific international actors, to claim normative priority for one set of international legal norms over alternative norms. Indeed, some go as far as characterizing the quest for legal unity

and security) *with* CME Czech Republic B.V. v. Czech Republic, UNCITRAL, Final Award (Mar. 14, 2003) (Stockholm tribunal, considering the same fact pattern, finds state action to constitute expropriation, to violate fair and equitable treatment, and to deny investor full protection and security).

[8] *See, e.g.,* International Law Commission, *Report of the International Law Commission on Long-term Programme of Work,* ILC (LII)/WG/LT/L.1Add. 1 (July 25, 2000) at 26.

through constitutional norms as "a hegemonic project."[9] Others counter that the search for ways to mediate among different values is simply recognition – common in the domestic sphere – of the inescapable need to make trade-offs between different values. Thus, one of the issues explored throughout this volume is whether and in what circumstances constitutionalization is a normatively desirable response to the challenges posed by fragmentation.

Although we have discussed globalization and fragmentation separately, the phenomena are related. Increased globalization generates pressures for greater numbers of international rules in more areas of international life. And a greater density of international norms in greater numbers of functionally separate international regimes heightens the dangers associated with the fragmentation of international law. Hence, two of the most important developments contributing to pressures for international constitutionalization are deeply connected.

II. The Functional Dimensions of International Constitutionalization: Enabling, Constraining, and Supplemental Constitutionalization

Just as the relations among globalization, fragmentation, and constitutionalization are complex, so, too, is the phenomenon of international constitutionalization itself. Hence, many of the essays in this volume devote considerable energies to the descriptive task of explaining the roles and functions of constitutional norms on the international plane. In this section, we begin to develop a functionalist approach to identifying and analyzing international constitutionalization.

Our functional methodology permits us to avoid the definitional conundrums that mark so much of the literature on constitutionalism beyond the state. A functionalist approach permits conceptual analysis that is not premised upon a definition setting forth a group of necessary and sufficient conditions which determine whether a given order is constitutional or not. This "check list" approach to constitutionalization tends to push discourse towards terminological disputes, and thereby divert attention from substantive analysis. The definitional approach can also mistakenly suggest that international constitutionalism is a binary, "all or nothing" affair. As this chapter suggests, constitutionalism consists of a type – rather than a quantum – of rules.

---

[9] Martti Koskenniemi, *Global Legal Pluralism: Multiple Regimes and Multiple Modes of Thought* 5 (2005) (unpublished manuscript, on file with authors).

Undoubtedly, our functional approach to global constitutionalization suffers from the lack of certainty that a check list or other bright line approach would provide. But a functionalist methodology has the virtue of directing attention to the appropriate inquiry: the purposes that international constitutional norms are intended to serve. Thus, we turn to a description of the three key purposes that international constitutional norms serve.

For current purposes, we highlight three important functions that international constitutional norms play: (1) enabling the formation of international law (i.e., enabling constitutionalization), (2) constraining the formation of international law (i.e., constraining constitutionalization), and (3) filling gaps in domestic constitutional law that arise as a result of globalization (i.e., supplemental constitutionalization). In this section, we explain these three functions. We draw a bright line between measures designed to achieve these three functions, on the one hand, and ordinary international law, on the other hand. To the extent that a measure performs these functions, it is a rule of international constitutional law.

After completing our discussion of these three functions, in section III we explain how each of these functions is implemented through seven mechanisms that are commonly associated with constitutionalization: (1) horizontal allocation of authority, (2) vertical allocation of authority, (3) supremacy, (4) stability, (5) fundamental rights, (6) review, and (7) accountability or democracy. Note that we assess these mechanisms with respect to how they implement the enabling, constraining, and supplemental constitutional functions. These mechanisms are distinct ways to achieve these functions, but in this chapter we do not develop a theory of the relationship and choice among these mechanisms.

A. Enabling Constitutionalization
First, some constitutional norms enable the production of ordinary international law (i.e., enabling constitutionalization). Treaty provisions that endow international bodies with the ability to create secondary international law fall into this category. For example, the treaties establishing the European Union set forth complex procedures for the creation of secondary union legislation. Similarly, the United Nations Charter, discussed by Bardo Fassbender and Michael Doyle in their contributions to this volume, empowers the Security Council, under certain circumstances, to establish norms that are binding upon UN member states. These are prominent examples of what we understand as enabling constitutionalization. International tribunals, as well, sometimes engage in enabling constitutionalization. Landmark European Court of Justice (ECJ) decisions, such as *Costa v. ENEL*, *Van Gend en*

Loos, and others discussed in Daniel Halberstam's contribution to this volume, are examples of international bodies effectively reallocating law-making authority both among various international actors and between national and supranational actors.

From the perspective of new institutional economics, including constitutional economics, enabling constitutionalization may be understood as an aggregate allocation of authority, in the sense that it allocates authority over multiple decisions at once, in a general or nonspecific way. Enabling constitutionalization determines allocations of authority rather than the content of the specific exercise of authority. Because of this aggregate nature, and because constitutional mechanisms operate over time, these are also allocations under a veil of uncertainty as to the distributive outcome of the aggregate allocation: the distributive consequences of the specific rules that will be established are not known in advance. The institutionalization associated with this allocation of authority becomes valuable when it enables relevant actors to cooperate more effectively: when it reduces either transaction costs or strategic costs of cooperation, or when it enables these actors to enter into cooperative arrangements that would otherwise have been unavailable.

B. Constraining Constitutionalization

Second, some international constitutional norms constrain the production of ordinary international law (i.e., constraining constitutionalization). Thus, for example, the European Court of Human Rights has consistently held that rules of the European Convention on Human Rights take precedence over other treaty commitments made by member states. The convention has a constitutional dimension insofar as it constrains the making or effect of inconsistent international law. Similarly, any number of foundational international legal norms – we might think of the constitutional commitment to state sovereignty,[10] and international norms of a *jus cogens* character – act as constraints on the production of ordinary international law.

Notably, enabling and constraining constitutionalization often appear together. Thus, for example, article 24(1) of the UN Charter confers certain powers on the Security Council; article 24(2) provides that, in exercising these powers, "the Security Council shall act in accordance with the Purposes and Principles of the United Nations." Thus, as Tom Franck notes in his preface to this volume, constitutionalized systems both authorize the exercise

---

[10] *See, e.g.,* IAN BROWNLIE, PRINCIPLES OF PUBLIC INTERNATIONAL LAW 287 (Oxford Univ. Press 6th ed. 2003) (characterizing the sovereignty and juridical equality of states the "basic constitutional doctrine of the law of nations").

of power and ensure that the exercise of power "does not go institutionally unchecked and unbalanced."

To the extent that constraining constitutionalization limits the scope of international law, it constrains the ability of states to use international law to effect certain purposes. In many instances, constraining constitutionalization preserves state autonomy and, to the extent international law would otherwise constrain individuals, individual autonomy. In other instances, where international law promotes individual liberties, as, for example, in connection with human rights law or certain types of international economic law, constraining constitutionalization may limit the scope of individual protections.

The notion of constraining constitutionalization outlined here suggests a rather different approach to the relationship between human rights law and international constitutionalization from that found in most of the literature. As Stephen Gardbaum points out in his contribution to this volume, most arguments over the constitutional nature of international human rights norms focus on the vertical dimension of human rights law and, specifically, the ways in which human rights norms empower individuals and protect them from certain forms of state action. For our purposes, however, much of this corpus of law should be considered ordinary international law, as it constrains domestic action. However, to the extent that international norms constrain international legal or international organizational action, they should be considered international constitutional law: constraining constitutionalization.[11]

With this understanding, it is ordinarily a category mistake to characterize as international constitutional law those forms of international law designed to constrain domestic action (but see our discussion of supplemental constitutionalization herein). Imposing constraints on state action is the function of ordinary international law, although it is certainly true, as Gardbaum

---

[11] For current purposes, we identify this category of international constitutional law but take no position on the debate over which, if any, human rights or other customary norms apply to specific international organizations. For a sense of the debate, *see, e.g.,* ILA Report of the 71st Conference, Berlin, Aug. 16–21, 2004, *Report of the International Law Association Committee on Accountability of International Organizations, available at* http://www.ila-hq.org/en/committees/index.cfm/cid/9 (last accessed March 10, 2009); ANDREW CLAPHAM, HUMAN RIGHTS OBLIGATIONS OF NON-STATE ACTORS (Oxford Univ. Press 2006) (discussing, inter alia, human rights obligations of the United Nations, World Bank, WTO, and other international organizations). For recent work on the international legal responsibility of international organizations, see Giorgio Gaja, *First Report of the Special Rapporteur,* U.N .Doc. A/CN.4/532 (2003); Giorgio Gaja, *Second Report of the Special Rapporteur,* U.N. Doc. A/CN.4/541 (2004); Giorgio Gaja, *Third Report of the Special Rapporteur,* U.N. Doc. A/CN.4/553 (2005) (draft articles).

suggests, that some of these ordinary international law norms may perform a constitutional function at the state level.

We expect to see greater demands for constraining constitutionalization as international law becomes more demanding and intrusive, and particularly with moves toward international law making without unanimous state consent. The European Union provides a striking example in this regard. Over time, various EC and EU treaties have shifted legislative authority away from the member-state-dominated Council and have increased the use of majority voting. We understand these developments as enabling constitutionalization. However, enabling moves will virtually inevitably prompt constraining moves. One notable constraining move is the Maastricht Treaty's subsidiarity clause, which provides that the European Community "shall take action . . . only if and in so far as the objectives of the proposed action cannot be sufficiently achieved by the member-States and can therefore, by reason of the scale or effects of the proposed action, be better achieved by the Community."[12] The subsidiarity principle is a critical reaction to gradual shifts in legislative authority to EC institutions and is intended to limit the reach of EU legislation and thereby preserve a degree of national and local regulatory autonomy.[13]

We also expect to see greater demands for constraining constitutionalization following the creation of strong forms of international adjudication. Here, the field of investment provides a good example. Before 1995, relatively few international investment disputes were submitted to international arbitration. However, in recent years, states have entered into more than one thousand investment treaties. All of these treaties grant investors a set of specific substantive rights, and virtually all of the treaties give investors a direct cause of action against the host state. As a result, the number of investment arbitrations has increased exponentially – as has the number of inconsistent or otherwise problematic awards – giving rise to what practitioners and commentators have characterized as a legitimacy crisis. Current debates over the need for a standing appellate body to correct legal errors and bring coherency to this body of law can be understood as calls for a form of constraining constitutionalization.[14]

---

[12] Treaty Establishing the European Community, art. 3b, Nov. 10, 1997, 1997 O.J. (C340) 3.

[13] *See* Edward T. Swaine, *Subsidiarity and Self-Interest: Federalism at the European Court of Justice*, 41 HARV. INT'L L.J. 1, 4–6 (2000).

[14] *See, e.g.*, Susan D. Franck, *The Legitimacy Crisis in Investment Treaty Arbitration: Privatizing Public International Law through Inconsistent Decisions*, 73 FORD. L. REV. 1521 (2005); William H. Knull III & Noah D. Rubins, *Betting the Farm on International Arbitration: Is It Time to Offer an Appeal Option?* 11 AM. REV. INT'L ARB. 531, 559–563 (2000). *See also* 19 U.S.C. § 3802(b)(3)(G)(iv) (2000) (grant of trade promotion authority to the president,

C. Supplemental Constitutionalization

Finally, we identify a third category of norms that seems to merit inclusion in international constitutional law. Some argue that the increasing scope and density of international norms reduces, or threatens to reduce, the effect of certain types of domestic constitutional law. A third category of international constitutional law thus consists of international legal norms that arise in response to domestic constitutional deficiencies, particularly where the deficiency either arises from or is exacerbated by increased globalization and the increasing density of international law. We call this third category "supplemental constitutionalization."[15] Perhaps the best way to understand supplemental constitutionalization is as a way to maintain a steady equilibrium of constitutional arrangements in the domestic setting, under globalization. To maintain such an equilibrium, it sometimes becomes necessary to protect or promote domestic constitutional values at the international level.

Supplemental constitutionalization can be distinguished from enabling and constraining constitutionalization because it represents a particular type of constitutional subsidiarity. Constitutional subsidiarity implies that under some changes in technological or social circumstances, the vertical level at which it is appropriate to guarantee certain constitutional values may change. Supplemental constitutionalization responds to gaps in the domestic law constitutional framework that are created or accentuated by globalization. These gaps may take the form of failure to apply constitutional rules to circumstances that are difficult to distinguish from those to which domestic constitutional rules ordinarily apply but that are outside the reach of domestic constitutional rules, conflicts between the constitutional rules of different states, or the possibility of unstable or inefficient competition between constitutional rules of different states. One response to these phenomena is to agree on rules determining the scope of application of different states' constitutional rules – we might call these "choice of constitutional law rules."[16] An alternative response to these phenomena is to harmonize constitutional law rules or to establish constitutional law rules at the international level.

requiring that future trade agreements have "an appellate body or similar mechanism to provide coherence to the interpretation of investment provisions in trade agreements"). For an argument that an appellate tribunal is unwise and unnecessary, see Steven R. Ratner, *Regulatory Takings in Institutional Context: Beyond the Fear of Fragmented International Law,* 102 Am J. Int'l L. 475 (2008).

[15] For an alternative approach to this general idea, *see* Anne Peters, *Compensatory Constitutionalism: The Function and Potential of Fundamental International Norms and Structures,* 19 Leiden J. Int'l L. 579 (2006).

[16] Elsewhere, Trachtman refers to these as "tertiary rules." Joel P. Trachtman, *The Constitutions of the WTO,* 17 Eur. J. Int'l L. 623 (2006).

Both types of supplemental constitutional response, as they act on domestic legal systems rather than regulate the international legal system, share some features with ordinary international law. However, to the extent that these international norms address issues heretofore addressed by domestic constitutional rules, we believe that it is appropriate to consider supplemental constitutionalization a form of international constitutionalization. In addition, some types of what we have called "constraining constitutionalization" may also be understood in terms of supplemental constitutionalization. That is, where constraining constitutionalization arises as a result of the increasing authority of international legislative or adjudicative institutions, perhaps at the expense of the authority of domestic institutions that were under domestic constitutional constraint, constraining constitutionalization may play a supplemental role.

A few examples illustrate the dynamic we have in mind. Consider, for example, several well-known interactions between the German Federal Constitutional Court (Bundesverfassungsgericht) and the ECJ. In *Solange I*, the German Federal Constitutional Court was faced with a claim that a European Community enactment violated rights guaranteed by the German Constitution. Although the ECJ had previously declared that Community law was supreme over domestic law, the German court held that it nevertheless had a duty to review Community enactments for consistency with the German Constitution, particularly in light of the absence of fundamental rights jurisprudence to constrain Community action.[17]

In response to the *Solange I* court's implicit suggestion that the Community internalize human rights norms, the ECJ began to review Community legislation for consistency with fundamental individual rights – despite the absence of any treaty provision defining those fundamental rights or authorizing the court to engage in this form of judicial review. We can understand this development as an example of an international regime responding to pressures for international constitutional norms that constrain the scope of international legal activity, and thus preserve spheres of state autonomy and individual rights. It is an example of supplemental constitutionalization, in which the rising capacity of international institutions induces demands to supplement domestic constitutions by establishing constitutional rules at the international level. It is also an example of constraining constitutionalization "arising from below," in that to ensure the reliability of international norms,

---

[17] Internationale Handelsgesellschaft v. Einfuhr- und Vorratsstelle für Getreide und Futtermittel (*Solange I*), 37 BVerfG 271 (1974), 2 COMMON MKT. L. REV. 540. *See also In re* Application of Wunsche Handelsgesellschaft (*Solange II*), 73 BVerfGE 339 (1987), 3 COMMON MKT. L. REV. 225.

the ECJ and later the European Union were impelled to develop a doctrine of fundamental rights at the EU level.[18]

Similar concerns have arisen in the context of UN Security Council actions imposing sanctions on individuals and firms suspected of involvement in terrorist activities. In 1999, Security Council Resolution 1267 created a committee that maintains a list of individuals and entities to which sanctions apply. The committee decides, by consensus, whether to add names to this list. However, this process was criticized for lack of transparency and due process in listing and delisting decisions.[19] In response to these criticisms, and various legal challenges to listing decisions, the committee established guidelines that set forth new standards for listing decisions, including a requirement for more detailed information about entities to be listed. However, domestic laws implementing committee decisions continue to be challenged as violating rights traditionally protected by domestic constitutions, including the right to a fair hearing, the right to respect for property, and the right to effective judicial review. Again, where international tribunals effect functions that have traditionally been the prerogative of domestic tribunals, we see demands for supplemental constitutionalization to maintain safeguards that have been developed in domestic constitutions. We can also understand these challenges as part of larger efforts to seek constraining constitutional-type norms that impose legal constraints on Security Council action in this area.

These issues have been litigated in the European Union. In an opinion released as this volume was going to press, the ECJ annulled a Council regulation giving effect to a Security Council resolution requiring that assets of those associated with Al-Qaeda of the Taliban be frozen. The court ruled that the regulation violated the right to be heard and the right to effective judicial review. Although the court carefully noted that it was reviewing the lawfulness of a Community act, and not the lawfulness of the Security Council decision itself, we can nevertheless understand this opinion as an example

---

[18] We borrow this phrase from Harold Koh, who emphasized the idea of constitutionalization from below at a presentation he delivered at the "Ruling the World?" book workshop.

[19] *See, e.g.*, Bardo Fassbender, *The Responsibility of the UN Security Council to Ensure That Fair and Clear Procedures Are Made Available to Individuals and Entities Targeted with Sanctions under Chapter VII of the UN Charter* (Mar. 2006) (study commissioned by the UN Office of Legal Affairs); Council of Europe, European Convention on Human Rights, Due Process and UN Security Council Counter-Terrorism Sanctions (Feb. 2006). For a detailed account of Security Council actions in this regard, *see* Ian Johnstone, *Legislation and Adjudication in the UN Security Council: Bringing Down the Deliberative Deficit*, 102 Am. J. Int'l L. 275 (2008).

of the resistance that can arise when international norms are perceived as inconsistent with domestic constitutional guarantees.[20]

Finally, consider various controversial U.S. actions in the war on terror that implicate transnational interests, including the extraordinary rendition of suspected terrorists to states accused of committing torture and the commission of human rights abuses against terrorist suspects by U.S. agents at sites outside of the United States. As of this writing, the extent to which U.S. constitutional protections apply to these acts has not been definitively resolved.[21] If domestic courts ultimately determine that domestic constitutional protections do not apply to these sorts of fact patterns, we would expect renewed pressure for supplemental international constitutional norms in these areas.[22]

Thus, international constitutionalization may arise (1) to enable or regularize the processes for making ordinary international law under circumstances where more efficient production of law seems desirable (i.e., enabling constitutionalization), (2) to constrain the production of ordinary international law, preserving a sphere of autonomy for the state or other actors

---

[20] Kadi and Al Barakaat v. Council and Comm'n, Joined Cases C-402/05 P and C-415/05 P, 2008 E.C.R. 299.

[21] *See, e.g.,* Boumediene v. Bush, 553 U.S. __ (2008) (Detainee Treatment Act unconstitutionally suspends rights of alien enemy combatants to petition for writ of habeas corpus); El-Masri v. United States, 479 F.3d 296 (4th Cir. 2007) (dismissing suit by individual allegedly detained as part of the Central Intelligence Agency's extraordinary rendition program and tortured on grounds that case could not proceed without disclosing state secrets), *cert. denied,* 128 S. Ct. 373 (2007); Arar v. Ashcroft, 532 F.3d 157 (2d Cir. 2008) (dismissing suit by alien against United States and government officials alleging that he was mistreated and then removed to Syria, where he was tortured).

[22] Disputes over the extraterritorial reach of fundamental rights and constitutional norms are not new. *See, e.g.,* The Insular Cases, 182 U.S. 1 (1901) (addressing whether U.S. Constitution applies in territory that is not a state). With globalization, increasing numbers of cases involving the extraterritorial application of fundamental rights are arising before international and domestic tribunals. *See also* Legal Consequences of the Construction of a Wall in the Occupied Palestinian Territory, 2004 I.C.J. Rep. (July 9) (ICCPR "is applicable in respect of acts done by a State in the exercise of jurisdiction outside its own territory); Case Concerning Armed Activities on the Territory of the Congo (Democratic Republic of the Congo v. Uganda, 2005 I.C.J. Rep. 168 (Dec. 19) (international human rights and humanitarian treaties apply to acts in occupied territories); Öcalan v. Turkey, 2005-IV Eur. Ct. H.R. 131 (Grand Chamber) (overseas arrest of separatist leader); Bankovic v. Belgium, 2001-XII Eur. Ct. H.R. 333 (Grand Chamber) (legality of NATO bombing of Serbia); Ben El Mahi v. Denmark, 2006-XV Eur. Ct. H.R. (aliens abroad injured by hate speech in Denmark); Munaf v. Geren, 128 S. Ct. 2207 (2008) (U.S. Constitution does not prohibit transfer of U.S. citizens detained by U.S. military in Iraq to Iraqi custody despite possibility of torture); Atamirzayeva v. United States, 77 Fed. Cl. 378 (2007), *aff'd,* 524 F.3d 1320 (Fed. Cir. 2008) (rejecting alien's claim for compensation when foreign government, with cooperation from U.S. government, took her land adjoining U.S. embassy).

(i.e., constraining constitutionalization), or (3) to supplement domestic constitutional protections (i.e., supplemental constitutionalization).

Some might argue, alternatively, that the critical functional feature of any constitution is a settlement regarding the fundamental structure of society. So, the type of inquiry that Rawls made in *A Theory of Justice*, for example, might be understood in this sense as not just an inquiry but as *the* constitutional inquiry. And the resulting structure of society might be understood as *the* constitution. However, for current purposes, it is analytically useful to treat this type of inquiry as meta-constitutional. That is, the basic decisions about the fundamental structure of society precede and determine the structuring of legal constitutions. We can understand legal constitutions as efforts to effectuate or instantiate the chosen fundamental social structures. Alternatively, we can understand the selection of the specific features of a constitution, both initially and dynamically, as an opportunity to (re)negotiate, implicitly or explicitly, fundamental social structures. The types of rules that are privileged, and the types of rule making that are facilitated, will no doubt play a role in determining these fundamental social structures. So, we understand that enabling, constraining, and supplemental constitutionalization will be harnessed to the process of establishing these fundamental social structures.

III. The Mechanisms of Constitutionalization

Having identified the functions of international constitutionalization, we turn our attention to the types of measures and institutional mechanisms used to implement enabling, constraining, and supplemental functions. The core functions performed, and the core metrics of evaluation, will continue to be the extent of enablement, constraint, and supplementation resulting from each mechanism. As we emphasize herein – and as the essays in the first part of this volume confirm – particular legal orders may exhibit various constitutional mechanisms in various degrees, and constitutionalization is a process. Hence, we believe that, at this relatively early stage of systematic inquiry into global constitutionalization, it is useful to identify and evaluate the institutional similarities and differences in various constitutional and quasi-constitutional orders.

Thus, our goal here is to set forth an analytic scheme that can provide both a vocabulary and a conceptual apparatus for the identification, classification, and comparison of different constitutional orders. As will become clear, this section builds on the prior section, as we evaluate each mechanism in terms of its relationship to enabling, constraining, and supplemental constitutionalization.

For current purposes, we offer the following, provisional list of constitutional mechanisms. For each mechanism described, we attempt to explain its potential role in enabling, constraining, and supplementary constitutionalization. In fact, any mechanism that performs these functions should be understood as constitutional.

1. *Creation of governance institutions and allocation of governance authority in a horizontal context.* Constitutions create institutions and mechanisms for governance and allocate authority among those bodies. Governance mechanisms typically are constructed with divided power, and this type of rule determines the allocation of authority among, for example, legislatures, executives, and judiciaries (horizontal separation of powers). Horizontal separation of powers often is designed to reflect comparative institutional strengths, as well as to reflect political divisions, including the vertical division between the center and the periphery; that is, some organs in a horizontal federal structure may be designed to represent certain constituencies, such as subnational units. In the international context, horizontal allocations of authority may combine elements of enabling constitutionalization and constraining constitutionalization. That is, they may be part of a grant of power to an international organization, with requirements that may constrain the exercise of that power.

2. *Allocation of governance authority in a vertical context.* In entities that are federal or have some measure of devolution, constitutions often establish the relationship between more and less centralized components of governance (vertical federalism). This can include not only clear allocations of authority according to specific rules but also standards to be applied by courts in determining allocation of authority in specific instances. As with horizontal allocations of authority, vertical allocations in the international context typically involve elements of both enabling and constraining constitutionalism: grants of authority to international organizations with specified limitations and procedural constraints.

3. *Supremacy.* Constitutional norms are ordinarily hierarchically superior to ordinary law, which is made through constitutionally approved processes. Thus, in the event of a conflict, a constitutional norm prevails over an inconsistent ordinary law norm. In the international constitutional context, supremacy serves as a form of constraining constitutionalization, constraining the scope of ordinary international law. (The fact that international law is supreme vis-à-vis domestic law, at

least within the international legal system, gives international law a constitutional-type role at the domestic level, but this type of international law is ordinary law at the international level.) Supremacy of certain types of rules, such as fundamental rights, may be motivated in part by supplemental constitutionalization. In the international setting, the main feature of jus cogens is supremacy over ordinary international law.

4. *Stability.* Constitutional norms are often entrenched in a way that ordinary norms are not. That is, it is more difficult to change a constitutional norm than to change ordinary law. As a result, constitutional norms are protected against temporary shifts in political power and enjoy a stability that ordinary law lacks. Stability in this sense is a critical component of fundamental rights, and of broad settlements regarding the structure of society and the structure of governance. The relative stability of constitutional norms, compared to that of ordinary law, serves, like supremacy, as a form of constraining constitutionalization, constraining the development of certain forms of ordinary law. Under the normal international legal rule of unanimity for treaty making, international law, once made, is highly stable: it is difficult to reverse a rule of international law. Thus, international treaty law is rather uniformly stable, and we see little difference between ordinary international law and constitutional international law in this regard. However, customary international law may exhibit a greater differentiation, as between ordinary customary international law and constitutional international law, such as *jus cogens* rules.

5. *Fundamental rights.* Modern constitutions typically purport to enshrine and protect fundamental human rights. The exact content and scope of these rights is subject to debate and varies widely across different constitutions. Some constitutions focus largely, if not entirely, on political and civil rights; others might protect social, cultural, or economic rights. As has already been noted, fundamental rights at the international level may serve as a form of constraining constitutionalization as well as a form of supplemental constitutionalization.

6. *Review.* Modern constitutions typically provide for one or more mechanisms designed to test the legal compatibility of laws and other acts of governance with the entrenched norms or fundamental rights expressed in the constitution. This activity might be understood as a component of horizontal separation of powers, but it serves a broader purpose. A review mechanism can serve as the guardian or arbiter of constitutional settlements, making them enforceable where they might

otherwise not be. By authoritatively determining whether particular acts are consistent with constitutional norms, based on a prior delegation of authority to do so, this type of review may solve information problems and thereby create a more stable political equilibrium. Supremacy is a precondition for this type of review, and review may have different effects depending on the degree of invocability, the remedies, and the other structural features of review. Review can have constraining effects where it limits the power of certain bodies. In addition, review can play an important role in supplemental constitutionalization, where review applies, at the international level, constitutional values or concerns that would ordinarily be applied at the national level. Again, review at the transnational level of member state or component legislation, as in the WTO's review of member state measures, seems to be a mechanism for enforcement of ordinary international law, and so is not on its face part of international constitutionalization. However, to the extent that international review entails a measure of judicial legislation, the grant of review power is a type of enabling constitutionalization.

7. *Accountability/democracy.* We assume that constitutions, like other law, exist to advance individual or collective goals. To ensure faithful execution of constituent wishes, and to determine whether satisfactory progress toward constitutional goals is being achieved, constitutions typically include mechanisms designed to provide some form of accountability to constituents. Importantly, the commitment to democratic governance is qualified by the fundamental rights and stability functions referenced above: constitutions serve, in part, as devices to establish precommitments that limit or channel the domain of democratic politics. In the international setting, accountability mechanisms may constrain constitutionalization by limiting the ability of international entities to act where they lack sufficient democratic credentials. However, accountability mechanisms may supplement constitutionalization by adding accountability to the international governance process in circumstances where that process is taking on greater responsibilities vis-à-vis member states.

Finally, one other less functional and more constructivist feature of constitutional orders deserves mention, although it differs considerably from the constitutional mechanisms identified earlier. A somewhat fanciful example, slightly modified from one developed by Frederick Schauer, helps illustrate this feature. Imagine that, after substantial deliberation, the contributors to this volume collectively drafted a "Constitution for the World." Suppose that this constitution – reflecting the considerable wisdom of its drafters – contained exquisitely designed provisions allocating powers along vertical and horizontal dimensions, set forth a highly developed list of fundamental rights, provided for an efficient and stringent mechanism for reviewing the constitutionality of norms, included well-designed accountability mechanisms, provided for just the right balance of stability and change, and declared itself supreme to all other forms of law. Imagine further that this document provided that it would become effective upon notice of its existence appearing in this book. Under these circumstances, the conditions for the document's claim to be a Constitution for the World would now be satisfied.[23]

Could one meaningfully claim that the world now had a (new) constitution? Surely not. As a pragmatic matter, a text's assertion of its own supremacy and authority cannot establish that supremacy and authority; the terms of a legal text cannot ultimately determine its own status. Rather, a constitution's authority – its status as fundamental law – ultimately rests not on textual provisions, or even on historical practice, but on "the Constitution's acceptance as authoritative in the present."[24] This acceptance, when it exists, rests on facts external to the constitution, which we might consider pre- or extra-constitutional.[25]

From this perspective, global constitutionalism is "[t]he extension of constitutional *thinking* to world order,"[26] and it is premised on ideas, convictions, and commitments as much as on politics or legal doctrine. The existence of this intersubjective understanding is one of the key markers that, from a constructivist perspective, distinguishes a constitutionalized international legal order from one that is merely highly legalized. The absence of that acceptance makes any purported constitution no more authoritative than the hypothetical Constitution for the World discussed previously. The status of a text or set

[23] This example appears, in slightly modified form, in Frederick Schauer, *Amending the Presuppositions of a Constitution, in* RESPONDING TO IMPERFECTION: THE THEORY AND PRACTICE OF CONSTITUTIONAL AMENDMENT 145, 147–148 (Sanford Levinson ed., 1995); Larry Alexander & Frederick Schauer, *Defending Judicial Supremacy: A Reply,* 17 CONST. COMMENT. 455, 465 (2000). For a sophisticated presentation, and critique, of this argument, *see* Frank Michelman, *Constitutional Authorship by the People,* 74 NOTRE DAME L. REV. 1605 (1998–1999).

[24] Alexander & Schauer, *supra* note 24, at 460.

[25] Stated more formally, "[C]onstitutions rest on logically antecedent presuppositions that give them their constitutional status." Frederick Schauer, *Amending the Presuppositions of a Constitution, in* RESPONDING TO IMPERFECTION: THE THEORY AND PRACTICE OF CONSTITUTIONAL AMENDMENT 145, 147–148 (Sanford Levinson ed., 1995).

[26] RICHARD FALK, THE PATHWAYS OF GLOBAL CONSTITUTIONALISM, IN THE CONSTITUTIONAL FOUNDATIONS OF WORLD PEACE 13, 14 (1993) (emphasis added).

of norms as constitutional in any particular society is thus a contingent social fact that can be usefully examined through historical, sociological, statistical, psychological, or other relevant evidence. This constructivist perspective differs from the functionalist perspective outlined herein. However, both perspectives would agree that a constitution is based on history and social context: enabling, constraining, and supplemental constitutionalization, for a functionalist, are based on a perceived need in a real social setting.

We believe that the intersubjective nature of constitutional orders beyond the state informs the discussions of a constitutional paradigm and constitutional sensibility that appear in many of the essays in this volume, including the contributions by Mattias Kumm and Andreas Paulus, as well as Neil Walker's suggestion that we understand constitutionalism as "a framing mechanism."

Given this necessarily brief explanation of our approach, a few cautionary comments are in order. First, we emphasize that the mechanisms identified above are provisional, and we expect that a more refined set of mechanisms can be developed as research on global constitutionalization progresses. That is, the various mechanisms identified here are intended to begin – rather than conclude – a dialogue about the most appropriate mechanisms to achieve international constitutionalization. Moreover, we emphasize that the mechanisms we identify apply to constitutions in general. Any particular constitutional order might exhibit various mechanisms in greater or lesser degrees. Indeed, we would expect that any particular constitutional order would have a unique, desirable combination of enabling, constraining, and supplemental constitutionalization, and that any particular legal setting would use a unique combination of mechanisms to achieve this type of constitutionalization. Each mechanism that we describe has effects that go beyond enabling, constraining, and supplementing, and we do not seek here to explain these other effects. We leave for future research an inquiry into the the choice among mechanisms, or the emphasis among mechanisms. But, for us, the choice among mechanisms is not constitutional, but incidental to the constitutional choice on which we focus attention.

As we examine specific international legal regimes, it is useful to examine whether the various features of those regimes fulfill the enabling, constraining, and supplemental functions and how they use the previously listed mechanisms to do so. Of course, any particular international legal regime could outsource some of these functions or mechanisms to domestic or other international systems, and this possibility would increase the difficulty of any analysis. However, with this analytical template, we are able to evaluate the degree and character of constitutionalization within any international regime. We also are able to begin to develop a qualitative measure of the degree of fulfillment of the enabling, constraining, and supplemental functions; future research may begin to align different degrees of fulfillment with other characteristics.

We also recognize that constitutions are dynamic and historically and socially contingent settlements that respond over time and space to varying needs. Constitutions must be understood in terms of path dependency: past constitutional structures may have continuing effects in allowing or limiting certain subsequent social developments, including constitutional developments. Constitutions may serve different functions, or serve them in different ways, depending on particular social needs. These social needs not only vary in different societies but also vary at different times in the same society. Constitutions are moving targets. In fact, this is one of their attractive design functions: constitutions mediate between stability and change. For this reason, gaps or variations in emphasis are not necessarily susceptible to straightforward normative response. In fact, some would say that this dynamic feature is a critical part, if not of a constitution, then of a constitutive process in a society. This dynamic and perhaps civic republican aspect of a constitution might be included in a list of constitutional functions or characteristics.

Finally, we fully recognize that any attempt to identify and categorize constitutional mechanisms is prone to underinclusiveness, overinclusiveness, and overlap. For example, some would argue that freedom of commerce is constitutional. Indeed, it is protected in a number of constitutional documents. But freedom of commerce can also be protected by ordinary law. One way of including commercial freedoms as constitutional under our framework is to define them as, to some extent, fundamental rights.[27] In this sense, freedom of international commerce may be understood in terms of supplemental constitutionalization: given globalization, purely domestic freedom of commerce becomes too limited and must be expanded to cover a broader sphere.

---

[27] Ernst-Ulrich Petersmann has explored the constitutional dimensions of a fundamental right to trade in a number of writings. *See, e.g.*, Ernst-Ulrich Petersmann, *Multilevel Trade Governance in the WTO Requires Multilevel Constitutionalism, in* CONSTITUTIONALISM, MULTILEVEL TRADE GOVERNANCE AND SOCIAL REGULATION (Christian Joerges & Ernst-Ulrich Petersmann eds., 2006); Ernst-Ulrich Petersmann, *Justice in International Economic Law? From International Law among States to International Integration Law and Constitutional Law*, 1 GLOBAL COMMUNITY Y.B. INT'L L. & JURISP. 105 (2006); Ernst-Ulrich Petersmann, *From Member-Driven Governance to Constitutionally Limited Multi-level Trade Governance, in* THE WTO AT TEN: THE CONTRIBUTION OF THE DISPUTE SETTLEMENT SYSTEM 86 (G. Sacerdoti et al. eds., 2006). For one type of response, *see* Philip Alston, *Resisting the Merger and Acquisition of Human Rights by Trade Law: A Reply to Petersmann*, 13 EUR. J. INT'L L. 815 (2000).

IV. Domestic and International Constitutionalization and Democratic Legitimacy

The constitutional mechanisms identified earlier are drawn largely from domestic experience. We do not assume that any of these mechanisms can be simply or unambiguously transposed to the international plane. Indeed, we are acutely aware that the international domain poses a distinct set of practical, analytic, and normative challenges, and that difficult problems of translation unavoidably accompany any effort to apply normatively rich and deeply contested concepts found in domestic constitutions to the international domain.[28]

Perhaps the greatest distinction between domestic and international political orders – and the greatest problem of translation – may be in connection with democratic legitimacy. Democracy is, of course, a highly contested concept, but virtually all theories of democracy require that the members of a political community decide for themselves the contents of the rules that govern their collective life. If this were true for ordinary law, then, a fortiori, democratic theory would demand that the members of the political community decide the most basic of constitutional principles.

Given the possibility that international legal norms may be more isolated from the democratic legitimation practices that we see on the domestic plane, many politicians, activists, and scholars have decried the democratic deficit that is said to be found in various international legal orders. As constitutional norms are both hierarchically superior to and more entrenched than ordinary international legal norms, we might expect the relationship between democracy and international constitutionalization to be even more problematic. For this reason, many of the essays in this volume – including particularly those by Samantha Besson and Mattias Kumm – devote substantial attention to the cluster of issues that comprise the "paradox of constitutional democracy."[29] One of the key goals of this volume is to examine whether this paradox exists in the international setting and, if so, to identify various ways this paradox can be addressed.

While concerns over democratic legitimacy are significant, it bears noting that to the extent that international constitutional law acts as a constraint

---

[28] *See, e.g.*, Neil Walker, *Postnational Constitutionalism and the Problem of Translation, in* EUROPEAN CONSTITUTIONALISM BEYOND THE STATE 27 (Joseph Weiler & Marlene Wind eds., Cambridge Univ. Press 2003); J. H. H. WEILER, THE CONSTITUTION OF EUROPE (Cambridge Univ. Press 1999).

[29] FRANK MICHELMAN, BRENNAN AND DEMOCRACY (1999). The issue has given rise to a substantial literature. For one response, *see* Jürgen Habermas, *Constitutional Democracy: A Paradoxical Union of Contradictory Principles*, 29 POL. THEORY 766 (2001).

on the domain and effect of ordinary international law, international constitutional law can ameliorate ordinary international law's democracy deficit. Whether international constitutional norms would in fact do so depends, in part, on the relations between and relative strength and quality of those dimensions of constitutionalization that enable and those that constrain ordinary international law. For example, while domestic constitutions may be understood in some contexts to constrain democracy, and while ordinary international law may also be understood this way, international constitutional norms and processes that either constrain ordinary international law, or that require its democratic legitimation, may be seen as enhancing democratic legitimacy overall. On the other hand, as Joel Trachtman suggests in his chapter, international constitutional norms might be considered inconsistent with democratic legitimacy to the extent that they constrain the formation of international law that would otherwise be democratically legitimate.

Thus, even if shifts in power and authority to international sites of governance impose costs on domestic democratic politics, it is not clear how serious those costs are. More important, it is not clear how to evaluate those costs in light of any benefits associated with international constitutionalization. The existing literature does not address the question of these possible trade-offs,[30] and one goal of this volume is to prompt explicit consideration of the diverse implications of relations between international and domestic constitutional structures.

V. A Preliminary Constitutional Matrix

The constitutional mechanisms identified above can form the basis for a constitutional matrix that attempts to identify which mechanisms are included in which international settings and how they perform particular constitutional functions in those settings, thereby facilitating comparison of different international regimes. We believe that it is useful, in a complex system of vertically and horizontally divided governments that overlap in various ways, as a first descriptive step to construct a matrix showing where, if anywhere, these mechanisms are located within the system (see Table 1.1).

We emphasize that a matrix – like the constitutional mechanisms and functions we identify here – is an analytical tool and not a normative argument. Thus, such a matrix cannot by itself tell us whether some gaps should be filled

---

[30] One notable exception is Allen Buchanan & Russell Powell, *Constitutional Democracy and the Rule of International Law: Are They Compatible?* 16 J. POL. PHIL. 326 (2008).

Table 1.1. *Constitutional matrix*

	International system	United Nations	European Union	World Trade Organization	Human rights
Horizontal allocation of powers	Without centralized legislative or administrative bodies, there is little need for horizontal allocation of powers; in a sense, fragmentation raises the issue of horizontal interfunctional allocation of power.	Charter delineates responsibilities of General Assembly, Security Council, ICJ, and other UN bodies. Simultaneous enabling and constraining constitutionalization. Security Council has created, inter alia, international tribunals that elaborate law and subsidiary bodies that make quasi-judicial determinations.	EU treaties delineate responsibilities of EU institutions, but in practice these are clarified through litigation before the ECJ. Simultaneous enabling and constraining constitutionalization.	WTO texts create various councils and other subsidiary bodies, but these bodies generally lack independent legislative capacity; AB does not yet exercise judicial review. Under member organization (interstate) model, neither enabling nor constraining constitutionalization.	Human rights treaties typically do not create bodies that can create subsidiary law but often create bodies that can interpret treaty provisions and generate soft law norms. Neither enabling nor constraining constitutionalization.
Vertical allocation of powers	Few principles that separate matters of international as opposed to domestic concern; legislation of international law can be understood as vertical allocation from states to international legal order. Law of treaty and law of formation of custom may be understood as enabling and constraining constitutionalization.	Charter delineates matters within UN ambit and those subject to national jurisdiction, but the area reserved exclusively for domestic jurisdiction has been eroded over time, and the line between the two domains has proved hazy. Simultaneous enabling and constraining constitutionalization.	Treaties delineate area of EU competence and state competence; four different forms of secondary EU law make different demands on national systems; formal doctrine of subsidiarity. Simultaneous enabling and constraining constitutionalization.	WTO texts do not explicitly set out principles for distinguishing areas within WTO competence from areas without; norms of negative integration give states wide leeway on implementation. More recent norms of positive integration (e.g., TRIPs) give less discretion. SPS provides quasi-legislative status to norms generated by Codex, IPCC, etc. Simultaneous enabling and constraining constitutionalization.	Legislation of international human rights law as vertical allocation of authority to international legal system and away from *domaine reserve*.

(continued)

Table 1.1 *(continued)*

	International system	United Nations	European Union	World Trade Organization	Human rights
Supremacy	Here, issue is supremacy vis-à-vis ordinary international law. Generally, jus cogens is considered supreme over ordinary international law. In a sense, rules regarding modification of custom or treaty are supreme over other international law.	The Charter provides that it is supreme in the event of conflicts with other treaties (art. 103), and that member states agree to follow Security Council decisions taken under chapter 7 (art. 25). Also, art. 2(6) provides that the United Nations "shall ensure" that nonmembers act in accordance with Charter principles.	Generally, the constitutive treaties are supreme vis-à-vis secondary legislation.	As a practical matter, WTO law may be understood as supreme over other international law that lacks strong dispute settlement mechanisms; the issue turns, in part, on whether and how panels and AB use non–trade law in disputes.	Other than jus cogens, there is no generally agreed-on hierarchy of human rights over other international law.
Stability	Difficult to establish or change jus cogens rules. Otherwise, under positivist views, law made or changed only with state consent. VCLT article 56 purports to limit state ability to exit treaty regimes but some state practice is to the contrary. Newly formed states are bound by rules of customary international law.	Amendment requires two-thirds vote of all members and ratification by two-thirds of members, including all permanent members of Security Council. Also, Charter has no provision for state withdrawal (in contrast to the League of Nations Covenant, which permitted withdrawal upon two years' notice).	EU treaties are de facto difficult to amend; secondary legislation is relatively easy to change. EU treaties are of perpetual duration and do not explicitly permit withdrawal.	Formal mechanism for amendment, but treaty norms informally require consensus to change; withdrawal possible upon six months' notice.	Resistance to change is no more or less than in other areas of treaty law. Many treaties permit withdrawal on notice (CAT, Rights of Child); others do not explicitly permit withdrawal (ICCPR; ICESCR). UN Human Rights Committee opined that it is not possible to denounce ICCPR. and whether withdrawal is permitted from other human rights treaties is contested.

Fundamental rights	As specified in general human rights law. Some international human rights law may be understood as supplemental constitutionalization.	Charter seeks respect for and observance of human rights but does not specify content. Various UN instruments, including the Universal Declaration of Human Rights, detail the content of human rights, and over time the UN has created various mechanisms for monitoring human rights violations.	Over time, ECJ has incorporated a strong set of fundamental human rights. May be understood as supplemental constitutionalization.	Treaties do not set out robust fundamental human rights; unclear whether fundamental rights enter WTO legal system. Some demands for supplemental constitutionalization.	Treaties set out strong fundamental human rights.
Review	No standing body with compulsory jurisdiction to review legality of actions by international actors.	ICJ has been extremely hesitant to review legality of acts of coordinate UN bodies.	ECJ jurisdictional provisions, including national referrals, provide for strong review.	WTO dispute settlement is an extraordinarily strong mechanism for reviewing national compliance, but there is no review yet of WTO acts.[a]	Varies by regime; some treaties provide for individual access to courts; others rely on various review bodies.
Accountability/ democracy	Depends on particular norms, ratification mechanisms in particular states.	Periodic concern over legitimacy of Security Council composition and decisions. Wide participation by all states in General Assembly and by nonstate actors in various UN bodies. Concern may be understood as claims for supplemental constitutionalization.	Persistent claims of democracy deficit; direct election to European Parliament. Supplemental constitutionalization.	Recent claims of democracy and legitimacy deficits can be understood as claims for supplemental constitutionalization.	Same characteristics as general international law.

[a] It may be that, in the future, the binding effect of a legislative act of the WTO would be challenged and reviewed within the context of a contentious case between two states.

or whether some constitutional features are unnecessary in some contexts. This matrix allows us to compare the constitutional development of different international regimes, but it does not allow us to identify strengths and weaknesses in various regimes.

An evaluative matrix would be more difficult to construct. An evaluative matrix would examine the match between existing constitutional provisions and actual constitutional needs. It would evaluate the social conditions, or social concerns, that each function or mechanism addresses, and it would examine whether that condition or concern is adequately addressed. An evaluative matrix also allows for consideration of whether some international regimes provide the constitutional functions or mechanisms that are needed in other parts of the international system. For example, does the WTO need its own fundamental rights function, or can it rely on the protection of fundamental rights elsewhere in the system?

VI. Constitutional Coordination, Constitutional Pluralism, and Constitutional Synthesis

Historically, international law has developed in regional and functional pockets – the law of diplomatic relations, human rights, norms on the use of force – all in the context of a set of background norms like *pacta sunt servanda*, the rules of state responsibility, and the like. This highly decentralized and non-hierarchical system renders constitutional coordination both necessary and problematic.

As has been noted, several of the chapters in this volume locate the constitutional turn in international legal discourse as, at least in part, a response to the anxieties induced by international law's fragmentation. In one strong sense of the term, the constitutional turn might suggest that the international community shares a universal set of values that can bring order and hierarchy to the disorder and uncertainty associated with fragmentation. However, many doubt that such a comprehensive set of universal values that can play such a role exists.

A softer version of constitutionalism might start from the premise that international law's various functional regimes are part of a larger system of general international law, such that gaps and incoherencies are addressed by implicit rules of hierarchy or conflict of laws. There is some doctrinal support for this perspective; international tribunals as diverse as the ECHR and the WTO's AB have emphasized the ways in which "specialized" international legal regimes are embedded within the larger system of public international law.[31] Moreover, this sense of international law's systemic reach finds support in various international legal contexts,[32] and informs Andreas Paulus's contribution to this volume. From this perspective, constitutionalization can provide a mechanism that can harmonize or coordinate the various components of the international legal system.

While this softer version of constitutionalism is attractive in many respects, the vision of systemic integration implicit in this understanding raises some difficulties. First, the vision of a unified, systemic international legal order that underlies this position remains controversial as a matter of both theory and practice, and it may be nearly as difficult to establish as the conditions for the stronger form of constitutionalism. Even though subregimes, such as trade or human rights, do not exist in isolation from general international legal norms, it is not always clear when or how norms from one regime apply within another regime or what hierarchy would be appropriate. Thus, for example, although the WTO's AB has often relied on rules of treaty interpretation found in the Vienna Convention on the Law of Treaties and customary international law, it has at other times declined to give effect to customary or treaty norms found in other international legal regimes. If general public international law were to provide rules for harmonizing or prioritizing otherwise conflicting norms found in various subregimes, a set of conflict rules would be an important constitutional element.

Thus, the increased density and reach of legal norms in a fragmented and multilevel system of global governance poses difficult questions of coordination. Notably, coordination questions are not limited to relations among regional and functional organizations but extend also to national and indeed

---

[31] In the *Bankovic* case (1999), the ECHR "recall[ed] that the principles underlying the Convention cannot be interpreted and applied in a vacuum. The Court must also take into account any relevant rules of international law when examining questions concerning its jurisdiction and, consequently, determine State responsibility in conformity with the governing principles of international law, although it must remain mindful of the Convention's special character as a human rights treaty. The Convention should be interpreted as far as possible in harmony with other principles of international law of which it forms part." *Bankovic v. Belgium*, 2001-XII Eur. Ct. H.R. 333, 351 (decision on admissibility), at para. 57 (references omitted). *See also* Appellate Body Report, *United States – Standards of Reformulated and Conventional Gasoline*, WT/DS2/AB/R (Apr. 29, 1996) (stating that WTO agreements "should not be read in clinical isolation from public international law").

[32] A recent ILC study group suggested as much. *See* "Fragmentation of International Law. Problems caused by the Diversification and Expansion of International law, Report of the Study Group of the International Law Commission." Finalized by Martti Koskenniemi A/CN4/L.682, at 65–101 (Apr. 13, 2006); "Fragmentation of International Law: Difficulties Arising from the Diversification and Expansion of International Law: Report of the Study Group of the International Law Commission," A/CN.4/L.702 at 7–25 (July 18, 2006).

subnational constitutions. Hence, the coordination function has both horizontal and vertical dimensions.

The existence of numerous constitutional orders produces the phenomenon of constitutional pluralism, a topic explored in detail in chapters by Daniel Halberstam and Miguel Poiares Maduro. With constitutional pluralism come questions regarding how different orders relate to one another, as well as the possibility of constitutional confrontations. These confrontations can be largely horizontal, as when Libya in effect asked the ICJ to declare a Security Council resolution to be *ultra vires* in the *Lockerbie* dispute,[33] or they can have a vertical component, as in the German constitutional court's *Solange* opinions, the ICJ and US Supreme Court opinions in the Vienna Convention on Consular Relations cases,[34] and the ECJ's *Kadi* decision. These confrontations may be mediated by a variety of mechanisms, including rules of dualism, rules of subsidiarity, or the passive virtues of courts. One of the most important functions that international constitutionalization can play is to provide mechanisms for addressing how different constitutions relate to one another and how they can be coordinated.

Finally, from a matrix evaluation of constitutional functions and mechanisms, identification of fragmentation, and the systematization of coordination may develop a kind of new constitutional synthesis. This new constitutional synthesis may develop in the international legal system as a whole or in specific subfields. Absent a large exogenous shock, any new synthesis will likely develop functionally, in fits and starts over time, just as the U.S. constitutional order changed over time as the United States evolved into a unified federal state, or as the European Union has since 1957 evolved into a quasi-federal entity fully capable of competing for authority with its member states. Any new synthesis on the international plane will no doubt be more complex than what we have seen before. But a constitutional synthesis should be susceptible to analysis using the matrix approach described above.

[33] Case Concerning Questions of Interpretation and Application of the 1971 Montreal Convention Arising from the Aerial Incident at Lockerbie (Libya v. United States), 1992 I.C.J. Rep. 114 (Apr. 14).

[34] *See, e.g.*, Medellin v. Texas, 554 U.S. __ (2008) (refusing to order stay of execution notwithstanding ICJ indication of provisional measures); Medellín v. Texas, 552 U.S. __ (2008) (ICJ orders are not directly enforceable as domestic law in state courts in United States); Request for Interpretation of the Judgment of 31 March 2004 in the Case Concerning Avena and Other Mexican Nationals (Mexico v. United States) (ICJ issues provisional measures ordering United States to take all measures necessary to ensure that Medellín is not executed pending judgment in this action); Case Concerning Avena and Other Mexican Nationals (Mexico v. United States), 2004 I.C.J. 12 (Mar. 31, 2004) (United States violated Vienna Convention and must give review and reconsideration to named Mexican nationals).

Conclusion

This volume joins a rapidly expanding literature on international constitutionalization.[35] While it is not possible to summarize the diverse, and sometimes contradictory, arguments found in the papers that follow, one can understand these essays as an extended and richly textured dialogue over a number of critical questions, including:

- What is international legal constitutionalization, and how is it measured?
- How does international legal constitutionalization relate to globalization and the fragmentation of international law ?
- What are the relationships between international legal constitutionalization and domestic constitutionalism?
- What are the relationships among international legal constitutionalization, fundamental rights, democracy and legitimacy?

However, this volume is not simply a sophisticated examination of these and related issues. It can also be understood as an important contribution to an emerging dialogue among three literatures: international constitutionalization, global administrative law, and legal pluralism. Each of these literatures arises in response to the enormous shifts in power and authority from the national to the international, and each presents itself as an appropriate legal response to the challenges of globalization, fragmentation, and global governance.

Although there are some overlaps among these three approaches, there are also important differences. The global administrative law (GAL) scholarship highlights the importance and variety of administrative practices in the implementation and elaboration of international regulatory regimes.[36] Like the constitutionalization literature, it explores the uses and limitations on the exercise of power in transnational settings. In some ways it takes a broader view of international processes than the constitutionalization literature. For example, GAL's attention to hybrid and private bodies is wider than constitutionalization's focus on more traditional, state-centric processes. On the other hand, in many ways GAL's ambit is much narrower than that found

---

[35] Important recent contributions include VICKI C. JACKSON, CONSTITUTIONAL ENGAGEMENT IN A TRANSNATIONAL ERA (2009); JAN KLABBERS, ANNE PETERS & GEIR ULFSTEIN, THE CONSTITUTIONALIZATION OF INTERNATIONAL LAW (2009).

[36] See, e.g., Benedict Kingsbury & Nico Krisch, Introduction: Global Governance and Global Administrative Law in the International Legal Order, 17 EUR J. INT'L L. 1 (2006); Benedict Kingsbury, Nico Krisch, Richard B. Stewart & Jonathan B. Wiener, Forward: Global Governance as Administration – National and Transnational Approaches to Global Administrative Law, 68 L. & CONTEMP. PROBS. 1 (2005).

in the constitutionalization literature. For example, unlike GAL writings, the constitutionalization literature does not limit itself to administrative exercises of power, but also examines legislative and judicial practices. Moreover, constitutionalization addresses a much broader array of normative issues. GAL scholarship tends to focus on the accountability and legitimacy concerns that accompany global administrative practices. While accountability and legitimacy are central constitutional values, the essays that follow illustrate many of the ways in which constitutionalization scholarship addresses a wider range of normative concerns that arise out of contemporary global governance.

Finally, and perhaps most importantly, insofar as the GAL scholarship examines administrative practices within regimes and compares administrative practices across regimes, it has little to say about the issues raised by fragmentation, which center on the institutional and normative relationships among regimes. To the extent that international legal constitutionalization is understood in terms of secondary or tertiary rules in the Hart sense – in terms of rules determining the scope of authority or allocating authority between different legal systems or between different constitutions – international legal constitutionalization responds to fragmentation. Where, for example, an overall constitutional rule allocates authority between the trade legal system and the environment legal system, this is one response to fragmentation. An international constitutional rule might also determine the scope of sovereignty – allocating authority a priori between the *domaine reservé* and the international legal system. Where the domestic system represents some substantive areas of concern while the international system represents others, this too is a response to fragmentation.

The legal pluralism scholarship highlights the fragmentation of the international legal system, but often downplays the desirability or possibility of bringing hierarchy to the resulting (dis)order. Many pluralists suggest that there is no meta-rationality that can be invoked to order a proliferating number of international institutions and norms. To the extent that some understandings of constitutionalization emphasize moves toward highly legalized and hierarchical relations among international legal regimes, these understandings can be sharply distinguished from pluralist approaches. Although this is the dominant understanding of constitutionalization, several of the essays in this volume make clear that constitutional approaches do not necessarily result in the introduction of determinate hierarchies. Many constitutional approaches – including the one set forth in this introduction – are fully consistent with notions of constitutional pluralism.

Under these understandings, mediation among different constitutional regimes requires either a kind of "tertiary rule" that would determine the relative domains of applicability of these constitutional regimes, or a judicial dialog that produces consensual "comity" between constitutional regimes. There may also be a degree of competition between constitutional regimes: seeking greater authority through the decisions that they make. In either event, these approaches focus more on mechanisms to channel and structure relations between different legal regimes than on the imposition of hierarchical order among various regimes.

Of course, scholars are only beginning to explore constitutionalist approaches to international law and global governance, not to mention the relations among constitutionalization, GAL, and legal pluralism. Our goal in this introduction is to provoke rather than conclude debates over international constitutionalization. Read in conjunction with the other chapters in this volume, this chapter seeks to provide readers with an incisive overview of the current state of the debates over constitutionalization beyond the state as well as a coherent analytical structure by which to advance these debates.

Is the International Legal System a Constitution for International Society?

2. The Mystery of Global Governance

DAVID KENNEDY

Introduction: How Little We Know

The workshop from which this volume emerged reflected in a variety of ways on constitutionalism as a way of thinking about global governance. In the past few years, many have experimented with the metaphor of a constitution to describe the legal order beyond the nation-state.[1] We have been encouraged to think of the UN Charter as a constitution, particularly when it comes to the use of force. Others have seen a constitutional moment in the emergence of human rights as a global vernacular for the legitimacy of power. Some trade scholars have proposed that we see the World Trade Organization (WTO) as a constitutional order. The WTO has rendered the General Agreement on Tariffs and Trade (GATT) more properly legal, strengthening dispute settlement and deepening engagement with national legal regulations. If, as Ernst-Ulrich Petersmann urges, we were to add human rights to what John Jackson famously termed the WTO's substantive legal "interface" between

---

[1] *See, e.g.,* Bardo Fassbender, *The United Nations Charter as Constitution of the International Community*, 36 COLUM. J. TRANSNAT'L L. 530 (1998), which discusses the notion of the UN Charter as a global constitution, noting similar ideas in ALFRED VERDROSS & BRUNO SIMMA, UNIVERSELLES VÖLKERRECHT: THEORIE UND PRAXIS (3d ed. 1984). *See also* Anne-Marie Slaughter & William Burke-White, *An International Constitutional Moment*, 43 HARV. INT'L L.J. 1 (2002); John O. McGinnis & Mark L. Movsesian, *Commentary: The World Trade Constitution*, 114 HARV. L. REV. 512 (2000); Ernst-Ultrich Petersmann, *Trade Policy as a Constitutional Problem: On the Domestic Policy Functions of International Rules*, 41 AUSSENWIRTSCHAFT 243 (1986); *The WTO Constitution and Human Rights*, 3 JOURNAL OF INT'L ECON. L. 19 (2000).

University Professor of Law and David and Mariana Fisher University Professor of International Relations, Brown University, and Manley O. Hudson Visiting Professor of Law, Harvard Law School. A version of this chapter was presented as the Kormendy Lecture at Ohio Northern University, Pettit College of Law, in January 2008. My thanks to the editors of the *Ohio Northern University Law Review* who have agreed to publish that version of the chapter in an upcoming volume of their review.

national regulatory systems, we might well see the result as a constitution, at least to the extent that we are willing to see the legal regime of the European Union in constitutional terms.[2] At the same time, others find the key to world public law in the relations among national constitutions. Comparative constitutional law is front and center in their accounts of how we are governed at the global level.

It is useful to remember as we begin considering these various constitutional ideas that constitutionalism is but one of many ongoing efforts to rethink how we are governed globally. Across the legal field, people are reimagining the nature of law outside of and among states. And, of course, we lawyers are not alone. Our colleagues throughout the social sciences, in economics, political science, sociology, anthropology, and more, are all thinking anew about global patterns of power and influence.

Undoubtedly, some of these efforts are more accurate and promising than others, but the simple fact that people are thinking anew is itself of real significance. It is significant because it reflects how little we in fact know about how we are governed.

We know very little, in fact, about the structure of global society. How is public power exercised, where are the levers, who are the authorities, and how do they relate to one another? Everywhere we can see the impact of things global, foreign, faraway. How does it all work? How do all the pieces fit together? Are the worlds of politics, markets, and cultural influence held together in a tight structure or is it all more loose and haphazard? Is there more than one global order – how much, in the end, is simply chaos, and how much the work of an invisible hand?

For some, questions about global governance arise first from substantive concerns. How is so much poverty sustained in a world of such plenty? How can security be achieved between and within the world's different cultures and nations? If we wanted to do something about poverty or the environment – if we wanted to complain or protest or simply participate – to whom should we address ourselves? What cleaves leading and lagging sectors, cultures or nations, from one another? How has knowledge about all this come to be so unequally distributed? If we understood the machinery by which inequalities and hierarchies of influence and wealth and knowledge are reproduced, we might know how to make the world a better place.

But the answers to such questions are not at all clear. It is not at all obvious how power is put together on the global stage, let alone how its exercise might

---

[2] *See* JOHN H. JACKSON, THE WORLD TRADING SYSTEM: LAW AND POLICY OF INTERNATIONAL ECONOMIC RELATIONS 178–79, 248–50 (2d ed. 1997).

be rendered just or effective. Indeed, we are only just beginning to unravel the mystery of global governance. Simply mapping the modes of global power and identifying the channels and levers of influence remains an enormous sociological challenge.

At the same time we must remember that not that long ago most in the legal profession thought they knew how it all worked. There was private law and public law, national law and international law, each with its own domain. Global governance was the sum of these well-known parts, each served by its own disciplinary experts. It is fascinating how quickly that confidence has disappeared and those disciplinary boundaries have broken down.

Not that long ago it was quite common to find leading public international lawyers simply dismissive of the world of international economic law and trade as far outside their concern. Internationalists on every faculty had something of the ghetto mentality. Each subfield defended its turf. The study of European law was a rather dramatic example precisely because it arose so recently, with tributaries in public international law, national business regulation, constitutional and administrative law, and more. But it soon enough became a world of its own.

When visiting law faculties in Europe and the United States today, one is struck by the extent to which all of that has been swept away. Specialists in every field – family law, antitrust, intellectual property, civil procedure, criminal law, banking and commercial law – have all come to see their subject in international or comparative terms. It is hard to think of a legal problem that does not cross disciplinary and national boundaries, and it is common for internationalists themselves to stretch across public and private law, to teach about trade and security and development, dipping into national and comparative law as they do. Off the top of my head I can think of numerous inventions that would have been unthinkable just a few years back – I am sure each of you can, as well. I know of at least two courses in international local government law, private law scholars coming out with a legal casebook on comparative Islamic modernization, a new program devoted to the law of empire and colonialism, and on and on.

Let me begin, then, with preliminary thoughts about moments such as this one – moments both of great unknowing and of disciplinary reinvention.

First, it would be surprising if the new order were waiting to be found rather than made. It could be, of course, that our world is already constituted, structured, governed, and we simply lack the vision to understand how it works. It seems more plausible to suppose that our conventional understanding has broken down because things in the world are changing – changing rapidly and in all sorts of different directions at once. If there is to be a new order,

legal or otherwise, it will be created as much as discovered. We will need to
think of our work on global governance not only as description but also as
program.

I expect that those most enthusiastic about constitutional metaphors
understand this all too well – they propose a constitutional interpretation
not only as a discovery but also as a project. Wouldn't things be better if the
world's legal order were constituted, whether the WTO or the UN Charter or
in some other way? And we know that in such matters saying it can sometimes make it so. That is why the effort to imagine a world constitution can
sometimes feel morally and politically so urgent. If you think constitutionalism has worked well at home, and that your own constitution may even be
threatened by global pressures of one sort or another, it can feel like a project
of the utmost seriousness and urgency to interpret the world in constitutional
terms.

At the same time, of course, our program will be but one among many
and will find itself pushed and pulled by the projects and priorities of all
the other actors in the field. We will need to think about global governance
as a dynamic process in which legal, political, and economic arrangements
unleash interests, change the balance of forces, and lead to further reinvention
of the governance scheme itself.

I suspect, moreover, that the changes underfoot are likely to swamp our
efforts to rethink the world by speaking to one another in the academy.
Like constitutional orders before it, a new global governance regime will be
imagined and built through collective hope, struggle, and disappointment.
It will be an order made and known through processes we can only dimly
see. My only consolation is the intuition – and perhaps the hope – that as the
world is reordered, law will be there, imagining it, making it, writing it down,
consolidating and contesting the new arrangements.

Of course, in the meantime, there is an enormous scholarly premium on
being able to see how things will turn out – and how they should turn out.
It is much less satisfying to seek to understand what is unknown, to identify
the powers that elude our grasp, the maps by which it is no longer wise to
navigate, the problems for which there are no ready solutions, or the solutions
long since out of alignment with today's problems. But I am afraid that is
where we are. All the rest remains, for the time, a wish.

My second preliminary observation is that knowledge about how we are
governed is very unevenly spread about the planet. This is also part, if you like,
of how we now find ourselves constituted. We should not be surprised to learn
that people in the global North and the global South understand the nature

of global power and order quite differently. It is common to imagine that our situations are parallel. One often hears that people in the South know as much as we do about how things work, but they simply have different objectives and interests; or that their knowledge, while different, is equal – they know local things, perhaps cultural things. If we have the luxury to generate theory, they have had the rough luck to inhabit the context where that theory will meet the road. In some sense, this is all certainly true. The insiders and the powerful certainly have their own characteristic blind spots and biases.

But we know the gains from the trade of theory for context are rarely distributed equally. Those in a system's center can sometimes, perhaps even quite often, see how the order is ordered, where the levers of power do and do not reside, in ways that are inaccessible at the periphery. Yes, they can resist and reinvent and appropriate – but so, then, can we, for we are also a context to be reckoned with. I worry about the disequilibriums introduced into the governance machinery by the unequal distribution of knowledge. All the more so when educational resources – resources of institutions like this one – are themselves so unevenly distributed. We all know from our own experience that when you are on the outside looking in, it can seem that the powerful know and intend all that they do. But when you are on the inside looking out, it is easy to feel buffeted by one thing after another. We will need to find ways to assist the intelligentsia at the margins of the world system in understanding how things look from the center, just as there will be much we will need to learn from them. It is easy to think of this as just educational policy, a matter for the Internet and cultural exchange – but it is more. The distribution of knowledge about the global order is also a constitutional issue.

A similar dynamic affects relations between the spheres of public and private power on the global level. In my own experience, I have certainly found that the corporate lawyers, investment bankers, and businesspeople of the global economy understand how to manage, instrumentalize, or simply operate within a plural and disaggregated global legal order far more instinctively than do their counterparts in national government service, diplomacy, or the world of international public institutions. In a similar fashion, for all the intense professionalism of our military today, I have found military professionals, including military lawyers, who have a far more difficult time thinking strategically about operations in a global battle space stretching across jurisdictions and characterized by wildly divergent interpretations of supposedly common rules and principles than do their counterparts in the world of transnational finance or business, for whom legal pluralism is an everyday matter of risk and opportunity.

The distribution of knowledge about strategic action in a fluid world is also a constitutional issue. That corporate and financial actors move so easily while every public authority is constituted around a territorial jurisdiction is a matter of law. We might well consider it constitutional, structuring the forms of political life. Whatever our conception of how the world is governed, we will need room for the dynamic effects of people living and struggling in that world not only with different interests and cultures and values but also with different knowledge, and different levels of knowledge, about how it all works.

Consider this broad-brush story about the past century. Over the past century, global labor was liberated from serfdom and slavery into citizenship but incarcerated into one or another nation-state. At first, capital was also largely a prisoner of territory. In some places there was an enormous capital shortage and development was difficult; in others a capital abundance and wages rose. As capital became able to move, the price of labor rose wherever development occurred, while capital became relatively scarce where wages remained high. The financial, intellectual, and business leaders deracinated themselves, floating freely about the globe. Those at the bottom detached from the formal market and the forms of political life to live in an informal world of illegal migration, remittance, and black market entrepreneurialism. Meanwhile, politics remained largely the prerogative of national states, lashed to the interests of a territorial middle class. The relative mobility of capital and rigidity of politics rendered each unstable. In the end political and economic leadership has everywhere drifted apart. Structurally they are linked to different interests, living under different conditions, responding to different constituencies. All this was no accident. Each of these moves was imagined, implemented, and resisted in legal terms.

You can get a good sense of this by traveling the world from one free trade zone to another, enclaves of informality and exceptions from bureaucratic rule, and then trying to adopt a child abroad or listen for the idea that Americans and Mexicans might share a common political future in the speeches of any American primary election campaign. All these territorial arrangements and attitudes are underwritten by law – and are part of how we are globally governed.

I am not sure how significant this story is, or even whether it is altogether correct. I offer it more as a warning. The world's political, economic, and social life is legally organized in ways we rarely find the opportunity to notice in routine discussions about global law and governance. We have built fault lines into the political economy of the world and placed forces in motion that will remake the habitual channels of global governance just as we are reaching to understand how it all works.

Earlier Efforts to Reimagine the Legal World and the World in Legal Terms

Before we assess the constitutionalist project, however, it will be helpful to place it in the context of alternative proposals for new thinking about how the global legal order coheres. First, we need to remember that the traditional legal disciplines – public international law, private international law, international economic law, comparative law, UN law – are all also projects of reinvention. Each began both as an effort to draw a more accurate map of the global regime and as a project to remake that regime, in part by reimagining and redescribing it. We might say that our first contemporary project of rethinking has been the project, under way for more than twenty years, to write new histories of these fields: histories that track their origin not to 1648 or the Roman Empire but to the mid- and late nineteenth century; histories that link our conventional legal disciplines to the imaginative political and ideological projects of particular people, inspired by one or another version of European liberalism and legalism, wed to the colonial endeavor; and histories that follow the repeated remaking of these traditions across the twentieth century in bursts of modernist revision. As projects of reimagination, reconstitution, and reform, our conventional disciplines have been pulled this way and that by political and ideological trends that have swept through society and the academy, perhaps most conspicuously in the past years by feminism and various postcolonialisms.

There remains much we can learn from exploring these conventional projects, although we have lost confidence in them both as maps of the world and as programs for liberal reform. Taken together, their picture of the way the world is governed is striking for its blind spots and biases. The pieces don't fit together or add up. But it is worth understanding why not and how they could have seemed so coherent for so long. The intellectuals who built them also sought to reconnect the global legal order with the social and psychological forces of their day, to codify that order, to capture it in principles, to structure it with new institutions, and to treat those new institutions as more than the sum of their parts. We can learn from their ambitions as well as their techniques. Broadly speaking, these were all humanist endeavors, extending what had been learned at home about humanism to the global stage. We can learn from the limitations and possibilities of a century of legal humanism on the world stage. Moreover, little that these conventional disciplines set in motion has been lost – it is all there, in fragments, built into this or that corner of our imagination and our institutional fabric. Their ideas and formulations continue to have currency.

In the excitement of new ideas and new developments, it is easy to lose sight of this history. This volume contains chapters on new governance in the European Union, on soft law and comitology and the open method of coordination. We need to remember that they stand on a long history of remaking not only the European Union's administrative machinery but also that of other international and national administrative bodies hoping to transform relations with social partners or civil society and to soften the need for interstate agreement. Think of the 1992 Program, the single European market, the new method of harmonization, the Europe of the citizen, variable geometry, the Europe of two speeds – and these just get us back to the Single European Act of 1985. It is hard to remember a time when the elites of the European Union were not preoccupied with the imminent reform of their procedures, new modes of engagement among member states, new styles of regulation and engagement with citizens and social groups – or when they felt adrift because the last reform seemed too many months back. Nor was the European Union the only place to experiment with soft law, regulatory negotiation, compliance incentives, and the rest – consider, for example, the new institutional arrangements for ad hoc multilateralism in the diplomatic world. They are only the latest in a long line of fashionable multilateral solutions to the problems of anarchy and order in the postwar era – think of regional intergovernmental organizations, security alliances and blocs, coalitions of the willing, and Uniting for Peace.

As we begin our discussions, then, I hope we will pause to recall these earlier efforts, if for no other reason than to remind ourselves that whatever we build will rest atop the often still-smoldering ruins of more than a century's worth of efforts to describe in new ways how the world is put together from the point of view, and for the purpose, of governance.

Indeed, even when we move away from the conventional disciplines, we find a history of renewal and reform. In the United States, three projects of reimagination stand out, each, oddly, associated with a particular university. We might see them as the mothers of all reinventions in the field of global governance. The first was the Yale project on World Public Order, pioneered by Myres McDougal and Harold Lasswell in the 1950s.[3] Rooted in the sociology

---

[3] The literature that I have in mind would include the following: Myres S. McDougal, *Law and Power*, 46 AM. J. INT'L L. 102 (1952); *The Comparative Study of Law for Policy Purposes: Value Clarification as an Instrument of Democratic World Order*, 1 AM. J. COMP. L. 24 (1952); *International Law, Power and Policy: A Contemporary Conception*, 82 HAGUE RECUEIL 137 (1953); *Peace and War: Factual Continuum with Multiple Legal Consequences*, 49 AM. J. INT'L. L. 63 (1955); *The Realist Theory in Pyrrhic Victory*, 49 AM. J. INT'L. L. 377 (1955); *Some Basic Theoretical Concepts about International Law: A Policy-Oriented Framework of Inquiry*, 4 J. CONFLICT RESOL. 337 (1960); MYRES S. MCDOUGAL & ASSOCIATES, STUDIES IN WORLD

and philosophy of the interwar period, their effort cast aside conventional disciplinary boundaries to reconsider the nature of public order from the ground up. At the base was not the politics of sovereignty – but neither was there a *Grundnorm*. There were procedures and values, modes of communication, persuasion, and compulsion. Everything was on a continuum, antiformal, requiring judgment and human ethical choice. Elites inhabited a policy process in which they would as often make as follow the law. Global governance was a work in progress, a terribly serious business, neither irrational politics nor rational law, but an ongoing project to choose a world public order of freedom and justice.

The second was something of a reaction, an alternative found for a generation in Manhattan, at Columbia and New York University, and associated with an astonishing group of figures – Thomas Franck, Wolfgang Friedmann, Louis Henkin, Oscar Schachter, and their many colleagues.[4] They were as antiformal

Public Order (Yale Univ. Press 1960); Myres S. McDougal & William T. Burke, The Public Order of the Oceans: A Contemporary International Law of the Seas (Yale Univ. Press 1962); Myres S. McDougal & Florentino P. Feliciano, Law and Minimum World Public Order: The Legal Regulation of International Coercion (Yale Univ. Press 1961); Myres S. McDougal & Harold D. Lasswell, *The Identification and Appraisal of Diverse Systems of Public Order*, 53 Am. J. Int'l L. 1 (1959); Myres S. McDougal, Harold D. Lasswell & Lung-chu Chen, Human Rights and World Public Order (Yale Univ. Press, 1980); Myres S. McDougal, Harold D. Lasswell & James C. Miller, The Interpretation of Agreements and World Public Order: Principles of Content and Procedure (Yale Univ. Press 1967); Myres S. McDougal, Harold D. Lasswell & Ivan A. Vlasic, Law and Public Order in Space (Yale Univ. Press 1963); Myres S. McDougal & W. Michael Reisman, *The Changing Structure of International Law: Unchanging Theory for Inquiry*, 65 Colum. L. Rev. 810 (1965); Richard A. Falk, Law, Morality and War in the Contemporary World (Praeger 1963); The Role of Domestic Courts in the International Legal Order (Princeton Univ. Press 1964); Legal Order in a Violent World (Princeton Univ. Press 1968); The Status of Law in International Society (Princeton Univ. Press 1970); *A New Paradigm for International Legal Studies: Prospects and Proposals*, 84 Yale L.J. 969 (1975); Rosalyn Higgins, The Development of International Law through the Political Organs of the United Nations (Oxford Univ. Press 1963); *Policy Considerations and the International Judicial Process*, 17 Int'l & Comp. L.Q. 58 (1968); *Policy and Impartiality: The Uneasy Relationship in International Law*, 23 Int'l Org. 914 (1969); Morton A. Kaplan & Nicholas deB. Katzenbach, The Political Foundations of International Law (Wiley 1961); W. Michael Reisman, Nullity and Revision: The Renewal and Enforcement of International Judgments and Awards (Yale Univ. Press 1971). *See also* Toward World Order and Human Dignity: Essays in Honor of Myres S. McDougal (W. Michael Reisman ed., Free Press 1976) and The Structure and Process of International Law: Essays in Legal Philosophy, Doctrine, and Theory (R. St. J. Macdonald & Douglas M. Johnston eds., Kluwer Boston 1983).

[4] Particularly notable contributions include the following: Thomas M. Franck, *The Courts, the State Department and National Policy: A Criterion for Judicial Abdication*, 44 Minn. L. Rev. 1101 (1960); *International Law: Through National or International Courts?*, 8 Vill. L. Rev.

and postrealist as Yale, but their emphasis was different. Rules seemed more necessary to restrain the cold war great powers. The United Nations loomed large, the Charter providing at once a set of restraints, a venue for multi-lateralism, and a ready vernacular and perspective for the legitimation and delegitimation of national power. For the Manhattan school, global governance was to be as much a work of the spirit, a work on the self, as a structure of rules and institutions. Most famously, perhaps, for Louis Henkin, the human rights regime matured into a global ideology, common to elites everywhere, limiting and channeling the exercise of public power automatically, without the machinery of enforcement. If he was right, Holmes and Hohfeld had been defeated. It was not all about remedies and every right no longer implied a correlative duty. Social order had been replaced – and ensured – by collective social practice and belief.

Human rights was not the only idea proposed for governance by consciousness. There were also democracy, human freedom, and the human propensity to truck and barter. Neoliberalism, after all, was not only the disciplining creed of a few international financial institutions and first-world governments – it was the spirit of an age, enforcing itself wherever two were gathered in its name, in city governments, corporate boardrooms, local central banks and dozens of national civil services. In this, the Manhattan school echoed Wilhelm Roepke's famous description of the liberal order of the nineteenth century, held together not by institutions of global governance but by a common appreciation of the "liberal" principle that governments should simply not allow the political to contaminate the economic. For Roepke, this "liberal spirit," plus the gold standard, constituted what he termed an "As-If-World-Government" more valuable and ethically compelling than the collectivist fantasies of both European and international lawyers after the

139 (1962–63) and later THE POWER OF LEGITIMACY AMONG NATIONS (Oxford Univ. Press 1990); FAIRNESS IN INTERNATIONAL LAW AND INSTITUTIONS (Oxford Univ. Press 1995); Wolfgang Friedmann, *Half a Century of International Law*, 50 VA. L. REV. 1333 (1964); THE CHANGING STRUCTURE OF INTERNATIONAL LAW (Columbia Univ. Press 1964); *United States Policy and the Crisis of International Law*, 59 AM. J. INT'L L. 857 (1965); *The Relevance of International Law to the Processes of Economic and Social Development*, 60 PROC. AM. SOC'Y OF INT'L L. 8 (1966); *Law and Politics in the Vietnamese War: A Comment*, 61 AM. J. INT'L L. 776 (1967); *The Reality of International Law – A Reappraisal*, 10 COLUM. J. TRANSNAT'L L. 46 (1971); LOUIS HENKIN, HOW NATIONS BEHAVE: LAW AND FOREIGN POLICY (Praeger 1968), INTERNATIONAL LAW: POLITICS AND VALUES (Kluwer Academic Publishers 1995) (from Henkin's general course at the Hague Academy of International Law, 1989); Oscar Schachter, *Dag Hammarskjöld and the Relation of Law to Politics*, 56 AM. J. INT'L L. 1 (1962); *The Uses of Law in International Peace-Keeping*, 50 VA. L. REV. 1096 (1964); *Scientific Advances and International Law Making*, 55 CAL. L. REV. 423 (1967); *Human Dignity as a Normative Concept*, 77 AM. J. INT'L. L. 848 (1983); *In Defence of International Rules on the Use of Force*, 53 U. CHI. L. REV. 113 (1986).

Second World War.[5] For the Manhattan school it was the activist spirit of Dag Hammarskjöld, working flexibly with great, if often contradictory, principles, along the boundaries of law and politics, East and West, guided by the imaginary perspective of an international community, an international judiciary, an international jury of his peers.

The third great project of reimagination was a bit of a reaction to the reaction. It is represented here today by Yale, in the person of Harold Koh. Though he might well trace his lineage to Philip Jessup, it is probably more accurate to locate the origins at Harvard, where Harold and I were classmates, home to the legal process tradition, to Det Vagts, Henry Steiner, Abe and Toni Chayes, and Anne Marie Slaughter.[6] For these thinkers, the key to global governance lay in national law, national courts, and the procedures for allocating authority among them. The state was opened up, broken apart, replaced by the shifting internal dynamics of national bureaucracies and local powers, as well as the distribution among them of the authority to resolve various issues. The focus shifted from keeping the peace, structuring coexistence, or facilitating projects of cooperation to dispute resolution and the chastening of political will that comes with exposure to the sands of international reaction. Their work was also interdisciplinary, drawing on public choice theories and new institutionalisms in both political science and economics.

No doubt these traditions overlapped and learned from one another. Each explicitly rejected conventional disciplinary boundaries, blurred public and

---

[5] *See* Wilhelm Roepke, *Economic Order and International Law*, 86 RECUEIL DES COURS, 203 (1954).

[6] *See* ABRAM CHAYES ET AL., THE INTERNATIONAL LEGAL PROCESS (Little, Brown 1968); THE CUBAN MISSILE CRISIS (Oxford Univ. Press 1974); ABRAM CHAYES & ANTONIA HANDLER CHAYES, THE NEW SOVEREIGNTY: COMPLIANCE WITH INTERNATIONAL REGULATORY AGREEMENTS (Harvard Univ. Press 1995); Harold H. Koh, *Transnational Legal Process*, 75 NEB. L. REV. 181 (1996), *Commentary: Is International Law Really State Law?*, 111 HARV. L. REV. 1824 (1998); *The Globalization of Freedom*, 26 YALE J. INT'L L. 305 (2001); Anne-Marie Slaughter, *Toward an Age of Liberal Nations*, 33 HARV. INT'L L.J. 393 (1992); *International Law and International Relations Theory: A Dual Agenda*, 87 AM. J. INT'L L. 205 (1993); *International Law in a World of Liberal States*, 6 EUR. J. INT'L L. 503 (1995); *Liberal International Relations Theory and International Economic Law*, 10 AM. U. J. INT'L L. & POL'Y 1 (1995); *The Accountability of Government Networks*, 8 IND. J. GLOBAL LEGAL STUD. 347 (2001); HENRY J. STEINER & DETLEV VAGTS, TRANSNATIONAL LEGAL PROBLEMS: MATERIALS AND TEXT (Foundation Press 1968) (this text is currently in its fourth edition, in relation to which Harold H. Koh has joined Steiner and Vagts as coauthor: HENRY J. STEINER ET AL., TRANSNATIONAL LEGAL PROBLEMS: MATERIALS AND TEXT (4th ed. 1994); Detlev F. Vagts, *The United States and Its Treaties: Observance and Breach*, 95 AM. J. INT'L L. 313 (2001); *International Law in the Third Reich*, 84 AM. J. INT'L L. 661 (1990); *The Traditional Legal Concept of Neutrality in a Changing Environment*, 14 AM. U. INT'L L. REV. 83 (1998).

private, national and international, and drew inspiration from colleagues elsewhere in the social sciences. For each, the legal order stood at the center of global order. Each rejected the pictures of law drawn by earlier schools of legal thought as they remembered them, whether naturalism or positivism, formalism or realism. And they rejected the images of law drawn by laypeople and colleagues in other disciplines looking at the legal regime from the outside. From that perspective, the fluidity and pluralism of the legal system, the immanence of value in legal order, as well as law's engagement with social and political processes were all not visible.

There is now a large literature assessing the weaknesses and limitations of these schools of thought. They have criticized one another and survived long enough to give rise to internal eddies of discontent and rethinking. I won't revisit here what went wrong. Like the disciplines that preceded them, they remain all around us, their central ideas and institutional and doctrinal innovations remain useful and are, in fact, used every day by courts and diplomats and activists and scholars. But we are gathered here, I think, talking about various new constitutionalisms, in part because at least in this sense the center has not held and these earlier efforts have lost their ability to inspire. We embark on the constitutionalization of the world not only atop the ruins of our conventional disciplines but also against the background of these earlier and still powerful efforts to rethink the legal order in unconventional ways.

As I am sure their proponents would agree, even at their best, the more recent traditions remain rudimentary and partial answers to the question, How are we governed at the global level? Much remains to be learned. Already when I began teaching international law, more than twenty years ago, it seemed sensible to look outside this lexicon for new approaches to international law. For years we found ourselves fully occupied simply understanding the history and limits of these earlier efforts to think in new ways about how the world is legally constituted.

The past few years have brought yet another group of large-scale proposals to reinterpret the world of law, all of them distinct from the constitutionalisms we will take up here. All stand on the legacy of our traditional disciplines, renewed by Yale and Manhattan and Harvard. Let me mention just a few, to give a sense for the scale and diversity of the efforts under way. We might start with the enormous project of legal sociology underway at Australian National University to map the world of regulation. Peter Drahos and John Braithwaite begin with the observation that an enormous number of rules are neither made nor enforced by states – and those that are will often have been written and may well be enforced by people in other states and other institutions.[7] They focus on private ordering, standard-setting bodies, the social practices and patterns of influence within industry and professional bodies. Their project is descriptive – who functions in this hidden world where rules are made, how do they become powerful, what kinds of rules and principles travel from one domain to another, and which are left behind? Their ambition is to share knowledge and access to the inner workings of global regulation more equitably, to empower those left out of the process.

Then there is the new project on global administrative law at New York University.[8] Richard Steward, Ben Kingsbury, and their colleagues seek to rethink public power as a form of administration, regardless of whether it is exercised by courts or private actors, integrated into a conventional hierarchy of public authority, or dispersed across the globe. Looked at this way, they ask whether conventional administrative law reforms – transparency, participation, opportunity to be heard, judicial review – might not offer a recipe for improving global governance.

In Frankfurt, we have the work of Gunther Teubner and others influenced by Niklas Luhmann's systems theory.[9] Perhaps, they argue, the world is ordered in a series of semiautonomous systems, loosely associated with industries or domain of social practice or belief, each with its own rules and

[7] JOHN BRAITHWAITE & PETER DRAHOS, GLOBAL BUSINESS REGULATION (Cambridge Univ. Press 2000). The project of which this work is a part (the Regulatory Institutions Network, or RegNet) has spawned a truly voluminous interdisciplinary literature over the past eight or so years that spans a diversity of topics. RegNet's past publications are detailed at http://regnet.anu.edu.au/program/publications/index.php.

[8] See Benedict Kingsbury, Nico Krisch & Richard Stewart, The Emergence of Global Administrative Law, 68 L. & CONTEMP. PROBS. 15 (2005); Benedict Kingsbury, The Administrative Law Frontier in Global Governance, 99 PROC. AM. SOC'Y OF INT'L L. (2005). See also the various papers included in Benedict Kingsbury, Nico Krisch & Richard Stewart (special eds.), The Emergence of Global Administrative Law, 68 L. & CONTEMP. PROBS. (Summer/Autumn 2005), and Benedict Kingsbury & Nico Krisch (special eds.), Symposium on Global Governance and Global Administrative Law in the International Legal Order, 17 EUR. J. INT'L L. (2006). For further bibliographical resources for the global administrative law literature, see A Global Administrative Law Bibliography, 68 L. & CONTEMP. PROBS. 365 (2005), and http://iilj.org/GAL/documents/GALBibliographyMDeBellisJune2006.pdf (last checked 1 March 2009).

[9] See Gunter Teubner & Andreas Fischer-Lescano, Regime-Collisions: The Vain Search for Legal Unity in the Fragmentation of Global Law, 25 MICH. J. INT'L L. 999–1046 (2004); GUNTHER TEUBNER, LAW AS AN AUTOPOETIC SYSTEM (1993); The King's Many Bodies: The Self-Deconstruction of Law's Hierarchy, 31 L. & SOC. REV. 763 (1997); Contracting Worlds: The Many Autonomies of Private Law, 9 SOC. & LEG. STUD. 399 (2000). See also the collected essays in GLOBAL LAW WITHOUT A STATE (Gunther Teubner ed., 1997). This literature draws strongly on Niklas Luhmann's system theory approach. See generally NIKLAS LUHMANN, SOCIAL SYSTEMS (John Bednarz & Dirk Baeker trans., Stanford Univ. Press, 1995); and NIKLAS LUHMANN, LAW AS A SOCIAL SYSTEM (Fatima Kastner et al. eds., Klaus A. Ziegert trans., Oxford Univ. Press 2004).

procedures, even constitutional procedures and principles, pursuing its own logic: a health system, a sports system, a trade system, a pharmaceutical system, and so on. Governments – or certainly diplomacy – would be but one system among many. The research objective is to identify these systems, to study their emergence and interaction, in search of a general model – what constitutes a system, how do systems change and interact with one another, how are conflicts resolved, and how are systems defended?

We also have an emergent body of literature proposing new-governance ideas developed domestically and in Brussels for the international order. Embracing tenets of democratic experimentalism and innovative institutional arrangements disconnected from more traditional modes of thinking about law and regulation, scholars of this school seek to wed notions of democratic legitimacy with economic efficiency in an ambitious project of renewal and change.[10]

One of the most interesting and sustained grand projects of reimagination has been the effort by a new generation to rethink the relationship between the international law and the third world. Sparked by the work of scholars like Tony Anghie, Makau Mutua, James Gathii, B. S. Chimni, and Balakrishnan Rajagopal, this intellectual movement is not associated with a university – participants have found footholds here and there, and only in London, at the School of Oriental and African Studies and the affiliated schools of the University of London, do you find a critical mass.[11] They are exploring the continuing significance of the colonial project for the structure of

[10]   See, e.g., Charles F. Sabel, A Quiet Revolution of Democratic Governance: Towards Democratic Experimentalism, in GOVERNANCE IN THE 21ST CENTURY (Organisation for Economic Co-operation and Development 2001); Michael Dorf & Charles F. Sabel, A Constitution of Democratic Experimentalism, 98 COLUM. L. REV. 267 (1998); Charles F. Sabel & William Simon, Destabilization Rights: How Public Law Litigation Succeeds, 117 HARV. L. REV. 1016 (2004); James Liebman & Charles F. Sabel, A Public Laboratory Dewey Barely Imagined: The Emerging Model of School Governance and Legal Reform (2003) 28 N.Y.U. REV. L. & SOC. CHANGE 183; Gráinne de Búrca, The Constitutional Challenge of New Governance, 28 EUR. L. REV. 814 (2003); LAW AND NEW GOVERNANCE IN THE EU AND THE US (Gráinne de Búrca & Joanne Scott eds., Hart Publishing 2006); Susan Strum, Second Generation Employment Discrimination: A Structuralist Approach, 101 COLUM. L. REV. 458 (2001); David M. Trubek & Louise G. Trubek, Hard and Soft Law in the Construction of Social Europe: The Role of the Open Method of Co-ordination, 11 EUR. L.J. 343 (2005). See also Orly Lobel, The Renew Deal: The Fall of Regulation and the Rise of Governance in Contemporary Legal Thought, 89 MINN. L. REV. 342 (2004), which provides a good overview of a large portion of the new governance literature. For some of my thoughts concerning the new governance approach, see David Kennedy, Remarks for the "New Governance Workshop" Harvard Law School (Feb. 25–26, 2005), available at: http://www.law.harvard.edu/faculty/dkennedy/speeches/Remarks.pdf (last accessed 1 March 2009).

[11]   For current scholarship associated with third-world approaches to international law, see Anthony Anghie, Francisco de Vitoria and the Colonial Origins of International Law, 5 SOC. & LEG. STUD. 321 (1996); Finding the Peripheries: Sovereignty and Colonialism in Nineteenth

global law and political life, identifying issues not solved by transforming the dominions into formal sovereigns that they might participate in the institutions of intergovernmental life and take responsibility for territorial government. As one might expect from the work of a broad network, the results are far more diverse in viewpoint and method than what has so far emerged from the parallel efforts at New York University or Australian National University or Frankfurt. What they share is the ambition to redraw the map of global governance from the periphery, placing altogether different issues and modes of rulership in foreground focus. And a dissatisfaction with their own intellectual forefathers in the era of decolonization is every bit as intense as that felt by the reinventions of the North about our conventional disciplines.

These are all powerful reconceptualizations. It is always tempting in this sort of situation to imagine that each has hold of one piece of the elephant. Each does, certainly. But each is also proposing a different elephant. Each offers a vision, more or less in the mode of our conventional disciplines before them, that it claims to be a more complete account, a plausible total or ground-level answer to the question of how we are governed, as a candidate to function as queen of the sciences when it comes to global governance. We ought not to dismiss these claims as misguided hubris. Constitutionalism,

---

Century International Law, 40 HARV. INT'L L.J. 1 (1999); *Colonialism and the Birth of International Institutions: Sovereignty, Economy and the Mandate System of the League of Nations*, 34 N.Y.U. J. INT'L L. & POL. 513 (2002); IMPERIALISM, SOVEREIGNTY AND THE MAKING OF INTERNATIONAL LAW (Cambridge Univ. Press 2005); Upendra Baxi, 'The War on Terror' *and 'The War of Terror': Nomadic Attitudes, Aggressive Incumbents and the 'New' International Law; Prefatory Remarks on Two Wars*, 43 OSGOODE HALL L.J. 7 (2005); Bhupinder Chimni, *International Institutions Today: An Imperial Global State in the Making*, 15 EUR. J. INT'L L. 1 (2004); James Gathii, *International Law and Eurocentricity*, 9 EUR. J. INT'L L. 184 (1998); *Alternative and Critical: The Contribution of Research and Scholarship on Developing Countries to International Legal Theory*, 41 HARV. INT'L L.J., 263 (2000); *Neoliberalism, Colonialism and International Governance: Decentering the International Law of Governmental Legitimacy*, 98 MICH. L. REV. 6 (2000); Balakrishnan Rajagopal, *Locating the Third World in Cultural Geography*, 1998–99 THIRD WORLD LEG. STUD. 1 (1999); INTERNATIONAL LAW FROM BELOW; DEVELOPMENT, SOCIAL MOVEMENTS AND THIRD WORLD RESISTANCE (Cambridge Univ. Press 2003); Makau Mutua, *What is TWAIL?*, 94 PROC. AM. SOC'Y OF INT'L L. 31 (2000); *Critical Race Theory and International Law: The View of an Insider-Outsider*, 45 VILL. L. REV. 841 (2000); *Savages, Victims, and Saviors: The Metaphor of Human Rights*, 42 HARV. INT'L L.J. 201 (2001); Karin Mickelson, *Rhetoric and Rage: Third World Voices in International Legal Discourse*, 16 WISC. INT'L L.J. 353 (1997); Obiora Chinedu Okafor, *Newness, Imperialism, and International Legal Reform in Our Time: A Twail Perspective*, 43 OSGOODE HALL L.J. 171 (2005); *The Third World, International Law and the Post 9/11 Era: An Introduction*, 43 OSGOODE HALL L.J. 1 (2005); Amr A. Shalakany, *Arbitration and the Third World: A Plea for Reassessing Bias under the Specter of Neoliberalism*, 41 HARV. INT'L L.J. 2 (2000). See also *Symposium: Globalization at the Margins: Perspectives on Globalization from Developing States*, 7 IND. J. GLOBAL LEGAL STUD. (1999).

of course, has claimed pride of place for years in our own legal academy –
as the study of process, civil procedure, and federal courts did a generation
before, or private law before that. The structure of governance has always
been both the sum of the disciplinary insights spawned in its name and a
struggle among perspectives claiming to be foundational.

If we are to embrace constitutionalism, we will need to explain not only
what it adds to the knowledge we have gleaned from, say, public international law or international economic law but also what it means to treat
constitutionalism as, well, constitutional. Each field, after all, carries with it a
disciplinary sensibility about what the problems are and where solutions lie.
Standing on each foundation, some problems will be easy to see, and others
harder. Some actors and authorities and perspectives will be foregrounded,
and others not. As we compare frameworks for thinking about global governance, we will need to assess their relative blindness and insight, and the
consequences of treating one rather than another as the base. What projects
of reform, what space for politics will be enabled setting off from one rather
than another of these various points of view?

Moreover, these are certainly not the only new ideas out there about how it
all fits together. The traditions of public choice and institutional economics,
imported into law by law and economics scholars, also propose new ways of
explaining global legal order.[12] I have mentioned only projects well known
in the English-language academy. But we must imagine there is rethinking

---

[12] William J. Aceves, *The Economic Analysis of International Law: Transaction Cost Economics
and the Concept of State Practice*, 17 U. PA. J. INT'L ECON. L. 955 (1996); DOUGLAS G. BAIRD
ET AL., GAME THEORY AND THE LAW (Harvard Univ. Press 1994); Eyal Benvenisti, *Collective
Action in the Utilization of Shared Freshwater: The Challenges of International Water Resources
Law*, 90 AM. J. INT'L L. 384 (1996); Robert D. Cooter, *Structural Adjudication and the New
Law Merchant: A Model of Decentralized Law*, 14 INT'L REV. L. & ECON. 215 (1994); Jeffrey
Dunoff & Joel Trachtman, *Economic Analysis of International Law*, 24 YALE J. INT'L L. 1
(1999); Jack L. Goldsmith & Eric A. Posner, *A Theory of Customary International Law*, 66
U. CHI. L. REV. 4 (1999); Moshe Hirsch, *The Future Negotiations over Jerusalem, Strategical
Factors and Game Theory*, 45 CATH. U. L. REV. 699 (1996); Jonathan R. Macey, *Chicken Wars
as a Prisoner's Dilemma: What's in a Game?* 64 NOTRE DAME L. REV. 447 (1989); William
B. T. Mock, *Game Theory, Signaling, and International Legal Relations*, 26 GEO. WASH. J.
INT'L L. & ECON. 33 (1992); Joel R. Paul, *The New Movements in International Economic Law*,
10 AM. U. J. INT'L L. & POL'Y 607 (1995); Paul B. Stephan, *Barbarians inside the Gate: Public
Choice Theory and International Economic Law*, 10 AM U. J. INT'L L. & POL'Y 745 (1995);
Accountability and International Lawmaking: Rules, Rents, and Legitimacy, 17 NW. J. INT'L
L. & BUS. 681 (1996–97); Alan O. Sykes, *Protectionism as a Safeguard: A Positive Analysis
of the GATT "Escape Clause" with Normative Speculations*, 58 U. CHI. L. REV. 255 (1991);
The Economics of Injury in Antidumping and Countervailing Duty Cases, 16 INT'L REV. L. &
ECON. 5 (1996); Joel P. Trachtman, *The Theory of the Firm and the Theory of the International
Economic Organization: Toward Comparative Institutional Analysis*, 17 NW. J. INT'L L. & BUS.
470 (1996–97).

underway as well in Moscow and Tehran and Beijing and – it will be a long list. And we are still looking only at the projects in law – there are every bit as energetic projects moving ahead across the social sciences.

Having multiplied things so far, I should probably come clean as having my own pet project of totalizing redescription. My own focus has been on the work of experts and the significance of expert knowledge in governing our world. Over the past several years, I have studied the work of various experts – international lawyers, human rights activists, military professionals, experts in economic development – to understand the nature of their expertise, the knowledge they bring to bear, their background consciousness about what is and is not part of their domain, the terms through which they argue for one or another position, and the channels through which they make what they know real. On the basis of these preliminary studies, I have proposed pieces of what I hope will become a general model of expertise and the work of experts in global governance.[13]

For now, let me simply say that I have become convinced that the role of experts is drastically understudied. We focus on statesmen and public opinion, and not enough on the ways in which their choices, their beliefs, are shaped by background players. After all, if for a generation everyone thinks an economy is a national input-output system to be managed, and then suddenly they all become convinced that an economy is a global market for the allocation of resources to their most productive use through the efficiency of exchange in the shadow of a price system, a lot has changed. That is also governance. At the same time, our ideas about experts and expertise are rarely realistic. We often overestimate their capacity and influence. We imagine that development economists know how to bring about development, or that lawyers know how to build an institution or draft a statute to bring about a desired result. What holds them back is the friction and resistance of context – or incompetence. At the same time, we rarely have a good picture of the blind spots and biases introduced by expertise, along the lines of the old adage that to a man with a hammer, everything looks like a nail. Indeed, experts rarely

---

[13] *See, e.g.,* David Kennedy, *Challenging Expert Rule: The Politics of Global Governance,* 27 SYDNEY. L. REV. 5 (2005); THE DARK SIDES OF VIRTUE: REASSESSING INTERNATIONAL HUMANITARIANISM (Princeton Univ. Press 2004); OF WAR AND LAW (Princeton Univ. Press 2006); *The Politics and Methods of Comparative Law, in* THE COMMON CORE OF EUROPEAN PRIVATE LAW: ESSAYS ON THE PROJECT 345 (Mauro Bussani & Ugo Mattei eds., Kluwer Law International 2003); *New Approaches to Comparative Law: Comparativism and International Governance,* 2 UTAH L. REV. 545 (1997); *Laws and Developments, in* LAW AND DEVELOPMENT: FACING COMPLEXITY IN THE 21ST CENTURY 17 (Amanda Perry-Kessaris & John Hatchard eds., Cavendish Publishing 2003); *The International Style in Postwar Law and Policy,* 1 UTAH L. REV. 7 (1994).

know what they don't know – and know a great deal that is fashion, that is borrowed, misunderstood, reduced to a slogan, or simply too contradictory to be applied or implemented straightforwardly.

It may be unwise to call what I am after "experts" and "expertise," for we are used to equating these terms with the work of the professions – scientists, technical people, doctors, and lawyers. My hypothesis is broader – that the relationships between power and knowledge that we can see in the professions most familiar to us, such as international lawyers or development professionals, are a model for the relationship between what both laypeople and leaders know and do. Politicians are also experts, of a sort, as are voters. It is not just that they have learned to think about international affairs from expert talking heads. It is that they also play roles and learn about their commitments and possibilities in social networks akin to disciplines or fields.

For all these people – technical experts, politicians, citizens – it is not at all obvious how ideas become policies or how the expertise of various fields or disciplines blend together in that process. But I am convinced that were we to understand the mutually constitutive relationship between professional practice and knowledge, we would have displaced the agent-versus-structure debate that has so paralyzed much of the social sciences with respect to international affairs. Rather than agents in structures, we might come to see people with projects, projects of affiliation and disaffiliation, commitment and aversion, and with wills to power and to submission. We would find these people organized in disciplines, speaking with one another in the vernacular perhaps of public international law or international economic law or constitutionalism. These disciplines would have a history – an intellectual history, and an institutional and political history.

Their knowledge would be less recipe than rhetoric. Their practice would often be best understood as assertion and argument, the vernacular of those arguments structured like any other language. Were we to pursue this approach, we would focus less on procedures or institutions – or even substantive norms and values. The constitution, if we could call it that, for global governance would be written in the disciplinary habits, including the habits of mind and patterns of argument, of people with projects operating with expertise.

Comparative Evaluation: Things We Should Be Sure to See

Against this background, I come to our discussion of constitutionalism in a skeptical and comparative frame of mind. Skepticisms: can it really be that we are so soon constituted? Do we know enough about the structure of global arrangements – whether legal or political, economic, cultural – to be confident that what we know domestically as constitutionalism is a good idea for the globe? What if the distances are so great, the forces so chaotic, and the differences in situation so profound that the constitution ratifies what ought rather to be transformed?

At the same time, constitutionalism, in all the varieties taken up in this volume, is but one project to reinterpret and remake global governance. How ought we to compare it to these others? Each has given rise to a specialized profession. Each offers a focal point for reform. In comparing their vices and virtues, we will each have our own list of issues and facts about the world we think it particularly critical to take into account, and we will each judge these various efforts in part by their ability to do justice to our own preoccupations. Let me share a few of my own – the checklist against which I would judge the constitutionalist, or any other, project to rethink global governance. A brief list of things to which I worry we have paid insufficient attention.

First would be the sheer density of rules and institutions in the global space. We often imagine that the world is an anarchic struggle or a deregulated market over which we have managed to throw but a thin net of rules. But the situation is more the opposite – law and regulation and rule at every turn. Economic globalization means legal globalization – every box travels with a packet of rights and privileges; every transfer relies on a network of institutions and rules. The internationalization of politics means the legalization of politics. Every agent of the state, of the city, of the region, acts and interacts on the basis of delegated powers, through the instrument of decision and rule and judgment. Indeed, globalization has fragmented both economic and political power, but it has not delegalized it. The contrary. Even war today – asymmetric war, high-tech war, war stretched across a global battle space, war of missiles and missives – is an affair of rules and regulations and legal principles. As a result, the problem is not to bring political or legal actors into law but to understand and, where necessary, rearrange the laws that constitute those actors, channel their interactions, and influence their relative powers.

Second, and related, is the disorderliness, the pluralism, the uncertainty, the chaos, of all those rules and principles and institutions. The globalization of law, the legalization of politics and economics, have brought with it a tremendous dispersion of law. All manner of rules, enforced and unenforced, may, as a matter of fact, affect any global transaction. And as a matter of law there are conflicting and multiplying jurisdictions, asserting the validity or persuasiveness of their rules, with no decider of last resort. Some of this disorder is structured in one or another way – various federalisms, multiple jurisdictions, choices of law provisions, even races to the top and bottom.

But some is also a matter of struggle and conflict, between legal orders, ideas, powers, and traditions. Our constitutional picture will need to have room for all this disorder – there is no use denying or overlooking it, pretending coherence. And it is not at all clear that the situation would be improved by a net reduction in the plurality of law – it might or it might not. Some would gain and others would lose. We will need to assess the dynamic and distribution effects of one or another attitude toward the disorderliness of global governance.

Third is a series of issues we might think of as the inverse side of law. I worry that our ideas about global governance pay too little attention to the informal and the clandestine – to customary norms, background patterns of private and public expectation, black markets, and illegal flows. We rarely distinguish carefully the many degrees of separation from the legal foreground – the clandestine, the informal, the illegal, the corrupt, and the black market may all be quite different. Moreover, as everyone exercising a prosecutor's discretion to bring charges well knows, those who govern often strategize about a residual of noncompliance to be tolerated. Under a regime of exchange controls, a black market may be more effective than a tariff, and so on. We will need to pay more attention to these back-side calculations and effects, and articulate more clearly how awareness of their significance alters our sense of the big questions – where and what is global power, how is politics organized, and where are the levers for change?

In a similar vein, we are prone to imagine that things that happen in the exceptions to rules are outside the law altogether. As if the exception were not also a rule. Guantánamo, for example, far from being a legal black hole, is one of the most regulated places on the planet – it is simply that different rules apply and different rules do not apply. Indeed, our pictures of global governance are woefully inadequate in their attention to the significance of legal privileges. We forget that law is a matter not merely of rights and duties but also of privileges to injure without compensation. When the UN High Commissioner for Refugees knocks on the door of a sovereign and asks that a refugee be admitted, the response will be rooted not only in sovereign power but also in legal privilege – the privilege to exclude, to define those one will admit, to defend and fence the national territory. Despoiling the rainforest is not only an economic decision – it is also the exercise of legal privilege. In our thinking about global governance, I worry that we focus too much on the fate of a few hundred detainees held here and there, while our legal order meanwhile wraps the violent wartime deaths of thousands in the "privilege" to kill on the battlefield and the comforting reassurance that all the collateral damage was proportional, necessary, and reasonable. It is customary to understand things we don't like – war or poverty or sovereign discretion – as facts or powers prior to law. But each is also a legal institution. A refugee is not simply a person who flees his or her homeland – a refugee is also a legal status and legal regime that governs those who flee, often radically transforming who may flee, where they may go, and even whom they will imagine themselves to be.

Fourth, as I have said, it is easy to think about global governance, particularly when thinking about it constitutionally, as a static plan, a machine to be turned on. But our various proposals and reinterpretations will fall into an ongoing and unruly process. They will strengthen forces and weaken others in ways that will change how they function. Global governance is already under way, and proposals for its improvement will need to think strategically about the forces that must be strengthened to ensure their success. Are we betting on the middle powers, on the great democracies, on those with the capacity to project force abroad, on the rising giants of India and China, South Africa or Brazil?

There is nothing unusual in the idea that a scheme for global governance ought to be conscious not only about who will win and lose but also about whom one expects to carry the program to victory. For the United Nations it was to be the United States, founder, host, and leading source of funds, along with the other Allied powers granted veto status in the Security Council. Powers changed, new players emerged, the Charter was amended, in practice if not in text. It is also easy to see that the expansion of the GATT depended upon harnessing the great trade blocs and dominant traders within its terms from the start, just as the European Coal and Steel Community, whatever its legal structure, depended upon cementing a core trade-off between France and Germany that could be expanded, both geographically and substantively. The interests to be engaged were not simply states – they were farmers and industrialists. Indeed, trade scholars have long understood that bargaining in the GATT or WTO – running a successful trade war, if you like – is all about placing pressure on domestic social and economic sectors that one suspects may be able to move public decision makers abroad, perhaps farmers or cheese makers or the automotive industry. The WTO offers a framework for gaming conflicts among interests internal to other states.

Of course, not all contemporary discussions of global governance are silent on their implicit political and economic strategy. But I must say I worry about the plausibility of the coalitions that many of today's most popular governance projects would place on the field to ensure their coming into being – nongovernmental actors, national judges, international media elites, foundations, corporations enacting newfound ideas about social responsibility, wrapped together and styled the "international community" or "international civil society." There is certainly power there. But it can also be a rather weak reed, can stimulate a backlash more powerful than what it can bring to the table in defense, and can lash a global governance system to a narrow vision of the interests and issues in need of focus. It is easy to overlook conflict and risk and alternative visions of society and justice when your constituents have styled you as the voice of the universal.

In a similar vein, I worry that our efforts to comprehend global governance have focused far too much on the authority of agents we see to act within structures we understand. We have paid too little attention to the myriad ways power flows through flows of finances, of resources, of arms. But many are patterns of belief, modes of knowledge, of affiliation and disaffiliation, the social movement of wills to power, the desire to submit, the experience of triumph and victimization, pride and shame. All these things move like a virus or a fad, but our epidemiology is weak, and our sociology of status convention and emulation at the global level is rudimentary.

In a sense, governance by knowledge is easy to picture. We know that the idea of a national economy or a nation-state can rise and fall, changing a great deal about how people govern and how they imagine themselves in community. Similarly, by tracing the rise and fall of endogeneity in economics, we might learn a great deal about what seems possible for policy in different places and times. But imagine a map of global governance that tracked the distribution of pride and shame across the world's economies, political configurations, social and cultural forms. I am convinced we would find that social power and submission and all the pleasures and rages that accompany them both on the global stage will also turn out to be matters of governance and law.

Fifth and finally, I worry that our projects to rethink global governance fail to grasp the depth of the injustice of the world today and the urgency of change. They are projects of moderate reform for which the normal is stable and sustainable. Even our best disciplinary maps make inequality and domination in the world system difficult to see. We imagine that poverty was and remains simply there, precursor to growth, fact, and context for policy, and we understand far too little about the dynamic relationship between growth and poverty. In a similar way, the relationship between rulership and exclusion remains as difficult to understand as that between global governance and the informal world of clandestine flows. The alchemy by which inequality becomes routinized through the vernacular of experts and hardens as law is tough to unravel – but the effects are everywhere on view. Just writing the history of domination and inequality – and their erasure – into the maps legal intellectuals have already produced will be a great work.

We will each come to debates about global governance with a sense for the challenges we face. The sustainability of our lifestyle and our environment surely makes the list. Then there is the demographic challenge, so pronounced in Europe and the ex–Soviet Union, but also here – or in Saudi Arabia – that will force a reckoning with immigration or security or both. There is the challenge posed by economic success in the third world – by the hundreds of millions of Chinese and Indian individuals who have emerged from poverty into our industrial present. Speaking loosely, and to put it in the starkest terms, with economic globalization and the continued loss of public capacity, large swaths of the world will, in twenty years, have whatever social security system, whatever environmental regime, whatever labor law, whatever wage rate, prevails in China.

And there is the parallel challenge posed by economic failure in the third world – by the revolution of rising frustrations among the hundred of millions of individuals who can see in but for whom there seems no route through the screen except through rebellion and spectacle. If you put just these threats together, we confront an accelerating social and economic dualism. A rumbling fault line between two global architectures, between an insider and an outsider class, between leading and lagging sectors, both within and between national economies and political units.

It is disheartening that while the world fractures so many of our debates about global governance are content merely to embroider the habits of the technical class, decorating their management with intellectual filigree. So much scholarship today is simply a brief for the significance and vitality of a narrow professional culture and sensibility. Its authors struggle for political rapprochement between a center-right attuned to market failures and a center-left that has lost faith in its own nostalgia for what it remembers as the potent regulatory and administrative state of earlier days. These political tendencies are status quo parties, timid about social conflict, hesitant about distribution, resigned to poverty, harnessed to a culture of warfare.

I would prefer we set out with questions of political economy in the foreground and that we came to global governance and the constitutionalization of the planet not as an opportunity to depoliticize world affairs but as the chance to pursue a new politics attuned to these challenges. How does the world remain so unequal; how are hierarchy and domination reproduced? What does law have to do with the organization of politics and economics? If you are an intellectual in the periphery of the world system – the intellectual, geographic, political, cultural, or economic periphery – what can you do to change things? Our work on global governance should aim to answer questions like those.

We know, for example, that bargaining power is also distributed by law – both between nations and across production chains. If the trading system is to be our world constitution, how does it distribute bargaining power in global markets? When small or medium-size enterprises in Vietnam compete with producers in Laos or Mexico and then bargain with globally networked purchasers, how does law allocate their powers? Who captures the rent? Not only developing governments and their employees seek rents – so do Wal-Mart and Toyota and Chevron. Moreover, how are regulatory powers allocated where economic factors other than labor move more freely than sovereign power? Why do property rights travel so securely when the extraterritorial reach of labor law or employment discrimination or environmental protection law continues to seem unreasonable? How do we decide whether a low-wage development strategy is an unfair subsidy or the extraterritorial application of labor law a nontariff barrier to trade? Indeed, it may well turn out that antitrust or contract is the new global constitutional law. Should we so conclude, we'll want to understand the industrial policy embedded within it.

In short, I worry that everywhere global public capacity is not only too anemic or irregular to confront the stakes of global poverty, conflict, injustice; it is also the instrument of that poverty, those conflicts, and that injustice. As a result, where our shared dreams about global governance remain rooted in the status quo, they risk lulling us into complacency. We need to remember, as we speak about these things, that all of us in the professional classes of the North confront the rest of humanity with our entitlements and lifestyle, and also with our talk about the international community and global governance. It is not enough any more to say that we favor better law or good governance. We will need to ask for whom we govern, for what form of political, social, and economic life do we propose a constitution?

Constitutionalism as Global Governance

The conference organizers labeled our discussion of constitutionalism "ruling the world" – tongue in cheek, certainly, but expressive also of the gravity of what we're about. I worry that those who work in the constitutionalist vernacular are often dressing up normative projects in sociological terms. There is no question we need better maps of the legal regime through which we are governed globally. If we could understand how the whole scheme was constituted, we would be ahead of the game. But I must say current constitutionalist discussions of global governance, although they begin as description, end up sounding far more like proposals to remake the world's political order by sacralizing the institutional forms with which they are most familiar.

It may be my background in American law, but I have always felt constitutionalism a rather weak sociology of the way power functions. The U.S. Constitution is fascinating as a meditation on the possible relationships among a series of legal authorities. As a text, it could be the stuff of normative imagination or political philosophy. I am sure it is sometimes a useful textual reference for interpretive practice in quite specific institutional settings. But it is a lousy description of power in American society and a quite inaccurate map of how Washington works. Private power and economic form are altogether missing from the story, as are the role of political parties and money, the dynamics of social dualism in American life, changing ethical and political fashion, the world of background norms, informal and customary arrangements, and much more. The document reads as if powers outside the territory and entities outside the text are irrelevant to public order. If we imagine the world it constitutes as our political world, we will miss a great deal.

Perhaps our fledgling international constitutionalisms are on to something, but I am worried by the extent to which people come to these debates carrying baggage from their national constitutional traditions. Most scholars of global governance think their own societies do work rather well, and many credit their constitution in some way. Even if this is all true, we would still be right to question whether these constitutionalist ideas are useful at the global level, mostly for the familiar reason that international society is altogether different – larger, more fragmented, lacking, as they say, *demos*. Take judicial review – it seems central, though many democratic constitutional traditions do not have it. As American lawyers, we're familiar with dozens of arguments about the uses and abuses of judicial review, all of which are expressed in very general terms – treating things like executive power, judicial independence, judicial activism, and even sound judgment as if they were universals we might place in an ideal relationship with one another rather than idealized descriptions of quite specific institutions in the particular context of American history and political life. Indeed, I have often thought it would be a useful heuristic in discussions of global governance here in the United States simply to ban the use of catchphrases and code words from American constitutional debates precisely so that we could better remember when we are speaking about general things and when about our own experience.

Moreover, I wonder whether our national constitution has done such a good job constituting us as a nation, or whether the American cult of the constitution has not also made us less able to see enduring divisions within our society or imagine links with people outside the territorial boundaries of the place we call the United States. As a tool for social justice, we would have to concede the record is rather mixed. There have been some astonishing successes and important, if more routine, pressure against governmental overreaching. But a great deal of injustice has also been routinized or legitimated. The inequality in education for citizens in side-by-side suburbs, one wealthy, the other poor, remains a scandal and is rooted in legal arrangements and ideas, about cities and property and taxation. Or take the Senate – by entrenching the power of the least populated states, the U.S. Constitution has continuously structured the nation's political economy. Constitutions are about focusing political attention, removing some things from routine political struggle, placing others front and center, arranging the powers to be taken lightly and those to be accorded great respect.

On balance, we might be quite satisfied with how that has gone here at home. Our European colleagues might well feel the same way, if for different reasons and with a different history. But imagine a person who came to the constitutional discussion at the global level from a country with a different history of constitutionalism at home – a country whose constitution removed different issues from contestation, or where the constitution was irrelevant to the political struggles of the nation, or enshrined ethnic or religious divisions or political ideological commitments with which he or she disagreed, or whose formal terms had been altogether swamped by other modes of power sharing, rent seeking, or corruption. It is not just that such a person might not understand or value the global constitution we proposed – for we would certainly offer the world our own more workable arrangements. It might be that as the global struggle among us unfolds we will find ourselves with a global constitution of a completely different kind than we might anticipate.

As a tool for thinking about global governance, the constitutionalist literature has some unfortunate biases. Perhaps most serious is the idea that the world is, in fact, constituted – that things do add up, one way or the other. We might think of this as a bias against the perception of disorder or contradiction. There is often what we might call a "purposive bias" – that elements in a constitutional order have a function; they are things you can do something with; they reflect social needs or have their justification one or another way in instrumental reason or in a progressive or evolutionary reading of history. Such a bias might well predispose us against mystery, against the aesthetic, the ritualistic, the accidental or path dependent, the neurotic, or simply the unknown in our governmental forms. In a similar way, it has been difficult to think of power and knowledge as mutually constitutive or as social and cognitive flows in a constitutionalist framework that names the players and the channels of their interaction.

Most global constitutionalist projects are centered on existing institutional arrangements – the United Nations, or the WTO, or the interactions of national constitutional courts and regimes. There is always the problem of selection – why these and not others? Are they at actually at the center? Would things be better if we all treated them as central rather than simply as one more or less significant organization? Each of these institutions carries with it a project and a history – to free trade, to settle disputes, to enforce the peace. They are often worthy projects, but it would be odd to organize governance for the whole around the procedures once thought workable for these more limited aims. Constitutionalizing our existing governance structures does aim to remove them from contestation and revision, to harden their division of power, and to freeze their political and legal players. If all this could be accomplished by interpretation – if we could contribute in some small way to the process by which the world's elites came to think of these institutions in constitutional terms, I do worry about the responsibility we would bear for foreclosing other projects and players and possibilities.

Global constitutionalist discussions also often have a proceduralist bias. It can be very difficult to uncover the substantive biases and political projects of proposals for global governance. They all present themselves in even-handed terms, as if they were, in fact, drafted behind a veil of ignorance. Sometimes it is easy to see the trick – treating all "states" equally is hardly to be even handed given the astonishing inequality of states. But more often it takes great work to understand who has been structured to win and who to lose in global legal and institutional arrangements.

At the same time, the entire project of global legal arranging offers itself as innocent of value and ideology and cultural predisposition. All that has been pushed down, below the line of sovereignty – a matter for each local or national community to decide for itself. The international legal order expresses questions of value as rights or principles that are at least aspirationally universal, treating everything else as an interest or an ideology of the part, the nation, the region, the culture. To speak substantively places you off the international plane, expressing something we understand to be an attribute of states and organizations and individuals and groups rather than qualities of the international legal order itself.

We imagine that better procedures will be good for everyone, forgetting that the international order may have a powerful substantive agenda of its own. Focusing on right process, on dispute resolution, on the proper authority of various actors, we forget how much of the status quo we legitimate and how we squeeze those who would change it to the margins of legitimate politics. There is a charming moment in the Kingsbury and Stewart manifesto for better global administrative law when they acknowledge what a generation of law reformers discovered in the development context – improving the machinery of government makes no sense if scoundrels rule, or if the entire global architecture has a substantive skew against the poor, against Russia, against the developing world, against Israel, or whatever. In such a situation, you might well not wish to improve the procedures through which global politics reproduces these tendencies.

Joseph Weiler argued something similar about Europe at the workshop that gave rise to this volume. He notes that the European Union places in private hands the power to ignite the judiciary against national democratic decisions in the name of rules and arrangements largely settled by a transnational technical class. It is not at all clear that constitutionalization of this arrangement will democratize – it may well tip things in quite the other way. At a minimum, we can see that the European legal order affects new and old members differently and brings with it a whole development policy and particular modes of economic and social life. In a similar way, the trade regime entrenches a whole range of distinctions between normal and abnormal traders and trading practices, as well as the hub-and-spoke bargaining arrangements that characterize bilateral dealing between more and less diversified and developed economies.

Constitutionalism may also bring with it what we might call a "settlement bias." Recasting our situation in constitutional terms can give us the feeling things are settled. The struggle is over and this is how it turned out. Each year, I ask my international law students how they see the project of their generation – is this 1648 or 1918, when the entire order needed to be remade; is it more like 1945, when the system needed to be put back together, reformed, under new leadership; or is it like 1989, when we felt finally all we needed to do was implement, enforce, and utilize the international system we had spent so long building in the garage. As you might expect, most usually choose the middle washing machine, precisely as marketing studies would predict. But the number who take the first has grown sharply in the past years, while the number who feel that what the world needs now is more of the same has shrunk to a handful.

Whether we choose to see these as prerevolutionary times or not, it certainly does seem that the situation is far from settled. Economic, political, and cultural competition of many kinds is under way. Although the situation may sort itself out peacefully, I expect deep struggles will probably continue, struggles it will be difficult to routinize into the normal institutional politics of one or another constitutional arrangement. Should that happen, I do worry that the constitutionalist frame will encourage us to take our eye off the ball.

Constitution or Not, Global Governance Will Be Transformed

The current appeal of constitutionalism among those who concern themselves with global governance is a puzzle. And it's not just the Europeans either, although we must admit that projects of constitutional governance, like enthusiasm for international adjudication, have become something of a game for intellectuals from the middle powers. It may have something simply to do with the lack of workable maps of global power. We may grab constitutional efforts because they are familiar and the promise us a map, some form of cognitive control over global political life. People may hang on to their favorite constitutional arrangements, down to the institutional details, less because they work as designed even at home, let alone can be expected to do so in the quite different context of global society, than because they are a familiar map and even an inaccurate map from another country can be a comfort when crossing into terra incognita.

Thinking about global governance, I don't think we ought to try to constitute the world anew. There is too much work we still need to do simply to understand how it works, how the forces and factors we have overlooked might be brought into the analysis. We will need to collaborate with many who are not here, place ourselves in a far more global network of research and inquiry, to map the modes of global power and right. Going forward, our most significant contribution to global order may simply be spreading that knowledge, sharing it more evenly, building an academy outside the elite institutions of the North and West where these things are seen as we can see them – and encouraging us to see also what can be seen there.

Things like governance do change. In Foucault's terms, there was the gallows and then there was the prison timetable. Or, if you prefer, an economy can cease to be something to be harnessed for national growth or development and become an international market, facilitating the flow of goods and capital. New ways to govern, new meanings for politics, new identities for subjects and rulers, for law, for the state, and for things like culture – all these things have to be thought up. And when they are built, their power must be wrought into knowledge.

Sometime between 1789 and 1900 – and as late as 1960 for much of the colonial world – governance was consolidated on a global basis around the national sovereign state. People were organized into territorial states, granted citizenship, and government was defined as what national public authorities did. Building a national public politics across the planet had a strong emancipatory dimension – slaves, women, workers, peasants, colonial dominions, obtained citizenship in relationship to the new institutional machinery of a national politics. New global governance – called "government" – centered on national parliaments, and offered new identities for sovereigns and subjects, status dissolved into nation and contract. The twentieth century also remade global governance – it was no longer all nations all the time. Law infiltrated the political. Sovereignty, like property, was disaggregated into bundles of rights. Corporatism, administration, public-private partnerships, management – boundaries eroded, merged. Federalism, power sharing, subsidiarity, devolution. Interdependence, social solidarity, policy management. Here, too, there were emancipatory elements and important humanitarian accomplishments. But here, too, there were dark sides and disappointments, just as there were winners and losers.

We can be confident that global politics will be remade in the twenty-first century – it is just very difficult to say how. There are a lot of forces out there that might well turn out to have the revolutionary energy to remake the way we are governed: the emergence of new leadership across Latin America, of tribal nationalism in so many places, of religious fundamentalism in the developed and developing world alike. We might see even the Iraq War as a revolutionary project by a confident American leadership supported by an American middle class experiencing its global vulnerability. The decline of the European project, the rise of China, the erosion of confidence in the West's recipes for humanism and development – any of these might be the sign of things coming loose.

As they do come loose, I'm afraid constitutionalism will not be up to the task of holding the fort any more than channeling peaceful change. The conflicts are too real, the status quo too unstable, our current institutions far too wedded to the details of technical management to constitute a new politics. The same, I'm afraid, may be said about proposals for more transparency, accountability, participation, good governance, or an improved administrative process. They may remake management of the regime but not the politics of the globe.

My own hope would be that we might quicken the pace and emotional tenor of decisions in the background institutions of life. Render the forces affecting people's lives more contestable, awaken a sense among actors outside the spotlight of leadership and the fishbowl of the international political system that they also govern, that they have discretion, that they can act to change their – and our – institutional arrangements. I have in mind less new procedures than a new spirit of management, encouraging the human experience of responsible freedom throughout the worlds of corporate, private, public, and technical expertise.

The objective would be to carry the revolutionary force of the democratic promise – of individual rights, of economic self-sufficiency, of citizenship, of community empowerment, and of participation in the decisions that affect one's life – to the sites of global and transnational authority, however local they may be; to multiply the sites at which decisions could be seen and contested, rather than condensing them in a center, in the hope for a heterogeneity of solutions and approaches and a large degree of experimentation, rather than an improved constitutional process or more stable settlement. As we open spaces for conflict and struggle, moreover, we ought to take a break from the search for a universal ethics. Constitutionalism offers an improved institutional platform from which global ethicists can speak for the universal against those who must be cast out from the community of the universal – just when we need conversation, heterogeneity, interaction, ethical pluralism.

There are a lot of institutional ideas lying around – utopian heuristics for a politics remade. Perhaps the new politics will be about experimentation and institutional diversity, protected by a reactivated sovereignty in the middle powers of the South. In such a vision, we might strengthen and defend small pockets of public sovereignty in cities and churches and corporations and nations that have the capacity to experiment, as shields for the weak, guarantors of policy diversity, and arenas for democratic political life. Perhaps the new politics will be about mobility. Imagine a grand bargain linking free trade in goods, free movement of capital, with free movement of persons – not only in Europe, where it is easy, but also globally. Imagine every person born not only into national citizenship but also with a once-in-a-lifetime five-year visa to the country of his or her choice.

Or perhaps a new politics will be about building a transnational political will. Imagine sovereignty as an open-ended promise of inclusion – not just a path to membership in the Europe Union for nations along the boundaries who can swallow the whole *acquis* – but much more. Alberta doing a deal with Montana, New York with Dubai, Palestine finding a place in the European home. Imagine every citizen holding three votes to cast in any election in the world. If the new politics is to be about empowerment, we might imagine citizens not only informed, consulted, their polling data serving as base line for expert management, but actually deciding. Imagine international policy juries – citizens empowered to decide for war or peace, for poverty here or poverty there.

All these may all be terrible ideas – at best they are useful heuristics, reminders of scale and possibility. What we do know is that global governance will be remade over the coming century. International law may get the chance to mop up – but I would rather we seized the opportunity to be present at the creation.

3. The International Legal System as a Constitution

ANDREAS L. PAULUS

I. Introduction

Constitutionalism and Fragmentation of the International Legal System

International lawyers have often construed international constitutionalism as an offspring of the institutionalization of international law. An international constitutionalism would be able to draw the conclusion of the increasing institutionalization of the international realm by applying principles known from domestic constitutional law to the international system, resulting in a universal Kantian "state of law," away from the "state of nature" or anarchy[1] of international relations.[2] In the same vein in which a constitution unifies the domestic polity in one legal superstructure, a developed, institutional reading of international law would unify the international community in a single coherent constitutional structure.

Today, this institutionalist reading of international law has fallen prey, in a certain regard, to its own success. While an increasing institutionalization and organization of international organization can hardly be doubted, the

---

[1] On the anarchy of the international system, *see, e.g.,* HEDLEY BULL, THE ANARCHICAL SOCI-ETY: A STUDY OF ORDER IN WORLD POLITICS (2d ed. 1995); KENNETH N. WALTZ, THEORY OF INTERNATIONAL POLITICS 89, 102–38 (1979); for critique of the equation of anarchy with lawlessness, *see* FRIEDRICH V. KRATOCHWIL, RULES, NORMS, AND DECISIONS: ON THE CONDITIONS OF PRACTICAL REASONING IN INTERNATIONAL RELATIONS AND DOMESTIC AFFAIRS 45–68 (1989); Alexander Wendt, *Anarchy Is What States Make of It: The Social Construction of Power Politics* 46 INT'L ORG. 391 (1992).

[2] *See* Immanuel Kant, *Die Metaphysik der Sitten, in* 4 WERKE 309, 474, § 61 (W. Weischedel ed., 1798); *see also* Immanuel Kant, *Zum ewigen Frieden: Ein philosophischer Entwurf, in* 6 WERKE 208–13 (W. Weischedel ed., 1983). It may, thus, not be by accident that many writers of this school came and still come from the German legal tradition, where law and state have developed a very close relationship, up to Kelsen's point that the state and its law are, legally speaking, identical; HANS KELSEN, GENERAL THEORY OF LAW AND STATE xvi, 182, 188–89 (1949).

general impression is one of fragmentation rather than constitutionalization of the international legal system.[3] In other words, the diverse and divergent institutions fail to come under a single scheme; rather, the systemic character of international law seems threatened by a multiplicity of international régimes without obvious coherence. The constitutionalization of partial régimes appears as antidote rather than confirmation of the constitutionalization of the international legal system as a whole.[4] Calls for a true constitutionalism that would put the different subsystem into order confirm this intuition.[5]

The absence of a single world constitutional order, however, should not blind us to the ever-increasing relevance of international cooperation and concomitant legal regulation for individual human beings. Ask only the recipient of state social support who did not receive his or her monthly paycheck because she was on the Security Council terror list.[6] On the other hand, even legal adjudication within one subsystem must take account of the existence of other legal orders when deciding individual cases reaching beyond one single subsystem.[7]

---

[3] *See* Martti Koskenniemi, President of the International Law Commission, *Fragmentation of International Law: Difficulties Arising from the Diversification and Expansion of International Law: Report of the Study Group of the International Law Commission*, U.N. Doc. A/CN.4/L.682 (Apr. 13, 2006), *available at* http://www.un.org/law/ilc/ (follow "Texts and Instruments" hyperlink and then "Sources of Law" at "1.9"); Martti Koskenniemi & Paivi Leino, *Fragmentation of International Law: Postmodern Anxieties?*, 15 Leiden J. Int'l L. 553 (2002); Bruno Simma & Dirk Pulkowski, *Of Planets and the Universe: Self-Contained Regimes in International Law*, 17 Eur. J. Int'l L. 483, 494–506 (2006); as well as the contributions to the symposium *Diversity of Cacophony? New Sources of Norms in International Law*, 25 Mich. J. Int'l L. 845 (2004).

[4] *But see* Joel P. Trachtman, *The Constitutions of the WTO*, 17 Eur. J. Int'l L. 623, 645–46 (2006); Constitutionalism, Multilevel Trade and Social Regulation (C. Joerges & Ernst-Ulrich Petersmann eds., 2006); Ernst-Ulrich Petersmann, Constitutional Functions and Constitutional Problems of International Economic Law: International and Domestic Foreign Trade Law and Foreign Trade Policy in the United States, the European Community, and Switzerland (1991); Deborah Cass, The Constitutionalization of the World Trade Organization (2005).

[5] *See, e.g.*, Trachtman, *supra* note 4, at 623.

[6] *Cf.* Case C-402/05 P and C-415/05 P, Kadi and Al Barakaat v. Council [2008] 3 C.M.L.R. 41; as well as, in the first instance, Case T-306/01, Yusuf v. Council, 2005 E.C.R. 3533, and Case T-315/01, Kadi v. Council 2005 E.C.R. 3649. For criticism from a human rights perspective, *see* Council of Europe rapporteur Dick Marty, *Provisional Draft Report on UN Security Council and European Union Blacklists* (Nov. 12, 2007), *available at* http://assembly.coe.int/ASP/APFeaturesManager/defaultArtSiteView.asp?ID=717 (last visited Nov. 15, 2007).

[7] For a more complete treatment, *see* Andreas L. Paulus, *From Territoriality to Functionality? Towards a Legal Methodology of Globalization, in* Governance and International Legal Theory 59 (I. F. Dekker & W. G. Werner eds., 2004).

International constitutionalism needs, thus, to be decoupled from the building of new international structures. Rather, what is called for is a constitutional mind-set (Martti Koskenniemi)[8] or a constitutional reading of the international legal foundations on which today's fragmentation of international legal rules rests. Rather than asking whether the constitutional structure of the Charter organs are sufficiently similar to those of the state, we will reflect on whether and how the international legal order fulfils the background principles for a constitutional order worthy of that name in the constitutional tradition.[9] If not, the resistance to international regulation will likely – and justifiably – grow, and the accommodation needed for international order will not be forthcoming.

The development of constitutional thought in twentieth-century international law moves from a formal concept of constitutionalism – such as the existence of a formal unity of international law derived from one single, hierarchically superior source – to a more substantive conception that deals with the emergence of formal and substantive hierarchies between different rules and principles of international law. In its first part, this contribution will retrace this development of constitutional perspectives of international law, from the early system building of Kelsenian positivists to the recent challenges of fragmentation. In this part, the definition of constitutionalism will largely follow a deductive methodology.

In the second part, this contribution will proceed to an analysis of the typical substantive elements of a constitution in the Western tradition. As yardsticks for a constitutional understanding of the international legal order, it refers to democracy, the rule of law or *Rechtsstaat*, the separation of powers, as well as the basic conditions of legal subjects, namely the basic rights of states, on the one hand, and human rights, on the other. Finally, we will look at the question of whether contemporary international law embodies something of solidarity between the states and human beings.

In line with the matrix used by the editors of this volume,[10] the notion of constitutionalism used in the second part attempts to combine comparatism

---

[8] Martti Koskenniemi, *Constitutionalism as Mindset: Reflections on Kantian Themes about International Law and Globalization*, 8 THEORETICAL INQUIRIES IN LAW 9 (2007).

[9] For an analysis of the terms *constitution* and *constitutionalism*, see Besson, in this volume, p. 376–80. *See also* J. H. H. Weiler & M. Wind, *Introduction to* EUROPEAN CONSTITUTIONALISM BEYOND THE STATE 1, 4 (J. H. H. Weiler & M. Wind eds., 2003); for the resort to constitutional principles rather than a single foundational act, *see* J. H. H. Weiler, *In Defence of the Status Quo: Europe's Constitutional Sonderweg, in* EUROPEAN CONSTITUTIONALISM, *supra*, at 13, 15.

[10] *See* Jeffrey L. Dunoff & Joel P. Trachtman, *A Functional Approach to International Constitutionalism*, in this volume, at 3, 27.

and functionalism. To identify the elements of a hard constitution, we look at the domestic ideal type. However, to transfer these concepts to the international realm, this contribution follows functionalist lines; namely, we ask whether or not domestic constitutionalism can fulfill similar functions at the international level. As we shall see, the transfer of domestic constitutional principles to international law is fraught with difficulty, in particular because international law must always take into account at least two levels of analysis: the interstate level of classical international law and the interindividual level of world citizens at large. In this substantive perspective, only an international order that reaches the level of individual human beings can be called "constitutional."

The result of this enterprise will show that, if read in a constitutional light, international law may well develop in a constitutional direction, or has at least enough of a constitutional potential. However, by balancing rights of individuals and states with those of the international community, and by limiting the power of central institutions, such a reading will not necessarily result in a centralization of the international legal system. Rather, limitations to any exercise of public power for the sake of individual rights are the basic conditions for legitimate rule in the constitutional tradition. Only a constitutionalism that embodies these principles will be able to maintain the legitimacy of the increasing demands of the international legal system toward states and individuals.

II. The System of International Law; or, The Formal Constitution

The very title of this contribution presupposes an understanding of international law as a system. It thus distinguishes itself from an understanding of the role of law in international relations that considers the existence of rules and institutions an exception to the rule of anarchy in the international system.[11] Before we can ask ourselves whether or not this system has a constitution, however, we must deal with the systemic coherence of the international system.

1. International Law as a System

The systemic qualities of international law were at the center of international legal debate in the foundational period of contemporary international law, after the advent of international organization after World War I. For positivists

---

[11] J. H. H. Weiler & Andreas Paulus, *The Structure of Change in International Law or Is There a Hierarchy of Norms in International Law?* 8 EUR. J. INT'L L. 545, 547 (1997).

such as the early Hans Kelsen, the unity of the legal system could be secured only by opting for the primacy of international over domestic law, thus rejecting a nationalist reliance on a single domestic legal order for establishing a hierarchy of norms.[12] For his disciple Alfred Verdross, who was the first to apply the term *constitution* to the law of the international community,[13] the derivation of international law from a single source constituted the core of its constitutional character. However, already in the interwar years, the substantive content of that constitutional order was in dispute. Whereas the Permanent Court of International Justice, in its famous *Lotus* judgment,[14] regarded state sovereignty as the decisive element for the completeness of international law, Hersch Lauterpacht found the unity of the international legal system in the benefit of the international community.[15]

From a theoretical point of view, the thesis of the completeness of international law is closely related to its quality as a coherent system: an incoherent mass of rules will not be able to give a determinate answer to the binary matrix of any legal system, namely, whether an act is to be regarded as legal or illegal. In the case of lacunae in international law, this question cannot be answered in all cases, and the answer must be left to the political choice of the decision maker.[16] Thus, the systemic qualities of international law are anything but apolitical. Rather, political choices will determine our viewpoint on the decisive element transforming disparate rules into a system. If law is the exception, and anarchy the rule, international law can hardly be said to possess a constitution.

[12] HANS KELSEN, REINE RECHTSLEHRE. EINLEITUNG IN DIE RECHTSWISSENSCHAFTLICHE PROB-LEMATIK, 147–54 (Leipzig 1934) (*see* English translation, INTRODUCTION TO THE PROBLEMS OF LEGAL THEORY 120–25 (Bonnie Litschewski Paulson & Stanley L. Paulson trans., 1992)) [hereinafter PROBLEMS OF LEGAL THEORY]; *but see* HANS KELSEN, GENERAL THEORY OF LAW AND STATE 388 (primacy of international or national law a question of politics rather than legal theory); HANS KELSEN, REINE RECHTSLEHRE, 343–47 (2d ed., Franz Deuticke 1960) (hereinafter REINE RECHTSLEHRE) (primacy question of Weltanschauung, or "world-view").

[13] A. VERDROSS, DIE EINHEIT DES RECHTLICHEN WELTBILDES AUF GRUNDLAGE DER VÖLKERRECHTSVERFASSUNG 101 (1923); A. VERDROSS, DIE VERFASSUNG DER VÖLKER-RECHTSGEMEINSCHAFT (1926).

[14] The Case of the SS *Lotus* (France v. Turkey), 1927 P.C.I.J. (ser. A) No. 10, at 18; *but see* Legality of the Threat or Use of Nuclear Weapons, Advisory Opinion, 1996 I.C.J. 270, ¶ 13, Declaration of President Bedjaoui (rise of an objective conception of international law).

[15] HERSCH LAUTERPACHT, THE FUNCTION OF LAW IN THE INTERNATIONAL COMMUNITY 123 (1933).

[16] For a conspicuous example, *see* Legality of the Threat or Use of Nuclear Weapons, *supra* note 14, ¶ 97 at 263 (no definitive conclusion on the legality or illegality of the use of nuclear weapons in an extreme situation of self-defense). On lacunae in international law generally, *see* U. FASTENRATH, LÜCKEN IM VÖLKERRECHT (1991); Lauterpacht, *supra* note 15, at 70–104.

While international legal theorists were striving to demonstrate the unity of international law, however, others were not quite convinced that international law amounted to a true legal system. To name a prominent example, H. L. A. Hart granted the legal quality of international law only for want of a better term – by default, so to speak. Nevertheless, in his opinion, international law was deficient where it mattered most: instead of a unity of primary and secondary rules, international law was composed of primary rules only.[17] Hart thus rejected Kelsen's view that a formal basic norm could be found in the customary behavior of states.[18] But the mere formality of Kelsen's answer does not tell us anything about the substantive characteristics of a complete legal system. Even from a formal standpoint, custom seems too diverse and unsystematic to unify a legal system. For the real coherence of the international legal system, a more than formal hierarchy between international rules and principles appears necessary.

In a formal sense, international law constitutes a system because it contains secondary rules (in the Hartian sense) on law making by sovereign states – the famous sources triad with all its ramifications – and on their implementation and consequences of their breach. Most of these rules are dispositive – that is, subject to modification by further agreement between states – and the system of international law will thus give much leeway to states to modify even the most basic rules for specific purposes or régimes.

In a formal understanding of the term, a constitution is the document or even point from which all other authority is derived; it is the center of a hierarchical system in which the lower rules derive their authority from higher ones, to the point where the constitution itself rests on an ultimate "rule of recognition" (Hart)[19] or *Grundnorm* (Kelsen)[20] that can be derived only from extralegal sources of legitimacy, either religious (God) or civic (the *pouvoir constituant* or people power or constitutional moment). However, such formal derivation is nothing new. It constituted the basis of Verdross's "Verfassung der Völkerrechtsgemeinschaft." It was a formal principle of derivation of a system of rules from a purely formal source of authority. In this sense, the systemic nature of international law is sufficient to found its constitutional structure.

---

[17] H. L. A. Hart, The Concept of Law, 213 *et seq.* (2d ed., 1994).
[18] *See* Kelsen, Problems of Legal Theory, *supra* note 12, at 108; but see Hans Kelsen, Das Problem der Souveränität und die Theorie des Völkerrechts, 284 (1928) (*pacta sunt servanda* as basic norm). Kelsen, Reine Rechtslehre, *supra* note 12, at 223, explains that the earlier theory presupposed that custom was based on tacit agreement.
[19] Hart, *supra* note 17, at 94–110.
[20] Kelsen, Reine Rechtslehre, *supra* note 12, at 196 *et seq.*

Some scholars have pointed out that while Hart may have been correct in the early 1960s, international law has moved toward a more complete system, in which secondary rules indeed do exist, from law making to criminal responsibility.[21] Others, notably Jean Combacau, regard the formal coherence of international law as dependent on the maintenance of its horizontal interstate quality, and thus reject attempts at a hierarchization as a threat to its systemic attributes.[22] Arguably, the unity of the international legal system was never as great as in the interwar years, when the Permanent Court of International Justice provided some systemic coherence, while the basic principle of state sovereignty could serve as the background norm – thus, the systemic qualities of international law may well be regarded as an antidote of its hierarchization and constitutionalization.[23]

But if the international legal system is supposed to have developed into a constitution, it must have found some superior unity that goes beyond a system of formal rules. A constitution, in this strong reading, is more than a mere system of deriving substantive rules from state consent, acquiescence, and general principles of law. In a more developed formalist sense, a constitution is a comprehensive order of the whole system that is hierarchically superior to all other legal rules, and it derives its legal source itself, formally speaking, from the ultimate rule of recognition or, substantively speaking, from the ultimate source of legitimacy, which is, in the domestic legal order of democratic states, the people in form of the pouvoir constituant. Constitutionalization would thus add a different, better quality to international law, instead of being a mere assertion of its bindingness.

2. Institutionalism and Constitutionalism
Whereas system building in international law does not require institutionalization, a constitution appears to presuppose at least a minimum of organization of a political realm by legal means. At the same time in which legal theorists of the Kelsenian school were building a system around the classical sources of an interstate international law, the state system was slowly

---

[21] See, in particular, THOMAS FRANCK, FAIRNESS OF INTERNATIONAL LAW AND INSTITUTIONS 3–6 (1995) (maintaining that the fairness of the content of international law, rather than its legal nature, is now in contention).

[22] Jean Combacau, Le droit international: bric-à-brac ou système? 31 ARCHIVES DE PHILOSOPHIE DU DROIT 85, 102–05 (1986); see also Prosper Weil, Towards Relative Normativity in International Law? 77 AM. J. INT'L L. 413, 422–23 (1989).

[23] For a reassertion of a classical view of international law as interstate law, see O. SPIERMANN, INTERNATIONAL LEGAL ARGUMENT IN THE PERMANENT COURT OF INTERNATIONAL JUSTICE, 79–126 (2005).

institutionalizing. The "move to institutions" (David Kennedy)[24] has been a determining influence on international law in the twentieth century, from the League of Nations to the United Nations, from the Hague Peace Conferences to the statutes of the Permanent Court of International Justice and the International Court of Justice (ICJ), from Nuremberg to the International Criminal Court (ICC), and from the International Labour Organization (ILO) and Bretton Woods to the World Trade Organization (WTO). By establishing an international organization, states not only create a new subject of international law but also allow for the impact of the rules emanating from these institutions on states and individuals alike. While individuals and nonstate actors do not thereby become subjects of international law in the sense of lawgivers in their own right, they become bearers of international rights and obligations of a secondary nature.

Thus, the alleged constitutionalization of international law is closely related to its institutionalization. A weak understanding of the term *constitution* regards it as another word for *statute* or *founding treaty*. In this sense, one can speak of the constitution of the ILO[25] or the World Health Organization (WHO).[26] But the existence of several constitutions of this kind is not what is meant by the claim of the constitutionalization of international law. Whereas the term *system* connotes coherence but not necessarily strength, *constitution* implies comprehensiveness, hierarchy, and judicial control. Labeling international law a "system" does not amount to a history of political progress but simply conveys the idea of a reasonable ordering. Arguing for a comprehensive constitutionalization of the international legal system, on the contrary, implies advocating a strengthening of international organization epitomized in a single international constitution that is not necessarily substituting but supplementing domestic constitutions.

The one international organization that has the potential to constitutionalize the whole system of international law in this sense is the United Nations.[27] Relating to the UN Charter, constitutionalism would imply that,

---

[24] David Kennedy, *The Move to Institutions*, 8 CARDOZO L. REV. 841, 849 (1987).

[25] *See* The Constitution of the ILO, (Oct. 9, 1946), 15 United Nations Treaty Series (U.N.T.S.) 35, last amended on June 8, 1972, 958 U.N.T.S. 167; for further amendments that are not yet in force, *see* http://www.ilo.org/public/english/bureau/leg/amend/index.htm (last visited Aug. 21, 2008). With its tripartite structure, by which each state is represented not only by its government but also by a representative of the employers and the employees, the ILO has, however, a constitutional feature by looking behind the corporate veil of the state.

[26] *See, e.g.,* Legality of the Use by a State of Nuclear Weapons in Armed Conflict, Advisory Opinion, 1996 I.C.J. 74, ¶ 18.

[27] Even one of the strongest advocates for a constitutionalization of the WTO, Ernst-Ulrich Petersmann, argues for a revitalized Charter after the WTO model, not for a WTO that

taken together, the UN Charter, and the secondary rules on law making contained in the ICJ Statute that is its "integral part,"[28] constitute a foundational ordering of international law as a whole and are hierarchically superior to it. In addition, we would expect the Charter to borrow some, if not all, of its features from the more established domestic constitutions. As to the substance of such a constitution, we may expect, in line with the Western constitutionalist tradition, a division of competences similar to the separation of powers among the legislative, executive, and adjudicative branches of domestic government, the regulation of the law-making procedure, and a protection of the constituent rights of the members of the community (e.g., states). While states are not natural but juridical persons, we might also need a definition of how to qualify as a member of the community, as well as some rules on the relationships between the one natural subject of all legal systems, the human individual, with his or her state and the international community at large. Thus, both states' rights and individual rights would need to feature in the document. We might also need some measure to protect the primacy of the constitution, from its hierarchical superiority over ordinary norms to a mechanism of control, ideally a court or other judicial body. Finally, an international constitution in the Weberian sense would also require a centralization of the legitimation of the use of force.[29]

Indeed, when we look at the rules of the UN Charter and the ICJ Statute, we may indeed come to the conclusion that the Charter system contains exactly such an ordering, from the separation of powers among the General Assembly, Security Council, and ICJ to the rules of law making in article 38 of the ICJ Statute.[30] The primacy of the Charter is guaranteed by its article 103, and while its judicial control is far from perfect, this is not so different from many domestic constitutions. The judicial power of the ICJ is a part of the Charter system, and by asking for advisory opinions, the General

---

constitutionalizes international law alone; see Ernst-Ulrich Petersmann, *How to Reform the UN System? Constitutionalism, International Law, and International Organizations*, 10 Leiden J. Int'l L. 421 (1997).

[28] U.N. Charter, art. 92.

[29] For the monopolization of the use of force in the state, *see*, famously, M. Weber, *Politik als Beruf, in* Gesamtausgabe I/17, 157, 159–60 (W. J. Mommsen & W. Schluchter eds., 1992); for its transfer to the international sphere, *cf.* Kelsen, Problems of Legal Theory, *supra* note 12, at 108–09 (decentralized ordering of the international community before 1945); *but see* Hans Kelsen, The law of the United Nations: a Critical Analysis of its Fundamental Problems 732–37 (1950) (UN enforcement measures as sanctions for violations of international law or political measures).

[30] *Cf.* Bardo Fassbender, *The United Nations Charter as Constitution of the International Community*, 36 Colum. J. Transnat'l L. 529 (1998); B. Simma, *From Bilateralism to Community Interest in International Law*, 250 Recueil des Cours 217, 258 *et seq.* (1994).

Assembly and Security Council can at least elicit an authoritative pronounce-ment as to the constitutional law of the Charter. Article 2 contains a more or less complete set of states' rights, whereas human and peoples' rights belong to the founding principles of the Charter and are delegated to other bodies for concretization (art. 55 (c)). Since Switzerland decided in favor of UN membership, all uncontested states in the world are members of the United Nations, leaving out only dubious cases such as Kosovo, Palestine, Taiwan, or Western Sahara. While Kelsen's claim that the international use of force was either an (unlawful) violation or a lawful sanction of international law was rather doubtful in the absence of a certain degree of institutionalization, the UN Charter has achieved at least a monopolization of the legitima-tion of the use of military force in the Security Council, except in cases of self-defense.

Thus, it is not by accident that some writers have compared, with consid-erable success, the Charter rules to those of domestic constitutions and have come to the conclusion that, in the words of Bardo Fassbender, "a compar-ison of the Charter with the ideal type of constitution reveals a similarity sufficiently strong to attribute constitutional quality to the instrument."[31]

However, this formal way of looking at the Charter appears too good to be true. While the defects of the international order with regard to typical domestic constitutions can indeed be overcome – for instance, the rules on rule making contained in article 38 of the ICJ Statute are not integrated into the Charter, article 103 of the Charter is drafted as a mere conflict rule between different treaties, and judicial review by advisory opinion is a shadow of constitutional adjudication of mutual rights and duties of state organs – by pointing out that hardly any constitution will comprise all of the ideal-typical elements of a constitution, the reality of international relations does not quite fit into a view of the Charter as the comprehensive document of international legal relations.

This notion of a constitution implies a comprehensive ordering. While social reactions – up to the street demonstrations against the Iraq War that Jürgen Habermas regarded as substitute for a formalized condemnation[32] – may be as effective as formal sanctions;[33] Blackstone's maxim that a right

---

[31] BARDO FASSBENDER, UN SECURITY COUNCIL REFORM AND THE RIGHT OF VETO: A CONSTI-TUTIONAL PERSPECTIVE 114 (1998), and Fassbender, in this volume, at 133. For views to the contrary, see M. Doyle, in this volume, at 113; S. Kadelbach & T. Kleinlein, *International Law: A Constitution for Mankind? An Attempt at a Re-appraisal with an Analysis of Constitutional Principles,* 50 GERMAN Y.B. INT'L L. 303, 319 (2008).
[32] JÜRGEN HABERMAS, DER GESPALTENE WESTEN 44 (2004).
[33] *See* MICHAEL BARKUN, LAW WITHOUT SANCTIONS (1968).

requires a remedy[34] is a characteristic of a fully developed – in other words, a constitutionalized – legal system.[35] However, the overarching structures of international law have remained, at best, weak; from the traditional decentralized law making to the UN system,[36] in which the weakest body, the Economic and Social Council, has never been able to discharge its function of oversight of special legal régimes provided for by articles 57, 63, and 64 of the UN Charter. The Bretton Woods Institutions have never quite recognized the primacy of the UN system,[37] and the WTO's or the ICC's cooperation agreements do not even mention the United Nations' oversight function.[38] Thus, the overarching nature of the Charter for the whole international legal system is very much in doubt. In addition, the conditions for membership under article 4 of the Charter do not sufficiently define the basic unit of the international legal system (e.g., the state), whereas articles 1 (c) and 55 (c) are far from any comprehensive definition of basic human rights or the self-determination of peoples. Finally, the UN Charter itself does not regulate the sanctioning of violations of international law but centers on the maintenance of international peace and security, of which the observance of international law is only one, and sometimes not the most important, element. In summary, the Charter relies on general international law rather than defining its basic parameters.

While the Security Council, according to the Charter, enjoys a monopoly of the legitimation of violence beyond the emergency case of self-defense,

---

[34] 3 WILLIAM BLACKSTONE, COMMENTARIES ON THE LAW OF ENGLAND 23 (1979): "it is a general and indisputable rule, that where there is a legal right, there is also a legal remedy by suit or action at law whenever that right is invaded." *See also* Marbury v. Madison, 5 U.S. (1 Cranch 1803) 137, 162–63.

[35] *See also* HART, *supra* note 17, at 213 *et seq.* (absence of secondary rules as sign for the lack of truly juridical quality of international law).

[36] *See* Statute of the International Court of Justice, art. 38.

[37] United Nations, Agreements between the United Nations and the Specialized Agencies and the International Atomic Energy Agency, U.N. Doc. ST/SG/14 (1961), at 53, 60, 88, 111. For an overview, *see* W. Meng, *Art. 63, in* THE CHARTER OF THE UNITED NATIONS: A COMMENTARY (Bruno Simma ed., 2d ed. 2002); for more recent information, *see* UN System Chief Executives Board for Coordination, *available at* http://www.unsystemceb.org (last visited Aug. 21, 2008).

[38] The WTO did not conclude an agreement with the United Nations but exchanged letters with the UN secretary-general, Letter from the [UN] Secretary-General to the President of ECOSOC (Oct. 24, 1995), U.N. Doc. E/1995/125 (1995), taken note by ECOCOC res. 1995/322 (establishing a "flexible framework for cooperation"). However, the WTO takes part in the Board for Coordination, *id.* The International Criminal Court has recently concluded such an agreement on the basis of strict equality, *see* Negotiated Relationship Agreement between the International Criminal Court and the United Nations of 4 Oct. 2004, U.N. Doc. ICC-ASP/3/25, 301, art. 2.

the United Nations lacks the means of using force by itself and needs to leave concrete action to its member states, even if it claims a monopoly on their authorization. In the absence of the UN forces provided for by article 43 of the UN Charter, the decision to use force is within the discretion of states, not the UN, which can only withhold legality but cannot use military force by itself.

Most important, however, the term *constitution* is not limited to certain formal characteristics of a legal system. It has also something to do with the acceptance of the ordering of a society by its legal subjects as a comprehensive political order, as a ground rule for their social activities that commands their allegiance in good as in bad times. In view of the disrespect for the Charter law coming from the privileged permanent members of the Security Council, from the U.S. attempt to establish a law-free zone at Guantánamo Bay to the Chinese disregard for civil and political rights and the Russian occupation of parts of Georgia, to name only a few recent examples, some early supporters of the idea of a constitution have reneged on their previous writings by pointing to the actual behavior of states in international relations. "This is not a way to treat a constitution"[39] – Bruno Simma's outcry on the occasion of the cavalier approach of North Atlantic Treaty Organization countries to the UN Charter in the wake of the Kosovo crisis have found ample confirmation ever since. Many states, also in the West, regard the United Nations as one out of many possible avenues to further their political objectives but not as the ultimate authority on the use of force, and even less so on other aspects of international relations.

Nevertheless, while the claims of Security Council backing for the war against Saddam Hussein were dubious,[40] it is remarkable that the main participants justified their behavior before the UN Security Council,[41] just as required by article 51 of the Charter. By pointing to previous resolutions, they apparently wanted to create the impression that they were executing the Charter rather than violating it. China has signed the International Covenants

---

[39] Bruno Simma, *Comments on Global Governance, the United Nations, and the Place of Law*, 9 FINNISH Y.B. INT'L L. 61, 65 (1998).

[40] For details, *see* Andreas L. Paulus, *The War against Iraq and the Future of International Law: Hegemony or Pluralism?* 25 MICH. J. INT'L L. 691 (2004), with further references.

[41] Letter from the Permanent Representative of the United States of America to the United Nations, addressed to the President of the Security Council (Mar. 20. 2003), U.N. Doc. S/2003/351 (Mar. 21, 2003); Letter from the Permanent Representative of the United Kingdom of Great Britain and Northern Ireland to the United Nations, addressed to the President of the Security Council (Mar. 20, 2003), U.N. Doc. S/2003/350 (Mar. 21, 2003). *See also* Attorney General Lord Goldsmith, Hansard (Mar. 17, 2003), Column WA 2–3.

on Civil and Political Rights and has ratified the Covenant on Social, Economic, and Cultural Rights, thus accepting, in principle, human rights standards beyond the Charter.[42] Finally, marching into Georgia and violating its territorial integrity, Russia felt compelled to present the case as one of humanitarian intervention.[43] As the ICJ has pointed out in its *Nicaragua* judgment,[44] it seems less important for the viability of a legal régime whether or not it is scrupulously observed or regularly sanctioned but whether the legal subjects justify their behavior under the law rather than openly defy it.

But it is doubtful whether claims to the observance of Charter law are akin to recognition of its constitutional character. Rather, many states seem to regard the conformity to the Charter only as one out of many legal justifications for the use of force. The best example is probably the opinion that humanitarian interventions are legal in spite of the Charter law to the contrary. Similar claims have been made regarding the preemptive use of force,[45] denying the basic principle of any system of collective security that uncertain threats need to be determined and countered collectively, not individually. It is particularly indicative that claims like these come from the pillars of the Charter system, the permanent members of the Security Council, that enjoy privileges both according to the Charter and to other international legal instruments, in particular the Treaty on Non-Proliferation of Nuclear Weapons (NPT).

Thus, the case for an international constitutionalism is doubtful not only compared to the domestic models – which may also be less perfect and comprehensive than the ideal model would suggest – but also with regard to its recognition by the subjects of the law. A further element of a formal constitutionalism, the idea of a complete derivation of the international legal system from one particular and concrete source, raises the specter of fragmentation rather than constitutionalization.

---

[42] On China, *see, e.g.,* HUMAN RIGHTS AND CHINESE VALUES: LEGAL, PHILOSOPHICAL AND ETHICAL PERSPECTIVES (Michael C. Davis ed., 1995); R. Peerenbom, *What's Wrong with Chinese Rights? Toward a Theory of Rights with Chinese Characteristics,* 6 HARV. HUM. RTS. J. 29 (1993).

[43] *See only* the statements of the Russian representative, Mr. Churkin, to the Security Council, S/PV/5952 (Aug. 8, 2008), at 3; S/PV/5953 (Aug. 10, 2008), 9. *See also* the more complete legal argument by the Russian ambassador to NATO, Dmitry Rogozin, *Washington's Hypocrisy,* INT'L HERALD TRIB., Aug. 18, 2008.

[44] Military and Paramilitary Activities in and against Nicaragua (Nicaragua v. United States), 1986 I.C.J. 14, ¶ 186 at 98.

[45] The National Security Strategy of the United States of America, September 2002, *available at* http://www.whitehouse.gov/nsc/nss.pdf (last visited Dec. 3, 2007), at 15.

3. Chaos or System: The Fragmentation Debate

Recently, Combacau's question of whether international law was "chaos or system" has received new attention.[46] This time, however, the debate centers less on the systemic qualities or the existence of hierarchies in international law and more on the increasing fragmentation of its content. In view of the proliferation of international law and the judicialization of international legal subsystems such as trade law and international criminal law or human rights law, but also with regard to the rise of non-state actors, the unity of international law appears increasingly fragile. In the debate on the fragmentation of international law, some are raising doubts on the very existence of general international law;[47] others suggest views of international law as a network of loosely connected rules rather than a coherent system.[48] Political scientists have found some signs of legalization and judicialization of the international legal system,[49] but they continue to view legal regulation of international relations as isolated islands of stability in a sea of international anarchy. Finally, Joseph Weiler has regarded the geology of international law as composed of three different layers that correspond to different levels of legal development.[50]

Partial constitutionalizations, whether in the WTO or in the human rights fields, are lacking a central feature of domestic constitutions, namely, a mechanism for balancing all the interests of all stakeholders beyond the narrow confines of trade or human rights. In the absence of judicial oversight at a higher, more general level, the subsystems need to do the balancing themselves. If they fail to do so, they risk not only the dissolution of international law but also their own authority with other jurisdictions. This does not necessarily imply, however, that fragmentation inevitably leads to the dissolution of the international legal system, as long as the subsystems do respect their partial nature and continue to relate to the rest of the system in respect of the limits of their own scope.

[46] *Cf.* Combacau, *supra* note 22.

[47] *See, in particular,* Gunther Teubner & Andreas Fischer-Lescano, *Regime-Collisions: The Vain Search for Legal Unity in the Fragmentation of Global Law,* 25 MICH J. INT'L. L. 999, 1045 (2004).

[48] *See* Simma and Pulkowski, *supra* note 3, at 494–506 (seeking a balance between the system and the particular subsystems); Dirk Pulkowski, *Structural Paradigms of International Law, in* THE SHIFTING ALLOCATION OF AUTHORITY IN INTERNATIONAL LAW 51, 54 (T. Broude & Y. Shany eds., 2008) (presenting a network view as one of several paradigms).

[49] Judith Goldstein et al., *Legalization and World Politics: A Special Issue of International Organization,* 54 INT'L ORG. 385 *et seq.* (2000).

[50] J. H. H. Weiler, *The Geology of International Law,* 64 ZEITSCHRIFT FÜR AUSLÄNDISCHES ÖFFENTLICHES RECHT UND VÖLKERRECHT 547 (2004); similarly Pulkowski, *supra* note 48, at 51, 54, 72–76.

But the contents of international legal rules – which are indeed as manifold as the reality to which they relate and that they intend to rule – needs to be distinguished from the formal sources of international law. It is doubtful that the "new world order"[51] of global bankers and state officials has fundamentally diminished the position of states as sole authoritative rule makers. Nongovernmental organizations (NGOs) have hardly gained the ability to make law of their own that they could impose on others with any claim of legitimacy, let alone superiority over states.[52] Also, NGO participation in international rule making, from the prohibition of land mines to the Kyoto Protocol, does not amount to law-making capacity, which has remained with states. Banking regulation continues to depend on the state for its implementation or needs to be based on authorizing legislation to be directly binding on banks and businesses. As long as the state remains the only legitimate legislator, and as long as it constitutes the main bearer of responsibility for breaches of international law, a new global law over or above state consent will have to wait for another day. Thus, the fiction that state will is not internally contradictory, and that therefore different emanations of the state will need to be interpreted in a way that brings them into a coherent framework of the whole, remains valid even at a time of fragmentation.

This is not meant to imply that the content of international legal norms is unimportant or negligible. Rather, we should be careful about what exactly we are saying: the rule-making function of states (and of international organizations regarding secondary rules), the implementation of international law, or the new quality of some international subsystems – for example, the WTO system – that are much more institutionalized and hierarchized. Indeed, whereas some subsystems appear legally stabilized in spite (or because) of permanent modifications, general international law as a whole lacks the same kind of judicial mechanisms. Thus, while states members of the WTO have accepted a form of binding adjudication with regard to multilateral trade, the number of states accepting the jurisdiction of the ICJ under the optional clause system is not making much progress,[53] and even traditional supporters of the system have strived, with partial success, to limit their exposure to the court

---

[51] Anne-Marie Slaughter, A New World Order (2004).
[52] Cf. Kenneth Anderson, The Ottawa Convention Banning Landmines, the Role of International Non-Governmental Organizations and the Idea of International Civil Society, 11 Eur. J. Int'l L. 91 (2000).
[53] The recent acceptance of the compulsory jurisdiction of the ICJ by Germany constitutes the exception rather than the rule; see Declaration under art. 36 (2) of the ICJ Statute of Apr. 30, 2008; see U.N. Doc. C.N.357.2008.TREATIES-1 (Depositary Notification) (May 6, 2008), which, however, excludes military matters.

by adding reservations.[54] And yet, the court has much more work to do than in the cold war era, and in matters of maritime and territorial delimitation, states choose the court even for tasks for which they could form an ad hoc tribunal or invoke the more specialized International Tribunal for the Law of the Sea.[55] Arbitral tribunals, including those dealing with investor-state litigation,[56] and domestic constitutional courts continue to rely on the ICJ for guidance on general legal issues.[57]

Indeed, international tribunals of all kinds do not see themselves or the law administered by them "in clinical isolation from international law," as the WTO Appellate Body put it in its first-ever decision,[58] but regularly draw on the problem-solving capacity of the general rules of the system, whether on human rights or humanitarian law, or apply the rules on state responsibility even to investment cases for which it was not developed.[59] Thus, a residual function of general international law can hardly be doubted. I find it disingenuous to claim that the subsystems developed their rules autonomously

---

[54] *See, e.g.*, Fisheries Jurisdiction (Spain v. Canada), 1998 I.C.J. 432, at 457, ¶ 61 *et passim* (accepting the admissibility of such limitations by a 12–5 vote).

[55] *See* art. 286 of the UN Convention on the Law of the Sea, Dec. 10, 1982, U.N.T.S. 1833, 3.

[56] *See, e.g.*, the ICSID decisions on Argentine debt, CMS Gas Transmission Co. v. Argentine Republic, ICSID Case No. ARB/01/8, Award of May 12, 2005, *available at* http://icsid.worldbank.org/ICSID [hereinafter "CMS award"], ¶¶ 315, 372 (relying on art. 25 on the ILC articles on state responsibility and the ICJ interpretation of it); *but see* CMS Gas Transmission Company v. Argentine Republic, ICSID Case No. Arb/01/08, Decision of the Ad Hoc Committee on the Application for Annulment of the Argentine Republic, 2007, *available at* http://icsid.worldbank.org/ICSID [hereinafter "Annulment Decision"], ¶¶ 125 *et seq.* (also relying on a different reading of public international law); *similarly* LG&E Energy Corp. v. Argentine Republic, ICSID Case No. ARB/02/1, Award of Oct. 3, 2006, *available at* http://icsid.worldbank.org/ICSID [hereinafter "LG&E award"], ¶ 245.

[57] *See, e.g.*, CMS Award, at ¶ 372, relying on Gabčíkovo-Nagymaros Project (Hungary v. Slovakia), 1997 I.C.J. 7, at 40, ¶¶ 51–52. The U.S. Supreme Court decision in Sanchez-Llamas v. Oregon, 548 U.S. 331, 352–57 (2006), which refused to follow the ICJ precedent regarding the effect of consular notification, constitutes the exception rather than the rule in this regard. The Supreme Court itself occasionally refers to the ICJ for guidance on international law; *see, e.g.*, Hamdan v. Rumsfeld, 548 U.S. 557, 631 n.63 (2006), indirectly citing to Nicaragua v. United States, 1986 I.C.J. 14, ¶ 218, 25 I.L.M. 1023 *and* Prosecutor v. Tadić, Case No. IT-94-1, Decision on the Defence Motion for Interlocutory Appeal on Jurisdiction, ¶ 102 (I.C.T.Y. App. Chamber, Oct. 2, 1995) for guidance on the meaning of common art. 3 of the Geneva conventions. For comparative analysis with the practice of the German constitutional court, *see* Carsten Hoppe, *Implementation of LaGrand and Avena in Germany and the United States: Exploring a Transatlantic Divide in Search of a Uniform Interpretation of Consular Rights*, 18 Eur. J. Int'l L. 317 (2007).

[58] Appellate Body Report, US: *Standards for Reformulated and Conventional Gasoline*, WT/DS2/AB/R (Apr. 29, 1996).

[59] *See, e.g., supra* note 56.

or "auto-poietically" rather than with regard to general international law,[60] in particular when a closer look reveals that they derive their authority from international sources or state authority and not from some functionalist claim of legitimacy based on an ultimately arbitrary division between different sub-systems.

Nevertheless, such residual function may not be sufficient for maintaining the unity of the international legal system. This article does not attempt to deny that an increasing institutionalization and the rising number of international legal rules binding on and enforced against individuals have transformed the character of much of international law. Indeed, there is some plausibility, for example, to the claim of the European Court of Justice that European law, in spite of being derived from international treaties, has reached "critical mass" and turned its greater density and stronger integration in the domestic legal systems into a new quality by constructing a new legal order rather than a regional branch of international law.[61] Different from the suggestions of Kelsen and Hart, the international legal nature of the founding document of an institution does not guarantee its belonging to a coherent legal system.

But as the recent report on fragmentation by the International Law Commission has demonstrated, the methods of general international law to bring seemingly contradictory demands of different legal régimes into accord in practice do not require a constitutional superstructure but simply the traditional technical skills and good-faith efforts of decision makers and their lawyers.[62] It is by means of prioritization (*lex posterior* and *lex specialis*), hierarchization (*jus cogens*, primary and secondary sources), and interpretation that international law maintains the coherence of its legal sources so that each subject of the law can ideally know what international law requires.

Certainly, to solve contradictions between legal subsystems, some writers have observed a shift from the application of rules to the balancing of

---

[60] *See* in this vein Teubner & Fischer-Lescano, *supra* note 47, at 1032–39 regarding jus cogens. For a more detailed discussion, *see* Andreas L. Paulus, *Comment to Andreas Fischer-Lescano & Gunther Teubner: The Legitimacy of International Law and the Role of the State*, 25 Mich. J. Int'l L. 1047, 1053 (2004).

[61] *See, in particular*, Case 26/62, Van Gend & Loos, 1963 E.C.R. 1 (direct effect); Case 6/64, Costa/ENEL 1964 E.C.R. 585 (supremacy over domestic law); Case 11/70, Internationale Handelsgesellschaft 1970 E.C.R. 1125, para. 3; on the constitutional nature of European law, *see* C. Möllers, *Pouvoir Constituant – Constitution – Constitutionalisation, in* Principles of European Constitutional Law 183 (A. Von Bogdandy & J. Bast eds., 2006).

[62] *See* Koskenniemi, *supra* note 3.

principles,[63] but this has not lead to an increasing demand for a comprehensive constitutionalization of international law. A constitution cannot solve the value conflicts of the founding principles of a legal order but may provide mechanisms for how to balance them in cases of clash to preserve the unity of international law in spite of the absence of a hierarchical order between the increasingly diverse international adjudicatory mechanisms.[64]

Indeed, while there have been divergences of interpretations of international law between different national and international courts and tribunals,[65] the number of cases discussed in this regard has been astonishingly small and appears not to be larger than within domestic jurisdictions. In general, international courts and tribunals of a specialized character have strived to maintain the unity of international law by taking the principles of other régimes into account.[66] Divergences of opinion with regard to the relationship between subsystems have, in general, not gone beyond differences regarding the application of any single subsystem. In other words, the partial hardening or even constitutionalization of more limited legal régimes, in particular the trade régime in the WTO and the regional human rights mechanisms, has not dissolved the unity of international law – which, except for a few norms of a jus cogens character, is based on the permissibility of consensual derogation.

But the coherence of international law – or, as others have maintained, the continuous existence of a network of international legal regulation[67] – is something other than the existence of a constitution. This contribution suggests that the debate on the constitutional character of the international

---

[63] *See* Kadelbach & Kleinlein, *supra* note 31, at 346; Paulus, *supra* note 7, at 94; Andreas L. Paulus, *International Adjudication, in* PHILOSOPHY OF INTERNATIONAL LAW (S. Besson & J. Tasioulas eds., 2007).

[64] On these, *see only* Benedict Kingsbury (ed.), *The Proliferation of International Tribunals: Piecing Together the Puzzle*, 31 N.Y.U J. INT'L L. & POL. 679 (1999); YUVAL SHANY, THE COMPETING JURISDICTIONS OF INTERNATIONAL COURTS AND TRIBUNALS (2003).

[65] For an example of insoluble differences between international communitarian principles and the state's right to survival, *see* Legality of the Threat or Use of Nuclear Weapons, *supra* note 14, at 266; for a clash between individual responsibility and state immunity, *see* Arrest Warrant of 11 Apr. 2000 (D.R. Congo v. Belgium), 2002 I.C.J. 3, 24, ¶¶ 59 *et passim*; Al-Adsani v. United Kingdom 34 Eur. Ct. H.R. 11 (2002); R. v. Bow Street Metropolitan Stipendiary Magistrate *ex p.* Pinochet (No. 3) (2000) A.C. 151 (U.K.). Note that in these cases, different branches of law and basic principles clash, in particular state and general human interests. These hard cases need to be distinguished from mere differences of opinion between different courts on points of law or fact.

[66] The most prominent example is possibly the Shrimp/Turtle case before the WTO Dispute Settlement Body, Appellate Body Report, *United States: Import Prohibition of Certain Shrimp and Shrimp Products*, WT/DS58/AB/R (Oct. 12, 1998), available in 38 INT'L LEGAL MATERIALS 1999, 121. For further analysis on these lines, *see* Paulus, *supra* note 7, at 80–86, with further references.

[67] Simma & Pulkowski, *supra* note 3.

legal system is less important than the debate on the substantive principles such a constitution should contain. In other words, the debate on the constitutionalization of international law should take a turn toward a debate on the substantive principles of the international legal system.[68]

Thus, this contribution suggests a move away from the question of theoretical unity or gap filling of special régimes to the substance of international law. While the question of the existence vel non of a system deals with the question of whether international law is coherent and whether different subrégimes derive their authority from following the basic systemic rules, the question of constitution should relate to the substance of international law. It is not content with some residual functions of a background system of formal legitimacy derived from the authority of sovereign states. Such a constitution needs substantive principles to stand on, not merely a formal derivation of all rules from a common source. The accordance of international law with substantive constitutional principles would enhance the legitimacy of international law and would thus make it easier for national legal systems to observe it. It is these constitutional principles to which we now turn.

III. Substantive Constitutional Principles and the International Legal System

The formal or systemic unity of international law that is based on its formal sources is not sufficient for its constitutionalization. A purely formal concept of legitimacy appears insufficient for founding an international constitution.[69] This chapter does not intend to analyze the UN Charter to find traces of constitutionalism there,[70] but rather attempts to go into the substantive principles of constitutionalism. It suggests that any claim of constitutionalization needs to talk not only about form but also about substance.

One might object that mingling constitutionalism and content amounts to a confusion of form and substance. However, it is precisely the argument of this chapter that with regard to a constitution, form and substance are

---

[68] For a similar argument, see Kadelbach & Kleinlein, *supra* note 31, at 337–47 (constitutional principles as general principles of law in the sense of art. 38 of the ICJ Statute). On the contrary, Besson, in this volume, at 379, regarding constitutionalism in a more essentialist sense as necessarily combining superiority and comprehensiveness.

[69] See also THOMAS FRANCK, THE POWER OF LEGITIMACY AMONG NATIONS, 24 (1990); and the critique by D. Georgiev, *To the Editor in Chief*, 83 AM. J. INT'L L. 551 (1989); *but see* FRANCK, *supra* note 21, at 6–9 (moving from formal legitimacy to substantive fairness).

[70] For such an analysis, see Fassbender, *supra* note 30; Simma, *supra* note 30, at 258–84.

inseparable. In other words, if a legal order has a constitution, there exists a substantive standard that needs to be fulfilled within the whole legal order. On the other hand, to be effective, a constitution also needs machinery for determining the constitutionality of any conduct. A set of substantive standards alone would be insufficient if it is not accompanied by a mechanism for decision making. Thus, most constitutions contain both: a set of general standards for the legal order and a machinery to implement them.

In the following, this contribution first looks to the existing principles in international law of a higher rank, in particular peremptory norms (jus cogens). Second, we will look at standards derived from domestic constitutions and ask how much of them can be found in, or incorporated into, contemporary international law. The result will be that – not surprisingly – international law does not meet the precise content of an ideal-type constitution. However, in view of the different scope of international and domestic law, a constitutional development of international law not only would be welcome but also might overcome some of the domestic objections against international law. Thus, while international law may never possess a constitution in the strict sense of domestic constitutions, international constitutionalism as an attempt to establish and control international power remains a worthy endeavor.

1. Jus Cogens and the Basic Principles of International Law

The usual place to look for the basic principles of international law is jus cogens or the peremptory norms of international law.[71] Jus cogens is a loose, objective standard of a purely negative character, however. In its original version codified in the Vienna Convention on the Law of Treaties,[72] it is established by the "international community of States as a whole" and voids any contrary international agreement. In spite of the uncertainty surrounding the "international community of States as a whole,"[73] there seems to develop a general agreement as to the contents of jus cogens – the prohibitions on the use of force and genocide, basic human rights such as not to be tortured, and the core rules of international humanitarian law are the main candidates

---

[71] On jus cogens generally, see, recently, with further references to an abundant literature, ALEXANDER ORAKHELASHVILI, PEREMPTORY NORMS IN INTERNATIONAL LAW (2006); THE FUNDAMENTAL RULES OF THE INTERNATIONAL LEGAL ORDER (Christian Tomuschat & Jean Marc Thouvenin eds., 2006). For a theoretical perspective, see S. KADELBACH, ZWINGENDES VÖLKERRECHT (1992); ROBERT KOLB, THÉORIE DU JUS COGENS INTERNATIONAL (2001). See also my own view in Andreas L. Paulus, Jus Cogens in a Time of Hegemony and Fragmentation – An Attempt at a Re-appraisal, 74 (3–4) NORDIC J. INT'I L. 297 (2005).

[72] Vienna Convention on the Law of Treaties, Jan. 27, 1989, 1155 U.N.T.S. 331.

[73] See Paulus, Jus Cogens, supra note 74, at 325–28.

commanding near-to-universal consent.[74] The ICJ also puts respect for the self-determination of peoples into the related category of *erga omnes* obligations.[75] The Inter-American Court and the Inter-American Commission on Human Rights have adopted a more expansive reading that integrates the larger part of human rights law into jus cogens, such as the prohibition on the death penalty against perpetrators younger than age eighteen, as well as the principles of equality and nondiscrimination.[76] As far as the present author can see, these precedents have not been followed elsewhere, however.

These mostly negative principles may be part of an international constitution broadly defined, but they do not by themselves ground a constitution. They limit state sovereignty only insofar as any legal régime worthy of this name would do. Outlawing the use of force or genocide does not a constitution make. On the other hand, not every peremptory norm not subject to interstate agreement necessarily belongs to the constitution.[77] Of the consensus candidates cited previously, the principle of self determination has such constitutional characteristics because it bears on the question of who is to be regarded as a legal subject. However, it is lacking any machinery of realization. It is almost alien to a system built on states as original subjects, which are classically defined by criteria of effectiveness, namely, the effective control over population and territory. Even the recent tendency to add democratic legitimacy to the tests of effectiveness does not condition statehood on legitimacy – otherwise, one may suspect that a great many states would not qualify.[78]

Article 2 of the UN Charter defines basic states' rights and duties, and some of them, such as the prohibition on the use of force, probably belong to jus cogens. Other norms of a jus cogens nature, such as the prohibition on genocide and the right not to be tortured, belong to human rights. However, these isolated elements are lacking coherence and comprehensiveness to be the basis of a constitution of the international community.

---

[74] *Id.* at 306, with further references. For a more extended list (which is apparently due to its nonconsensual character), *see* ORAKHELASHVILI, *supra* note 71, at 50 *et seq.*

[75] East Timor (Portugal v. Australia), 1995 I.C.J. 90, at 102, ¶ 29.

[76] For the execution of minors, *see Inter-American Commission of Human Rights,* Roach and Pinkerton v. United States, *Res. No. 3/1987,* 8 HUM. RTS. L.J. 353 (1987), ¶ 56; *confirmed in* Domingues v. United States, Rep. No. 62/2002, ¶¶ 84–85, *available at* http://www.cidh.org (last visited Aug. 18, 2005); for equality and equal protection before the law and nondiscrimination *see* Inter-American Court for Human Rights (IACtHR), *Juridical Condition and Rights of the Undocumented Migrants,* Advisory Opinion, OC-18/03 (Sept. 17, 2003), ¶ 101.

[77] ORAKHELASHVILI, *supra* note 71, at 9–10.

[78] *Cf.* Thomas Franck, *The Emerging Right to Democratic Governance,* 86 AM. J. INT'L L. 46 (1992).

While some have undertaken a heroic effort to bring conceptual coherence to jus cogens,[79] there is no escape from the necessity to demonstrate a consensus of the international community of states as a whole both for the substantive content and the legal effects of jus cogens. Such a constitutional consensus seems to have eluded the international community at least since the San Francisco Conference of 1945; and as far this consensus goes, it has not produced a complete ordering but rather a piecemeal result in some areas that cannot be extended to others by logical implication alone.[80] Thus, rules of a jus cogens nature will be part of any list of constitutional elements of international law, but they are neither necessary nor sufficient for a constitutionalization of the system of international law.

2. From Form to Substance: Constitutional Principles

This contribution proposes a different approach. To evaluate the progress and potential of constitutionalization in general international law, it suggests using established principles of domestic constitutions and asking whether they can be fulfilled by the international legal order. Obviously, it is far from evident that an international constitutionalism would have to be similar in content to domestic constitutions. On the other hand, the development of domestic constitutions constitutes the outcome of several centuries, if not millennia, of constitutional thought, and should thus not be discarded lightly.[81]

At a time when, in the wake of globalization, the regulatory power of the state seemed to wane,[82] a great many of decisions relevant for human

---

[79] See, in particular, ORAKHELASHVILI, supra note 71.

[80] See the criticism by Michael Byers, Book Review (Orakelashvili, Peremptory Norms in International Law), 101 AM. J. INT'L L. 913 (2007). But see Alexander Orakhelashvili, Letter to the Editors in Chief, 102 AM. J. INT'L L. 309 (2008). In his treatment, see ORAKHELASHVILI, supra note 71, at 38, 44, 49, 50, Orakhelashvili fails to take account of the difference between the rationale of jus cogens – embodying community interests that may not be derogated from by individual states – and the positive validation of jus cogens by the international community of states as a whole.

[81] Christoph Möllers, supra note 61, at 185, speaks in this regard of the "French-American tradition" creating "a specific democratic stock of traditions" that combines law with politics. For the example of the European Union, see PRINCIPLES OF EUROPEAN CONSTITUTIONAL LAW (Armin von Bogdandy & Jurgen Bast eds., 2006).

[82] For an analysis of this development, see, e.g., SUSAN STRANGE, THE RETREAT OF THE STATE: THE DIFFUSION OF POWER IN THE WORLD ECONOMY (1996); for an account of the consequences for law in general, see NEIL MacCORMICK, QUESTIONING SOVEREIGNTY (1999); GLOBAL LAW WITHOUT A STATE (Gunther Teubner ed., 1997). For constitutional law in general, see Neil Walker, The Idea of Constitutional Pluralism, 65 MOD. L. REV. 317 (2002); C. Walter, Constitutionalizing (Inter)national Governance: Possibilities for and Limits to the Development of an International Constitutional Law, 44 GERMAN Y.B. INT'L L. 170 (2001);

beings are taken at the international level. To cancel out this development, Anne Peters has advocated a "compensatory constitutionalism" at the international level.[83] Others have regarded the appeal to international norms as a means to redeem democratic control of international decisions.[84] Even if a compensation for the decline of domestic constitutionalism may overestimate the impact of international norms, it seems difficult to contest that, if and to the extent that power is delegated to or exercised by international institutions and decisions, they require the same restrictions and safeguards of individual rights – be they state or human rights – as do domestic executive decisions. In addition, to the extent international decisions are subject to similar constraints as domestic decisions, their legitimacy and thereby their compliance pull may be enhanced.[85] In the last resort, the argument in favor of international constitutionalism closely resembles the argument in favor of domestic constitutionalism, and thus there is at least a presumption for the application of similar principles. However, as we shall see, the fate of these principles on the international plane will require a considerable number of adjustments.

If international law conforms to those principles, one may argue that, while there may be no single written constitution in international law, there is effectively already a constitution in place. If the answer is in the negative, we may at least get an idea about how international law would have to change to constitutionalize in the domestic sense. Finally, if and to the extent that the answer lies somewhat in the middle, we will be able to approach the two most important questions in this regard: namely, how domestic constitutionalism needs to be modified to be applicable in the international realm of today, barring some revolutionary changes for the better; and how international law can be developed further to realize its constitutional potential. In other words, while we may not believe that an international constitutionalism is in the position to copy domestic constitutions, I do not think that we can have an international constitutionalism worthy of that name that would not even remotely take up the insights of several centuries or so of domestic development of constitutional principles.

---

see also M. Kumm, in this volume, at 258; for Europe, see European Constitutionalism, supra note 9.

[83] Anne Peters, *Compensatory Constitutionalism: The Function and Potential of Fundamental International Norms and Structures*, 19 Leiden J. Int'l L. 579 (2006).

[84] Eyal Benvenisti, *Reclaiming Democracy: The Strategic Uses of Foreign and International Law by National Courts*, 102 Am. J. Int'l L. 241 (2008). *See also* Dunoff & Trachtman, *Introduction to this volume*, at 14–18.

[85] On the compliance pull of legitimate norms, *see* Franck, *supra* note 69, at 25 *et passim*.

The criteria we propose here are the most basic principles of domestic constitutional orders. The French Declaration of the Rights of Man and the Citizen reads in article 16: "Toute société dans laquelle la garantie des droits n'est pas assurée, ni la séparation des pouvoirs déterminée, n'a point de constitution."[86] The constitution of Germany lists them in its article 20 and bars any amendments taking them away.[87] The U.S. Constitution does not list these basic principles explicitly, but they are contained in the machinery and principles established by it. The British constitution does not have an explicit core but arguably conforms to these principles where it counts, in domestic reality.[88]

The principles this contribution thereby derives from the Western constitutional tradition are democracy, separation of powers, rule of law and Rechtsstaat, as well as states' rights and human rights. Democracy answers the question about the ultimate source of legitimacy, namely the people. The rule of law or, in a slightly different meaning, the Rechtsstaat principle, is not so much about the ruler him- or herself but about the limits of rule, from the equality of subjects under the law to the legal constraints on the exercise of power. The separation of powers combines both principles and secures freedom by dividing power and preventing dictatorship, but it also allows for the exercise of democratic power in the first place.[89]

[86] "A society in which the observance of the law is not assured, nor the separation of powers defined, has no constitution at all." Déclaration des Droits de l'Homme et du Citoyen (Arthur W. Diamond Law Library at Columbia Law School trans.), *available at* http://www.hrcr.org/docs/frenchdec.html (last visited Nov. 29, 2007).

[87] Art. 20 of the German Constitution reads:

(1) The Federal Republic of Germany is a democratic and social federal state.
(2) All state authority is derived from the people. It shall be exercised by the people through elections and other votes and through specific legislative, executive, and judicial bodies.
(3) The legislature shall be bound by the constitutional order, the executive and the judiciary by law and justice.
(4) All Germans shall have the right to resist any person seeking to abolish this constitutional order, if no other remedy is available.

1949 Fed. Gaz. 1 (Inter Nationes trans.), *available at* http://www.iuscomp.org/gla/statutes/GG.htm#20 (last visited Dec. 3, 2007). Art. 79, para. 3, immunizes art. 20 against constitutional amendments.

[88] A recent constitutional law manual derives the following basic ideas from the British Constitution: democracy, parliamentary sovereignty, rule of law, separation of powers, and accountability; *see* C. TURPIN & A. TOMKINS, BRITISH GOVERNMENT AND THE CONSTITUTION, 33–137 (6th ed. 2007). Of these, only the sovereignty of parliament does not fit to the international realm, whereas accountability may qualify as general principle of law.

[89] *See* Eyal Benvenisti, *The Future of International Law Scholarship in Germany: The Tension between Interpretation and Change*, 67 ZEITSCHRIFT FÜR AUSLÄNDISCHES ÖFFENTLICHES RECHT UND VÖLKERRECHT 585, 590–91 (2007); Möllers, *supra* note 61, at 190 (*see also* 191, 203), speaks of the limitation and the shaping of power, and a process of juridification as well as democratization.

The latter two principles, human and states' rights, recognize that, in international law, we are dealing with at least two levels of government: interstate and individual. While a constitutional order needs to define the members of a community and the relationship between community and members, states are the original subjects of international law. An international constitution would need to define the qualifications to become its subjects. On the other hand, the ultimate beneficiary of all legal ordering are human beings; and a legal order made for states only would not appear legitimate.[90]

In addition, while the British and U.S. constitutions do not contain a formal constitutional principle of solidarity, a basic form of solidarity among the members of a community belongs to any legal system. The principle of solidarity is indeed indispensable to international law, as it is to any domestic legal constitution. A basic principle of solidarity already exists under international law.[91] Others regard a global principle of solidarity as the necessary consequence of Rawlsian ethics.[92] Some domestic constitutions contain similar principles (e.g., the social state principle deduced from art. 20, para. 1, of the German Grundgesetz).[93] For Immanuel Kant, because of a worldwide communal bond, the violation of the law in one corner of the Earth was felt everywhere.[94] On the other hand, a lack of strong bonds of solidarity may be regarded as the decisive feature distinguishing the international from national societies, and globalization has as much put into question the Kantian vision as it has contributed to its realization.[95]

---

[90] The skepticism expressed by S. A. Watts, *The International Rule of Law*, 36 GERMAN Y.B INT'L L. 15, 21 (1993), regarding human rights as part of the rule of law stems from the primary responsibility of the state for the observance of human rights, and thus does not relate to the substance but to the question of direct effect.

[91] *See, e.g.*, U.N. Millennium Declaration, G.A. Res. 55/2, U.N. Doc. A/RES/55/2 (Sept. 18, 2000); on the right to development, in particular, *see* Vienna Declaration and Programme of Action, U.N. Doc. A/CONF.157/23, 32 INT'L LEGAL MATERIALS 1661 (1993), ¶ 10; M. Kotzur, *Soziales Völkerrecht für eine solidarische Völkergemeinschaft?* 63 JURISTENZEITUNG 265 (2008).

[92] *See, e.g.*, THOMAS W. POGGE, REALIZING RAWLS, 244 *et seq.* (1989); for a balanced view, *see* STANLEY HOFFMANN, DUTIES BEYOND BORDERS: ON THE LIMITS AND POSSIBILITIES OF ETHICAL INTERNATIONAL POLITICS 156–59 (1981).

[93] *See supra* note 87.

[94] IMMANUEL KANT, ZUM EWIGEN FRIEDEN (Perpetual Peace), 216–17 (1795, 46). *But see also*, from about the same time, JOHANN GOTTFRIED HERDER, IDEEN ZUR PHILOSOPHIE DER GESCHICHTE DER MENSCHHEIT (original ed. 1784–81; 1966) (preferring concrete solidarity over cosmopolitanism).

[95] For a philosophical argument in favor of global solidarity, *see* HAUKE BRUNKHORST, SOLIDARITY: FROM CIVIC FRIENDSHIP TO A GLOBAL LEGAL COMMUNITY (2005). For a critical evaluation of the relationship between globalization and inequality, *see* Andrew Hurrell &

However, it is by no way obvious that these elements of domestic constitutions can be transferred to the international realm. In the following, we will look at them one-by-one.

a. Democracy

The most basic and most important constitutional principle enshrined in domestic constitutions is the principle of democracy. It is not only a principle of government but also a principle for the foundation of government. In the international realm, however, the "democratic deficit" appears endemic and incontrovertible.[96] In other words, in the term coined by Kalypso Nicolaïdes, is democracy possible for an association of multiple *demoi*, a "demoi-cracy"?[97]

Democracy requires an agreement of the minority that it will abide by the decisions of the majority. The acceptance of majority decisions presupposes a general agreement on the framework in which democratic decision making can take place. In the absence of a global demos, international law has difficulty in commanding respect from democratically elected representatives of the nation-state or a local community.[98] In other words, cosmopolitan morality alone appears insufficient as a basis for the creation of rights and obligations that would overrule local or national democratic decisions. Therefore, it should surprise no one that the democratic deficit is held against international law, in particular when it requires changes in national policies and laws going beyond narrowly tailored functional regulation. Democracy in a meaningful sense of the term appears possible only within a nation-state or local setting, not on the world stage.

Ngaire Woods, *Globalisation and Inequality*, 24 Millennium 447 (1995); for a very measured evaluation, *see* Andrew Hurrell, On Global Order: Power, Values, and the Constitution of International Society, 194–215, 298–308 (2007).

[96] *Cf.* Weiler, *supra* note 50, at 561 (rejecting a "simplistic application of the majoritarian principle in world arenas").

[97] Kalypso Nicolaïdes, *Our European Demoi-cracy: Is This Constitution a Third Way for Europe?* in Whose Europe? National Models and the Constitution of the European Union, 137, 144 (Kalypso Nicolaïdes & Stephen Weatherill eds., 2003); Samantha Besson, *Institutionalizing Global Demoi-cracy*, in International Law, Justice and Legitimacy (L. Meyer ed., 2007); Besson, in this volume, at 387.

[98] *See* J. Isensee, *Nachwort. Europa – die politische Erfindung eines Erdteils*, in Europa als politische Idee und als rechtliche Form 103, 133 (J. Isensee ed., 2d ed. 1994); P. Kirchhof, *Der deutsche Staat im Prozeß der Europäischen Integration*, in 7 Handbuch des Staatsrechts 855, ¶¶ 33, 39, 46, 52 *et passim* (J. Isensee & P. Kirchhof eds., 1992); *cf.* the *Maastricht* decision of the German Constitutional Court, 89 BVerfGE 155, 186, which substitutes Kirchhof's and Isensee's *never* with a *not yet* and requires limits to European integration; see also 83 BVerfGE 37; 83 BVerfGE 60 (communal right to vote of foreigners); partial English translation in D. P. Kommers, The Constitutional Jurisprudence of the Federal Republic of Germany 197–99 (2d ed., 1997).

In the United States, in particular, some of the opposition to the decisions of international bodies is grounded in an apparent lack of democratic control over those institutions. Law without democracy, the argument goes, is not much more than an imposition that needs to be judged on the individual merits of the law in question, not on any inherent legitimacy of international law. In the words of Jack Goldsmith and Eric Posner, international law "can have no democratic pedigree because there are no international institutions that reliably convert the world public's needs and interests into international law and that can change existing international law when the world public's needs and interests change."[99]

Democratic legitimacy depends on the representation of the principal stakeholders. Representation by a non–democratically elected government or NGO at the international level may be preferable to no representation at all, but it is hardly equivalent to the representation by an elected government. A global majority rule that would rely on a weighing of international votes according to the sizes of the respective population would fail to respect the inherent limitation of democracy, namely, that it presupposes a consensus that the minority will accept the rule of the majority. To put it mildly, such an international consensus is internationally not forthcoming. It could lead to a directorate of some great powers (e.g., China, India, Russia, the United States) to the exclusion of Europe, Africa, or Latin America. While the current composition of the Security Council may be regarded as unjust, its competences are limited to the maintenance of international peace and security and thus do not encroach upon the national sovereignty over the main distributional struggles within societies.[100]

However, more and more decisions, both at the international and at the domestic level, appear to affect a great number of people without regard to the boundaries of nation-states, and many tasks cannot be realized at the national level only, from free trade to the fights against terrorism, climate change, global poverty, and AIDS.[101] Thus, national democratic processes cannot solve the problem of legitimacy of the collective answer that is required to tackle these problems. On the one hand, decisions taken, or not taken, at the domestic level affect the citizens not only of a single state but also of humanity at large, from the provision of AIDS medication to the waging of wars. On the other hand, international decisions have different effects on different national or international constituencies. Thus, the democratic deficit of international decisions cannot be balanced by domestic democratic processes alone. In

[99] Jack L. Goldsmith & Eric A. Posner, The Limits of International Law 199 (2005).
[100] U.N. Charter arts. 24, 25, 39.
[101] On these community interests, see Simma, supra note 30, at 233–43.

other words, domestic democratic processes do not represent outsiders, and international processes are not democratic and thereby truly representative.

In the current system of international law, representation goes through states. This two-level system is under threat from liberal ethicists and sovereignists alike. While the latter reject any long-term international decision making not subject to domestic ratification, the former demand the construction of something akin to a world democracy by introducing domestic constitutional processes in international decision making.[102] None of them has been successful. The improvement of the legitimacy of international decisions seems to require both a strengthening of the domestic representativeness of states as well as a more open, transparent process of decision making at the international level that would include the voices and accommodate the interests of all stakeholders. Models of deliberative democracy may be helpful in this regard.[103] However, democracy is not only about deliberation but also about rule by the people.[104] Deliberation is thus necessary but by no means sufficient for democracy.

Thus, democracy may indeed constitute an argument in favor of leaving decisions at the lowest possible level.[105] It does not, however, point against the attempt of construing multilateral institutions that are capable of inter- and supranational decision making, if the task in question requires an answer that goes beyond the purview of the nation-states. Thus, the democratization of global institutions, as limited as it may be, is preferable to a return to domestic regulation. When global decisions are concerned, the democracy of domestic decisions alone is undemocratic when seen from the perspective of outsiders.

This, of course, is not a sufficient argument as to the democratic nature of international decision making itself. In an ideal world, we would possibly not live in a world state but would have democratic decision making in

---

[102] *See, in particular,* COSMOPOLITAN DEMOCRACY: AN AGENDA FOR A NEW WORLD ORDER (Daniele Archibugi & David Held eds., 1995); DAVID HELD, DEMOCRACY AND THE GLOBAL ORDER (1995). For a more moderate version, *see* O. HÖFFE, *DEMOKRATIE IM ZEITALTER DER GLOBALISIERUNG* (1999); Besson, *supra* note 97; Besson, in this volume, at 389–90.

[103] On deliberative democracy in general, *see* DELIBERATIVE DEMOCRACY AND ITS DISCONTENTS (Samantha Besson & Jose Luis Martí eds., 2006); DELIBERATIVE DEMOCRACY (Jon Elster ed., 1998); DAVID HELD, MODELS OF DEMOCRACY 231–55 (3d ed., 2006); for its transfer to the international level, *see* Joshua Cohen & Charles Sabel, *Directly-Deliberative Polyarchy*, 3 EUR. L.J. 313 (1997); Held, *id.*

[104] The Greek term δμος means "people" and κρατία means "rule."

[105] For a more comprehensive treatment, *see* Andreas L. Paulus, *Subsidiarity, Fragmentation and Democracy: Towards the Demise of General International Law? in* THE SHIFTING ALLOCATION OF AUTHORITY IN INTERNATIONAL LAW: CONSIDERING SOVEREIGNTY, SUPREMACY AND SUBSIDIARITY 193 (Tomer Broude & Yuval Shany eds., 2008).

each state and a consensus procedure internationally, with a slight dose of majoritarianism regarding individual holdouts; as well as direct participation of citizens and NGOs at the global stage to prevent a cartel of state leaderships against the interests of their populations. Regionally, we might wish for more regional groups of democratic states with closer integration, such as the European Union. In the end, international legal ordering should not be democratic if this implies majority rule. On the other hand, it could become much more democratic when its basic actors enjoy more of a democratic legitimacy at home.

A basic feature of a domestic democracy eludes the international realm, however: a change of government is only possible within states and at the helm of international organizations. Because democracy internationally will continue to rely on indirect representation via states, the changes of government will be limited to the state level.

Thus, an international democracy cannot and will not look similar to a state. But that should not imply that it is impossible to render the international community more democratic.

b. Rechtsstaat and Rule of Law

The other pillar of any constitutional order is the rule of law. Without rule of law, the very attempt to establish a comprehensive legal order according to a few guiding principles and institutions is lacking authority. While there is no consensus on the precise meaning of the rule of law and Rechtsstaat,[106] the Rechtsstaat emphasizes the establishment of institutions by legal means, whereas the rule of law deals with the constraints on the state and due process of law. Nevertheless, the core of the two terms seems identical: it is possibly best captured by John Adams's phrase, the "government of laws, and not of men."[107] In other words, as all humans are created equal, rule itself is conditioned on rules that are equal for everybody. Human beings of equal

---

[106] In particular, the rule of law has procedural and substantive aspects – the latter being denied by some. For a substantive view in the common law, *see*, recently, Lord Bingham, *The Rule of Law* 66 CAMBRIDGE L.J. 67 (2007); Paul Craig, *Formal and Substantive Conceptions of the Rule of Law: An Analytical Framework*, 1997 PUBLIC LAW 467, with further references. According to Watts, *supra* note 90, the rule of law is "not a concept with any easily identifiable content." *But see* his list of criteria, id., at 26–40 (completeness and certainty of the law, equality before the law, absence of arbitrariness, effective application of the law, in particular judicial control); *cf.* J. M. FARRALL, UNITED NATIONS AND THE RULE OF LAW 40–41 (2007), (transparency, consistency, equality, due process, proportionality). This article limits itself to the regulation and judicialization of the use of force, in a formal rather than substantive way. The other constitutional elements take up the substantive aspects of the rule of law.

[107] 1774 BOSTON GAZ., no. 7. *See also* A. V. DICEY, INTRODUCTION TO THE STUDY OF THE LAW OF THE CONSTITUTION 188 (9th ed. Macmillan, 1956): "[T]he rule of law is contrasted

dignity may accept rules of behavior for living together but no permanent rule of one of them over the other. Thus, as Rechtsstaat, the state is based on legal rules and procedures, and is also bound by them (rule of law).

Internationally, the rule of law appears both as a precondition for any legal – and even more so constitutional – ordering of the international realm and as permanently threatened by the lack of comprehensive judicialization. Political science has claimed for a long time that the international realm is one of anarchy, whose legal regulation is effectively limited to special régimes.[108]

The state monopoly of the use of force – or at least the central monopoly of its legitimation – constitutes the basic feature of a state in the Weberian sense. In this sense, the constitutionalization of international law hinges on the rule of law rather than on the rule of force.[109] Internationally, the constitutionalization of the use of force appears only insufficiently based on legal criteria. However, from the tests of article 39 of the Charter for Security Council action – a threat to the peace, breach of the peace, or act of aggression – only the latter is (incompletely) legalized.[110] While the Charter provides for a monopolization of the legitimation of the use of force, it gives the Security Council almost full discretion on this legitimation[111] – leading to a rule by the Security Council, and not by the law. A constitutionalization would thus at least imply a narrow reading of the discretion of the council under article 39 of the UN Charter. On the contrary, regarding individual self-defense, article 51 of the UN Charter seems to respect armed force only as the very last resort, giving priority to the collective security system of the Charter. Self-defense is limited to emergency measures "if an armed attack occurs," and does not give the attacked states much discretion.

Another central element of the rule of law is the judicial protection of individual rights. In this regard, both the UN system and the individual use of force by states are insufficiently judicialized, at best. In principle, horizontal disputes between states are today resolved in the same manner as in the nineteenth century, the World Court or "principal judicial organ of the

---

with every system of government based on the exercise by persons in authority of wide, arbitrary, or discretionary powers of constraint"; cf. Craig, supra note 106, at 471.

[108] See, e.g., INTERNATIONAL REGIMES (Stephen D. Krasner ed., 1983).

[109] Similarly Watts, supra note 90, at 25.

[110] However, even the "definition of aggression" (G.A. Res. 3314 (XXIX), at 142, Annex, U.N. Doc. A/9631, U.N. GAOR, 29th Sess., Supp. No. 31 (1974)) opens the way for purely political decisions by the Security Council; see art. 2 (Security Council not bound to declare anything an aggression) and art. 4 (definition not exhaustive).

[111] U.N. Charter, art. 39; for a discussion of the limits of the Security Council's discretion, see, e.g., Jochen Frowein & Nico Krisch, Introduction to Ch. VII, paras. 25–31, in THE CHARTER OF THE UNITED NATIONS, supra note 37, at 701, 710.

United Nations" (art. 92 of the UN Charter) being a permanent court but lacking compulsory jurisdiction. As far as the Charter law itself is concerned, advisory opinions according to article 96 are only a very incomplete substitute for constitutional litigation on the extent and the limits of UN competences. Only some special areas, such as world trade law and international criminal law, benefit from a denser system of adjudication. However, only investment tribunals and regional human rights courts know of binding adjudication between states and individuals.

Thus, the deficiency of the rule of law in international affairs is, in the first place, due not to a lack of rules but to a lack of adjudication of these rules. Progress of constitutionalization would thus be tied to a rise of adjudication. However, even then the question arises of how the different mechanisms relate to one another. Recent divergences, if not clashes between the ICJ and the International Criminal Tribunal for the Former Yugoslavia (ICTY), on the one hand,[112] and the ICJ and the U.S. Supreme Court, on the other,[113] have shown that a multiplicity of courts and tribunals will also result in a multiplicity of judicial outcomes. In the absence of a formalized hierarchy, the success of international adjudication will depend on an atmosphere of mutual deference and respect between courts and tribunals.[114]

However, the argument often used against international adjudication, namely, that it is not sufficiently under democratic control,[115] appears unwarranted. International adjudication is used only when and to the extent that a problem cannot be solved within the domestic realm. The basis of classical international adjudication lies less in democracy but in a protection of states' rights – in other words, in the delineation of interests among several states, democracies, or otherwise. Thus, international adjudication could be controlled only by a global democracy – hardly the outcome the critics want. As shown previously, the critics' alternative – letting domestic democracy decide – is, however, at least as undemocratic as the adjudication of international claims by an international court or tribunal. Constitutionalizing and democratizing the international rule of law can be achieved only by improving the democratic legitimacy of all the actors involved, not by unilateral decision-making.

---

[112] See Application of the Genocide Convention (Bosnia-Herzegovina v. Serbia and Montenegro), 2006 I.C.J (Feb. 26), *available at* http://www.icj-cij.org (last visited Dec. 3, 2007).
[113] See Sanchez-Llamas v. Oregon, 126 S.Ct. 2669 (2006).
[114] See Anne Marie Slaughter, *A Global Community of Courts*, 44 Harv. Int'l L.J. 191 (2003).
[115] In this sense, *see* Eric A. Posner & John C. Yoo, *Judicial Independence in International Tribunals*, 93 Cal. L. Rev. 1, 27 (2005); against them, *see* Laurence R. Helfer & Anne-Marie Slaughter, *Why States Create International Tribunals: A Response to Professors Posner and Yoo*, 93 Cal. L. Rev. 899, 905 (2005).

c. Separation of Powers

Since John Locke, we regard any rule as conditioned by the respect for individual rights and freedoms; and to safeguard liberty, power must be shared between different branches of government. Thus, the notion of the rule of law is closely related to the separation of powers, which lies at the heart of any constitutional system.

It is, however, difficult to apply the separation of powers to the international realm. The UN Charter itself does not provide for a legislator in the true meaning of the term. On the other hand, the Security Council as the rough equivalent of an executive branch has a formally strong arm as far as peace and security are concerned, but with all the practical weaknesses stemming from the lack of an armed force of its own. Nevertheless, the Security Council has begun to broaden its jurisdiction to legislate itself, thus combining a policing with a norm-setting function that would be anathema to a well-ordered constitutional state.[116] The judicial realm is even more wanting, fragmented in various different parts and, the ICJ notwithstanding, lacking one single authoritative judicial authority that can interpret and apply the rules and principles of international law to all states and individuals alike.[117]

However, in the view of the particularities of the international realm and the absence of a world state, such a mechanical transfer of the notions of a domestic constitution to the international sphere appears anachronistic and illusory. Thus, it is not the point whether the separation of powers between the Security Council and the General Assembly is similar or different to the one between a domestic parliament and the executive branch. Rather, it is important that all power is checked by other powers, both horizontally, at the center, and vertically, between center and subjects.

A constitutional reading would thus be skeptical of the recent broadening of the sanctioning practice of the Security Council, for example, the drawing up of terror lists without any individual control or individual procedure of

---

[116] Stefan Talmon, *The Security Council as World Legislature*, 99 Am. J. Int'l L. 175 (2005); Ian Johnstone, *Legislation and Adjudication in the UN Security Council: Bringing Down the Deliberative Deficit*, 102 Am. J. Int'l L. 275 (2008). Johnstone's attempt to use models of deliberative democracy falls directly into the trap described in note 104 and accompanying text, namely to substitute democracy by mere deliberation without real decision making, see *id.*, at 283–94. For critique, *see, e.g.*, Martti Koskenniemi, *The Police in the Temple. Order, Justice and the UN: A Dialectical View*, 6 Eur. J. Int'l L. 325 (1995); Andreas Zimmermann & Björn Elberling, *Grenzen der Legislativbefugnisse des Sicherheitsrats*, 52 Vereinte Nationen 71 (2004).

[117] For an enormously rich literature on the fragmentation of the international judicial system, *see* Kingsbury (ed.), *supra* note 64; Shany, *supra* note 64, with further references.

redress,[118] because this amounts to a blatant disregard of the human rights of the individuals involved as long as they do not have any judicial or quasi-judicial means to show their innocence. In my view, those who justify the council by pointing to its emergency competence[119] seem to disregard the fact that any emergency procedure would require some sort of judicial control after the fact, which is absent at the international level.[120] When the basic point of constitutional governance relates to the protection of individual rights against governmental power, even in emergencies, the constitutional tradition suggests the necessity of mechanisms of legal control, in whose absence the procedure should be regarded as contrary to the principles of the international legal order, to which due process and a right to a hearing certainly belong.

Thus, a constitutional reading of the Charter does not necessarily entail a broadening of the power and competencies of the international realm but rather implies its limitation in the same way as constitutional government limits the executive branch domestically.

d. From State Rights to World Federalism?

A constitutional understanding of international law, in particular a "multi-level constitutionalism," would suggest an international definition of the tasks of the different levels. Indeed, the division of competences is a central task of any domestic constitution or the statute of an international organization.

International law continues to be based on states.[121] As a constitutional system, it would have to clearly delimit the competences of the international realm. Whereas earlier international law contained sovereignty as a default rule,[122] recent jurisprudence has been doubtful whether such an

---

[118] See Bardo Fassbender, *Targeted Sanctions Imposed by the UN Security Council and Due Process Rights* 3 INT'L ORG. L. REV. 437 (2006). *Cf.* Kadi v. Council, *supra* note 6. For criticism from a human rights perspective, *see* Marty, *id.*

[119] See, *in particular*, the European Court of the First Instance in Yusuf, *id.*

[120] For recent attempts to that effect, *see* Fassbender, *supra* note 118. Less skeptically, *see* Johnstone, *supra* note 116, at 299–307, who makes important concessions by relying on deliberative processes rather than individual rights – a concept inimical to the rule of law.

[121] For criticism, *see, recently*, ALLEN BUCHANAN, JUSTICE, LEGITIMACY, AND SELF-DETERMINATION: MORAL FOUNDATIONS FOR INTERNATIONAL LAW (2004), and Fernando R. Tesón, *The Kantian Theory of International Law*, 92 COLUM. L. REV. 53 (1992) (both arguing for a basis in human rather than states' rights).

[122] See, *in particular*, The Case of the SS *Lotus* (France v. Turkey), 1927 P.C.I.J. (ser. A) No. 10, at 18.

easy solution is still appropriate when dealing with issues concerning the whole international community, such as the protection of the environment or nuclear proliferation.[123]

In its article 2, the UN Charter contains the basic international protections and obligations of states, including sovereign equality and a right of non-interference in domestic affairs by the United Nations. However, paragraph 7 of Article 2 contains only a loose standard for protection of State sovereignty from interference by the UN, in particular because of a dominant interpretation that defines the domain reserved to states in accordance with the ever-progressing development of international law instead of using an objective minimum standard.[124] In addition, the provision explicitly excludes measures taken by the Security Council for the maintenance of international peace and security under chapter VII of the UN Charter. In light of the ever-growing use of chapter VII for a broad range of measures, from the ad hoc solution of political crisis to long-term measures against terrorism, the Charter draws only very loose limits for collective action. Thus, an application of the principle of subsidiarity to the international sphere appears warranted.[125]

The horizontal relationship between states is also partly defined in article 2 of the Charter, including, in particular, the prohibition on the use of force. However, international law does not provide for one centralized mechanism of enforcement, not even in cases involving a blatant disregard for the most basic protections such as military invasions or the annexation of territory. Judicial control remains predicated on the previous consent of states. As we have seen, the criteria for Security Council intervention are political rather than legal – with the effect that states cannot rely on the council to protect them from outside threats.

Thus, while international law in general, and the UN Charter in particular, contain the basic rights of states, the mechanisms for their protection are at best inadequate from a constitutional standpoint. An organized structure of a

---

[123] See, in particular, Legality of the Threat or Use of Nuclear Weapons, supra note 14, at 270, ¶ 13.

[124] See Georg Nolte, Art. 2 (7), para. 29, in THE CHARTER OF THE UNITED NATIONS, supra note 37.

[125] On subsidiarity in international law, see Christian Calliess, Susidiaritätsprinzip und Solidaritätsprinzip als rechtliches Regulativ der Globalisierung von Staat und Gesellschaft – dargestellt am Beispiel von EU und WTO, 20 RECHTSTHEORIE BEIHEFT 371 (2002); Ulrich Fastenrath, Subsidiarität im Völkerrecht, 20 RECHTSTHEORIE BEIHEFT 475 (2002); THE SHIFTING ALLOCATION OF AUTHORITY IN INTERNATIONAL LAW: CONSIDERING SOVEREIGNTY, SUPREMACY AND SUBSIDIARITY 193 (Tomer Broude & Yuval Shany eds., 2008); Kumm, in this volume, pp. 291–95.

quasi-federal nature, as the one to be found, at least in nuce, in the European Union, is absent from international law.

e. Human Rights: Toward Protection before International Organizations

The multilevel structure of the international realm and the, at best, imperfect protection of human rights at the domestic level have rendered the central regulation of human rights protection necessary. The protection of human rights of individuals even against their own state in cases of crass abuse is one of the greatest achievements of contemporary international law.

Why should, however, democratic states accept the supervision of international institutions when nondemocratic states violate human rights? And why should nondemocratic states accept an obligation to protect human rights when the very concept is so much tied to the concept of a Western, liberal, and democratic tradition?

To both of these questions there exists a classic – and superficial – answer: namely, state consent. All UN member states have agreed, in principle, on the obligation contained in article 1, paragraphs 3 and 55, of the UN Charter to promote respect for human rights. Many states, with some notable exceptions, have accepted or at least signed the UN covenants as well as the conventions against discrimination against women and for racial grounds. Most, but by no means all, also accept the supervisory role of the treaty bodies of the respective instruments, in some cases including individual applications.

As to the effect of international human rights within the domestic legal system, the times of terrorism and of the so-called war waged on it, have shown that this last line of defense for the human being also provides important outside checks and balances on executive measures of democratic states – domestic or international – that affect human rights.[126] On the other hand, the submission of democratic states to international procedures contributes to their claim of authority with regard to other states as well. International human rights embody the historical experience of many states containing the indispensable core of human rights for the protection of individuals. They also contribute to the international and national legitimacy of the claims of the state toward allegiance of its citizens. Even democracies may be tempted to forgo the protection of individuals for the sake of the majority; and the international demarcation of the limits of the submission of individuals to majority rule may thus be an important outside yardstick. In other words, listening to the experience of others is not only a virtue for undemocratic

[126] On the domestic uses of international law in this respect, *see* Benvenisti, *supra* note 84, at 253–58.

states, provided that the international obligations remain realistic – or, to paraphrase Justice Jackson's famous words, do not "convert the [international] Bill of Rights into a suicide pact."[127] As a safeguard for individual rights, the borders between human rights and the imposition of a suicide pact should also be subject to judicial determination and supervision, both domestically and internationally.

State consent alone may not explain the effect of international law on individuals. Current international human rights law does not provide for supremacy and direct effect of international law on individuals within the domestic legal order.[128] That is why supranationality in the narrow sense of the term is eluding the United Nations – different from the European Union.[129] Rather, it merely establishes a minimum standard. Only two regional systems, the European and the Inter-American systems, know of a functioning judicial protection of individuals against their home state.

But what appears most problematic from a constitutional standpoint is the lack of control of the international organizations and actors themselves. Recent reports on abuses committed by UN peace-keepers, but also the continuing debate on the terror lists set up by the Security Council, demonstrate the point. It is also interesting – and regrettable – that the debate within the European Union seems to disregard the extent to which the UN Charter itself contains human rights standards (i.e., art. 1, para. 3; art. 24, paras. 2 and 25), to allow for individual control of Council decisions from a human rights perspective.[130] Whereas we are moving toward an independent human rights control of the European Union by the European Court of Human Rights, the latter's *Behrami* judgment virtually exempting international administrations

---

[127] Terminiello v. Chicago, 337 U.S. 1, 37 (1949) (Jackson, J., dissenting). In the same logic, the ICJ has opined that the right to self-defense, when the survival of a state is at stake, may remove the illegality of the threat or use of nuclear weapons; see Legality of the Threat or Use of Nuclear Weapons, *supra* note 14 at 263, para. 96–97. For a provocative demonstration of the dangers of such an approach that eschews absolute rights, *see* RICHARD A. POSNER, NOT A SUICIDE PACT: THE CONSTITUTION IN A TIME OF NATIONAL EMERGENCY (2006).

[128] For a recent summary of the effect of international treaties in domestic law, *see* THE ROLE OF DOMESTIC LAW IN TREATY ENFORCEMENT: A COMPARATIVE STUDY (Derek Jinks & David Sloss eds., Cambridge Univ. Press, 2009).

[129] Van Gend & Loos, 1963 E.C.R. 1 (direct effect); Case 6/64, Costa/ENEL 1964 E.C.R. 585 (supremacy over domestic law). Both were created by the case law of the European Court of Justice, whose authority as the final adjudicator of community law under art. 220 TEC is thus decisive. See also Gardbaum, in this volume, at 233. For a broader use of the concept of supranationality, see M. Doyle, in this volume, at 113.

[130] *See, e.g.*, Farrall, *supra* note 106, at 244; C. Tomuschat, *Case Note (Kadi, Yusuf)*, 43 COMMON MKT. L. REV. 537 (2006).

from human rights control is certainly a step in the wrong direction.[131] The European Court of Justice, in the *Kadi* case, has denied a control of the international legality of UN sanctions, relying instead on the separateness of the European legal order to demand the divulsion of information on the evidence for the inclusion in the terror list. It thus provided a way for improving the sanctions régime to make it acceptable under the guarantees of human rights under Article 6 of the Treaty on European Union, but did not solve the lack of control of the *international* legality of the UN measures, as the European Commission had proposed.[132] A mechanism that would allow for a human rights control not only of states but also of international organizations would be a necessary step toward the meaningful constitutionalization of international law. Otherwise, the domestic rule of law would be supplanted by a superpower or Security Council rule, and this change would hardly be one for the better. Another, albeit inferior, alternative is a direct effect of international law conditional on the implementation of core international rights.[133]

Again, it appears that constitutionalization in the sense of a direct effect of international law on the individual is not fully realized. On the other hand, the impact of international law on the relationship between the individual and his or her own state is anything but negligible.

f. Equality and Solidarity

Finally, and in view of the communal feeling binding the international community together, it remains questionable whether the solidarity toward far-away people and peoples is comparable to the communal bond between conationals of a single state. The latter allegiance will be different from person to person, and from state to state, corresponding to the degree to which citizenship is perceived as freely entered or coerced and also to wealth and individual freedoms or levels of social and national security. Nevertheless,

---

[131] Behrami v. France, Application No. 71412/01, Grand Chamber judgment of May 2, 2007, *available at* http://www.echr.coe.int/echr (last visited Dec. 3, 2007). For harsh – and richly deserved – criticism, *see* Marko Milanovic & Tatjana Papic, *As Bad as It Gets: The European Court of Human Rights Behrami and Saramati Decision and General International Law*, 58 Int'l Comp. L.Q. (2008).

[132] *See Kadi, supra* note 6, paras. 287, 326, 345, 371 *et passim*. For a similar critique of the ECJ judgment, see Joseph Weiler, *Editorial*, 19 Eur. J. Int' L. 895–96 (2008); Andrea Gattini, *Comment*, 46 C.M.L. Rev. 213–14, 226–27 (2009); Daniel Halberstam and Eric Stein, *The UN, the EU, and the King of Sweden*, 46 C.M.L. Rev. 13, 71–72 (2009); see also the position taken by the European Commission in *Kadi*, paras. 269–70; but see Bjørn Kunoy and Anthony Dawes, *Plate Tectonics in Luxembourg*, 46 C.M.L. Rev. 73, 103–04 (2009).

[133] This is the logic of the European Court of Human Rights, see *Bosphorus v. Ireland* [2005] ECHR-VI. For a more extensive discussion of its relevance in the context of UN sanctions, see Gattini, *supra* note 132, at 233–34.

national feelings of solidarity tend to be thicker than international ones.[134] The mere existence of an immediate affection with the plight of suffering people watched on television, for example, cannot be associated with a readiness to sacrifice. This is why distributive rights in the international sphere will remain more controversial than at the domestic level, not to speak of the problems of effectiveness and efficiency involved.[135] This is also why democratic states will remain reluctant to risk the lives of their soldiers and the tax money of their constituents for causes in which their own material interests are of an altruistic nature only.

While international law recognizes a right to sovereign equality of states (art. 2, sec. 1, of the UN Charter) that equals the domestic equality before the law, and human rights law contains principles of nondiscrimination and equality before the law that at least one international court has held to belong to jus cogens,[136] these rights do not amount to a right to positive assistance or international subsidies. The right to development that is internationally recognized as a "third generation human right" does not specify what kind of redistribution it mandates beyond the mere duty of states to cooperation.[137] Part IV of the GATT contains special rules for, and the 1979 Enabling Clause allows for preferential treatment of developing countries deviating from GATT rules but are of dubious effectiveness.[138]

Thus, international solidarity as a right has not quite entered the operational phase. However, that does not imply a denial of increasing efforts, for example, in the wake of the Millennium Declaration of 2000,[139] to exercise solidarity in practice. A constitutionalization remains, sixty years after the introduction of the Economic and Social Council into the Charter of the United Nations, elusive, however.

g. Conclusion

The conclusion of our enterprise is mixed at best: domestic constitutional principles do have international equivalents, but their realization remains precarious. On the one hand, the two-tiered structure of the international legal ordering means that some characteristics of a domestic constitutional order – namely, providing for individual rights or balancing the rights of the

[134] MICHAEL WALZER, THICK AND THIN: MORAL ARGUMENT AT HOME AND ABROAD (1994).
[135] For an ethical argument to this effect in the Rawlsian tradition, see Pogge, supra note 92.
[136] See IACtHR, supra note 76.
[137] See supra note 91.
[138] See, e.g., PETER-TOBIAS STOLL & FRANK SCHORKOPF, WTO: WORLD ECONOMIC ORDER, WORLD TRADE LAW (2006) paras. 89, 309–10; PETROS C. MAVROIDIS, TRADE IN GOODS (2007) at 137–48, 450.
[139] See supra note 91.

majority (democracy) and individual rights – need to take account of at least two levels for the distribution of rights and obligations. On the other hand, the more the international order resembles the constitutional characteristics of a nation-state, the more it may clash with the same structure at the domestic level. Identical principles of constitutional ordering do not necessarily lead to identical decisions. Nevertheless, only an international order that is subject to some of the same checks and balances as the domestic legal order will be recognized as legitimate.

A constitutional, deductive model of international order would need to devise a strict division of competences between the international and domestic constitutional spheres. However, the European example demonstrates how difficult and conflict rich such a division of competences is. But the division of competences can also constitute an additional mechanism of control. At times, the real control of international law will thus come from the measure of compliance at the domestic level. In other words, an international constitutional order that is not assured of its domestic effect will have to take care that it does respect its own limits. The inductive approach to international law making (e.g., the necessity to ground any rule in the consent, treaties, or acquiescence, custom, of states) ensures that the powers of international law and organizations will remain limited.

Where, however, the international constitutional order itself resembles in effectiveness and coercion the domestic legal order – as the example of the terror lists of the Security Council has shown – international law needs to respect similar limitations to its power. As in the domestic sphere, constitutionalization may lead to a limitation rather than an extension of international power.

IV. Conclusion and Outlook: From Formal to Substantial Constitutionalism

Understandings of constitutionalism vary, and thus the international legal system may or may not be found to have a constitution. In the first part, this contribution has intended to show that it is possible to maintain that international law constitutes a system of law, in spite of the leeway it leaves to its members. In this sense, international law is a system insofar as it is bound together by the application of a limited set of formal sources and of instruments to apply them, such as rules of interpretation, as well as a few basic principles such as *pacta sunt servanda* or responsibility for wrongdoing. In the formal sense, international law can be regarded as a system but hardly as a constitution, however: the constitutional characteristics of the UN Charter are incomplete, at best; and, as the fragmentation debate has shown, an over-all international constitution that would balance the different subsystems toward a coherent whole is largely absent. There is little hope for an ultimate judicial decision of clashes among different values, principles, or subsystems once and for all. Balancing of rights and obligations under different sub-systems substitutes for the lack of a comprehensive judicial structure or an unequivocal judicial hierarchy.[140] Only the strict and formalist positivists of the early twentieth century would regard such a system a constitution.

Rather, as the second part of the chapter has demonstrated, a full constitu-tionalism demands more, namely, the respect for substantive constitutional principles, in particular democracy and the rule of law, as well as some further principles, such as the separation of powers, the respect for human rights, and the existence of a bond of solidarity among the members of the international community. In the multilevel system that an international constitutionalism would entail, these criteria need to be modified. Even then, however, the international legal system does not appear to follow them, in spite of recent advances in the law – from the partial constitutionalization of trade law and the emergence of international criminal law to the monopolization of the legitimation of interstate violence.

As long as a strong constitution in this sense is lacking, two options stand out: One option would lead back to the domestic control of international organizations, either by regional or by domestic courts. However, this is not a promising route, because it implies a divergence of protection between different states or regions and thus contradicts the very need for international regulation in the first place. Thus, a second option appears to be more promising: namely, a constitutional reading of the constitutive instruments of international organizations. Such an understanding of international rule, both by political and judicial bodies, could lead the way toward the very checks and balances and respect for human rights and state freedoms that the Western constitutional tradition embodies. By limiting rather than extending the power of international institutions, it would not run into the risk of further strengthening the international at the cost of the domestic legal realm; by binding the exercise of international power to legal rules, it might get us nearer to the rule of law in international affairs. Finally, while an international "demoi-cracy" is yet to be established, the strengthening of deliberation and the inclusion of the individual stakeholders in international decision making may lead to a better legitimacy and therefore an increased acceptance of international decisions at the domestic and individual levels.

[140] For a more extensive argument in this regard, *see* Paulus, *supra* note 7.

What is more important than labels is the insistence on constitutionalism as, in the words of Martti Koskenniemi, mind-set,[141] as a way to look at international regulation with the goals and principles of domestic constitutionalism in mind, both defining and limiting the use of power. Defining international power according to the competences extended by international instruments on the basis of state consent or acquiescence to international institutions; limiting international power by balancing international competences with the individual and state rights recognized by the same or other sources of international law. In this sense, constitutionalization is also a means for daring to think big, so to speak, to break out of the ghetto of individual disciplines toward more comprehensive thinking.[142]

In the age of globalization and functionalization, the very idea of a comprehensive ordering of any legal realm becomes ever-more illusory. One may well read the insistence of domestic courts on their constitutional prerogatives, in the strong version of the U.S. Supreme Court or the weaker one of the German Bundesverfassungsgericht, as the heroic but ultimately futile attempt to stop the clock, as an attempt to save what can be saved of democratic constitutionalism at a time when the ability of any government to regulate the world according to the wishes of their electorates appears to be waning.

A constitutional reading of international law should avoid the parochial view of domestic law, but also of the international legal subsystems; rather, it should strive for a more comprehensive balancing of rights and interests beyond the narrow confines of a specific subsystem. It should use the potential for checks and balances to hold all holders of public power accountable, whether state representatives or international civil servants. It should allow for the protection of human rights against both state and international holders of power. Finally, a constitutional understanding of the UN Charter would have us strive to improve the international system in a way that would lead it closer to our ideas of an ideal constitution, render it more democratic, more respective of individual rights, more consonant with the rule of law.

In a globalized but fragmented world, the very idea of a comprehensive, even totalizing constitution of any social realm may be bound to fail, domestically as well as internationally. Constitutionalization as a principle of legal ordering, however, continues to have great potential to rule the world as a rule of law rather than the rule of power.

---

[141] Koskenniemi, *supra* note 8; *see also* Kumm, in this volume, at 321.
[142] *See* David Kennedy, in this volume, at 67.

PART II: THE CONSTITUTIONAL DIMENSIONS OF SPECIFIC INTERNATIONAL REGIMES

The United Nations

4. The UN Charter – A Global Constitution?

MICHAEL W. DOYLE

Is the UN Charter a constitution? Answering that question depends on what we mean by a constitution and to what alternative we are contrasting a constitution.

If the relevant contrast is to the U.S. Constitution – the constitution of a sovereign state – the answer is clearly no. The United Nations was not intended to create a world state. As the Charter's preamble announces, it was created for ambitious but specific purposes: "to save succeeding generations from the scourge of war," to "reaffirm faith in fundamental human rights," to "establish conditions under which justice and respect for the obligations arising from treaties and other sources of international law can be maintained," and to "promote social progress and better standards of life in larger freedom." The United Nations, moreover, is an organization based on the "sovereign equality of all its members" (art. 2.1), its membership being open to all "peace-loving states" (art. 4.1). This contrasts strikingly with the U.S. Constitution's much more general, sovereign-creating purposes: "to form a more perfect union, establish justice, insure domestic tranquility, provide for the common defence, promote the general welfare and secure the blessings of liberty to ourselves and our posterity."[1]

The UN Charter lacks at least two of the three key attributes that the Constitutional Court of South Africa identified as essential to a constitution.

---

[1] U.S. Const. pmbl.; *see* José E. Alvarez, International Organizations as Law-makers 67–68 (2006).

Harold Brown Professor of International Affairs, Law and Political Science, Columbia University. This chapter has benefited from the excellent research assistance of Geoffrey S. Carlson at Columbia Law School, Abbas Ravjani at Yale Law School, and Svanhildur Thorvaldsdottir of the International Peace Institute. I am especially grateful for the extensive comments of Steven Ratner at the Temple conference and Brian Graf at a seminar at Rutgers organized by Jack Levy, and for suggestions from Jeffrey Dunoff, Joel Trachtman, and Samantha Besson.

In *Pharmaceutical*, the court averred that a constitution is a unified system of law: "There is only one system of law. It is shaped by the Constitution which is the supreme law, and all law, including the common law, derives its force from the Constitution and is subject to constitutional control."[2] The Charter lacks what Frank Michelman, in commenting on the case, has called the attributes of, first, "pervasive law" (i.e., "all law is subject") and, second, "basic law" (i.e., "derives its force").[3] The UN Charter, instead, reflects what Laurence Helfer calls the "disaggregated and decentralized" character of the international order.[4] Neither is all international law subject to the United Nations nor is the Charter the legal source of all international law. Much international law precedes the Charter and has been developed in parallel to it, including fundamental elements of international law such as the Genocide Convention, which requires its signatories (and as *jus cogens*, all states) to prevent, stop, and punish genocide seemingly irrespective of whether genocide is an "essentially" domestic matter under article 2 (7) and whether the Security Council (hereinafter, "Council") has authority to act in matters beyond "international peace and security." The Charter does, however, have a degree of the third attribute of a constitution: supremacy.

If we contrast the Charter to a standard contract-like treaty, the differences are also clear.[5] The UN Charter is a treaty but a special treaty. Like a constitution, it has supremacy (art. 103) even over treaties that would normally supersede it by "the last in time" rule (Vienna Convention art. 30). This supremacy covers not all international law (it is not pervasive or basic) but only the aspects of the Charter in which it imposes "obligations," most particularly, peace and security. Like the U.S. Constitution (*U.S. v. White*), moreover, the Charter is perpetual; it cannot be revoked by its constituents. Indeed, while states can be expelled, there is no provision for resignation. Moreover, the Charter binds all states, whether members or not, in matters of peace and security (art. 39). Like a constitution, it is "indelible," in Thomas Franck's terminology.[6] Unlike most treaties, no reservations can limit its

---

[2] In re Pharm. Mfrs. Ass'n of S.A. 2000 (3) BCLR 241 (CC) at para. 44 (S. Afr.).

[3] Frank Michelman, *What Do Constitutions Do That Statutes Don't (Legally Speaking)? in* THE LEAST EXAMINED BRANCH: THE ROLE OF LEGISLATURES IN THE CONSTITUTIONAL STATE 273 (Richard Bauman & Tzvi Kahana eds., 2006).

[4] Laurence R. Helfer, *Constitutional Analogies in the International Legal System*, 37 LOY. L.A. L. REV. 193, 207–08 (2003).

[5] *See* Thomas Franck, *Is the UN Charter a Constitution? in* VERHANDELN FUR DEN FRIEDEN 95 (Jochen Frowein et al. eds., 2003) for a discussion of these differences. *See also* Bardo Fassbender, *The United Nations Charter as Constitution of the International Community*, 36 COLUM. J. TRANSNAT'L L. 529 (1998) for a wide-ranging survey of the debate on Charter constitutionalism.

[6] Thomas Franck, *op. cit.*, supra at 5.

effects on states that ratify it. And it is very hard to amend. Amendments require an international conference and a two-thirds affirmative vote of the entire membership, including all five permanent members of the Council (the "Permanent Five") (art. 109).

Last and most important, it has institutional, for lack of a better word, "supranationality" in the sense that it permits authoritative decisions without continuous consent.[7] Like many constitutions, it does so by dividing powers between constituents and the constituted institution.[8] The Charter establishes a division of powers among the functional components of governance – the Council, General Assembly (hereinafter, "Assembly"), Secretariat, International Court of Justice (ICJ), and so on – which have quasi-executive, legislative, administrative, and judicial functions. The UN Secretariat is pledged to international independence in the performance of its duties (art. 100). Crucially, the United Nations makes or is authorized to make decisions without the continuous consent of its member states. Budgets can be adopted by a two-thirds vote, and the ICJ has held them as binding on all the members, including those who voted against the substantive measures that the budget funds (ICJ *Expenses Case*). Council decisions taken under chapter 7 in matters of international peace and security – those with at least nine out of fifteen votes, including no vetoes by the Permanent Five – are binding on all states (arts. 25 and 48). The Charter has also been interpreted flexibly to make "necessary and proper" functions viable. The requirement that Council votes on substantive matters pass with affirmative votes of the Permanent Five, for example, has been flexibly interpreted to mean no negative votes (vetoes), allowing permanent members to abstain without vetoing.[9]

This supranationality might be seen as, first, simple agency on behalf of the member states, second, a delegation of specific functions to be administered independently, and third, a transfer of sovereign powers to a central and

---

[7] I do not mean that the United Nations is sovereign over the member states; the United Nations is an organization of the member states. Groping for a label, in an earlier draft I called this "governmentality." Thomas Franck calls this "institutional autochthony," stressing the independence (*competenz competenz*) of the institution. That is part of what I want to convey, but even more I want to highlight its ability of some member to bind all without explicit, case-by-case consent from each member.

[8] States, for example, have reserved "essential" domestic jurisdiction for themselves, and granted the United Nations international jurisdiction, in article 2.6.

[9] The late Oscar Schachter of Columbia Law School is widely credited for this creative, constitutional interpretation made when he was UN deputy legal adviser. *See* Leo Gross, *Voting in the Security Council: Abstention from Voting and Absence from Meetings*, 60 YALE L.J. 209 (1951), and Myres S. McDougal & Richard N. Gardner, *The Veto and the Charter: An Interpretation for Survival*, 60 YALE L.J. 258–92 (1951) for further discussion of this topic.

independent institution, as Dan Sarooshi explicates in his valuable recent study of the question.[10] In this chapter, I add three elements to the issue.

First is the way in which in the United Nations' key Charter powers mix these three categories of delegation and how they do so asymmetrically vis-à-vis different member states, particularly with regard to peace and security.

Second is the manner in which seemingly pure administrative agency becomes inherently political and delegates executive powers, as Secretary-General (hereinafter, "SG") Dag Hammarskjöld famously anticipated they would.

Third is the way in which delegation of duties to the Secretariat leads to inadvertent transfers of authority within the wider UN system, as illustrated by the evolution of the peacekeeping and the Millennium Development Goals (MDGs).

In each case I will be looking at the rationale for the supranationality and the struggle that ensues between those authorized to act multilaterally and the efforts of states to restrict the authority granted. The UN Charter, like so many constitutions before it, is an invitation to struggle.[11]

The UN Charter: Supra over Some and Less So for Others

Supranationality in the Charter affects the responsibilities of all member states, but it affects some much more so than others. All states are affected by the UN's possession of a legal "personality" that permits it to undertake responsibilities and act on behalf of the membership. It can sue a member without the consent of the member and be sued by members without the consent of other members. In the *Reparations Case* involving reparations for the assassination of a UN official, Count Bernadotte, the ICJ declared that the United Nations

> [I]s at present the supreme type of international organization and it could not carry out the intentions of its founders if it was devoid of international personality. It must be acknowledged that its Members, by entrusting certain functions to it, with the attendant duties and responsibilities, have clothed it with the competence to enable those functions to be effectively discharged.[12]

---

[10] DAN SAROOSHI, INTERNATIONAL ORGANIZATIONS AND THEIR EXERCISE OF SOVEREIGN POWERS (2005).

[11] There are, of course, a number of other ways to explore the constitutionality of the UN system, including, for example, comparing the United Nations to other regional and international organizations, analyzing the separation of powers among its principal organs, and exploring the role played by the ICJ as a constitutional interpreter. Some of these examples are taken up by other authors in this volume.

[12] Reparations for Injuries Suffered in the Service of the United Nations, Advisory Opinion, 1949 I.C.J. 174, 179 (Apr. 11).

The management of UN finances illustrates a more substantial facet of supranationality, and again one that bears on all members. In articles 17 and 18 the Assembly is given the authority to "consider and approve" the budget and the members undertake to bear those expenses "as apportioned by the General Assembly." The budget being an important matter, a two-thirds vote thus binds – in effect, taxes – the members to support the expenses of the organization. This differs notably from the League of Nations, where unanimity ruled.[13] The UN budget assessments, moreover, are enforced by the provision in article 19 whereby any member will lose its vote in the Assembly if it is two years or more in arrears.

In December 1961, following the controversy over payment for the UN Expeditionary Force in the Sinai and the UN operation in the Congo, and in particular the vehement rejections of financial responsibility by France and the Soviet Union, the Assembly requested an advisory opinion from the ICJ on whether the expenses the organization had "incurred" were obligatory under article 17. In its *Expenses Case* opinion of July 1962, the court's majority ruled expansively. Noting that even though some of the policy authorizations were made by the Assembly and not by the Council (which had "primary" responsibility for peace and security), the ICJ found that the Council did not have exclusive responsibility for peace and security. Furthermore, the obligatory character of the expenses, if properly approved by the Assembly, did not rest on the legitimacy of the underlying substantive purpose of the resolution.[14] This seemed to imply that the Assembly could legally tax where the United Nations could not otherwise legally oblige.[15]

But as interesting as the legal judgments were, political forces determined the outcome of the financing controversies. As early as 1946, money talked as the United States set limits on what it was prepared to pay (at 40 percent), whatever a pro rata estimate would indicate. When the Soviet Union fell two years in arrears in 1964 and 1965, the United States led a campaign to deprive the Soviet Union of its Assembly vote.[16] When this failed, the United States announced that it would also assume a right to regard the budget as nonbinding (i.e., the Goldberg Reservation). The Assembly then moved to a procedure that recognized functional consensus (will the taxpayers pay?)

---

[13] Leland Goodrich & Edvard Hambro, Charter of the United Nations: Commentary and Documents 183–91 (1949).

[14] *See* Certain Expenses of the United Nations (art. 17, ¶ 2, of the Charter), Advisory Opinion, 1962 I.C.J. 151 (July 20).

[15] *See* Stanley Hoffmann, *A World Divided and a World Court Confused: The World Court's Advisory Opinion on UN Financing, in* International Law and Political Crisis 251 (Lawrence Scheinman & David Wilkinson eds., 1968) for an illustrative interpretation.

[16] Ruth Russell, *United Nations Financing and the Law of the Charter*, 5 Colum. J. Transnat'l L. 68, 83–85 (1966).

as the basis for budgeting. In practice, this allowed the eight countries that, on average, paid 75 percent of the budget to have a veto equivalent to the other 180-plus members. The United States, regarding the budget as advisory, then regularly withheld assessments as leverage to promote institutional and other changes it sought to impose on the organization. Political pushback thus effectively amended the Charter in a pragmatic – but far from organizationally effective – direction as a wide range of states each adopted a bargaining veto vis-à-vis the biennial budget negotiations.

The most striking governmental features of the Charter system are of course the provisions of chapter 7 with regard to international peace and security. Here the United Nations is both supranational and discriminatory. In matters of international peace and security (art. 39), Council decisions bind all UN members (arts. 25 and 48) when they garner the requisite nine votes, including no vetoes by the Permanent Five. Nine members can govern the whole. But the Permanent Five – the United States, the United Kingdom, France, Russia, and China – have the unequal right to remain unbound unless they concur or abstain. The working interpretation that abstentions by the Permanent Five do not count as vetoes reinforces their special status, allowing them the unique discretion not to veto without necessarily affirming and establishing informal precedents they might not want to recognize.[17]

In the *Lockerbie Case*, the ICJ majority held that Council Resolution 748 trumped the provisions of the Montreal Convention that allowed Libya at its discretion to either extradite or try suspected criminals (*aut dedere aut judicare*). In doing so it affirmed the supremacy of Council resolutions over conflicting international law.[18] Statements by the ICJ judges left open the

[17] See fn x, supra.
[18] Case Concerning Questions of Interpretation and Application of the 1971 Montreal Convention Arising from the Aerial Incident at Lockerbie (Libya v. United Kingdom; Libya v. United States), Provisional Measures, 1992 I.C.J. 114 (Apr. 14). *See also* Michael Plachta, *The Lockerbie Case: The Role of the Security Council in Enforcing the Principles of Aut Dedere aut Judicare*, 12 Eur. J. Int'l L. 125 (2001). Recent European jurisprudence affirms similar Council authority in counterterrorism. There are currently 359 people on the Council's counterterrorism list. Described as "punishment without trial" by German lawyer Gul Pinar (who represents one of the people named on the list), Council procedures allowed no court process before someone is added to the list and no appeal afterward, other than through national processes that might lead the individual's home government to petition to have the individual removed from the list. If an individual's home government used Council Resolution 1267 or 1373 procedures to condemn, for example, a dissident, there was no recourse. Named individuals were banned from international travel, had their bank accounts frozen, and suffered other restrictions on economic activity. The Council of Europe has determined that Resolution 1267 procedures do not meet the standards of the European Convention on Human Rights. For a discussion of these issues, *see* David Crawford, *The*

possibility that Council resolutions might be held ultra vires by the ICJ if a relevant case were put before the court, but the overall weight of the opinion strongly reinforced the supranationality of the United Nations in peace and security vis-à-vis all member states, whether or not they had approved the particular Council decision.

This led some to question just how legitimate and representative the Council was when considered as a world governmental body.[19] But the more usual sovereign pushback was the refusal to negotiate agreements under articles 43 to 47 to allocate forces under the direct command of the Council. The original Charter conception involved division-sized forces of aircraft, naval, and ground forces, all subject to the Council and commanded by the postwar equivalent of the World War II Allied joint command, a military staff committee appointed by the Council. Absent such "special agreements," states retained the right to refuse to deploy forces at the call of the Council, which was reduced to negotiating with potential troop contributors to form, in Brian Urquhart's phrase, the UN equivalent of a "sheriff's posse."[20] In this way sovereignty was reaffirmed.

The International Civil Servant as Neutral Man

Secretary-General Dag Hammarskjöld began his famous 1961 lecture "The International Civil Servant" (hereinafter, the "Oxford lecture") with a reference to and quotation from a then recent interview with Chairman Nikita Khrushchev in which the Soviet leader stated that "while there are neutral

---

Black Hole of a U.N. Blacklist, WALL ST. J., Oct. 2, 2006, at A6, and a reply by Ambassador John R. Bolton, *Letter to the Editor: U.N. Rightly Imposed Sanctions on Terrorists*, WALL ST. J., Oct. 6, 2006, at A15. *See also* David Dyzenhaus, *The Rule of (Administrative) Law in International Law*, 68 LAW & CONTEMP. PROBS. 127 (2005). Two recent developments have improved the rights of those accused of terrorist connections. First, while affirming the nonreviewability of Council resolutions other than by jus cogens standards (the *Yusuf* and *Kadi* cases), the European Court of First Instance held that European Community decisions that interpret and apply Council resolutions are reviewable (the *Ayadi* and *Hassan* decisions). It then overturned, on European human rights grounds, the Community regulations implementing Council Resolution 1373. Second, Council Resolution 1730 (Dec. 19, 2006) created a review process that gives individuals a right to submit petitions to, but not participate in, an appeal at the Sanctions Committee. Governments, however, must consent if their nationals are removed from the sanctions list. Chia Lehnardt, *European Court Rules on UN and EU Terrorist Suspects*, ASIL INSIGHT, Jan. 31, 2007, *available at* http://www.asil.org/insights/2007/01/insights070131.html.

[19] *See* Derek Bowett, *The Impact of Security Council Decisions on Dispute Settlement Procedures*, 5 EUR. J. INT'L L. 1 (1994); *see also* Michael Reisman, *Constitutional Crisis in the United Nations*, 87 AM. J. INT'L L. 83 (1993).

[20] Brian Urquhart, *Beyond the Sheriff's Posse*, 32:3 (May–June, 1990) SURVIVAL, 196–205.

countries, there are no neutral men."[21] The chairman had become concerned that the SG was harming, or at least not promoting, Soviet interests in the Middle East and Africa. This led him to propose a troika leadership for the United Nations – three co-SGs, one appointed by Moscow, able to veto one another's actions. Then, he hoped, Soviet interests would be suitably protected from an interested, political administration.

The founders of the United Nations imbued the role of SG and the Secretariat with various tensions. The essence of the position was to be administrative. The SG was the "chief administrative officer of the Organization" (art. 97). He or she was to administer the various tasks assigned by the political principal organs (e.g., the Council, Assembly, Economic and Social Council) and direct the Secretariat. The founders at San Francisco debated whether to "elect" the SG but instead chose the word *appoint* to emphasize the administrative, nonpolitical character. Rejecting a three-year term as too short and subject to too much control, they favored a longer term to encourage independence from the Permanent Five, whose approval would be needed for selection.[22] They embodied these principles in the requirement that the Secretariat be independent – of "an exclusively international character" – and that it would neither seek "instructions" from the members nor would the members seek to "influence" it (art. 100). The Secretariat, moreover, would be chosen for "efficiency, competence, and integrity" with due regard being paid to recruitment "on as wide a geographical basis as possible" (art. 101).

Responding to the pressure of sovereign pushback, the effective independence of the Secretariat was curbed. It soon became the norm that Secretariat positions would be allocated by national quotas. At the higher reaches, leading member states would insist on holding specific posts and in some instances filling them with nationals whom they would specifically name.[23] All of this limited the administrative independence of the Secretariat. For the SG the most consequential effect was the inability to form a governmental cabinet of like-minded followers, such as a typical prime minister or president would do.[24] The SG chooses only his or her small executive office.

---

[21] Dag Hammarskjöld, *The International Civil Servant in Law and Fact*, Oxford Lecture (May 30, 1961), in DAG HAMMARSKJÖLD: SERVANT OF PEACE 329 (William Foote ed., 1962) [hereinafter SERVANT OF PEACE].

[22] Report of Rapporteur of Committee I/2 on Chapter X (The Secretariat), 3–4, Doc. 1155 I/2/74(2), 7 U.N.C.I.O. Docs. 386 (1945).

[23] SG Annan waged a quiet campaign to persuade member states to present three nominees for "their" open posts. He did not usually succeed. For a valuable survey of the role, see SECRETARY OR GENERAL: THE UN SECRETARY GENERAL IN WORLD POLITICS (Simon Chesterman ed., 2007).

[24] Dag Hammarskjöld, *The Development of a Constitutional Framework for International Cooperation*, in SERVANT OF PEACE, *supra* note 21, at 259.

The SG had more success in transcending a purely administrative understanding of his role. Hammarskjöld, in the Oxford lecture, made a powerful case for neutrality as the ideal of the international civil servant. But he also noted that he could neither be neutral "as regards the Charter" nor "as regards facts."[25] Moreover, he was bound to become nonneutral, and inevitably political, when an organ of the United Nations assigned him responsibilities that conflicted with the interests of one or more member states.[26] In addition, he had one more key responsibility. Article 99 reads, "The Secretary-General may bring to the attention of the Security Council any matter which in his opinion may threaten the maintenance of international peace and security." This was an inherently political capacity and an important responsibility.

Though rarely invoked, article 99 was the foundation for the ever-increasing political role of the SG as mediator and, to some, "world's chief diplomat." Apart from their role with the Council, SGs saw themselves as representatives of the entire Untied Nations (the so-called Peking formula), particularly when the Council was locked in a confrontation with a state, as it was with China in the 1950s when Hammarskjöld began a delicate series of negotiations to free captured U.S. airmen.[27]

Transitional Peace Operations Authority

Supranationality to one degree or another is nearly inevitable in the complicated UN-managed transitions from war to peace and often, simultaneously, from autocracy to democracy and from state to market.

A transitional peace operation usually needs two authorizations: one is international and the other domestic. The two need not be always connected. An internationally authorized humanitarian intervention could proceed without host-state authorization (but it will not succeed unless it wins the support of significant majority of the local population). And a sovereign government can invite foreign forces to assist it without recourse to the United Nations or a regional organization for authorization. But the two usually are connected. (It is worth noting that even the forcible interventions in Somalia, Haiti, and Kosovo each had prior domestic authorizations, albeit each under duress, and in the Somali case from factions rather than from a functioning national government).

---

[25] The International Civil Servant, *supra* note 21, at 351–52.

[26] *Id.* at 344.

[27] See Ian Johnstone, *The Role of the Secretary-General: The Power of Persuasion Based on Law*, 9 GLOBAL GOVERNANCE 441, 443 (2003); Mark Zacher, *The Secretary-General and the United Nations' Function of Peaceful Settlement*, 20 INT'L ORG. 724, 728 (1966).

From the international point of view, peace operations – which intrude upon the domestic sovereignty of states – come to be established in two ways. First, under chapter 6 of the UN Charter, they reflect the negotiated consent of the parties and then are governed by a series of status-of-forces agreements that specify the legal terms for the presence of foreign forces. Or, second, they are established under chapter 7, which permits the overriding of domestic jurisdiction (arts. 2–7) without consent of the local parties. These enforcement operations draw upon the authority of article 42, which permits the Council to "take such action by air, sea, or land forces as may be necessary to maintain or restore international peace and security"; article 25, under which member states "agree to accept and carry out the decisions of the Security Council"; and article 43, in which they agree to "make available to the Security Council, on its call, . . . armed forces, assistance and facilities." Troop-contributing countries in these cases negotiate in detail the terms of the participation of their forces: either under UN command and thus with the SG in charge (as in El Salvador or Cambodia): with a regional organization authorized as delegated in chapter 8; or with the leader of a multinational "coalition of the willing" authorized under chapter 7 (as was the case of U.S. leadership of the Unified Task Force in Somalia). Many operations draw on combinations of authorizations: peace treaties among factions, backed up or supplemented by other measures authorized (e.g., arms embargoes, no-fly zones) under chapter 7, as did the various UN Protection Force and Implementation Force operations.[28] "Chinese Chapter 7" – as employed to authorize the use of force for the UN Transitional Administration for Eastern Slavonia – has emerged as a new signal of firm intent to enforce a chapter 6 operation, though in essence it reaffirms the Katanga rule of the UN Operation in the Congo: the traditional principle that force can be used both in self-defense of peacekeeping troops and of the mission (mobility of the force).

From the domestic point of view, a local authority (or authorities) shares temporarily and, usually, conditionally some of its (or their) own legitimacy with the international peace operation. Domestic authority can be examined in the light of the classic types of authorization and imperative coordination. Max Weber outlined three ideal types of imperative coordination: traditional, charismatic, and rational.[29] The first two types of authority may be rare in civil war transitions. Traditional authority – an established belief in

---

[28] For a valuable discussion of the international law on the use of force and its bearing on authority for peace operations, *see* Karen Guttieri, *Symptom of the Moment: A Juridical Gap for U.S. Occupation Forces*, 13 INT'L INSIGHTS 131 (Fall 1997).

[29] MAX WEBER, THE THEORY OF SOCIAL AND ECONOMIC ORGANIZATION 324–33 (A. M. Henderson & Talcott Parsons trans., 1947).

the sanctity of immemorial traditions and of the status of those exercising authority under them – has often broken down. Under the pressures of economic growth and social mobilization, tradition tends to erode and traditional states collapse. Charismatic authority – resting on devotion to the sanctity, heroism, or exemplary character of the individual leader and the order ordained by him or her – is often in excess supply, claimed by each of the faction leaders. Usually, therefore, rational authority – the legality of patterns of normative rules and the right of those elevated under such rules to exercise commands – has to do the work of reconstruction, and often in competition with preexisting but weakened traditional and charismatic sources of authority. Transitional authority must be constructed through painstaking negotiation, taking some cognizance of widely recognized international human rights norms and endorsed through negotiated schemes of power sharing or popular elections.

It is difficult, for example, to imagine the success, limited as it is, that Cambodia has achieved without the leadership of King Sihanouk. He repeatedly served as a catalyst for difficult decisions and a bridge between competing factions that would only contact each other under his auspices. The charismatic authority enjoyed by Nelson Mandela was an equally vital part of the difficult transition under way in South Africa. Lacking these forms of unifying authority in Somalia, El Salvador, Guatemala, and Bosnia, peace operations had to rely on enforceable or continually renegotiated agreements, which made the quality of international transitional authority a key component of success or failure.

Straightforward as these authorizations are, each leaves room for unanticipated but inevitable instances where delegated authority turns into what Ian Johnstone called "open-ended consent."[30] In chapter 7 enforcement operations, authority derives from a Council resolution, but no committee of fifteen can anticipate or manage the ensuing process of reconstructing domestic authority thousands of miles away. Even chapter 6 operations that rest on a painstakingly negotiated peace treaty cannot anticipate the myriad operational circumstances that will require decisions.[31] Special representatives, exercising command from the saddle, then learn to treat their Council mandates as either ceilings that cannot be breached or floors that support extended action, depending on the local circumstances. Should, for example,

---

[30] Ian Johnstone, Rights and Reconciliation in El Salvador (1995).

[31] See generally Steven Ratner, The New UN Peacekeeping: Building Peace in Lands of Conflict (1995). For varying discussions of types of transitional authority, see Jarat Chopra, Peace Maintenance (1999) and Michael Doyle, Transitional Authority, in Ending Civil Wars 71 (Stephen Stedman et al. eds., 2002).

the peace process continue if one or more of the parties has breached the peace agreement by not disarming, as occurred in the middle of the Cambodian peace? Special Representative Yasushi Akashi, with the support of the Council and some, but not all, Cambodian parties decided to continue, contained the spoilers, and succeeded in organizing a (barely) free and fair election that legitimated a new sovereign government of Cambodia. Reginald Austin, head of the Cambodian peace's electoral component, recognized a similar choice and degree of discretion when he asked:

"What are the "true objectives of [the UN Transitional Authority in Cambodia]: Is it a political operation seeking the immediate solution to an armed conflict by all means possible? Or does it have a wider objective: to implant democracy, change values, and establish a new pattern of governance based on multipartism and free and fair elections?"[32]

Extensive and open ended as this delegated authority is, inevitably here, too, one finds significant sovereign pushback against supranationality. Noted earlier was the insistence by China to constrain the independent exercise of coercive force by peacekeeping operations ("Chinese Chapter 7"). But even more significant in shaping contemporary peacekeeping is pushback by two other key participants: the peace-kept and the troop contributors.

Peace operations are political. Spoilers resist the terms of peace treaties, and agreements tend to be fluid. In the new civil conflicts, leaders are reluctant to give up power, and where they are willing to share power, they find that they often lack the ability to maintain a difficult process of reconciliation leading to a reestablishment of national sovereignty. The South West African People's Organization in Namibia, the Farabundo Martí Liberation Front in El Salvador, and the Khmer Rouge in Cambodia all defected from (or failed to implement) crucial elements of the peace within months and, in some cases, days.[33] Nearly equal challenges arise in managing peace operations by coordinating rivalrous international agencies or mobilizing government contingents. Each participant in the combined effort wants a lead role, and few are prepared to be led or coordinated.[34]

---

[32] For a discussion of these themes see DR. REGINALD AUSTIN, UNTAC, CHIEF ELECTORAL OFFICER'S ELECTORAL EVALUATION: SUMMARY REPORT 14 (1993); MICHAEL DOYLE, THE UN IN CAMBODIA: UNTAC'S CIVIL MANDATE (1995).

[33] See Stephen Stedman, Policy Implications, in ENDING CIVIL WARS, supra note 31, at 663; Page Fortna, Does Peacekeeping Keep the Peace?, 48 INT'L STUD. Q. 269 (2004). See also MICHAEL DOYLE & NICHOLAS SAMBANIS, MAKING WAR AND BUILDING PEACE (2006).

[34] See Bruce Jones, The Challenges of Strategic Coordination, in ENDING CIVIL WARS, supra note 31, at 89; TERJE ROED-LAURSEN & RICK HOOPER, COMMAND FROM THE SADDLE (1999).

The MDGs: Road Map to Confrontation

Supranationality also appears in legislative delegation by the General Assembly. In the United Nations, as in most institutions, principals delegate to agents (e.g., member states to the Secretariat) because implementation is too detailed an activity to be managed by 192 states. The agents' job becomes problematic, controversial, and sometimes supranational when the program outlined by the principals is ambiguous or contested (i.e., other than unanimous among the principals). Then the Secretariat is inherently engaged in supranational governance. This is what happened when the "Road map" report to implement the Millennium Declaration was delegated to the Secretariat.

At the UN Millennium Summit in September 2000, the members formally dedicated themselves to a redefinition of goals and means. Since its inception the United Nations has been an organization by, for, and of states – and so it remained. But in 2000, under the leadership of SG Kofi Annan, it set out to acquire a parallel identity, a new model of itself. It was redefining the meaning of global good citizenship for our time by putting people rather than states at the center of its agenda. The Millennium Declaration set this agenda.[35]

At the Millennium Summit, world leaders agreed to a set of breathtakingly broad goals that are global, public commitments on behalf of "we the peoples" to promote seven agendas:

Peace, security and disarmament,
development and poverty eradication,
protecting our common environment;
human rights democracy and good governance;
protecting the vulnerable;
special needs of Africa;
and strengthening UN institutions.

Promising an agenda for action – the international community's marching orders for the next fifteen years – the member states blithely transferred responsibility for designing a road map to implement these goals to the SG. "The Follow-up to the Outcome of the Millennium Summit" requested "the Secretary-General urgently to prepare a long-term 'road map' towards the implementation of the Millennium Declaration within the UN system and to submit it to the General Assembly at its 56th session [nine months later]."[36]

---

[35] United Nations Millennium Declaration, G.A. Res. 55/2, U.N. Doc. A/RES/55/2 (Sept. 8, 2000), *available at* http://www.un.org/millennium/declaration/ares552e.pdf.

[36] G.A. Res. 55/162, ¶ 18, U.N. Doc. A/RES/55/162 (Dec. 18, 2000). SG Kofi Annan assigned me the task of putting together this report when I arrived at the UN as his special adviser

This report was to incorporate annual monitoring focusing on "results and benchmarks achieved," to recognize that the primary responsibility for success lay with the member states of the UN themselves, to reflect the capacities of the entire UN system including the World Trade Organization and Bretton Woods institutions, and to outline practical measures to meet the ambitious targets.

A small coordinating team in the Executive Office of the SG, the Strategic Planning Unit, set about collecting from all the United Nations' agencies and programs information on what the UN system was already doing to promote these goals and what next steps seemed practicable to advance them. Once compressed and simplified, this encyclopedic list became the Roadmap Report.[37] The striking part of the report was the treatment of the development goals, which came to be called the MDGs.

Drawn from the development and environment chapters of the Millennium Declaration, the MDGs defined common aspirations in the worldwide effort to alleviate poverty and promote sustainable economic and social development. They pledged to "spare no effort to free our fellow men, women and children from the abject and dehumanizing condition of extreme poverty" and "to create an environment – at the national and global levels alike – which is conducive to development and the eradication of poverty." The eight MDGs that an interagency UN team crystallized from the two chapters of the Millennium Declaration were the following:[38]

1. Eradicate extreme poverty and hunger
   Target for 2015: Halve the proportion of people living on less than a dollar a day and those who suffer from hunger.
2. Achieve universal primary education
   Target for 2015: Ensure that all boys and girls complete primary school.
3. Promote gender equality and empower women
   Targets for 2005 and 2015: Eliminate gender disparities in primary and secondary education preferably by 2005, and at all levels by 2015.
4. Reduce child mortality
   Target for 2015: Reduce by two thirds the mortality rate among children under five.

in April, 2001, four months after the GA authorization. Dr. Abiodun Williams, head of the Strategic Planning Unit, managed the information collection process of UN experience in addressing the many goals in Millennium Declaration and Jan Vandermoortele of UNDP cochaired with me the meeting of UN experts who developed the indicators for the MDGs.

[37] U.N. Doc. A/56/326 (Sept. 6, 2001).
[38] Report of the Secretary-General, *Road Map towards the Implementation of the UN Millennium Declaration*, A/56/326 (6 September, 2001).

5. Improve maternal health
   Target for 2015: Reduce by three-quarters the ratio of women dying in childbirth.
6. Combat HIV/AIDS, malaria and other diseases
   Target for 2015: Halt and begin to reverse the spread of HIV/AIDS and the incidence of malaria and other major diseases.
7. Ensure environmental sustainability
   Targets:
   • Integrate the principles of sustainable development into country policies and programs and reverse the loss of environmental resources.
   • By 2015, reduce by half the proportion of people without access to safe drinking water.
   • By 2020 achieve significant improvement in the lives of at least 100 million slum dwellers.
8. Develop a global partnership for development
   Targets:
   • Develop further an open trading and financial system that includes a commitment to good governance, development and poverty reduction – nationally and internationally.
   • Address the least developed countries' special needs, and the special needs of landlocked and small island developing States.
   • Deal comprehensively with developing countries' debt problems.
   • Develop decent and productive work for youth.
   • In cooperation with pharmaceutical companies, provide access to affordable essential drugs in developing countries.
   • In cooperation with the private sector, make available the benefits of new technologies – especially information and communications technologies.

The MDGs soon became controversial and allegedly ultra vires bureaucratic impositions that went beyond what the member states had authorized as goals in the Millennium Declaration. The United States[39] refused to acknowledge

---

[39] The actual source of U.S. discontent seemed to me to be a policy disagreement. The Bush administration was launching the Millennium Challenge Account, which made governance reform (e.g., marketization, private enterprise, fiscal balance, open current accounts for international finance, democratization) the precondition for foreign aid. Once the political appointees in the administration had come into office in late 2001, they saw the MDGs as a reflection of the "old ideology" of northern responsibility for southern poverty and an ideological platform to make the shortfall in foreign aid the excuse for development failures. My response was that the MDGs were a thermometer designed to measure progress, not

the MDGs as such, referring to them instead as the "internationally recognized development goals in the Millennium Declaration," making the United Nations' effort to promote and brand the goals difficult. The crescendo of attack peaked with the rhetoric of Ambassador John Bolton, who used them as one more reason to reject the outcome consensus on UN reform in the summer of 2005, until at last he was overridden by President George W. Bush, who accepted the MDGs by word and title in his September 2005 speech.

The MDG goals, targets, and indicators in reality had three sources. The interagency team from the entire UN system that met over the spring and summer of 2001 drew first and most importantly on the Millennium Declaration. Contrary to the U.S. critics, every goal had a textual source with painstaking provenance in the declaration's text. Every significant commitment in the declaration's development chapter found a place in the MDGs as goal, target, or indicator. But the MDGs were not a verbatim copy of the declaration. The development chapter of the declaration, for example, had fourteen bulleted goals; the MDGs, eight. Some declaration goals were specific, time bound, and targeted; others were vague and aspirational. All the MDGs had a similarly mandatory and exhortatory character.

The second source was the preexisting development goals of the international community, most particularly the seven International Development Goals (IDGs). First developed in 1996 by the Organisation for Economic Co-operation and Development (OECD), they won the endorsement of the World Bank, OECD, International Monetary Fund (IMF), and UN SG Kofi Annan in the June 2000 report *Better World for All: Progress Towards the International Development Goals* (hereinafter, "BWfA Report"). The IDGs included goals and targets to reduce extreme poverty, and to promote education and maternal health – all of which reappeared in the Millennium Declaration.

The BWfA Report soon became shrouded in controversy. Many developing states and many in the world of development nongovernmental organizations rejected the seemingly one-sided program to monitor third-world progress without an equivalent measure of the contribution the wealthy countries were making to global progress. Some countries (Catholic and Muslim and, after January 2001, the United States under the Bush administration) objected

---

a strategy. There was no reason not to portray the MCA as the best (U.S.) strategy for meeting the MDGs. This argument was welcomed in the U.S. Treasury, but not in the State Department.

to the "reproductive health goal," which seemed to endorse birth control and possibly abortion services. The developing world critics soon tagged the report with the title "Bretton Woods for All." Nonetheless, key development actors, including the Bretton Woods institutions and the influential U.K. Department for International Development (DFID), had a stake in the viability of the IDGs and the principles of multidimensional, human-centered, output-oriented, and measurable development they embodied.

The UN system interagency team adopted the framework of the IDGs, replaced "reproductive health" from the IDGs with "HIV/AIDS " from the Millennium Declaration, and added an eighth goal – a "global partnership for development" that assembled a variety of commitments in trade, finance, and development aid made by the wealthy countries and embodied in the Millennium Declaration. The result was the new eight that in late June 2001 they decided to call "The Millennium Development Goals."[40]

The third source was a determination to overcome generations of dispute among the Bretton Woods institutions, the UN Development Programme (UNDP), the UN Conference on Trade and Development, and other UN agencies. Each had grown into the habit of criticizing the others' reports and strategies, producing a cacophony on what development meant, how it should be measured, and whether progress was being made. The UN system interagency team assembled to create a road map of the development section of the Millennium Declaration was a team of experts, particularly involving the heads of the statistical services within the respective organizations. Acutely aware that agreed indicators would shape development policy coordination and determine the high-priority statistics that national and international statistical agencies would collect, they took great care in choosing – within the usual confines of agency stakes and commitments – the best forty-eight indicators then available to measure eighteen targets that defined the eight goals.

In addition to rejecting the MDG framework in general, the Bush administration later objected that one of the forty-eight indicators proposed by officials of the World Bank, the IMF, and the UN Secretariat to measure progress on the goals and targets mentions the international goal of seven-tenths of 1 percent of wealthy nations' gross domestic products for development

---

[40] I took considerable effort to discuss drafts of the emerging MDGs with various UN delegations, including the G77 developing country caucus, the European Union caucus, and the U.S. delegation during the summer of 2001 in order to make sure that the necessary votes for approval would be forthcoming when the road map was presented to the General Assembly in the coming September.

assistance. The United States (i.e., the Bush administration) itself affirmed this internationally agreed target at the Monterrey Conference in 2001. But the larger source of U.S. concern was that the goals reflected a hardening of soft law. Unlike the other Millennium Declaration goals in peace and security and humanitarian protection, the Millennium *Development* Goals (MDGs) had moved from very soft law – an Assembly resolution – to hard international public policy endorsed officially by operative institutions such as the World Bank, the IMF, the World Health Organization, and others – bypassing an interstate treaty or agreement.

If we measure the hardness of law by how obligatory and either delegated or precise it is,[41] then the MDGs have significantly hardened the issues they cover in the Millennium Declaration. The Millennium Declaration started out as a soft Assembly resolution: vague, hortatory, and undelegated in substance. When the member states delegated the formulation of the road map to the Secretariat, they set in motion a hardening process that resulted in the MDGs. While all eight MDGs have textual support in the principles and authority provided by various parts of the declaration, now they have become precise targets and measurable indicators. More important, they have become the template for development for the World Bank, IMF, and United Nations. They shape the World Bank's Poverty Reduction Strategy Papers and the UN Development Assistance Frameworks that measure the progress of developing countries seeking development grants and loans from the World Bank, IMF, and the UNDP. They increasingly influence bilateral donors. In effect, the MDGs are quasi legislative in the developing world, a long step from the rhetoric they appeared to be in September 2000.

If the pushback from sovereign states was most striking in the U.S. campaign to undermine the MDGs and in Ambassador Bolton's perfervid rhetoric, the more subtle and important pushback came from a much more important source. The goals were hortatory; the key source of implementation was national, not the UN system. Whether the developing countries would actually adopt them in practice and whether the developed world would respond with a genuine partnership to create additional international opportunities for growth were the two decisive factors in what has become the MDGs' mixed record of success.[42] This was soon reflected in the natural development of country-level MDGs that mixed existing development

---

[41] *See* Kenneth Abbott & Duncan Snidal, *Hard and Soft Law in International Governance*, 54 INT'L ORG. 421 (2000) (drawing these distinctions).
[42] *See* the annual MDG reports of SG, *available at* www.un.org/documents/repsc.htm.

planning with the MDG framework. In some national development plans, the MDGs served as rhetorical window dressing; in others, they played an operational role and became the operative framework for assessing the World Bank's Poverty Reduction Strategy Papers and the UNDP's UN Development Assistance Framework.[43]

Conclusion

Supranationality is a key element of a constitutional order that separates a constitution from an ordinary treaty. It opens the door to complex agency on behalf of the member states in which authoritative decisions are taken without continuous sovereign consent.

It is worth recalling, however, that these decisions are inherently asymmetric, different for some than for other states. This is clearly the case in Charter-based allocations of rights and responsibilities in peace and security, but it appears whenever the underlying circumstances of state inequality cannot be rectified by the formal equality of multilateral institutions.

In addition, supranationality appears in the manner in which seemingly pure administrative agency becomes inherently political when it delegates executive powers. Secretary-General Dag Hammarskjöld famously anticipated this, and the practice of SGs in active mediation in international disputes has confirmed it.

Supranationality also emerges in the delegation of duties to the Secretariat when it leads to inadvertent transfers of authority within the wider UN system, as illustrated by the operation of peacekeeping and the evolution of the MDGs.

Sometimes, in world politics, the constitutions of international organizations deepen supranationality. Where the stakes are high, where a small group of leading states is closely connected, there supranational solutions to cooperation problems sometimes grow.[44] The evolution from the General Agreement on Tariffs and Trade to the World Trade Organization, from a veto to implement to a veto to prevent the enforcement of a trade ruling, is a classic instance. But where the constitution reflects a hegemonic constitutional

---

[43] See, e.g., IMF, PRSP Factsheet (Apr. 2008), available at http://www.imf.org/external/np/exr/facts/prsp.htm (last visited April 14, 2008) ("PRSPs aim to provide the crucial link between national public actions, donor support, and the development outcomes needed to meet the United Nations' Millennium Development Goals (MDGs)").

[44] See MANCUR OLSON, THE LOGIC OF COLLECTIVE ACTION (1965); Duncan Snidal, The Limits of Hegemonic Stability Theory, 39 INT'L ORG. 579 (1985).

moment, as the UN Charter did with the predominance of the United States at the end of World War II, then the evolution tends to go in the opposite direction.[45] Supranationality generates sovereign pushback. Weak as it was and is, the UN "constitution" of 1945 still authorizes more than the members are now prepared to cede.

[45] *See* ROBERT KEOHANE, AFTER HEGEMONY (1984); JOHN IKENBERRY, AFTER VICTORY (2001).

5. Rediscovering a Forgotten Constitution: Notes on the Place of the UN Charter in the International Legal Order

BARDO FASSBENDER

"[I]t would be surprising," David Kennedy said in his very perceptive contribution to this volume, "if the new [constitutional] order were waiting to be found rather than made.... If there is to be a new order, legal or otherwise, it will be created as much as discovered."[1] I felt caught *in flagrante delicto* because that was exactly what I had tried to show some ten years ago in an article titled "The UN Charter as Constitution of the International Community" – that we can rediscover a constitutional quality of the Charter that had been there right from the start but that had fallen into oblivion in the meantime. In the words of my article:

> Good arguments support the view that the Charter has had a constitutional quality *ab initio.* In the course of the last fifty years the "constitutional predisposition" of the Charter has been confirmed and strengthened in such a way that today the instrument must be referred to as the constitution of the international community.[2]

If the failed European Constitution of 2004 was a "treaty which masqueraded as a constitution,"[3] the UN Charter is a constitution in the clothes of a treaty, because no other garment was available in 1945.

However, David Kennedy's skepticism is understandable. Whenever a rather small group of people claims to see something invisible to all the

---

[1] David Kennedy, *The Mystery of Global Governance*, in this volume, Chapter 2.

[2] *See* Bardo Fassbender, *The United Nations Charter as Constitution of the International Community*, 36 COLUM. J. TRANSNAT'L L. 529, 531 (1998). For a new and more extensive analysis along the lines of this article, *see* BARDO FASSBENDER, THE UNITED NATIONS CHARTER AS THE CONSTITUTION OF THE INTERNATIONAL COMMUNITY (2009).

[3] *See* Joseph H. H. Weiler, *A Rapid Snapshot of Constitution and Constitutionalism in the European Union*, presentation at Ruling the World book workshop, Temple Law School, Dec. 7, 2008.

Professor of International Law, University of the Armed Forces (Universität der Bundeswehr), Munich, Germany.

others, suspicion is well founded. A contemporary oracle of Apollo seems to be at work, a body of priests and priestesses revealing a truth that only they themselves understand. If that truth is the so-far-undiscovered existence of an international constitution, the revelation is especially astonishing because a constitution really was meant to be something generally known and accepted as such. "Failing to recognize itself as a society, international society has not known that it has a constitution,"[4] Philip Allott once wrote (admittedly having a different idea of an international constitution than the one developed by me). But is this possible – an international society (or community) not recognizing itself and, accordingly, not knowing its own, existing, legal structure? A scientific truth, like the law of gravity or the fact that Earth revolves around the sun, existed before it was discovered. Can the same be said about a constitution as a set of human-made legal rules?

An Almost-Forgotten Constitution and the Keeper of the Truth

The answer I have suggested is that, in 1945, and for a few years thereafter, there was indeed an awareness of the break the UN Charter meant in the history of international law and relations, and of the Charter's quality as the foundational document of a new age. President Harry Truman had no difficulty comparing the Charter to the U.S. Constitution: "The Charter, like our own Constitution, will be expanded and improved as time goes on."[5] And his description of the success of the U.S. Constitution expressed his hopes for the new Charter: "And upon it there was built a bigger, a better, and a more perfect union."[6] But with the return to old-style power politics in the unfolding cold war, this idea of the Charter became more and more implausible until it was almost forgotten.

Some voices, it is true, kept on pronouncing the old truth, which regained some credibility after the turn in world history of 1989. How could the international society continue to be so deaf? A part of the answer may be that the explanation of the idea of the Charter as a constitution was indeed often oraclelike: ambiguous or obscure, inconsistent or indecisive. In any case, it would be an exaggeration to claim that scholars have engaged in a searching debate over whether, and how, to understand the UN Charter as a

[4] PHILIP ALLOTT, EUNOMIA: NEW ORDER FOR A NEW WORLD 418 (1990).
[5] See Harry S Truman, Speech at the final session of the San Francisco Conference (June 26, 1945), in 1 DOCUMENTS OF THE UNITED NATIONS CONFERENCE ON INTERNATIONAL ORGANIZATION 680 (1945).
[6] Id.

constitutional charter for the international community. A debate deserving that name has only just begun.[7] What we had before were individual statements of scholars, few and far between, and not taking note of, or responding to, one another. They were usually prompted by specific purposes and left behind once the desired effect had been achieved or not achieved. When ten years ago I tried to compile and organize the use of constitutional arguments with regard to international law and, particularly, the United Nations (and the UN Charter), I found that the constitutional language was rarely based on any coherent idea of constitutionalism.[8] Only few authors of the twentieth century had made an effort to explain systematically both the reasons for and the consequences of their adopting such language, and the three major schools of thought that I identified (the one founded by the Viennese jurist Alfred Verdross, the New Haven school formed at Yale University, and the international community school) not only had nothing in common but also largely ignored one another. It was only in my writing that I tried to engage them in a late conversation.

The mutual disregard was not simply an expression of intellectual self-importance but more so a result of the fact that the foundational works of the three schools date from very different periods and, accordingly, addressed different questions arising from different circumstances. Verdross, a disciple of Hans Kelsen and initially a follower of his doctrine of legal positivism, started writing on the subject in the late 1920s (it is no coincidence that these were the "good" years of the League of Nations). Myres McDougal and Harold Lasswell in New Haven conceptualized their "world public order" in the 1950s,[9] with the unfolding cold war increasingly leaving a mark on their work. The more heterogeneous "doctrine of international community," as I called it, can be traced to the lectures Judge Hermann Mosler delivered in the

---

[7] *See, in particular,* TOWARDS WORLD CONSTITUTIONALISM: ISSUES IN THE LEGAL ORDERING OF THE WORLD COMMUNITY (Ronald St. John Macdonald & Douglas M. Johnston eds., 2005), THE PARADOX OF CONSTITUTIONALISM: CONSTITUENT POWER AND CONSTITUTIONAL FORM (Martin Loughlin & Neil Walker eds., 2007), and TRANSNATIONAL CONSTITUTIONALISM: INTERNATIONAL AND EUROPEAN PERSPECTIVES (Nicholas Tsagourias ed., 2007). *See also* the special issue "Focus on Constitutionalism and International Law," 19 LEIDEN J. INT'L L., with contributions by Anne Peters, Erika de Wet, and Ernst-Ulrich Petersmann. Of the older literature, I mention THE CONSTITUTIONAL FOUNDATIONS OF WORLD PEACE (Richard A. Falk, Robert C. Johansen & Samuel S. Kim eds., 1993).

[8] *See* Fassbender, *The UN Charter as Constitution, supra* note 2 at 538–41.

[9] For a brief self-description of the New Haven school, *see* Myres S. McDougal & W. Michael Reisman, *International Law in Policy-Oriented Perspective, in* THE STRUCTURE AND PROCESS OF INTERNATIONAL LAW: ESSAYS IN LEGAL PHILOSOPHY, DOCTRINE AND THEORY 103 (R. St.-J. Macdonald & Douglas M. Johnston eds., 1986). For more bibliographic references, *see* Kennedy, *The Mystery, in* this volume, *supra* note i, Chapter 2.

Hague in 1974,[10] but it really flourished only in the hopeful years after the end of the cold war.[11]

In my approach, I integrated arguments of all three schools in order to develop more fully and substantiate a claim made by Verdross, at the age of eighty-six, and his young coauthor Bruno Simma, in the 1976 edition of his textbook of international law – the claim that today the constitutional law of the universal community (of states) has its foundation in the UN Charter.[12] In the past, the authors explained, one had to distinguish "general international law" from the law of the Charter, the latter applying only to a part of the community (i.e., those states that had joined the United Nations). "But since the UN [now] includes almost all states and the few states remaining out-side have recognized its fundamental principles, *the UN Charter has gained the rank of the constitution of the universal community of states.*"[13]

"The Charter-as-constitution view informs and determines the entire system of his [Verdross'] last treatise," Simma wrote later in an essay honoring his mentor.[14] The main consequence of this view was to give up the traditional distinction between "general international law" and the law of the Charter. Instead, the presentation of the former (e.g., the subjects and sources of international law, the law of state responsibility) was integrated into that of the latter. The authors began with a comprehensive analysis of "the constitution of the United Nations," and only then presented the standard subject matters of an international law textbook under the title "The Reception and Transformation of the Traditional Rules of International Law by the UN Charter."[15] This integrative approach was surely a big step forward, compared to the average textbook, which still mentions the United Nations in passing as an example of an "important" international organization,[16] as if its existence was an almost ignorable detail of contemporary international law. But the Verdross and Simma approach turned out to be largely programmatic. The

[10] *See* Hermann Mosler, *The International Society as a Legal Community*, 140 Recueil des Cours (1974-IV). A revised version was published as a book under the same title in 1980.

[11] *See, in particular,* Christian Tomuschat, *Obligations Arising for States without or against Their Will*, 241 Recueil des Cours 195 (1993-IV).

[12] *See* Alfred Verdross & Bruno Simma, Universelles Völkerrecht: Theorie und Praxis 5 (1976).

[13] Alfred Verdross & Bruno Simma, Universelles Völkerrecht: Theorie und Praxis vii–viii (3d ed. 1984) (emphasis added).

[14] Bruno Simma, *The Contribution of Alfred Verdross to the Theory of International Law*, 6 Eur. J. Int'l L. 33, 43 (1995).

[15] *See* Verdross & Simma, Universelles Völkerrecht, *supra* notes 12–13, part 3.

[16] *See, e.g.,* Ian Brownlie, Principles of Public International Law 60 (6th ed. 2003). According to the index, the UN Charter is first being dealt with on pp. 292–94 – almost halfway through the book – in the context of domestic jurisdiction of states. As far as I see, the Verdross and Simma approach has remained unique.

authors shied away from drawing those conclusions that alone appear to be logical.[17] They oscillated between their novel constitutional approach and a traditional perception of the Charter as a treaty governed by the rules of general international law. Christian Tomuschat, a leading representative of the international community school, even held outright that in international law the concept of constitution is "no more than an academic research tool suited to focus attention on the substantive specificities of a particular group of legal norms," and that "[n]o additional legal consequences may be attached to the characterization of a rule of international law as pertaining *ratione materiae* to the constitution of humankind."[18] I do agree with this idea of a heuristic value of the constitutional approach,[19] but a constitution only going as far as that would be a rather poor thing.

The UN Charter as a Constitution: A Functionalist Approach

In my own work, I have tried to give the idea of an international constitutional law a more consistent and also a more concrete meaning. To borrow language from Neil Walker, this has been an effort to invoke the UN Charter "as a point of reference for the work of reform and re-imagination of international constitutionalism" and to create, on the global level, "a suitably focused context of action."[20] A principal reason for my suggesting that the UN Charter must be understood as *the* constitution of the international community was the intention to get "out of the fog" of an indistinct constitutional rhetoric by turning to one visible document as an authoritative statement of the fundamental rights and responsibilities of the members of the international community and the values to which this community is committed – a document that is also the basis of the most important community institutions.[21]

---

[17] I tried to demonstrate this inconsistency in the authors' treatment of amendments to the Charter, on the one hand, and action taken by the Security Council against non–member states, on the other hand. *See* BARDO FASSBENDER, UN SECURITY COUNCIL REFORM AND THE RIGHT OF VETO: A CONSTITUTIONAL PERSPECTIVE 44–45, 90–94 (1998).

[18] *See* Christian Tomuschat, *International Law: Ensuring the Survival of Mankind on the Eve of a New Century* (General Course on Public International Law), 281 RECUEIL DES COURS 9, 88 (1999).

[19] *See generally* Mattias Kumm, *Constitutionalism as a Form of Legal Analysis*, in this volume, Chapter 10.

[20] *See* Neil Walker, *Making a World of Difference? Habermas, Cosmopolitanism and the Constitutionalization of International Law*, *in* MULTICULTURALISM AND LAW: A CRITICAL DEBATE 219 (O. A. Payrow Shabani ed., 2005).

[21] For a thoughtful analysis of the meaning of the concept of international community and of the problem of the constituent power in that community, *see* Samantha Besson, *Whose Constitution(s)? International Law, Constitutionalism, and Democracy*, in this volume, Chapter 13, § 3.

In the mid-1990s, when I turned my attention to the issue of a reform of the UN Security Council, I approached the problem of an international constitutional law with a rather practical or concrete question in mind: Is a reform of the Council purely a matter of political decision making, with governments having a free hand to reorganize the Council and its procedure as they wish, or are there, to the contrary, certain legal standards binding on UN member states? And where could one find such standards? I could not find them in general international law, or the law of treaties, but I found them by understanding the Charter as a constitution, and by taking this qualification seriously. On that basis, I was able to put forth an outline of a constitutional right of veto (i.e., a proposal for a reform of the veto power in accordance with constitutional standards and concepts). But, so I found, a constitutional reading of the Charter allowed me not only to answer that practical question but also to better understand other aspects of the Charter that had puzzled me (and others) – like its impressive opening formula "We the Peoples of the United Nations," with which the drafters replaced the traditional standard opening of an international treaty,[22] or the meaning of "sovereign equality" of states (art. 2, para. 1),[23] or the claim of the Charter that its principles are binding on non–member states (art. 2, para. 6), or the fact that the Charter – different from conventional treaties and also from its predecessor, the League of Nations Covenant[24] – does not provide for its termination or the possibility of a member leaving the organization.[25]

In the terms suggested by Jeffrey Dunoff and Joel Trachtman,[26] I used a functionalist approach in order to determine whether the UN Charter can be regarded as a constitution, both of the UN as an organization and of the international community in a broader sense. To answer the anteceding question (what types of functions do constitutions generally fulfill?), I followed a comparative method, examining typical features of existing (state) constitutions. Taking those features together, and drawing on a method

---

[22] See Bardo Fassbender, 'We the Peoples of the United Nations': Constituent Power and Constitutional Form in International Law, in THE PARADOX OF CONSTITUTIONALISM, supra note 7, at 269–90. See also Weiler, A Rapid Snapshot, supra note 3.

[23] See Bardo Fassbender, Sovereignty and Constitutionalism in International Law, in SOVEREIGNTY IN TRANSITION 115 (Neil Walker ed., 2003).

[24] See art. 1, para. 3, of the Covenant (withdrawal from the League).

[25] However, the UN founding conference agreed in a declaration that in certain exceptional circumstances a member could not be forced to remain in the organization. See Wolfram Karl et al., Article 108 of the UN Charter, in II THE CHARTER OF THE UNITED NATIONS: A COMMENTARY 1341, 1355 (Bruno Simma et al. eds., 2d ed. 2002).

[26] See Dunoff & Trachtman, A Functional Approach to Global Constitutionalization, in this volume, Chapter 1.

developed by Max Weber, I established an ideal type of constitution as a point of reference.[27] Weber's ideal type – "ideal" not in the sense of perfect or best, but as opposed to "real" – is built by intensifying and combining certain features of a phenomenon or development to form a consistent theoretical construct which "is neither historical nor 'true' [but] . . . a purely ideal, or imagined, border-notion (*Grenzbegriff*), a yardstick or standard to which reality is compared in order to elucidate certain significant elements of its empirical substance."[28]

I arrived at an ideal type of constitution characterized by a number of features (most of them, indeed, functions). A constitution is a set of fundamental norms about the organization and performance of governmental functions in a community, and the relationship between the government and those who are governed. It shall, in principle for an indefinite period of time, provide a legal frame as well as guiding principles for the political life of a community. It is binding on governmental institutions and the members of the community alike, and it is paramount (or supreme) law in the sense that law of lower rank must conform to the constitutional rules.[29]

If one compares that list of constitutional features with the constitutional mechanisms identified by the editors of this book in their introduction,[30] one finds that it fully corresponds to the items *a* to *d* of the latter. These features are neutral in the sense that they apply to every constitution regardless of the substance of the fundamental rules that it comprises. In other words, in terms of their contents those rules may follow a liberal or a Marxist model; they may

---

[27] *See* Fassbender, *The UN Charter as Constitution, supra* note 2, at 570.

[28] *See* Max Weber, *Die "Objektivität" sozialwissenschaftlicher und sozialpolitischer Erkenntnis* (1904), *reprinted in* Max Weber, Gesammelte Aufsätze zur Wissenschaftslehre 146, 190–94, 202 (Johannes Winckelmann ed., 7th ed. 1988). For a similar method of constructing "analytical-synthetic generalizations" in the form of "generic principles which are shared by all the constitutions of all societies," *see* Allott, Eunomia, *supra* note 4, at 167–70.

[29] *See* Fassbender, *The UN Charter as Constitution, supra* note 2, at 569–70. *See also id.* at 536–37. Similarly, Thomas Franck described a "constitutive instrument" of a community as distinguished by the characteristics of (1) perpetuity, (2) indelibleness, (3) primacy, and (4) institutional autochthony. *See* Thomas M. Franck, *Is the U.N. Charter a Constitution? in* Verhandeln für den Frieden – Negotiating for Peace: Liber Amicorum Tono Eitel 95, 96–99 (Jochen A. Frowein et al. eds., 2003). For an insightful application of the constitutional ideal type to the 1982 United Nations Convention on the Law of the Sea, see Shirley V. Scott, *The LOS Convention as a Constitutional Regime for the Oceans, in* Stability and Change in the Law of the Sea: The Role of the LOS Convention 9, 14–20 (Alex G. Oude Elferink ed., 2005).

[30] *See* Dunoff & Trachtman, *supra* note 27, in Chapter 1. For another constitutional checklist, based on what typically counts as constitutional in terms of a juridical, political-institutional, authorizing, social, and discursive frame, *see* Neil Walker, in this volume, Chapter 6, § B, "Constitutional Framing."

establish a democratic system of governance or a communist system, and so on. In that sense, the features *a* to *d* are elementary, or primordial. In contrast, the items *e, f,* and *g* of the Dunoff and Trachtman list (i.e., fundamental rights, judicial review, and accountability/democracy) are an expression of liberal and democratic values. They follow European and American political ideals as they were pursued in the French and American revolutions of the eighteenth century. These ideals have given the formal notion of constitution a specific substantial meaning, which by now (after the demise of Soviet-style communism) has become an almost universal standard. The UN Charter, too, is standing in that tradition, as especially evidenced by its preamble as a "statement of identity and aims" of the international community.[31]

Applying the features of my ideal constitution to the UN Charter, I saw that the Charter is indeed characterized by those essential features.[32] In particular, it establishes a horizontal and vertical system of governance, it defines the members of the constitutional community, it claims supremacy over "ordinary" international law (art. 103), and it aspires to eternity. The Charter was the result of a "constitutional moment,"[33] it was intentionally given a name denoting an especially elevated class of legal instruments, and it is universal in the sense that it applies without exception to all members of the community. "In a constitution," Joseph Weiler said, "one wants to find . . . a statement of identity, of ideals, of the type of society and polity one not only is but one wants to believe one is."[34] With this in mind, read again the preamble and articles 1 and 2 of the Charter.

In the meantime, other authors have used a similar methodology and have arrived at conclusions that, in principle, endorse my position. (In fact, to my knowledge nobody examining the UN Charter along a list of constitutional features has thus far denied its constitutional quality.) Let me here quote only two – but eminent – voices, the first of an international lawyer, and the second of a social theorist and philosopher. Thomas Franck wrote in 2003:

---

[31] See Ronald St. John Macdonald, *The International Community as a Legal Community, in* MACDONALD & JOHNSTON, TOWARDS WORLD CONSTITUTIONALISM, *supra* note 7, at 853, 860.

[32] See Fassbender, *The UN Charter as Constitution, supra* note 2, at 573–84.

[33] *Id.* at 573–74. *See also* Anne-Marie Slaughter & William Burke-White, *An International Constitutional Moment,* 43 HARV. INT'L. L.J. 1 (2002). H. Brunkhorst sees the events of 1945 as the "beginnings of the first global legal revolution (*Rechtsrevolution*)" or of "a global revolution of international law," respectively. *See* Hauke Brunkhorst, *Die globale Rechtsrevolution, in* RECHTSTHEORIE IN RECHTSPRAKTISCHER ABSICHT: FREUNDESGABE ZUM 70. GEBURTSTAG VON FRIEDRICH MÜLLER 9, 12 (Ralph Christensen & Bodo Pieroth eds., 2008).

[34] Weiler, *A Rapid Snapshot, supra* note 3.

Perpetuity, indelibleness, primacy, and institutional autochthony [by which he understands a system of governmental power]: these four characteristics of the UN Charter relate that unique treaty more proximately to a constitution than to an ordinary contractual normative arrangement. But does it make a difference? Indeed it does. Whether or not the Charter is a constitution affects the way in which the norms of systemic interaction are to be interpreted by the judiciary, the political organs and by the Secretary-General.... [T]he question – is the UN Charter a constitution? – is not one of purely theoretical interest.... Indeed, how it is answered may well determine the ability of the Organization to continue to reinvent itself in the face of new challenges, thereby assuring its enduring relevance to the needs of states and the emergence of an international community.[35]

In a recent book, *The Divided West*, Jürgen Habermas has also taken up my analytical effort by identifying three "normative innovations" that provide the UN Charter with a constitutional quality and make it possible to interpret the Charter as a global constitution: (1) the explicit combination of the goals of safeguarding world peace and protecting human rights, (2) the coupling of the prohibition of the use of force with a realistic threat of sanctions and criminal prosecution, and (3) the inclusiveness (*Inklusivität*) of the United Nations and the universality of UN law.[36] Habermas concluded that the UN Charter "is a framework in which UN member states no longer *must* understand themselves exclusively as subjects bringing forth international treaties; they rather can now perceive themselves, together with their citizens, as the constituent parts of a politically constituted world society."[37]

Rules of Positive International Law Recognizing the UN Charter

The unique position of the UN Charter in the present international legal order is recognized and reflected by many rules of positive international law, especially treaty law. They are mainly intended to secure, in the context of a particular regime, the primacy of the Charter over "any other international agreement" (article 103 of the Charter). By way of example, I mention article 102 of the Charter of the Organization of American States (OAS) of 1948:

---

[35] Franck, *Is the U.N. Charter a Constitution? supra* note 29, at 102, 106. See also Macdonald, *The International Community as a Legal Community, supra* note 31, at 859–68 (describing characteristic features of the UN Charter as "the global constitution").

[36] See Jürgen Habermas, *Hat die Konstitutionalisierung des Völkerrechts noch eine Chance?* [Does the constitutionalization of international law still have a chance?], *in* JÜRGEN HABERMAS, DER GESPALTENE WESTEN 113, 159 (2004) (THE DIVIDED WEST 115, 160–61 (C. Cronin trans., 2006)). For a critical discussion of Habermas's turn to constitutionalism in the context of his cosmopolitan position, *see* Walker, *Making a World of Difference? supra* note 20.

[37] *Id.* at 159 and 161, respectively.

"None of the provisions of this Charter shall be construed as impairing the rights and obligations of the Member States under the Charter of the United Nations."[38] According to article 1, paragraph c, of the Statute of the Council of Europe of 1949, "Participation in the Council of Europe shall not affect the collaboration of its members in the work of the United Nations." Article 7 of the North Atlantic Treaty (NATO Treaty) of 1949 provides that "[t]he Treaty does not effect, and shall not be interpreted as affecting, in any way the rights and obligations under the [UN] Charter . . . , or the primary responsibility of the Security Council for the maintenance of international peace and security." At the very end of its codification of the law of state responsibility, the International Law Commission made a general reservation in favor of the UN Charter: "[t]hese articles are without prejudice to the Charter of the United Nations."[39] The definition of the crime of aggression envisaged in article 5, paragraph 2, of the Rome Statute of the International Criminal Court of 1998 "shall be consistent with the relevant provisions of the Charter of the United Nations." Other rules shall ensure the effective discharge of duties of the Security Council under the UN Charter. For instance, according to article 16 of the Rome Statute, no investigation or prosecution may be commenced or proceeded with after the Security Council has made a request to the court to that effect.

In the Treaty on European Union, as amended by the 2007 Treaty of Lisbon, the UN Charter is prominently referred in the article about the aims of the European Union: "In its relations with the wider world, the Union . . . shall contribute to peace, security, the sustainable development of the Earth, . . . as well as to the strict observance and the development of international law, including respect for the principles of the United Nations Charter."[40] In addition, the Charter appears in the articles of the treaty about the union's external action, the Common Foreign and Security Policy and the Common Security and Defence Policy. According to article 21, paragraph 1, of the treaty, "The Union's action on the international scene shall be guided by . . . respect for the principles of the United Nations Charter and international law."[41]

---

[38] *See also* Vienna Convention on the Law of Treaties art. 30(1), May 23, 1969, 1155 U.N.T.S. 331; Vienna Convention on Treaties with and between International Organizations, art. 30(6), Mar. 21, 1986, 2 U.N. Doc. A/CONF.129/14 (determining the rights and obligations of states parties to successive treaties "[s]ubject to Article 103 of the Charter of the United Nations").

[39] *See* Articles on Responsibility of States for Internationally Wrongful Acts, art. 59, G.A. Res. 56/83, Annex, U.N. Doc. A/56/49(Vol.1)/Corr. 4 (Dec. 12, 2001).

[40] Treaty on European Union, art. 3(5), May 9, 2008, Official Journal of the EU no. C 115.

[41] *See also id.* art. 21 (2) (c), arts. 41 (1) & (7).

In addition, there are myriad bilateral and multilateral treaties, the preambles of which refer to the UN Charter. In the OAS Charter, for example, the American states "[r]esolved to persevere in the noble undertaking that humanity has conferred upon the United Nations, whose principles and purposes they solemnly reaffirm."[42] The states parties to the Vienna Convention on Diplomatic Relations of 1961 declared to have in mind "the purposes and principles of the Charter of the United Nations concerning the sovereign equality of States, the maintenance of international peace and security, and the promotion of friendly relations among nations."[43] The states parties to the 1982 Convention on the Law of the Sea proclaimed they believed "that the codification and progressive development of the law of the sea achieved in this Convention will contribute to the strengthening of peace, security, cooperation and friendly relations among all nations . . . in accordance with the Purposes and Principles of the United Nations as set forth in the Charter."[44]

One may conclude that states, as the principal authors of public international law, hold the UN Charter in higher esteem than do many scholars of international law. States have constantly and consistently affirmed the unique place of the Charter in the present structure of international law – accepting, in fact, the existence of an "international legal order *under the United Nations.*"[45] And they have done so not only when the political costs of a commitment to the Charter were low (as in the time of the East-West confrontation, when many of its norms could not be enforced) but throughout the life of the Charter – in the early days, before the cold war developed fully, as much as in the 1990s or today. With the exception of the defeated "enemy" states, virtually all states existing in 1945 agreed to the Charter. Today, the United Nations is the first organization in world history that has achieved the acquisition of a universal membership of states.[46] No state has ever withdrawn from

---

[42] *See* Charter of the Organization of American States preamble, April 30, 1948 (as amended), 119 U.N.T.S. 48.

[43] Vienna Convention on Diplomatic Relations preamble, April 18, 1961, 500 U.N.T.S. 95.

[44] United Nations Convention on the Law of the Sea preamble, Dec. 10, 1982, 1833 U.N.T.S. 3.

[45] This is an expression used by the [European] Court of First Instance in its *Kadi* judgment of Sept. 21, 2005 (Case T-315/01, Yassin Abdullah Kadi v. Council of the European Union and Commission of European Communities (2005) ECR II-3649, ¶¶ 178, 180) (emphasis added).

[46] Today the United Nations has 192 member states, the newest member being Montenegro (2006). Only the state of the Vatican City by free choice remains an observer. Taiwan tried to become a member but failed because of the one-China policy of the People's Republic of China. The independent statehood of a few other entities (e.g., Palestine, Northern Cyprus, and Kosovo) is controversial.

the United Nations;[47] it has been the first effort of every newly independent
state to join the organization; and never through sixty years it has been even
tried to establish an alternative. States – in their formation as "the international community as a whole" – have recognized the authority of the Charter
as the ultimate source of legitimacy in international law to a degree that it
is difficult to imagine what would happen to that law if the foundational
layer that the Charter represents ceased to exist. To stay with this geologic
metaphor for a second, one could say that for states the Charter has been a
layer of basalt whereas for many lawyers it has only been a layer of quicksand.

Interpretation of the Primary Role of the UN Charter by Legal Science

If states have thus consented to a primary role of the UN Charter in international law, it is the task of legal science task to interpret properly that
role. This task, however, has given legal science a hard time. Back in 1988,
Ronald Macdonald, the eminent Canadian jurist and champion of a constitutional view of the Charter,[48] concluded that "the majority of international lawyers would probably classify the Charter as something more
than a treaty yet less than a world constitution."[49] About a decade later,
Pierre-Marie Dupuy called the Charter "a treaty without an equivalent (*un
traité sans équivalent*),"[50] while Christian Tomuschat styled it a "world order
treaty."[51] In the present volume Michael Doyle addresses the Charter as "a
treaty, but a special treaty."[52]

The problem with the notion of more than a treaty or a special treaty is
that it is no more enlightening than the sui generis classification in which
lawyers usually take refuge for lack of something better. The notion reflects
a certain lack of imagination. It is a sign of a legal theory that is a captive

---

[47] For the case of Indonesia's temporary withdrawal of 1965 and 1966, *see* FASSBENDER, UN
SECURITY COUNCIL REFORM, *supra* note 17, at 153–54.

[48] *See* R. St.-J. Macdonald, *The United Nations Charter: Constitution or Contract?* in THE
STRUCTURE AND PROCESS OF INTERNATIONAL LAW, *supra* note 9, at 889.

[49] *See* Ronald St. John Macdonald, *The Charter of the United Nations and the Development
of Fundamental Principles of International Law*, in CONTEMPORARY PROBLEMS OF INTER-
NATIONAL LAW: ESSAYS IN HONOUR OF GEORG SCHWARZENBERGER 196, 197 (B. Cheng &
E. D. Brown eds., 1988).

[50] *See* Pierre-Marie Dupuy, *L'unité de l'ordre juridique international* (Cours général de droit
international public), 297 RECUEIL DES COURS 9, 217 (2002). For a further evaluation of
the constitutional idea, *see* Pierre-Marie Dupuy, *Taking International Law Seriously: On the
German Approach to International Law*, 50 GERMAN Y.B. INT'L L. 375 (2008).

[51] *See* Tomuschat, *Obligations for States, supra* note 11, at 248. See also Tomuschat, *International
Law, supra* note 18, at 79: "the special character of the UN Charter."

[52] *See* Michael W. Doyle, *The UN Charter – A Global Constitution?* in this volume, Chapter 4.

of the traditional triad of sources of international law as listed in article 38 of the International Court of Justice (ICJ) Statute: treaties, custom, general principles of law – full stop. But we are certainly not prohibited from going beyond that narrow catalog, as much as international law itself has moved into new spheres since 1945.

It is not suggested that a qualification of the Charter as a constitution is the only possible answer to the problem of identifying its place in the international legal order of today. But I believe that in comparison it is the most plausible answer offered so far. Constitution is an accepted notion of law and political philosophy that, in particular, can explain the supremacy of the Charter. For lack of a better alternative, the idea of constitutionalism encapsulates much of what contemporary international law, guided by the UN Charter, is striving for – an organization and allocation of authority and responsibility on the international plane that is commensurate with the present-day threats to international peace and security.

To regard the Charter as the constitution of the international community does not mean to equate it with a national constitution, such as that of the United States, or the constitution of a highly integrated regional association of states, like the European Union. In spite of its partial extrapolation from domestic constitutional law, the constitutional idea in (global) international law must be understood as an autonomous concept. In accordance with subsidiarity as a principle that can guide the allocation of competencies in a multilevel system of governance, a constitution of the international community shall, and need not, replicate a national or regional constitution. Instead, its contents depend on the specific tasks and responsibilities of the international community. As those tasks and responsibilities are different from those of a national body politic organized for civil rule and government or of a regional association with a focus on a common market, the respective constitutional rules must differ.

The Charter is a part of a more inclusive constitutional process. It must be seen together with other customary and treaty law of a fundamental nature that I have called the "constitutional bylaws"[53] of the international community, in particular the two International Covenants on Human Rights, the Convention on the Elimination of all Forms of Racial Discrimination, the Convention on the Prevention and Punishment of the Crime of Genocide, and the Rome Statute of the International Criminal Court (ICC).[54] In this

---

[53] See Fassbender, *The UN Charter as Constitution, supra* note 2, at 588–89.
[54] For a characterization of the 1982 U.N. Law of the Sea Convention as a by-law to the Charter and a constitution in its own right, see Scott, *The LOS Convention, supra* note 29, at 20.

sense, the Charter can be understood as the framework constitution[55] of the international community, which is supplemented and completed by other constitutional rules.

It is true, at the beginning of the twenty-first century, that both the position and the role of the United Nations in international affairs find themselves under great stress. Fundamental rules of the Charter, especially the ban on the use of force,[56] are challenged, and the legitimacy of the Security Council, as the organization's institutional backbone, is called into question. The members of the international community are far away from uniting their strength in an effort to give new life and vigour to the Charter system of international governance, as is evidenced by the unsuccessful attempts of fifteen years at reforming the membership and the voting procedures of the Security Council.[57] A law student reading the Charter today must have a feel of encountering a distant past, of traveling through time right into black-and-white photos of Franklin Roosevelt and Winston Churchill that he or she may have seen in a schoolbook. The old age of the U.S. Constitution evokes the student's reverence, but that of the Charter only a feeling of datedness. Being told that this old Charter occupies a central place in a constitutional structure of the present international community, the student will react with amazement and disbelief, and very understandably so.

On the other hand, many critics of the United Nations are little familiar with the actual day-to-day work of the organization, its range and intensity. They are astonished when they read, for instance, an average monthly agenda of the Security Council and realize that more often than not the Council is not the paper tiger for which they had taken it. They are astonished to see their home governments taking for granted the centrality of the United Nations in the system of international diplomacy and, yes, increasingly also governance. Certainly, rules of the Charter are violated, but so are the rules, say, of the U.S. Constitution (as is demonstrated by an endless stream of Supreme Court rulings) without anybody questioning their constitutional character. So far, no state has denied the binding force of the rules of the Charter. As H. L. A. Hart wrote about international law in general, "When

---

[55] See Bardo Fassbender, *The UN Charter as Framework Constitution of the International Community, in* 1 SELECT PROCEEDINGS OF THE EUROPEAN SOCIETY OF INTERNATIONAL LAW 377, 381 (Hélène Ruiz Fabri, Emmanuelle Jouannet & Vincent Tomkiewicz eds., 2008).

[56] For an overview, see Christine Gray, *A Crisis of Legitimacy for the UN Collective Security System?* 56 INT'L & COMP. L.Q. 157 (2007).

[57] See Bardo Fassbender, *Pressure for Security Council Reform, in* THE UN SECURITY COUNCIL: FROM THE COLD WAR TO THE 21ST CENTURY 341 (David M. Malone ed., 2004); and *On the Boulevard of Broken Dreams: The Project of a Reform of the UN Security Council after the 2005 World Summit,* 2 INT'L ORG. L. REV. 391 (2005).

the rules are disregarded, it is not on the footing that they are not binding; instead efforts are made to conceal the facts."[58] Many international lawyers apply to the Charter standards of compliance and enforcement that today in a domestic context no lawyer would apply to criminal law or tax law or, indeed, constitutional law.

To see the UN Charter, in terms of international law, as the constitution of the international community is not meant to whitewash the instrument, the UN organization, or international law in general. It should not imply that any of the three has reached a state of perfection or anything close to it. It is not an exercise in self-congratulation of the legal community. Much more modestly, it is an effort to identify and interpret the deep structural change of the international legal order that has taken place since 1945 and to draw the appropriate conclusions. In other words, labeling the Charter a "constitution" does not make the world a better place. Taking the constitutional character of the Charter seriously can, however, be a starting point for moving toward conditions in which the values pronounced in the Charter – life in peace and tolerance, the protection of human rights and freedoms, justice, social progress, equality of states and peoples – are better and more evenly realized. "The use of the term 'constitutional' in a descriptive way . . . will have a normative connotation, implying a commitment to managing public affairs in accordance with fundamental values and through certain formally legitimate procedures."[59]

Coldplay's great new song "Viva La Vida" opens with the line, "I used to rule the world." And the third verse says: "One minute I held the key / Next the walls were closed on me. / And I discovered that my castles stand / Upon pillars of salt, and pillars of sand."[60] Apparently, a king is speaking, or an archetype of king. Only an international lawyer listening to the song could get the idea that the *I* could also be the UN Charter. Whatever the fate of the Charter will be in the years to come, whether it will be rediscovered as a constitution or not – one thing is for sure: in retrospect, the Charter of the United Nations will be acknowledged as the twentieth century's most important contribution to a constitutional history of the world.

---

[58] *See* H. L. A. HART, THE CONCEPT OF LAW 215 (1961).

[59] *See* Herman Belz, *Changing Conceptions of Constitutionalism in the Era of World War II and the Cold War*, 59 J. AM. HIST. 640, 669 (1972).

[60] COLDPLAY, *Viva La Vida, on* VIVA LA VIDA OR DEATH AND ALL HIS FRIENDS (EMI Records, 2008).

The European Union

6. Reframing EU Constitutionalism

NEIL WALKER

A. Introduction: Disputing the European Constitution

In the summer of 2007 the European Council announced its decision to "abandon" the "constitutional concept" it had endorsed so optimistically only four years previously on the occasion of receiving a draft of a first constitutional treaty for the European Union from the Convention on the Future of Europe.[1] After the trials and tribulations of the 'no' votes to the 2005 French and Dutch referenda on the (duly promulgated) constitutional treaty, and in light of its dubious popularity and unratified status in some other member states, Europe's leaders finally opted to jettison the new and return to the more familiar vehicle and modest agenda of a "Reform Treaty."[2] This move seemed to pay a very quick political dividend, with agreement reached as early as Lisbon summit of December 2007 and implementation (in the event of successful ratification) of this new "postconstitutional Treaty" initially scheduled for the beginning of 2009.[3] The subsequent rejection of the new Treaty by the Irish electorate in June 2008, however, disrupted that optimistic timetable and threatened the new initiative with the same fate as the old. At the time of writing, therefore, Europe's juridical future remains unresolved.

Not the least irony of the protracted and ultimately terminal difficulties encountered by the project to adopt a documentary constitution has been that they coincided with the more widespread acceptance of some kind of constitutional status for the European Union – even if this tends to be seen

---

[1] Presidency Conclusions, Brussels European Council (June 21–22, 2007).11177/1/07 Rev 1 Conc 2.

[2] Treaty of Lisbon amending the Treaty on European Union and the Treaty establishing the European Community, Dec. 13, 2007, 2007 O.J. (C 306) 01 [hereinafter Treaty of Lisbon].

[3] Alexander Somek, *Postconstitutional Treaty*, 8 GERMAN L.J. 1121, 1121–32 (2007).

in "small 'c'" rather than documentary "big 'C'" terms.[4] Yet this is no mere coincidence. For one of the consequences of the extensive debate over the constitutional treaty has been to encourage those interested in the European Union – practitioners and theorists alike – to cast, or in some cases to recast, their understanding of the European Union's existing attributes (as opposed to its projected design) in constitutional terms. There are various reasons why this might be so. From the perspective of the big *C* constitutional enthusiast, the reconceptualization of the new legal and political order as an accomplishment that already amounts to an unwritten constitution is intended as ballast in support of the case for a written constitution.[5] Conversely, from the perspective of the big *C* constitutional skeptic, such a historical reconstruction supports quite the opposite inference. To highlight the maturity of the existing constitutional *acquis* might suggest not that a written text is unobjectionable but that it is simply redundant. More forcefully, to stress the organic development and complex richness of a mature acquis might argue for the intrinsic difficulty or premature timing of its reduction to a single self-contained documentary constitution.[6] Or, in a further variation of the skeptical theme, resort to constitutional language might be with a view to dramatize the gap between those modest aspects of constitutionalism that are deemed appropriate to the supranational domain and those that are familiar from the state tradition, and so to accentuate the deep incongruence – or "category error"[7] – of a fully fledged written constitution in this new domain. Whatever the balance of strategic purposes, we can see why the constitutional tone has become more insistent than once it was. And, tellingly, we can see why this change says as much about the deep disputability of what is properly conceived of as constitutional in the postnational domain as it does about any prospect of agreement.

The aim of the present contribution is to show what is at stake in this emergent, multisourced, and many-sided supranational constitutional narrative. In what sense, if at all, can we meaningfully talk about the European Union as already possessing a constitution, and in what sense not? And what does the complexly nuanced and highly conflicted picture this investigation reveals tell

---

[4] Neil Walker, *Big "C" or Small "c"?* 12 EUROPEAN L.J. 12, 12–14 (2006).

[5] *See infra* discussion of pro–constitutional treaty strategies in section C of this chapter.

[6] *See, e.g.,* Joseph Weiler, *In Defence of the Status Quo. Europe's Constitutional Sonderweg, in* EUROPEAN CONSTITUTIONALISM BEYOND THE STATE (Joseph Weiler & Marlene Wind eds., 2003); Stephen Weatherill, *Is Constitutional Finality Feasible or Desirable? On the Case for European Constitutionalism and a European Constitution*, 7 CONWEB (2002), *available at* http://www.bath.ac.uk/esml/conWEB/Conweb%20papers-filestore/conweb7–2002.pdf.

[7] *See, e.g.,* Andrew Moravcsik, *Europe without Illusions: A Category Error*, PROSPECT, July 2005, at 22–26, at 22.

us both about the present state of debate and about the longer-term prospects of supranational constitutionalism?

The method I have chosen to pursue this topic, drawing upon and developing earlier work,[8] is to conceive of constitutionalism as a series of separable but mutually reinforcing frames through which political community is both recognized and constructed. These two features – the key idea of a constitution as a multifaceted framing mechanism and the supplementary notion that what it frames is in some sense both already constituted and always under construction – provide what we might call the "basic structure" of the constitutional idea. As we shall see, each structural characteristic is vital in accounting for one crucial aspect of the deep disputability of the idea of transnational constitutionalism. The first characteristic directs us to the open-endedness of constitutionalism as an object of knowledge – and so refers us to the cognitive dimension of disputability. The second deepens our insight into the intimacy of the connection between description and (preferred) prescription in constitutional affairs – and so refers us to the motivational dimension of disputability.

We can illuminate these two basic structural characteristics by tracing the etymology of the term *constitution*. Originating in the Latin verb *constituere* ("to establish") and its associated noun *constitutio*, and at more distant removal in a cluster of similar predecessor concepts in ancient Greece, the idea of constitution was gradually extended from its original field of reference in the material and physical world to the world of the "body politic."[9] Whether in the natural or the political world, the term *constitution* necessarily implied, and implies, the existence of a discrete and self-contained entity – a polity or political community – as the object of constitutional reference.

Of course, the idea of politics as an activity that takes place within and with reference to particular bounded contexts – within and between particular polities, in other words – is so deeply entrenched within our dominant contemporary social imaginary that it may appear entirely unremarkable. But that should not blind us to the particularity of the constitutional way of conceptualizing the world. At its most elementary, this particularity embraces our first basic structural element – a framing logic. There are two aspects and two steps within this framing logic. First, the idea of constitution proceeds on the assumption that politics is an activity capable of being located within

---

[8] *See especially* Neil Walker, *European Constitutionalism in the State Constitutional Tradition, in* 59 Current Legal Probs 51 (Jane Holder & Colm O'Cinneide eds., 2006); Neil Walker, *Taking Constitutionalism beyond the State*, 56 Pol. Stud. 519–543 (2008).

[9] *See, e.g.,* Dieter Grimm, *The Constitution in the Process of Denationalization*, 12 Constellations 447, 447–63 (2005).

certain clearly differentiated containers of social space. Second, the idea of
constitution sets out, in various different registers, to engage in the practices
necessary to recognize and shape just such a demarcation and organization
of social space. That is to say, the constitutional way of thinking understands
itself and projects itself as setting the very framework within which and in
accordance with which we engage in the collective forms of practical reasoning
we call "politics." And in so doing it provides a distinctive mechanism for
meta-level practical reasoning – a presumptive answer to the question: How
to decide how to decide?

These different framing registers are juridical, political-institutional,
authorizing, social, and (as a kind of frame of frames) discursive. In their
very multiplicity and variety, these registers demonstrate how easily we can
mean diverse things by the term *constitution*, and how much scope that allows
for disagreement over what is or is not properly constitutional or over what
is more or less maturely constitutional. But before we pursue this through a
detailed examination of each frame and their relationship inter se, we should
note how the kind of relationship the activity of framing has with the object
framed also alerts us to the second deep structural element of our root sense
of constitution.

As one writer puts it, the idea of constitution, and so also the notion of
framing so deeply inscribed within the idea of constitution, "seems to cut
across the essentialist-nonessentialist distinction."[10] On the one hand, an act
or process of constitution is not a matter of pure invention. 'To constitute'
presupposes an entity to be constituted – something that already exists in
some ideal or material form prior to its being constituted. On the other hand,
through constitutive framing, we also necessarily re-present and modify that
prior thing.[11] So constitutionalism refers both, passively, to determining and
recording the nature and character of some discrete object that already possess
an innate character and, actively, to constructing that object as a kind of conventional artifact. Here, then, we find the origins of the historically resilient
double focus of constitutionalism on what is already in place, or constituted
on the one hand, and what is a matter of projection or constituting on the
other.[12] And while, as we shall see, the descriptive element is more prevalent

---

[10] Donald Lutz, Principles of Constitutional Design 188 (2006).
[11] See, e.g., Hans Lindahl, *Sovereignty and Representation in the European Union, in*
Sovereignty in Transition 87 (Neil Walker ed., 2003).
[12] This is a highly complex distinction and relationship, and certainly not reducible to any
simple dichotomy. Some writers map the descriptive and prescriptive elements of constitutionalism onto (given) fact and (aspirational) value, respectively; others map description
and prescription more specifically onto *gubernaculum* (governing capacity) and *jurisdictio*

in premodern constitutionalism and the actively prescriptive element in modern constitutionalism, all constitutional forms, given the Janus-faced dynamic of framing, remain in some measure ambivalently poised between the two. Both what is and what ought to be – fact and norm – are inescapable and indivisible features of thinking constitutionally, and it follows that what *is* always in some sense conditions what ought to be. That, indeed, is why – as we have already noted in passing and as we shall develop more fully in due course – European thinkers who disagree over the constitutional future so often begin by discussing and disagreeing over the constitutional past.

B. Constitutional Framing

In this section we look at each of the five constitutive frames separately and in combination, before turning in the following sections to their current application and developmental prospects in the EU context. In the most general terms, each of these frames already expresses the historically embedded double focus of constitutionalism as concerned with both description and prescription – with the recognition of the already-constituted body politic as well as with the constitutive representation or projection of an ideal model of political community. What typically counts as constitutional in terms of the juridical frame is the idea of a mature rule-based or legal order – one that claims and demonstrates a certain level of independent efficacy and aspires to a certain standard of virtue that we associate with legal orderliness and the rule of law. What typically counts as constitutional in political-institutional terms is the presence of a set of organs of government that provide an effective instrument of rule across a broad jurisdictional scope for a distinctive polity and seek a fair form of internal balance between interests and functions. What typically counts as constitutional in terms of authorization is a developed sense of self-authorization, one in which the legal and

---

(principled limitation of governing capacity), respectively (*see, e.g.,* Giovanni Sartori, *Constitutionalism: A Preliminary Discussion*, 56 AM. POL. SCI. REV. 853, 853–64 (1962)); while others still tend to reverse the fact-value sequencing and see in the descriptive dimension a deep rendering of the existing mores and customary order and in the prescriptive element a more instrumental and pragmatic approach to legal and political order (*see, e.g.,* CHARLES MCILWAIN, CONSTITUTIONALISM, ANCIENT AND MODERN (1947); JAMES TULLY, STRANGE MULTIPLICITY: CONSTITUTIONALISM IN AN AGE OF DIVERSITY (1995)). The point to be stressed is that under the basic duality of description and prescription all of these ways of imagining the dynamic of constitutionalism are possible, and indeed are often linked to competing ideologies of constitutionalism, but none can reduce constitutionalism as a form of practical reasoning about the operation of a polity either to pure description or to pure prescription.

political-institutional complex may plausibly be attributed to some *pouvoir constituant* that is both original to and distinctive of that polity and qualified to claim a legitimate pedigree or authorial title. What typically counts as constitutional in social terms is a community sufficiently integrated to be the subject of legal regulation and institutional action that is both plausibly effective in terms of collective implementation and compliance and capable of locating and tracking some meaningful sense of that community's common good. And finally, what typically counts as constitutional in discursive terms is the balance of the existing ideological power struggle between selfish interests and the ongoing normative 'battle of ideas' entailed in the labelling of certain phenomena or prospects under the binary logic of constitutional/unconstitutional with all that that implies in terms of the constitutional status and worthiness of the phenomena so framed.

Let us now look more closely at these five framing dimensions in turn. To begin with legal order, this refers to the circumstances under which we may conceive of a certain domain of law qua legal order, as something systemic and self-contained.[13] The fine details may be viewed differently across jurisprudential schools, but the very idea of legal order is commonly understood as a necessary incident, or at least precondition, of any constitutional system. Legal order involves a cluster of interconnected factors; in particular self-ordering, self-interpretation, self-extension, self-amendment, self-enforcement, and self-discipline. The quality of self-ordering refers to the ability of a legal system to reach and regulate all matters within its domain or jurisdiction, typically through its successful embedding of certain law-making secondary norms as a means to generate and validate a comprehensive body of primary norms.[14] The quality of self-interpretation refers to the ability of some organ or organs internal to the legal order, typically the adjudicative organ, to have the final world as regards the meaning and purpose of its own norms. The quality of self-extension refers to the ability of a legal system to decide the extent of its own jurisdiction – otherwise known as *kompetenz-kompetenz*. The quality of self-amendment refers to the existence of a mechanism for changing the normative content of the legal order, which is provided for in terms of that order and that empowers organs internal to that order as the agents of the process of amendment. The quality of self-enforcement refers to the ability of the legal order, through the development of a body of procedural law and associated sanctions, to provide for the application and implementation of its own norms.

---

[13] *See, e.g.,* JOSEPH RAZ, THE CONCEPT OF A LEGAL SYSTEM (1980).
[14] H. L. A. HART, THE CONCEPT OF LAW 79–99 (2d ed. 1997).

The quality of self-discipline refers to the positively evaluative and aspirational dimension of legal order, for which the first five dimensions provide a necessary, if insufficient, platform. Once the legal order reaches a certain threshold of certainty and reliability in its production and of comprehensiveness in its coverage of its primary norms (self-ordering); once it has reached a certain threshold of effectiveness in its rules of standing, justiciability, and liability (self-enforcement); once it has obtained the ability to adjust or correct its own normative structure and provided it can guarantee sufficient autonomy from external influences in these systemic endeavours (self-amendment, self-interpretation, and self-extension), it is then in a position to achieve two related aspects of self-discipline. In the first place, it can offer a certain level of generality and predictability in the treatment of those who are subject to its norms, and in so doing help cultivate a system-constraining cultural presumption against arbitrary rule. Second, and more specifically, the consolidation of a legal order with mature claims to autonomy, comprehensiveness, and effectiveness provides the opportunity and helps generate the expectation that even the institutional or governmental actors internal to the legal order need and should not escape the discipline of legal restraint in accordance with that mature order. Indeed, these two core ideas – of the "rule of law, not man," and of a "government limited by law,"[15] – provide a key element of all Western legal traditions, whether couched in the language of rule of law or *état de droit* or *Rechtsstaat*, and so supply a cornerstone of constitutionalism understood as a value-based discourse.

Whereas this first building block of modern constitutionalism can be traced back to the Roman roots of civilian law, albeit its rule-of-law characteristics developed later, the second feature was one of the distinctively novel features of the modern state as it emerged as a new form of political domination in Continental Europe in response to the confessional civil wars of the sixteenth and seventeenth centuries. What we are here concerned with is the establishment and maintenance of a comprehensive political-institutional framework understood as a system of specialized political rule. This is a development that achieved an early stylistic maturity in the form of the French and American documentary constitutions of the late eighteenth century. For such a system neither its title to rule nor its ongoing purpose flows from prior and fixed economic or status attributes or concerns (of the type that in the constitutional thought of classical and medieval polities tended to exclude some actors from the polity or grade and degrade them within it) or from some notion of traditional or divine order external to the system itself (as

---

[15] *See, e.g.,* Brian Tamanaha, On the Rule of Law 114–126 (2004).

in premodern constellations of political power generally). Instead, authority rests upon a putative idea of the individual as the basic unit of society and as the (presumptively equal) source of moral agency, with the very idea of a political domain built upon and dedicated to that secular premise – one that develops its own authoritative yardsticks for conflict resolution and its own mechanisms for collective decision making.[16]

This development speaks to a new stage in the differentiation of social forms, one in which there is for the first time a separate sphere of the public and political that in its operative logic is distinctive both from the society over which it rules and from some notion of transcendental order. Such a specialized system has the dual attributes of immanence and self-limitation. On the one hand, it purports to be self-prescribing and self-legitimating. The justification of the continuing claim to authority of the autonomous political domain and the higher order rules through which that authority is inscribed rests not upon the external force and discipline of a metaphysical or a reified-through-tradition order of things, but upon the operation of the political domain itself and the secular interests it serves. On the other hand, as the flip side of this, there emerges a general sphere of purely private action and freedom that lies beyond either the autonomous domain of politics or the now-redundant special mixed regimes of public and private right and obligation based upon prior forms of privilege or natural order.[17] The regulatory structures of the new specialist political order echo its distinctive attributes. Positively, and reflecting the quality of immanence, they take the form of third-order institutional rules and capacities for making (legislature), administering (executive), and adjudicating (judiciary) the second-order legal system norms through which the coordination of first-order action and the resolution of first-order disagreement within a population is secured. Negatively, and reflecting the quality of self-limitation, they take the form of checks and balances and monitoring mechanisms – of constitutionalism as limited government – aimed to protect a separate sphere of private individual or group freedom, one safe from incursions at the third-order level of public authority or infraction at the second-order level of the substantive norms of the legal system.

The idea of a specialized system of political rule also carries with it certain assumptions about the kind and intensity of normative concern properly

---

[16] *See, e.g.,* Ian Loader & Neil Walker, Civilizing Security 35–72 (2007); Martin Loughlin, The Idea of Public Law 32–52 (2003).

[17] *See, e.g.,* Grimm, *supra* note 9, at 452–53; Jürgen Habermas, *Constitutional Democracy: A Paradoxical Union of Contradictory Principles,* 28 Pol. Theory 766–781 (2001).

considered constitutional. There are again two aspects to this, mirroring those affecting the institutional dimension. On the one hand, there is the idea of the normative system providing a "comprehensive blueprint for social life"[18] – of recognizing no externally imposed substantive limits to its ability to regulate each and all areas of social policy with which it may be concerned, and to do so in a joined-up manner. On the other hand there is the recognition of an internally imposed constraint – the protection of the very sphere of private autonomy that underpins the idea of a secular political order in the first place. In turn this entails formal or informal catalogs of individual rights – constitutionalism as fundamental rights protection – to add substance to the institutional or structural checks referred to previously.

The institutionalization of a separate and specialist sphere of political contestation and decision and a correspondingly broad and deep political jurisdiction stands in a close relationship to the legal-order dimension already considered. Indeed, it is this basic relationship that Luhmann had in mind when he talked about the constitution as operating within both legal and political systems and providing a mechanism for their linking, or structural coupling, with the institutions of the political system both dependent upon – instituted under – a legal pedigree and implicated as key agents in the processes of self-ordering, self-interpretation, self-extension, self-amendment, self-enforcement, and self-discipline through which the legal order is sustained and developed.[19] Yet the idea of a specialized political system, still less that of an autonomous legal order, does not necessarily imply, within the third framing register of constitutionalism, a type of authorization that claims either a democratic founding or a continuing democratic warrant. Rather, the operational autonomy, specialist nature, and expansive normative scope of the political sphere may be consistent with a set of arrangements in which the original authorization comes from beyond the system, as in many of the subaltern constitutions of imperial systems;[20] or in which the original authorization is located within the system but is presented as a top-down monarchical or aristocratic grant or bequest rather than a bottom-up popular claim.[21]

---

[18] Christian Tomuschat, *International Law: Ensuring the Survival of Mankind on the Eve of a New Century: General Course on Public International Law*, 63 RECUEIL DES COURS DE L'ACADÉMIE DE DROIT INTERNATIONAL 9, 281 (2001).

[19] NIKLAS LUHMANN, DAS RECHT DER GESELLSCHAFT (1993); *see also* Kaarlo Tuori, *The Failure of the EU's Constitutional Project: A Cultural Discrepancy*, No FOUNDATIONS, June 2007, at 37, 37–48.

[20] PETER C. OLIVER, THE CONSTITUTION OF INDEPENDENCE (2005).

[21] As in many of the *constitutions octroyées* of the nineteenth century (*e.g.*, the French Charters of 1814 and 1830, the Italian *Statuto Albertino* of 1848).

So the autonomy and capaciousness of the political sphere need not imply
that all those affected by the operation of the system participate or be represented in its, institution or even in its subsequent homologation. It need
imply merely that, within the third framing register, an understanding of
political title should prevail, whether this be presented in terms of raison
d'état or salus populi or some other version of the collective good, which is
adequate to the constitutional polity's claim and character, within the second
framing register, as a special and encompassing sphere of political action –
one where there is no transcendental or otherwise overriding external justification as well as freedom from special social or economic interests. Yet the
specialized system of political rule, just because it introduces the idea of a
sphere of authority that must construct itself and provide for its own secular
justification, cannot indefinitely avoid the very question, How to decide how
to decide? – and still less its even more starkly indeterminate derivative, Who
decides who decides?[22] – that it bring into sharp relief for the first time.
Therefore, at least in the developing state tradition, constitutionalism tends
to be a precarious achievement unless and until joined by a claim of collective
self-authorization.

Within constitutional thought in that state tradition, this third authorizing
frame gradually comes to be conceived in terms of the idea of constituent
power, or the ultimate sovereignty of the people.[23] Again, the documentary form that centers modern state constitutionalism directly engages this
dimension, with such texts normally claiming to be not only for the people
but also of the people, and their drafting procedures – typically through the
involvement of constituent assemblies and popular conventions – dramatize a
commitment to substantiate that claim of popular authorship.[24] So prevalent,
indeed, is the ethic of democratic pedigree in modern state constitutionalism – of democracy as a metavalue in terms of which other governance values
are understood and articulated[25] – that debate tends to center not on the
question of its appropriateness but only on the adequacy of its instantiation.
This may manifest itself in the critique of those constitutional settlements
that lack a founding documentary episode, or at least a plausible narrative
of subsequent popular homologation,[26] or in the claim that the constitution

[22] Miguel Maduro, *Where to Look for Legitimacy?* in CONSTITUTION MAKING AND DEMO-
CRATIC LEGITIMACY, 5 ARENA REPORT 81, 91 (Erik O. Eriksen, John E. Fossum & Agustin J.
Menendez eds., 2002).
[23] *See, e.g.*, Andreas Kalyvas, *Popular Sovereignty, Democracy and the Constituent Power*, 12
CONSTELLATIONS 223, 223–44 (2005).
[24] *See, e.g.*, ANDREW ARATO, CIVIL SOCIETY, CONSTITUTION AND LEGITIMACY (2000), ch. 7.
[25] *See, e.g.*, JOHN DUNN, SETTING THE PEOPLE FREE: THE STORY OF DEMOCRACY (2005).
[26] On the British case, *see* ADAM TOMKINS, OUR REPUBLICAN CONSTITUTION (2005).

has betrayed its popular foundations, or in the criticism that for all its derivative concern with democracy in the everyday framework of government, the constitution is not autochthonous but instead remains dependent upon the constituted power of another polity or polities.

But modern (state) constitutionalism is not only about the generation through an act and continuing promise of democratic self-authorization of the wherewithal for the operation of a self-sufficient legal order underpinned by its own institutional complex and normatively expansive framework of secular political rule. Alongside these internal frames, given the increased emphasis upon the prescriptive over the descriptive work of the constitution that the idea of an autonomous and self-authorizing political sphere inevitably brings, the modern state constitution also either presupposes or promises (and typically both), as a fourth, external, framing achievement, a degree of societal integration on the part of the constituency in whose name it is promulgated and to whom it is directed.[27] Unless there is already in place some sense of common cause to endorse those interests or ideals that the constitutional text has identified as being well served by being put in common and to affirm and so vindicate the capability of the institutional means that the constitution deems instrumental to the pursuit of these common interests or ideals, then the constitution conceived of as a project of political community is in danger of remaining a dead letter. What this prior propensity to put things in common or basic sense of political community amounts to is an issue of much controversy, and in any event it is something better conceived of as a matter of degree. As a basic minimum, however, it refers to a sense of common attachment or common predicament within the putative demos sufficient to manifest itself in three interrelated forms. It should be sufficient to ensure that most members demonstrate the minimum level of sustained mutual respect and concern required to reach and adhere to collective outcomes that may work against their immediate interests in terms of the distribution of common resources and risks. Reciprocally, it should be sufficient to ensure that each is prepared to trust the others to participate in the common business of dispute resolution, decision making, and rule following on these same other-respecting terms. Finally, this web of mutual respect and trust should be strong enough to sustain a political culture that, just because of the accomplishment of its core common commitment, can acknowledge and accept difference beyond this core commitment.[28]

---

[27] See, e.g., Dieter Grimm, *Integration by Constitution*, 3 INT'L J. CONST. L. 193, 193–208 (2005).
[28] See, e.g., DAVID MILLER, ON NATIONALITY (2005); MARGARET CANOVAN, NATIONHOOD AND POLITICAL THEORY (2006).

Yet just because it cannot guarantee the necessary social supports of respect and concern, trust, and mutual toleration merely through normative enunciation does not mean that the constitution is incapable of influencing the measure of social integration necessary to its effective application and can do no more than passively presuppose the prior existence of the requisite measure of social integration. To begin with, its normative framework of political rule seeks to provide a settled template for living together in circumstances free from despotism or intractable conflict, and to that extent it offers an incentive to all who are attracted by such a template to secure the floor of common commitment necessary for its effective implementation. Second, the act of making the constitution may have a mobilization dividend that goes beyond agreement on the particular text in question. The value of the process is not exhausted by its textual product,[29] but it may extend to the generation or bolstering of just these forms of political identity necessary to the successful implementation of the text. Third, as constitutions in the modern age are typically viewed as the expression and vindication of the constituent power of a people, the successful making of a constitution has come to assume a special symbolic significance as a totem of peoplehood. So powerful, indeed, is the chain of signification developed under the modern banner of popular, nation-state constitutionalism that, regardless of how it came into existence, the very fact that a constitution exists is typically understood and widely portrayed as testimony to the achievement, the sustenance, or – as in the case of the new Central and Eastern European states after 1989 – the restoration of political community. Fourth, insofar as the constitution crystallizes such general common ends or values as are the subject of agreement in the constitution-making moment and as may also be already present in the preconstitutional ethical life of the relevant social constituency, it may have a "double institutionalization" effect.[30] The addition of the constitutional imprimatur may amplify the importance of and the extent of common subscription to these common values and ends, and in so framing and reinforcing a common political vernacular, strengthen the societally integrative relationship between that common political vernacular and the mutual respect, concern, trust, and tolerance that is indispensable to political community. Fifth and last, we may look beyond the founding moment of the constitution to see how it can become an ongoing source of intensification of

[29] See, e.g., Wojciech Sadurski, Conclusions: On the Relevance of Institutions and the Centrality of Constitutions in Post-Communist Transitions, in 1 Democratic Consolidation in Eastern Europe 455, 455–72 (Jan Zielonka ed., 1991).
[30] Paul Bohannan, The Differing Realms of the Law, in Law and Warfare: Studies in the Anthropology of Conflict 43, 43–56 (Paul Bohannan ed., 1967).

the social foundations necessary to its effective implementation. This operates in at least two ways. On the one hand, the constitution may function as a reminder of community. Insofar as common political identity often develops alongside and feeds off the collective memorialization of claimed common events, achievements, and experiences, constitutional history provides one such stream of sanctified tradition. The constitution may thus write itself into collective history.[31] On the other hand, the constitution may provide a resilient but flexible structure for political-ethical debate, an anchor for a continuing conversation about the meaning of political community that operates in a Janus-faced manner to strengthen that political community. Looking back, it supplies a token not only of the supposed depth and extension of common experience but also of the weight of accumulated practical knowledge. Looking forward, the constitution may be sufficiently open ended and sufficiently understood as a work of transgenerational authorship for its structures and values to be capable of being inflected in ways that retain the symbolic gravitas of accumulated wisdom, yet are adaptable to contemporary forms of political vernacular and understandings of trust, solidarity, and tolerance. In other words, the constitution may provide a repository, and so a standing corroboration of the viable ethical threshold of political community, as well as a vehicle for its continuous adaptation.[32]

Let us finally turn to "constitution talk" – and so to the discursive frame. Some aspects of this we have already considered under the symbolic aspect of the social dimension. Constitutional discourse is not unique in its reference to legal order, specialized political system, extensive normative capacity, constituent power, or political community, but it provides a unique imaginary frame in its potential to join these elements together in a singular discourse about a polity.[33] That is to say, it is capable of proving an encompassing and self-reflexive vocabulary for imagining the polity in political-ethical terms. Of course, constitution talk can also be used ideologically and strategically. As

---

[31] Avishai Margalit, The Ethics of Memory 12 (2002).

[32] See, e.g., Jürgen Habermas, On Law and Disagreement: Some Comments on "Interpretative Pluralism," 16 Ratio Juris 187,187–199 (2003).

[33] Constitutionalism thus tends to be more comprehensive in remit and more explicitly polity based than its transnational juridical competitors, such as human rights or the recently popular idea of global administrative law (see, e.g., Benedict Kingsbury, Nico Krisch & Richard Stewart, The Emergence of Global Administrative Law, 68 Law & Contemp. Probs. 15, 15–61 (2005)), each of which tends (1) to focus only or predominantly upon the legal dimension of social relations and (2) to take the traditional view of polities as exclusively or largely restricted to states, and stress the importance and independent legitimacy of juridical relations that cut across different (state) polities. See also Neil Walker, Beyond Boundary Disputes and Basic Grids: Mapping the Global Disorder of Normative Orders, 6 Int. J. Const. L. 373–396 (2008).

we have seen in our discussion of its societal dimension, such a socially resonant discourse is constantly invoked as a way of reinforcing particular claims
and judgements, whether positive or negative – constitutional or unconstitutional – about particular political acts or practices or categories of political
acts or practices. Indeed, its ethical centrality and its susceptibility to ideological exploitation and strategic manoeuvre are two sides of the same coin –
accounting for the status of constitutionalism as a "condensing symbol,"[34]
to whose terms a whole series of debates about how we do and should live
together are continuously reduced.

C. The EU Constitutional Frame

It is clear that the European Unoin's constitutional credentials are distributed
unevenly across the frames. In both legal and political-institutional terms it
registers strongly – though, as we shall see, by no means unproblematically –
on the constitutional scale. The first has been enough for many lawyers to
talk up the constitutional credentials of the European Union, and increasingly so, while the second has been enough for many institutionally oriented
political scientists to do likewise. Yet in terms of self-authorization and social
integration, it registers weakly. It is these weaknesses in the self-authorization
and societal frames, respectively, that lie behind the oft-heard criticisms that
the European Union lacks a pouvoir constituant and has no demos, and so
can be described under present conditions as possessing merely a "low intensity" constitutionalism.[35] It is against this backdrop of uneven and truncated
constitutionalism that we can begin to makes sense of the EU documentary
constitutional project of recent years – both its attraction and its contestation. Indeed, we can identify three main strategic clusters – intensification,
nominalization, and refinement – associated with the nonskeptical camp
within the documentary constitutional project, each of which is vulnerable
to skeptical challenge.

In the first place, there is the ambitious strategy of intensification, based
upon the premise that the European Union is capable of becoming a thick
constitutional frame in self-authorizing and social terms as well as in legal
and political-institutional terms, and that the documentary constitution

---

[34] Victor Turner, Dramas, Fields and Metaphors: Symbolic Action in Human Society
(1974).

[35] *See* Miguel Maduro, *The Importance of Being Called a Constitution: Constitutional Authority
and the Authority of Constitutionalism*, 3 Int'l. J. Const. L. 332, 340 (2005); *see also* Mattias
Kumm, *Beyond Golf Clubs and the Judicialization of Politics: Why Europe Has a Constitution
Properly So Called*, 54 Am. J. Comp. L. 505 (2006).

offers an important contribution and catalyst to that end.[36] As regards self-authorization, the documentary constitutional moment is viewed as providing an opportunity for a democratic baptism. As regards social integration, the act of constitution making is proposed as important both as an event in the mobilization of commitment and as an anchor for the development over time of an acquis of common constitutional achievement – an acquisition that represents a dividend as well as a reinforcing source of mutual trust, respect, and tolerance within the developing supranational political community. Against this, on the skeptical side we find the view that there is no democratic need and can be no democratic mandate for such a self-authorization – either because there is still a delegated democratic authority from states,[37] or because the kind of expertise or impersonal authority required for many EU functions do not depend upon and indeed may be corrupted by democratic voice.[38] And as regards societal integration, the claims of the integrative potential of a constitutional process, formal baptism, and sustained conversation are likely to be dismissed as fanciful or at least as unduly optimistic.[39]

In the second place, there is the strategy of nominalization – the gambit that the very formal act of labeling (within the discursive frame) the canonical text(s) as a constitution and no longer just as a treaty – would itself provide a significant and self-legitimating token of the maturity of the EU polity. In its naked form this naming strategy seeks nothing more than the added value of a symbolic "vindication"[40] of the constitutional-achievement-to-date within the other frames, and as such is bound to place a strong emphasis on the backward-looking aspect of the constitutional Janus face. Indeed this helps explain why, in the early stages of the Convention at least, many seemed content with a constitution that would leave the vast majority of the treaty

[36] Academically, closely associated with the position of Jürgen Habermas. See supra notes 17 and 32. See also the essays collected in JÜRGEN HABERMAS, THE POSTNATIONAL CONSTELLATION (Max Pensky ed. & trans., 2001) and, more recently, in JÜRGEN HABERMAS, THE DIVIDED WEST (2006). For discussion, see JAN-WERNER MULLER, CONSTITUTIONAL PATRIOTISM (2007), ch. 3.

[37] See, e.g., Andrew Moravcsik, Is There a "Democratic Deficit" in World Politics? A Framework for Analysis, 39 GOV'T & OPPOSITION 336, 336–63 (2004); Peter Lindseth, Delegation Is Dead, Long Live Delegation: Managing the Democratic Disconnect in the European Market-Polity, in GOOD GOVERNANCE IN EUROPE'S INTEGRATED MARKET 139, 139–63 (Christian Joerges & Renaud Dehousse eds., 2002).

[38] See, e.g., GIANDOMENICO MAJONE, DILEMMAS OF EUROPEAN INTEGRATION: THE AMBIGUITIES & PITFALLS OF INTEGRATION BY STEALTH (2005).

[39] See, e.g., Andrew Moravcsik, What Can We Learn from the Collapse of the European Constitutional Project? 47 POLITISCHE VIERTELJAHRESSCHRIFT 2 (2006); Karl-Heinz Ladeur, "We, the European People . . . " – Relâche? 14 EUR. L.J. 147, 147–67 (2008).

[40] For discussion of this strategy in the Convention, see Neil Walker, Europe's Constitutional Momentum and the Search for Polity Legitimacy, 3 INT'L J. CONST. L. 211, 228–30 (2005).

substance untouched. Gradually, the nominalization strategy became more associated with either intensification or refinement strategies, and so with the more constructive tendency of each of these, but the backward-looking vindication dimension remained (unsurprisingly) influential in the ideological politics of an entity whose most visible sign of common cause lay not in the dimension of societal culture but in its fifty-year-old institutional acquis. On the skeptical side, however, this kind of symbolic strategy has always been liable to criticism and dismissal as a form of constitutional misrepresentation or inflation[41] – as cynical as the strategy of intensification is naive.

In the third place, then, there is the strategy of refinement. The aim here is less radical than intensification in accordance with a statist model but less conservative than a merely nominal approach. Rather, the aim is to edit and adjust those aspects of the more accessible frames of postnational constitutionalism, namely, the basic legal and political-institutional frames of constitutionalism that, in comparison to state constitutions at least, remain in some respects unresolved or out of balance. At root, these unresolved features may be traced to the distinctive structural position of the European Union as a "relational" polity within the developing post-Westphalia configuration.[42] In the novel plural or compound configuration where states exist alongside a range of emergent poststate political sites[43] (of which the European Union is only the most powerful), unlike in the simple or one-dimensional Westphalian configuration, the relevant units are no longer mutually exclusive territories with mutually exclusive jurisdictions and citizenries. Rather, the new species of poststate polity in general, with the European Union in the vanguard, increasingly overlaps the states in terms of geographical reach, competence, and the political identity of its citizens. It follows that the relationship between these different orders of polity is best conceived of as "osmotic"[44] – as a generalized process of mutual infiltration – rather than as the negotiation and maintenance of clear boundaries, as in the case of traditional interstate relations. This relational quality has direct consequences for both the legal order and the political-institutional frames, each of which speaks in its different way and in accordance with its distinctive systemic logic to the new porosity of the post-Westphalia polity. The relational quality has the effect, first,

---

[41] *See, e.g.,* Weiler, *supra* note 6.

[42] *See* Walker, *supra* note 8, at 70.

[43] Alongside other regional organisations such as the North American Free Trade Agreement and global organizations such as the World Trade Organization. *See generally* Walker, *supra* note 33.

[44] Ulrich Preuss, *The Constitution of a European Democracy and the Role of the Nation State,* 12 RATIO JURIS 417, 417–28 (1999).

of making the legal order nonexclusive and, second, of attributing to the political-institutional structure the character of a "mixed" or a nonunitary polity.[45] And it is with the difficulties and adjustments attendant upon these characteristics that the strategy of refinement is concerned.

Take first the nonexclusive legal order. If we look again at the various features of a mature legal order – self-ordering, self-interpretation, self-extension, self-amendment, self-enforcement, and self-discipline – the EU legal order shows itself to be nonexclusive in two closely complementary and overlapping senses. On the one hand, it provides an incomplete authority system, reliant upon other legal orders for the perfection and pursuit of its normative order. On the other hand, it provides a contestable authority system, one whose authority is challengeable by other legal orders at certain key points. That is to say, as a legal order it both requires and is vulnerable to other legal orders within a broader pluralist configuration,[46] and in neither sense can it exclude them. In terms of self-ordering and self-interpretation the EU legal order comes closest to being a fully self-contained and exclusive order in that it provides for its own internal hierarchy of norms and of instruments – a capacity dependent upon a governing idea of the supremacy or primacy of its norms in general over the norms of other legal systems – and has its own authoritative supreme court in the European Court of Justice (ECJ). But even here, the dependence upon national instruments for implementation on the one hand, and the lack of an appeal (as opposed to a reference) procedure that would give the ECJ the final power "to decide what to decide" on the other,[47] compromises these features at the margins. As regards self-extension, through the doctrine of implied powers and an expansive reading of its own necessary-and-proper clause,[48] the ECJ makes some claim to determine the extent of its own competence, but in the final analysis this is limited by its dependence upon (textually) conferred powers and by the readiness of national supreme courts in Germany, Spain, Denmark, Poland, and so on, to challenge what they see as practices of self-expansion.[49]

---

[45] See, e.g., Giandomenico Majone, Delegation of Regulatory Powers in a Mixed Polity, 8 EUR. L.J. 319 (2002).

[46] The literature on so-called constitutional pluralism in the European Union is now extensive. For an excellent overview, see MONICA CLAES, THE NATIONAL COURTS' MANDATE IN THE EUROPEAN CONSTITUTION (2006).

[47] Treaty Establishing the European Community, art. 234, Nov. 10, 1997, 1997 O.J. (C 340) 3 [hereinafter EC Treaty].

[48] Id. at art. 308.

[49] On recent developments in the case law, see, e.g., Wojciech Sadurski, 'Solange, Chapter 3': Constitutional Courts in Central Europe-Democracy-European Union, 14 EUR. L.J. 1, 1–35 (2008).

The power of legislative self-amendment is entirely lacking, and instead the EU legal order is reliant upon a mechanism external to its own institutional working order – namely, the Intergovernmental Conference – for formal change. Notwithstanding the doctrine of the direct effect (of EU norms in national legal orders), which operates in close combination with primacy, the self-enforceability of the EU legal order is restricted. Even within the limited range of those supranational rules that are considered sufficiently clear, precise, and unconditional to be domestically justiciable, the cooperation of national judges is patently necessary. And beyond that limited range of directly effective provisions, the EU legal order is dependent upon national authorities both for the legislative transposition and for the executive and (again) judicial application of non–directly effective norms – with the gradual expansion of the doctrine of state liability as a way to plug the gaps in this system itself only a selectively effective sanction.[50] Finally, self-discipline in the sense of the rule of law applying comprehensively to the institutions of the European Union itself, elevated to the litmus test of constitutional status by the ECJ in their coining of the small-c word in *Les Verts*,[51] has remained vulnerable to the nonjusticiability or limited justiciability of certain areas of EU law, notably in the so-called flanking pillars of justice and home affairs and common foreign and security policy.

Take next the nonunitary political-institutional system. Patently, the European Union boasts its own specialized and well-established political system – Council, Commission, European Parliament, ECJ, and so on – and today that system also embraces a very broad normative scope, much wider that its original market-making remit under the 1957 Treaty of Rome, and since 2000 incorporating a Charter of Rights. Yet whereas the primary axis of division within the state polity tends to be based upon the range of governmental function – legislative, executive, or judicial – within a basically unitary polity, within the EU system it tends to be based upon the representation of diverse interests or "estates"[52] – European (Commission and ECJ), citizenry (European Parliament) and national (Council, European Council, national Parliaments, national courts). Reflecting this structural underpinning, the notion of nonunitary institutional balance vies with the idea of clearly demarcated separation of powers under some version of the unitary

---

[50] *See, e.g.,* Case C-224/01, Kobler v. Austria, 2003 E.C.R. I-10239.

[51] Case 294/83, Parti Ecologiste (Les Verts) v. European Parliament, 1986 E.C.R. 1339. For discussion, *see* Neil Walker, *Opening or Closure? The Constitutional Intimations of the ECJ, in* THE ECJ AFTER 50 YEARS (Miguel Maduro and Loic Azoulay eds., forthcoming). 2009.

[52] *See* Majone, *supra* note 45.

logic of parliamentarianism or presidentialism as the key operational principle of the political system.[53]

It is important to stress that the detailed strategy of refinement of the nonexclusive nature of the legal order and the nonunitary nature of the political-institutional system are controversial not only within the category of those favorable to a more state-like and so integration-friendly conception of these two constitutional frames as respectively more exclusive and more unitary but, as with the strategies of intensification and vindication, also between integration-friendly and integration-skeptic perspectives. So the perfectibility of the legal system and its protection from and trumping over external influence is a conflicted issue between different general conceptions of the European supranational polity, just as is the possibility of a shift away from a nonunitary and interest-based toward a more unitary political order. Indeed, many of the specific amendments to the existing treaty structure made in the constitutional text reflect this controversy and the compromises made in its settlement. For example, at the level of legal order, the statutory restatement of the principle of primacy,[54] and the extension of the ECJ's jurisdiction in the area of the third pillar (whose abandonment as a separate pillar was also proposed as part of the same process of assimilation and leveling up)[55] can be seen as moves toward a more exclusive sense of legal order, while the reiteration of the restraining principle of (textually) conferred powers[56] and the retention of a largely externalized constitutional amendment process[57] showed the continuing significance of a more relational and nonexclusive model.

So, too, at the level of the political-institutional system, we see a kind of double contestation – both about the balance of interests or estates and about the general appropriateness of a model based on the balance of interests.

---

[53] See, e.g., Paul Magnette, *Appointing and Censuring the European Commission: The Adaptation of Parliamentary Institutions to the Community Context*, 7 EUR. L.J. 292, 292–310 (2001).

[54] Treaty Establishing a Constitution for Europe, art. I-6, Dec. 16, 2004, 2004 O.J. (C 310/1) [hereinafter Constitutional Treaty]; and see similarly now Annex to the Treaty of Lisbon. Declarations concerning provisions of the Treaties, 17 – declaration concerning primacy.

[55] See generally Constitutional Treaty, pt. 3, tit. 6, ch. 1, sec. 1(5). And see similarly now under the Treaty of Lisbon; pt. 6, tit. 1, ch. 1, sec. 5 of the new Treaty on the Functioning of the European Union, May 9, 2008, 2008 O.J. (C 115/49) [hereinafter Treaty on the Functioning of EU], replacing with amendments the equivalent provisions on the ECJ in the EC Treaty, pt. 5, tit. 1, sec. 4.

[56] Constitutional Treaty, art. I-11. And see similarly now under the Treaty of Lisbon; Treaty on the Functioning of EU, new art. 3B

[57] Constitutional Treaty, art. IV-443. *And* see similarly now under the Treaty of Lisbon; Treaty on the Functioning of EU, amended art. 48.

On the one hand, many of the key tensions and controversial innovations concerned the shifting interest-based balance of power toward a stronger Council (and one, in voting terms, more dominated by the larger states),[58] and the empowerment of national parliaments,[59] and even some general limiting of supranational power in the name of the long constitutional pedigree of a Charter of Rights[60] and a competence catalog.[61] Yet on the other hand, this very model of struggle and balance between the estates is also in tension with the separate attempt to increase the responsibility of the Commission toward an elected European Parliament (by requiring the election of the Commission president to take account of the results of the parliamentary elections),[62] and to provide for a clearer demarcation between legislation and executive action more generally (particularly, through distinguishing instruments with different methods of promulgation and different effects),[63] within a more unitary separation of powers model of constitutional architecture.

What we may observe, in short, is a constitutional debate that takes place in the shadow of deep disputation. None of the approaches of intensification, nominalization, or refinement – or indeed the combined strategies that they allow, in particular intensification and nominalization versus refinement and nominalization – is neutral between different conceptions of constitutionalism. Intensification is based on a controversial understanding of the adaptability of a statist conception of the pedigree and motivation of political community to the supranational level. Nominalization turns on the range and resonance of the constitutional signifier. Refinement, despite its more modest profile, as we have seen, begs the very questions of the proper trajectory of a poststate polity that the larger question of high-intensity versus low-intensity constitutionalism raises more directly. But equally, the various forms of skepticism that we find on the other side of these positions are not neutral either. The denial of a strategy of intensification is a denial of the relevance and ambition of a more democratically grounded and

[58] Constitutional Treaty, art. I-25. *And* see similarly now under the Treaty of Lisbon; Treaty on the Functioning of EU, new art. 9A.
[59] Constitutional Treaty Protocol 1 on the role of national parliaments in the European Union. *And see similarly* now under the Treaty of Lisbon; Treaty on the Functioning of EU, new art. 8A.
[60] Constitutional Treaty, pt. 2. *And see similarly* now under the Treaty of Lisbon; Treaty on the Functioning of EU, amended art. 6.
[61] Constitutional Treaty, arts. I-12 to I-17. *And see similarly* now under the Treaty of Lisbon; Treaty on the Functioning of EU, pt. I, tit. 1.
[62] Constitutional Treaty, art. I-27. *And see similarly* now under the Treaty of Lisbon; Treaty on the Functioning of EU, new art. 9D(7).
[63] Constitutional Treaty, pt. 1, tit. 5, ch. 1. *And see similarly* now under the Treaty of Lisbon; Treaty on the Functioning of EU, pt. 6, tit. 1, ch. 2.

socially penetrative brand of constitutionalism at the EU level, whereas the denial of nominalization suggests both that there is a true test of constitutionalism and that the EU definitively fails it. Finally, to argue that refinement should be concerned only to retain and entrench those features that emphasize the historical sui generis quality of the European Union – the pronounced and distinctive nonexclusiveness of its legal order and the pronounced and distinctive nonunitary character of its political structure – is to affirm a highly conservative, supranational, constitutional culture, one that permits only modest claims even within those modest frames where it is well developed.

D. Framing the Future

We should not be surprised that such a deeply disputed and polyvalent constitutional project fell foul of the ratification process.[64] But what happens now? Clearly there is no compelling case for an ambitious strategy of intensification or of nominalization or of refinement and adjustment, just as there is no compelling case for any of the skeptical and conservative alternatives to these. None of these options, as we have seen, is constitutionally neutral in the sense of either standing above the constitutional struggle or alighting upon an incontestably one best constitutional way. The openness and internal variety of the constitutional idea simply does not allow for any such definitive conclusion.

Might we instead, then, simply adopt a pragmatic approach, and say that the constitutional process and substance that survives and prevails is by dint of that very fact the fittest for the purpose? There have been many points since the failure of the French and Dutch referenda where even such a limited ambition would have appeared to be in jeopardy. At various junctures it has been unclear that the atmosphere of deep disputation would produce anything other than recurrent blockage, with all process options capable of undermining the others but none – whether active initiative or default positions – strong enough to win out.[65] The signing of the Lisbon Treaty – a nominally nonconstitutional initiative that proceeded on the same intergovernmental basis as all of its predecessor treaties since the Treaty of Rome but retained the vast majority of the substantive constitutional strategies of adjustment and refinement of the legal order and institutional system previously found

---

[64] See, e.g., Renaud Dehousse, The Unmaking of a Constitution: Lessons from the European Referenda, 13 CONSTELLATIONS 151 (2006).

[65] See, e.g., JACQUES ZILLER, IL NUOVO TRATTATO EUROPEO (2007).

in the Constitutional Treaty[66] – provided some short-term reassurance to the pragmatic position, although, in light of the subsequent Irish no-vote, it remains very much an open question whether this new measure will survive even a ratification process downgraded and rendered almost (but, crucially, not quite!) (referendum proof)[67] by the very expedient of declining to call it a constitution.[68] But even if the pragmatic argument did gain some short-term succor, it can no more on that account claim the popular high ground than it can assume objective constitutional rectitude. For the successful promulgation of the new treaty is a function of the process chosen for its deliberation and promulgation – which itself was neither widely inclusive nor popularly endorsed. What we are left with, then, in the absence of a trumping argument in either objective or popular and intersubjective terms, is just the iterative play of claim and counterclaim, the unpredictable pattern of stalemate and strategic opening.

What, then, in these inhospitable circumstances, are the prospects and possible justifying grounds for the renewal of a big-C project of constitutional framing in the short or longer term? If such a case can be made at all, it must be as constructive as it is critical. It must be one that not only recognizes the inadequacies of all present candidate solutions and of the manner in which they vie with one another but that finds the seed of a deeper justification of a constitutional solution in the fact and character of that general inadequacy. Such a justification, it is submitted, is possible only if we can find something in the constitutional idea that somehow stands both as a critical diagnosis and as a means of transcendence of the present predicament. In turn, this requires us to refocus on the idea of constituent power under the third, self-authorizing frame, and to explore how this connects with and serves the idea of "democratic iteration."[69]

By "democratic iteration" we refer to the sense in which democracy as a principle cannot be exhausted by and limited to its present, and typically presupposed, institutional representations. If these representations are not available, or are no longer adequate, the idea of democratic self-authorization itself does not become redundant but must provide the catalyst for the discovery

---

[66] See supra notes 54–63.

[67] Following much pressure by other member states and the European institutions in the months after the referendum defeat in June 2008, the Irish government intends to hold a further referendum on the Treaty of Lisbon in the Autumn of 2009.

[68] See Neil Walker, Not the European Constitution, 15 MAASTRICHT J. EUR. & COMP. L. 71–78 (2008).

[69] See, e.g., SEYLA BENHABIB ET AL., ANOTHER COSMOPOLITANISM (2006), ch. 2.

of new and more appropriate institutional forms. This may apply, for example, in the case of an argument for national secession, or, conversely, for the merger of two states, cases where the demos must be reimagined – reiterated – before institutionalized forms of democracy can get going again. The case in pure democratic theory for a new democratically constitutive foundation for the European Union is similar. Again, we should recognize that the democratic principle remains relevant even if the existing institutional forms of democracy are inadequate, and, indeed, that it becomes all the more relevant just because these institutional forms are no longer adequate. Simply put, the range of autonomous authority available to the European Union is now so great that the case in democratic principle for a purely path-dependent, state-delegated and internationalist conception of democratic pedigree and form in the European Union is arguably no longer sufficient, and the need for a new and direct democratic grant of supranational authority alongside the continuing spheres of (undelegated) national democratic authority has become more profound.[70]

What is more, such an argument is not weakened by counterclaims either of irrelevance or of self-contradiction. As regards irrelevance, supranational democracy is not rendered beside the point by the fact that a significant amount of what the European Union does in policy and administrative detail, from competition regulation to the specification of food safety standards and the setting of transnational interest rates, is best done by experts and impartial players. Indeed, the case against quotidian democracy in these areas merely underlines the importance of a broader democratic imprimatur for and control over such a wholesale removal from popular control. A broadly engaged and deliberated constitutional founding serves such a function, independently of whatever additional argument might be made about the mobilization and settlement of a strong sense of societal integration and the role of constitutionalism in its fourth framing function as an instrument of such mobilization and settlement.

Equally, and crucially, as regards self-contradiction, the case for a democratic founding is not defeated by the mere fact of deep democratic disagreement over the proper constitutional form for Europe and its proper balance with other national constitutional forms. Rather, the argument from democratic iteration would hold that we have to find the optimal metapolitical container in Europe to focus our controversial debate on the proper

---

[70] *See further* Neil Walker, *Post-Constituent Constitutionalism, in* THE PARADOX OF CONSTITU-TIONALISM 247–68 (Martin Loughlin & Neil Walker eds., 2007).

constellation of political containers. And provided that, unlike the intensification strategy, it does not presume too much of the answer in advance, the taking of a big-*C* constitutional initiative as a way of providing that open-ended metapolitical container is preferable to a position that avoids the common question and represses controversy by simply reverting to the default of twenty-seven national constitutional constituencies.

None of this implies, however, that it can confidently be predicted that any future European constitution will suffer a better fate than its predecessor. Rather, three sets of difficulties impeding any fresh initiative in supranational constitutionalism may be identified.[71] The first difficulty is conceptual. We lack even an ideal understanding of the supranational conception of constituent power within a more relational postnational configuration. That is to say, if, against the skeptic, it can be demonstrated that European constituent power is not merely derivative of national constituent power, we nevertheless still must acknowledge the national legacy of its foundations and, alongside the newer supranational authority, the resilience of the original national constituent powers. The 'people' of second-order supranational understanding can never be just like the otherwise politically unencumbered and unmediated 'people' of our first-order state imaginary; the second-order people necessarily describes a compound structure. Various formulations in the aborted Constitutional Treaty hinted at these complex origins. In the preamble and article 1, "the citizens [singular] and States" were referred to as the ultimate authors, but elsewhere in the preamble the "peoples [plural] of Europe" are also invoked. And in more recent official communications concerning the constitution and the question of democratic renewal more generally, especially from the European Commission,[72] we often find the people reduced to the singular alongside the states. So what is emerging is a vague sense of a dual constituent power, and indeed regular references in political discourse to "dual legitimacy,"[73] but disagreement and uncertainly as to the identity of its components, and little sense of the relationship between the two. Unlike other pluralist group-based understandings of the ingredients of constituent

---

[71] *Id.*

[72] *See*, as just one of many examples, the frequent slippage between plural and singular in *A Constitution for Europe: Presentation to Citizens*, an information document produced by the Commission in the wake of the signing of the CT in 2003: European Commission, *A Constitution for Europe: Presentation to Citizens*, *available at* http://www.europa-kommissionen.dk/upload/application/9babda99/udl.pdf (last visited September 22, 2008).

[73] Not least by the president of the Constitutional Convention: *see, e.g.*, Valéry Giscard d'Estaing, *The Convention and the Future of Europe: Issues and Goals*, 1 INT'L J. CONST. L. 346 (2003).

power at the state level,[74] where the groups in question tend to belong to the same category or conceptual order (e.g., community of affinity, language, or territory), this is not true of states and people(s). How we forge a meaningful sense of constituent power out of such a hybrid of incommensurables – one that does not collapse into its component parts and/or presumptively favor one component over the other – remains a key puzzle.

The second difficulty is symbolic. While much has been invested in the idea of constitutionalism as a way of articulating and operationalizing constituent power, the sheer variety of ways in which constitutionalism is invoked suggests, as we have stressed, that it is a deeply and increasingly contested currency. The ability of constitutions to do the various kinds of symbolic work discussed here may be resilient and adaptable, but unlike the claims of the idea of democratic iteration they seek to serve, they are not timeless; the symbolic capital of constitutionalism is itself a contingent and precarious achievement of social construction manifesting implicit agreement that written constitutions can frame political community in the various ways we have suggested, including, most pertinently, providing a discursive frame for the very reflexive debate over the nature of the political community in question. But for how long can this conviction survive such a diversity of constitutional strategies, especially on the unfamiliar terrain of postnational constitutionalism?[75]

The third and most grounded difficulty is political and returns us to the practical dimension of the problem of deep disputability. Although support for a European constitution was – and may perhaps again be – generated from the critique of the anachronistic inadequacy of a state-based indirect foundation, states will not willingly divest themselves of authority – witness the retention of their amendment and ratification powers in the aborted Constitutional Treaty.[76] And even if they did, the difficulties of authenticating an alternative and uncontained constituent power are profound. At this point the conceptual puzzle of dual legitimacy set out above shades into a problem of political capability: Who decides who decides? becomes a deep problem

---

[74] *See, e.g.,* Tully, *supra* note 12 (on first nation constitutionalism); Simone Chambers, *Democracy, Popular Sovereignty, and Constitutional Legitimacy,* 11 CONSTELLATIONS 153 (2004) (on South Africa); Michel Rosenfeld, *Constitution-Making, Identity Building and Peaceful Transition to Democracy* 19 CARDOZO L. REV. 1891 (1998) (on Spain).

[75] On the exhaustion of constitutional language, *see, e.g.,* Ulrich Haltern, *Pathos and Patina: The Failure and Promise of Constitutionalism in the European Imagination,* 9 EUR. L.J. 14 (2003); Ladeur *supra* note 39.

[76] Constitutional Treaty, arts. IV-443 and IV- 447. And see also under the new Treaty of Lisbon; Treaty on the Functioning of EU, amended art. 48.

of initiative.[77] We see this even in some of the failed attempts to resuscitate the first Constitutional Treaty. In response to the invitation of the European Council in the summer of 2005 – renewed the following year[78] – to undertake a period of reflection on the future of the constitutional project in the light of the referendum no votes in France and the Netherlands, many institutional efforts simply disappeared into the authority vacuum. To give but one example: although, on behalf of the (people) of Europe, the European Parliament sought during the first months of the reflection period to seize the revivalist initiative, many of the national parliaments, acting on behalf of the (peoples), quickly refused this initiative.[79]

What is more, even if the luxury of a duly ratified text were available, the problem of foundations would not disappear. A successful constitution is not just an open set of possibilities for the fluid negotiation of the constituencies represented in the constituent power but also a textually grounded set of institutional facts. And it is possible to use constructivist techniques to develop and sustain the idea of a distinctive supranational self-authorization only to the extent that these textual reference points provide the appropriate cues. But as we have already noted, the aborted Constitutional Treaty, and indeed any conceivable successor, have a textual content reflecting a complex compromise that does not offer an unqualifiedly positive basis for promoting and sustaining a distinctive sense of authorship. That is to say, the deep structural controversy over the very idea of postnational constituent power left its mark on the text just as much as it subsequently did on the process of its adoption, and we can envisage similar problems with any future explicitly constitutional text. So while we find modest but to some extent innovative recognition of the European people as drafters (in the Convention design), as subjects (citizens)[80] and as editors (through the involvement of the Convention mechanism in any further major amendment),[81] and some strengthening of their role through Parliament as legislators,[82] the people are neither the final authors,[83] nor even invoked as the narrators of this text.[84]

---

[77] Maduro, *supra* note 22.
[78] Presidency Conclusions, Brussels European Council ¶¶ 42–49 (June 15–16, 2006).
[79] *See, e.g.,* Mark Beunderman, *National Parliaments Rebuff MEPs on Constitution,* Jan. 17, 2006, *available at* http://euobserver.com/9/20700.
[80] Constitutional Treaty, art. I-10; though this merely repeated existing treaty provisions under EC Treaty, arts. 17–22.
[81] Constitutional Treaty, art. IV-443.
[82] Constitutional Treaty, art I-20; *see also* arts. I-45 to I-52.
[83] Treaty on the Functioning of EU, art. 48 (intergovernmental conference required to prepare final text); Constitutional Treaty, art. IV-447 (requirement of unanimous national ratification).
[84] Again the states, or high contracting parties; see preamble to Constitutional Treaty.

Do these sobering thoughts mean that, in conclusion, we are forced after all to answer the question of self-authorizing constituent power in the European Union in the negative? I do not believe this to be the case. The debate over the first constitution may not have created the practical conditions for its own success, but it has, paradoxically, succeeded in encouraging its indefinite recurrence. One consequence of the emphasis upon posing the constitutional question in terms of achievement over the first fifty years and the vindication of that achievement, with such powerful reference being made to the preconstitutional acquis, is that failure has been as apt as success would have been in leaving that preconstitutional acquis looking inadequate, while simultaneously making it more difficult to undertake further institutional change. That is to say, if one message of nonratification was to question the basic reaffirmation of the acquis, another and equally powerful message was to endorse the idea that the acceptability of further large-scale reform of the European Union could never again be taken for granted, and if attempted again would demand the same level of popular scrutiny as succeeded in demonstrating its unacceptability last time round. This, indeed, is why the like-for-like replacement Lisbon Treaty, even if it ultimately completes its reduced ratification process, is trapped in such a narrow bind. On the one hand, its success may offer a partial homologation of the reprocessed substance of the constitutional treaty, provided the modest and largely conservative character of that substance continues to be stressed. On the other hand, as is indicated by the deafening silence over further treaty reform, for the first time since the Single European Act twenty years ago, the European Union is loath to style itself as in the midst of a "semi-permanent" revision process, for to do so would inevitably reawaken the unwelcome specter of the kind of process it has just purported to abandon.[85]

To make the same point more positively, we may suggest that simply by launching the constitutional initiative once, the European Union has demonstrated sufficient common resolution and generated sufficient common expectations to deny to itself in any future scenario of significant reform any preconstitutional or nonconstitutional comfort zone. But this is merely to indicate an opening to return to the constitutional drawing board, not to show that this opening will be taken. What will in fact transpire when the calls for further major institutional change do eventually come – as they inevitably will given the continuing and deep-rooted structural tensions affecting both

[85] Bruno de Witte, *The Closest Thing to a Constitutional Conversation in Europe: The Semi-Permanent Treaty Revision Process, in* Convergence and Divergence in European Public Law 39–57 (Paul Beaumont, Carole Lyons & Neil Walker eds., 2002).

the legal order and political system frames – remains obscure. Indeed, whether that eventuality will provide the impetus for serious reengagement with the idea of a supranational constituent power, or whether it will provoke an existential crisis for the European Union beyond our known or imagined capacity of constitutional framing, is perhaps the deepest question surrounding the European Union's uncertain future.

The World Trade Organization

7. The Politics of International Constitutions: The Curious Case of the World Trade Organization

JEFFREY L. DUNOFF

I. Introduction

Not terribly long ago, conventional wisdom held that ours was an "age of rights."[1] But perhaps ages lack the staying power that they used to, for we now seem to be entering an "age of international constitutions" – at least, if legal scholarship is to be believed. In addition to this volume, a raft of new books address the topic,[2] and international law scholarship seems fixated on analyzing and critiquing various constitutional orders said to be found in diverse international legal regimes.[3]

The constitutional turn has been particularly pronounced in writing about international trade,[4] with much of this literature detailing particular visions

---

[1] Louis Henkin, The Age of Rights ix (1990).

[2] See, e.g., Vicki C. Jackson, Constitutional Engagement in a Transnational Era (2009); Jan Klabbers, Anne Peters & Geir Ulfstein, The Constitutionalization of International Law (2009); Transnational Constitutionalism (Nicholas Tsagourias ed., 2007); Constitutionalism, Multilevel Trade Governance and Social Regulation (Christian Joerges & Ernst-Ulrich Petersmann eds., 2006).

[3] See, e.g., Symposium: Rethinking Constitutionalism in an Era of Globalization and Privatization, 6 Int'l J. Const. L. 371 (2008).

[4] Important contributions include Joel Trachtman's contribution to this volume and Richard H. Steinberg, Judicial Lawmaking at the WTO: Discursive, Constitutional and Political Constraints, 98 Am. J. Int'l L. 247 (2004); Neil Walker, The EU and the WTO: Constitutionalism in a New Key, in The EU and the WTO: Legal and Constitutional Issues 31 (Gráinne

This chapter extends ideas contained in *Constitutional Conceits: The WTO's 'Constitution' and the Discipline of International Law*, 17 European Journal of International Law 647 (2006). Earlier versions of this chapter were presented at the *Ruling the World* book workshop at Temple Law School, a faculty workshop at Harvard Law School, and at a Law and Public Affairs Seminar at the Woodrow Wilson School at Princeton. I am extremely grateful to participants at these events and to Bobby Ahdieh, Bill Alford, Kristen Boon, Ryan Goodman, Bob Keohane, Ernst-Ulrich Petersmann, Mark Rahdert, Kim Lane Scheppele, Joel Trachtman, and Mark Tushnet, for helpful critiques and suggestions.

of the development, nature and features of the World Trade Organization's (WTO) constitution. These writings presuppose precisely the question this paper addresses: is the trade regime properly understood as a constitutional entity? As demonstrated in this chapter, neither WTO texts nor practice support this understanding.

The curious disjunction between trade scholarship and trade practice presents a puzzle: why would prominent trade scholars devote their energies to debating the WTO's (nonexistent) constitutional features? As developed more fully below, the leading scholarly accounts of the WTO's constitution highlight the trade regime's increasing legalization, but underplay or elide the effect that constitutionalization would have on the nature and quality of world trade politics. Stated more starkly, the constitutional turn in much trade scholarship can be understood as a mechanism for withdrawing controversial and potentially destabilizing issues from the parry and thrust of ordinary politics to a less inclusive constitutional domain. Paradoxically, however, the call for constitutionalization has sparked precisely the contestation and politics that it seeks to preempt. Hence, one goal of this chapter is to illuminate the self-defeating nature of the constitutional turn in trade scholarship.

But this analysis raises an even larger puzzle: if there is no world trade constitution, and if calls for such a constitution trigger the very politics that constitutionalism seeks to avoid, why do international trade scholars continue to employ constitutional discourse? Exploration of this question will lead us to deeper and more troubling questions about the current status of the discipline of international law.

International legal scholarship is in a period of heightened doctrinal and methodological ferment. This time of disciplinary critique, confusion, and rethinking reflects, in part, diverse aspects of the current geopolitical landscape which have highlighted persistent concerns over international law's relevance and efficacy. In this paper, I wish to consider whether the constitutional turn can be understood as a reaction to this context. More specifically, might the scholars' invocation of constitutional discourse be understood as a response to deep disciplinary anxieties about international law's perceived marginality and lack of normative force? Could the use of constitutional discourse at the WTO – and elsewhere in international law – be a rhetorical strategy designed to invest international law with the power and authority that domestic constitutional structures and norms possess?

de Búrca & Joanne Scott eds., 2001); Robert Howse & Kalypso Nicolaïdis, *Legitimacy and Global Governance: Why Constitutionalizing the WTO Is a Step Too Far*, in EFFICIENCY, EQUITY, AND LEGITIMACY: THE MULTILATERAL TRADING SYSTEM AT THE MILLENNIUM 227 (Roger B. Porter et al. eds., 2001).

To explore these issues, this chapter proceeds as follows. Part II examines the WTO's constitutional status in light of the functional analysis of international constitutionalization developed in the introduction to this volume. Part III turns from the WTO to writings about the WTO. It reviews the three leading understandings of the WTO's constitution developed in trade scholarship. These conceptions understand the WTO's constitution as institutional architecture, as the privileging of a set of normative values, and as a process of judicial mediation among conflicting norms, respectively. Part III then examines whether any of the leading conceptions of the WTO's constitution find significant expression in WTO law or practice. Part IV discusses whether there are commonalities among the apparently divergent understandings of the WTO's constitution. It explores whether the various constitutional visions can be understood as standing in opposition to an expansive and inclusive vision of international trade politics. Given the disjunction between institutional practice and trade scholarship, Part V examines three different potential explanations for why leading scholars might analyze the WTO through a constitutionalist lens. It explores the allure of constitutional discourse and suggests that the constitutional turn may reflect a disciplinary anxiety over international law's current status and role. Part VI briefly outlines some inquiries that future scholarship in this area might pursue. A short conclusion follows.

II. Is the WTO a Constitutionalized Regime?

Given the scholarly attention devoted to constitutionalism at the WTO, it is appropriate to inquire into the nature, scope, and features of the organization's supposed constitution, or processes of constitutionalization. But any such inquiry immediately confronts a curious difficulty. Unlike in the European Union, at the WTO there has not been – and is not currently – an ongoing political process of crafting a constitutional instrument, nor is there any likelihood of such a process in the foreseeable future. There is no constitutional court, no constitutional assembly, and no readily identifiable constitutional moment.

Moreover, on their face, the Uruguay Round Agreements creating the WTO lack virtually all of the features commonly associated with constitutions and constitutional entities. Thus, for example, the instruments establishing the WTO do not expressly announce themselves to be a constitution for world trade; they do not create institutions empowered to create norms that are legally binding upon WTO members; they do not explicitly set out a system of separation of powers or checks and balances among the trade regimes' various institutional components; they do not explicitly enshrine any fundamental rights; they make no claim that the norms they contain are hierarchically superior to other international norms; and the agreements do not have a formal stability that is greater than that enjoyed by ordinary international legislation. Thus, the instruments creating the trade regime lack virtually all of the features that are normally associated with constitutionalized regimes.

The quest to identify and analyze the WTO's constitution fares little better when we shift our attention from constitutional features to constitutional functions. As explained in the introduction to this volume, international constitutional norms serve three primary functions, which we have labeled "enabling," "constraining," and "supplemental" constitutionalization.[5] Applying this framework to the WTO reveals little evidence that, at present, the trade system should properly be considered a constitutionalized regime.

A. Enabling Constitutionalization

Enabling constitutional norms authorize or facilitate the production of ordinary international law. They can do so by allocating authority over certain subject areas or decisions to specific bodies, or by creating bodies that can promulgate legally binding norms. Important examples include the treaties creating the European Union, which create institutions and set forth rules for the production of secondary EU legislation, and international norms empowering the Office of the UN High Commissioner for Refugees to issue rulings on individuals' refugee status.

The WTO lacks a strong form of enabling constitutional norms. Notably, the WTO agreements neither create a world trade legislature nor vest autonomous legislative or regulatory authority in a WTO body. Instead, although the WTO treaties provide for majority vote in some circumstances, as a matter of long-standing practice the WTO operates by consensus. As a result, there is virtually no capacity for secondary legislation, and small numbers of states can and do block significant political and legislative initiatives. Joel Trachtman discusses why the consensus system is theoretically problematic; recent developments dramatically illustrate its practical difficulties.[6]

To be sure, it would be an exaggeration to claim that the WTO is wholly without the capacity to generate normative claims upon member states. For example, there is an extensive system of WTO Councils and Committees,

---

[5] Jeffrey L. Dunoff & Joel P. Trachtman, *A Functional Approach to International Constitutionalization*, Chapter 1 in this volume.

[6] *See, e.g.*, Stephen Castle & Mark Landler, *After 7 Years, Talks Collapse on World Trade*, N.Y. Times, July 30, 2008 at p. 1.

and these have proved useful for creating consensus around disputed issues and reaching informal understandings. Indeed, in at least some respects, these informal mechanisms have been more effective at generating shared understandings and at resolving certain types of problems than the WTO's more formalized processes.[7] On balance, however, there is little doubt that the WTO's legislative capacity is underdeveloped, in comparison either with the WTO's highly developed dispute resolution system or with the legislative capacity found in some other international organizations.

Given the lack of legislative capacity, it is instructive to examine the WTO's powerful dispute settlement processes. The WTO has a highly legalized dispute system, and there can be little doubt that WTO dispute panels and the Appellate Body (AB) occasionally engage in judicial law making. Sometimes dispute panels fill gaps in treaty language or clarify textual ambiguities; on other occasions the law-making function has been more expansive.[8] Tracht-man observes that to the extent the WTO's dispute settlement mechanism is "authorized, explicitly or implicitly, to interpret or craft . . . rules of negative integration, th[is] authorization may be understood as a kind of enabling constitutionalization."[9]

However, to the extent that the WTO's dispute system possesses elements of enabling constitutionalization, it bears noting that these elements are highly constrained. First, the dispute system possesses no explicit authority to craft rules of negative integration. To the contrary, WTO panels are explicitly denied the authority to interpret or craft rules of negative integration. The relevant treaty text expressly provides that panels "cannot add to or diminish the rights and obligations provided for in the covered agreements."[10] Second, to the extent that panels are perceived as engaged in law making, this activity often triggers strong criticism from WTO members and efforts to constrain dispute panels.[11] For example, as discussed in Part III.C. below, members

---

[7] *See, e.g.,* Jeffrey L. Dunoff, *Lotus Eaters: The Varietals Dispute, the SPS Agreement, and WTO Dispute Resolution, in* HEALTH REGULATION IN THE WTO 153 (George Bermann & Petros Mavroidis eds., 2006) (comparing ability of WTO's Sanitary and Phytosanitary Committee to resolve food safety disputes with AB's ability to do so).

[8] Steinberg, *supra* note 4.

[9] Joel P. Trachtman, *Constitutional Economics of the World Trade Organization,* in this volume Chapter 8.

[10] Understanding on Rules and Procedures Governing the Settlement of Disputes, Apr. 15, 1994, Marrakesh Agreement Establishing the World Trade Organization, Annex 2, arts. 3.2 & 19.2.

[11] As Steinberg notes, during the first eighteen months of negotiations over dispute settlement reform, "concern about instances of or proposed solutions to judicial lawmaking by WTO panels or the Appellate Body had been raised seventy seven times by representatives of fifty-five members." Steinberg, *supra* note 4, at 256. In addition, confidential notes from meetings

sometimes seek to override controversial panel or AB decisions, and powerful states, including the United States, have advanced proposals designed to rein in dispute panels' powers. These political pressures, as well as the textual constraints identified earlier, constrain the ability of dispute panels to make new law. On balance, WTO dispute settlement represents only a weak form of enabling constitutionalization.

B. Constraining Constitutionalization

Constraining constitutionalism refers to international norms and mechanisms that limit the production of ordinary international law. International norms that are hierarchically superior to other international norms are a good example. Thus, *jus cogens* norms limit the production of ordinary international law, as states cannot lawfully enter into agreements that violate such norms.

There is little in WTO texts or practice to suggest that trade norms are hierarchically superior to international legal norms deriving from other sources. Indeed, no provisions to this effect are found in any WTO treaty. In this respect, the WTO agreements can be usefully contrasted with the UN Charter, which explicitly provides that its provisions trump inconsistent terms found in other treaties. Similarly, WTO panels and the AB have carefully avoided any claim that trade norms are superior to other international law norms. This doctrinal approach can be contrasted with that of, say, the European Court of Human Rights, which has stated that human rights provisions of the European Convention trump inconsistent norms found in other treaties, and the European Court of Justice, which has held that "the obligations imposed by an international agreement cannot have the effect of prejudicing the constitutional principles of the EC Treaty."[12]

Fundamental rights are another form of constraining constitutionalism. Although there has been substantial debate over whether the WTO should include a social charter, the WTO currently contains no explicit provisions protecting fundamental rights. Similarly, review mechanisms are frequently used as a form of constraining constitutionalization. These mechanisms review ordinary international law to ensure its consistency with constitutional rules and values, and hence constrain ordinary international law. Although the WTO has a very highly developed system of review, it is not a form of constitutional review. That is, WTO panels review the conformity of domestic measures with ordinary WTO norms; they do not review the legality of

---

of the DSU Reform Group "reveal that judicial lawmaking was considered at almost every meeting during the period for which notes are available." *Id.*

[12] Kadi v. Council, C-402/05 P, at para. 285 (Sept. 3, 2008).

acts by WTO councils, committees, or other bodies to ensure their consistency with other WTO norms. Hence, other than the constraints on panel lawmaking discussed above, there are few, if any, examples of constraining constitutionalization at the WTO.

C. Supplemental Constitutionalization

The third function of international constitutionalization is supplemental constitutionalization. These international norms are produced in response to concerns that international developments threaten domestic constitutional arrangements and values. Hence, these norms supplement domestic constitutional orders that seem unable to adequately protect values traditionally addressed by domestic constitutional law.

Although many critique the WTO for addressing various policy issues formerly addressed on the domestic plane, such as environmental or food safety laws, these issues are generally not considered constitutional issues on the domestic plane. Thus, because the WTO does not threaten domestic constitutional orders, there is virtually no pressure for, and no examples of, supplemental constitutionalization at the WTO.

In short, along virtually every constitutional metric discussed in the introduction to this volume, the WTO represents, at best, a very weakly constitutionalized order. Nevertheless, constitutional discourse has moved to the center of trade scholarship. One purpose of this chapter is to explore the reasons for this disconnect between trade scholarship and practice. Before doing so, however, it will be useful to briefly review some of this scholarship so that we might better understand what scholars mean when they discuss the WTO's "constitution."

III. Competing Conceptions of the WTO's Constitution in Trade Scholarship

Despite the texts and practice discussed above, constitutional discourse has moved to the center of academic writing about the WTO.[13] This scholarship uses the terms *constitution, constitutionalism,* and *constitutionalization* in different ways. Nevertheless, it is possible to characterize the most prominent of this scholarship as falling into one of three different categories. As described immediately below, the most influential trade scholarship understands the WTO constitution to consist of (1) the WTO's institutional architecture, (2) a

[13] As noted subsequently, a handful of scholars have discussed constitutionalism at the WTO for many years. However, the level of attention to and political and scholarly salience of constitutional arguments have greatly increased in recent years.

set of normative commitments, or (3) a process of judicial mediation among conflicting values. However, as we shall see, none of these understandings finds significant support in WTO texts or practice.

A. Institutional Architecture as Constitution

One influential strand of trade scholarship understands the WTO constitution primarily in institutional terms, and the most prominent advocate of this understanding is Professor John Jackson.[14] As Jackson's constitutional vision has been thoroughly and ably discussed elsewhere,[15] I offer here only a very brief summary of his arguments.

In *Restructuring the GATT System*,[16] Jackson set out the case for conferring a constitutional status upon, and creating a constitutional structure for, the international trade system. Jackson argued that a constitutional structure would serve as a pragmatic means of addressing the General Agreement on Tariffs and Trade's (GATT) famous "birth defects," including the provisional nature of GATT obligations, a losing party's ability to veto adverse dispute settlement reports, and the doctrinal and practical difficulties resulting from multiple GATT agreements and understandings.

In addition to these characteristically pragmatic arguments, Jackson advanced a striking historical-descriptive – and normative – claim: "To a large degree the history of civilization may be described as a gradual evolution from a power oriented approach, in the state of nature, towards a rule oriented approach."[17] Jackson argued that, in the economic context, only a rule-oriented approach could provide the security and predictability necessary for decentralized international markets to function. Jackson claimed that this new rule-based approach could best occur through a constitution creating a new international organization – the WTO.

Jackson's post–Uruguay Round writings continue to focus on the theme of institutional architecture as constitution. In recent years, Jackson has critiqued the WTO's institutional structure, focusing on the strengths and limitations of the WTO's innovative dispute resolution system and on the

---

[14] Constitutional arguments run through much of Jackson's international trade scholarship. For a sampling, *see, e.g.,* JOHN H. JACKSON, THE WORLD TRADE ORGANIZATION: CONSTITUTION AND JURISPRUDENCE (1998); JOHN H. JACKSON, RESTRUCTURING THE GATT SYSTEM (1990); JOHN H. JACKSON, WORLD TRADE AND THE LAW OF GATT (1969); John H. Jackson, *The WTO "Constitution" and Proposed Reform: Seven "Mantras" Revisited,* 4 J. INT'L ECON. L. 67 (2001); John H. Jackson, *The Birth of the GATT-MTN System: A Constitutional Appraisal,* 12 LAW & POL. INT'L BUS. 21 (1980).

[15] *See, e.g., A Tribute to John Jackson,* 20 MICH. J. INT'L. L. 95 (1999).

[16] JACKSON, RESTRUCTURING THE GATT SYSTEM, *supra* note 14.

[17] *Id.* at 52.

institutional obstacles to rule making at the WTO. While Jackson's immediate concerns have, of course, shifted over time, and he sometimes uses the terms *constitution* and *constitutionalism* in different ways, as a general matter his writings continue to focus on questions of the trade regime's institutional architecture.

However, although the WTO does have a complex institutional structure, it does not have a highly constitutionalized structure. Indeed, the leading AB report discussing the WTO's institutional architecture clearly rejects a constitutional vision or understanding of this institutional structure.

The most prominent dispute in this regard is India–Quantitative Restrictions on Imports of Agricultural, Textile, and Industrial Products (India-QRs).[18] That dispute involved a challenge to certain trade measures imposed, India claimed, for balance-of-payments purposes. India argued that the panel had only limited competence to examine the issue, as "jurisdiction over this matter [had] been explicitly assigned" to other WTO bodies, notably the Balance of Payments (BOP) Committee and the General Council. More broadly, India argued that a principle of institutional balance mandated that the dispute panel adopt a limited and deferential role lest it upset "the distribution of powers between the judicial and the political organs of the WTO."[19]

In advancing these arguments, India urged the AB to adopt an understanding of the WTO architecture akin to a separation of powers understanding of domestic governmental systems. Indeed, India explicitly invoked domestic separation of powers systems and argued that

> the drafters of the WTO Agreement created a complex institutional structure under which various bodies are empowered to take binding decisions on related matters. These bodies must cooperate to achieve the objectives of the WTO, and can only do so if each exercises its competence with due regard to the competence of all other bodies. In order to preserve a proper institutional balance between the judicial and the political organs of the WTO with regard to matters relating to balance-of-payments restrictions, review of the justification of such measures must be left to the relevant political organs.[20]

Notably, the AB flatly rejected India's approach. After reviewing the relevant WTO texts and prior panel reports, the AB concluded, "India failed to advance any convincing arguments in support of a principle of institutional balance that requires panels to refrain from reviewing the justification of balance-of-payments restrictions." Instead, the AB relied upon the text of the Dispute Settlement Understanding and a footnote to the BOP Understanding that explicitly provided for dispute settlement mechanisms to be available "with

[18] WT/DS90/AB/R (Aug. 23, 1999).   [19] Id.
[20] Id.

respect to any matters arising from the application of restrictive import measures taken for balance of payments purposes."[21]

In one sense, of course, the India-QR report addresses issues at the heart of a Jacksonian constitutional vision: the relationships among different parts of the WTO's institutional architecture. However, what is more significant for current purposes is the AB's explicit and unequivocal rejection of the invitation to adopt a theory of separation of powers, or to articulate anything approaching a constitutional theory concerning the relationships between the WTO's political and judicial organs. The AB decision turns on a close textual analysis of a footnote, and the AB does not understand – or at least declare – itself to be articulating a constitutional vision of the relationships among coordinate branches of an overarching institution or to be policing the jurisdictional lines that separate those coordinate branches.[22] In short, there is little to suggest that relevant WTO actors understand the organization's institutional structure in constitutional terms.

B. The Constitutional Entrenchment of Normative Values

A second strand of scholarship views constitutionalization at the WTO as consisting of the entrenchment and privileging of a set of normative commitments. Perhaps the most prominent advocate of this position is Professor Ernst-Ulrich Petersmann.[23] For Petersmann, constitutionalism has less to do

---

[21] Id.

[22] To be sure, on occasion the AB does evidence a concern over horizontal division-of-powers issues. For example, the AB refused to address the sequencing issue that arose in the Bananas litigation and indicated that the issue should be addressed by the WTO's political organs. But statements like these are a far cry from setting out a full-blown constitutional theory of how the various entities that make up the WTO interrelate.

[23] An incomplete listing of Petersmann's writings linking constitutionalism with international economic law includes *Multilevel Trade Governance in the WTO Requires Multilevel Constitutionalism, in* Joerges & Petersmann, *supra* note 2, at 5; *Justice in International Economic Law? From the "International Law among States" to "International Integration Law" and "Constitutional Law,"* 1 GLOBAL COMMUNITY Y.B. INT'L L. & JURIS. 105 (2006); *Time for a United Nations "Global Compact" for Integrating Human Rights into the Law of Worldwide Organizations: Lessons from European Integration,* 13 EUR. J. INT'L L. 621 (2002) [hereinafter Petersmann, *Time for a United Nations "Global Compact"*]; *The WTO Constitution and the Millennium Round, in* NEW DIRECTIONS IN INTERNATIONAL ECONOMIC LAW: ESSAYS IN HONOR OF JOHN H. JACKSON 111 (Marco Bronckers & Reinhard Quick eds., 2000); *The WTO Constitution and Human Rights,* 3 J. INT'L ECON L. 19 (2000); *Constitutionalism and International Organizations,* 17 Nw. J. INT'L L. & BUS. 398 (1996) [hereinafter Petersmann, *Constitutionalism and International Organizations*]; *How to Reform the UN System? Constitutionalism, International Law, and International Organizations,* 10 LEIDEN J. INT'L L. 421 (1997) [hereinafter Petersmann, *How to Reform the UN System*]; *How to Constitutionalize the United Nations? Lessons from the "International Economic Law Revolution," in* LIBER AMICORUM GUNTHER JAENICKE 313 (1998) [hereinafter Petersmann, *How to Constitutionalize the UN System*]; CONSTITUTIONAL FUNCTIONS AND CONSTITUTIONAL PROBLEMS OF INTERNATIONAL ECONOMIC LAW (1991).

with institutional arrangements than it does with the elevation of a set of normative values designed to protect against both government overreaching and shortsighted decisions by the population: constitutions consist of precommitments to norms that "effectively constitute and limit citizen rights and government powers."[24]

Constitutions are thus premised upon a series of normative values, including, inter alia, the rule of law, substantive rules that constrain governments by subjecting government actions that restrain "individual freedoms (including the right to import and export)" to the tests of "necessity" and "proportionality,"[25] and horizontal and vertical separation-of-powers principles designed to produce "rule-oriented rather than power-oriented settlement of international disputes."[26] Finally and, for Petersmann, most importantly, constitutional systems recognize and protect inalienable human rights, 'market freedoms,' and other fundamental rights as nonderogable limitations on government powers.

Perhaps most controversially, Petersmann has argued that economic freedoms lie at the core of his conception of fundamental human rights. Petersmann emphasizes the fundamental importance of "economic freedoms" such as the freedom "to produce and exchange goods," and he argues that "market freedoms are indispensable" for human autonomy and self-determination.[27] Repeatedly, Petersmann praises European integration law for "fully recogniz[ing]" that "transnational 'market freedoms' for movements of goods, services, persons, capital and related payments" are judicially enforceable "transnational citizen rights,"[28] and he urges the WTO and other international organizations to follow Europe's lead in this regard.

Thus, Petersmann's understanding of constitutionalism can be sharply distinguished from Jackson's. While Petersmann does not ignore institutional issues, his understanding of constitutionalism is centered on a precommitment to the elevation and protection of certain normative values. Human rights are central to these values, which in Petersmann's understanding should encompass economic rights – including the freedom to trade.

However, the WTO treaties do not enshrine a series of fundamental rights, much less a fundamental freedom to trade. The Uruguay Round Agreements

---

[24] *Id.* at 13.

[25] Petersmann, *Constitutionalism and International Organizations*, at 431.

[26] Petersmann, *How to Reform the UN System*, at 427. Thus, Petersmann shares some of Jackson's focus on institutional architecture.

[27] Ernst-Ulrich Petersmann, *How to Constitutionalize International Law and Foreign Policy for the Benefit of Civil Society?* 20 MICH. J. INT'L L. 1, 17 (1998).

[28] Ernst-Ulrich Petersmann, *Theories of Justice, Human Rights, and the Constitution of International Markets*, 37 LOY. L.A. L. REV. 407, 457 (2003).

are silent on this question. Although the existence of such a freedom has never been squarely presented in a WTO dispute, the panel report in the Section 301 dispute provides the most relevant discussion of whether the WTO establishes an individual freedom to trade. In a passage obviously intended to distinguish the WTO's legal order from the EU's, where Community law can create individual rights, the panel stated:

> Neither the GATT nor the WTO has so far been interpreted by GATT/WTO institutions as a legal order producing direct effect [i.e., as creating legally enforceable rights and obligations for individuals]. Following this approach, the GATT/WTO did not create a new legal order the subjects of which comprise both . . . [m]embers and their nationals.[29]

The panel goes on to state that "it would be entirely wrong to consider that the position of individuals is of no relevance to the GATT/WTO legal matrix," for a primary purpose of the GATT/WTO is "to produce market conditions" that permit "individual activity to flourish."[30] The panel therefore opines that it may be convenient "in the GATT/WTO legal order to speak not of the principle of direct effect but of the principle of indirect effect."[31]

While the Section 301 report is surely an important acknowledgment that international trade occurs primarily among private parties and that the system therefore serves the interests of these parties, it rejects any theory that the primary WTO texts create individual rights,[32] let alone a judicially enforceable freedom to trade. No other WTO panel or AB report has discussed the "direct effect" (or indirect effect) of WTO law on individuals or an individual freedom to trade. In brief, neither WTO texts nor dispute panels or the AB has adopted the freedom to trade that Petersmann urges.

C. Constitutionalization through Judicial Mediation

Perhaps the most common conception of constitutionalization found in the literature highlights the mediating and norm-generating elements of WTO dispute settlement as the engine of constitutional development. This strand of thought envisions an incremental, common law form of constitutionalism – not the product of a constitutional moment, but rather the result of a gradual and incremental judicially led process.

---

[29] *United States – Sections 301–310 of the Trade Act of 1974*, WT/DS152/R, para. 7.72 (Jan. 27, 2000). The panel report was not appealed.

[30] *Id.* at para. 7.73.   [31] *Id.* at para. 7.78.

[32] Some less important WTO texts do confer rights upon private parties. For example, the Agreement on Preshipment Inspection provides that private party exporters shall have access to procedures to appeal decisions made by preshipment inspection entities.

Thus, for example, Professor Deborah Cass argues that the WTO's AB "is the dynamic force behind constitution-building by virtue of its capacity to generate constitutional norms and structures during dispute resolution."[33] Cass argues that the AB generates these constitutional norms through four distinct processes: the AB borrows constitutional rules, principles, and doctrines from other systems and amalgamates them into the AB's own case law; the AB generates rules on burdens of proof, fact-finding, and participation by nonstate actors that "are constitutive of a new system of law"; the AB addresses issues traditionally viewed as within national constitutional processes, such as public health; and the AB "associates itself with deeper constitutional values" in the ways that it carefully crafts and justifies its decisions. Cass argues that, taken in the aggregate, these four features comprise the mechanisms through which "the emerging jurisprudence of the WTO is beginning to develop a set of rules and principles which share some of the characteristics of constitutional law; and that this in turn is what contributes to the constitutionalization of international trade law."[34] In short, for Cass, the AB is "building . . . a constitutional system by judicial interpretations emanating from the judicial dispute resolution institution."[35]

By way of example, Cass highlights the AB's "choice of fact-finding method" as illustrating how the AB advances the "constitutionalization process." Her argument rests upon the premise that different modes of fact-finding – such as inquisitorial or adversarial – have deep implications for the legal system as a whole; thus, for Cass, "fact-finding rules can code for one form of system characterization."[36] Cass argues that, in a line of cases, the AB has generated a "procedurally relatively informal system whereby information can be elicited from a variety of sources, and the tribunal is not hemmed in by any strict rules of evidence and procedure."[37] In this regard, Cass places special emphasis on the AB report in the Shrimp-Turtle dispute, which held that panels have authority to accept information from non-state actors. She notes that this decision "lend[s] credence to the constitutionalization claim and ha[s] significance from a democratic and constitutional design perspective."[38] It does so, in part, by potentially expanding the participants in the trade system

---

[33] Deborah Z. Cass, The "Constitutionalization" of International Trade Law: Judicial Norm-Generation as the Engine of Constitutional Development in International Trade, 12 Eur. J. Int'l L. 39, 42 (2001). Cass expanded and updated her arguments in The Constitutionalization of the World Trade Organization (2005).

[34] Id. at 52. Cass is careful not to argue that these four features automatically make a system constitutional. Rather, it is that the AB is generating "constitutional-like" doctrine and that this doctrine is being understood in the literature as constitutional in nature.

[35] Id. at 52.   [36] Id. at 60.

[37] Id. at 60.   [38] Id. at 61.

beyond states to corporations, nongovernmental organizations (NGOs), and civil society. This increased participation, in turn, may increase the perceived levels of the legitimacy and fairness of the trade system.

However, Cass's arguments substantially overstate the ability of the AB to generate new norms. As noted above, WTO texts and various formal and informal pressures limit the AB's law-making abilities. These pressures are particularly pronounced when the AB approaches issues that may have 'constitutional' dimensions. Hence, one of the key examples Cass relies upon to illustrate "the way the[AB's] decisions herald a constitutionalization process" actually highlights the severe constraints on the AB's ability to play this role.

Cass highlights the AB's report in the Shrimp-Turtle dispute permitting amicus submissions from non-state actors, including NGOs, as an example of "constitutionalization" through AB decisions.[39] No doubt, this decision is dramatic and controversial. However, close examination of panel and AB practice tends to problematize Cass's thesis about the constitutional dimensions of judicial norm-generation.

The Shrimp-Turtle dispute involved, inter alia, the question whether non-state actors could participate in WTO dispute settlement. The background to this issue is that, from time to time, non-state actors have attempted to submit amicus briefs to dispute panels. In Shrimp-Turtle, the panel held that such amicus briefs were inadmissible as a matter of WTO law.[40] On appeal, the AB explicitly rejected the panel's legal conclusion that amicus briefs were inadmissible and held that panels had discretionary authority to accept the briefs.[41]

In a subsequent case involving a Canadian challenge to a French ban on asbestos, it became apparent that many NGOs wished to submit briefs. *Sua sponte*, the AB issued a "communication" with a procedure for interested parties to request leave to file amicus briefs.[42] Several developing states requested a special meeting of WTO members to discuss this communication and the larger issue of amicus briefs. An overwhelming majority of states that spoke

---

[39] Notably, Jackson also thinks this report is of constitutional dimension. *See, e.g.*, John H. Jackson, *International Economic Law: Complexity and Puzzles*, 10 J. INT'L ECON L. 3, 4 (2007) (discussing the "Shrimp-Turtle case, which may be the most profound 'constitutional' case of the system"); John H. Jackson, *The Varied Policies of International Juridical Bodies – Reflections on Theory and Practice*, 25 MICH. J. INT'L L. 869 (2004) (characterizing Shrimp-Turtle dispute "as perhaps the most interesting constitutional case").

[40] *United States – Import Prohibitions of Certain Shrimp and Shrimp Products*, WT/DS58/R (May 15, 1998).

[41] *United States – Import Prohibitions of Certain Shrimp and Shrimp Products*, WT/DS58/AB/R (Oct. 12, 1998).

[42] *European Communities – Measures Affecting Asbestos and Asbestos-Containing Products, Communication from the Appellate Body*, WT/DS135/9 (Nov. 20, 2000).

at this meeting severely criticized the AB for issuing this communication. The chair of the meeting announced he would forward a note to the AB urging it to exercise "extreme caution" on this issue.[43] The AB denied each of the seventeen requests to file amicus briefs that were submitted in the asbestos appeal. Since then, in virtually every dispute involving amicus briefs, panels and the AB have only addressed the arguments presented in NGO briefs when a party to the dispute appended the amicus brief to its own submission.

Thus, WTO practice belies the claim that the AB has played a constitutional, norm-generating role here. In practice, a large number of WTO members strongly objected to the new norm that the AB tried to generate. After member states communicated their displeasure, the AB retreated from the supposedly constitutional norm it had created.

In short, over a decade's worth of WTO practice, including panel and AB decisions, reveals that none of the leading accounts of the WTO's constitution is descriptively accurate. Few dispute settlement reports address the issues of institutional architecture that Jackson's scholarship would suggest is central to the WTO's "constitution," and given the opportunity the AB declined to endorse a constitutionalist framework. Few address and none adopt a theory of individual rights, let alone the controversial individual "freedom to trade," that Petersmann would have at the heart of the WTO's constitution. The only report to even address the issue finds that individual rights do not exist under WTO law. And few authoritatively resolve the sorts of disputes that Cass claims are central to the constitutionalization process, such as whether non-state actors will have access to WTO dispute resolution. Thus, we are left with a puzzle. Sophisticated and experienced trade scholars develop increasingly elaborate theories of the WTO's constitution. But neither WTO text or practice support any of the specific constitutional conceptions found in the scholarly literature, let alone a move to constitutionalization in general. How can we account for the disquieting disconnect between WTO scholarship and practice?

IV. What Is the Relationship between Constitutionalization and International Trade Politics?

The preceding discussion illustrates just some of the diverse ways that trade scholars have characterized the WTO's supposed constitution – as well as

---

[43] WTO General Council, Minutes of WTO General Council Meeting, WT/GC/M/60 (Nov. 22, 2000).

the curious disconnect between this scholarship and WTO practice. Should we conclude that the scholars surveyed here are referring to dramatically different constitutions? Or is there a conceptual, or even ideological, link between these competing conceptions of the WTO's constitution?

The analysis above demonstrates that none of the leading understandings of the WTO's constitution accurately reflects WTO law or practice. So perhaps at this point in the development of the WTO system we should understand discussions of the WTO's "constitution" in a metaphorical, rather than a literal, sense. For current purposes, this metaphor's significance lies not only in its imagery, but in its implications. That is, if we accept the metaphor that life is a journey, then the implication is that we should expect obstacles and seek movement toward a destination. What implications would flow from a claim that the WTO is a constitutional system?

In the U.S. setting, constitutional practice, precedent, discourse, and scholarship frequently emphasize the distinction between the constitutional and the political. Political decisions, in this view, are often driven by legislative pandering and self-interest or reflect pork-barrel bargaining among legislators or constituents. Constitutional decisions, on the other hand, are said to reflect principle rather than partisanship, and reasoned deliberation rather than special interest pleading. Thus, "[a] higher law background runs deep in our constitutional thinking... [in which] the Constitution is understood to stand above and against politics, a legal constraint on the power of democracy and elected officials."[44] A large and influential scholarly literature elaborates on the various ways that constitutional and political decisions can be distinguished.[45]

Within traditions that distinguish constitutional decisions and norms from those resulting from ordinary politics, one of the virtues of constitutional processes is thought to be that, by removing issues from the political arena,

---

[44] Keith E. Whittington, *Extrajudicial Constitutional Interpretation: Three Objections and Responses*, 80 N.C. L. REV. 773, 774 (2000).

[45] *See, e.g.*, BRUCE ACKERMAN, WE THE PEOPLE, TRANSFORMATIONS (1998) (detailing a theory of constitutional dualism whereby "We the People" express our sovereign will in transformative and rare constitutional moments that thereafter constrain the actions of legislative agents engaged in "ordinary" politics); PHILIP BOBBITT, CONSTITUTIONAL INTERPRETATION (1991) (identifying and distinguishing six modalities of argumentation that distinguish constitutional discourse from political and moral argument); ALEXANDER BICKEL, THE LEAST DANGEROUS BRANCH (1962) (constitution represents "enduring values" as distinguished from "the current clash of interests" that inform and drive ordinary politics). This distinction also appears in the literature on international constitutionalism. *See, e.g.*, Jan Klabbers, *Constitutionalism Lite*, 1 INT'L ORG. L. REV. 31 (2004) ("one of the main attractions of constitutionalism is to suggest that there is a sphere beyond every day politics comprising values that cannot... be affected or changed").

constitutionalism can promote the principled and authoritative settlement of divisive issues.[46] While this settlement function is a critical aspect of all types of law, it is particularly notable and important in a constitutional context, given the supremacy of constitutional norms over other forms of law. Authoritative constitutional settlement is useful, in part, because continuous reconsideration of the same issues is wasteful, unsettling, and potentially destructive of social stability. Authoritative constitutional settlement can also help solve collective action problems and promote common interests. In addition, finality can provide the stability and certainty that are particularly important in certain contexts, such as planning economic activities.

For current purposes, I am less interested in the descriptive accuracy of the distinction between constitutional practice and ordinary politics than in its prominence and influence in legal discourse.[47] The question posed is whether the three leading accounts of the WTO's constitution outlined above are trading on this feature of constitutional thought – and whether this feature provides a common link among the otherwise disparate visions.

Consider Jackson's understanding of the WTO's constitution. As noted, Jackson urged creation of an institutional architecture that would support a rule-based system to replace the preexisting power-based trade system. Jackson is explicit that, at bottom, the new rules based system is designed as an antidote to the corrupting influence that the exercise of power – that is, the "diplomatic process" marked by bargaining among states with wide disparities in power, influence and resources[48] – has heretofore exerted on the international trade system. Thus, Jackson's constitutional vision is centrally concerned with substituting law for ordinary processes of international trade politics.

Petersmann similarly offers the constitutional turn as a necessary corrective to the pathologies of politics: "[c]onstitutionalism emerged in response to negative experiences with abuses of political power in order to limit such abuses through rules and institutions."[49] Or, as Petersmann memorably

---

[46] See, e.g., Larry Alexander & Frederick Schauer, *On Extrajudicial Constitutional Interpretation,* 110 HARV. L. REV. 1359 (1997).

[47] To be clear, in invoking this conventional distinction, I do not mean to suggest that constitutional principles are somehow apolitical or that political entities with strong constitutional traditions cannot or do not also engage in "normal" politics.

[48] Jackson explicitly equates a power-oriented system with the diplomatic process. *See, e.g.,* John H. Jackson, *Fragmentation or Unification among International Institutions,* 31 N.Y.U. J. INT'L L. & POL. 823, 826–27 (1999).

[49] Ernst-Ulrich Petersmann, *Constitutionalism and International Adjudication: How to Constitutionalize the U.N. Dispute Settlement System?* 31 N.Y.U. J. INT'L L. & POL. 733, 758 (1999).

suggests, constitutionalism's foundational insight is that the central political question is not who shall govern, but rather "how must laws and political institutions be designed . . . so that even incompetent rulers and politicians cannot cause too much harm."[50]

As noted, Petersmann would constitutionally enshrine and elevate economic freedoms, including an individual freedom to trade. However, Petersmann's arguments about the need to integrate market freedoms into human rights law reflects one very particular – and highly contested – vision of human rights.[51] There is a much larger debate, or political struggle here, both within and among nations, about the appropriate balance among economic and noneconomic policy goals. We can understand efforts to constitutionalize one controversial view of that balance as, in effect, efforts to preempt that debate and that struggle.

Cass and others who focus upon judicial processes similarly present a vision of constitutionalization that can be understood in opposition to more inclusive sites of political contestation. Their focus is on the generation of constitutional norms by the WTO dispute settlement process. While WTO dispute resolution is a highly deliberative and rationalized form of dispute settlement, it is hardly a site for participatory or democratic politics.

Moreover, Cass's version of constitutionalization would center constitutional power and authority on the WTO's judicial actors. But, as noted above, it is not reasonable to expect panels and the AB to authoritatively resolve highly contested issues. Expecting it to do so risks undermining what is otherwise a highly functioning dispute system.[52]

Thus, a common link among the three different understandings of the WTO's constitution is that, for each of the scholars surveyed, the constitutional turn can be understood as an element of a larger turn away from politics. That is, for each of the scholars surveyed, the constitutionalization of the WTO can be understood as a corrective or replacement for unruly and potentially destructive trade politics.

Ironically, however, in this sense the constitutional turn can be understood more as a step backwards than a step forwards. During GATT's early years, the trade system worked on a "club model" of international cooperation.[53]

---

[50] Petersmann, *How to Reform the UN System?*

[51] *See, e.g.,* Philip Alston, *Resisting the Merger and Acquisition of Human Rights by Trade Law: A Reply to Petersmann,* 13 Eur. J. Int'l L. 815 (2002); Robert Howse, *Human Rights in the WTO: Whose Rights, What Humanity?,* 13 Eur. J. Int'l L. 651 (2002).

[52] *See, e.g.,* Jeffrey L. Dunoff, *The Death of the Trade Regime,* 10 Eur. J. Int'l L. 733 (1999).

[53] Robert O. Keohane & Joseph S. Nye, *The Club Model of Multilateral Cooperation and the World Trade Organization: Problems of Democratic Legitimacy, in* Efficiency, Equity, and Legitimacy, *supra* note 4, at 264.

That is, during this time, a relatively small number of like-minded diplomats and economists from a relatively small number of like-minded states worked quietly to make trade policy. The GATT "club" operated for decades without much input or oversight from legislators or publics.[54] As Weiler explains:

> The GATT successfully managed a relative insulation from the 'outside' world of international relations and established among its practitioners a closely knit environment revolving around a certain set of shared normative values (of free trade) and shared institutional (and personal) ambitions situated in a matrix of long-term first-name contacts and friendly personal relationships. GATT operatives became a classical 'network'.... Within this ethos there was an institutional goal to prevent trade disputes from ... spilling out into the wider circles of international relations: a trade dispute was an 'internal' affair which had ... to be resolved ("settled") as quickly and smoothly as possible within the organization.[55]

For a variety of reasons, over time this "club" approach to managing trade relations broke down.[56] As GATT (and then WTO) membership expanded dramatically, and as the trade system expanded its reach beyond traditional issues such as tariffs and quotas into, for example, intellectual property and services, the trade system came under intensive and sustained public scrutiny. By the time of the "Battle in Seattle" at the WTO's Ministerial Conference in December 1999, the trade regime was widely understood to be at the heart of an evolving system of global economic governance. Moreover, it was clear that there could be no return to the era of trade relations being quietly managed by a small group of trade cognoscenti. The political developments and pressures that undermined the club model similarly resist the constitutional turn, or at least the types of constitutionalization on offer from Jackson, Petersmann and Cass.

V. The Allure of Constitutional Discourse

In championing a constitutionalist understanding of the WTO, constitutional advocates implicitly trade on established theories of constitutionalism on the domestic plane. In particular, constitutional advocates seem to share a desire to channel political conflict into a constitutional domain, where contentious disputes can supposedly be more easily resolved. But efforts to

[54] For an insightful discussion, see Robert Howse, *From Politics to Technocracy – and Back Again: The Fate of the Multilateral Trading Regime*, 96 Am. J. Int'l L. 94 (2002).
[55] Joseph Weiler, *The Rule of Lawyers and the Ethos of Diplomats: Reflections on the Internal and External Legitimacy of Dispute Settlement* in Efficiency, Equity, and Legitimacy, *supra* note 4, at 334, 336–37.
[56] For differing accounts, compare Keohane & Nye, *supra* note 53, with Howse, *supra* note 54.

authoritatively resolve contentious political issues through constitutionalized decision making simply create a different type of politics and can reinforce and aggravate the underlying conflicts. This paradox raises an even more difficult mystery than the ones we have explored: given the self-defeating nature of constitutional discourse – and the manifest absence of a true world trade constitution – why are so many trade scholars preoccupied with debating constitutionalism at the WTO *now*?

A. Responding to Fragmentation: International Trade Law as First among Equals?

A dominant explanation for the constitutional turn is as a response to globalization and the increased density of international norms, and associated concerns over the fragmentation of international law.[57] In the WTO context, the fragmentation concern has several different dimensions. One dimension relates to the substantive reach of WTO rules. What issue areas are properly considered within the trade system? The WTO already has rules on topics that are not primarily, or at least exclusively, about trade, including rules on intellectual property, service industries, and health and safety measures. Should there be WTO rules on, for example, environment, human rights, competition, labor, and other topics?

A related dimension of the debates over the relationship between trade and other bodies of international law focuses on the status and use of non-WTO law in WTO dispute settlement proceedings. Although GATT panels rarely used public international law in their reports, WTO panels and the AB have invoked multilateral treaties, bilateral agreements, customary international law, and nonbinding international legal instruments. Trade scholars have engaged in a spirited debate over whether the Uruguay Round Agreements confer upon panels the legal competence to apply non–trade law to resolve trade disputes,[58] and whether it is normatively desirable that they do so.[59]

A third dimension of the debate over the relationship between trade and other bodies of international law focuses on the relationship between the

---

[57] *See, e.g.*, Dunoff & Trachtman, *supra* note 5; Andreas Paulus, *The International Legal System as a Constitution*, in this volume; Mattias Kumm, *The Cosmopolitan Turn in Constitutionalism: On the Relationship between National Constitutions and Constitutionalism beyond the State*, in this volume.

[58] *See, e.g.*, JOOST PAUWELYN, CONFLICT OF NORMS IN PUBLIC INTERNATIONAL LAW: HOW WTO LAW RELATES TO OTHER RULES OF INTERNATIONAL LAW (2003); Joel P. Trachtman, *Book Review of Conflict of Norms in Public International Law: How WTO Law Relates to Other Rules of International Law*, 98 AM. J. INT'L L. 855 (2004).

[59] Jeffrey L. Dunoff, *The WTO in Transition: of Constituents, Competence and Coherence*, 33 GEO. WASH. INT'L L. REV. 979, 1009–12 (2001).

WTO and other international organizations. In its early years, the GATT had relatively little interaction with other international organizations. Over time, the development of informal consultations and working linkages eventually led to the conclusion of formal agreements with the World Bank, the International Monetary Fund, the World Intellectual Property Organization, and specialized bodies such as the World Health Organization and Food and Agriculture Organization. However, relations with several other international organizations, including the International Labour Organization and international environmental bodies, have been considerably more problematic. Thus, while there is broad consensus on the desirability of increased coherence and coordination of the WTO with other international organizations, there is no consensus on which bodies the WTO should cooperate with or what form that coordination should take.

All of these issues raise questions of institutional and doctrinal coherence.[60] They are particular instantiations of larger questions about whether the decentralized international legal order will be marked by increasing fragmentation or increased unity and coherence. To claim that the WTO is a constitutional entity is to suggest a certain approach to these types of questions. A constitutional perspective seems to envision a relatively broad substantive scope for WTO norms. Moreover, as constitutional norms are superior to other legal norms, a constitutionalist approach implies a certain outcome when WTO norms conflict with other legal norms. Finally, the approach suggests that other international organizations should accord some measure of deference to the WTO when they interact. In short, the constitutional turn can be understood as a strategic move in the context of debates over the status and reach of WTO norms vis-à-vis other international norms and bodies.

B. A Strategy of Resistance: Constraining the Trade Regime

The paragraphs above suggest several reasons why WTO enthusiasts might use constitutional rhetoric as a mechanism for elevating and expanding the reach of WTO norms. The WTO's critics have a decidedly different view of the trade regime. As vividly illustrated by protesters at the "Battle in Seattle" and unrest at subsequent WTO Ministerial meetings, many criticize the WTO for overriding decisions reached through domestic democratic processes, and

---

[60] Trachtman addresses these issues under the rubric of "intersectoral coherence." I read his observation that the WTO has developed a "modest approach to intersectional coherence" and his prediction that "[o]ver the next [fifty] years, we may expect to see . . . an effort to develop more nuanced means to integrate different global values" as implicitly acknowledging that no constitutional mechanism currently exists in the WTO to address institutional and doctrinal coherence.

more broadly for threatening sovereignty and representative government on the domestic plane. From this perspective, the WTO and its dispute system raise the question of who will control trade policy – electorally accountable national officials, or unelected and unaccountable trade bureaucrats and Appellate Body members?[61] Paradoxically, individuals or groups who oppose globalization or trade liberalization, or who otherwise wish to limit the WTO's substantive reach, might also decide to analyze the WTO through a constitutional register. The critics might embrace the idea of a trade constitution as a tool for constraining, rather than enabling, the WTO's power and authority.

Although a constitutional turn by the WTO's critics may currently appear rather remote, it will be useful to recall the trajectory of debates over the EU's constitution.[62] During the early stages of the debate, most Euroskeptics opposed the constitutional undertaking. However, over time, some of these opponents came to support the drafting project. For many, this switch reflected an emerging understanding that the constitution could be viewed as a policy-limiting device, rather than a polity-making or policy-consolidating device. Thus, for example, groups such as the German Lander became strategically reconciled to the constitutional process as a way of limiting the federalist agenda. Similarly, some Euroskeptics supported a Charter of Rights as a way to limit, rather than expand, EU power.

To be sure, critics of the trade system have heretofore generally rejected, rather than embraced, the use of constitutional discourse at the WTO. However, this should be understood as a strategic choice made to advance certain substantive or political values in light of historically contingent circumstances. As these circumstances change, the critics' strategies may change as well, and it is possible to imagine that in the future it could well be the WTO's critics, rather than its champions, that advance constitutional claims.

C. A Compensatory Mechanism?

In virtually all of the scholarship addressing constitutional developments at various sites of transnational governance, the constitutional turn is understood as a reaction to various developments in international relations and international law. But it might be useful to reverse the usual line of analysis. That is, instead of looking to recent developments to explain the constitutional

---

[61] See, e.g., Philip R. Trimble, *International Trade and the "Rule of Law,"* 83 MICH L. REV. 1016, 1029 (1985) (posing the question in this form).

[62] I draw this account from Neil Walker, *After the Constitutional Moment, in* A CONSTITUTION FOR THE EUROPEAN UNION: FIRST COMMENTS ON THE 2003 DRAFT OF THE EUROPEAN CONVENTION (I. Pernice & M. Maduro eds., 2004).

turn, we might consider what the constitutional turn can tell us about recent developments in international law.

This reversal of the usual perspective suggests yet another possible explanation for the rise of constitutional discourse. Specifically, it invites consideration of whether the constitutional turn is less a sign of international law's flourishing than of it being in a discipline under severe pressure. A constellation of events in the 1980s and 1990s – the end of the cold war, the fall of the Berlin wall, the apparent revitalization of the United Nations – gave rise to heady claims about the reality and promise of international law. The creation of the WTO was just one of many developments that led prominent scholars to declare that international law had finally entered a "post-ontological" age.[63]

But international law's triumphalist moment quickly faded, and today the discipline faces severe challenges, both from within and without. From within, empirical studies raise serious questions about international law's effectiveness,[64] and a revisionist literature attacks international law's premises and foundations.[65] Contemporary critics challenge not simply specific doctrines or principles, but international law's coherence and legitimacy.

At the same time, many recent developments in international relations raise questions concerning whether international law and institutions are adequate to confront current challenges. International processes and institutions have, to date, proved largely ineffective in addressing pressing environmental challenges such as climate change. The current global economic meltdown has sparked a number of calls for fundamental restructuring of the institutions of global economic governance. And various actions related to the "war on terror," not to mention recent developments in many long-standing regional conflicts, have placed sustained pressure on numerous international legal norms. In short, contemporary international law is a discipline under severe stress.

The WTO is not immune from these developments. The spectacular collapse of the Doha Round trade negotiations is only the most recent setback; as one former negotiator observed, "[t]he stature of the WTO itself has suffered incalculable collateral damage by seven years of fruitless, arcane negotiations, and more recently by the petty bickering and blame-games of national trade

---

[63] THOMAS M. FRANCK, FAIRNESS IN INTERNATIONAL LAW AND INSTITUTIONS 6 (1995).

[64] See, e.g., Oona A. Hathaway, Do Human Rights Treaties Make a Difference? 111 YALE L.J. 1935 (2002).

[65] See, e.g., JACK L. GOLDSMITH & ERIC A. POSNER, THE LIMITS OF INTERNATIONAL LAW (2005).

ministers."[66] Indeed, in recent years, a succession of high-level panels and blue-ribbon commissions have been convened in efforts to chart a new path for the WTO[67] – perhaps the surest sign of the deep dissatisfaction that surrounds the institution. The institution's malaise has not, of course, escaped scholarly notice.[68]

Might we understand efforts to "constitutionalize" the WTO as a move to address these regime-specific concerns, as well as broader concerns about the discipline of international law? A constitutionalized WTO would possess a strength and vigor that other international legal norms may lack; a constitutionalized WTO would have a stability that other treaty norms lack; and a constitutionalized WTO would no longer be understood as "a complex, messy negotiated bargain of diverse rules, principles and norms" but rather as a coherent, integrated structure.[69] In short, to constitutionalize the WTO is to give it "the legitimacy of higher law – irreversible, irresistible, and comprehensive."[70]

Moreover, it is not surprising that constitutional advocates focus prominently on the WTO. There can be little doubt that "[w]hatever its flaws, the [WTO] is the envy of international lawyers who are more familiar with less efficient and more compliance-resistant legal regimes, including those within the International Labour Organization (ILO), United Nations (UN) human rights bodies, and other adjudicative arrangements such as the World Court or the ad hoc war crimes tribunals."[71] Hence, if any international legal regime would possess constitutional qualities, it would appear to be the WTO.

From this perspective, it is misleading to understand the constitutional turn in international legal scholarship as being simply an effort to more accurately map the international legal order. That is, constitutionalist writings are not simply scholarly efforts to uncover or reveal the UN's or the WTO's constitution, but are better understood as a sustained "project to interpret the world as constituted, as held together in constitutional terms."[72] Seen in this way, the constitutional enthusiasts are engaged in an effort that is less

---

[66] Claude Barfield, *The Doha Endgame and the Future of the WTO*, available at http://www.voxeu.org/index.php?q=node/2806.
[67] *See, e.g.,* THE WARWICK COMMISSION, REPORT ON THE FUTURE OF THE MULTILATERAL TRADE REGIME; Consultative Board to the Director-General Supachai Panitchpakdi *Addressing Institutional Challenges in the New Millennium* (2005).
[68] *See, e.g.,* Debra P. Steger, *The Culture of the WTO: Why It Needs to Change*, 10 J. INT'L ECON. L. 483 (2007).
[69] Howse & Nicolaides, *supra* note 4, at 239.   [70] Id.
[71] Jose E. Alvarez, *How Not to Link: Institutional Conundrums of an Expanded Trade Regime*, 7 WIDENER L. SYMP. J. 1 (2001).
[72] David Kennedy, *The Mystery of Global Governance*, Chapter 2 in this volume.

descriptive than it is prescriptive. In the WTO context, the constitutionalist project is perhaps best understood as an effort to bridge the gap between the WTO's perceived power, and the lack of a broad popular basis for exercise of that power.

In recent years, constitutional advocates have occupied substantial scholarly space. However, to date, they have not persuaded a critical mass of trade officials or citizens that the WTO should be considered a constitutional entity. But this does not mean we should simply dismiss the constitutionalist project as misguided or failed advocacy. The WTO is a relatively young international organization, and it is probable that current understandings will evolve. Moreover, the EU and UN experiences demonstrate that constitutional claims and understandings can fall in and out of favor at various points in time. Hence, it is much to early to assess the legacy of the constitutional project.

VI. Toward a New Wave of Constitutionalism Scholarship

Despite the critique set out in this chapter, international law scholars in general, and trade scholars in particular, are likely to continue to invoke constitutional rhetoric and imagery. Indeed it appears that the use of constitutional discourse in discussions of transnational governance, if anything, is becoming more common.[73] I have argued that the most influential scholarship on constitutionalization at the WTO has, to date, employed a conception of constitutionalization that would have the effect of closing down, rather than opening up, political debate and contestation. However, this does not mean that alternative conceptions are unavailable. Indeed, trade scholars can articulate forms of constitutionalization designed to open up spaces for political dialogue and contestation, rather than preempt such discourse. While the articulation of such a vision is beyond the scope of this article, it may be useful to offer a few preliminary thoughts that might help inform the next stage of scholarship.

This chapter has attempted to foreground one aspect of the debates that has received insufficient attention: the political dimensions of constitutional discourse. My goal has been to identify, rather than exhaust, this topic, and I hope that this paper will encourage others to extend, or correct, the arguments set out above. Similarly, future scholarship should explore the distributional consequences of different conceptions of constitutionalism. Like

---

[73] Indeed, as this volume goes to press, an international and interdisciplinary group of scholars, including several contributors to this volume, is attempting to found a new journal entitled "Global Constitutionalism."

other important legal and political institutions, different constitutions would privilege different constituencies. Trade scholars have not addressed who is advantaged and who disadvantaged, who empowered and who disempowered, under different constitutional conceptions.

Moreover, future scholarship on constitutionalzation at the WTO would benefit greatly from more direct engagement with the growing literature on post-national constitutionalism. This scholarship foregrounds yet another issue that has remained submerged in the trade literature: the "problem of translation." This term refers to the difficulties raised by the transposition of the key normative concepts associated with constitutionalism from a state-centric setting to a supranational or post-national setting.[74] As writings on post-national constitutionalism properly emphasize, the central concepts and categories associated with constitutionalism have been debated and refined for centuries within the context of the sovereign state. The transfer of these concepts, including separation of powers, subsidiarity, and human rights, to the transnational plane is neither simple nor straightforward. While national and post-national forms of governance may well face many of the same puzzles of governance, it should not be assumed that strategies effective on the domestic plane can be easily replicated in a very different institutional and political context. Of course, this general idea is hardly late-breaking news to trade law scholars; but the constitutional scholarship has paid insufficient attention to this difficulty. Future scholarship would benefit from explicitly and self-consciously addressing the problem of translation, for it would help illuminate both the possibilities and the limitations of constitutionalization at the WTO.

Relatedly, constitutional analysis should address the interplay of domestic constitutional structures, WTO norms, and general international law. This analytic move highlights a reality that Daniel Halberstam and Miguel Maduro explore in their contributions in Chapters 11 and 12 this volume but that has been underappreciated in the trade literature, namely, that we inhabit a world of "constitutional pluralism."[75] As Neil Walker explains

> Constitutional pluralism . . . is a position which holds that states are no longer the sole locus of constitutional authority, but are now joined by other sites,

---

[74] *See, e.g.,* Neil Walker, *Postnational Constitutionalism and the Problem of Translation, in* EUROPEAN CONSTITUTIONALISM BEYOND THE STATE 27–54 (J. H. H. Weiler & Marlene Wind eds., 2003).

[75] Daniel Halberstam, *Constitutional Heterarchy: The Centrality of Conflict in the United States and Europe, in* Chapter 11; Miguel Poiares Maduro, *Courts and Pluralism: Essay on a Theory of Judicial Adjudication in the Context of Legal and Constitutional Pluralism, in* Chapter 12.

or putative sites of constitutional authority, most prominently . . . and most relevantly . . . those situated at the supra-state level, and that the relationship between state and non-state sites is better viewed as heterarchical rather than hierarchical.[76]

Finally, constitutional scholarship should engage the global administrative law (GAL) scholarship. Like the constitutional scholarship, GAL purports to provide a conceptual framework for understanding contemporary global governance, including the trade system. Hence, GAL scholars have explored, inter alia, aspects of WTO dispute settlement practice, as well as practice within WTO committees. However, to date, trade scholars have not engaged in a comparative analysis of these two approaches. Doing so could, for example, help highlight the strengths and limits of each approach and illuminate the range of issues that each can usefully explain.

These topics are just a few that are underdeveloped in the literature, and are offered to illustrate some of the paths yet to be taken. Exploration of these and related topics will aid understanding of constitutionalism's possibilities and limits, both in the context of the WTO and in other international regimes.

Conclusion

Trade scholars are preoccupied with the debate over the WTO's constitution. While this term is used in many different ways, I have tried to demonstrate that constitutional discourse is almost always used as a way to characterize the dense legalization of the trade system, and also almost invariably would be a mechanism to defuse or resolve potentially destabilizing political conflicts. However, the constitutional turn cannot preempt or displace political debate on controversial issues. Paradoxically, the constitutional turn is self-defeating as it creates precisely the sort of politics that it seeks to preempt.

But if the constitutional turn triggers the very world trade politics that it seeks to avoid, why do leading trade scholars engage in this discourse? This question prompts inquiry into the conditions that have given rise to the constitutional debate at the WTO. I have suggested that the timing and prominence of this debate may shed light on the current status of the discipline of international law. In short, the constitutional turn may reflect a deep disciplinary anxiety about the nature and value of international law that has been heightened in recent years. Constitutional discourse may be a defensive

---

[76] Neil Walker, *Late Sovereignty in the European Union, in* SOVEREIGNTY IN TRANSITION 4 (Neil Walker ed., 2003). See also Neil Walker, *The Idea of Constitutional Pluralism*, 65 MOD. L. REV. 317 (2002).

reaction of international lawyers who perceive that international law is under severe stress.

However, the arguments developed above should not be understood as a categorical rejection of the constitutional turn. To claim that the WTO today should not be understood as a constitutionalized entity is not to say that it could never be understood as such. Moreover, despite the analysis set out above, constitutional analysis of the WTO continues. As the discussion above suggests, constitutions can come in many different forms. The forms most prominent in the trade scholarship to date seem designed to preempt political debate and contestation. But other constitutional understandings might be designed that invite political debate and contestation, or empower democratic and deliberative decision making. Institutional architecture can be used to support or to undermine broader political participation and contestation. Many scholars have suggested ways for the WTO to be more open and inclusive. Similarly, to the extent the emerging trade constitution is understood as privileging certain values over others, or as the result of judicial decision making, those values and decisions can be directed toward openness and participation. As a result, as a general theoretical matter, there is no simple answer to normative questions about the desirability of constitutionalizing the WTO.

8. Constitutional Economics of the World Trade Organization

JOEL P. TRACHTMAN

This chapter examines the World Trade Organization (WTO) from the social scientific perspective of constitutional economics. This chapter thus seeks to identify the causes and consequences of constitutionalization. Assuming that states act with intentionality and accuracy in their establishment of organizational features, the cause of constitutionalization is the desire to effect the consequences of constitutionalization, so the focus here is on the potential consequences of constitutionalization in and in connection with the WTO.

1. The WTO in the World

The constitutional aspects and context of the WTO cannot be examined without laying out first the factual setting in which the WTO exists and operates. This section will locate the WTO within the process of globalization and regulation.

a. Globalization

For a number of years, the WTO has served as a lightning rod for criticism of globalization, and many concerns regarding globalization are expressed in terms of the adequacy of the structure and function of the WTO: of both its process and its results. This identification of globalization with the WTO seems correct, insofar as the WTO is an instrument of globalization, where globalization is defined as increasing international economic integration. Of course, the WTO is not the only instrument of globalization, and the WTO

This chapter develops some ideas introduced in my *The Constitutions of the WTO*, 17 Eur. J. Int'l L. 623 (2006). I am grateful to Anne van Aaken, Jeffrey Dunoff, and Anne Peters for comments on an earlier draft, as well as participants at the book workshop for *Ruling the World*, for their helpful comments. I thank Jeremy Leong for his dedicated research assistance.

even limits international economic integration in important ways, so a more nuanced perspective must examine the WTO within a broader context.

The WTO secretariat personnel and others seek to deflect this type of criticism of the WTO by pointing out that the WTO is a member organization. This argument, building in part on realist international relations theory, points out that the WTO itself has no power but is merely a conduit for the exercise of member states' power. Therefore, the argument proceeds, it is not appropriate to blame the WTO, either for sins of omission or for sins of commission, because the WTO is no more than a conduit for member-state action. This argument never provided great protection from criticism, largely because, even conceding its force, it leaves the possibility to criticize a type of member-state action in the form of WTO action or inaction. Moreover, this argument proves too much, for if the WTO were merely a conduit for member-state action, there would be no need to cloak member-state action in the WTO.

However, increasing economic integration both makes increasing disciplines on national regulatory autonomy useful and exposes lacunae in the international regulatory structure. Thus, as the ability to generate new international legal rules to discipline national regulation or to fill lacunae becomes important, globalization gives rise to calls for "enabling international constitutionalization" (as defined in the Introduction to this volume) in order to facilitate legislation of welfare-improving restrictions on protectionist or other inefficient domestic regulation. "Enabling international constitutionalization" at the WTO – structures that facilitate the production of law – would mean the end of the WTO as a member organization in which each member (in formal terms) retains veto power.

To the extent that the WTO becomes an actor itself – albeit accountable to its member states as a group – it will engage responsibility for its acts. It would be analogous to a national legislature, in the sense that, while composed of individual representatives of different subgroups of people, it would be seen to act as a corporate entity while remaining also decomposable into its separate representatives.

There are rising demands for enabling international constitutionalization, not just to restrain protectionism but also to complement restraints on protectionism. At the same time, there are rising concerns regarding the accuracy and accountability of efforts to increase disciplines on national regulatory autonomy, as well as concerns regarding the ability of these efforts to encompass the full scope of public policy desiderata, giving rise to calls for "constraining international constitutionalization" (also as defined in the Introduction).

Constraining international constitutionalization might take the form of
restrictions on the scope of law making at the international level, either in
terms of subject matter or in terms of procedural limitations. Subject-matter
limitations might take the form of requirements for supermajorities (relative
to legislation on other subject matters) or of carved-out national rights that
are, in effect, inalienable, or at least unalienated.[1]

Finally, the lacunae exposed by globalization give rise to calls for "supplemental constitutionalization," in some cases in the context of the WTO.[2]
With greater economic integration comes the possibility of greater regulatory
arbitrage and increasing pressure on domestic regulatory preferences.

And yet the WTO is but one component of a variegated and increasingly dense tapestry of global governance. So, it would be wrong to examine the WTO separately from the institutional context in which it exists.
Furthermore, while it is possible that acts of enabling constitutionalization, constraining constitutionalization, and supplemental constitutionalization may best take place within the organizational confines of the WTO,
it is equally plausible that they would best take place in other parts of
the international legal system. Here, there are two critical questions. The
first is a question of a type of horizontal and vertical constitutional subsidiarity – where should the constitutional function best be addressed? The
second is that of coherence – how do the different constitutional functions fit
together?

b. Unbalanced Demand for International Law

The demand for additional international law is the driving force behind
enabling international constitutionalization. This demand for additional
international law can arise from the demand for liberalization (which in turn
is caused by other social forces, including changes in technology, changes
in the structure of production, and changes in economic understanding),
but the production of law to enhance liberalization has two types of knock-
on effects: (1) a resulting demand for other types of international law and,
(2) where the initial liberalization measures take the form of negative integration, a resulting demand for positive integration. We see both of these types
of knock-on effects in the history of the European Union.

[1] *See* Dennis Mueller, *Rights and Liberty in the European Union*, 13 Sup. Ct. Econ. Rev. 1
(2005). Mueller explains that the difference between a rule of unanimity and a right is that
a right cuts off wasteful negotiation and lobbying to reach unanimous agreement, where it
is possible to decide in advance that such negotiation and lobbying will be fruitless.
[2] *See* Anne Peters, *Compensatory Constitutionalism: The Function and Potential of International
Norms and Structures*, 19 Leiden J. Int'l L. 579 (2006).

One of the factors giving rise to criticism of the WTO is a possible imbalance in the production of different types of international law. This occurs for three reasons.

First, business interests often are able to lobby in a concentrated and effective way for government action that provides them with benefits. So it is not surprising that some types of liberalization measures, such as reductions of barriers to trade and disciplines on national regulatory measures that restrict trade, would achieve greater saliency in national politics, and consequently in international politics, than other types of measures. It is also worth noting that business interests also lobby against liberalization, but the overall tendency since the 1940s has been toward liberalization. Moreover, the increasingly nuanced rules of liberalization that result entail the production of increasing volumes of international law, and of international legal institutions. This production of international trade law has demonstration effects: showing environmentalists, human rights activists, and other constituencies that it is possible to establish new international law addressing their concerns. Perhaps most important, the establishment of more binding dispute settlement at the WTO than existed prior to 1994 has suggested that more binding dispute settlement, and more binding international law, may be possible in these other areas. Indeed, the move toward more binding dispute settlement at the WTO has upset a preexisting equilibrium of bindingness in international law, causing reexamination of the binding nature of other areas of law.

Second, liberalization itself gives rise to recognition of lacunae in the substantive or jurisdictional coverage of national regulation, or to the possibility of adverse regulatory arbitrage. Environmental, human rights, tax, competition, and other types of regulation are thus challenged by liberalization, and relevant constituencies seek responsive redress. Increasing liberalization gives rise to increasing demands for regulatory harmonization, or regulatory rules of prescriptive jurisdiction. Some of these demands are based on a perception of regulatory competition that is accentuated by liberalization.

Third, in the "embedded liberalism" sense explained by Karl Polanyi and John Ruggie,[3] liberalization has distributive effects that make it necessary, in order for liberalization to be sustained, to effect redistributive regulation.

---

[3] John G. Ruggie, *International Regimes, Transactions, and Change: Embedded Liberalism in the Postwar Economic Order*, 36 INT'L ORG. 379 (1982). Ruggie modernizes and adapts a perspective earlier elucidated by Karl Polanyi, *The Great Transformation: The Political and Economic Origins of Our Time* (1944). Dani Rodrik has considered the application of this perspective to modern global markets. Dani Rodrik, *Has Globalization Gone Too Far?* 7 (Peterson Institute 1997). *See also* Robert L. Howse, *From Politics to Technocracy – and Back Again: The Fate of the Multilateral Trading Regime*, 96 AM. J. INT'L. L. 94 (2002).

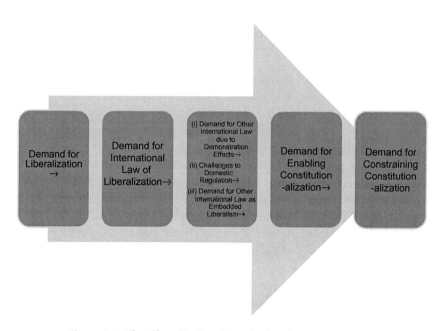

Figure 8.1. The Liberalization-Constitutionalization Cascade.

Thus, the demand for liberalization sets off a cascade of demands for the production of other international law. The demand for both liberalization and other international law may more easily be satisfied with greater enabling international constitutionalization. And, as noted previously, the establishment of enabling international constitutionalization creates a demand for nuanced controls in the form of constraining international constitutionalization. This cascade might appear as shown in Figure 8.1.

One method of discipline on national regulatory measures is the type of negative integration provision that establishes a legal standard, enforced and articulated through adjudication, prohibiting certain types of national measures that may create excessive barriers to trade. The most common type of negative integration standard is national treatment-type nondiscrimination. In a sense, these rules against protectionism are specialized rules of dynamic subsidiarity. They contingently remove power from the state under a specified range of circumstances. Interestingly, these rules may be understood as serving a constraining constitutionalization role at the domestic level: they constrain the production of ordinary law. But at the international level, they are ordinary international law. On the other hand, to the extent that international judges are authorized, explicitly or implicitly, to interpret or craft these rules of negative integration, the authorization may be understood as a kind of enabling constitutionalization.

These types of adjudicative standards used in negative integration compete with legislative solutions to the same problems. Legislative solutions – known in this context as positive integration – might develop regimes of harmonization or recognition, or blended regimes of harmonization and recognition, as in the European Union's "essential harmonization" program.[4] These legislative solutions could enjoy greater political support than judicial decisions addressing the same issues.

It is in this regard that negative integration devices, such as those in the WTO, that may be used to strike down domestic regulatory regimes may create demand for positive integration devices, such as those associated with majority voting. Deregulation through negative integration may create demand for re-regulation at the central level through majority voting-based legislative capacity. This results in demand for enabling constitutionalization in terms of legislative capacity. Majority voting among states might give rise to demands for greater democratic accountability: a kind of countervailing constraining constitutionalization. Pascal Lamy has called for a WTO parliamentary consultative assembly for just this reason.[5]

So the causal chain here might appear as shown in Figure 8.2, where the conjectural causal chain shows a link between adjudication and legislation. In this model, the power of adjudicative negative integration gives rise to a need for the check of legislative capacity for positive integration. The possibility of centralized legislation gives rise to the need for centralized democratic accountability. This diagram elides much nuance, but it is intended to provide a suggestion of how the commencement of economic integration may set off a cascade of governance demands along a predictable path.

---

[4] *See* Joel P. Trachtman, *The Domain of WTO Dispute Resolution*, 40 HARV. INT'L L.J. 333 (1999).

[5] Pascal Lamy, European Commissioner for Trade, Conference on the Participation and Interface of Parliamentarians and Civil Societies for Global Policy: Global Policy without Democracy (Nov. 26, 2001) *available at* http://europa.eu/rapid/pressReleasesAction.do?reference= SPEECH/01/586&format=HTML&aged=0&language=EN&guiLanguage=en. *See also* Gregory Shaffer, *Parliamentary Oversight of International Rule-Making: The Political and Normative Context*, *available at* http://papers.ssrn.com/sol3/papers.cfm?abstract_ id=434420; Richard Falk & Andrew Strauss, *On the Creation of a Global Peoples Assembly: Legitimacy and the Power of Popular Sovereignty*, 36 STAN. J. INT'L L. 191 (2000); Robert L. Howse, *How to Begin to Think about the Democratic Deficit at the WTO*, in INTERNATIONAL ECONOMIC GOVERNANCE AND NON-ECONOMIC CONCERNS: NEW CHALLENGES FOR THE INTERNATIONAL LEGAL ORDER (Stephan Griller ed., 2003).

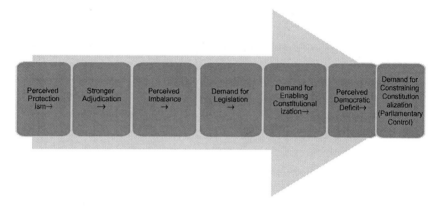

Figure 8.2. The Negative Integration-Positive Integration Cascade.

c. The Demand for Enabling International Constitutionalization and the Demand for Constraining International Constitutionalization

In the prior subsection, we began to see a model of the relationship between the demand for law to effect liberalization, the demand for other international law, and the demand for international constitutional law. There is also an interesting relationship between enabling constitutionalization and constraining constitutionalization. Enabling constitutionalization and constraining constitutionalization are two sides of the same coin. As a sculptor adds clay with one tool and cuts it away with another, so enabling constitutionalization adds to the powers of the international legal system, while constraining constitutionalization refines the grant of powers, and artfully, and often conditionally, cuts back on it.

2. Constitutional Economics

Constitutional economics brings a positive analytical perspective to constitutions. Under this approach, constitutions are simply instruments of human interaction: mechanisms by which to share authority in order to facilitate the establishment of rules. In Buchanan's phrase, they are instruments to facilitate gains from trade – not from trade in the conventional sense but from transactions in authority. In a transaction cost or strategic model, constitutions are assumed to be designed to overcome transaction costs or strategic barriers to Pareto superior outcomes. Once this is accepted, it follows that constitutional rules are not natural law; instead, they are political settlements designed to maximize the achievement of individual citizens' preferences. Enabling constitutionalization, constraining constitutionalization, and supplemental constitutionalization can all be understood in these terms.

Thus, from this perspective, if there were no potential value to be obtained from cooperation, constitutions would be unimportant and would not exist. Constitutional economics assumes that constitutions exist to resolve transaction costs and strategic problems that would otherwise prevent the achievement of efficient exchanges of authority. Where there is value to be obtained by agreement, constitutions may be used to facilitate the realization of this value by reducing transaction costs and strategic costs, such as the problem of states holding out or defecting from their commitments.

Much of the political science literature has been skeptical of the possibility for cooperative international constitutional solutions.[6] Garrett argues, "In situations in which there are numerous potential solutions to collective action problems that cannot easily be distinguished in terms of their consequences for aggregate welfare – and the [EU] internal market is one – the 'new economics of organization' lexicon conceals the fundamental political issue of bargaining over institutional design."[7] Brennan and Buchanan respond to this criticism by explaining that bargaining over institutional design is cooperative in nature and that the aggregate increased value will provide incentives for agreement.[8] They compare such constitutional bargaining with ordinary politics. First, they agree that in ordinary politics: "the Pareto-optimal set would be exceedingly large."[9] They continue as follows: "[t]his prospect is dramatically modified, however, when the choice alternatives are not those of ordinary politics but are, instead, rules or institutions within which patterns of outcomes are generated by various nonunanimous decision-making procedures."[10]

The indirectness and broadly reciprocal nature of the distributional consequences of constitutional bargaining erect a Harsanyian veil of uncertainty that provides incentives for agreement on efficient institutions. This argument based on a veil of uncertainty suggests that bargaining problems can be overcome in connection with the decision to form an international organization, which can then make decisions in ordinary politics terms. This veil of uncertainty is limited because those who negotiate constitutions

---

[6] See Stephen D. Krasner, Global Communications and National Power: Life on the Pareto Frontier, 43 WORLD POL. 336, 340 (1991) ("the problem is not how to get to the Pareto frontier, but which point along it will be chosen"); Geoffrey Garrett, International Cooperation and Institutional Choice: The European Community's Internal Market, 46 INT'L ORG. 533, 541 (1992).

[7] Garrett, supra note 6, at 541.

[8] GEOFFREY BRENNAN & JAMES M. BUCHANAN, THE REASON OF RULES: CONSTITUTIONAL POLITICAL ECONOMY 28–32 (1985). See also James M. Buchanan, The Domain of Constitutional Economics, 1 CONST. POL. ECON. 1 (1990).

[9] Id. at 29.   [10] Id.

can predict some of the distributive consequences of constitutional-type bargains.

Constitutional economics allows us to place a number of features associated with constitutionalization into an overall context and show the relations among them. Importantly, constitutional economics is not predicated upon or even related to economic constitutionalism: the belief that liberalism is threatened by the state and must be protected through constitutional means, including international law that plays a constitutional function in the domestic system.

Constitutional economics, like economics in general, is agnostic as to the types of preferences that will be articulated or the way that individuals will value each preference. It assumes only that each individual has a utility function and enters society in order to maximize his or her preferences. While the utility function is by no means limited to the material, constitutional economics does not accept generally preemptive values such as human rights, environmental protection, or wealth maximization. It would accept that some of these preferences are valued more greatly than others, or that it makes sense to make some of these preferences preemptive, for strategic or transaction cost reasons. For example, assuming that core human rights are so highly valued that they rarely are trumped by other values, it may be appropriate to establish them as preemptive in order to avoid the costs of evaluation in specific cases.

Some of the essays in this volume may suggest that legitimacy is a better metric by which to assess constitutional structures than the normative individualist focus on individual preferences of constitutional economics. Yet normative individualism sees even the concept of legitimacy through a preference metric. Legitimacy, if it is to be understood in rational terms, is no more than the satisfaction of preferences or, again in constitutional economics terms, the acceptance of reduced satisfaction of preferences pursuant to a structure that was agreed ex ante because of the anticipation of maximization of preferences. This is the Harsanyian, and Rawlsian, concept of stochastic symmetry. In other words, legitimacy is no more than the acceptance ex post of the results of a mechanism that was designed and accepted, ex ante, to maximize aggregate preferences. "In Constitutional Economics, rules are assumed to be legitimate if rational individuals seeking to maximize utility (can) unanimously agree to them."[11]

[11] Anne van Aaken, *Deliberative Institutional Economics, or Does Homo Oeconomicus Argue? A Proposal for Combining New Institutional Economics with Discourse Theory, in* DELIBERATION AND DECISION: ECONOMICS, CONSTITUTIONAL THEORY, AND DELIBERATIVE DEMOCRACY 3, 7 (Anne van Aaken, Christian List & Christoph Luetge eds., 2004).

I might add that each of us labors under bounded rationality, and so legitimacy may also include the extent to which we are made aware that our preferences are maximized in the way I have described. This is the public relations, or marketing, function that is so important to legitimacy in practice.

Constitutional economics can be understood as a commitment, as a theory, as a methodology, and as a policy orientation. As a commitment, it is predicated upon normative individualism, holding that institutional arrangements are to be established in order to maximize individual welfare in the eyes of the individual. As a theory, it postulates that citizens in a constitutional moment will agree on a constitution that maximizes their collective welfare. As a methodology, it derives hypotheses based on this theory and tests them empirically. As a policy orientation, it advises that the task of framers of constitutions, and of analysts, is to engage in comparative institutional analysis[12] – even if the reference is historical or hypothetical – in order to determine which institutional features will maximize the net achievement of preferences.

In our context, the policy question asked by constitutional economics is, Which international constitutional features will maximize the net achievement of global individual preferences? We might begin by comparing the status quo with postulated alternative international constitutional structures. Interestingly, in the international constitutional setting, we do not have multiple global systems existing at once, to be used to structure a comparison. So, any comparative method will be based on historical experience, cross-functional comparison (as, for example, between the WTO and the International Labour Organization [ILO]), or hypothetical alternatives.[13]

Constitutional economics recognizes the possibility of constitutional moments. A "constitutional moment" in the Buchanan and Tullock[14] sense is an historical moment at which a Harsanyian "veil of uncertainty" allows individuals, or in our case, states, to agree on constitutional change even though they are uncertain of the possible future implications. Constitutional moments generally result from a shift in the concerns, or perception of concerns, of constituents: an exogenous shock that disturbs a constitutional equilibrium.

---

[12] NEIL KOMESAR, IMPERFECT ALTERNATIVES (1995); Joel P. Trachtman, *The Theory of the Firm and the Theory of the International Economic Organization: Toward Comparative Institutional Analysis*, 17 Nw. J. INT'L L. & Bus. 470 (1997).

[13] JOEL P. TRACHTMAN, THE ECONOMIC STRUCTURE OF INTERNATIONAL LAW (2008).

[14] JAMES M. BUCHANAN & GORDON TULLOCK, THE CALCULUS OF CONSENT, LOGICAL FOUNDATIONS OF CONSTITUTIONAL DEMOCRACY (1962).

Furthermore, a constitution may produce its own demand: once established, by reducing transaction costs and strategic costs of international arrangements, constitutions would be expected to make attractive a host of arrangements that were otherwise unattractive. There may be a path-dependency characteristic to constitutional development, with tipping points that result in lumpy movement or punctuated equilibria. Thus, once a centralized legislative and parliamentary feature is established for one purpose, it may make it easier to use it for other purposes.

Of course, the existing international legal constitution provides that collective decisions are made by unanimity of states – the somewhat contestable consent rule. (Customary international law is not predicated upon unanimity per se.) The consent rule has certain important characteristics. Some would say that it is perfectly democratic (at least among states, as opposed to individuals), insofar as new rules cannot be made unless all consent. On the other hand, it is just as easily understood as perfectly undemocratic, allowing the tyranny of the minority to reign, insofar as the smallest minority can block collective action. The rising importance of global collective goods shows the strategic inadequacy of the consent rule. Of course, under formal requirements of unanimity, informal coercion or logrolling can reduce the inhibitive effect of unanimity.

So, assuming that a state is behaving like an individual in determining whether to move from a rule of unanimity, we would expect the state to calculate its position as follows: The state would maximize its expected utility by a cost-benefit analysis, based on its understanding of the probabilities that it would get what it wants from future decision making. Of course, depending on the issue, it may want action or it may want inaction (eliding the choices in between). If the state could specify a rule of unanimity for the decisions where it prefers inaction, and a rule of the easiest possible approval in areas where it prefers action, this would be its ideal outcome. But it is not possible to predict all the issues that may arise, or all the consequences of each issue, with great accuracy. This is fortunate, because under a veil of uncertainty, it becomes possible for states to reach agreement, whereas under certainty they would experience a greater likelihood that negotiations would break down over the division of the gains.

3. Application of the Method of Constitutional Economics to the WTO

This section suggests some of the ways in which constitutional economics may be applied to certain aspects of the WTO. Of course, as noted previously, it is appropriate to view the WTO not as a self-contained constitutional entity but as a part of a broader international legal system, and in its relation to national and regional legal systems.

a. WTO Decision Making

The WTO's decision making is generally effected by consensus, despite provisions of the WTO Charter that permit decision making by majority. Furthermore, most significant decisions, aside from dispute settlement, are effected through treaty amendment, which requires unanimity. If we ignore the differences between a requirement of consensus (no objection) and a requirement of unanimity (express assent), these methods are consistent with the general system of treaty making and amendment in international law. These methods are also consistent with the pre–Single European Act (1987) method for legislation in the European Community: unanimity, or at least no objection, was required for legislation. Interestingly, in both the European Community prior to 1987 and in the WTO today, formal provisions for majority voting are ignored in favor of rules of unanimity.

I have suggested that there may be a kind of dynamic imbalance, or cascade, leading from strong dispute settlement to greater capacity for legislation: from one type of enabling constitutionalization to another. There is a dynamic relationship between enabling constitutionalization of the judicial type and enabling constitutionalization of the legislative type. Strong dispute settlement at the international level might not immediately be recognized as enabling international constitutionalization. However, to the extent that strong international dispute settlement is understood as contributing to the capacity to make law at the international level, its establishment must be understood as a type of enabling international constitutionalization.

Thus, in 1995, at the inception of the WTO, including its Dispute Settlement Understanding, the global community engaged in a type of enabling international constitutionalization. In fact, in functional terms (as opposed to formal terms), the WTO exhibits no other significant features of enabling international constitutionalization. That is, its main transnational (as opposed to intergovernmental) feature is dispute settlement.

Consensus or unanimity-based decision making presents a significant formal limitation. By *limitation* I do not mean to convey a negative judgment: it may be that this limitation is normatively attractive in particular contexts. The limitation is that unanimity, especially in a multilateral context, makes legislation exceedingly difficult. In formal terms, any legislative measure must present benefits to each state: there is no room to achieve legislative transactions that are Kaldor-Hicks efficient but that harm one state, even a small state, and even mildly. Thus, much welfare is left on the table. This formal limitation thus cries out to be overcome. In fact, we might say that a formal unanimity-based system involves no enabling international constitutionalization at all: all decisions are still dependent on each member's determination.[15] There are formal and informal methods by which to overcome this limitation. The formal method is to amend the WTO constitution to provide for majority voting. The informal method is to engage in logrolling-type transactions, or package deals that, on a net basis, benefit all parties. In a sense, enabling constitutionalization may be understood simply as a particularly broad package deal.

As I have already suggested, unanimity-based decision making cannot be defended by a reference to democracy. It can only be defended by such a reference to the extent that the national desire is negative, or defensive – to the extent that the goal is to defeat legislation that may be adverse, in contrast to a goal to pass legislation that is beneficial. This can easily be seen where a single state has the ability to block decisions that are desired by the overwhelming majority of states.[16] This cannot be explained in terms of democracy.

Furthermore, for a similar reason, unanimity-based decision making cannot be defended by a reference to rights or to national autonomy. We might begin by saying that a decision rule of unanimity in international law protects national autonomy, just as a supermajority or unanimity rule in municipal legislation protects individual autonomy. Yet, again, this is seen purely from a defensive standpoint, where autonomy means being left alone and does not include the ability to influence the behavior of others. For, assuming for a moment that a state has equal interests in avoiding constraints on its behavior and procuring constraints on other states' behavior, any voting rule should be equally attractive to any other voting rule. What you lose in legislation constraining others, you gain in autonomy, and vice versa. But if there is a surplus to be gained from making a certain amount of international law, a constitutional arrangement that results in a less than optimal amount of international law is undesirable.

---

[15] On the other hand, if we take a step farther back, we might understand the rule of *pacta sunt servanda* as a type of enabling international constitutionalization.

[16] A good example is the 2008 rejection by Ireland of the proposed Treaty of Lisbon, establishing a constitutional structure for the European Union. In response, German Interior Minister Wolfgang Schäuble made the following statement: "Of course we have to take the Irish referendum seriously, but a few million Irish cannot decide on behalf of 495 million Europeans." Stephen Castle & Judy Dempsey, *Rejection of Treaty Hints at Split in EU*, INT'L HERALD TRIB., June 16, 2008 at 1.

Of course, where you expect to be in the minority more often – where you expect the costs of lost autonomy to exceed the benefits of constraints on others – that reduced capacity to legislate becomes attractive. Under these circumstances, a rule of unanimity or a supermajority rule would be desirable. But it may be even more desirable for other states to compensate you in advance for your willingness to accept an arrangement that is otherwise efficient.

This perspective explains constitutional moments. A constitutional moment would occur when an exogenous shock changes constituent perceptions of the value of legislation. Constituents would be expected to engage in enabling constitutionalization when the anticipated value of constraint on others rises in relation to the anticipated cost of lost autonomy.

And yet, assuming that logrolling, package deals, linkage, side payments, or vote buying are possible without transaction costs, we would expect the efficient level of constraint and autonomy to emerge under any voting rule, just as an efficient allocation of property rights would arise in domestic society under zero transaction costs. So the choice of a voting rule must be based on differential transaction costs. How is this transaction cost–based explanation consistent with the idea, expressed in the prior paragraph, that constitutional moments arise from changes in the value of legislation – from transaction benefits? Constituents would examine the combination of transaction benefits and transaction costs; an increase in transaction benefits would justify greater transaction costs, and a decrease in transaction costs would enable the achievement of transaction benefits that were otherwise out of reach. Changes in transaction benefits result from changing technology, preferences, social structures, or other factors, which are not likely to be immediately malleable through purposive action. On the other hand, the transaction cost component of the equation may be addressed through purposive action, in the form of enabling constitutionalization, assuming that changes in voting rules have effects on transaction costs.

Therefore, in theory, while enhanced dispute settlement may increase the possibility that enhanced legislative capacity at the WTO would be desirable, much depends on the question of whether sufficient impetus in the form of transaction cost improvements would motivate states to move toward some form of voting. This type of shift seems to have taken place in the 1980s in the European Union.[17]

Interestingly, a move toward enabling international constitutionalization in the form of enhanced legislative capacity would demand a move toward

---

[17] See Trachtman, *supra* note 12.

constraining international constitutionalization. In this case, constraining international constitutionalization might take the form of restrictions on the subject matter of legislative capacity exercised at the WTO, as well as human rights limitations on the types of measures that could be legislated.

b. Accountability and the Democratic Deficit

Accountability is a subtle concept, as is the idea of a democratic deficit. The subtlety arises from the conundrum of positive legislative capacity versus negative (or blocking) legislative capacity. The principle is that democracy in the sense of majority rule is not necessarily enhanced by supermajority provisions, or by other devices that constrain international governmental action, because these devices prevent the majority from achieving its goal. This issue is at the core of most claims of American unilateralism – many of these are claims that the United States fails to join a multilateral treaty, such as the Kyoto Protocol or the Rome Statute of the International Criminal Court, thereby defeating the will of the majority.

Here, it is necessary to link the WTO's constitution to its member states' constitutions. To the extent that the WTO is truly a member organization – an international as opposed to a transnational organization – perhaps the democracy deficit critique is misguided, and the real question is one of member-state democracy. Thus, under circumstances of decision making by unanimity, direct accountability at the international level would not serve as constraining international constitutionalization, as there is little capacity at the international level to constrain. It might be understood as a type of supplemental constitutionalization: addressing an accountability issue that arises with globalization. The accountability issue under these circumstances of decision making by consensus must be that the national government is not sufficiently accountable at home, in connection with the commitments it accepts at the WTO.

Alternatively, if the concern is that even under a rule of unanimity, some member states lack sufficient influence in the WTO, perhaps the democracy deficit would be addressed through empowerment of those states rather than the addition of parliamentary control at the WTO level. Indeed, it may be that the Uruguay Round was concluded through threats of exclusion from the "single undertaking" in a way that gave weaker states insufficient influence.

However, under (hypothetical) circumstances of decision making by majority, where the WTO would no longer be considered a member organization, arrangements for direct accountability may be understood differently, as a type of constraining constitutionalization. As constraining constitutionalization, accountability measures would ensure that decision making is accountable to constituents. Constituents desire procedures that ensure that their voices are heard, especially under majority voting, where they have accepted that their preferences may not hold sway.

In this context also, under majority voting, concern for fundamental rights serves as a form of constraining international constitutionalization, specifying areas into which international legislation may not infringe. Thus, if majority voting were implemented at the WTO, it would seem appropriate also to implement a set of human rights constraints on the decisions taken by majority vote. A similar process took place in the European Union, where the *Solange* decisions gave rise to the establishment of an EU human rights capacity.

On the other hand, one might argue that since the WTO dispute settlement system already holds significant legislative power – as there was a move toward enabling constitutionalization in 1994 – the WTO should already be subjected to human rights constraints. One response to this argument lies in the textualism of the WTO dispute settlement system. Under an interpretative approach that sees itself as constrained by text, there is reduced scope for significant legislative action under the mantle of dispute settlement, and so reduced legislative authority. According to this argument, WTO law comprises more specific "rules" rather than more general "standards" with minimal judicial discretion.[18]

Of course, another response to this argument that the WTO system has legislative power by virtue of its authority to adjudicate is again the claim that the WTO is a member organization, and that each of its members is already subject to a broad set of human rights obligations. Combined with this response is the argument that, so long as the human rights are implemented somewhere, they need not be implemented at the WTO per se. This latter point is based on a broader vision of the international legal system rather than on an isolated vision of the WTO. This argument puts great pressure on the relationship between WTO law and human rights law – on coherence. If there were sufficient coherence, there would be no need for supplemental constitutionalization in this context. A further response is that there already is a somewhat uncertain relationship between WTO dispute settlement and human rights, within WTO dispute settlement. Certainly under article 31 of the Vienna Convention on the Law of Treaties, at least universal human rights rules would be used in the interpretation of WTO law. Some argue that

---

[18] *See* Trachtman, *supra* note 4.

human rights rules would be directly applicable, as law, within WTO dispute settlement, but this argument is increasingly untenable.

c. WTO Dispute Settlement, Supremacy, and Direct Effect

The preceding paragraph already addresses a critical issue in connection with WTO dispute settlement: the extent to which it may be understood as a form of legislative action. There is an important quasi-legislative role for dispute settlement to play at the international level. Often this role is one of elaboration and application of general standards set by legislatures, as opposed to more specific rules.

Often, in connection with EU legal affairs, supremacy and direct effect are noted as features of constitutionalization. Indeed, these features, along with judicial review, are seen as the central features of constitutionalization, or at least of judicial constitutionalization. However, these features of EU law must be understood primarily as constitutionalization at the domestic level: they enabled EU law to have constitution like power at the domestic level in the EU context. They act to restrict the scope of ordinary law at the domestic level, and thus play a quasi-constitutional role at that level. The same would be true in the case of supremacy and direct effect of WTO law. Interestingly, of course, WTO law, as international law, is already supreme over municipal law within the international legal system (of course, the same was true of the Treaty of Rome). However, it is within the domestic legal system that this supremacy, and effect, is contested. So, in connection with supremacy and direct effect, the interesting international aspect is the source of the domestic constitutional rule: whether it is a matter of domestic law or a matter of international law. But the main point is that supremacy and direct effect are generally constitutional only in the domestic legal system and not in the international legal system.

But before we move on, concluding that the discussion of supremacy and direct effect as international constitutional issues is merely a category mistake, we must note that there is another, more subtle, effect that can be understood in terms of international constitutionalization. Under the prevailing horizontal structure of the international legal system, with only limited mandatory adjudication, and where even such adjudication as exists cannot generally form the basis for strong enforcement, international law often lacks the compliance force of municipal law. But direct effect allows the international legal system, and such international law as is directly effective, to take advantage of the strong compliance force provided by the municipal legal system. In this sense, direct effect is a component of enabling international constitutionalization: it provides legislative capacity to the international system by lending the relevant international law greater force than it would otherwise have. Supremacy within the municipal setting plays a similar role.

d. Fragmentation and the WTO

Fragmentation – the phenomenon of diverse functional sources of international law and diverse tribunals applying international law – is not necessarily a problem. There are components of fragmentation that must be understandable as benevolent functional pluralism. On the other hand, there may be fragmentation that results from inadequate integration of different functional goals. While globalization is an integrated phenomenon, with complementarities and spillovers, most legal instruments have been developed in single-issue contexts.

The constitutional issue here is one of allocation of subject matter, or jurisdictional, authority among functional entities. The rules that make this allocation are termed by Hart *secondary rules,* to distinguish them from ordinary laws, which are termed *primary rules.* In our context, relating the WTO to the United Nations, the United Nations Environment Programme, the World Intellectual Property Organization, the ILO, and the UN Conference on Trade and Development, and so on, can be understood as relating different constitutional structures to one another. Hence, I have called the rules that would allocate authority among these entities "tertiary rules." These tertiary rules allocate authority among constitutions: among state constitutions, between state constitutions and international organization constitutions, and among international organization constitutions. It should be noted at the outset that the structure of the international legal system itself might be understood as the one true constitutional structure, with all of these functional entities, and states, being mere substructures. However, the residual authority in this system is not clearly allocated, unlike, for example, the U.S. federal structure in which the central government seems under current historical circumstances to be the residual authority.

Thus, we operate in an era of uncertainty as to the residual authority among international organizations or different functional sources of international law. However, this uncertainty is not necessarily inefficient. If conflicts between these rules were not sufficiently frequent and important, we would not expect states to expend the negotiation resources to establish either specific rules or more general standards by which to resolve these conflicts. The establishment of these rules would be an important component of both enabling constitutionalization and of constraining constitutionalization, as it would enable and constrain the legislative authority of different functional entities in the international legal system.

Thus, another facet of constitutionalization addresses the extent to which broad social values are integrated with one another, and more specifically, the way in which market concerns are integrated with nonmarket concerns. It is striking that both the United States and the European Union began with emphases on commercial relations and developed broader capacities over time. It is also striking that each domestic government has the institutional capacity to deal with interfunctional trade-offs.

It is in this sense that constitutionalization is concerned with capacities: here the capacity to integrate diverse values. Functional subsidiarity counsels against aggregating all multilateral power to the WTO, while increasing functional linkage makes some kinds of intersectoral coherence useful.[19] In order to assess the degree of coherence, we must look both within and without the WTO.

Within the WTO, we can see the development of a modest approach to intersectoral coherence in the WTO's reference to standards promulgated by international standards organizations. We can also see it in the Appellate Body's *Shrimp-Turtle* decision, which referred to an international environmental agreement in order to assist in interpreting some of the exceptional provisions of the WTO agreements. But the international community may need to develop more complete and predictable mechanisms to promote coherence between trade policy and other policies. These will not necessarily result in a perfect hierarchy or in uniform enforceability of all international law. States need flexibility to create both harder and softer international law, and indeed to avoid answering some questions. This counsels against blanket calls both for direct effect of WTO law in domestic legal orders,[20] and for the enforcement of other international law in WTO dispute settlement. Each legal rule, and its binding effect based on the institutional structure available to implement it, respond to a specific social setting and set of incentives. Given diverse social settings, it would be wrong to prescribe uniformity of institutional structure or binding effect.

Developing countries have been reluctant to bring human rights, labor rights, or environmental protection inside the WTO more directly, for fear that social clauses will be used as bases for protectionism. Implicit in this position is the assumption that social clauses cannot today be used as bases

---

[19] *See* Joel P. Trachtman, *Transcending "Trade and . . . " – An Institutional Perspective*, 96 Am. J. Int'l L. 77 (2002). Robert L. Howse & Kalypso Nicolaïdes, *Enhancing WTO Legitimacy: Constitutionalization or Global Subsidiarity*, 16 Governance 73 (2003), refer to the same concept as "horizontal subsidiarity."

[20] Joel P. Trachtman & Philip Moremen, *Whose Right Is It Anyway? Private Parties in EC-U.S. Dispute Settlement at the WTO*, 44 Harv. Int'l L.J. 221 (2003).

for protectionism. In order to advance coherent policy making in these areas, at levels that will satisfy the wealthier states, it will be necessary to establish mechanisms to guard against protectionism. It may also be necessary to provide compensation to poorer states in exchange for their willingness to accept standards that may otherwise be inappropriate, or simply too costly, for their society or level of development. Compensation could be provided through trade liberalization or even through direct monetary settlements.

Outside the WTO, the broader international system responds to the problem of coherence, but perhaps in too limited a fashion. The broader international system is characterized by decentralized global law making and decentralized global adjudication. This decentralized system does not satisfactorily respond to the need, under circumstances of varying and shifting legislative sources, to resolve conflicts between rules.

Conflicts between rules are the legal face of conflicts between different values. The core issue is a choice of law problem, not between states in a horizontal legal order, nor between component political entities and a central government. Rather, it is an interfunctional choice of law problem, between law that arises in different sectors of the international legal system, from different functional and institutional contexts – indeed from different constitutional structures. These contexts overlap like tectonic plates, and sometimes collide with one another, causing discontinuity and disruption.

The current structure of the international legal system for dealing with diverse legal rules from diverse sources is certainly imperfect, utilizing formal last-in-time rules or perhaps a *lex specialis* rule to address some of the most important normative issues faced by international society. These problems of policy integration are not susceptible to simple solutions. For example, even a rule to the effect that human rights trumps other international law, if it existed, would not solve the problem, partly because the rights revolution has asserted many rights that conflict with one another. While we may delegate the policy integration job to judges, we do not do so wholesale in the domestic sphere. So there is little reason to expect that judges will make all these decisions in the international sphere.

Over the next fifty years, we may expect to see more negotiations in an effort to develop more nuanced means to integrate different global values, such as trade, environment, and human rights. These negotiations will take place in response to perceptions of real conflict and will result in nuanced rules and institutional development. They will no doubt reduce the indeterminacy arising from wide variation in the arrangements for adjudication in different subject areas – from functionally decentralized international adjudication. But they will not eliminate it. Thus, in order to mediate and deal with conflicts in the allocation of authority among international organizations, and indeed between different rules of international law, we can expect development of interfunctional constitutionalization both within and without the WTO legal system. The tertiary rules developed may be of the nature of either rules or standards, and to the extent that standards are utilized it may indeed be appropriate to delegate the application of these standards to judges.

Interfunctional constitutionalization can thus be understood in terms of constitutional economics. Interfunctional constitutions facilitate intersectoral trade-offs among different categories of preferences. In terms of the theory of the firm, they bring within a single institution the different categories of preferences that otherwise would intersect in the market of the general international legal system. This theoretical perspective provides a ready understanding that there will be some functional areas that should be addressed together within a single international organization and others that will be better addressed separately.[21]

e. Trade and Redistribution

The work of John Rawls fits well into the constitutional economics tradition.[22] His "veil of ignorance" can be understood as a means to simplify negotiations of constitutional principles by putting the particular distributive consequences in the background. He uses this mechanism to speculate on the principles that would be agreed. One of the principles relevant here is the difference principle, which holds that economic inequality can be justified only to the extent that it redounds to the benefit of the poorest. To the extent that trade liberalization may cause increased economic inequality, it would appear appropriate to develop a redistributive mechanism in order to ensure that an appropriate portion of the benefits from free trade are redistributed to the poor.

This constitutional principle could be converted into positive constitutional law through negotiations. Constitutional reforms may be a necessary part of a redistributive settlement at the WTO. These constitutional reforms may include a modification of decision making that would provide more power to the poor, or the establishment of rights that effect redistribution to the poor. At the WTO, the main focus for the poor in the near future will be on mechanisms to produce greater liberalization in sectors in which the poor could compete.

---

[21] For arguments regarding the scope of issues that might be addressed within the WTO, *see* Andrew T. Guzman, *Global Governance and the WTO*, 45 HARV. INT'L L.J. 303 (2004).

[22] *See* Mueller, *supra* note 1.

However, it is not necessary that these negotiations, or their results, be located within the WTO. It would not be impossible for the WTO to evolve into the ministry of efficiency for the world, while some other organization, such as the World Bank, the UN Development Programme, or something else evolved into the ministry of redistribution.

Similarly, the embedded liberalism concept of Karl Polanyi and John Ruggie may also be understood within the constitutional economics tradition. Under this concept, mechanisms for redistribution through regulation are a price to be paid to those who would otherwise lose from liberalization, in order to ensure the continuity of the benefits of liberalization. The WTO is both a result and a cause of greater global interdependence, and of the development of global society. To avoid disruption of this global society, by démarches in trade, economic catastrophes or violent upheavals in member states, or terrorism, it is morally and politically necessary to develop mechanisms to enhance the position of the poor.[23]

f. The WTO Demos?

Is it necessary to have a demos in order to have a constitution, and does the WTO have one? Joseph Weiler points out that the European Union itself lacks a "constitutional demos," and so is not rooted in a central federal-type power.[24] The WTO has much less of a constitutional demos. Claims of existence of a demos are based on a type of cultural or ethnic affinity that motivates loyalty to a social structure. Indeed, a shared history, with its attendant values, concerns, and camaraderie, may be understood in institutional economics terms itself, and may indeed shape behavior. These informal institutions may be seen as complements or substitutes for formal constitutional structures, depending on the circumstances.

While constitutional economics tends to highlight formal institutions, and would not ordinarily be demos-dependent, it is open to the possibility that cultural or ethnic factors may enter its analysis, either as informal institutions as has been discussed here or as preferences of two types. First, we may prefer a society composed of our compatriots in a cultural or ethnic sense. Second, we may have a greater preference for altruism vis-à-vis our cultural or ethnic compatriots than vis-à-vis others.

---

[23] Joel P. Trachtman, *Legal Aspects of a Poverty Agenda at the WTO: Trade Law and "Global Apartheid,"* 6 J. INT'L ECON. L. 3 (2003).

[24] Joseph H. H. Weiler, *Federalism without Constitutionalism: Europe's Sonderweg,* FED. VISION, Nov. 2001, at 54–71; *See also* Jürgen Habermas, *So, Why Does Europe Need a Constitution?* 11 NEW LEFT REV., Sept.-Oct. 2001.

Constitutional economics is allied with the concept of constitutional patriotism: it highlights not the exogenous cultural or ethnic causes of constitutional loyalty but the structural and contextual reasons why a constitution allows the greater satisfaction of individual preferences. But constitutional economics recognizes the place of shared experience and shared characteristics, in terms of informal institutions and preferences.

So, the lack of a WTO demos, today, does not stand in the way of the existence of a WTO constitution, but it does suggest that a WTO constitution would be different, in terms of the informal complements and in terms of preferences for solidarity, from a typical image of a national constitution. To the extent that the informal institutions of a demos are substitutes for other forms of constitutionalization, the lack of such a demos at the WTO would suggest a place for greater constitutionalization at the WTO than at the national level.

4. Conclusion: The Level of Analysis Problem

The preceding discussion shows that the international legal system indeed has a constitution, with enabling, constraining, and supplemental features. There is also no doubt that the WTO constitution is a part of this broader constitution, and that it too has enabling, constraining, and supplemental features vis-à-vis states, other international organizations, and the international legal system in general. Indeed, it is these enabling, constraining, and supplemental features that define – that constitute – the WTO in relation to these other entities.

A constitutional matrix is a useful tool of taxonomy, but it cannot answer the question, at any particular level, of what constitutional features are needed. Rather, it is constitutional economics that provides the answer to this question. Constitutional economics examines the existing structure for decision making and evaluates the existing structure in comparison to other potential structures as a device for producing legal rules. It recognizes that it may be costly to fail to produce legal rules that could benefit citizens, and that it also may be costly to produce legal rules that harm citizens. So, constitutional economics assumes that states, in the international constitutionalization process, use enabling constitutionalization, constraining constitutionalization, and supplemental constitutionalization to establish the types of international constitutions that are optimal. Optimal constitutions are those that maximize the benefits of production of international law, net of transaction costs.

Of course, there is a public choice critique of this rosy picture: the establishment of constitutional rules is an exercise of power, and constitutional discourse may constrain the good and enable the bad.[25] Yet one may respond that this is the human condition, and it applies to all law: men and women have found it good to depart anarchy and to establish constitutional rules in many contexts.

The most difficult work will be at the margins: at the places where different constitutions engage one another. These places will require delicate management. Delicate management does not necessarily require formal, specific, legal rules; in fact, it seldom does in the most important areas. Rather, it is not unusual to find these marginal areas ruled by comity in the form of mutual deference, by muddy rules that give rise to negotiations in specific cases, by threats, and by conflict. This is true even in the domestic setting. For example, there are many areas in U.S. constitutional law of give-and-take, of uncertainty, and of conflict. If such murkiness were simply wrong, or inefficient, would it not have been addressed by now?

Where rules, or standards, are developed in order to mediate between the constitutions of different international organizations, or between the constitutions of international organizations and those of states, we might understand these as tertiary rules. Constitutional economics can provide a perspective and a set of tools that can be brought to bear on whether tertiary rules are needed, and what their structure should be. For example, the perspective of constitutional economics would endorse a rule of constitutional subsidiarity, allocating constitutional functions at the constitutional level that may address the relevant issue most efficiently. Furthermore, a kind of interfunctional rule of constitutional subsidiarity, allocating authority to the international organization best able to address the relevant issue, is also consistent with constitutional economics.

---

[25] *See* Jeffrey Dunoff's contribution to this volume, Chapter 7.

PART III: CROSSCUTTING ISSUES

Exploring the Relationships among International and Domestic Constitutions

9. Human Rights and International Constitutionalism

STEPHEN GARDBAUM

I. Introduction

Gerald Neuman starts an important essay as follows: "Two leading systems exist today for protecting the fundamental rights of individuals: constitutional law and [international] human rights law.... For liberal states that actively enforce constitutional norms, the relationship between these two systems assumes increasing importance."[1] Neuman explores this relationship by focusing on the institutional consequences and mutual interactions of the two systems.

In trying to both clarify and evaluate the role of human rights law in discussions about international constitutionalism, my focus in this chapter will be less on the relationship between these two legal systems than on their differences and respective functions. I will ask and address two threshold questions. First, how different are the two systems? Second, why have both systems?

Whatever the general degree of analogy or dissimilarity between constitutional law and international law,[2] domestic bills of rights and international human rights law undoubtedly perform the same basic function of stating

---

[1] Gerald L. Neuman, *Human Rights and Constitutional Rights: Harmony and Dissonance*, 55 STAN. L. REV. 1863, 1863–64 (2003).

[2] *See, e.g.,* Laurence R. Helfer, *Constitutional Analogies in the International Legal System*, 37 LOY. L. REV. 193 (2003); Jack L. Goldsmith III & Daryl J. Levinson, *Law for States: International Law, Constitutional Law, Public Law*, 122 HARVARD L. REV. (forthcoming, 2009).

Professor of Law, UCLA School of Law. This chapter was presented at the book workshop "Ruling the World? Constitutionalism, International Law & Global Government," held on December 6–7, 2007 at Temple University School of Law. Thanks to Jeff Dunoff and Joel Trachtman for organizing the workshop and for inviting me to participate in the project. Thanks also to Samantha Besson and Michael Perry for extremely helpful comments on an earlier draft, and to Gerry Neuman for valuable and incisive commentary on my paper at the workshop.

limits on what governments may do to people within their jurisdictions.[3]
Indeed, in "liberal states that actively enforce constitutional norms," international human rights law tends to place similar limits on the very same
governments. So what are the major differences between the two beyond the
obvious one of source? In particular, is there anything "constitutional" about
international human rights law? Should one conclude from the similarity
of function and substance that international human rights law is primarily
meaningful in, or addressed to, nonliberal or non-Western states? Or are there
perhaps other – distinctive – functions performed by international human
rights law in protecting fundamental rights everywhere? What additional
contribution, if any, does human rights law make to the general development
of constitutionalism?

As many have commented, the four related terms *constitutional, constitutionalism, constitution,* and *constitutionalization* have tended to be used
in a vague, fuzzy, or interchangeable way within the international constitutionalism literature (though not only here), which often obscures rather than
clarifies the precise claim being advanced – whether descriptive or normative.
Rather than offer my own necessarily abstract definitions or stipulations, I
think the more helpful task is to frame questions and claims with sufficient
precision and specificity that the distinct – if related – ideas expressed by
these terms become clear in context. At least, this is what I shall try to do.

Let me end my introductory comments with what is perhaps a paradox.
Although human rights law is at the forefront of the developments driving
the most general of the international constitutionalist claims – that international law should replace its traditional, horizontal paradigm of the sovereign
equality of states with a more vertical, constitutionalist paradigm – it is in
some ways exceptional within this overarching narrative. One central part
of this narrative is the loss of state governance power within its territory
in the face of such forces as globalization, privatization, federalization, and
supranationalism so that state constitutions are no longer "total constitutions." Some of this lost power has been transferred to the international level,
which has taken on increasing governance functions. A second part of the
narrative is the normative problem of the legitimacy of international law that
results from this increased governance function. Here, constitutionalism at
the international level, as a form of "compensatory constitutionalism," has
been proposed as a solution.[4]

---

[3] I do not intend to suggest in either case that this is the only function or, in the case of
international human rights law, the only basic function.

[4] Anne Peters, *Compensatory Constitutionalism: The Function and Potential of Fundamental
International Norms and Structures,* 19 LEIDEN J. INT'L L. 579 (2006).

Yet neither the loss of state power story nor the legitimacy problem of international law applies very obviously or directly to international human rights. Although conceptually international human rights law has contributed to the former by piercing the veil of sovereignty, in practice the major barrier to developing a more effective system of protecting and enforcing fundamental rights at the international level is still too much state power, not too little. Similarly, whatever other problems beset international human rights law, its general legitimacy is not high on the list.[5] No one talks of a democracy deficit in the European Convention on Human Rights.

II. How Different Are the Two Systems?

One obvious similarity between the two systems of constitutional law and international human rights law is their age. Although, to be sure, there were important precursors and subsequent developments in each system, both were essentially created after 1945 as responses to the massive violations of fundamental rights immediately before and during World War II. This filled what was a major gap in the coverage of *both* domestic law and international law.

A slightly less obvious but very important similarity is their general content and structure. Taken as a whole, and with the most notable exception of parts of the International Covenant on Economic, Social and Cultural Rights (ICESCR) and the Convention on the Elimination of All Forms of Discrimination against Women (CEDAW), the rights contained in the major international human rights treaties are very broadly similar in substance to the rights contained in most modern constitutions.[6] Both typically include such civil and political rights as the right to the liberty and security of the person; rights against torture, cruel and inhumane punishment, and slavery; the right to vote; rights to freedom of expression and religious practice; and rights to be free from state discrimination on the basis of race, ethnicity, national origin, and sex. Many domestic bills of rights also include some or most of the core social and economic rights contained in the ICESCR, such as the rights to education, health care, choice of work, and basic standard of living.

---

[5] Even the most direct recent attack on the international human rights system as a form of Western imperialism, in the name of "Asian values," takes pains not to deny the general legitimacy of international human rights law but rather how it is currently institutionalized and organized.

[6] Certain parts of the ICESCR and CEDAW are exceptional because they include more detailed and extensive social and economic rights than are found even in those domestic bills of rights that contain the greatest number of such rights.

Moreover, both systems generally share a common structure of rights. Thus, a few rights in each system are treated as categorical or peremptory norms, permitting no limitations or derogations. Apart from these, the primary conception of rights is as presumptive shields rather than as absolute trumps, permitting them in principle to be justifiably limited or overridden where necessary to promote important but conflicting public policy objectives. Such limits tend to be expressed in either or both derogation during national emergency clauses and special or general limitations clauses. Most of the rights in each system apply directly only against governments and not private actors, although in various ways – including where they are understood to impose positive duties on those governments – many of the rights *indirectly* regulate private relations.[7] In that they frequently contain a general duty to enact legislative or other measures necessary to give practical effect to all protected rights, human rights treaties typically impose more extensive positive duties than domestic bills of rights. Overall, it is because of these general similarities that the three main international human rights instruments are often collectively referred to as the "international bill of rights" and that one can talk about two systems for protecting the same thing: namely, the fundamental rights of individuals.

Beyond these important similarities of function, age, substance, and structure, a well-known but very important institutional difference between the two is their respective methods of enforcement. Thus, while the tremendous growth in the number of constitutional courts exercising full powers of judicial review and compulsory jurisdiction over their governments has led to the recent coining of such terms as *juristocracy* and *juridification*, international human rights courts with similar powers remain the exception rather than the rule, especially at the global level.

A more complex issue is that bills of rights typically – though not always – have constitutional status within domestic legal systems (hence Neuman's categorization). Accordingly, in thinking about human rights law as an international bill of rights without quotation marks, the question I want to raise and address in the remainder of this section is whether this fact points to a major difference between the two legal systems or whether, to the contrary, the difference between them is further reduced because international human rights law is also, or has become, constitutional in some significant sense.

---

[7] On the difference between direct and indirect effect of constitutional rights on private actors, as well as the variety of types of indirect effect, see Stephen Gardbaum, *The "Horizontal" Effect of Constitutional Rights*, 102 MICH. L. REV. 387 (2003).

There is undoubtedly something inherently constitutional in the very nature and subject matter of international human rights law, in that one of its primary functions is to specify limits on what governments can lawfully do to people within their jurisdictions. This is a central constitutional function; indeed, it is arguably the most direct and straightforward constitutional function performed by any type of international law – in that international law does not (EU supranationalism apart) clearly organize and empower any general political authority.

But beyond this central function that inheres in the very existence of international human rights law, is there anything constitutional about the international human rights system in some more specific sense? I think there are three more specific claims that either can be or have been made, and need to be distinguished in order to assess the difference between the two systems and the contribution (or limitations) of international constitutionalism in the area of human rights. The first is that the international human rights system has become one of constitutional law in its own right, thereby creating twin systems of domestic and international constitutional law protecting fundamental rights. In other words, the legal status of the protected rights has become similar within each system. The second claim is that regardless of the precise legal status of the protected rights vis-à-vis other types of international law, the human rights system itself can properly be characterized as a constitutionalized regime *of* international law in the same way that some other international regimes – most notably the European Union – are understood to be. The third claim is that the development of international human rights law is a critical part of the general case for rejecting the traditional, horizontal paradigm of international law based on the sovereign equality of states, and replacing it with a more vertical, constitutionalist, or public law paradigm.

In further clarifying and evaluating these three claims about what is constitutional about human rights law, it may be helpful to refer to two different processes of constitutionalization that have, on the whole, been separately discussed by comparative constitutional and international lawyers, respectively. The first process concerns the legal status of fundamental rights within a given regime and, in particular, the shift from ordinary to higher law status of rights that has characterized so many domestic systems since 1945. Relatively recent examples of such internal constitutionalization of rights are Canada's Charter of Fundamental Rights and Freedoms that superseded its statutory Bill of Rights in 1982, and the United Kingdom's Human Rights Act of 1998 that created a comprehensive bill of rights within the domestic legal system, albeit by "constitutional statute," for the first time (at least in three hundred years).[8] Accordingly, the first claim – that human rights law is international constitutional law – raises the issue of whether a similar shift has taken place.

The second process of constitutionalization, which has mainly concerned international lawyers, is the transformation of a particular international law regime from a purely treaty-based entity to a constitutional one. Here, the European Union presents the paradigmatic case, and a good part of the international constitutionalism debate consists of asking whether other international regimes can be said to have followed suit. So the second claim addresses the issue of whether the human rights system has itself become a constitutionalized regime of international law in this sense, and the third, whether and how human rights has contributed to the constitutionalization of international law as a whole.

A. Is Human Rights Law International Constitutional Law?

Although there is undoubtedly something inherently constitutional about human rights law in that it functions to limit what governments can do to persons within their jurisdictions, the precise question for consideration here, however, is whether this "something" currently amounts to giving human rights the specific legal status of constitutional law. Obviously, limits on governments can and do take a variety of legal and nonlegal forms; in the purely domestic context, they may be constitutional, statutory, common law, administrative, conventional, or simply political and/or pragmatic. As constitutional law is law of a particular type, this question has, at least in part, an unavoidably formal content – although, to be sure, this content must be abstracted away from the purely domestic context. Indeed, because the European Union is now almost universally acknowledged to have constitutional law (even without a formal constitution), of which its human rights law is part, this type of law is no longer in practice, and so cannot be conceptualized as, limited to the national.

What are the defining characteristics of constitutional law, in the sense exemplified by (though not limited to) the first legal system for protecting fundamental rights? That is, putting to one side the purely functional sense of constitutional law as any law containing one or more metarules for the organization and ordering of political authority, as traditionally employed in the United Kingdom.

First, it is law made by a special, episodic, and self-consciously constituent power – however real, nominal, or hard to identify in practice – as compared

---

[8] I analyze these two examples and suggest that they present a new, alternative model of constitutionalism in Stephen Gardbaum, *The New Commonwealth Model of Constitutionalism*, 49 AM. J. COMP. L. 707 (2001).

to the ordinary, continuous law-making processes. In some cases, this power is institutionalized in a specially appointed constituent assembly, a special ratification or decision-making process, or simply the same body wearing a different hat, as with the Israeli Knesset; in others, it may be less institutionalized than manifested in the quality and length of deliberation.[9] Second, constitutional law is higher law and typically occupies the highest position in the hierarchy of norms comprising all types of positive law, trumping such other law in case of conflict. Third, constitutional law is entrenched against ordinary methods of amendment or repeal that apply to statutes and other forms of law by means of some type of additional procedural or supermajority requirement. As the highest form of law emanating from a special constituent authority, constitutional law can be amended or repealed only by that same law-making authority or its equivalent. (Of course, in practice constitutional law can be changed – if not amended or repealed – by judicial interpretation.)

Although distinctive of domestic constitutional law protection since 1945, special methods of enforcement – particularly through judicial review – are not strictly required. There is a clear and meaningful sense in which the Netherlands protects fundamental rights by constitutional law – and the United Kingdom and New Zealand do not – despite the express absence of judicial review in its constitution.[10] Whether fundamental rights are effectively protected without some form of judicial review is a separate, if practically very important, question, especially in the context of international human rights, where there is a significant difference between regional and global systems in this regard.

Determining whether, or to what extent, international human rights law satisfies these various criteria is complicated by two obvious and well-known factors: (1) as just mentioned, there is no single international human rights system but regional and global ones that overlap and interact in complex ways; and (2) there is no single international legal source of human rights law, and many of the sources also overlap. So although the most common method of

---

[9] Even if one accepts Jed Rubenfeld's distinction between "democratic constitutionalism" in the United States and "internationalist constitutionalism" in Europe, between self-government and the protection of one or more universal human rights, such as dignity, as the foundational normative basis of a constitution, this does not mean that European constitutions were not equally the products of a (democratic) constituent power. Thus, the Basic Law of Germany only came into effect upon ratification by two-thirds of the Länder, as required by article 144(1); not so very different from the U.S. Constitution's requirement in article 7 of ratification by "the Conventions of nine [out of thirteen] States." See Jed Rubenfeld, *Unilateralism and Constitutionalism*, 79 N.Y.U. L. REV. 1971 (2004).

[10] Article 120 of the Netherlands Constitution states: "The constitutionality of Acts of parliament and treaties shall not be reviewed by the courts."

legalizing human rights has been international treaties, some human rights law – including many rights also incorporated into treaties – has its source in custom and, arguably, also in general principles. Moreover, when the small subset of human rights that have achieved *jus cogens* status (and also, if larger, the subset imposing *erga omnes* duties) is factored in, certain human rights norms, such as the ban on genocide, may fall into every category.

Indeed, more generally, one might doubt whether the question of the international constitutional status of human rights law has very much traction. As is well known, there is much disagreement about whether any general hierarchy of norms in international law exists. Even if it does, it is relatively rare in practice for there to be a conflict between a state's human rights obligations and another, subsequent international law obligation – perhaps the only type of situation where international constitutional status would matter in practice. This contrasts with the much more common situation of a conflict between a state's human rights obligation and either (1) its own purely domestic law or action or (2) its international conduct that is not undertaken as a matter of international obligation. And even where there is such a conflict, international human rights monitoring or enforcement bodies do not generally have jurisdiction to resolve it as such, but rather only to determine whether the human rights they are empowered to enforce have been violated. This means that faced with such a conflict, an international human rights court, for example, would tend to frame the issue as whether the subsequent international obligation justifies the limitation of the right as far as the human rights treaty is concerned. In other words, the court will tend to assume its priority. Arguably, only a more general international court would have the jurisdiction genuinely to resolve the conflict by deciding which international law obligation takes priority.

Nonetheless, I think the question worth pursuing for what it may reveal, positively or negatively, about the human rights system. Admittedly, for the reasons just given, it may frequently be the case that not very much of direct practical significance turns on the answer. But apart from such practical reasons, domestic bills of rights are also typically granted constitutional status – and often placed at the beginning of a constitutional text – for expressive reasons, to reflect a collective commitment to fundamental rights as the most important legal norms within that system. It is a useful exercise to explore whether, or to what extent – rhetoric aside – the international legal system currently expresses a similar commitment. Moreover, if there is international constitutional law at all, which is certainly one claim that international constitutionalists make, then one would expect international human rights law to be part of it.

Let me begin by testing the criteria in a different international context and asking how they apply in the case of EU law, where it is generally understood that both the Treaty of Rome and EU human rights principles operate as constitutional law within the EU legal system. Primarily this is because of their higher law status. Thus, both the Treaty itself and the European Court of Justice's (ECJ) human rights jurisprudence trump all other types of EU law in cases of conflict. Indeed, arguably EU human rights law would trump the Treaty if such a conflict were ever found, although (until such time as the Charter of Fundamental Rights is made binding and incorporated into the Treaty) the ECJ would likely rationalize this situation to the effect that as general principles of law, EU human rights law is authorized by, and so part of, the Treaty itself. Although supremacy is the most important reason for attributing constitutional status, it is not the only relevant criterion – at least as far as the Treaty is concerned. The iterative and highly deliberative process of promoting European integration though law that culminated in the 1957 Treaty is plausibly viewed as amounting to a constitutional moment, as, too, are certain subsequent amendments and additions. Moreover, the cumbersome amendment process of convening an intergovernmental conference and the requirement of unanimous ratification before its proposals take effect entrenches the Treaty of Rome by comparison with many other treaties, including some human rights ones.

How do the three criteria apply to international human rights law? With respect to constituent power, the methods of international law-making – treaties aside – are notoriously hard to specify with any precision. Moreover, there is no general conception of a constituent power at the international legal level. Nonetheless, the UN Charter and the two general global human rights treaties that it authorized and that took twenty years to negotiate have credible claims, like the Treaty of Rome, to be products of constitutional moments – of a constituent authority – in a way that much other international law does not.

Whether there is a hierarchy of norms within international law in general, whether this is a question worthy of further inquiry, and whether human rights law is superior to other types of international law in particular are all matters of significant disagreement and debate inside and outside the international constititutionalist literature.[11] There is perhaps general agreement that a small but critical core of the most important human rights law has

---

[11] See, e.g., the disagreement on this score between Anne Peters, *supra* note 4, and Christian Walter, *Constitutionalizing (Inter)national Governance – Possibilities for and Limits to the Development of an International Constitutional Law*, 44 GERMAN Y.B. INT'L L. 170 (2001). On the value of the enterprise, *see* J. H. H. Weiler & Andreas Paulus, *The Structure of Change*

achieved jus cogens and, thus, higher law status as binding treaty makers and probably also trumping conflicting custom (if such a conflict is a conceptual possibility), although there is less consensus about how – the process by which – norms achieve this status, which may prevent the list from being added to. Some argue that a next tranche of human rights law imposes erga omnes duties on states, although neither which these are nor the precise hierarchical implications of this is very clear. Finally, article 103 of the UN Charter supplies a form of supremacy clause. It provides that "[i]n the event of a conflict between the obligations of the Members of the United Nations under the present Charter and their obligations under any other international agreement, their obligations under the present Charter shall prevail." Yet the Charter itself, of course, includes no specific human rights obligations, and the extent to which article 103 incorporates subsequent human rights measures mandated or authorized under the Charter's general auspices remains an uncertain question. Within the context of human rights treaties (as distinct from the category of jus cogens generally), rights expressly stated to be nonderogable are sometimes claimed to be hierarchically superior to derogable ones, but whether there is a hierarchy among human rights is not directly relevant to whether (all or some) human rights are superior to other types of international law.

At the regional human rights level, the European Court of Human Rights has consistently engaged in the practice of treating the European Convention on Human Rights (ECHR) as supreme over other international treaty obligations of the member states. This is manifested not only by framing infringements of convention rights based on subsequent international obligations as questions of justified limitations under the ECHR (the previously mentioned assumption that the ECHR governs) but also by its general statements about the very nature of the ECHR. Thus, the court has referred to the guarantees of the convention as having a "peremptory character,"[12] and to the ECHR as a "constitutional instrument of European public order."[13] Most directly, it has affirmed that member states "retain Convention liability in respect of treaty commitments subsequent to the entry into force of the Convention."[14]

Another factor surely relevant to its constitutional status is that human rights law is not generally understood to bind international organizations.

---

in *International Law or Is There a Hierarchy of Norms in International Law?* 8 Eur. J. Int'l L. 545 (1997).

[12] Case 45036/98, Bosphorus Hava Yollari Turzim ve Ticaret Anonim Sirketi v. Ireland, para. 154.

[13] Case 15318/89, Loizidou v. Turkey (preliminary objections), para. 75.

[14] *Bosphorus*, para. 154.

This is because such organizations are not parties to human rights treaties, are not clearly subjects of international law for jus cogens purposes, and/or because nonstate actors are square pegs in the hermeneutic circle of customary international law. Again, in comparison with both domestic law and supranational constitutional law, this is a significant limitation on constitutional status. It is hard to conceive of bills of rights not binding the political institutions created by a constitution. And would we still talk about the constitutional status of the Treaty of Rome, or of EU human rights law, if they did not bind the EU institutions?

Finally on supremacy, the "suprapositive,"[15] or preexisting and independent, normative force of human rights law, most obviously captured (but not exhausted) by that subset accorded jus cogens status, distinguishes human rights treaties from other treaties.[16] It is also undoubtedly part of what distinguishes human rights law from other international law on the issue of legitimacy. How this substantive factor plays out in terms of supremacy is less clear, but it is, I think, suggestive of a form of hybrid status somewhat akin to that of countries adopting (what I have termed) the "new commonwealth model of constitutionalism"[17] in the domestic context: a legal status for fundamental rights that largely straddles the normal dichotomy of constitutional versus nonconstitutional law. Like certain "super" or "constitutional statutes" in domestic contexts, which are granted higher than ordinary statute status by means of an interpretive rule requiring subsequent statutes to be read consistently with them if possible and also an ouster of implied repeal, at least some international human rights treaties can be thought of as constitutional treaties in this sense, enshrining a form of quasi-constitutional law at the international level.

Turning to the third characteristic: is international human rights law entrenched? For the small number of core human rights that have achieved the status of jus cogens, they are ipso facto entrenched against treaty amendment or repeal. On the other hand, to the extent that as a matter of positive law the very category of jus cogens derives from an international treaty (art. 53 of the Vienna Convention), this treaty is amendable by the ordinary procedures it stipulates. To the extent that either the category of jus cogens or which norms have this status is a matter of custom or general acceptance, these arguably may be modfied in the same way in which they were established.

---

[15] See Neuman, supra note 1, at 1868–69.

[16] See id.; see also Martti Koskenniemi, The Pull of the Mainstream, 88 Mich. L. Rev. 1946 (1990).

[17] See supra note 7.

With respect to other human rights norms contained in the major inter-national treaties, these treaties themselves typically contain a formal amend-ment process that is somewhat more onerous and specific than the general or default international law of treaty amendments contained in the Vienna Convention, which permits amendment by, and insofar as there is, "agree-ment between the parties." On multilateral treaties in particular, the Vienna Convention requires only that

> any proposal . . . must be notified to all the contracting States, each one of which shall have the right to take part in: (a) the decision as to the action to be taken in regard to such a proposal; and (b) the negotiation and conclusion of any agreement for the amendment of the treaty.[18]

So, for example, the ICCPR requires (1) the convening of an amendment conference upon at least one-third of states parties favoring one following a proposed amendment, (2) a majority vote at the resulting conference, (3) approval of the proposed amendment by the General Assembly, and (4) ratification by a two-thirds majority of the states parties.[19] In both cases, amendments only bind states that have accepted them, but relative to the default rule, the ICCPR is partially entrenched by the specified procedures. Note, however, that there is no unanimity requirement before amendments enter into force, as in the European Union. In other words, states have an "immunity veto" rather than a blocking veto.

On the issue of withdrawal from human rights treaties, the ICCPR in particular has been interpreted as more entrenched than a typical, non–human rights treaty. Under the Vienna Convention, "the termination of a treaty or the withdrawal of a party may take place: (a) in conformity with the provisions of the treaty; (b) at any time by consent of all the parties," or (c) where there is no provision, the intent to permit withdrawal is established or "may be implied by the nature of the treaty."[20] The ICCPR contains no provision on termination or withdrawal, and the Human Rights Committee in General Comment 26 of 1997 declared that there was no such intent, so that a state may not withdraw from it. In so doing, the committee distinguished the permanent protection afforded by the "International Bill of Rights" as a whole from the more temporary character of many other treaties. By contrast, both the ECHR and the American Convention expressly permit denunciations after five years. Trinidad and Tobago exercised its right to denounce the latter in 1998.

---

[18] Vienna Convention on the Law of Treaties, art. 40.
[19] ICCPR, art. 51.   [20] Vienna Convention, arts. 54 & 56.

B. The Human Rights System as a Constitutionalized Regime of International Law

Let's now turn to the other senses, or ways, in which there may be something constitutional about international human rights law. At the outset, it is important to distinguish among legalization, judicialization, and constitutionalization. Certainly there can be no doubt that the human rights system, like the international trade system, has become increasingly legalized and, to a lesser extent, judicialized. But constitutionalization is not simply the sum of these two processes.

As mentioned previously,[21] there are at least two different processes of constitutionalization relevant to discussions about international constitutionalism. The first, discussed in the previous section, is the process by which fundamental rights achieve the legal status of constitutional law – whether domestically or internationally. Here, the key contrast is between ordinary law and higher law. The second, to be discussed in this and the following section, is the process by which a particular international law regime makes a transition from being a horizontal, intergovernmental entity to a more vertical, supranational, or autonomous entity. Here the key contrast is between treaties and constitutions. In this section, I discuss the possible constitutionalization of the human rights system itself, and in the next, the role of the human rights system in the possible constitutionalization of international law as a whole. This latter reflects the most general claim made under the umbrella of international constitutionalism.

If the contrast in this second process of constitutionalization is between treaty-based and constitution-based international entities, what is the difference between them? While there is, of course, no watertight division here but rather a spectrum, I think there are two main differences in this context, either of which is sufficient to ground plausible claims of a constitutionalized regime of international law. The first is that, in very general terms, treaty-based regimes operate primarily at the international level, whereas constitution-based regimes penetrate domestic legal systems to some significant degree and thereby structure a relationship between the two levels. This is constitutionalization as federalization, or what might be thought of as the move from dualism to federalism. The second difference is that whereas treaty-based regimes impose legal obligations on states that are both fixed at the outset and consensual, constitutional entities have the ability to impose obligations on states that are neither. Such new obligations may be imposed by a governance structure with autonomous law-making powers acting by

---

[21] On page 8, in the introductory material at the beginning of Part II.

some version of majority vote and may be enforced by an adjudicatory body with compulsory jurisdiction. In this process of constitutionalization, the shift is from consent to compulsion.

The European Union is the paradigm of a constitutionalized regime of international law because uniquely it has moved far in both directions. Thus, its supranational status is a function of (1) the federalization of EU law and (2) a governance structure in which new legal obligations are both created by a form of majority decision making and enforced by an international court with compulsory jurisdiction, as well as by domestic courts.

The story of the transformation of the European Union from a treaty-based to a supranational entity is now, of course, too familiar to require details.[22] In the constitutionalization as federalization part of the story, the critical role was played by the doctrine of direct effect, which, when applicable, means that EU law operates of its own force within the domestic legal system without the need for any national legislative or other measures and regardless of the domestic constitutional status of treaty law. In combination with the traditional doctrine of the supremacy of international law over domestic law, direct effect created a system of hard EU law on which citizens could rely in national court and against which member states were powerless to act at the domestic level. Hence, their sovereignty was limited and partially transferred to a vertical, supranational system of international law. In this transformation, human rights famously played no intrinsic role but rather only an instrumental or pragmatic one as the sugar helping certain member state courts to swallow the pill. The result is that with only a few exceptions – the most prominent being that EU human rights law does not generally bind the member states – the structure of EU law (if not its institutions and processes) is essentially identical to that of federal law within a domestic federal system.

How do regional and global human rights regimes compare? The ECHR has arrived at a roughly similar point of constitutionalization as federalization, albeit via a different route. In addition to its developing constitutional supremacy over other sources of international law, as discussed in the previous section, the ECHR is also quite far along the path of developing *federal* supremacy over the domestic laws of member states. Unlike EU law, in which direct effect is one of its central constitutional principles, the ECHR does not formally require that its provisions themselves are invocable in, and

---

[22] Almost as familiar is the fact that the seminal work here was done by Joseph Weiler; *see, e.g.,* Weiler, *The Transformation of Europe*, 100 YALE L.J. 2403 (1991).

penetrate, the domestic legal system – only that individuals whose rights have been violated "shall have an effective remedy before a national authority."[23] But there is, at it were, de facto rather than de jure direct effect in that at this point all forty-seven member states have incorporated the ECHR into domestic law in one legal form or another,[24] and thus permit individuals to invoke its provisions in national court. Moreover, when so invoked, several countries require domestic judges to consider or take into account the interpretation of the relevant convention right given by the European Court of Human Rights.[25] Similarly, the ECHR has achieved de facto supremacy over domestic law in that whatever the particular internal hierarchy of norms may be vis-à-vis the incorporated right, at least where there is a successful recourse to the Strasbourg court, member states generally abide by that decision as required by article 46 and, where necessary, amend or repeal their domestic laws and/or policies, including their constitutions. In this only slightly attenuated way in comparison with the European Union, the ECHR operates within the member states' legal systems as an invocable and supreme law and, accordingly, can be understood as a federalized or constitutionalized regional human rights system.

The American Convention on Human Rights also penetrates domestic systems in a broadly similar fashion, at least structurally if not necessarily always in practice. Although, as with the ECHR, (1) there is no principle of direct effect per se and (2) states parties are not required to incorporate the treaty itself into domestic law, most have in fact done so thereby rendering it invocable by individuals in national court. Some countries, including Argentina and Venezuela, have granted the convention (as well as other human rights treaties) constitutional rank; others, including Costa Rica and Paraguay, grant it legal status below the constitution but above statutes; and still others give it equal rank with statutes. In addition, unlike the ECHR, article 2 of the American Convention does mandate some substantive (i.e., nonremedial) domestic legal effects of the treaty by imposing a duty on the states parties "to adopt . . . such legislative or other measures as may be necessary to

[23] ECHR, art. 13.
[24] Variations include incorporating the ECHR as having higher status than the constitution (the Netherlands), equal status to the constitution (Austria), below the constitution but above statutes, and equal status as statutes (Germany).
[25] In the United Kingdom, section 2 of the Human Rights Act requires British judges to "take into account" European Court of Human Rights interpretations; in Germany, a similar duty was imposed on lower courts by the Federal Constitutional Court. See Görgülü v. Germany, 2 BVG 1481 (2004).

give effect" to the protected rights.[26] Where this duty is fulfilled, individuals are indirectly invoking the convention when they rely on the resulting legislation in national court, in much the same way as with properly transposed directives in the European Union.

Overall, the global human rights system has not yet progressed as far in this process of constitutionalization as federalization. On the one hand, of their own force, several major international human rights treaties, including the ICCPR and CEDAW, contain an equivalent provision to article 2 of the American Convention mandating domestic legislative and other measures to give effect to the rights. Although again not required, several countries have incorporated global treaties into domestic law either generically (because of a general monist approach) or specifically (incorporating either all ratified human rights treaties or particular ones). On the other hand, the rate of such incorporation is significantly lower than with either the ECHR or the American Convention, and both reservations and statements of non-self-executing nature are more frequent at the global level. Finally, it is more common for domestic judges to consider or rely on regional treaties to which their state is a party than global ones for the purpose of interpreting their own constitutions.

As has been discussed, the second type of treaty to constitution shift, from consent to compulsion, is also typified by the European Union. Thus, there is the compulsory element of qualified majority voting in its general governance structure and the ECJ has compulsory jurisdiction over all member states as a condition of membership. Elsewhere within international law generally, a compulsory governance structure is far more partially embodied in the United Nations, given the limited subject-matter jurisdiction of the Security Council, and compulsory adjudication in the World Trade Organization's (WTO) Appellate Body and the European Court of Human Rights. Apart from the European Union, the model of constitutionalization via compulsory governance structure seems most relevant to functionally self-contained international regimes, such as the WTO, rather than to the human rights system, which necessarily applies to and cuts across all governmental functions. Moreover, bills of rights, of course, do not purport to constitute any governance structure but rather to limit those brought into, or already in, existence. Compulsory jurisdiction of human rights courts, in the strong sense as a condition of membership, remains limited to the European Court of Human Rights. With respect to its contentious caseload, the Inter-American Court of Human Rights has compulsory jurisdiction only over those states

---

[26] American Convention on Human Rights, art. 2.

parties that have chosen to accept it: currently twenty-one out of twenty-four countries.

C. Human Rights and the Constitutionalization of International Law

A third and final claim that there is something constitutional about human rights focuses less on the human rights system in isolation – as a particular regime of international law – than its wider role in the constitutionalization of international law as a whole. The growth of the human rights system is a critical part of the case for those who argue that fundamental changes have taken place in international law that justify a shift in overall paradigm from a horizontal conception of sovereign equality to a more vertical, constitutionalist conception.

Perhaps the most general of these fundamental changes is that individuals have become subjects of contemporary international law in addition to states. That is, individuals and no longer only states have rights and duties under international law. Just as in 1963, the ECJ cited this precise characteristic of EU law as the basis of its famous statement in *Van Gend en Loos* that EU law forms "a new legal order of international law,"[27] so, too, since 1963 can it be said that this characterization now applies to international law as a whole. Human rights law, which was essentially relaunched just a few years later with the opening of the two international covenants for signature, is of course the major source and manifestation of the rights side of the transformation, while the rapid development of individual liability under international criminal law in the past decade is arguably the major source and manifestation of the duties side. This transformation in the basic subjects of international law can be thought of as constitutional in nature because it represents a shift from the private law model of international law as exclusively regulating horizontal relations among sovereign equals to the public law model of also regulating vertical relations between states and individuals: in other words, a shift from contractual to constitutional functions.

Among other developments in international law that have been adduced in support of this claim of implicit constitutionalization are the growth of nonconsensual state obligations (e.g., forms of binding majority decision making and compulsory adjudication of international courts), the general objective of securing the common interests of humanity rather than simply the individual or aggregate interests of states, and the establishment of the United Nations, the European Union, and perhaps also the WTO as systems

---

[27] Van Gend en Loos v. Nederlandse Administratie der Belastigen, Case 26/62, [1963] ECR 1, at recital 12.

of international governance. This descriptive claim also has a normative variant, as expressed by German Constitutional Court Judge Brun-Otto Bryde, "a constitutionalist concept of international law tries to bind these actors [states and international organizations] ... to substantive constitutional principles, especially the rule of law and human rights."[28] By contrast, the role of human rights is far less central in the claim of explicit constitutionalization of international law, which views the UN Charter as the constitution of the international community.[29] This is due to the low profile of human rights in that document.

Because it performs both the general public law function of regulating relations between the state and individuals and the particular constitutional function of limiting governmental power, the contemporary human rights system is undoubtedly one of the strongest parts of this general constitutionalist claim. Indeed, it is *the* strongest part of the claim to the extent that the United Nations is not seen as successfully fulfilling the other primary constitutional function of creating an autonomous governance structure.

Nonetheless, there are also certain weaknesses in this claim about the role of human rights in constitutionalizing international law. First, as Joseph Weiler has noted, the human rights system makes individuals objects, or recipients, of rights – like endangered species or the environment – rather than truly subjects of them in the authorial sense.[30] This, of course, lessens the claim of a fundamental change in international legal subjecthood – as it does not apply to states – and also stands in contrast to most modern constitutions, which typically claim their legitimacy from being the active, engaged handiwork of "we the people."

Second, the human rights system does not generally bind governments against their will and so, in this regard, exists in some tension with the other factors driving the nonconsensual, constitutionalist paradigm. With the exception of human rights norms that have customary international law or general principle status, the treaty basis of much modern human right law requires state consent, as of course the U.S. failure to ratify several illustrates. Moreover, under a purely positivist reading of jus cogens as deriving exclusively from the Vienna Convention, such norms primarily function to restrict a state's treaty-making power but do not directly impose the substantive duty on an unwilling state.

---

[28] Brun-Otto Bryde, *International Democratic Constitutionalism, in* Towards World Constitutionalism 106 (Ronald St. John MacDonald and Douglas M. Johnston eds., 2005).

[29] *See* Bardo Fassbender, *The United Nations Charter as Constitution of the International Community*, 36 Colum. J. Transnat'l L. 529 (1998).

[30] Joseph Weiler, *The Geology of International Law – Governance, Democracy and Legitimacy*, 64 ZaöRV 547, 558 (2004).

Third and finally, because of this still dominant consensual model of state subjects of international law in this area, international human rights do not generally bind international organizations or the constituted structures of international governance. Such organizations and structures are not parties to, but rather often creations of, human rights treaties. This is surely a significant limitation on the constitutionalist model, distinguishing the global human rights system not only from domestic bills of rights, the primary function of which is to bind the constituted political authority, but also from the human rights system of the European Union. It is the equivalent of a bill of rights in a federal system only binding state governments and not federal, or EU human rights law only binding the member states and not the EU institutions – the reverse of the actual situation.

From the perspective of the constitutionalist paradigm of international law, there is thus a disjunction between the substance of the human rights system and its scope. Within the confines of a human rights regime itself, which does not purport to have an autonomous governance structure in the first place, this disjunction does not arise. But once human rights are conceptualized as part of a broader system of international governance, this limitation in the scope of coverage becomes a highly visible lacuna. This is particularly so when the creation and expansion of international organizations is heralded as part of the evidence that international law is developing goals beyond those of merely serving state interests. Accordingly, calls among international constitutionalists for human rights to bind international organizations are highly appropriate, but this must be the full panoply of human rights and not simply a selection – whether just economic rights or any other.[31]

III. Why Have Two Systems?

With respect to international law itself, the development of the human rights system closed a huge gap in coverage in that previously, due to the doctrine of nonintervention in internal affairs, it concerned itself almost exclusively with a state's external conduct – conduct outside its territory and/or regarding foreign nationals. But since 1945, this same internal space – previously largely unregulated by either constitutional law or international law – has also and increasingly been regulated by domestic bills of rights. Accordingly, if domestic bills of rights and international human rights perform the same

---

[31] By the "full panoply of human rights," I mean that no type or category of human right should be excluded. Clearly, given the variety and range of human rights, certain particular ones are not plausibly applicable or transferable to international organizations.

primary function of protecting fundamental rights and placing limits on how governments may treat their own populations, why is there a need for both systems? From the perspective of constitutional subsidiarity, are there any fundamental rights-protecting functions that either cannot be or typically are not adequately performed at the national, or perhaps, regional level?

Most straightforwardly, the international human rights system performs the instrumental function of filling a number of important gaps in the constitutional law system. These perhaps mostly fall into the category of rights-protecting functions that are contingently, rather than necessarily, unperformed at the national level. But, in addition, the human rights system performs at least two additional and unique functions, even in "liberal states that actively enforce constitutional norms." These are that it marks a new, external stage in the development of constitutionalism, and it also enshrines and clarifies a distinct normative basis for fundamental rights.

In terms of gap filling, most obviously there is no duplication of function with respect to those domestic systems lacking either de jure or de facto constitutional protection of fundamental rights. That is, either where there is no constitutional bill of rights – as, for example, in the United Kingdom and (Kelsenian) Austria prior to its constitutional incorporation of the ECHR – or for the many more countries in which there is no effective protection of the constitutional rights formally granted. Here, the international system may be said to substitute for, rather than duplicate, the domestic. The challenging issue, of course, is what nonduplicative functions human rights play in countries outside this category; for some human rights skeptics, the answer is essentially none.

But there are other significant gaps that human rights help to fill. First, even where domestic bills of rights exist and are generally enforced, they often do not bind, or fully bind, governments acting outside their territories. By contrast, international human rights law in principle should, and in practice does, have significant degrees of extraterritorial application. Although (1) this is not an issue that has been fully resolved by international courts, monitoring bodies, or commentators, and (2) the extent of a state's extraterritorial human rights obligations may vary depending on such factors as relevant treaty language and degree of control,[32] human rights obligations have been

---

[32] Thus, article 2 of the ICCPR states that "[e]ach State Party . . . undertakes to respect and to ensure to all individuals *within its territory and subject to its jurisdiction* the rights recognized in the present Covenant" (emphasis added). By contrast, most other human rights treaties omit the reference to "territory" and bind states to respect and secure rights to everyone "within their jurisdiction," giving them a potentially broader territorial scope.

interpreted to include substantial extraterritorial application.[33] So, for example, the U.S. Constitution has been generally interpreted by the Supreme Court to protect U.S. citizens but not others outside the territorial limits of the country; hence, the presumed rationale for the Bush administration's employment of various offshore detention centers, including Guantánamo Bay in Cuba.[34] By contrast, given the degree of control exercised by the U.S. government over Guantánamo, there is little doubt that its international human rights obligations, including those under the ICCPR and the Torture Convention, apply there and perhaps also to centers in Iraq and Afghanistan.

Second, international human rights law undoubtedly applies to a government's treatment of noncitizens inside its territory, whereas a bill of rights may not apply either at all or fully and equally. So, for example, constitutional antidiscrimination norms sometimes permit forms of discrimination against resident noncitizens that would be prohibited in the case of citizens.[35] Third, human rights law may bind governments in situations where they jointly create an international organization and claim immunity for it under domestic constitutional law. Finally, in addition, of course, to the fact that particular bills of rights and human rights instruments may specify somewhat different fundamental rights for protection, human rights treaties tend to use the protective method of imposing positive duties on governments more generally or frequently than is true of domestic constitutions. Thus, as has been noted, several human rights treaties contain a blanket obligation on states not only to "respect" the included rights but also to "ensure" them by adopting legislative and other measures necessary to give the rights practical effect.[36] Such measures may in turn impose duties on private actors. Even

---

[33] See generally John Cerone, Jurisdiction and Power: The Intersection of Human Rights Law & the Law of Non-International Armed Conflict in an Extraterritorial Context, 40 ISR. L. REV. 72 (2007).

[34] The recent U.S. Supreme Court decision in Boumediene v, Bush, 553 U.S._(2008), holding by five votes to four that, as an exception to this general principle, the Constitution protects aliens held at Guantánamo because of the U.S.'s de facto sovereignty over the base of course undermined this presumed rationale – and also reduced the contrast between the U.S. bill of rights and international human rights in this specific case.

[35] A striking example of this difference is that, applying the international human rights provisions of the ECHR as incorporated under the Human Rights Act, the UK's House of Lords declared the indefinite detention provisions of the Anti-Terrorism, Crime and Security Act of 2001 (which applied only to foreigners) as unlawful discrimination against aliens living in the UK. By contrast, the U.S. Supreme Court stated in 2003 that on the issue of preventive detention, the Constitution permits treatment of aliens living in the U.S. that would not be permissible in the case of citizens. See A and others v. Secretary of State for Home Department [2004]; Denmore v. Hyung Joon Kim, 538 U.S. 510, 522 (2003).

[36] See, e.g., the ICCPR and the American Convention.

where positive duties exist in domestic systems, they tend to be specific to particular individual rights and not of this blanket nature.

But apart from filling these largely contingent gaps, international human rights law also performs three functions that cannot be performed by domestic bills of rights. The first and most concrete is that in addition to imposing legal limits on how a state may treat its own population (a function it shares with bills of rights), international human rights law gives states a cognizable legal interest in how other populations are treated by their governments. That is, one should not forget that, although human rights law has helped to make individuals subjects of international law, it also renders states the objects of legitimate scrutiny and action by other states as well as by international and nongovernmental organizations.

Related to this point, a second unique function is that international human rights law creates a new, external stage in the institutional development of constitutionalism. Even where there is in practice a complete overlap between the two systems, human rights creates a second set of legal limits that, unlike the first, is not exclusively specified or enforced by the state itself. Under domestic bills of rights, limits on government are self-generated and self-imposed and, whatever the internal degree of separation of powers or procedural/institutional mechanism for enforcing them, a state is still ultimately and inevitably the judge in its own case. Where bills of rights are judicially enforced, judges may be independent of the other branches of government but are still themselves government officials and so in a broader picture part of the accused state[37] – as typically acknowledged in both domestic constitutional and international law.

By contrast, the human rights system adds a third layer of greater independence. Limits on the state are no longer exclusively created or enforced internally but also externally. This division of authority over fundamental rights between internal and external systems, between constitutional law and human rights law, adds an important international dimension to separation of powers/checks and balances, and creates the possibility of a more genuinely impartial or independent adjudication that does not violate the principle of *nemo judex in causa sua*. Here, it is helpful (though not precisely analogous) to think of the difference between a claim under the ECHR being brought against a member state before a national court of that state with the final word in the case and a claim brought under the existing system with its possibility

---

[37] The one exception to this would be where a domestic constitutional court has foreign members, as in Bosnia and Herzegovina. Under its constitution, three of the nine members of the constitutional court are nominated by the president of the European Court of Human Rights and cannot be citizens of the country.

of appeal from the national court to the European Court of Human Rights. By adding a final layer incorporating greater independence and impartiality, the ECHR system enhances constitutionalism – and the international human rights system globalizes this phenomenon.

In this way, the human rights system can be thought of as a further stage in the historical development of the idea of constitutionalism. In the preconstitutionalist order, sovereignty was conceptualized as absolute and indivisible, and located in the person of the monarch (*l'état, c'est moi*). In the first stage of constitutionalist thought, sovereignty is still conceptualized as absolute and indivisible but is now located in the people and delegated to their representatives (popular sovereignty). This in turn implies certain moral and/or political limits on the exercise of power, most famously enforced through Locke's right of rebellion. In the second stage of constitutionalism, limits on the exercise of power are legalized and also often both judicialized and constitutionalized, but all such limits and enforcement mechanisms are internally generated (domestic constitutionalism). In the new third stage, legal limits are now imposed by international law and may also be interpreted and applied by – or in the shadow of – international rather than domestic state actors (global constitutionalism).

Of course, some individual countries may have skipped the second stage (and possibly also the first) so that human rights supplies the only layer of legal limits. But either way it represents a growth in constitutionalism. Moreover, this growth in global constitutionalism occurs whether or not the human rights system is properly understood as form of international constitutional law. This is because constitutional law and constitutions are neither necessary nor sufficient for constitutionalism; global constitutionalism does not require global constitutional law.

A third unique function of the international human rights legal system is that it enshrines – and clarifies – the distinct normative basis for the protection of fundamental rights as rights of human beings rather than as rights of citizens. Thus, the ECHR, for example, is properly thought of as specifying the rights of humans as recognized, legalized, and applied in Europe and not simply the rights of Europeans. In specifying this function as "unique," however, it is important to specify the precise difference between bills of rights and international human rights law in this regard, and not to overstate it. Undoubtedly the fundamental rights protected by constitutional law in some countries are conceived of as human rights. Here one might think, for example, of the Declaration of the Rights of Man that has been incorporated by the *Conseil constitutionnel* into the Constitution of the Fifth French Republic. But in other countries, bills of rights are conceptualized as protecting the more particularized rights of citizenship in that country. Perhaps instructive in this regard is the contrast between the American Declaration of Independence, which speaks in the voice of the rights of man, and the U.S. Constitution, which seems to take a narrower, rights-of-citizenship perspective. The point is that, uniquely, international human rights law can *only* be conceptualized as protecting human rights and, in so doing, it clarifies the normative basis of these rights as rights all humans have simply in virtue of being human.

More concretely, even countries with a self-understanding of constitutional rights as human rights may find themselves struggling with the issue of whether to extend such rights to (legal and illegal) immigrants, a distinction that is normatively irrelevant under a human rights analysis. The fact that the protection of a particular international human rights law may attach to the rights of citizenship in Country A and not Country B, because A has ratified a human rights treaty and B has not, does not detract from this point. Citizenship in Country A is not the normative, but simply the legal, basis for the rights in question.

The distinct normative basis of human rights, as enshrined in international human rights law, has several implications. First, whatever the general legitimacy problem that international law faces due to its changing nature as a structure of governance does not attach to the human rights system. International human rights law may have an enforcement problem, and perhaps also an identification or specification problem, but not a general legitimacy problem. Second, the fundamental rights of U.S. or Brazilian citizens are historically and context specific so that it makes perfect sense to think of their content changing over time in a way that is not so obviously true of human rights given their different normative basis. Finally, unlike bills of rights, the inherently universalistic basis of human rights, as rights all humans have simply in virtue of being human, necessarily casts a shadow over the resolution of such issues as extraterritorial application, even if the specific form and content of their legalization places certain limits on their scope.

IV. Conclusion

Let me conclude by summarizing the answers to my two threshold questions. How different are the two systems of constitutional law and international human rights law? In terms of basic function, age, content, and structure, we have seen that there are substantial similarities. The most obvious differences seem to be in legal status and methods of enforcement, but probing the former leads us to ask: What, if anything, is constitutional about international human rights law? Here there are plausible arguments that certain parts of it satisfy at least some of the conditions for being considered international constitutional (or quasi-constitutional) law, particularly those of constituent power and entrenchment. Moreover, there is an ongoing process of implicit constitutionalization in both the human rights system itself and international law as a whole, although both are constrained by the still important role of state consent within human rights and the failure of human rights generally to bind international organizations. These developments in the human rights system have combined to further and promote global constitutionalism.

This last point suggests one reason why the human rights system does not simply replicate domestic bills of rights – or substitute for them where lacking – for by externalizing the limits in significant ways it takes constitutionalism to a new stage in its historical development. I have argued that international human rights law also functions to enshrine and clarify the distinct normative basis for the protection of fundamental rights as rights of human beings rather than as rights of citizens. From a human rights perspective at least, increasing understanding of these differences and similarities between domestic and international bills of rights is perhaps the greatest gain of the constitutional turn in international legal scholarship.

10. The Cosmopolitan Turn in Constitutionalism: On the Relationship between Constitutionalism in and beyond the State

MATTIAS KUMM

I. Introduction

1. Constitutionalism beyond the State? The Skeptic's Challenge

The language of constitutionalism has become widespread among international lawyers. International law as a whole[1] or specific international regimes[2] are described using constitutional language. Yet from the perspective of many national constitutional lawyers – not only, but particularly, in the United States – the application of constitutional language to international law is viewed with skepticism. A constitution, in the modern tradition, is generally understood as the supreme law of a sovereign state. The constitution is a written document, imagined as constituting and authorized by "We the People," enforced, if need be, by the coercive power of the state. International law, on the other hand, is conventionally imagined as the law among states, founded on the consent of states, and addressing questions of foreign affairs. Within this dualist paradigm, any talk of constitutionalism beyond the state is deeply

---

[1] See in this volume Andreas Paulus, *The International Legal System as a Constitution*, Chapter 3. For a brief history of constitutional language in international law, *see* Bardo Fassbender, *"We the Peoples of the United Nations": Constituent Power and Constitutional Form in International Law, in* THE PARADOX OF CONSTITUTIONALISM 270–73 (Martin Loughlin & Neil Walker eds., 2007).

[2] The focus of discussion has been on the United Nations, the European Union, the World Trade Organization, and the international human rights regime. *See* Jeffrey Dunoff & Joel Trachtman, *A Functional Approach to International Constitutionalization*, Chapter 1, and their contributions to Part II of this volume.

Besides Jeffrey Dunoff and Joel Trachtman and the participants of the workshop on "Ruling the World" in October 2007 in Philadelphia I thank the conveners and participants of the workshop at the Wissenschaftskolleg in May 2008 in Berlin on "The Twilight of Constitutionalism?" and in particular Dieter Grimm, Martin Loughlin and Alexander Somek for their critical comments and questions as well as Jack Goldsmith and Daryl Levinson and the participants of the Harvard Public Law workshop in February 2009.

implausible. Whoever uses the language of constitutionalism in relation to public international law is suspected of effectively advocating some version of a constitutional world state. Given the central role that sovereign states play and are likely to continue to play in the international system, such ideas, whatever their merit from a purely moral point of view might be,[3] are easily dismissed as hopelessly out of touch with reality and certainly of little value for the analysis and assessment of international law as it exists today.

Of course most international lawyers embracing the language of constitutionalism do not see themselves as committed to a grand institution-building project that will lead to the establishment of a federal world state.[4] The way that international lawyers use constitutional language to describe facets of international law is, at least on the surface, more modest. Their project is conventional: to describe and analyze international law or some part of it as a coherent legal order. Constitutional language is helpful for this purpose, because there are structural features of international law that bear some resemblance to features associated with domestic constitutional law. In part these are formal: there are elements of a hierarchy of norms in international law. They range from *jus cogens* norms to article 103 of the UN Charter, establishing the priority of the UN Charter over other norms of international law. In part they are functional: there are multilateral treaties that serve as regime-specific constitutional charters for institutionally complex transnational governance practices. And in part they are substantive:[5] human rights obligations have long pierced the veil of sovereignty that kept the relationship between the state and its citizens from the purview of international law. The individual has long emerged as a subject of rights and obligations under international law. There are international human rights courts established by treaties that authorize individuals to vindicate their rights before international courts. International law even criminalizes certain types of particularly serious human rights violations. These are features more characteristic of modern constitutional systems than of the traditional paradigm of international law as the law among states.

To the extent that constitutional language is used to describe international law in these contexts, it appears to be used in a different way from in the

---

[3] From a moral point of view, too, the idea of a federal world state is controversial. Immanuel Kant famously associated such a state with despotism, whereas others embrace it.

[4] In fact, no contributor in this volume conceives of constitutionalism in international law in this way.

[5] *See, e.g.,* Erika de Wet, *The Emergence of International and Regional Value Systems as a Manifestation of the Emerging International Constitutional Order*, 19 LEIDEN J. INT'L L. 611 (2006).

domestic context. Domestic constitutionalism and international constitutionalism appear, on the surface, to be homonyms. There is constitutionalism
with a "big *C*" (constitutionalism properly so called, or domestic constitutionalism) and there is constitutionalism with a "small *c.*" Constitutionalism
properly so called is linked to the establishment of ultimate legal authority in
the form of a written constitution, in the service of "We the People" people
governing itself democratically and supported by the coercive powers of the
state. Constitutionalism with regard to international law is constitutionalism
with a small *c*: the project to describe international law or parts of it as a
coherent legal system that exhibits some structural features of domestic constitutional law, but that is not connected to the establishment of an ultimate
authority, not connected to the coercive powers of state institutions and not
connected to the self-governing practices of a people.

Even when those distinctions are clear and confusion is avoided, there are
serious problems with the use of constitutional vocabulary beyond the state.
If legal practices are described in constitutional terms, the aura of legitimacy
and authority associated with big-*C* constitutionalism tends to be bestowed
on international practices. This tends to cover up a number of problems that
are said to plague international law. The idea of constitutional order suggests
coherence, when in fact there is a deeply pluralist and fragmentized international legal practice.[6] It suggests effectiveness, when in fact compliance
issues are a central problem to at least some of the areas of international
law most associated with the use of constitutional language.[7] And it suggests
legitimacy in exactly those areas of international law not firmly grounded in
state consent, where legitimacy concerns are most serious.[8] Small-*c* constitutionalism appears as little more than legitimating rhetoric for a discipline of
international law that is in crisis, after having partially unmoored itself from
the firm and reliable anchor of state consent. Constitutional language has the
double function of assuaging disciplinary anxieties about international law
and helping co-opt national constitutional actors, national courts in particular, to lend their support to a cosmopolitan project of transnational integration whose legitimacy and efficacy are questionable. It stands in a fraught

---

[6] *See Report of the Study Group of the International Law Commission: Fragmentation of International Law: Difficulties Arising from the Diversification and Expansion of International Law*,
U.N. Doc. A/CN.4/L.682, Apr. 13, 2006.

[7] *See* JACK GOLDSMITH & ERIC POSNER, THE LIMITS OF INTERNATIONAL LAW (2005), for a
recent attempt to establish what kind of international law matters and what kind does not.
Literature on compliance has recently mushroomed.

[8] *See* JEREMY RABKIN, THE CASE FOR SOVEREIGNTY (2004).

relationship with the idea of constitutional self-government.[9] It should therefore be abandoned.

That is the core of the skeptic's challenge.

The following can be read as a thought experiment. What if the real puzzles, pathologies and peculiarities are connected to the way national constitutional lawyers imagine constitutional law, rather than the way international lawyers imagine international constitutionalism? What might domestic constitutionalism be, if it was imagined not within the conventional statist paradigm, but within a cosmopolitan paradigm? What if the idea of sovereignty as ultimate authority, a conception of constitutional law tied to the coercive institutions of the state and a conception of legitimacy and democracy reductively tied to the self-governing practices of "We the People", is deeply flawed and implausible? What might it mean to reconstruct the legal and political world without reference to the conventional conceptualizations, idealizations and assumptions connected to the paradigm of statehood and sovereignty? What might it mean and what would one be able to see if one analyzed the relationship between international and national law using a cosmopolitan paradigm? How would one describe and analyze the structural changes that international law has experienced after WWII and the Cold War? How might one make sense of the structure of human rights and constitutional rights practice across liberal democracies, with the principle of proportionality playing such a central role, and the increasingly intimate relationship between national and international rights practice, both of which are not easily reconciliable with a conventional account of constitutional law?

The following is an attempt to articulate as clearly as possible an argument that, if plausible, would propose as significant a revolution in legal thinking, as the emergence of modern constitutionalism in the 18th century, perhaps even as significant as the emergence of the statist paradigm associated with the Westphalian settlement in the 17th century. To even attempt something of that sort in an essay rather than a book length work rich in historical detail, legal analysis and theoretically informed reflection might suggest an unfortunate if not uncommon combination of megalomania and lack of sophistication. But the thought experiment, which here takes the form of an

---

[9] For an overview of the issues, *see* Mattias Kumm, *The Legitimacy of International Law: A Constitutionalist Framework of Analysis*, 15 EUR. J. INT'L L. 907 (2004). In Europe, where national constitutional practice has opened itself to transnational law to a significant extent, and the density of transnational legal practice is high, revisionist sensibilities are articulated in more defeatist, nostalgic tones. There is talk of the "twilight" of constitutional law and the demise of the modern constitutional tradition.

argument for radically reimagining the legal world in order to assess whether
that improves our understanding of it, is not only successful, if it proves to
be correct. There might be a great deal to learn even from its failure. For that
reason, at least, I hope that the reflexive disbelief of the more sophisticated of
the skeptics will be suspended to allow for serious engagement.

To further encourage the suspension of disbelief a clarifying disclaimer is
in order: As transformative as the project to be undertaken might appear to
be on the conceptual level, its claims are focused on how best to understand
the law as it is, not to make an argument about what the law should be.
Cosmopolitan constitutionalism, as it is presented here, is a jurisprudential
account claiming to describe the deep structure of public law as it is. It tries
to make sense of a series of basic structural features of international and
domestic constitutional law practices in liberal constitutional democracies
that remain a peculiarity within the statist paradigm of constitutionalism,
but can easily be accounted for within the cosmopolitan paradigm. More
specifically the cosmopolitan paradigm provides a unifying framework for
the analysis of four phenomena: the increasingly complex structure of doctrines that concern the management of the interface between national and
international law (conventionally described as the constitutional law of foreign affairs), the proliferation of internally complex governance structures
within international law (focused on, for example, by the Global Administrative Law project) and the functional reconceptualization of sovereignty,
as well as basic structural features of contemporary human rights practice,
including the global spread of proportionality analysis and the increasing
interaction between national and transnational human rights adjudication.
The central claim is that a cosmopolitan paradigm is better able than a statist
paradigm to make sense of contemporary public law practice, to provide a
plausible reconstructive account that both fits that practice and shows it in its
best light.[10] The adoption of a cosmopolitan cognitive frame for imagining
public law is not conceptually connected to *any* political project relating to
institutional architecture and certainly does not entail a commitment to a
world state. On the contrary, those who insist on the desirability of establishing a world state tend to be caught up in statist thinking in the same way as

[10] The basic jurisprudential assumptions informing this project are unspectacular: 1. Law,
conceived from the internal point of view of a participant in the practice of making legal
claims, has a normative structure; 2. the identification of legal norms is at least in part a
matter of conventions; 3. the identification and interpretation of the relevant conventions
to some extent requires engagement with moral arguments, that is arguments about what is
efficient, fair, legitimate or just. All three assumptions are shared among others by Ronald
Dworkin, who has specifically coined the 'best fit' formula. The first two are shared also by
modern positivists such as H. L. A. Hart, Joseph Raz, Jules Coleman or Leslie Green.

traditional statists. They too endorse big *C* constitutionalism. They just want big '*C*' constitutionalism on the global scale.

2. Clarifying the Stakes: A Clash of Constitutional Paradigms

The skeptic's challenge, I will argue, fails. In fact, its failure is complete and deep. It fails for reasons that go right to the heart of the understanding of national constitutionalism. Many of the conventional assumptions underlying domestic constitutional practice, particularly as it relates to international law, are misguided. It is not the discipline of international law that has misleadingly appropriated the vocabulary of constitutionalism; it is the discipline of national constitutional law that has, at least to the extent that it makes use of the cognitive frame informing the skeptic's challenge, inappropriately narrowed, morally misconstrued, and falsely aggrandized national constitutionalism by analytically connecting it to a statist paradigm of law. The skeptic's challenge points to an important point: big-*C* constitutionalism is incompatible with a meaningful conception of constitutionalism on the international level. But it does not follow that the language of constitutionalism should be restricted to the domain of the national. Instead something is wrong with the conception of big-*C* constitutionalism: I will argue that it is necessary to rethink the basic conceptual framework that is used to describe and interpret national constitutional practice in order to make sense of the idea of constitutionalism beyond the state. There is no deep divide between big-*C* constitutionalism and small-*c* constitutionalism beyond the state. There is only constitutionalism in different institutional contexts. Constitutionalism does not require the framework of a state to be meaningful. The meaning of the institutional framework of the state is to be determined by principles of constitutionalism. Constitutionalism, then, needs to take a Copernican turn. The statist paradigm of constitutionalism needs to be replaced by a cosmopolitan paradigm of constitutionalism. Within the cosmopolitan paradigm, both national constitutional practice and international law can be meaningfully analyzed and assessed within the same conceptual framework, notwithstanding their different institutional structure. Conceived in this way, constitutionalism becomes a universally applicable conceptual framework for the analyses and assessment of the institutions, procedures, and decisions of public authorities.[11] To put it another way: *Cosmopolitan constitutionalism*

---

[11] For a conceptual approach that has a similar structure, *see* Miguel P. Maduro, *From Constitutions to Constitutionalism: A Constitutional Approach for Global Governance, in* GLOBAL GOVERNANCE AND THE QUEST FOR JUSTICE – VOLUME 1: INTERNATIONAL AND REGIONAL ORGANISATIONS (Douglas Lewis ed., 2006).

establishes an integrative basic conceptual framework for a general theory of
public law that integrates national and international law.

The debate about constitutionalism in international law is not appropriately understood exclusively as a debate internal to the discipline of public
international law. It is also a debate that concerns national constitutional
law and its conception of legitimate constitutional authority.[12] The debates
about constitutionalism in international law are complemented by highly
contentious debates within national constitutional law about how domestic institutions should relate to the structural changes of international law,
given national constitutional commitments. Just as the language of constitutionalism is contested on the international level, the constitutional law of
foreign affairs has become a highly contested field of law in many liberal
democracies.[13] When international lawyers discuss the development of governance structures on the transnational level, domestic constitutional lawyers
discuss the nature of domestic constitutional commitments that guide and
restrict domestic institutions as they engage these practices. Questions that
arise include the following: Does the constitution authorize the transfer of
public authority to transnational institutions? If so, under what conditions?
Does enforcement of international legal obligations require specific endorsement by national political institutions or should they be legally enforceable
by domestic courts, even in the face of political resistance? What does it mean
and who gets to decide whether international obligations are self-executing?
Should national judges, when interpreting national constitutional rights provisions, refer to international human rights? If so, what weight, if any, should
be attached to them? What is at stake in these debates is not only the resolution
of this or that doctrinal issue or the appropriateness of this or that interpretative strategy. There are patterns of arguments that repeat themselves across
doctrinal areas and methodological debates that point to a deeper conflict.
On the one hand there are doctrines, interpretative strategies, and arguments
supporting an open constitution that encourage the progressive development
of international legal authority and reflect a cosmopolitan paradigm of constitutionalism. On the other hand there are revisionists who are seeking to
ensure that national political institutions remain in effective control over

---

[12] *See* Samantha Besson, *Whose Constitution(s)? International Law, Constitutionalism, and*
Democracy, Chapter 13 in this volume.

[13] Whereas in Europe integration has created significant dynamism in the field, generally
leading up to a greater opening of constitutional legal orders to transnational law (for an
overview, see The European Courts & National Courts (Anne-Marie Slaughter, Alec
Stone Sweet & Joseph Weiler eds., 1998)), in the United States, revisionists have pushed
in the opposite direction. Among those leading the revisionist charge are Professors Curtis
Bradley, Jack Goldsmith, and John Yoo.

the generation and enforcement of an international law that is and should remain firmly grounded in state consent. What is at stake here is the clash between two competing constitutional paradigms, which influence both the understanding of national constitutional law as it relates to foreign affairs and the understanding of international law more generally.

The skeptic's challenge is articulated within a statist paradigm of constitutionalism: the constitution establishes the supreme legal norms of the national legal system. It constitutes the legal system of the sovereign nation-state. That rank is justified with reference to "We the People," the demos as the *pouvoir constituant*, and the foundation of constitutional authority. The statist paradigm establishes an analytical link among the constitution as a legal document, democracy as a foundational value, and the sovereign state as an institution. The conception of legitimate constitutional authority it establishes insists on the importance of a chain of legitimation that traces the legitimate authority of any law, including international law, to the national constitution and the democratic practices it establishes. The more attenuated that link, the greater is the concern about its legitimacy. Given those presuppositions, there can be no legitimate global legal order that does not tie effective control of the generation and application of international law firmly tied back to the states' consent. Within the statist paradigm of constitutionalism, the skeptic's challenge succeeds. There is certainly no space for big-C constitutionalism beyond the state. And it is unclear what small-c constitutionalism achieves, beyond providing a legitimating rhetoric that covers up a democratic deficit. But the statist paradigm of constitutionalism is contested. At the heart of many contemporary debates, internationally and nationally, lies a struggle between the statist paradigm of constitutionalism and those that seek to transcend it.

In order to transcend the statist paradigm, it is not sufficient to embrace the language of *post* and *beyond* (sovereignty, the state, the nation) that has become so prominent in international scholarship. Nor is it sufficient to attach the label "constitution" to any treaty that establishes some elements of public authority and some degree of hierarchical ordering, or to use the language of governance to describe certain transnational practices of an administrative character. Such language is symptomatic of a crisis. Its virtues lie in the fact that it brings into focus some features of transnational practice that conventional statist descriptions of international law tend to neglect or downplay. But because of its lack of a theoretical grounding and its disconnection from domestic constitutional practice, it is too easy to dismiss or ignore as unpersuasive idealistic rhetoric, not rooted in how we normally think of law. It does not provide an alternative to the statist paradigm for making intelligible the legal and political world. A serious alternative to the statist paradigm would have to provide what the statist paradigm provides: the conceptual tools for the description and analysis of the basic structure of the legal world as a whole, connected to the basic structure of an account of legal and political authority. Furthermore, such an alternative paradigm would be successful only if it were able to make better sense of legal and political practice as it currently exists than does the statist paradigm of constitutionalism. Is there such an alternative? If so, what are its basic features and implications? And what makes it more attractive than the statist paradigm?

The core purpose of this chapter is threefold. First, it analyzes the central role that cognitive frames or paradigms play in constitutional law. Second, it presents a cosmopolitan paradigm of constitutionalism as a competitor to the statist paradigm and traces its implications for the construction of the relationship between national and international law. As will become apparent, many of the more persistent disagreements and major debates in constitutional and international law can be traced back to differences in the choice of cognitive frame. Third, it argues that the cosmopolitan paradigm better fits existing practice and should replace the statist paradigm, where it still has a strong hold. A Copernican turn in constitutionalism is not only possible but also necessary. The cosmopolitan paradigm can make better sense of many of the core structural features of contemporary legal and political practice than can the statist paradigm. It also provides a morally more convincing account of constitutionalism than the statist paradigm and allows for an empirically more grounded account of public law. The statist paradigm has become a central stumbling block for the intelligent and context-sensitive assessment of international law and the constitutional law of foreign affairs.

3. The Idea of a Constitutional Paradigm and Its Connection to Constitutional Practice

A constitutional paradigm provides a cognitive frame that makes intelligible the legal and political world. It establishes a basic conceptual framework for the construction of public authority. Conceptual frameworks are the basic building blocks for theories of public law. In national constitutional law the cognitive frame guides and structures debates about the appropriate interpretative methodologies and the substantive principles underlying various areas of constitutional law. In international law, where there is no constitutional text, the cognitive frame is central for helping to identity, to structure, and to interpret the relevant legal materials. This chapter focuses on the implication of the choice of cognitive frame for constructing the relationship between national and international law. But the choice of cognitive frame has more general implications.

A constitutional paradigm provides a cognitive frame for the construction of public authority. In jurisprudential terms, it provides a thin account for the grounds of what positivists describe as the rule of recognition,[14] or *Grundnorm*.[15] It provides an answer to the question of why we should, for example, look to the constitution to provide us with guidance when assessing, say, whether an act of the legislature should be enforced. "It's the supreme law of the land and the legislature is bound by it," a lawyer might say. But how do we know that? Of course it is not sufficient to say that the constitution says so. The fact that a document says that it is the supreme law of the land does not make it so. What the constitution says is only relevant once we already know that this is where we should look to for guidance. If you and I draw up a document and establish solemnly in article 1 that "this document and everything its authors in their infinite wisdom formally declare to be good and just is the supreme law of the land," that does not make it the supreme law of the land. Furthermore, many constitutions have no explicit supremacy clause, yet they are recognized as the supreme law of the land. A supremacy clause, then, is neither necessary nor sufficient to establish a constitution as the supreme law of the land. We might, of course, say that the constitution is in fact recognized as a supreme law of the land, and as lawyers, that is all we need to know. The Why? question often has a legally sufficient answer when we can point to established conventions. But in some contexts that presumption might be challenged. That was the case, for example in Europe, when national highest courts of European Union Member States one day found themselves confronted with the claim by the European Court of Justice, that European law is not only self-executing but requires national courts to ignore national constitutional provisions precluding the enforcement of EU Law. But even if the supremacy of the national constitution is settled, we might still want to know what reasons there are to accept the constitution as the supreme law of the land, because those reasons might be relevant when it comes to *the interpretation* of the constitution. Questions of interpretative methodology as well as questions concerning the guiding principles that underlie the different areas of constitutional law – rights provisions, federalism provisions or the provisions governing the constitutional law of foreign affairs – call for answers that ultimately make reference to the moral grounds for legitimate constitutional authority. Here constitutional paradigms provide the resources to guide and structure debates in constitutional practice.

To provide some illustrations, it might be helpful to go right to the two paradigms that are the protagonists of this chapter. According to the statist

---

[14] H. L. A. Hart, The Concept of Law (1960).
[15] Hans Kelsen, Reine Rechtslehre (2d ed. 1960).

paradigm, the authority of the constitution rests on its authorization by "We the People." The constitution is seen as the legal framework through which a political community governs itself as a sovereign nation. For the cosmopolitan paradigm, the authority of the constitution rests on its authorization by the formal, jurisdictional, procedural, and substantive principles of cosmopolitan constitutionalism. The cosmopolitan paradigm also requires that the national constitution be justified to those it seeks to govern. But there are two core differences. First, that justification has to meet a complex standard of public reason,[16] established by the principles of cosmopolitan constitutionalism, not by the will of a demos. Second, this complex standard of public reason requires taking into account legitimate concerns of outsiders. The legitimate authority of a constitution depends at least in part how it relates to the wider international community of which it is an integral part. Much will be said about these principles, their connection to public reason, and their operation in concrete contexts later. The point here is that within the cosmopolitan paradigm, a complex standard of public reason, which includes reference to jurisdictional and procedural principles, replaces the equally complex idea of a collective will or democracy as the basic point of reference for the construction of legal authority.

The choice of paradigm for the construction of public authority has implications for the structure of debates concerning both interpretative methodologies and interpretative outcomes.

According to the statist paradigm, the constitution is required to be interpreted so as to best reflect the will of "We the People." After all, if that is the source of the constitution's authority, it should also guide its interpretation. Debates about interpretative methodologies are debates about how to understand that requirement. Even though there is considerable space for disagreement about when "We the People" act in a constitutionally relevant way,[17] and what is to count as the people's will,[18] characteristically different versions of originalism play a central role in debates that are framed within

[16] Public reason here refers to reasons that are appropriate for the justification of law in liberal democracies. This conception of public reason shares many of the features described by John Rawls. See JOHN RAWLS, POLITICAL LIBERALISM (1993). But it is developed here in a way that includes reference to jurisdictional and procedural concerns.

[17] Bruce Ackerman famously argued in the U.S. context that "We the People" as the nation's *pouvoir constituant* have acted not only at the time of the founding but at least on two other constitutional revolutions in conjunction with the Civil War and the New Deal. See BRUCE ACKERMAN, "WE THE PEOPLE": FOUNDATIONS (1993).

[18] *Compare* ROBERT BORK, THE TEMPTING OF AMERICA (1990) (focusing on original intent) *with* ANTONIN SCALIA, A MATTER OF INTERPRETATION (1997) (focusing on the original understanding).

this paradigm. The open engagement with public reason, on the other hand, reflected in open-ended tests like proportionality, tends to be looked upon skeptically,[19] and cabined if not marginalized.[20] Within the cosmopolitan paradigm, on the other hand, constitutions are interpreted to best reflect the principles of cosmopolitan constitutionalism. Here, too, there is some space for disagreement on interpretative methodologies, but characteristically public-reason-oriented, purposive interpretations and the proportionality requirement play a central role and are openly endorsed. Questions regarding the judicial role are more often framed as problems with specific understandings of the proportionality test and the role of courts adjudicating them.

Besides debates about interpretative methodology, debates about the desirability of interpretative outcomes are also assessed within different frameworks. Within the statist paradigm, the assessment of those outcomes is ultimately focused on the degree to which they enable and reflect the more perfect realization of democracy: "We the People" governing themselves. The central problem of rights-protecting judicial review, for example, is its democratic legitimacy. If and to the extent it is legitimate, it must be so because it helps to more fully realize democracy. Perhaps democracy is more perfectly realized because rights judicially recognized are representation reinforcing.[21] Perhaps the right conception of constitutional democracy is itself internally committed to the protection of certain substantive rights.[22] Perhaps the constitutionalized rights reflect a particular historical commitment of the self-governing community.[23] Whatever the case may be, the statist paradigm makes democracy the standard for assessing institutional arrangements and outcomes. It is not possible to argue that a particular solution may or may not be compatible with democracy but that it has other virtues that take precedence under the circumstances. Whatever virtues those might be, they have to be shown to be an integral part of an attractive conception of democracy.

Within the cosmopolitan paradigm, on the other hand, outcomes are more openly assessed in terms of their public reasonableness. Concerns about

---

[19] *See* T. Alexander Alenikoff, *Constitutional Law in the Age of Balancing*, 96 YALE L.J. 943 (1987).

[20] The only way that the use of open-ended moral principles as standards for the adjudication of rights claims can be justified within this paradigm is to insist that that was what the framers originally understood to be authorizing courts to do. For such an attempt, *see* Ronald Dworkin, *Originalism and Fidelity*, in JUSTICE IN ROBES 117–39 (2006).

[21] *See* J. H. ELY, DEMOCRACY AND DISTRUST (1981).

[22] *See* RONALD DWORKIN, FREEDOM'S LAW (2000).

[23] *See* JED RUBENFELD, FREEDOM AND TIME (2001); Lawrence Lessig, *Fidelity in Translation*, 71 TEX. L. REV. 1165 (1993).

democratic legitimacy tend to be debated in terms of the appropriate degree of deference that should be accorded to legislative decisions, when assessing the substantive justification of a decision within the proportionality framework. Of course, political decision making connected to electoral accountability should play a central role given the fact of reasonable disagreement on questions of rights and public policy. But not all disagreements are reasonable. The real issue is not the legitimacy of judicial review. The real issue is the legitimacy of a decision by public authorities that imposes burdens on individuals when that decision is not susceptible to a plausible justification within a framework of public reason.

Note how these differences in construction do not map onto different views of the role of the judiciary as an institution in a simple way. Within both paradigms it is possible to make the case for or against an active judiciary, depending on how the comparative merits of the judiciary over the legislative branches are assessed.[24] The real differences lie in the structure of the arguments that need to be made to justify one position or another and the different structure of the doctrines that result. At the same time there is a comparative collectivist bias underlying the statist paradigm that assesses institutional arrangements and outcomes in terms of democracy. Conversely, there is a comparative individualist bias underlying the cosmopolitan paradigm that assesses institutional arrangements and outcomes in terms of public reason.

The purpose of these examples was merely to illustrate how constitutional paradigms structure debates about basic constitutional questions. The relationship between constitutional paradigms and constitutional practice needs to be further clarified in three respects. First, paradigms should not be confused with constitutional theories. Constitutional theories are elaborations of constitutional paradigms. They tend to be thicker, in that they provide a richer and more fully developed account of the relevant values, their relationship to one another, and their institutional and doctrinal implications. Constitutional paradigms are cognitive frames that merely provide a general conceptual structure within which basic constitutional issues are contested and resolved. A constitutional practitioner may not think of him- or herself as having much of a constitutional theory. But even the most pragmatic judges will have their reasoning be informed by one or another constitutional paradigm that provides them with a general sense of what they are doing.

---

[24] Jeremy Waldron's wholesale skepticism about judicial review, for example, is articulated within a cosmopolitan rights-based paradigm. *See, e.g.,* JEREMY WALDRON, LAW AND DISAGREEMENT (1999); Jeremy Waldron, *The Core Case against Judicial Review,* 115 YALE L.J. 1346 (2006); Jeremy Waldron, *A Right-Based Critique of Constitutional Rights,* 13 OXFORD J. LEGAL STUD. 18 (1993).

Second, constitutional paradigms as cognitive frames help structure debates. They do not determine specific outcomes. But even though they do not determine outcomes, the choice of structure focuses debates in a certain way and gives certain types of arguments greater force while weakening others. The choice of cognitive frames tends to effect the pattern of outcomes. Third, in constitutional debate these frames are rarely made the subject of explicit analysis and assessment. They often remain part of the legal unconscious. But without being made explicit, cognitive frames can never be the conscious subject of an informed choice. When disagreements based on competing cognitive frames remain unanalyzed, they often give an impression of being based on incommensurable premises. Such disagreements tend to become shrill once it becomes clear that they will remain unresolved by further argument and that it is not even clear why the other side is emphasizing the arguments they are emphasizing while being seemingly impervious to the arguments of the other side. When the stakes in these debates are high in political and legal terms, the sociologically dominant side finds it easy to brand the other side as ideological. More generally, disagreement on constitutional paradigms tends to foster camp mentalities: you're either with us or against us. Making explicit what is too often implicit in constitutional debates about the relationship between national and international law, this chapter is also an effort to provide a deeper understanding of the nature of the disagreement in order for that disagreement to be engaged more intelligently.

In the following, the core structure of the cosmopolitan paradigm of constitutionalism will be analyzed, and its link to legal practice, particularly as it relates to international law, described and contrasted with the statist paradigm (Section II). That description seeks to make explicit the basic features of an understanding of constitutionalism that has implicitly shaped many of the doctrinal developments and scholarly writings on constitutionalism in international law as well as national constitutional law of foreign affairs. It seeks to provide the bare-bones structure and theoretical grounding for the proliferation of the language of constitutionalism on the international level. But it also seeks to provide a theoretical ground for the opening up of national constitutional orders to international law that characterizes many constitutions and constitutional interpretations after World War II, not just in Europe. The cosmopolitan paradigm repositions national constitutional practice as an integral part of a global practice of law and reconceives public international law in light of constitutional principles. National constitutional law and public international law are reconceived as reflecting a common commitment to basic constitutional principles. Instead of "We the People," statehood, and sovereignty as the foundations of a practice of constitutional law that imagines itself as focused on the interpretation of one text, diverse legal materials are identified, structured, and interpreted in light of principles that lie at the heart of the modern tradition of constitutionalism. Ultimate authority is vested not in "We the People" either nationally or globally, but in the principles of constitutionalism that inform legal and political practice nationally and internationally. A third section will discuss some counterarguments to the cosmopolitan paradigm, also to provide a better understanding of its core legal, moral, and empirical assumptions.

II. The Structure of Cosmopolitan Constitutionalism

The following consists of three parts. Each part addresses prominent features of contemporary public law practice that are difficult to make sense of within the statist paradigm of law. The first addresses the relationship between national and international law and the unconventional doctrinal structures that courts use to engage legal practices outside their jurisdiction. This part spells out the implications of the cosmopolitan paradigm of constitutionalism for the idea of constitutional legality and the construction of legal authority. Here the formal, jurisdictional, procedural, and substantive principles of the cosmopolitan paradigm of constitutionalism are introduced and their implications for the construction of legal authority described. The principles give rise to a structure of legal authority that is described as constitutional pluralism: it is not monist and allows for the possibility of conflict not ultimately resolved by the law, but it insists that common constitutional principles provide a framework that allows for the constructive engagement of different sites of authority with one another.

The second part focuses on some central features of international law: The increasing divorce of international law from state consent, either in the form of relatively autonomous governance practices, the increasing divorce of customary international law from time honored custom that might plausibly serve as a proxy for implict consent and the ever expanding domain of international law. This part addresses the legitimacy issues such practices raise, and will provide a discussion of the jurisdictional principle of subsidiarity and the general procedural principle of due process, which, in the domestic context, takes the form of a commitment to democracy and on the international level translates into a complex requirement of good governance. The cosmopolitan paradigm provides an original perspective on what conventionally is perceived as the structural legitimacy problems that plague international law not closely tied to state consent. The core concern is not that international public authorities are not subject to electoral accountability. Significantly more serious is the capture of the international jurisgenerative process by states, in particular the state's executive branches. The current legal structure, in which powerful states can too easily sabotage effective collective action, tends to impose unreasonable burdens on the development of processes and norms that ensure appropriately wide participation and help guide and constrain state action in order to and effectively realize global public goods. And it has led to an international law that authorizes states to harm others without effective legal remedies being provided. These are the problems that debates about legitimacy should be focused on. Questions of democratic legitimacy of transnational governance practices, on the other hand, are widely overstated. Once freed from statist assumptions of what makes democracy legitimate, these concerns translate into the important, but relatively mundane demand to ensure that appropriate forms of transparency, participation, representativeness, and accountability become an integral part of governance practice.

The third part focuses on some structural features of human and constitutional rights practice, such as the pervasiveness of the proportionality requirement and the increasing mutual engagement of international and national human rights practice. This practice structurally connects rights discourse with the idea of justifiability in terms of public reason. It also establishes strong links between national constitutional rights practice and international human rights practice, which are conceived of as part of a joint, mutually engaging, cooperative enterprise. Together these interlocking and mutually reinforcing elements describe a coherent paradigm of constitutionalism. As will become clear, the cosmopolitan paradigm not only provides a description and assessment of national and international constitutionalism within a common conceptual framework; its defining feature is its insistence that questions of legal authority and legitimacy have to be discussed in a way that takes into account the structural connections between national and international law. Constitutionalism, to the extent that it is concerned with the establishment and maintenance of legitimate public authority, has to be conceived within a cosmopolitan, not a national, frame.

1. The Construction of Legal Authority: Cosmopolitan Constitutionalism as a Framework for Legal Pluralism

Cosmopolitan constitutionalism carves out a distinct position beyond monism and dualism to describe the relationship between national and international law: constitutional pluralism.[25] Constitutional statists are right

---

[25] The idea of constitutional pluralism has played a central role for understanding the relationship between national and EU law. *See* Neil Walker, *The Idea of Constitutional Pluralism*, 65 Mod. L. Rev. 317 (2002); Miguel Poiares Maduro, *Contrapunctual Law: Europe's Constitutional Pluralism in Action*, in Sovereignty in Transition 501–37 (Neil Walker ed., 2003);

that it is a mistake to imagine the world of law as a hierarchically integrated whole, as monism does. But it is also a mistake to imagine national and international law as strictly separate legal systems that follow their own ultimate legal rules with only contingent secondary connections between them, as dualism does. Instead, common principles underlying both national and international law provide a coherent framework for addressing conflicting claims of authority in specific contexts. These principles will sometimes favor the application of international rules over national – even national constitutional – rules. At other times they will support the primacy of national rules.

So what are the principles governing the construction of legal authority? To begin with, there is the principle of legality. The principle of legality, in its thinnest interpretation,[26] establishes that wherever public authority is exercised, it should respect the law. If there is a law that governs an activity, public authorities are under an obligation to abide by it. If there are competing and contradictory laws or interpretations governing that activity, the legal system established by the constitution provides the resources to determine which law ought to govern an actor's behavior. The question is: What does respect for the law mean in a situation where national law conflicts with international law? What if, for example, a UN resolution imposes legal obligations on member states to impose severe economic sanctions on blacklisted individuals, when compliance with such an obligation would require a state to disregard national constitutional guarantees?[27] What does legality require of public authorities in these types of situations?

a. Beyond Monism and Dualism: Constitutionalism as a Principled Framework for Legal Pluralism

Within the framework of the statist paradigm, this is not a difficult question. The national constitution, reflecting a commitment of "We the People" governing themselves, is the supreme law of the land. The only kind of legality

---

Mattias Kumm, *The Jurisprudence of Constitutional Conflict: Constitutional Supremacy in Europe before and after the Constitutional Treaty*, 11 Eur. L.J. 262 (2005). For a critical discussion, *see* Julio Baquero Cruz, *The Legacy of the Maastricht-Urteil and the Pluralist Movement*, 14 Eur. L.J. 389 (2008).

[26] There are considerably more demanding conceptions of legality or the rule of law. That is not surprising. As Joseph Raz points out: "When a political ideal captures the imagination of large numbers of people its name becomes a slogan used by supporters of ideals which bear little or no relation to the one originally designated." Joseph Raz, The Authority of Law 210 (1979).

[27] This question is currently at a heart of a number of cases before the ECJ. *See* Yusuf and Al Barakaat C-415/05 P and Kadi C-402/05 P.

that ultimately matters is national constitutional legality. The idea of legality is interpreted within a statist paradigm of constitutionalism and leads to a classical dualist account of the legal world: if the national constitution is the supreme law of the land, international law matters only if and to the extent the national constitution so determines. All public authority that becomes effective on the state's territory must ultimately be justified in terms prescribed by the national constitution. All legality properly so called is ultimately legality as defined by national constitutional standards. When faced with a choice to violate either international law or national constitutional law, public authorities are required to respect the national constitution and violate international law. Of course national constitutions often grant international law a certain status in domestic law. National constitutional conflict rules typically focus on the sources of international law. Characteristic for the statist paradigm is a constitutional rule that determines that treaties have the same status as domestic legislation,[28] particularly when national legislative institutions were involved in the ratification process. Furthermore, rules of customary law might also be assigned a status under the constitution.[29] But within the statist paradigm the lack of specific and clear state consent as a necessary requirement for the emergence of a rule of customary international law means that it is difficult to justify a status for customary international law in domestic law that would make it immune from override by national political decisions. At any rate, whatever the status that international law has as part of domestic legal practice is circumscribed by the national constitution, which serves as the ultimate point of reference for determining international law's authority in domestic practice. Legality as constitutional legality does not depend on requirements of international law. On the contrary, whether compliance with international law is legal depends on the requirements of the national constitution, whatever the constitutional legislator has determined them to be. Violations of international law compatible with the national constitution are not violations of the principle of legality, because what legality properly so called requires is constitutional legality. This is the classical dualist understanding of the relationship between national and international law: independent systems of national law and international law. A violation of international law may trigger the responsibility of the state as a matter of international law, but national constitutional legality provides its own distinct

---

[28] For a comparative overview concerning the rules governing treaties, *see* THE EFFECT OF TREATIES ON DOMESTIC LAW (Francis Jacobs & Shelley Roberts eds., 1987).

[29] For an overview, *see* Luzius Wildhaber & Stephan Breitenmoser, *The Relationship between Customary International Law and Municipal Law in Western European Countries*, 48 ZEITSCHRIFT FÜR AUSLÄNDISCHES ÖFFENTLICHES RECHT UND VÖLKERRECHT 163 (1988).

criteria for legality, the specifics of which depend on the requirements established by the national constitution.

But notwithstanding deeply engrained habits of thought linked to the statist paradigm, why should one think of legality in this somewhat schizophrenic way, sharply separating international from domestic legality? If legality reflects an important commitment, what sense is there in limiting it to whatever constraints domestic law imposes on the enforcement of international law? Why should the idea of legality not generally require that the law be taken seriously, whether it is domestic or international law? Why discriminate against international law in this way? Is there no alternative conception of legality that is more attractive? After all, like all law, international law in part seeks to effectively address collective action problems and achieve coordination benefits, thus ensuring the provision of global public goods for the global community. Those functions are more effectively fulfilled if the requirement of legality is not, from the perspective of national public authorities, restricted to national constitutional legality.

An argument along those lines is at the heart of a competing conception of legality that has been at the center of jurisprudential debates about the relationship between national and international law in the twentieth century: international legal monism.[30] According to it international law and domestic law form one hierarchically integrated whole, with international law as the supreme law. Public authorities are never faced with an option to break one law or another, just as a state judge within a federal legal system is not required to break state law in order to comply with federal law. Instead the legal system provides for a clear conflict rule – the primacy of international law – that helps public authorities determine what their legal obligations really are. International law recognizes states and authorizes them to govern themselves through national constitutions, but only within the limits of international law. National constitutional law can never legally be used to set aside provisions of international law. Of course the constitution remains supreme national law. It trumps ordinary legislation, administrative regulations, municipal ordinances, and so on. But it is not the supreme law governing public authorities and individuals; international law is. The national supremacy claim is linked only to the limited authority delegated by international law to the national community to govern itself through national law. The idea of legality is tied to a monist construction of the legal authority.

---

[30] The classic literature on the monist side includes the Vienna school, with HANS KELSEN, GENERAL THEORY OF LAW AND STATE 363–80 (1945); ALFRED VERDROSS, DIE EINHEIT DES RECHTLICHEN WELTBILDES AUF GRUNDLAGE DER VÖLKERRECHTSCERFASSUNG (1923); and HERSCH LAUTERPACHT, INTERNATIONAL LAW AND HUMAN RIGHTS (1950).

International legal monism is a conception of legality that has the advantage of not artificially dividing up the world into two fundamentally separate legal systems, the national and the international. It appropriately extends the idea of legality beyond the realm of the state. But the idea of legality is insufficient to carry the heavy burden of justifying a categorical rule that international law should always trump domestic law when the two are in conflict. The idea of legality – respect for the rule of law – and the functional considerations that support extending it to the international level plausibly provide for a presumption of some weight: that international law should be respected by public authorities, national law to the contrary notwithstanding. But in liberal democracies, legitimate authority is not tied to the idea of legality alone. It is also tied to procedural and substantive requirements that are reflected in constitutional commitments to democracy and the protection of rights. That does not mean that the authority of international law, from the perspective of national law, should be determined exclusively by national constitutions, as suggested by dualists. Both legal monism and the dualist conception of the legal world provided by the statist version of national constitutionalism ultimately provide one-sided and thus unpersuasive accounts of the principle of legality. What it suggests instead is that the presumption in favor of applying international law can be rebutted if in a specific context, when international law violates countervailing principles in a sufficiently serious way. More will be said about these principles later. Here it must suffice to name them: besides the principle of legality, which establishes a presumptive duty to enforce international law, the potentially countervailing principles are the jurisdictional principles of subsidiarity, the principle of due process, and the substantive principle of respect for human rights and reasonableness.

The basic building blocks of a conception of legality that is tied to a framework of cosmopolitan constitutionalism are now in place: international law should presumptively be applied even against conflicting national law, unless there is a sufficiently serious violation of countervailing constitutional principles relating to jurisdiction, procedure, or substance.

Note how these sets of principles do not simply replace national constitutional provisions that establish rules regarding the engagement with international law. Clearly the fact that the national constitutional legislator has established constitutional rules that limit the application of international law will itself be a legally relevant fact that weighs against the application of international law, because of its connection to ideas of procedural legitimacy. But this does not mean that national constitutional rules are conclusive. True, national courts will rarely, if ever, be required to say that national constitutional rules are trumped by the presumption of international law's

legality established by the cosmopolitan paradigm. But this is not because
the constitution effectively establishes the supreme law of the land when it
comes to the determination of the status of international law. There are three
reasons why the possibility of a direct conflict between the requirements
of the cosmopolitan paradigm and national constitutional rules relating to
international law remains a theoretical possibility only. First, the cosmopolitan paradigm does not itself provide hard-and-fast conflict rules, but just
background principles, in light of which the terms of engagement between
national and international law should be specified. Often enough, national
constitutional rules can be reconstructed as plausible interpretations of the
requirements of the cosmopolitan paradigm. If they can be reconstructed
in this way, it strengthens their authority. Second, national constitutional
rules relating to international law are often highly indeterminate and incomplete. The U.S. Constitution, for example, establishes that treaties are part
of the supreme law of the land, but it does not say whether they trump
congressional legislation or whether they are superior to it or whether the
constitution trumps treaties or whether they have the same rank.[31] Furthermore the constitution says nothing about when the treaty is to be enforced
by domestic courts without further political endorsement. Does that mean
that treaties should be judicially enforced like domestic law without further
endorsement by the political branches? If treaties are to be enforced only if
they are self-executing, when are they self-executing, and who gets to make
that determination?[32] The constitutional text is silent on all these questions.
Finally, the constitutional text also says nothing about the status of customary
international law generally, though it does acknowledge its existence as law.
Clearly, within such a textual framework, constitutional practice is strongly

[31]   The U.S. Constitution states in art. VI (2): "This Constitution, and the Laws of the United
States which shall be made in Pursuance thereof; and all Treaties made, or which shall be
made, under the Authority of the United States, shall be the supreme Law of the Land." That
is today translated into the following conflict rule: "An act of Congress supersedes an earlier
rule of international law or a provision of an international agreement as law of the United
States if the purpose of the act to supersede the earlier rule or provision is clear or if the act
and the earlier rule or provision cannot be fairly reconciled." See Restatement (Third) of
Foreign Relations Law of the United States § 115(1)(a) (1987).
[32]   Restatement (Third) of Foreign Relations Law of the United States § 111(4) (1987) states
the governing rules as follows: "An international agreement of the United States is non-self-
executing (a) if the agreement manifests an intention that it shall not become effective as
domestic law without the enactment of implementing legislation, (b) if the Senate in giving
consent to a treaty, or Congress by resolution, requires implementing legislation, or (c) if
implementing legislation is constitutionally required." These complex rules, which are not
very stable in practice, are the result of relatively freestanding constructive exercises by courts
and scholars over time.

guided by background principles of interpretation, which are drawn either from the statist or from the cosmopolitan paradigms, each of which tend to lead to a very different structure of doctrines. Third, even if there are clear and specific restrictive constitutional rules, their scope of application can be reduced by not applying them in certain types of cases, such as where the reasons supporting international legality are particularly strong. In Europe there were several states that simply did not apply the general constitutional rule that treaties have only the same status as domestic legislation to laws of the European Union, even though those laws were generated by institutions established by treaties.[33] The functional reasons supporting greater weight in favor of the effective and uniform enforcement of EU law led courts to devise doctrines that effectively give greater deference to EU Law. Seen as a whole, constitutional practice that relates to engagement with international law often bears only an attenuated connection to constitutional provisions, perhaps in part exactly because it is understood that the national constitutional legislator's authority in this area is limited by prerogatives of the international legal system.

This results in a conception of legality that is not monist in that it allows for legal pluralism: potential for legally irresolvable conflict between national and international law remains. But it is not simply dualist either: the relationship between national and international law is reconceived in light of a common set of principles that play a central role in determining the relative authority of each in case of conflict, thus ensuring legal coherence.[34] The following section provides an example that illustrates how such a conception of legality can operate not only to mitigate potential conflicts between national and international law but also to ensure coherence within the increasingly fragmentized practice of international law.[35]

b. Constitutional Pluralism in Context: The European Court of Human Rights, the European Union, and the United Nations

International institutions, from the European Union to the United Nations, have an increasingly important role to play in global governance. States have

---

[33] For an overview of the reception of EU law in member states and the doctrinal dynamics that were an integral part of this process, see THE EUROPEAN COURTS AND NATIONAL COURTS (Anne-Marie Slaughter, Alec Stone Sweet & J. H. H. Weiler eds., 1998).

[34] The existence of a common unifying conceptual framework of norms makes it possible to describe cosmopolitan constitutionalism as monist, even if the institutional practices it justifies might have a pluralist structure. I thank Alexander Somek for clarifying this point.

[35] For a more elaborate discussion of the framework, see Mattias Kumm, *Democratic Constitutionalism Encounters Constitutional Law: Terms of Engagement, in* THE MIGRATION OF CONSTITUTIONAL IDEAS 256–93 (Sujit Choudhry ed., 2006).

delegated authority to these institutions in order to more effectively address the specific tasks within their jurisdictions.[36] The institutions make decisions that directly effect people's lives. Increasingly, this gives rise to situations in which the constitutional or human rights of individuals are in play. When these decisions are enforced domestically, should national courts apply to them the same constitutional rights standards they apply to acts by national public authorities?

Here there are two opposing intuitions in play. The first focuses on the nature of the legal authority under which international institutions operate. International institutions are generally based on treaties concluded between states. These treaties are accorded a particular status in domestic law. If these treaties establish institutions that have the jurisdiction to make decisions in a certain area, these decisions derive their authority from the treaty and should thus have at most the same status as the treaty as a matter of domestic law. Because in most jurisdictions treaties have a status below constitutional law, any decisions enforced domestically must thus be subject to constitutional standards.

The opposing intuition is grounded in functional sensibilities. Constitutions function to organize and constrain domestic public authorities. They do not serve to constrain and guide international institutions. Furthermore, international institutions typically function to address certain coordination problems that could not be effectively addressed on the domestic level by individual states. Having states subject decisions by international institutions to domestic constitutional standards undermines the effectiveness of international institutions and is incompatible with their function. So both the function of the domestic constitution and the function of international institutions suggest that domestic constitutional rights should not be applied to decisions by international institutions at all.

In its *Bosphorus* decision,[37] the European Court of Human Rights (ECHR) had to address just this kind of question, and it did so by developing a doctrinal framework that can serve as an example of the application of the framework presented here. To simplify somewhat, the applicant, Bosphorus, was an airline charter company incorporated in Turkey that had leased two 737-300 aircraft from Yugoslav Airlines. One of these Bosphorus-operated planes was impounded by the Irish government while on the ground in Dublin airport.

[36] DELEGATING STATE POWERS: THE EFFECT OF TREATY REGIMES ON DEMOCRACY AND SOVEREIGNTY (Thomas M. Franck ed., 2000).
[37] Bosphorus Hava Yollari Turizm ve Ticaret Anonim Sirketi v. Ireland, App. No. 45036/98 Eur. Ct. H.R. 30 (2005).

By impounding the aircraft, the Irish government implemented EC Regulation 990/93, which in turn implemented UN Security Council Resolution 820 (1993). UN Security Council Resolution 820 was one of several resolutions establishing sanctions against the Federal Republic of Yugoslavia in the early 1990s, designed to address the armed conflict and human rights violations taking place there. It provided that states should impound, inter alia, all aircraft in their territories in which a majority or controlling interest is held by a person or undertaking in or operating from the Federal Republic of Yugoslavia. As an innocent third party that operated and controlled the aircraft, Bosphorus claimed that its right to peaceful enjoyment of its possessions under article 1 of Protocol No. 1 to the convention had been violated.[38]

The ECHR is, of course, not a domestic constitutional court, but itself it is a court established by a treaty under international law. But with regard to the issue it was facing, it was similarly situated to domestic constitutional courts. Just as the UN Security Council or the European Union – the two international institutions whose decisions led to the impounding of the aircraft – are not public authorities directly subject to national constitutional control, they are not directly subject to the jurisdiction of the ECHR either. Just as only national public authorities are generally addressees of domestic constitutions, the ECHR is addressed to public authorities of signatory states.

The ECHR began by taking a formal approach: at issue were not the acts of the European Union or the United Nations, but the acts of the Irish government impounding the aircraft. These acts unquestionably amounted to an infringement of the applicant's protected interests under the convention. The question is whether the government's action was justified. Under the applicable limitations clause, the government's actions were justified if they struck a fair balance between the demands of the general interest in the circumstances and the interests of the company.[39] Government's actions have to fulfill the proportionality requirement. It is at this point that the court addresses the fact that the Irish government was merely complying with its international obligations when it was impounding the aircraft. The ECHR

---

[38] Art. 1 of Protocol No. 1 to the Convention reads:

Every natural or legal person is entitled to the peaceful enjoyment of his possessions. No one shall be deprived of his possessions except in the public interest and subject to the conditions provided for by law and by the general principles of international law.

The preceding provisions shall not, however, be in any way impair the right of a State to enforce such laws as it deems necessary to control the use of property in accordance with the general interest or to secure the payment of taxes or other contributions or penalties.

[39] See *Bosphorus* para. 149.

held that compliance with international law clearly constituted a legitimate interest. The ECHR recognized "the growing importance of international co-operation and of the consequent need to secure the proper functioning of international organizations."[40] But that did not automatically mean that a state could rely on international law to completely relieve itself from the human rights obligations it had assumed under the convention. Instead, the ECHR "reconciled" the competing principles – ensuring the effectiveness of international institutions and the idea of international legality on the one hand and outcome-related concerns (the effective protection of human rights under the convention) on the other – by establishing a doctrinal framework that strikes a balance between the competing concerns.

First, the ECHR held that state action taken in compliance with international legal obligations is generally justified "as long as the relevant organization is considered to protect fundamental rights, as regards both the substantive guarantees offered and the mechanisms controlling their observance, in a manner which can be considered at least equivalent to that for which the Convention provides."[41] If an international institution provides such equivalent protection, this establishes a general presumption that a state has not departed from the requirements of the convention when it merely implements legal obligations arising from membership of such an international institution. If no equivalent human rights protection is provided by that international institution, the ECHR will subject the state action to the same standard as it would if it were acting on its own grounds, rather than just comply with international law. When a general presumption applies, this presumption can be rebutted in the circumstances of the particular case, when the protection of convention rights was manifestly deficient.[42]

Under the circumstances, the ECHR first established that the international legal basis on which the Irish government effectively relied was the EC regulation that implemented the UN Security Council resolution and not the UN Security Council resolution itself, which had no independent status as a matter of domestic Irish law. It then engaged in a close analysis of the substantive and procedural arrangements of the European Community as they relate to the protection of human rights. Given, in particular, the role of the European Court of Justice (ECJ) as the enforcer of last resort of human rights

---

[40] *Id* at para 150.

[41] *Id.* at para. 155. *Bosphorus* further develops the ECHR's case law in this respect. *See* Case 13258/87, M. & Co. v. Federal Republic of Germany (1990) 64 DR 138, and Case 21090/92, Heinz v. Contracting States also Parties to the European Patent Convention, (1994) 76A DR 125.

[42] *See Bosphorus* para. 156.

in the European Community, the ECHR concluded that the European Community was an international institution to which the presumption applied. Because this presumption had not been rebutted in the present case, it held that the Irish government had not violated the convention by impounding the aircraft.

This approach may be generally satisfactory with regard to legislative measures taken by the European Community and reflects sensibilities toward constitutionalist principles. But in an important sense it dodges the issue. In this case the European Community itself had merely mechanically legislated to implement a UN Security Council resolution. And it is very doubtful that the ECHR would have held that UN Security Council decisions deserve the same kind of presumption of compliance with human rights norms as do EC decisions. It is all very well to say that European citizens are adequately protected against acts of the European Community generally. But this just raises the issue of what adequate protection amounts to when the substantive decision has been made not by EC institutions but by the UN Security Council. How should the ECJ go about assessing, for example, whether EC Regulation 990/93, which implemented the UN Security Council resolution, violated the rights of Bosphorus as guaranteed by the European Community? Should the ECJ, examining the EC regulation under the European Community's standards of human rights, accord special deference to the regulation because it implemented UN Security Council obligations?

There is no need to make an educated guess about what the ECJ would do. The ECJ had already addressed the issue. Bosphorus had already litigated the issue in the Irish courts before turning to the ECHR. The Irish Supreme Court made a preliminary reference to the ECJ under article 234 of the EC treaty, to clarify whether or not EC law in fact required the impounding of the aircraft or whether such an interpretation of the regulation was in violation of the human rights guaranteed by the European legal order. In assessing whether the regulation was sufficiently respectful of Bosphorus's rights to property and its right to freely pursue a commercial activity, the ECJ ultimately applied a proportionality test.[43] The general purposes pursued by the European Community must be proportional under the circumstances to the infringements of Bosphorus's interests.

How, then, is it relevant that the EC regulation implemented a UN Security Council resolution? Within the proportionality test, the ECJ emphasized that the EC regulation contributed to the implementation at the European

---

[43] Case C-84/95, Hava Yollari Turizm ve Ticaret Anonim Sirketi v. Minister for Transport, Energy and Communications and Others [1997] ECR I-2953, paras. 21–26.

Community level of the UN Security Council sanctions against the Federal Republic of Yugoslavia. But, unlike the ECHR, the ECJ did not go on to develop deference rules establishing presumptions of any kind. Instead, the fact that the EU regulation implemented a Security Council decision was taken as a factor that gave further weight to the substantive purposes of the regulation to be taken into account. The principle of international legality was a factor in the overall equation. The purpose to implement a decision by an international institution added further weight to the substantive purpose pursued by the regulation to persuade the Yugoslav government to change its behavior and help bring about peace and security in the region. But a generous reading of the decision also suggests that, beyond formal and substantive considerations, jurisdictional considerations were added to the mix: the ECJ emphasized the fact that the concerns addressed by the Security Council pertained to international peace and security and to putting an end to the state of war. The particular concerns addressed by the UN Security Council went right to the heart of war and peace, an issue appropriately committed to the jurisdiction of an international institution such as the United Nations. Jurisdictional concerns, then, give further weight to the fact that the United Nations had issued a binding decision on the matter. Under these circumstances the principle of international legality has particular weight. The ECJ concluded: "as compared with an objective of general interest so fundamental *for the international community*... the impounding of the aircraft in question, which is owned by an undertaking based in ... the Federal Republic of Yugoslavia, cannot be regarded as inappropriate or disproportionate."[44]

Within the framework used by the ECJ, both the principle of international legality and jurisdictional considerations were factors that the ECJ relied on in determining whether, all things considered, the EU measures as applied to Bosphorus in the particular case were proportionate. Outcome-related concerns did not disappear from the picture. Indeed, within proportionality analysis substantive concerns – striking a reasonable balance between competing concerns – framed the whole inquiry and remained the focal point of the analysis. But what counts as an outcome to be accepted as reasonable from the perspective of a regional institution such as the European Union is rightly influenced to some extent by what the international community, addressing concerns of internal peace and security through the United Nations, deems appropriate. Though it may not have made a difference in this particular case, sanctions by the European Union enacted under the auspices of the UN Security Council may be held by the ECJ to be proportionate, even when the

---

[44] *Id.* at para. 26 (emphasis added).

same sanctions imposed by the European Union unilaterally may be held to be disproportionate and thus in violation of rights.

The approaches by the ECHR and the ECJ both reflect engagement with the kind of moral concerns already highlighted here. The ECHR's more categorical approach is preferable with regard to institutions such as the European Union that have relatively advanced human rights protection mechanisms. With regard to such an institution, a presumption of compliance with human rights seems appropriate, preventing unnecessary duplication of functions and inefficiencies. On the other hand, even when such a presumption does not apply, there are still concerns relating to the principle of international legality in play. Here the kind of approach taken by the ECJ in Bosphorus seems to be the right one.

But the case of UN Security Council resolutions may help bring to light a further complication. It is unlikely that UN Security Council resolutions would be held by the ECHR as deserving a presumption of compatibility. Procedurally, UN Security Council decisions involve only representatives of relatively few and, under current rules, relatively arbitrarily selected, states.[45] Their collective decision making is frequently, to put it euphemistically, less than transparent.

Council resolutions enacted to combat terrorism in recent years in particular illustrate the severity of the problem.[46] These resolutions typically establish the duty of a state to impose severe sanctions on individuals or institutions believed to be associated with terrorism: assets are frozen and ordinary business transactions are made impossible because an individual or an entity appears on a list. The content of the list is determined in closed proceedings by the Sanctions Committee established under the resolution. Until very recently, this internal procedure did not even require a state that wanted an entity or individual to be on the list to provide reasons.[47] If a state puts forward a name forward to be listed, it would be listed, unless there were specific objections by another state. There is no meaningful participatory process underlying UN Security Council resolutions, and there is no process within the Sanctions Committee that comes even close to providing the kind

---

[45] The UN Security Council composition, particularly with regard to the permanent members, reflects post–World War II standing in the international community. Current reform proposals are focused on creating a more representative body including a stronger South American, Asian, and African presence.

[46] See Kim Lane Scheppele, *The Migration of Anti-Constitutional Ideas: The Post 9/11 Globalization of Public Law and the International State of Emergency, in* THE MIGRATION OF CONSTITUTIONAL IDEAS 347 (Sujit Choudhry ed., 2006)

[47] A weak reason giving requirement has been established by S.C. Res. 1617, U.N. Doc. S/RES/1617 (July 29, 2005).

of administrative and legal procedural safeguards that are rightly insisted upon on the domestic level for taking measures of this kind.

These deficiencies are not remedied by more meaningful assessments during the implementation stage in Europe. The implementation of the Council Resolution by the European Community does not involve any procedure or any substantive assessments of whether those listed are listed for a good reason.[48] Implementation is schematic. The fact that a name appears on the list as determined by the UN Security Council is regarded a sufficient reason to enact and regularly update implementation legislation. As the Sanctions Committee of the UN Security Council decides to amend the list of persons to whom the sanction are to apply, the European Union amends the implementation regulation, which is the legal basis for legal enforcement in member states, accordingly.[49] The EU member states have frozen the assets of about 450 people and organizations featured on this list.

Furthermore, there is no administrative-type review process and no alternative legal review procedures that provide individuals with minimal, let alone adequate, protection against mistakes or abuse by individual states that are represented in the Sanctions Committee. The only "remedy" originally available to individuals and groups who found their assets frozen was to make diplomatic representations to their government, which could then make diplomatic representations to the Security Council Sanctions Committee to bring about delisting, if the represented member states unanimously concur.

This was the context that provided the backdrop to the ECJ's recent ruling in Kadi,[50] which involved a challenge to the EU Regulation implementing the UN Security Council decision. The decision is complex and multifacetted and can't be described in great detail here. Here it must suffice to point out some of its core structural features. The Kadi decision overturned the decision by the European Court of First Instance (ECFI).[51] Unlike either

---

[48] See Commission Regulation 881/2002 (EC).

[49] See, e.g., Commission Regulation 1378/2005 (EC), amending for the fifty-second time the original implementation Regulation 881/2002 (EC). In order to satisfy the reason giving requirement under art. 253 of the ECT, the Commission stated only: "On 17 August 2005, the Sanctions Committee of the United Nations Security Council decided to amend the list of persons, groups and entities to whom the freezing of funds and economic resources should apply. Annex I should therefore be amended accordingly."

[50] See Joined Cases C-402/05 P and C-415/05 P Yassin Abdullah Kadi and Al Barakaat International Foundation v. Council and Commission.

[51] See Case T-306/01, Yusuf and Al-Barakaat Int'l Found. v. Council and Comm'n, 2005 E.C.R. II-03649. See also Case T-315/01.

the ECJ or the ECHR in Bosphorus, the ECFI adopted a straightforward monist approach.[52] It began stating the trite truth that UN Security Council resolutions were binding under international law, trumping all other international obligations. But it then went on to derive from this starting point that "infringements either of fundamental rights as protected by the Community legal order... cannot affect the validity of a Security Council measure or its effect in the territory of the Community."[53] The only standards it could hold these decisions to were principles of *jus cogens*, which the European Court of First Instance held were not violated in this case.[54] The ECJ, in overruling the ECFI, adopted what on the surface looks like a conventional dualist approach. It insisted on the primacy of EU constitutional principles and explicitly rejected applying those principles deferentially, even though the EU Regulation implemented the UN Security Council Resolution. But on closer examination it becomes apparent that a great deal in that decision reflects cosmopolitain constitutionalist analysis: First, the court specifically acknowledges the function of the UN Security Council as the body with the primary responsibility to make determinations regarding the maintenance of international peace and security.[55] Second, the court examines the argument

---

[52] One reason for the reluctance of the European Court of First Instance to adopt anything other than a monist position was no doubt the introduction of art. I-3 s(4) of the Constitutional Treaty, which establishes that "the strict observance and the development of international law, including respect for the principles of the United Nations Charter" as an EU objective. The constitutional convention that drafted the Constitutional Treaty was deliberating these clauses in the context of what was widely regarded as the blatant disregard of the United States for international law and the United Nations specifically in the context of the Iraq War, which generated mass demonstrations in capitals across Europe, including London, Rome and Madrid. The Constitutional Treaty is unlikely to be ratified in the present form, following its rejection in French and Dutch referenda, but its provisions may still exert a moral pull that informs the interpretation of the current law of the European Union. A commitment to international legality, in particular in the security area, may well have become a central part of a European identity.

[53] Case T-306/01, para. 225.

[54] There are traces of constitutionalist thinking evident in the Court's innovative understanding of jus cogens. The Court acknowledged that the right to access to the courts, for example, is protected by jus cogens, but that as a rule of jus cogens, its limits must be understood very broadly. In assessing the limitations the Court essentially applies a highly deferential proportionality test attuned to the principles of the constitutionalist model: Given the nature of the Security Council decision and the legitimate objectives pursued, given further the Security Council's commitments to review its decisions at specified intervals, in the circumstance of the case the applicants' interest in having a court hear their case on the merits is not enough to outweigh the essential public interest pursued by the Security Council (see paras. 343–45). Even if the approach taken by the Court to jus cogens is plausible, the results it reached are not.

[55] Kadi, Recital 297.

whether it should grant deference to the UN decisions and rejects such an approach only because at the time the complaint was filed there were no meaningful review procedures on the UN level and even those that had been established since then[56] still provide no judicial protection.[57] Only after an assessment of the UN review procedures does the court follow that full review is the appropriate standard. This suggests that, echoing the ECHR's approach in Bosphorus, a more adequate procedures on the UN level might have justified a more deferential form of judicial review. This is further supported by the ECJ's conclusion that under the circumstances *the plaintiffs right to be heard and right to effective judicial review were patently not respected*. This language suggests that even under a more deferential form of review, the court would have had to come to the same conclusion. This section of the opinion indicates that the court was fully attuned to constitutionalist sensibilities. It just turns out that the procedures used by the Sanctions Committee were so manifestly inappropriate given what was at stake for the black-listed individuals, that any jurisdictional considerations in favor of deference were trumped by these procedural deficiencies, thus undermining the case not just for abstaining from review altogether, but also for engaging in a more deferential review. Third, the court shows itself attuned to the functional division of labor between the UN Security Council and itself when discussing remedies: The court does not determine that the sanctions must be lifted immediately, but instead permits them to be maintained for three months, allowing the Council to find a way to bring about a review procedure that meets fundamental rights reaquirements. Finally during all of this the court is careful to emphasize that nothing it does violates the UN Resolution, given that international law generally leaves it to the states to determine by which procedures obligations are enforced. Though it is still too early to tell, it seems as the forceful judicial intervention has had a salutary effect, with serious reform proposals being discussed on the UN level. Taking international law seriously does not require unqualified deference to a seriously flawed global security regime.[58] On the contrary, the threat of subjecting these decisions to meaningful review might help bring about reforms on the UN level. Only once these efforts bear more significant fruit will the ECJ have reasons not to insist on meaningful independent rights review of individual cases in the future.

---

[56] *See* S.C. Res. 1730, U.N. Doc. S/RES/1730 (Dec. 19, 2006); S.C. Res. 1735, U.N. Doc. S/RES/1735 (Dec. 22, 2006); S.C. Res. 1822, U.N. Doc. S/RES/1822 (June 30, 2008).

[57] Kadi, Recital 321, 322.

[58] *See* Scheppele, *The Migration of Anti-Constitutional Ideas, supra* note 46.

c. The Structure of Legal Authority: The Techniques and Distinctions of Graduated Authority

Cosmopolitan constitutionalism establishes a normative framework for assessing and guiding courts in their attempt to engage international law in a way that does justice both to their respective commitments and to the increasing demands of an international legal system. There are three interesting structural features that characterize any set of doctrines that reflect a commitment to a conception of legality conceived within the framework of cosmopolitan constitutionalism.

First, such courts take a significantly more differentiated approach than traditional conflict rules suggest.[59] Treaties are not treated alike, even if constitutionally entrenched conflict rules suggest that they should be. Instead, doctrines used are sensitive to the specific subject matter of a treaty and the jurisdictional considerations that explain its particular function. Furthermore, the example of the ECHR's engagement with international institutions illustrated how outcome-related considerations are a relevant factor in assessing the authority of its decisions.

Second, the kind of doctrinal structures that come into view suggests a more graduated authority than the statist idea of constitutionally established conflict rules suggests. The doctrinal structures in the example illustrated a shift from rules of conflict to rules of engagement. These rules of engagement characteristically take the forms of a duty to engage, the duty to take into account as a consideration of some weight, or presumptions of some sort. The old idea of using international law as a canon of construction points in the right direction but does not even begin to capture the richness and subtlety of the doctrinal structures in place. The idea of a discourse between courts is, too, a response to this shift. That idea captures the reasoned form that engagement with international law frequently takes. But it too falls short conceptually. It is not sufficiently sensitive to the graduated claims of authority that various doctrinal frameworks have built into them. The really interesting questions concern the structures of graduated authority built into doctrinal frameworks: who needs to look at what and give what kind of consideration to what is being said and done.[60]

---

[59] See W. Michael Riesman, *The Democratization of Contemporary International Law-Making Processes and the Differentiation of Their Application, in* DEVELOPMENTS OF INTERNATIONAL LAW IN TREATY-MAKING 15 (Rüdiger Wolfrum & Volker Röben eds., 2005).

[60] There are two other ways in which the discourse-between-courts paradigm is not helpful. It downplays the significance of the distinction between international law and foreign law. Outside of the area of human rights, the reasons supporting judicial engagement with

Finally, the practice is jurisprudentially more complex than the statist models suggest. The traditional idea that the management of the interface between national and international law occurs by way of constitutionally entrenched conflict rules that are focused on the sources of international law is deeply committed to dualist legal thinking. It suggests that the national constitution is the source of the applicable conflict rules. Furthermore, these constitutional conflict rules are themselves typically organized around the sources of international law: treaties and customary international law are each assigned a particular status in the domestic legal order. Both ideas are seriously challenged by actual practice, which is attuned to cosmopolitan constitutionalism. Principles relating to international legality, jurisdiction, procedures, and outcomes have a much more central role to play in explaining and guiding legal practice. These principles are not alien to liberal constitutional democracy, appropriately conceived. And they are not alien to international law. But their legal force derives not from their canonical statement in a legal document but from their ability to make sense of legal practice and help guide and constrain it in a way that is morally attractive.

2. Complex Procedural Legitimacy: Subsidiarity, Due Process, and Democracy

The cosmopolitan conception of procedural legitimacy includes a jurisdictional and a procedural prong in the narrow sense. First, the jurisdictional prong consists of the principle of subsidiarity. Second, the procedural prong consists of a principle of due process that, on the domestic level, emphasized the role of electoral institutions at the heart of the political process. Both prongs are internally connected: overall procedural legitimacy can be assessed only by also taking into account jurisdictional concerns. Third, questions relating to jurisdiction are central to procedural legitimacy. This means that national legislation enacted in perfect democratic processes on the domestic level can raise serious legitimacy issues, if that legislation creates serious externalities and addresses issues that should be addressed by the international community. And it means that less-than-democratic

---

foreign law are generally considerably weaker than the reasons supporting engagement with international law. Not surprisingly, in many jurisdictions these differences are reflected in the different doctrinal structures concerning engagement with international law. Furthermore the idea of discourse between courts is too court focused. The spread of constitutional courts and international courts and tribunals clearly is a factor that furthers the tendencies described here. But this shift is not just about courts engaging other courts. It is about courts engaging the various institutions that generate and interpret international law.

international processes might in some cases be superior to domestic democratic processes in terms of overall procedural legitimacy.

a. Jurisdictional Legitimacy: From Sovereignty to Subsidiarity

The principle of subsidiarity helps structure and guide meaningful debates about the appropriate sphere of state autonomy or sovereignty, defined as the sphere in which a state does not owe any kind of obligations to the international community and can govern itself as it deems fit. Turned around, it is also a principle that helps define the appropriate scope of international law and thus guides and limits the interpretation and progressive development of international law. The principle of subsidiarity helps give constructive meaning to debates on sovereignty that permeate international law. On the one hand, claims to sovereignty tend to be made by state actors against the interpretation or progressive development of international law whenever an important national interest is at stake. On the other hand, there is the formalist legal rejoinder that, as a matter of international law, the limits of sovereignty are defined by international law, whatever it happens to be. The principle of subsidiarity can help transform competing and incommensurable claims about sovereignty into a constructive debate about the appropriate delimitation of the sphere of the national and the international in specific legal and political debates.

Sovereignty is invoked as an argument in international law in a variety of ways. When the UN Security Council decides, for example, whether government behavior violates human rights in such a way as to legitimate sanctions under chapter 7 of the UN Charter, those who do not favor such intervention often invoke sovereignty as an argument. This can be understood as an argument that concerns the interpretation of the competencies of the UN Security Council and the meaning of "threat to the peace" and "restoration of international peace and security" in article 39 of the UN Charter more specifically. Here sovereignty is invoked as an argument that is supposed to carry some weight in the context of interpreting international law, thus restricting its reach. Sovereignty is also invoked as an argument against assuming certain types of potentially intrusive international obligations. More specifically it is often invoked as a reason not to enter into a particular international legal commitment, for example, to sign and ratify a multilateral treaty that establishes am international institution and provides it with some degree of potentially intrusive decision-making authority.[61] Here the argument from sovereignty

---

[61] For an overview of such regimes, see Thomas Franck, Delegating State Powers: The Effect of Treaty Regimes on Democracy and Sovereignty (2000).

is invoked as a political argument. It may be of legal relevance, however, when made in the context of domestic constitutional debates about the proper constitutional limits for the 'delegation' of authority to international institutions. Often national constitutions do not contain any provisions that either explicitly authorize or explicitly prohibit or impose constraints on the delegation of authority to international institutions. But in those cases sovereignty serves as an argument to read implicit restrictions into vague national constitutional provisions.[62] Connected to the idea of sovereignty is the idea of "matters essentially within the domestic jurisdiction of a state" (art. 2(7) of the UN Charter). In both cases the invocation of sovereignty is tantamount to making the claim that that the issue discussed is an issue that properly concerns only the state and that requires no international regulation, intervention, or even justification to the international community. To put it another way, the international community does not have jurisdiction to address the issue because the issue pertains to the exclusive jurisdiction of the state. In that sense sovereignty refers to the domain over which a national community may govern itself without regard to the international community.

The idea of sovereignty does not, however, in and of itself provide any indication whatsoever of how large that domain should be or even how to meaningfully structure debates about the boundaries of sovereignty. In practice, the invocation of sovereignty is typically little more than a way of expressing a political will in legal language. When a representative of a state says that something is within that state's sovereign right, he or she means to say that the state's behavior pertains to a domain that is of no legitimate concern for the international community without having provided any kind of reason why that should be so. The idea of sovereignty adds nothing. The idea of sovereignty becomes meaningful only in the context of a particular theoretical paradigm that provides an account of how the debates about the boundaries of sovereignty should be structured. Without it, the invocation of sovereignty might seem like an empty rhetorical gesture.

The reason why sovereignty is not merely an empty rhetorical gesture in political life but one that is widely understood and widely resonant is that the language of sovereignty has traditionally been connected to the statist

---

[62] In France, for example, the Conseil Constitutionnel has held that transfers of authority that "violate the essential conditions for the exercise of national sovereignty" require constitutional amendment and not just the ordinary majorities usually sufficient for the ratification of treaties. See Conseil Constitutionnel, Apr. 9, 1992, Maastricht I. Other constitutions establish more demanding ratification procedures for treaties that authorize international institutions to exercise public authority, requiring supermajorities rather than the ordinary majorities needed for treaty ratification.

paradigm that does give it a specific meaning. Within the statist paradigm, any discussions relating to jurisdiction are biased in favor of the central level of the state. Besides the claim to establish an ultimate legal authority, the universal, all-encompassing claim to jurisdiction is a defining feature of sovereignty. Constructively, the national or state level is the level where all decision making is originally located. Of course a state might enter into treaties, even multilateral treaties that establish international institutions and delegate some authority to them. But if international law is to impose any obligations on states, it will presumptively have to trace those firmly back to the states' consent.[63] Presumptively, the state has jurisdiction. International law has jurisdiction only if and to the extent that a restriction of that sovereignty can be traced back to the state's consent.

Today the language of subsidiarity has to some extent replaced the language of sovereignty. In the law of the European Union, the language of subsidiarity has completely replaced the language of sovereignty. The principle of subsidiarity found its way into contemporary debates through its introduction to European constitutional law in the Treaty of Maastricht. In Europe it was used to guide the drafting of the European Constitutional Treaty, whose operational provisions are mostly identical to the Treaty of Lisbon. It is a principle that guides the exercise of the European Union's power under the treaty. And it guides the interpretation of the European Union's laws. As such, it is a structural principle that applies to all levels of institutional analysis, ranging from the big-picture assessment of institutional structure and grant of jurisdiction to the microanalysis of specific decision-making processes and the substance of specific decisions. The principle is also one of the principles that governs the relationship of the European Union with the larger international community.[64] Furthermore, some national constitutions have specifically adopted the principle of subsidiarity as a constitutional principle that determines whether and to what extent the transfer of public authority to international institutions is desirable.[65]

But even to the extent that the language of sovereignty remains alive, the concept of sovereignty is today sufficiently unsettled to open up the

---

[63] For a leading case that exemplifies such an understanding, see the SS *Lotus* case (France v. Turkey), 1927 P.C.I.J. (ser. A) No. 10 (Sept. 7).

[64] See art. 21 of the Lisbon Treaty, which establishes that the relationship between the European Union and the international community is to be governed by the same basic principles as the principles central to the evolution of the European Union.

[65] Grundgesetz für die Bundesrepublik Deutschland (federal constitution), art. 23, states: "To realize a United Europe, the Federal Republic of Germany cooperates with others to develop a European Union that is committed to . . . the principle of subsidiarity."

possibility to redescribe it in terms of a commitment to subsidiarity.[66] Sovereignty should be, and to some extent already has been, reinterpreted within a cosmopolitan paradigm, which has given it a different meaning. On the one hand, the idea has gained ground that a state can claim sovereignty only under the condition that it fulfills its responsibilities toward citizens. According to a high-level UN report, that means at the very least

> that states are under an obligation to protect citizens from large scale violence. . . . When a state fails to protect its civilians, the international community then has a further responsibility to act, though humanitarian operations, monitoring missions and diplomatic pressure – and with force if necessary, though only as a last resort.[67]

But the idea of *conditioning sovereignty on a state's ability to effectively fulfill functions* might also be extended to its role within the international system more generally. In effect this would mean *that the scope of sovereignty should be determined by the principle of subsidiarity*. What exactly would that mean?

At its core, the principle of subsidiarity requires any infringements of the autonomy of the relatively local level by the relatively centralized level to be justified by good reasons.[68] The infringement of a state's autonomy can take the relatively weak form of an international duty to justify state actions or have them monitored and subject to assessment in an international forum or the stronger form of being subject to restrictive substantive rules of international law. The principle of subsidiarity requires any international intervention to be justified as a concern appropriately addressed by actors, institutions, or norms beyond the state. There has to be a reason that justifies the international community's involvement; a reason against leaving the decision to be addressed conclusively by national institutions. Any norm of international law requires justification of a special kind. It is not enough for it to be justified on substantive grounds by, say, plausibly claiming that it embodies good policy. Instead, the justification has to make clear what exactly would be lost if the assessment of the relevant policy concerns was left to the lower level. With exceptions relating to the protection of minimal standards of human rights, only reasons connected to collective action problems – relating

---

[66] John Jackson labeled a similar idea "sovereignty-modern." *See* John H. Jackson, *Sovereignty-Modern: A New Approach to an Outdated Concept*, 97 Am. J. Int'l L. 782 (2003).

[67] *See A More Secure World: Our Shared Responsibility, Report of the Secretary-General's High-Level Panel on Threats, Challenges and Change*, U.N. Doc A/59/565, Executive Summary 4 (Dec. 2004).

[68] For a discussion of how the principle of subsidiarity operates, *see* Mattias Kumm, *Constitutionalizing Subsidiarity in Integrated Markets: The Case of Tobacco Regulation in the European Union*, 12 Eur. L.J. 503 (2006).

to externalities or strategic standard setting giving rise to race-to-the-bottom concerns, for example – or reasons relating to nontrivial coordination benefits are good reasons to ratchet up the level on which decisions are made. And even when there are such reasons, they have to be of sufficient weight to override any disadvantages connected to the preemption of more decentralized rule making. On application, subsidiarity analysis thus requires a two-step test. First, reasons relating to the existence of a collective action problem have to be identified. Second, the weight of these reasons has to be assessed in light of countervailing concerns relating to state autonomy in the specific circumstances. This requires the applications of a proportionality test or a cost-benefit analysis that is focused on the advantages and disadvantages of ratcheting up the level of decision making. This means that on application, this principle, much like the others, requires saturation by arguments that are context sensitive and most likely subject to normative and empirical challenges. Its usefulness does not lie in providing a definitive answer in any specific context. But it structures inquiries in a way that is likely to be sensitive to the relevant empirical and normative concerns. The principle of subsidiarity provides a structure for legal and political debates about the limits of sovereignty.

There are good reasons for the principle of subsidiarity to govern the allocation and exercise of decision-making authority wherever there are different levels of public authorities. These reasons are related to sensibility toward locally variant preferences, possibilities for meaningful participation and accountability, and the protection and enhancement of local identities, which suggest that the principle of subsidiarity ought to be a general principle guiding institutional design also in federally structured entities. In this way, it could also be put to fruitful use in the reconstruction of federalism rules and doctrines. But the principle has particular weight with regard to the management of the national-international divide. In well-established constitutional democracies, instruments for holding accountable national actors are generally highly developed. There is a well-developed public sphere allowing for meaningful collective deliberations grounded in comparatively strong national identities. All of that is absent on the international level. That absence, in conjunction with the danger of smaller states being dominated by the major powers in the international arena,[69] strengthens the prima facie case for state autonomy and raises the bar for the justification of international requirements being imposed in states.

---

[69] Benedict Kingsbury, *Sovereignty and Inequality*, 9 EUR. J. INT'L L. 599 (1998).

b. Due Process I: The Connection between Subsidiarity and Democracy
Discussions of the democratic deficit are often informed by a statist paradigm
of legitimacy, which tends to inappropriately focus legitimacy concerns on
electoral accountability. Because meaningful electoral accountability can take
place only on the national level, this casts a general cloud of suspicion over
all international law that does not take the form of treaties that establish in
relatively concrete and specific terms what the rights and obligations of the
parties are, thus ensuring democratic input at the time of treaty ratification.
Modern customary law or the kind of activities involving international institutions that are part and parcel of global governance all fall under a cloud of
suspicion. There is a plausible core underlying these sensibilities, to be sure:
basic political decisions properly made by the state should presumptively be
made by institutions that can be held accountable in an electoral process.
Furthermore, decisions appropriately made on the domestic level should
not be made on the international level, exactly because those processes are
linked to citizens' participation and concerns in a more attenuated way. It
is clearly not always an indication of human progress to have a problem
resolved by international institutions rather than democratically resolved in
the more open national processes. But questions of procedural legitimacy –
or input legitimacy – have to be tied to jurisdictional questions to be plausible. Dogmatic insistence on democratic accountability is misguided, to the
extent that it is conceived in terms of meaningful electoral accountability.
Many cases falling under the rubric of global governance concern the production of global public goods and make possible the participation of a wider
range of actors. They lead to enhanced representation of the relevant wider
community in the legal process, thus improving input legitimacy. The alternative of leaving decisions with significant externalities to states raises serious
legitimacy issues, even when the national process is democratic. Instead of
focusing exclusively on the legitimating virtues of the electoral process on the
national level that are absent on the international level, the central questions
are whether, to what extent, and following which procedure the international
community ought to have an effective say in decisions of public policy with
significant externalities made by states. That effective say might take the form
of imposing requirements on the state to justify its actions in a way that takes
into account outside interests. It might involve the articulation of certain
global minimum standards. Or it might involve a thicker set of regulations
that preempt national regulations.

    This way of framing the issue leads to a change of focus. Rather than
exclusively focusing on the legitimacy of activities by international actors, the
inactivity of international actors and the underdevelopment of institutional

capacities on the international level come into view as serious legitimacy concerns. Law can raise legitimacy concerns not only because of the restrictions it imposes but also because of what it fails to restrict. International law's permissive rules, its authorization of harmful state behavior without imposing duties to compensate, deserves to become a central concern for those concerned with law's legitimacy.[70] Given a background rule that sovereign states can do as they please unless a rule of international law proscribes a particular behavior, the focus should turn on the procedural rules that enable the international community to intervene and secure the provision of global public goods. Are the rules governing the jurisgenerative process on the international level – in more traditional parlance, the sources of law[71] – structured in a way that allows the international community to adequately address common concerns? Which interpretation of, say, the requirements of customary international law best serves this purpose? Is the international community best served by an understanding of state practice that includes or excludes declaration made by states or international bodies? What degree of support, what duration of time, and what level of consistency are required for customary international law to best serve its purpose? Should this depend on context? And how should the general principles of law be conceived of?

Furthermore, if treaty making remains at the heart of the international rule-making process and states remain the central institutions charged with the enforcement of treaties, then national constitutional rules regarding the negotiation, ratification, and enforcement of treaties have an important constitutional function in the international system. States do not just establish an institutional framework through which a national community governs itself. States also serve as legislators and enforcers of international law. They are an integral part of an international system through which the international community governs itself. Because of this double function,[72] national constitutional rules raise serious legitimacy concerns when they impose unreasonable burdens on the development of an effective and legitimate international legal order. Treaties under the U.S. Constitution, for example, require the ratification by two-thirds of the Senate. This makes it unusually difficult for the state to effectively commit itself internationally, even though its actions, more than that of any other nation, affects others. That may have been defensible in an age when the need for international engagement and international

---

[70] This point is made by DAVID KENNEDY, OF WAR AND LAW (2006).
[71] Conventionally the point of reference here is art. 38 of ICJ Statute, itself a provision of a treaty.
[72] Georges Scelle called this "dédoublement fonctionnel," or role splitting. See 1 PRÉCIS DE DROIT DES GENS. PRINCIPES ET SYSTEMATIQUE (1932).

interdependencies were comparably low. But under modern circumstances there might be good constitutional grounds to interpret extensively the power of the president to enter into international law treaties by concluding executive-congressional agreements, for which simple majorities suffice.[73] This type of concern deserves to be central to the assessment of constitutional rules and their interpretation by national courts.

The principle of subsidiarity, then, is not a one-way street. If there are good reasons for deciding an issue on the international level, because the concerns that need to be addressed are best addressed by a larger community in order to solve collective action problems and secure the provision of global public goods, then arguments from subsidiarity can support international intervention. Subsidiarity related concerns may, in certain contexts, strengthen either the legal case for interpreting the competencies of an international institution expansively or the political case for engaging in ambitious projects of international capacity building. And even though the principle generally requires contextually rich analysis, there are simple cases. The principle can highlight obvious structural deficiencies of national legislative processes with regard to some areas of regulation.

Imagine that in the year 2015, a UN Security Council resolution enacted under chapter 7 of the UN Charter imposes ceilings and established targets for the reduction of carbon dioxide emissions aimed at reducing global warming. Assume that the case for the existence of global warming and the link between global warming and carbon dioxide emissions has been conclusively established. Assume further that the necessary qualified majority in the Security Council was convinced that global warming presented a serious threat to international peace and security and was not appropriately addressed by the outdated Kyoto Protocol or alternative treaties that were negotiated and opened for signature following the Kopenhagen conference in late 2009, without getting the necessary number of ratifications to make them effective. Finally, assume that formal cooperation mechanisms between the General Assembly and the Security Council have been established, securing a reasonably inclusive deliberative process, and that a robust consensus has developed such that permanent members of the newly enlarged and more representative UN Security Council were estopped from vetoing a UN resolution if four-fifths of the members approved a measure.[74]

---

[73] See BRUCE ACKERMAN & DAVID GOLOVE, IS NAFTA CONSTITUTIONAL? (1995) (providing a historical embedded argument that embraces this type of argument).

[74] Assume that current proposals had become law and that it included as new permanent members an African state (Nigeria or South Africa), two additional Asian states (Japan and India or Indonesia), a South American state (Brazil), and an additional European state (Germany), as well as five new non–permanent members.

Now imagine that a large and powerful constitutional democracy, such as the India, has domestic legislation in force that does not comply with the standards established by this resolution. The domestic legislation establishes national emission limits and structures the market for emissions trading, but it goes about setting far less ambitious targets and allowing for more emissions than do the international rules promulgated by the Security Council. Domestic political actors invoke justifications linked to lifestyle issues and business interests.[75] National cost-benefit analysis, they argue, has suggested that beyond the existing limits, it is better for the nation to adapt to climate change rather than incur further costs preventing it. After due deliberations on the national level, a close but stable majority decides to disregard the internationally binding Security Council resolutions and invoke the greater legitimacy of the national political process. Yet assume that the same kind of cost-benefit analysis undertaken on the global scale has yielded a clear preference for aggressive measures to slow down and prevent global warming along the lines suggested by the Security Council resolution.

In such a case, the structural deficit of the national process is obvious. National processes, if well designed, tend to appropriately reflect values and interests of national constituents. As a general matter, they do not reflect values and interests of outsiders. Because in the case of carbon dioxide emissions there are externalities related to global warming, national legislative processes are hopelessly inadequate to deal with the problem. To illustrate the point: the United States produces nearly 25 percent of the world's carbon dioxide emissions, potentially harmfully affecting the well-being of people worldwide. Congress and the Environmental Protection Agency currently make decisions with regard to the adequate levels of emissions. Such a process clearly falls short of even basic procedural fairness, given that only a small minority of global stakeholders is adequately represented in such a process.[76] It may well turn out to be the case that cost-benefit analysis conducted with the national community as the point of reference suggests that it would be preferable to adapt to the consequences of global warming rather than incur the costs of trying to prevent or reduce it. In other jurisdictions, the analysis

---

[75] For an argument of this kind in respect to the U.S. position on the Kyoto Protocol, see Bruce Yandle & Stuart Buck, *Bootleggers, Baptists and the Global Warming Battle*, 26 HARV. ENVTL. L. REV. 177, 179 (2002) (contending that "the Kyoto Protocol would have been a potentially huge drag on the United States' economy" while producing minimal environmental benefits).

[76] Procedural requirements to take into account external effects in cost-benefit analysis have in part been established to mitigate these concerns. *See, e.g.,* Benedict Kingsbury, Richard B. Stewart & Nico Krish, *The Emergence of Global Administrative Law*, 68 LAW & CONTEMP. PROBS. 15 (2005); Richard B. Stewart, *Administrative Law in the Twenty-First Century*, 78 N.Y.U. L. REV. 437 (2003).

could be very different.[77] More important, cost-benefit analysis conducted with the global community as the point of reference could well yield results that would suggest aggressive reductions as an appropriate political response. The jurisdictional point here is that the relevant community that serves as the appropriate point of reference for evaluating processes or outcomes is clearly the global community. When there are externalities of this kind, the legitimacy problem would not lie in the Security Council issuing regulations. Legitimacy concerns in these kinds of cases are more appropriately focused on the absence of effective transnational decision-making procedures and the structurally deficient default alternative of domestic decision making.

The principle of subsidiarity, then, is Janus-faced. It not only serves to protect state autonomy against undue central intervention but also provides a framework of analysis that helps to bring into focus the structural underdevelopment of international law and institutions in some policy areas. In these areas, arguments from subsidiarity help strengthen the authority of international institutions engaging in aggressive interpretation of existing legal materials to enable the progressive development of international law in the service of international capacity building.[78]

What should also be clear is the link between jurisdictional and procedural principles of legitimacy: the jurisdictional principle of subsidiarity determines whether and to what extent an issue is a legitimate concern of the larger community or whether an issue is best determined autonomously by the state (or subnational local authorities within the state). If it is an issue in which the international community has a dominant interest, and in which national institutions effectively prevent the international community from addressing the issue, national decisions suffer from a legitimacy problem, no matter how democratic the procedure used to address it might be from a national point of view. Without the commitment to an international legal

---

[77] For example, the island of Tuvalu, situated in the Pacific Ocean, is in danger of disappearing entirely. On this issue, the governor-general of Tuvalu addressing the UN General Assembly on September 14, 2002, stated the following: "In the event that the situation is not reversed, where does the international community think the Tuvalu people are to hide from the onslaught of sea level rise? Taking us as environmental refugees is not what Tuvalu is after in the long run. We want the islands of Tuvalu and our nation to remain permanently and not be submerged as a result of greed and uncontrolled consumption of industrialized countries." See address of Governor General Sir Tomasi Puapua, Sept. 14, 2002, available at http://www.un.org/webcast/ga/57/statements/020914tuvaluE.htm (last accessed March 10, 2009).

[78] For the judicial interpretation of customary law in this respect, see Eyal Benvenisti, Customary International Law as a Judicial Tool for Promoting Efficiency, in THE IMPACT OF INTERNATIONAL LAW ON INTERNATIONAL COOPERATION: THEORETICAL PERSPECTIVES 85 (Eyal Benvenisti & Moshe Hirsch eds., 2004).

system that is able to effectively identify and address concerns of the international community, national constitutionalism suffers from a structural legitimacy deficit. National constitutionalism is legitimate only if and to the extent that it conceives of itself within a cosmopolitan paradigm.

This means that there is a statist or nationalist bias in identifying legitimacy of legal practices with democratic legitimacy. To focus debates on democratic legitimacy is misleading in two ways. First, democratic legitimacy is very plausibly a necessary condition for the legitimacy of domestic constitutional practice, but it is not sufficient. A further necessary criterion for the legitimacy of domestic constitutions is the commitment to an international legal system that is able to effectively identify and address concerns of the international community. Call this criteria cosmopolitan legitimacy. Constitutional rules that make the ratification of treaties prohibitively difficult, that generally preclude ratification of treaties that transfer regulatory authority to international institutions, or that preclude the effective enforcement of international law by the central government might raise serious legitimacy concerns. Second, given the structure of the international community and the nature of the decisions made on the international level, it is unreasonable to insist on democratic legitimacy of international institutions, at least if democratic legitimacy refers to meaningful electoral accountability on the international level. What is appropriate is to insist on compliance with the principle of subsidiarity, complemented by compliance with principles of good governance. This requires further elaboration.

c. Due Process II: Procedural Standards of Good Governance
Even when international law plausibly meets jurisdictional tests, it could still be challenged in terms of procedural legitimacy. The procedural quality of the jurisgenerative process clearly matters. Electoral accountability may not be the right test to apply, but that does not mean that there are no standards of procedural adequacy. Instead, the relevant questions are whether procedures are sufficiently transparent and allow for the fullest possible participation and representation of those affected under the circumstances.[79] Some aspects of

---

[79] See Grainne de Burca, *Developing Democracy Beyond the State*, 46 COL. J. TRANT'L L. (2008), providing a useful introduction to debates about the legitimacy of transnational governance practices. De Burca's distinction between a '*compensatory*' approach to democracy and a '*democracy-striving*' approach, however, is both overdrawn and misleading. It is overdrawn, to the extent it may not point to more than differences in semantics with regard to some of the authors she cites: Those differences mainly concern the question whether the term democracy should be restricted to describe processes that at a minimum include electoral accountability, whatever else they might require. If you do not believe that it is helpful to use the language of democracy to describe processes that are not

procedural legitimacy concern the basic structure of the institutional environment in which decisions are made and may raise serious concerns. The role and structure of the UN Security Council, for example, points to significant procedural legitimacy concerns: Given the increasing role of the UN Security Council, should it be required to cooperate more closely with the General Assembly, thereby ensuring a higher degree of inclusiveness? Is it legitimate for there to be some states that are permanent members and others that are not? If so, which criteria should be applied to determine who they should be? Is it acceptable that permanent membership comes with a veto right? Should the requirement of blocking decisions not be set higher? Here there is a great deal of space for reform. But besides procedural questions that concern the basic structure of the institution, many procedural questions concern more mundane questions that nonetheless are of considerable practical significance. When, for example, the UN Security Council establishes a Sanctions Committee that manages a blacklist that contains the names of persons against whom severe economic sanctions are to be applied, how should the procedure for listing and delisting be structured to ensure adequate due process? For these types of questions concerning the day-to-day decision making of international institutions, mechanisms and ideas derived from domestic administrative law may, to some extent, be helpful to give concrete shape to ideas of due process on the transnational level.[80] Furthermore, principles and mechanisms described by the EU Commission's 2001 white paper could also

---

anchored in electoral politics, then you'll insist on procedural requirements that compensate for the absence of democracy on the international level. If you embrace a more capacious notion of democracy, you will insist that, on the international level, too, democracy needs to be striven for. It is not clear, whether either approach produces different standards of legitimacy. More importantly both of these approaches, as de Burca describes them, seem to have in common that they do nothing to undermine the misleading premise that national democracy serves as the appropriate paradigm for legitimacy, a paradigm that international governance practices can at best compensate or strive for. Compared to national democratic law international law is always deemed to be comparatively deficient in some way. Some of those who endorse a 'compensatory approach' seek to reframe the issue: international law, appropriately structured, might help to compensate for the democratic deficit of national decision-making to the extent outsiders are effected in qualified ways. This idea is central to the comensatory approach developed, for example, by Anne Peters, *Compensatory Constitutionalism: The Function and Potential of Fundamental International Norms and Structures*, 19 Leid. J. Int'l L. 579 (2006), or Mattias Kumm, *The Legitimacy of International Law: A Constitutionalist Framework of Analaysis*, 15 Eur. J. Int'l L. 907 (2004). De Burca does however identify plausible criteria of procedural adequacy for international governance practices. On those see also Joshua Cohen & Charles F. Sabel, *Global Democracy?*, 37 N.Y.U. J. Int'l L. & Pol. 763 (2005).

[80] *See, e.g.*, Richard B. Stewart, *U.S. Administrative Law: A Model for Global Administrative Law?* 68 Law & Contemp. Probs. 63 (2005).

provide a useful source for giving substance to the idea of transnational procedural adequacy.[81] This is an area that has spawned an important research program focused on the development of global administrative law.[82]

The complex idea of procedural legitimacy that underlies the cosmopolitan paradigm thus has three core features. It replaces or reinterprets the jurisdictional idea of sovereignty using the principle of subsidiarity. It insists on connecting democracy concerns to jurisdictional concerns when assessing questions of procedural legitimacy. And it establishes standards of good governance when electoral accountability cannot reasonably be demanded.

3. Substance: A Cosmopolitan Conception of Human and Constitutional Rights

International human rights are generally the rights guaranteed by international treaties. Constitutional rights are the rights guaranteed by the national constitution. The cosmopolitan conception of human rights can give a plausible account of some core characteristic shared by both and their relationship to one another. As the preambles of many national constitutions and many human rights instruments indicate, the positive law of human and constitutional rights domestically and internationally sees its foundation in a universal moral requirement that public authorities treat those who are subject to their authority as free and equal persons endowed with human dignity. This helps explain three prominent features of contemporary human and constitutional rights practice: (1) the open-ended structure of reasoning about rights that connects rights discourse to public reason, (2) the engagement and mutual interaction between national courts and political institutions, and (3) the internal connections and mutual references between national constitutional and international human rights practice. Here nothing more than a very abbreviated rough sketch of each of these points can be given.

a. Rights and Public Reason

First, there is a close connection between the idea of rights and the idea of public reason. It is true that some human and constitutional rights are simply relatively clear and specific rules that define minimum standards that public authorities are required to respect. These are rules that reflect settled agreements on the concrete content of rights guarantees and can be found in

---

[81] See *The European Commission's White Paper on European Governance* (2001), *available at* http://eur-lex.europa.eu/LexUriServ/site/en/com/2001/com2001_0428en01.pdf (last accessed March 10, 2009).

[82] See Kingsbury, Stewart & Krish, *The Emergence of Global Administrative Law, supra* note 76.

constitutional texts, international human rights instruments, or settled judicial doctrine. Their application and interpretation requires nothing more than run-of-the-mill legal techniques. But a great deal of modern human and constitutional rights practice has a different, less legalistic structure. At the heart of much of human and constitutional rights adjudication is an assessment of the justification of acts of public authorities in terms of public reason. This is reflected doctrinally by the prevalence of proportionality tests[83] and related multitier tests,[84] which tend to be used to give meaning to highly abstract rights provisions invoking freedom of speech, privacy, freedom, religion, and the like in concrete contexts. These tests tend to provide little more than checklists for the individually necessary and collectively sufficient conditions that need to be fulfilled in order for an act to be justifiable in terms that are appropriate in a liberal democracy.[85] In this way, human and constitutional rights practices give expression to and operationalize the idea that the exercise of legal authority, to the extent it infringes on important individual interests, is limited to what can be demonstratively justified in terms of public reason. In a system that allows for individual judicial review – most liberal democracies and some regional human rights treaties – individuals are empowered to contest acts by public authorities and have them reviewed by a court to provide an impartial assessment of whether the acts plausibly meet the standards of public reason.

Within the statist paradigm, on the other hand, constitutional rights are rights whose authority is traced back to the will of the national constitutional legislator. To the extent that rights provisions have an open-ended structure, courts are under pressure to interpret them in line with national traditions or emerging accepted standards. Critical debates about democratic legitimacy of judicial review are endemic, as are methodological debates and insecurities about constitutional interpretation. These features are characteristic of a conception of law that is tied to the will of a people, governing itself within the framework of a constitutional state. If the foundation of law is a formally articulated will, then the judge's engagement with public reason is an anomaly, narrowly circumscribed by the original meaning of the act of constitutional legislation and further put in question by the legislative will of current majorities. The cosmopolitan conception, on the other hand,

---

[83] *See* ROBERT ALEXY, A THEORY OF CONSTITUTIONAL RIGHTS (2002); DAVID M. BEATTY, THE ULTIMATE RULE OF LAW (2004).

[84] *See* RICHARD FALLON, IMPLEMENTING THE CONSTITUTION (2000).

[85] For a more developed argument, *see* Mattias Kumm, *Institutionalizing Socratic Contestation, The Rationalist Human Rights Paradigm, Legitimate Authority and the Point of Judicial Review*, 1 EUR. J. LEGAL STUD. (No. 2) 1 (Dec. 2007).

takes as basic a commitment to rights-based public reason and interprets acts by the democratic legislator as an attempt to spell out what that abstract commitment to rights amounts to under the circumstances addressed by the legislative act. The will of the legislator – even the constitutional legislator[86] – is interpreted within a framework of rights-based public reason; rights are not interpreted within the framework of an authoritative will.

b. Rights, Courts, and Legislatures

Given the open structure of rights provisions, the contested nature of many rights claims and the relative indeterminacy of public reason, such a conception of rights seems to put a great deal of faith in the powers of the judiciary. But even though the old chestnut of the legitimacy of judicial review cannot be addressed here,[87] the problem is at least mitigated by the second feature of the cosmopolitan conception of rights. Rights practice is a highly cooperative endeavor in which courts and other politically accountable institutions are partners in joint enterprise and different institutions assume different roles. Courts, as veto players, are junior partners in a joint deliberative enterprise.[88] Judicial review within such a paradigm has been aptly characterized as a kind of quality-control process in which decisions already made by other institutions are subjected to a further test of public reason.[89] The definition and concretization of rights are not an activity that courts hold a monopoly on, even when courts claim to have the final say. Courts, legislators, and administrative agencies are conceived of as partners in a joint enterprise to give meaning to the abstract rights guarantees in concrete contexts. Perhaps the most obvious illustration of this is the fact that national-level courts generally accord the democratic legislator or administrative agencies some

---

[86] Taken to the extreme, it means that even the enactment of a bill of rights or a charter of fundamental rights has only epistemic, not constitutive, significance. Such an understanding is not alien to at least a part of contemporary rights practice. The preamble to the European Charter of Fundamental Rights specifically establishes that the charter has epistemic significance only: to clarify and make more visible the rights that the European citizens already have and that the European Court of Justice already protects, even without a written charter. Somewhat less radical but leaning in the same direction are national constitutions that entrench highly abstract basic principles relating to human rights, prohibiting their partial or complete abolition.

[87] See Kumm, Institutionalizing Socratic Contestation, supra note 85.

[88] For an overview of theories that emphasize the dialogic, cooperative nature of the relationship between courts and other political actors, see Christine Bateup, The Dialogic Promise: Assessing the Normative Potential of Theories of Constitutional Dialogue, 71 BROOK. L. REV. 1109 (2006).

[89] For such an understanding of the role of courts as it relates to rights in the U.S. constitutional tradition, see LAWRENCE G. SAGER, JUSTICE IN PLAIN CLOTHES (2004).

degree of discretion, particularly when it comes to assessing competing policy considerations within the proportionality framework. A court sees its task not to provide what it might consider the best, most efficient, or most just solution to an issue, but to merely to ensure that public authorities have not transgressed the boundaries of the reasonable.

c. The Relationship between National and International Rights Practice

This partnership relationship is not just one that is confined to the national institutions that interpret and concretize rights. International and national human and constitutional rights courts also see themselves as engaged in a joint, mutually engaging enterprise.[90] International courts like the ECHR, for example, leave member states considerable margins of appreciation in many contexts. The degree of that margin of appreciation depends at least in part on whether there is a widespread consensus in many of the other states on how a particular rights issue should be resolved.[91] If there is, the court is less likely to defer to a member state then in a situation of widely divergent national practices. More generally, an international court is well positioned institutionally to draw on the experience of other member states and thereby enrich legal analysis. For example, when the British government argued that reasons concerning the operative effectiveness of the armed forces justified preventing gays from serving in the military, the Strasbourg court was able to draw on experiences in a number of other European jurisdictions where armed forces had recently opened themselves up to gays and experienced very little disruption. This cast doubt on the force of that argument and in effect ratcheted up the burden of proof to a level that the British government was unable to meet.[92]

Similarly, international human rights practice guides and constrains the development of domestic constitutional practice in various ways. Besides having played an important role in the drafting of national constitutions in the past decades, human rights treaties also have played a central role in the context of the interpretation of national constitutional provisions.[93] National courts often refer to international human rights practice as persuasive

---

[90] *See* Gerald Neumann, *Human Rights and Constitutional Rights: Harmony and Dissonance*, 55 STAN. L. REV. 1863 (2003); Grainne de Burca & Oliver Gerstenberg, *The Denationalization of Constitutional Law*, 47 HARVARD INTERNATIONAL LAW JOURNAL 243 (2006). *See also* Stephan Gardbaum, *Human Rights and International Constitutionalism* (in this volume).

[91] Eyal Benvenisti, *Margin of Appreciation, Consensus, and Universal Standards*, 31 N.Y.U. J. INT'L L. & POL. 843 (1999).

[92] Lustig-Prean & Beckett v. United Kingdom, 29 Eur. Ct. H.R. 548 (1999).

[93] For a helpful overview, *see* T. Franck & Arun K. Thiruvengadam, *International Law and Constitution-Making*, 2 CHINESE J. INT'L L. 467 (2003).

authority.[94] There is a good reason for this. International human rights treaties establish a common point of reference negotiated by a large number of states across cultures. Given the plurality of actors involved in such a process, there are epistemic advantages to engaging with international human rights when interpreting national constitutional provisions. Such engagement tends to help improve domestic constitutional practice by creating awareness for cognitive limitations connected to national parochialism. At the same time such engagement with international human rights law helps to strengthen international human rights culture generally.

Human rights treaties can be relevant to the domestic interpretation of constitutional rights in a weak way or a strong way. International human rights can be relevant in a weak way by providing a discretionary point of reference for deliberative engagement. This is the way that some recent U.S. Supreme Court decisions have referred to international human rights law. In *Roper v. Simmons*, Justice Kennedy writing for the Court used a reference not to specific international human rights instruments,[95] but to an international consensus more generally, as a confirmation for the proposition that the Eighth Amendment prohibition of cruel and unusual punishment prohibits the execution of juvenile offenders. And in *Grutter v. Bollinger*, the Court made reference to a treaty addressing discrimination issues to provide further support for the claim that the equal protection clause does not preclude certain affirmative action programs.[96] In the United States, engagement with

---

[94] Persuasive authority as understood here refers to any "material . . . regarded as relevant to the decision which has to be made by the judge, but . . . not binding on the judge under the hierarchical rules of the national system determining authoritative sources." Christopher McCrudden, *A Common Law of Human Rights? Transnational Judicial Conversations on Constitutional Rights*, 20 OXFORD J. LEGAL STUD. 499, 502–3 (2000).

[95] He could have cited art. 6(5) of the International Covenant on Civil and Political Rights, New York, Dec. 16, 1966, in force Mar. 23, 1976, 999 U.N.T.S. 172, as well as art. 4(5) of the Convention of the Rights of the Child, New York, Nov. 20, 1989, in force Sept. 2, 1990, 1577 U.N.T.S. 3, and art. 37(a) of the American Convention of Human Rights, San José, Costa Rica, Nov. 22, 1969, in force July 18, 1978, 1114 U.N.T.S. 123. These obligations were not binding on the United States as treaty obligations because the United States had not signed on (Rights of the Child Convention), had signed but not ratified the treaty (in the case of the American Convention), or had signed and ratified the treaty but with reservations concerning the juvenile death penalty (the case of the International Covenant on Civil and Political Rights). Having signed two of these treaties and having failed to meet the persistent objector requirements, the United States was, however, under an obligation to comply with this prohibition as a matter of customary international law.

[96] Grutter v. Bollinger, 539 U.S. 306, 345 (2003) (O'Connor, J., concurring) (citing the Convention on the Elimination of All Forms of Racial Discrimination and the Convention on the Elimination of All Forms of Discrimination against Women); International Convention on the Elimination of All Forms of Racial Discrimination, Dec. 21, 1965, 660 U.N.T.S. 195; Convention on the Elimination of All Forms of Discrimination against Women, Dec. 18, 1979, 1249 U.N.T.S. 13.

international human rights, to the extent that it takes place at all, is regarded as discretionary. It is something that a federal court facing a constitutional rights question may or may not find helpful under the circumstances.[97] And even when engagement takes place, the existence of international human rights law governing a question does not change the balance of reasons applicable to the correct resolution of the case. Reference to international human rights merely has the purpose to confirm a judgment or make the Court aware of a possible way of thinking about an issue. In this way, the U.S. Supreme Court, and indeed much of the literature, does not distinguish between the use of foreign court decisions concerning human rights and references to international human rights law. Both have a modest role to play as discretionary points of reference for the purpose of deliberative engagement.

Second, international human rights law can be relevant to constitutional interpretation in a stronger sense. Foremost, instead of leaving it to the discretion of courts, some constitutions require engagement with international human rights law. A well-known example of a constitution explicitly requiring engagement with international human rights law is the South African Constitution. It establishes that the Constitutional Court "shall . . . have regard to public international law applicable to the protection of the rights" guaranteed by the South African Constitution.[98] Whereas engagement with the practice of other constitutional courts is merely discretionary,[99] engagement with international human rights law is compulsory. Next, a clear international resolution of a human rights issue may be treated not only as a consideration relevant to constitutional interpretation but also as a rebuttable presumption that domestic constitutional rights are to be interpreted in a way that does not conflict with international law. The existence of international human rights law on an issue can change the balance of reasons applicable to the right constitutional resolution of a case.

Such an approach has been adopted, for example, by the German Constitutional Court. Unlike the South African Constitution, the German Constitution makes no specific reference to international human rights law as a source to guide constitutional interpretation. Under the German Constitution, treaty law, once endorsed by the legislature in the context of the ratification process, generally has the status of ordinary statutes. Yet in a recent decision concerning the constitutional rights of a Turkish father of an

[97] Even the strongest supporters of transnational deliberative engagement on the court insist on that point. *See* STEPHEN BREYER, ACTIVE LIBERTY: INTERPRETING OUR DEMOCRATIC CONSTITUTION 180 (2005).
[98] South African Constitution (1996), art. 35.
[99] The Court "may have regard to comparable foreign case law." *Id.*

"illegitimate" child who had been given up for adoption by the mother, the Constitutional Court developed a doctrinal framework that exemplifies how international human rights can be connected to constitutional interpretation in a strong way.[100] In *Görgülü* a lower court had decided the issue in line with the requirements established by the ECHR as interpreter of the European Convention of Human Rights, granting certain visitation rights to the father. The lower court schematically cited the necessity to enforce international law in the form of the ECHR's jurisprudence and held in favor of the father. On appeal, the higher court dismissed the reliance on the ECHR on the grounds that the ECHR as treaty law, ranking below constitutional law, was irrelevant for determining the constitutional rights of citizens. The Constitutional Court held that both approaches were flawed. Instead, it held that "both the failure to consider a decision of the ECHR and the enforcement of such a decision in a schematic way, in violation of prior ranking [constitutional] law, may violate fundamental rights in conjunction with the principle of the rule of law."[101] The Court postulated a constitutional duty to engage: "the Convention provision as interpreted by the ECHR *must be taken in to account* in making a decision; the court must at least *duly consider* it."[102] The Court even held that there was a cause of action available in case this duty to engage was violated: "A complainant may challenge the disregard of this duty of consideration as a violation of the fundamental right whose area of protection is affected in conjunction with the principle of the rule of law."[103] Beyond the duty to engage the European Convention when interpreting the constitution, the Court also had something to say about the nature of that engagement: international law and especially the international human rights law of the European Convention establish a presumption about what the right interpretation of domestic constitutional law requires. "As long as applicable methodological standards leave scope for interpretation and weighing of interests, German courts *must give precedence* to interpretation in accordance with the Convention."[104] This presumption does not apply in cases where the constitution is plausibly interpreted to establish a higher level of protection than that of the ECHR. The standards established by the ECHR provide a presumptive floor but not a presumptive ceiling.

This is not the place to analyze the relative merits of the weak and strong ways of engaging with international human rights law in the context of domestic constitutional interpretation. Nor is it the place to analyze the

---

[100] Görgülü v. Germany (2004) 2 BvR 1481/04.
[101] *Id.* at para. 47.   [102] *Id.* at para. 62 (emphasis added).
[103] *See id.* at para. 30.   [104] *Id.* at para. 62.

differences in the legal, political, and cultural contexts that explain and, to some extent, justify the differences in approach of the U.S. Supreme Court and the German Constitutional Court. Here it must suffice to point out that within the cosmopolitan paradigm some form of cooperation between national and international courts is a natural corollary to a conception of rights that is universal and connected to public reason. Within the statist paradigm, on the other hand, it is not obvious what justifies making reference to transnational human rights practice. If rights are authoritatively connected to the authority of "We the People," engagement with transnational human rights practice is at the very least a peculiar anomaly that requires special justification.[105] The heated debates underlying the reference to international practice in the context of constitutional rights adjudication, even in the weak form that it takes in the United States, are difficult to make sense of in terms of its immediate practical implications. Those appear to be marginal. Looked at in pragmatic terms this debate might seem like a tempest in a teacup. The reason why such a practice could raise not just scholarly but also political passions is that it brings to the fore a clash of constitutional paradigms.

III. Criticisms and Challenges to Cosmopolitan Constitutionalism

The cosmopolitan paradigm describes the practice of national law and international law within a holistic cognitive frame. This cognitive frame establishes an internal connection between national and international law. That internal connection extends to the construction of legal authority, the standards of procedural legitimacy, and the practice of human and constitutional rights.

Obviously, the preceding sketch of the structure of cosmopolitan constitutionalism leaves a great many questions unanswered. It neither developed a theoretical grounding nor spelled out concrete implications for a wide range of specific issues. But that was not its point. Its point was to describe and analyze the central features of the cosmopolitan constitutional paradigm and the cognitive frame that is central to it by showing what it is that comes into view when such a paradigm is used to engage constitutional practice. It was not its point to develop a full-blown theory of public law or take a position on a concrete doctrinal issue. The sketch is successful if it threw light on many

---

[105] Those justifications might be linked to genealogy ("We the People" sought to continue a tradition of rights protection that first developed in the United Kingdom, so it might be helpful to look at how the rights were understood there), or they might be justified as refuting particular empirical claims (e.g., referring to the European Union as an empirical example that proves that that having states implement federal programs does not necessarily weaken federalism, see J. Breyer in Printz).

features of contemporary legal practice that remain peripheral, puzzling, and problematic when assessed within a statist paradigm but make perfect sense within the cosmopolitan paradigm. The following takes up a number of challenges to the cosmopolitan paradigm of constitutionalism and, in beginning to address them, provides some clarifications that concern the paradigms' theoretical foundations and assumptions.

1. Is Cosmopolitan Constitutionalism "Hard Law" or Just an Ideal?

Cosmopolitan constitutionalism does not just articulate an ideal. The argument presented here is a legal argument: it concerns the basic conceptual framework to be used for the interpretative reconstruction of an existing public law practice. It is not a political program to establish a particular kind of institutional architecture. Like its central competitor the statist paradigm, the cosmopolitan paradigm seeks to provide a conceptual framework that helps organize legal materials and structure legal debates, guiding and constraining them. That does not mean that normative ideals have nothing to do with the choice of conceptual paradigms. The correct paradigm is the one that best fits legal practice. All conceptual paradigms trying to reconstruct legal practice from an internal point of view necessarily have an idealizing element that complements the conventional element.[106] That idealization is an internal feature of the legal practice that they are trying to reconstruct.[107] Sovereignty, states, "We the People" as the constituent power – none of these concepts refer to a natural kind. They are a way of constructing the legal world that is informed by a host of ideas and assumptions about what is accepted, what is attractive, and what works. The idealizing element is shared by the statist and the cosmopolitan paradigm, even if the respective ideas and the conceptual structures that give expression to them are quite different. The question is which ideas and which conceptual structure best fit the legal world we inhabit. The criticism of the cosmopolitan paradigm would thus have to be reformulated: whatever the merit of the idealizing elements that it includes, does it actually fit practice?

Even though a great deal more would have to be said, the illustrations provided suggest that there are many features of the contemporary legal world that a cosmopolitan paradigm can help make better sense of. These range from

---

[106] In this regard, interpretative questions regarding the choice of basic conceptual paradigms are no different from other legal issues. Generally I follow the interpretative approach of Dworkin. *See* RONALD DWORKIN, LAW'S EMPIRE (1986).

[107] *See* JOSEPH RAZ, THE AUTHORITY OF LAW (1979) (claiming that law necessarily makes a claim to legitimate authority). *See also* ROBERT ALEXY, THE ARGUMENT FROM INJUSTICE (2002) (arguing that the law necessarily makes a claim to correctness).

the particular doctrinal structures that national courts in liberal democracies tend to use to manage the interface between national and international law to the evolution of sources doctrine or the understanding of sovereignty in international law or the basic structural features of human and constitutional rights practice. Many of these features remain contested. They are more widely accepted in some constitutional jurisdictions and more contested in others. But even when they are contested, they are contested at least in part because of the conflict of paradigms that lie at the heart of these disagreements. In that case the articulation of the cosmopolitan paradigm as a contrast to the statist paradigm of constitutionalism helps provide a deeper understanding of these debates by pointing to the source of disagreement.

Furthermore, when making a judgment about fit, that judgment is comparative. The level of fit required for a constitutional paradigm to best fit legal practice depends in part on the level of fit of competing paradigms. The statist paradigm, the chief competitor, however, does not fit constitutional practice very well. It is for that reason that reassertions of the statist paradigm come in the form of revisionist or, more accurately, reactionary approaches. These approaches react to established doctrines that have moved away from what they perceive as the old and better way of thinking about the relationship between national and international law. It is exactly because the statist paradigm does not fit practice that research agendas have been articulated around the idea of constitutionalism in international law, global governance, global administrative law, international public authority, and so on: their point is to focus and assess developments in international law that are difficult to make sense of within the traditional statist paradigm. Many of these efforts are complementary to and provide support for, rather than articulate alternatives to, the cosmopolitan paradigm described here. Their claims are more modest and their focus is more limited. Cosmopolitan constitutionalism provides a more comprehensive framework and deeper grounding for many of these efforts by providing an account of how various aspects of legal practice are connected, helping to overcome the fragmentation of international law, and building a bridge between international and national constitutional practice. Without such an overarching framework, these projects face the perpetual risk of either being marginalized (think of the general thrust of the skeptic's challenge), misdirected (think of the debates about democratic legitimacy of global governance), or unduly apologetic (fiddling while Rome burns). An important function of the cosmopolitan constitutional paradigm is to provide an overarching conceptual framework on the same basic level and fulfilling the same function as the statist paradigm.

The articulation of that alternative paradigm helps sharpen the awareness that, first, there is nothing inevitable about the choice of basic frameworks, and, second, it is necessary to have such a basic framework. The language of *post* and *beyond* in conjunction with the state, the nation, and sovereignty nicely fits postmodern sensibilities and its skepticism of overarching conceptual frameworks and grand narratives. And the virtues of modesty and narrow focus resonate strongly in a professional culture that is both cynical and attuned to serving the powerful and that prizes abstraction only when it comes in the form of economic models. But the powerful cognitive role of basic conceptual frameworks for guiding our sense of what is important and what is not, what is normal and what is not, and what is possible and what is not, only tends to become stronger if it is left unacknowledged and unreflected. This is a terrain that deserves to be a central focus of legal scholarship. It should not be left to deeply engrained habits of thought – the legal unconscious – or entrepreneurial political ideologues. Furthermore, the critical analysis of cognitive frames plays to a lawyer's comparative advantage. It requires analyzing conceptual structures and the moral and empirical presuppositions that make them meaningful, as well as tracing their implications for the structure and content of doctrines across areas of legal practice.

2. Is It Morally Attractive, Given the Normative Commitments That People Actually Have?

Even if the cosmopolitan paradigm can be understood as a legal paradigm rather than just a moral one, is it really morally attractive? One reason why it might not be morally attractive is that nations are central to political life. There are many reasons for this.[108] One of the most important ones is that nations enable meaningful political practices of collective self-government. Meaningful democracy is not possible without a certain kind of civic friendship and solidarity that generally do not exist beyond the state. One important advantage of the statist paradigm is that it provides a conceptual framework for the idea that at the heart of modern political life is necessarily the nation. Even to the extent that there is disagreement about the virtues and vices of nationalism, it must surely be of considerable moral significance that a great many people actually think of themselves primarily as national citizens. Of course there are also some who primary think of themselves as tribe or clan members. Where that happens it raises serious problems for state

---

[108] *See* DAVIS MILLER, ON NATIONALITY (1995).

building. But rarefied, and arguably not particularly enviable, is the group who primarily thinks of itself as cosmopolitan. If that is so, is cosmopolitan constitutionalism not a mere elitist project out of touch with the values citizens hold dear? Is the frequent reference to the international community not deeply problematic? Does a commitment to democracy not entail a commitment to a statist paradigm of constitutionalism, which ultimately connects all legal and political authority to "We the People"? And doesn't statism already misdescribe the paradigm in a biased way? Should it not be referred to as the sovereign democracy paradigm?

This type of criticism is largely based on a category mistake. There is much that could be said about these claims, concerning both the morality of nationalism and the empirical questions relating to commitments and identities that people in liberal democracies actually have. But here I will accept, for argument's sake, both the moral claims relating to the central virtues of nationalism and the empirical claims about the preponderance of strong national identities in democracies as a matter of fact. The core point is this: it is simply a mistake to assume that the thing that most people care most about should be the foundation of constitutional practice. If it were otherwise, the case for establishing Christianity and its teaching as the supreme law of the land in the United States would be strong. The reasons against making a commitment to a sovereign nation the foundation of constitutional practice, as in the statist paradigm, have a similar structure as the reasons against establishing Christian theology as the cognitive frame for U.S. constitutional practice. First, the reasons why constitutional practice is not based on what most people care most about has nothing to do with an elitist critical judgment about what people should or should not hold dear. Just as the establishment clause and a commitment to freedom of religion does not denigrate belief in a Christian God, the cosmopolitan paradigm of constitutionalism does not denigrate patriotic commitments to the nation and national self-government. On the contrary, just as religion can flourish in a country that refuses to establish an official religion and guarantees freedom of religion, so national patriotism and democratic self-government can flourish within a national constitutional framework that is conceived within a cosmopolitan paradigm. Second, the reason why neither Christian theology nor the idea of a sovereign nation should be the cornerstone of constitutional practice is that these tend to lead to pathologies that ultimately undermine both the values people care most about and the integrity of a constitutional practice that takes as basic the idea of free and equals governing themselves. Just as religious fervor, fear, and enthusiasm tends to mix badly with political ambition, so national fervor, fear, and enthusiasm mix badly with the idea of ultimate authority unconditionally grounded in "We the People." Third, excluding Christianity and the sovereign nation as the ultimate orientation and cornerstone of constitutional practice is nevertheless not a value neutral decision. Even though it is a decision that is not directed against Christianity or the idea of a sovereign nation generally, it does preclude certain conceptions of Christianity and of the sovereign nation. Just as theocratic conceptions of Christianity are effectively ruled out as unconstitutional by modern constitutions, certain forms of nationalism are effectively incompatible with a cosmopolitan conception of constitutionalism. Cosmopolitan constitutionalism requires that a commitment to the nation is conceived of as part of a constitutional framework that has due regard for the wider international community built into it. Imperially ambitious or autistically callous conceptions of the national self-government, for example, are incompatible with cosmopolitan constitutionalism.

But its possible to take the argument one step further. Any conception of national constitutionalism that takes as basic the idea of free and equals governing themselves is internally connected to a cosmopolitan paradigm of constitutionalism. It is ultimately not possible to make sense of the idea of constitutional self-government of free and equals within the statist paradigm. Within liberal democracies citizens are encouraged to conceive of themselves as free and as equals and to reflect on the legitimate limits of their individual freedom to do as they please within a framework that takes other persons seriously as free and equal. Furthermore, a universal framework of public reason is central to the determination of the limits of collective self-government as it relates to individual rights within the national community. It is difficult to see what would make plausible not using such a framework to determine the limits of national collective self-government with regard to citizens of other states, who are also conceived as self-governing equals and as fellow members of the international community. The idea of collective self-government that underlies the modern liberal-democratic constitutionalism is internally connected to a universalist frame of reference. The idea of self-governing free and equals cannot be plausibly developed within a statist paradigm without artificially imagining the national community radically separated from and independent of the self-governing practices of others and without giving up on the horizon of a liberated humanity, which is at the heart of the American and French constitutional traditions. Where resistance to a cosmopolitan paradigm of constitutionalism exists, it might well have its source in a commitment to a nationalism that itself is in tension with the idea of free and equals governing themselves within the framework established by the constitution.

3. Even If Cosmopolitan Constitutionalism Fits Practice and Is Generally Morally Attractive, Are the Assumptions It Makes about International Law Realistic?

Even if the cosmopolitan paradigm is, in principle, morally attractive, does it not rely on empirical assumptions about the working of the international system that are implausible? The question is somewhat puzzling because it is unclear what exactly the problem is supposed to be. What has been presented is a conceptual framework that helps reconstruct existing practice, not an institutional proposal for how the world should be governed. To the extent that it is a conceptual framework that succeeds in reconstructing actual legal practice, the assumptions it makes must evidently be compatible with it.[109]

But there is nonetheless a feature of international law, certainly of international law conceived of in constitutionalist terms, that seems to raise concerns. Many of the more powerful states in the world are not liberal democracies – China, Russia, and Iran, for example – and are unlikely to guide their practice by the types of concerns that are central to the cosmopolitan paradigm. And even countries that are liberal democracies tend to generally pursue their national interests, rather than embracing a humanity embracing mindset. Does it not follow that the paradigm is unrealistic?

The short answer is no. The fact that national political actors define and act upon what they conceive to be in their interest and very rarely reflect upon the world in the cosmopolitan framework presented here does not undermine it. It is not at all implausible to claim that liberal democracies, generally, have an interest to develop and support an international legal order that exhibits the kind of structure that the cosmopolitan paradigm describes. It projects the basic values underlying liberal democracy onto the global level, while creating a framework for mutually beneficial coordination and cooperation with other states. And given the hegemonic dominance of liberal democracies, even non-liberal democracies might well have an interest to participate in such a system, rather than staying outside of it or seeking to undermine it. They might not like the liberal democratic baggage that comes with it and might seek to minimize its impact. But they have an

---

[109] Perhaps the concern is targeted at the idea of the international community, which is frequently invoked as a reference within the cosmopolitan paradigm. Is there actually such a thing? What are the sociological presuppositions that justify using such language? The idea of an international community, as it is used here, makes no sociological presuppositions whatsoever. It refers to a legal concept that is defined in terms of jurisdiction. Just as in domestic constitutional law the people are simply those over whom domestic institutions have jurisdiction and to whom domestic institutional arrangements and decisions are addressed, so the idea of an international community simply refers to the larger community that falls under the jurisdiction of international law and to which it is addressed.

interest to reap the coordination and cooperation benfits that such a system provides. Such a system is further be stabilized by the NGOs and various actors of civil society and interest groups that attach themselves to various international institutions and their policies, helping to shape public debates and perceptions that help anchor more deeply a cosmopolitan understanding of politics and of national identity. Furthermore the participation in the various networks and regimes by public officials,[110] journalists, and citizens is more generally likely to lead to a strengthening of cosmopolitan sensibilities.

Since the end of the cold war liberal constitutional democracies have been ideologically hegemonic forces, without a serious global competitor. The existence of Islamic fundamentalism, as an ideological force that has captured some states, poses a threat in others and plays a central role in enabling the scourge of terrorism. But it is not currently and is unlikely to develop in the future as a global competitor to cosmopolitan constitutionalism,[111] nor is it able to seriously undermine it. More of a challenge to cosmopolitan constitutionalism is a resurgent nationalism of major powers, which have in the past and might continue to use the rhetoric of sovereignty, often in conjunction with democracy, to justify regional or global hegemonic ambitions.[112] But even actors who would not generally be inclined to take the perspective required by cosmopolitan constitutionalism will often have reasons to support an international system committed to it: it might be the best available alternative given actual power relationships and serve as an important instrument of national foreign policy. In many cases concrete results may reflect national interests. Even when they do not, reputational concerns will often push toward compliance, and bureaucratic inertia connected to standard operating procedures might stabilize existing settlements, as might internal interest group pluralism that ensures that some powerful faction will start to throw its weight around to insist on keeping previously made bargains. In some jurisdictions, public or professional cultures of legalism might further support compliance, as might perceptions of legitimacy. Of course, none of this means that international law will always be effectively applied by those

---

[110] ANNE-MARIE SLAUGHTER, A NEW WORLD ORDER (Princeton 2004).

[111] The deep political pluralism of the states inhabited by Muslim majorities, often misleadingly referred to as "the Islamic world," is a fact often underestimated. Indonesia, Bangladesh and Turkey, to take some of the largest states, are not Islamic, even though their populations are. And Iranian Shia theocracy is worlds aprt from both Sunni Wahhabi Saudia Arabia or the Taliban.

[112] Paradigmatic in this context is the rise of Putinism in Russia, which has given rise to a youth movement that is called "ours" and has an official ideology called "sovereign democracy." On the level of official rhetoric there are significant structural analogies between Russian nationalism under Vladimir Putin and U.S. nationalism under George W. Bush.

bound by it. It is obviously not, and, to the extent it is not, it is a concern that lawyers need to be attentive to. Issues concerning compliance should always be part of the equation when legally analyzing public institutions and the policies they adopt in specific contexts. But nothing in the cosmopolitan paradigm suggests that legal analysis should not take seriously and incorporate these concerns. What it does suggest is that whatever those concerns might be in particular contexts, they do not justify the claim that international law reaches its limits whenever it is not closely tied to the specific consent of each state to be bound. They certainly do not justify giving up the very idea of an internal account of international law that is necessarily informed by its own ideals. Any plausible conception of public law will have to acknowledge the absence of universal agreement about its foundations as well as its concrete manifestations and will have to recognize some degree of noncompliance.

That leads to a second point. Unwarranted wholesale skepticism about the use of moral categories to describe international law is the flip side of an equally unwarranted wholesale idealization of national constitutional law. International law has traditionally been burdened by the idea of states facing one another in the pose of gladiators waiting to do battle, giving rise to the question how international law can be law properly so called, absent a global sovereign. Constitutional law in liberal democracies, on the other hand, is traditionally conceived of in august terms as "We the People" governing themselves democratically within the framework of a national constitution. Both ideas are part and parcel of the statist paradigm of constitutionalism and the nationalism it provides intellectual cover for. The legal literature on national constitutional law is full of invocations of abstract moral ideals such as self-government, the idea of citizens constituting a community of free and equals, and so on. These and other ideas help make sense of constitutional practice on the national level, guiding and constraining the work of national courts in the elaboration of doctrine. In the domain of political rhetoric, this type of language is also used by politicians on the stump or on festive occasions and when concrete policy priorities are publicly defended to the whole national community. But such language, appropriate and useful as it is for analyzing and assessing public law and public policy from an internal point of view, must not conceal the fact that there is an alternative, no less appropriate way to characterize national political practice in constitutional democracies. Besides the quotidian struggles for power between competing interest groups, there are deep rifts in most societies along lines of class, race, nationality, religion, or other denominators. There is ideological and political struggle over entitlements and distributive claims; there are struggles for recognition of various groups, minorities fighting for greater autonomy in federal systems, asymmetric federal accommodations, minority rights, threats of independence, and sometimes civil war. Dealing with all that is part of the practice of the democratic constitutional tradition. Examples of what may at times appear to be irreconcilable conflict, deep divisions, ignorance, and mutual misunderstanding are not confined to the realm of the international. Nor are solutions to those problems involving power politics, violence, and disregard for law. When questioning international law it is important not to ignore these features of domestic practice, idealizing constitutional conventions notwithstanding. There is a widespread tendency, directly attributable to the prejudices associated with the statist tradition, to adopt idealizing prose when thinking about domestic constitutional practice while insisting on a hard-nosed realist vocabulary when describing the world of international affairs. A less distorting perspective would recognize and acknowledge the role of legal ideals in the practice of international legal practice, as well as the role of power politics and compliance concerns as central elements of domestic constitutional practice. More generally this suggests that no account of public law in and among liberal democracies is plausible that dogmatically excludes as irrelevant the ideals that inform it and reconstructs it as nothing more but the tools of the powerful.[113] And no conception of law is plausible if it does not recognize and reflect upon the fact that it is also the subject of manipulation, evasion, disregard, or openly hostile contestation by some of those it seeks to bind. Law is both a depository of ideals and an instrument of power and political struggle. Both features of public law practice are an integral part of the conditions of modern constitutionalism.

But there is a third way in which the statist paradigm of constitutionalism distorts legal and political realities. It inappropriately downplays the empirical relationship between successful constitutional self-government on the national level and the international environment, of which any state is a part. There are international legal and political environments that encourage the spread of liberal democracies and there are those that undermine it. The cold war proved to be a bad environment for serious democratic reforms in many states – think of Hungary, Czechoslovakia, Iran, or Nicaragua. In Europe after the cold war, on the other hand, with a perspective on membership in the European Union – a highly integrated regional transnational community governing itself within a treaty-based framework – has had the effect of encouraging democratic reforms and stabilizing liberal

---

[113] A 1930 article on constitutionalism in ENCYCLOPEDIA OF SOCIAL SCIENCES begins: "Constitutionalism is the name given to the trust which men repose in the power of words engrossed on parchment to keep a government in order." The author of the article makes clear that such trust ought to be regarded with contempt. See Richard S. Kay, *American Constitutionalism, in* CONSTITUTIONALISM: PHILOSOPHICAL FOUNDATIONS 16 (Larry Alexander ed., 1998).

constitutional democracy against internal challenges.[114] In the United States, on the other hand, the very imagination to live in a dangerous world that requires fighting a "global war on terror" whose territorial, temporal, and personal scope is unlimited has not just undermined confidence in international law. It has also undermined confidence in the U.S. Constitution as an instrument that can effectively restrain a committed president and commander in chief. If the success of liberal constitutional democracy on the national level depends at least to some extent on the structure of the international legal system of which it is a part, the converse is also true: the effectiveness and structure of international law depend to some extent on the domestic constitutional structures of states. A world dominated by liberal states will allow for a different international legal system than a world in which there are only great power rivalries, whose conflicts of interests are deepened and made more threatening by their connection to deep ideological conflict.[115]

To summarize: the conceptual structure of the statist paradigm, with its sharp and basic distinction between state law and international law, tends to distort complex legal and political realities. Those structural cognitive distortions operate on three levels. First, on the international level they tend to underestimate the significance of legal ideals for the analysis, assessment, and functioning of international law. Second, on the national level they tend to idealize national constitutional practice. And third, they tend to downplay the significance between the relationship between the domain of the national and the international. The cosmopolitan paradigm avoids these distortions. It insists on the central significance of idealization as an internal feature of legal practice and public policy debate. But it is open for considerations relating to effectiveness and compliance to play a role in the contextual analysis and assessment of specific legal issues or legal regimes. And it will include as relevant in that analysis the complex structure of the relationship between national and international practice. Serious context-focused inquiry is not precluded by unconvincing and overbroad generalizations about either national constitutional law or international law.

4. What Makes the Cosmopolitan Paradigm Constitutional Properly So Called?

But what exactly is constitutional about the cosmopolitan paradigm of constitutionalism? After all, it is not primarily focused on a constitutional text that

---

[114] That did not, of course, prevent the dissolution of and civil war in Yugoslavia.

[115] *See, e.g.,* Anne-Marie Slaughter, *International Law in a World of Liberal States,* 6 EUR. J. INT'L L. 503, 507 (1995). *See also* Andrew Moravcsik, *Taking Preferences Seriously: A Liberal Theory of International Politics,* 51 INT'L ORG. 513, 516–24 (1997).

codifies the rules that make up the supreme law of the land, either nationally or internationally. Why not simply call it a cosmopolitan paradigm of public law, for example, or the modern jus gentium paradigm?

The reasons why the cosmopolitan paradigm is a constitutional paradigm properly so called are twofold.

At the heart of constitutionalism is not a constitutional text but a constitutional cognitive frame. It is true that in the national context constitutional texts play a role that they do not on the international level. But if the argument presented here is plausible, constitutional texts get their meaning to a significant extent through the cognitive frames that are used to engage them. That is true independent of whether the cognitive frame is that of the statist or the cosmopolitan paradigm. At the heart of the modern tradition of constitutionalism is not primarily the idea of a formal constitutional text. It is the adoption of a particular cognitive frame for the construction of legitimate authority.[116] A constitutional text symbolically supports and anchors that cognitive frame in the public imagination, but it is not a necessary feature of constitutionalism. Were it otherwise, the prevalence of constitutional language in countries that do not have a written constitution, such as the United Kingdom, would be puzzling. Even when there is a constitutional text, a great deal of constitutional practice is linked to the text only in a highly attenuated way.[117] What international lawyers have understood intuitively is that at the heart of constitutionalism lies not a constitutional text but a cognitive frame. The cosmopolitan paradigm helps establish a connection and provide a deeper normative foundation to a significant part of the writing

[116] *See* Martti Koskiennemi, *Constitutionalism as Mindset: Reflections on Kantian Themes about International Law and Globalization*, 8 THEORETICAL INQUIRIES L. 9 (2007).

[117] In many constitutional traditions, the text seems to be of central significance primarily for the establishment of national institutions and the procedures they use to make decisions. It is considerably less significant for questions of federalism, foreign affairs, or human rights. This phenomenon, if corroborated by further research, might be explained in part by the fact that the authority of "We the People" as a collective is arguably greatest when it comes to establishing the institutions through which the people are to govern themselves. When it comes to foreign affairs, legitimate claims of the international community tend to undermine the authority of national texts, in due course putting pressure on national institutions to ignore or reinterpret them. When it comes to federalism, the federal government is often shackled by restrictions that are meaningfully connected not to subsidiarity concerns but to the preservation of power of state governments, who are often veto players in the constitution-giving process. Federal governments often successfully liberate themselves from these constraints in the course of affairs. When it comes to rights, the lists that adorn constitutions are generally of no predictive significance for actual practice. In part that may be because courts, pushed by individual litigants and faced with texts that are often highly indeterminate anyway, have become confident to assess actions of public authorities in terms of public reason.

on constitutionalism in the field of international law. Much of that writing is informed by ideas and sensibilities that the cosmopolitan paradigm and its cognitive frame can help make explicit. There is no big-C and small-c constitutionalism, only constitutionalism in different contexts.

But if at the heart of the modern constitutional tradition is the adoption of a particular cognitive frame, what makes a cognitive frame a constitutional cognitive frame? What are its defining features? What is it that the statist and cosmopolitan paradigms have in common as constitutional paradigms? For a cognitive frame to be constitutional in the modern sense it has to fulfill four requirements. First, it must provide a conceptual structure that allows for the *holistic* construction of legitimate public authority. Constitutionalism seeks to provide a comprehensive framework for all relevant considerations relating to the establishment and exercise of legitimate authority that falls within its scope. Second, that cognitive frame is of foundational significance. It is not derived not from the ordinary legal construction of a positively enacted legal text. Similarly, it is not subject to ordinary legal change by means of positive enactments. Ultimately, changes in legal and political practice can bring about a change of cognitive frame. The evolution of domestic and international practices that were highlighted in this essay may have undermined the statist paradigm and inspired and paved the way for the adoption of a cosmopolitan cognitive frame. But there can be no positively enacted legal rules that determine how and when such a shift occurs. Constitutional cognitive frames serve as the basic for the construction of legal authority, including sources doctrine. Third, the normative point of this holistic foundational construction of public authority is its reference to the *idea of free and equal persons.* Constitutionalism in the tradition of the American and French revolutions is tied to the idea of free and equals governing themselves individually and collectively through and within a framework of laws. Public authority cannot be derived from a god, the superior quality of a master class destined to rule, or from ancient history. Public authority has to be derived in some way from those who are governed by it. It is imagined as a human construct, the result of human choice and susceptible to reasoned assessment and change. Only a holistic perspective provides a point of view that allows for an informed critical judgment of whether a particular decision, the procedure that was used to enact it, and the background structure of the institutional arrangements meet the requirements of being justifiable in terms that all those subject to them might reasonably accept as free and equals. The difference between the statist and the cosmopolitan paradigms is merely that the statist paradigm narrows the perspective and focuses only on the national level, whereas the cosmopolitan perspective recovers constitutionalism's universal perspective.

Within the cosmopolitan paradigm, legitimate constitutional authority on the national level depends in part on its relationship to the international community, of which it is an integral part. Fourth, a constitutional cognitive frame must be able to integrate and structure in some way debates about three core concerns, all of which are internally connected to the idea of free and equals governing themselves through and by law.[118] First, constitutionalism is about constituting, guiding and constraining the exercise of public authority *through law*. A constitutional cognitive frame must be able to generate an account of legality. Second, it needs to be able to generate an account of legitimate procedures. Formal legality matters at least in part because of the moral significance of the procedures that generated the law in the first place. And third, it must provide some account of the substantive constraints and guiding norms for the exercise of public authority, to be fleshed out in terms of human or constitutional rights. These criteria are fulfilled by the statist and the cosmopolitan paradigms, respectively. Both are constitutional paradigms, properly so called. But if the argument in this chapter is correct, the cosmopolitan paradigm is significantly more attractive.

IV. Conclusions

The skeptic's challenge, then, is based on wrong premises and leads to wrong conclusions. The skeptic's challenge is articulated within a statist paradigm that imposes an unconvincing cognitive frame on the legal and political world. That cognitive frame aggrandizes, narrows, and misconstrues national constitutional law and fails to provide a plausible framework for the analysis of contemporary international law. This leads to a general tendency to idealize national law and to cast a general shadow of suspicion on international law. There is no deep conceptual difference between national and international constitutionalism. There are no special legitimacy problems connected to international law that are not shared by constitutional law. Nor are there compliance problems that are radically distinct from similar problems that tend to be standard fare in domestic practice. These biases are corrected by the cosmopolitan paradigm of constitutionalism that provides a cognitive frame that ultimately allows for a conceptually more refined, morally more attuned, and empirically more informed account of national and international public law practice.

---

[118] Jeremy Waldron, *Can There Be a Democratic Jurisprudence?* (Mar. 2004) (unpublished paper, on file with the author), rightly points out that the analytical distinction among rules of recognition, secondary rules, and primary rules is plausibly connected to an underlying normative commitment connected to liberal democracy.

But there is another virtue of the cosmopolitan paradigm. Constitutional paradigms do not just make intelligible and help interpret the present legal and political world. They also shape how we imagine its future. It is not unlikely that from the perspective of fifty years from now, contemporary juristic preoccupations will be recognized as a manifestation of a complacent, historically bound, yet peculiarly presentist legal consciousness. Images of what global law might be and discussions of the challenges that humanity faces are strangely absent from the reflective horizon of contemporary debates.[119] One advantage of the cosmopolitan paradigm is that it not only helps interpret existing constitutional practice in a way that shows it in its best light. True to its revolutionary constitutional heritage, it also conceptually places legal and political practices within the open horizon of a liberated humanity and thus opens up a perspective on further radical transformations of the global legal order.

---

[119] For criticism along those lines and some creative reform ideas regarding the future, *see* David Kennedy's contribution in this volume. Kennedy's mistake, however, is to implausibly connect this criticism with a criticism of constitutionalism as a cognitive frame that remains ultimately too apologetic of the status quo and too wedded to the structures that happen to be in place. Constitutional cognitive frames serve a double function. They provide a cognitive frame for guiding an existing legal practice. But they also structure a normative horizon within which the future can be imagined and contested. The cosmopolitan paradigm could be put to good use to assess the proposals that Kennedy introduces for illustrative purposes.

Navigating Constitutional Pluralism

11. Constitutional Heterarchy: The Centrality of Conflict in the European Union and the United States

DANIEL HALBERSTAM

I. Introduction

In the debates about whether to take constitutionalism beyond the state, the European Union invariably looms large. One element, in particular, that invites scholars to grapple with the analogy between the European Union and global governance is the idea of legal pluralism. Just as the European legal order is based on competing claims of ultimate legal authority among the European Union and its member states, so, too, the global legal order, to the extent that we can speak of one, lacks a singular, uncontested hierarchy among its various parts. To be sure, some have argued that the UN Charter provides for a basic ordering of the international legal system akin to a constitutional charter.[1] Others urge us to view the World Trade Organization as the foundation for global constitutional order.[2] And yet legal and institutional fragmentation among the various regimes in the international arena broadly persists, as in the unsettled relationship among, say, trade, environmental, and human rights regimes.[3] Moreover, with regard to the basic normative hierarchy as between domestic and international legal orders, the old debate

---

[1] *E.g.*, Bardo Fassbender, *The United Nations Charter as Constitution of International Community*, 36 COLUM. J. TRANSNAT'L L. 529 (1998).

[2] *E.g.*, Ernst-Ulrich Petersmann, *The WTO Constitution and Human Rights*, 3 J. INT'L ECON. L. 19 (2000); Ernst-Ulrich Petersmann, *How to Reform the UN System? Constitutionalism, International Law and International Organizations*, 10 LEIDEN J. INT'L L. 421 (1997).

[3] *E.g.*, Martti Koskenniemi, *Fragmentation of International Law: Difficulties Arising from the Diversification and Expansion of International Law*, 58th Sess., Int'l Law Comm'n (2006).

Eric Stein Collegiate Professor of Law and Director, European Legal Studies Program, University of Michigan. Thanks to Bruce Ackerman, Marco Bronckers, Don Herzog, Ellen Katz, Doug Laycock, Miguel Maduro, Eric Stein, and the participants in the workshop for this volume, in the George Washington Law School Roundtable on Comparative Constitutionalism, and in the University of Michigan's Fawley Workshop Series for comments and discussion. Thanks also to Sean Powers for research assistance.

between monism and dualism has run its course and the practical result is a tie. The international legal order claims autonomy from, and authority over, the state, whereas the state, in turn, claims primacy in the creation, direction, and implementation of international law.

With regard to the European Union itself, some take the lack of conclusive ordering as a sign of the absence of constitutionalism. Constitutionalism, for such scholars, depends on the existence of either a new *Grundnorm* or a fully fledged demos, or both.[4] Constitutional skeptics believe that, even in the European Union, talk of constitutionalism (whether invoked innocently or deployed strategically) is a solecism that taps into an understanding of political community that does not (yet) exist; ignores the quintessentially intergovernmental character of the political enterprise; or is incompatible with the general lack of hierarchy, order, and grand settlement that currently mark the Union.[5] Many scholars are skeptical about global constitutionalism for similar reasons.[6]

Those who pursue a constitutional understanding of the Union, however, have done so despite persistent discontinuities between traditional state-based constitutional systems and the project of European integration. A growing number of European constitutionalists have embraced the idea of constitutional pluralism, that is, the idea of competing claims of constitutional authority within a single system of governance.[7] Broadening their inquiry further, scholars have begun to consider pluralism within the European Union as a model from which to glean more general principles applicable to pluralism and constitutionalism elsewhere.[8] If we can find constitutionalism within the pluralist system of the European Union, so the argument goes, perhaps we can find constitutionalism within the international legal system as well.

This chapter takes a fresh look at constitutionalism and pluralism by bringing heterarchy home. In so doing, it explores a comparison that has been uniformly overlooked in the scholarly literature. This chapter examines the similarities between the pluralism that lies at the core of European constitutionalism and aspects of pluralism in U.S. constitutional practice. The

---

[4] *E.g.*, Trevor C. Hartley, *International Law and the Law of the European Union – A Reassessment*. 72 Brit. Yb. Int'l L. 1 (2001) (J. Crawford and V. Lowe eds., 2002).

[5] *See* Dieter Grimm, *Integration by Constitution*, 3 Int'l J. Const. L. 193, 208 (2005); Andrew Moravcsik, *In Defense of the "Democratic Deficit": Reassessing Legitimacy in the European Union*, 4 J. Common Mkt. Stud. 603 (2002).

[6] *See, e.g.*, Jeffrey L. Dunoff, *Constitutional Conceits: The WTO's "Constitution" and the Discipline of International Law*, 17 Eur. J. Int'l L. 647 (2006).

[7] The classic exposition of the idea is in Neil MacCormick, Questioning Sovereignty (1999); Neil Walker, *The Idea of Constitutional Pluralism*, 65 Mod. L. Rev. 317 (2002).

[8] *See, e.g.*, Mathias Kumm, Miguel Maduro, and Neil Walker, in this volume.

conflicts that are the focus of this chapter are not the pervasive background of social and cultural contestation that scholars such as James Tully have highlighted.[9] Nor are they the conflict of ordinary politics in Max Weber's felicitous turn of phrase.[10] Instead, this chapter focuses on concrete institutional and intergovernmental contestation in times of deep disagreement about final legal authority within constitutional systems.

By investigating the parallels of constitutional conflict in the United States and the European Union, this chapter exposes and explores the centrality of conflict in the constitutional operation of each system. With regard to these two systems, the chapter makes the following three claims. First, in both systems, important questions of final legal authority remain unsettled. This lack of settlement is neither a defect nor a temporary inconvenience but, instead, forms an essential characteristic of each system. Second, in both systems, this absence of hierarchy of legal authority does not lead to chaos but constitutes a system of order. This nonhierarchical order – call it heterarchy – reflects the spontaneous and decentralized mutual accommodation among the various constitutional actors. Third, the management of constitutional conflict and the resulting accommodation turn on what I claim are the three primary values of constitutionalism: voice, expertise, and rights.

Reaching beyond these two systems, the comparative inquiry pursued here helps answer what may be the most pressing question for those who seek to understand global governance in the language of constitutionalism. The question has repeatedly been asked: what can the idea of constitutionalism add to governance beyond the state, other than perhaps a mistake in translation?[11] What emerges from the proposed comparative analysis is a glimpse of the answer. By examining constitutionalism in the crucible of contestation in these two very different systems, we see what constitutionalism means. The comparison reveals that constitutionalism does not depend on traditional hierarchy among systems or interpretive institutions. Instead, constitutionalism can be realized within a system of heterarchy. Constitutionalism stands for a project of governance in which actors endeavor to realize the primary values of voice, expertise, and rights. And it is these three values that the idea

---

[9] JAMES TULLY, STRANGE MULTIPLICITY: CONSTITUTIONALISM IN AN AGE OF DIVERSITY (1995).

[10] MAX WEBER, PARLIAMENT AND GOVERNMENT IN GERMANY UNDER A NEW POLITICAL ORDER, *reprinted in* WEBER, POLITICAL WRITINGS 130, 173 (Peter Lassman & Ronald Speirs eds., 1994) ("the essence of all politics . . . is conflict").

[11] *See, e.g.,* J.H.H. WEILER, THE CONSTITUTION OF EUROPE: "DO THE NEW CLOTHES HAVE AN EMPEROR?" AND OTHER ESSAYS ON EUROPEAN INTEGRATION 270 (1999); Neil Walker, *Postnational Constitutionalism and the Problem of Translation, in* EUROPEAN CONSTITUTIONALISM BEYOND THE STATE 27 (J.H.H. Weiler and Marlene Wind eds., 2003).

of constitutionalism, if taken seriously, aims to vindicate at the global level of governance as well.

II. Constitutionalism and Pluralism: The European Union and the United States Compared

Comparative scholarship examining the relationship between the European Union and its member states has traditionally compared and contrasted that vertical relationship with the one between the United States and its several states. The parallel is both obvious and fruitful. On the basis of this comparison, scholars have examined a host of general questions about federalism.[12] Indeed, this comparison of principles of federalism in the European Union and the United States has been of interest not only to committed comparatists but also to others as a means of better illuminating important questions that scholars of one or the other system had previously examined only in isolation.[13]

In one important sense, however, the relationship between the European Union and its member states is, of course, different from that between the United States and the several states. In the United States, the relationship between federal and state law, and, in particular, between the federal Supreme Court and the state judiciary, is fully ordered. There is no real practical or theoretical doubt about federal legal supremacy in the United States – at least there has not been since the Civil War, which dispelled any remaining confederate conceptions (or illusions) about the nature of the U.S. Constitution.[14] Since the Civil War and Reconstruction, there has been no reasonable doubt that the U.S. Constitution establishes a single (federal) legal order that

---

[12] See, e.g., Daniel Halberstam, *Comparative Federalism and the Role of the Judiciary, in* THE OXFORD HANDBOOK OF LAW AND POLITICS (Keith Whittington et al. eds., 2008); THE FEDERAL VISION: LEGITIMACY AND LEVELS OF GOVERNANCE IN THE UNITED STATES AND THE EUROPEAN UNION (Kalypso Nicolaïdes and Robert Howse eds., 2001); INTEGRATION THROUGH LAW: EUROPE AND THE AMERICAN FEDERAL EXPERIENCE (Mauro Cappelletti, Monica Seccombe & Joseph Weiler eds., 1986). This tradition was begun by TERRANCE SANDALOW & ERIC STEIN, COURTS AND FREE MARKETS: PERSPECTIVES FROM THE UNITED STATES AND EUROPE (1982).

[13] See, e.g., Daniel J. Meltzer, *Member State Liability in Europe and the United States*, 4 INT'L J. CONST. L. 39 (2006); James Pfander, *Member State Liability and Constitutional Change in the United States and Europe*, 51 AM. J. COMP. L. 237 (2003).

[14] See, e.g., Charles Warren, *Legislative and Judicial Attacks on the Supreme Court of the United States*, 47 AM. L. REV. 1, 1, 161 (1913). In the aftermath of *Brown v. Board of Education*, 347 U.S. 483 (1954), the old doctrines of interposition and nullification briefly reared their head, provoking the Supreme Court's unprecedented assertion of interpretive supremacy in *Cooper v. Aaron*, 358 U.S. 1 (1958).

comprises both state and federal law.[15] The U.S. Constitution expressly makes the Constitution, federal law, and U.S. treaties directly effective within, and supreme over, the constitutions and laws of the several states. To the extent that there is a multiplicity of legal systems in the United States, then, it is a strictly ordered multiplicity, in that the legal systems of the several states are nested within the overarching system of law created by the U.S. Constitution.

In the European Union, by contrast, the relationship between the central and component state legal orders is fundamentally unsettled. On the one hand, the European Community claims normative superiority of Community law over the law of the member states. According to the European Court of Justice (ECJ), for instance, the Community is an autonomous legal order, directly effective within, and supreme over, the legal orders of the member states, and grounded in a constitutional charter of its own.[16] On the other hand, there is an equally persistent (and conceptually coherent) claim on the part of the member states regarding the ultimate primacy of their own legal orders. In the view of the German and Polish constitutional courts, as well as the Danish Supreme Court, for example, the European legal order is a treaty-based member state creation, and continued membership and participation in European integration on the part of the member states is subject to the control and limitations of the member state's own constitutional orders.[17]

In contrast to the historical state resistance to federal power in the United States, the unsettled relationship between the European and member state legal orders and their respective judiciaries is an enduring and essential part of the European legal order. First, as a matter of fact, the unsettled nature

---

[15] Indeed, strictly speaking, even interposition and nullification did not necessarily depend on challenging the idea of a unified legal system but focused instead on challenging the federal government's (and, in particular, the Supreme Court's) claim of final authority regarding the interpretation of the Constitution. *See, e.g.,* Barry Friedman, *The History of the Countermajoritarian Difficulty, Part One: The Road to Judicial Supremacy,* 73 N.Y.U. L. Rev. 333 (1998).

[16] *See* Case 294/83, Les Verts–Parti Ecologiste v. European Parliament, 1986 E.C.R. 1339, para. 23; Case 106/77, Amministrazione delle Finanze dello Stato v. Simmenthal SpA, 1978 E.C.R. 629; Case 6/64, Flaminio Costa v. E.N.E.L., 1964 E.C.R. 585; Case 26/62 NV Algemene Transport–en Expeditie Onderneming van Gend & Loos v. Netherlands Inland Revenue Administration, 1963 E.C.R. 1. *Cf.* Koen Lenaerts & Damien Gerard, *The Structure of the Union According to the Constitution for Europe: The Emperor Is Getting Dressed,* 29 Eur. L. Rev. 289, 299–300 (2004).

[17] *See* K 18/04 of May 11, 2005 (Poland's Membership in the European Union – The Accession Treaty), *English summary available at* http://www.trybunal.gov.pl/eng/summaries/documents/K_18_04_GB.pdf; Carlsen v. Rasmussen, [1999] 3 C.M.L.R. 854 (Danish Supreme Court) (English extract only); Bundesverfassungsgericht [BVerfG] [Federal Constitutional Court] 1993, 89 Entscheidungen des Bundesverfassungsgerichts [BVerfGE] 155 (F.R.G.) (hereinafter "Brunner").

of the hierarchy among legal systems in the European Union will continue for the foreseeable future. There is no sign that member states have any intention of giving up their claim of ultimate primacy within the foreseeable future. Not even the ambitious constitutional treaty sought to change this in any radical way.[18] Indeed, the very nature of that instrument – a treaty establishing a constitution for Europe – was designed to preserve the fundamentally unsettled nature of the relationship between the European Union and its member states. Second, as a matter of theoretical conceptualization of the European Union, the unsettled nature of hierarchy in Europe is not a troubling disturbance of the rule of law, as state defiance of federal rule was in nineteenth-century America. The uneasy relationship between European and member state legal orders is not a matter of constituent state recalcitrance to be overcome, as it was in the United States.[19] Instead, the unsettled nature of hierarchy within the Union, which Neil MacCormick and Neil Walker have dubbed "constitutional pluralism," is an essential characteristic of the European legal order.[20]

On this view, the federalism parallel with the United States becomes suspect, and we must look elsewhere for comparative insights for understanding the relationship between the competing constitutional authorities in the European Union. To be sure, we can still consider specific doctrines of federalism or structures of federalism theory and practice that span these two variations on shared rule. But if we are interested specifically in insights about the unsettled nature of hierarchy in the European Union, and, by extension, if we are interested in understanding the unsettled nature of hierarchy in the global arena, the domestic legal order of the United States seems irrelevant.

Not so fast. To be sure, if we search the United States for an analogue to Europe's essential characteristic of unsettled legality and finality, we cannot find it in the relationship between the federal government and the states. But we can find something similar elsewhere – in the separation of powers at the federal level of governance. Here, a similar terrain of contestation and lack of finality operates in the United States among the various branches of the federal government, that is, among the president, the Congress, and the Supreme Court of the United States. According to some, it even extends to

[18] For a careful analysis, see Mattias Kumm, *The Jurisprudence of Constitutional Conflict: Constitutional Supremacy in Europe before and after the Constitutional Treaty*, 11 EUR. L. J. 262 (2005).
[19] For an examination that juxtaposes the history of component state resistance in the two systems, see FRANZ C. MAYER, KOMPETENZUEBERSCHREITUNG UND LETZTENTSCHEIDUNG (2000).
[20] *See* MACCORMICK, *supra* note 7; Neil Walker, *supra* note 7.

"the people themselves."[21] Each of these actors has a plausible claim to being the final arbiter of legality within the American constitutional system.

This is not the place for an extended defense of this assertion, which remains controversial. Suffice it to say that the departmental or coordinate view of authority to interpret the constitution has significant support despite the insistence by some on the idea of judicial supremacy. Revived perhaps most controversially by President Reagan's attorney general, Edwin Meese,[22] some version of coordinated, as opposed to exclusively judicial, power to interpret the Constitution is now accepted by a broad range of scholars from a variety of political and methodological backgrounds. For present purposes, let us put to one side the most highly charged question whether the president and Congress have the constitutional authority to defy a Supreme Court judgment and order in a given case in which the federal government is a party before the Court (although there is even some precedent for that within the history of the American republic).[23] With regard to the more general question as to whether, as a matter of constitutional law, the Supreme Court's interpretation of the Constitution formally binds other actors within the system, there seems to be a growing consensus that the answer is no.[24]

A brief contrast with Continental systems illustrates the point. The standard European model of judicial review formally privileges a specialized tribunal with final authority over constitutional interpretation. As originally conceived of by Hans Kelsen, these constitutional courts would operate outside and, indeed, above the remainder of the legal system, rendering decisions that bind the constitutional judgment of all other actors throughout the system.[25] Although several features of Kelsen's model have been modified, the formal recognition of the legitimacy of judicial review by a specialized constitutional court remains. As Alec Stone Sweet has summed it up: "New

---

[21] LARRY D. KRAMER, THE PEOPLE THEMSELVES: POPULAR CONSTITUTIONALISM AND JUDICIAL REVIEW (2004); Mark Tushnet, *Popular Constitutionalism as Popular Law*, 81 CHI.-KENT L. REV. 991, 991 (2006).

[22] Edwin Meese III, Attorney General, Separation of Powers: Legislative-Executive Relations (April 30, 1986). *See* Meese, *The Law of the Constitution*, 61 TUL. L. REV. 979 (1987); Robert D. Sloane, *The Scope of Executive Power in the Twenty-First Century: An Introduction*, 88 B.U. L. REV. 341 (2008).

[23] *See* Michael Stokes Paulsen, *The Most Dangerous Branch: Executive Power to Say What the Law Is*, 83 GEO. L.J. 217 (1994) (defending the president's independent power to interpret the Constitution even in defiance of a direct Supreme Court order).

[24] For a quick sense of the depth of general acceptance of some form of departmentalism, see, e.g., the disclaimers in Larry Alexander & Frederick Schauer, *Defending Judicial Supremacy: A Reply*, 17 CONST. COMMENT. 455 (2000).

[25] *See* Hans Kelsen, *Wesen und Entwicklung der Staatsgerichtsbarkeit*, 5 VERHANDLUNGEN D. DEUTSCHEN STAATSRECHTSLEHRER 30 (1929).

European constitutions expressly provide for the supremacy of constitutional courts with respect to constitutional interpretation. European academics and constitutional judges will state as much in one breath, and then move on to more interesting issues."[26]

In the United States, by contrast, the unsettled nature of the relationship among the president, the Congress, and the Supreme Court is considered very interesting indeed. To be sure, Alexander Bickel's "countermajoritarian difficulty" of judicial review is, by now, stale, banal, and overwritten.[27] But the unsettled nature of the relationship among the president, the Congress, and the Supreme Court (and even the people themselves) in matters of constitutional interpretation is ever fresh and challenging.[28] Indeed, one scholar has dubbed this problem the "central obsession of constitutional theory" in the United States.[29] This aspect of U.S. constitutional practice – the lack of settlement of final interpretive authority – is not simply a glitch in the rule of law but, instead, an essential characteristic of the U.S. legal system. Let us call this feature of the U.S. system interpretive pluralism, in the sense that multiple institutions compete as authoritative interpreters of the U.S. Constitution.

To be sure, in ordinary times, a general practice of deference to the Supreme Court's interpretation of the Constitution prevails.[30] And that is as it should be. After all, a basic function of a legal system is to enable individuals to realize their projects, plans, and goals within a reasonably predictable framework for social order. And a basic function of a constitution is to create reliable enabling rules for the daily political conflict of ordinary politics. Absent a habit of accommodation resulting in a basic level of stability, then, our constitutional system would be a failure.

Nevertheless, throughout the history of the American republic, U.S. constitutional theory and practice have allowed multiple competing institutions to lay claim to being authoritative interpreters of the Constitution. Such

---

[26] Alec Stone Sweet, *Why Europe Rejected American Judicial Review: And Why It May Not Matter*, 101 MICH. L. REV. 2744, 2779 (2003).

[27] ALEXANDER M. BICKEL, THE LEAST DANGEROUS BRANCH (1962).

[28] So, for example, Robert Post and Reva Siegel recently developed this idea with regard to section 5 of the Fourteenth Amendment in *Legislative Constitutionalism and Section Five Power: Policentric Interpretation of the Family and Medical Leave Act*, 112 YALE L.J. 1943 (2003).

[29] Barry Friedman, *The Birth of an Academic Obsession: The History of the Countermajoritarian Difficulty, Part Five*, 112 YALE L. J. 153 (2002).

[30] *See, e.g.*, Walter E. Dellinger, Assistant Attorney General, Presidential Authority to Decline to Execute Unconstitutional Statutes (Nov. 2, 1994) (Memorandum for the Honorable Abner J. Mikva Counsel to the President), *available at* http://www.usdoj.gov/olc/nonexcut.htm.

constitutional conflict differs from the conflict of daily politics in that the framework for governance becomes the subject of dispute. At the same time, such constitutional conflict differs from revolutionary conflict, in that the dispute is not about whether the framework should be altered or discarded but about how the framework should be understood best. Constitutional conflict in the United States, then, is premised on competing claims of fidelity to the overall system and its underlying values. The object is victory within the system, not victory over the system. And the goal is to find a proper form of conflict resolution and thus, ultimately, a point of mutual accommodation within what remains a common project of governance.

The unsettled nature of the relative authority of the president, the Congress, and the Supreme Court in matters of constitutional interpretation, that is, the centrality of both conflict and accommodation within our system, is as old as judicial review itself. Only six days after *Marbury v. Madison*[31] proclaimed the great principle that the Supreme Court would review the constitutionality of legislative and executive action, *Stuart v. Laird*[32] upheld a constitutionally questionable attack on the Court by the political branches. *Stuart* and *Marbury* were part of the same pitched battle between the Federalists, who had lost control over the presidency and Congress in the election of 1800, and the new administration of Thomas Jefferson.[33] Although *Marbury* is usually celebrated and *Stuart* largely forgotten, the immediate practical importance of *Stuart* was, in many ways, greater than that of its famous twin. *Marbury* involved the idiosyncratic case of a single signed, sealed, but undelivered judicial commission. *Stuart*, by contrast, involved the imposition on the individual justices of an onerous duty to ride circuit and decide cases in courts of appeal, which left the justices less time to tend to the Supreme Court's own work. But lacking the votes to deal a second blow to the Jeffersonians after *Marbury*, the great chief justice simply recused himself in *Stuart* and allowed Associate Justice William Paterson to pen a perfunctory opinion upholding the objectionable law.[34]

Marbury and *Stuart* thus inaugurated a pragmatic American tradition of constitutional accommodation lasting to this very day. Over the course of U.S. constitutional history, the political branches have frequently squared off against the Supreme Court in seeking to vindicate their own vision of

[31] Marbury v. Madison, 5 U.S. (1 Cranch) 137 (1803).
[32] Stuart v. Laird, 5 U.S. (1 Cranch) 299 (1803).
[33] *See* GEORGE LEE HASKINS & HERBERT A. JOHNSON, FOUNDATIONS OF POWER: JOHN MARSHALL, 1801–15 (1981).
[34] *See* BRUCE ACKERMAN, THE FAILURE OF THE FOUNDING FATHERS 163–198 (2005).

constitutional meaning.[35] From Andrew Jackson's constitutionally based veto of the Bank Bill and Lincoln's emancipation address to Franklin D. Roosevelt's court-packing plan and George W. Bush's frequent signing statements, presidents have asserted a right – indeed, an obligation – of independent executive branch constitutional interpretation.[36] Congress, too, has asserted its own understanding of the Constitution, whether in supporting the president's political initiatives, as in Jefferson's and FDR's attacks on the judiciary, or in historical or contemporary efforts to strip the judiciary of jurisdiction, or by pushing for its vision of the constitutional right to equality.[37] Important in all this is that the president, the Congress, and the Court each has won these battles on some occasions and lost on others. Or, perhaps more to the point, in each case, the various branches ultimately reached states of pragmatic accommodation to solve the constitutional standoff.

Europe shares this lack of settlement and practice of accommodation with the United States, although there are certainly differences between the two. In Europe, what has been dubbed "constitutional pluralism" pertains to a plurality of constitutional systems with legal norms and sources that stand in a complex relation of mutual recognition and conflict with one another. The American brand of pluralism is also constitutional in nature but involves, by contrast, a single constitutional system within which a plurality of interpretive institutions stand in a complex relationship of mutual recognition and conflict with one another.

We might be tempted to conclude that the European Union is beset by interpretive pluralism as well. After all, within the European Union, member state courts – especially constitutional and supreme courts – appear to assert an independent power to serve as final arbiters of the meaning of the European treaties within their own territories. On closer inspection, however, it becomes clear that member state courts are not threatening to interpret the meaning of Community law as such in opposition to the ECJ but only trying to prevent Community law, under certain interpretations, from taking effect within their territory. To be precise, then, when Germany's Bundesverfassungsgericht, for instance, threatens to interpret the Maastricht Treaty at variance with the interpretation given by the ECJ, it is telling Germans not what the treaty means for Europe, but what the treaty can legitimately mean in Germany to

---

[35] *See generally* G. Edward White, *The Constitutional Journey of* Marbury v. Madison, 89 Vᴀ. L. Rᴇv. 1463 (2003); Christopher L. Eisgruber, *The Most Competent Branches: A Response to Professor Paulsen*, 83 Gᴇᴏ. L.J. 347 (1994).

[36] See Paulsen, *supra* note 23.

[37] *See, e.g.*, Post & Siegel, *supra* note 28 (on the dialogue between the Court and Congress on constitutional sex equality).

accord with the limitations that Germany's constitution places on Germany's continued membership in the project of European integration.[38] Accordingly, this clash of interpretive institutions within the European Union is at its core a manifestation of the plurality of systems.

Finally, with regard to the interpretation of European Union law itself, the ECJ indeed stands in a privileged position, much as its Kelsenian constitutional court counterparts do. As a matter of treaty law, the ECJ is the only institution formally charged with "ensur[ing] that in the interpretation and application of this treaty, the law is observed."[39] In its horizontal relations with the political branches of the European Union, the ECJ can well draw on a special mandate that provides it with superior authority in the interpretation of the treaty. Similarly, with respect to member state institutions, the ECJ can, strictly as a matter of EU law, equally draw on this formal delegation of superior interpretive authority. In Europe, then, it is, properly speaking, not the plurality of interpretive institutions that is the source of constitutional conflict but ultimately the plurality of constitutional systems.

Despite these differences among the American and European brands of constitutional pluralism, one basic fact remains: the unsettled nature of final legal authority is an enduring and essential characteristic of each system. As we shall see in the next section, the two systems also share deep similarities in the way in which they manage this lack of settlement by finding order within pluralism.

III. Managing Pluralism in the European Union and the United States

The United States and the European Union are both functioning legal systems. Neither the lack of settlement regarding the hierarchy of legal systems in Europe nor the lack of settlement regarding the hierarchy of institutions in the United States leads to anarchy or chaos. Instead, each system is a system of order. By definition, however, order within pluralism cannot be the product of central command and control. Order in the face of pluralism must, if at all, arise spontaneously within the decentralized interactions among the various actors involved. And that is what we find in both systems. The U.S. president does not routinely threaten to pack the Court whenever he disagrees with the

---

[38] *See* Brunner, *supra* note 17.

[39] Treaty Establishing the European Community, art. 220, 1992, 1997 O.J. (C340) 145. *Cf.* Treaty on European Union, art. 19, 2008 O.J. (C115) 13 (as modified by the Treaty of Lisbon) (not in force) (expanding "this Treaty" to "Treaties").

Court's interpretation of the Constitution, nor does the Bundesverfassungs-gericht routinely threaten to interpose German constitutional values to block the effectiveness of EU law within Germany. Instead, we find in both systems a habit of deference and accommodation that enables each system to function as a stable and predictable system of constitutional governance. Let us call this kind of constitutional order in the absence of hierarchy constitutional heterarchy.

Constitutional heterarchy is a system of spontaneous, decentralized order-ing among the various actors within the system. But it is more than that. Constitutional heterarchy is not merely conflict and accommodation based on raw power differentials or random fortuity of positions of relative advan-tage. Instead, constitutional heterarchy reflects the idea that the coordination among the various actors is based on constitutional considerations, that is, in the values of constitutionalism itself. Because conflict and accommodation are ordered in this way, constitutional heterarchy helps crystallize what these values are. Actors will base their respective claims of superior authority on their relative ability to vindicate the values of constitutionalism. And even when actors make what appears to be a naked bid for power, they will phrase their claims in terms of constitutional principle.[40] Put another way, those normative and interpretive conflicts are carried out in what Neil Walker has called a "constitutional register."[41]

Examining constitutional conflict in the two systems reveals that the inter-systemic engagement in Europe and interinstitutional engagement in the United States surround three primary values – call them voice, expertise, and rights. In the pitched battles of confrontation, as well as in the mundane practice of coexistence, the three values emerge as central to the pragmatic accommodation that sustains constitutionally based pluralism in both sys-tems. Put crudely, I want to define the first as asking which actor has the better claim of representing the relevant political will; the second as asking which actor has the better claim of knowledge or instrumental capacity; and the third as asking which actor has the better claim of protecting individual rights.

In the European Union and the United States, we observe that none of these values is exclusively or even reliably associated with one or another of

---

[40] Let us put to one side for the moment the debate about whether this rhetorical frame is mere window dressing or whether it reflects or affects the actual substantive claims that are made. Cf. Jon Elster, *Arguing and Bargaining in Two Constituent Assemblies*, 2 U. Pa. J. Const. L. 345, 371–419 (2000).

[41] Neil Walker, *Legal Theory and the European Union: A 25th Anniversary Essay*, 25 Oxford J. Legal Stud. 581, 599 (2005).

the contending actors. At different times, different actors can lay claim to be vindicating any one or more of these values. If an actor can maximize all three values in any given case, that actor's claim to authority within the system becomes paramount. If, as is more frequently the case, different actors can lay only partial claim to one or the other of these values, the stage is set for constitutional confrontation. Such confrontation can, of course, pit claims to different combinations of the three values against one another. The remainder of this section, however, will highlight constitutional confrontation that surrounds only one or another of these values to demonstrate that each actor can lay claim to vindicating each of the three primary values of constitutionalism.

A. Voice

One might be tempted to think that, in a reasonably well-functioning democracy such as the United States, the political branches invariably do better than courts in representing the relevant political will on any given matter. Indeed, this is the assumption that underlies the traditional understanding of the countermajoritarian difficulty and the usual justification for only limited judicial review.[42] On this view, the political branches create and represent the political will of the polity, whereas courts look out for rights. This suggests that courts should interfere with the political branches' expression of will, if at all, only to vindicate the autonomy rights of individuals against invasion by the majority. That view, however, is mistaken.

There are numerous ways of understanding the judiciary as, at times, vindicating the relevant political will better than the political branches do. As an initial matter, we may understand many aspects of constitutional law as enabling the creation of a collective political will, as opposed to guarding the autonomy rights of individuals against incursion on the part of the collectivity. There would be no coherent will of the community absent the procedures and institutions that allow for its creation.[43] Moreover, even many rights provisions – from provisions regarding jury trials to those protecting speech, debate, and even religion – can be understood as revealing a strong constitutional commitment to vindicating political majorities.[44] On this view, constitutional adjudication can be central to the reliable creation of majority

---

[42] See, e.g., BICKEL, supra note 27; James Bradley Thayer, The Origin and Scope of the American Doctrine of Constitutional Law, 7 HARV. L. REV. 129 (1893).

[43] Cf. Stephen Holmes, Precommitment and the Paradox of Democracy, in CONSTITUTIONALISM AND DEMOCRACY (Jon Elster & Rune Slagstad eds., 1988).

[44] See AKHIL REED AMAR, THE BILL OF RIGHTS (1998).

will and to vindicating that will against the capture of government by a small detached and self-interested political elite.

More broadly, as Bruce Ackerman has most prominently argued, judicial review can be understood not as a countermajoritarian difficulty, but as an intertemporal difficulty, with democratic claims on both sides of the ledger.[45] To the extent that the Constitution itself is grounded in the expression of a considered, legitimate political will, constitutional adjudication vindicates the constitutional politics of the past against incursion by a simple parliamentary majority of the present. Coupled with the idea of a relatively high degree of citizen mobilization in times of constitutional norm creation as compared with general citizen apathy in everyday politics, Ackerman lays out a basic democratic argument in favor of judicial review. Indeed, Ackerman's theory of constitutional moments brings the grand battles over shifts in constitutional meaning entirely back to the single value of voice, that is, the question of which actor has the better claim of representing the will of the people.

Even beyond the great interinstitutional conflicts of constitutional review, we may often see the judiciary as vindicating the value of voice against the potentially unrepresentative actions of the presently constituted political institutions. Some of the Court's clear statement rules serve this function. For example, courts have protected federalism or the adherence to international treaty obligations by requiring that Congress and the president speak clearly before committing the nation to actions contrary to these more particular constitutional values.[46] The underlying substantive judgment can run the other way, of course, as in the recent Supreme Court majority's insistence that Congress and the president indicate rather clearly when an international treaty is to be self-executing.[47] In these cases, courts are ostensibly not engaging in judicial review; that is, they are not formally challenging the political branches' constitutional interpretation. Instead, they are engaged in interpreting Congress's (or the president's) intent. And yet as we all know, ever so often, the project of statutory interpretation turns into a judicial challenge

---

[45] BRUCE ACKERMAN, WE THE PEOPLE (1993).

[46] See, e.g., Gregory v. Ashcroft, 501 U.S. 452 (1991) (refusing to extend federal Age Discrimination in Employment Act to state judges absent clear statement); U.S. v. Palestine Liberation Organization, 695 F. Supp. 1456 (S.D.N.Y.1988) (holding that federal Antiterrorism Act did not supersede UN Headquarters Agreement). To be sure, some clear statement rules may serve values other than voice, as in the requirement to state clearly the elements of a crime in order to provide notice to defendants. But even here the Supreme Court has used, for example, the rule of lenity as an indirect means to ensure democratic deliberation about extensions of federal power. See, e.g., Jones v. United States, 529 U.S. 848 (2000) (holding that federal arson statute does not cover arson to owner-occupied dwelling).

[47] See Medellin v. Texas, 552 U.S. __, 128 S.Ct. 1346 (2008).

that the political branches have failed to consider properly the protection of particular constitutional values.[48] The result of these decisions is, however, not to strike down the measure absolutely but to demand more transparent, deliberate, or inclusive politics on the particular constitutional value at hand. In short, it is a demand for voice.

Turning to constitutional pluralism in the European Union, one might similarly be tempted to think that the value of voice invariably favors the member states, not Europe. After all, traditional democratic processes, such as parliamentary elections, the formation of governments, and the creation and maintenance of a participatory public sphere, are reasonably well established at the nation-state level in most member states. At the European level of governance, by contrast, the analogues to these processes – to the extent they exist at all – are still in their infancy. But this jaundiced view of voice at the European level, or overly romantic view of voice at the level of the member states, would be mistaken as well.

As an initial matter, the European Union contains a plurality of collective wills (which Kalypso Nicolaïdis has aptly termed a "demoi-cracy") that requires an assessment of the relative legitimacy of each.[49] In addition, others have pointed out the frequent failure within the European Union and elsewhere of state-based structures of democratic governance to serve adequately the goals of self-governance, especially in light of the fact that decisions of one polity increasingly have significant effects on the members of another.[50] The value of voice, then, understood as the value of self-governance or as participation in the policy decisions that affect one's life, may not always be vindicated best at the level of the state.

Accordingly, arguments based on the voice of those affected by political choices need not favor the member states but may, at times, favor Europe instead.[51] Borrowing from federalism theory, for example, there are several

---

[48] *See* William M. Kelley, *Avoiding Constitutional Questions as a Three Branch Problem*, 86 CORNELL L. REV. 831 (2001). For a critical review, see William N. Eskridge Jr. & Philip P. Frickey, *Quasi-Constitutional Law: Clear Statement Rules as Constitutional Lawmaking*, 45 VAND. L. REV. 593 (1992).

[49] Kalpyso Nicolaïdis, *"We, The Peoples of Europe..."* 83 FOREIGN AFFAIRS 97–110 (2004); Samantha Besson, *Europe as a Demoi-cratic Polity*, 1/116 RETFAERD – NORDISK JURIDISK TIDSSKRIFT 3 (2007).

[50] *See, e.g.,* JO SHAW, THE TRANSFORMATION OF CITIZENSHIP IN THE EUROPEAN UNION (2007); Gráinne de Búrca, *Developing Democracy beyond the State*, 46 COLUM. J. TRANSNAT'L L. 221 (2008); Miguel Poiares Maduro, *Europe and the Constitution: What If This Is as Good as It Gets? in* EUROPEAN CONSTITUTIONALISM BEYOND THE STATE 74, 81–86 (J.H.H. Weiler & Marlene Wind eds., 2003).

[51] *See* Daniel Halberstam, *The Bride of Messina: Constitutionalism and Democracy in Europe*, 30 EUR. L. REV. 775, 797 (2005).

systematic reasons for preferring a central (or more comprehensive) represen-tation of voice over its more local counterparts. In particular, central processes of decision may better reflect the interests of the relevant affected parties in the face of what we may call interjurisdictional difficulties, such as overcom-ing externalities and other collective action problems that bedevil processes of decentralized decision making. Conversely, by virtue of the greater diversity of participating actors at the central level, central institutions may counteract the problem of intrajurisdictional difficulties, that is, the neglect or oppres-sion of politically disempowered groups within decentralized jurisdictions.[52]

Moreover, in the case of Europe, this recognition of the legitimacy of a collective voice beyond the state is not a foreign imposition but can be traced instead to the deliberate openness of member states' own constitutional sys-tems to supranational integration. Put another way, European constitutional pluralism – and the recognition of the legitimate claim of a supranational voice – is itself the product of specific member state commitments to accom-modate a collective political will beyond the state. As a result, the decision to resolve even a simple conflict between the European and national legal orders may, at least in part, almost always be brought back to a calculus of voice.

We can see a calculus of voice – especially in this latter sense – being played out in several important doctrines regarding the conflict between the supra-national and national legal orders. Take, for example, the European Com-munities Act of 1972, which implements British accession to the European Community.[53] By this act, the U.K. Parliament gives precedence to Com-munity law in general while reserving the possibility of national supremacy in cases in which the national legislator specifically expresses the intention to deviate from European norms. By imposing a heavy presumption against interpreting current legislation as abrogating European obligations, the act reflects an accommodation of constitutional pluralism based on voice.

As with the intertemporal difficulty in the United States, voice here figures on both sides of the ledger. The European Communities Act discounts the current voice of ordinary politics as compared to an earlier, presumably deeper, more considered, more transparent, and more participatory decision to join the European Union. It thus privileges one voice over another on the the assumption that the two are not of equal weight in representing the relevant political will. The act (and adherence to the act on the part of subsequent parliaments and courts) reflects the view that, all things being

---

[52] For a discussion of inter- and intrajurisdictional difficulties, see Halberstam, *Comparative Federalism, supra* note 12.

[53] European Communities Act of 1972, 1972, chap. 68.

equal, the expression of preference of any given Parliament with regard to a particular sectoral policy subsequent to the passage of the act is more likely the product of interest-group capture than was the broad-based preference for accession to the European Union. In the United Kingdom, this calculus of voice takes on added constitutional significance, given that it taps into the very same calculus of voice that underpins the national constitutional system itself. Put another way, without a formal documentary constitution spelling out national constitutional norms, the United Kingdom's national constitution depends, at least in part, on a similar calculus of voice that discounts present politics against the politics that led to, for example, the Magna Carta and the Bill of Rights.

We can see a similar calculus of voice at work in the Italian and German accommodation of Community primacy. In *Granital*,[54] for example, the Italian constitutional court allowed lower courts to disapply Italian law in favor of Community law with two exceptions. One of these exceptions is where the national law seems to threaten the very essence of the Community legal regime, in which case the question must be submitted to the constitutional court. I submit that we can see in this exception the very same reservation based on voice that we just saw in the United Kingdom's Act of Accession. The Italian Constitutional Court accommodates constitutional pluralism by presuming, as a general matter, that the Italian legislator did not intend to violate Community law. In cases where the Italian law challenges the very essence of Community law, however, we can no longer apply this presumption. In those cases, the question of the continued participation in the Community in the face of the purported violation of Community law must come before the highest constitutional tribunal itself.

The German *Maastricht* opinion,[55] for all its faults, can also be understood as coming to an accommodation of the two legal orders on the basis of voice. The decision upholds Germany's accession to the Maastricht Treaty against the challenge that the treaty undermines the individual's constitutionally protected participation in the control of the political process. It holds that the Community's powers remain sufficiently circumscribed as to leave member state parliaments with sufficient tasks and member state citizens with a sufficient voice in the process of policy making. More specifically, the opinion explains its imposition of constraints on European integration by linking the legitimacy of supranational law to the need for a European public sphere that is commensurate with the scope of European decision making.

---

[54] Corte costituzionale, June 8, 1984, No. 170, 21 C.M.L. REV. 756 (Granital).
[55] *See* Brunner, *supra* note 17.

Although the opinion is wooden in its conception of possible futures, and remarkable for its failure to see any current democratic deficit in the European Union, the calculus of accommodation here, too, is ultimately based on voice.

Finally, the recent row over the European Arrest Warrant (EAW) seems also to be managed at least in part based on voice (i.e., the depth of commitment of the Community and the member states to their respective positions on the matter). The EAW came about in the frenzy immediately after September 11, 2001. The idea for such an instrument had been previously raised and rejected but was hastily resurrected and quickly passed in the immediate aftermath of the terrorist attacks.

When the matter came before the Polish Constitutional Tribunal,[56] that court was confronted with a clear constitutional provision to the contrary (i.e., specifically prohibiting the extradition of its nationals). Although the Polish court could not ignore this clear expression of the national will, it nonetheless muted the national voice by delaying the effectiveness of its opinion for eighteen months to allow Parliament to change the constitution. Subsequently, Parliament changed the constitution to allow the extradition of Polish nationals in general, but the constitutional amendment did not accommodate the EAW in its entirety. As a result, differences between what Poland permits and what the EAW appears to require remain.

Similarly, Germany's highest constitutional court struck at the EAW, assailing not the act itself but only Germany's particular method of implementation.[57] Here, too, the constitutional court tempered its ruling in the face of Germany's background choice for participation in Europe.[58] The Community, for its part, has failed to challenge this resistance politically. Even after becoming empowered under the treaty of Lisbon to bring enforcement actions against Poland and other member states for failure to transpose the EAW, the Commission may well hold back because of the realization that its hasty decision to embrace the EAW in the fall of 2001 now confronts a highly deliberate decision on the part of member states to resist certain aspects of that mandate.

---

[56] Polish Constitutional Tribunal, P 1/05, April 27, 2005, *available at* http://www.trybunal. gov.pl/eng/summaries/summaries_assets/documents/P_1_05_full_GB.pdf (Polish European Arrest Warrant Decision).

[57] BVerfG, July 18, 2005, *available at* http://www.bverfg.de/entscheidungen/rs20050718_ 2bvr223604en.html (German European Arrest Warrant Act Decision).

[58] For an excellent comparative analysis of the German, Czech, and Polish responses to the EAW, see Zdeněk Kühn, *The European Arrest Warrant, Third Pillar Law and National Constitutional Resistance-Acceptance*, 3 Croatian Yb. Eur. L. & Policy 99 (2007).

B. Expertise

The second realm of contestation is that of expertise. I use this term broadly here to encompass knowledge-based capacity as well as bureaucratic capacity and instrumental rationality. In short, expertise here stands for expert judgment as well as effective administration and the capacity to deliver otherwise defined results. Expertise, understood in this sense, is an important aspect of modern liberal governance that brings us beyond the usual dichotomy of negative and positive liberty. To be sure, liberal constitutionalism must give citizens a voice in governance and protect individuals from abuses of power.[59] But liberal constitutionalism must do more. It must get certain things right and get the job of governance done. As we shall see, this value of expertise figures prominently in the constitutional conflict in both systems.

In the United States, relative institutional capacity is frequently the subject of dispute in asking whether judicial review of a given matter is appropriate or whether judging the constitutionality of any given course of action is better left to the Congress, the president, or even the people themselves. The basic argument in favor of judicial review in the United States has traditionally been one of expertise, that is, an argument based on the bureaucratic, professional, apolitical, and scholarly virtues of the judiciary.[60]

This claimed position of privilege is, however, frequently under attack. The first of the challenges denies the relevance of expertise entirely and insists on bringing us back to voice. Such critics assert that the judiciary, far from being removed from politics, is deeply enmeshed in the business of conducting politics by indirection.[61] The fundamentally realist challenge denies the claim of judicial expertise (and, in the extreme, the relevance of expertise in the crafting of public policy more generally) and recasts the interinstitutional battle simply in terms of voice. A second argument, more specific to the adjudication of rights, is that the judiciary should refrain from balancing values or interests in the adjudication of rights and should focus, instead, on smoking out government's illegitimate motives or purposes.[62] In contrast to the first critique, this argument distinguishes between a legitimate

---

[59] *Cf.* Stephen Holmes, Benjamin Constant and the Making of Modern Liberalism (1984).

[60] Bickel, *supra* note 27.

[61] *See, e.g.,* Karen Alter, Establishing the Supremacy of European Law 45–52 (2001); Keith E. Whittington, *Taking What They Give Us: Explaining the Court's Federalism Offensive,* 51 Duke L.J. 477, 480–487 (2001).

[62] *See* Joseph Raz, Practical Reason And Norms 178–199 (1990); Richard H. Pildes, *Avoiding Balancing: The Role of Exclusionary Reasons in Constitutional Law,* 45 Hastings L.J. 711 (1994).

realm of judicial involvement based on expertise (i.e., eliminating government actions based on unconstitutional considerations) and an illegitimate realm of judicial involvement in which the voice of the political branches should control (i.e., balancing various competing interests).

For present purposes, let us put aside these arguments that pit voice against presumed expertise, and let us focus briefly on a third critique. Here, the idea is that expertise may well matter pervasively to constitutional judgment but that judicial expertise in several areas, such as federalism, foreign affairs, or national security judgments, is lacking. This critique does not juxtapose the court's expertise with the voice of the political branches but argues, entirely on expertise-based grounds, that the court simply lacks the institutional capacity to judge the constitutionality of government policies any more reliably than the political branches can do themselves.[63] This critique, then, acknowledges the role of expertise generally in constitutional judgment while suggesting that the Court should either abstain from judgment or take an extremely deferential stance to the political branches, in areas where the president or the Congress have the more reliable institutional expertise. What is interesting, then, is that, once again, each institution of government can lay claim to furthering the value of expertise.

The management of interpretive pluralism in the United States often reflects the expertise-based claims of the various branches. Invoking his expert judgment, for example, Andrew Jackson vetoed the Bank Bill on constitutional grounds, claiming superior knowledge that the law, which seemed necessary to Congress and would have passed Supreme Court review was, in fact, not necessary but harmful.[64] Even apart from vetoes, which more recently have been based on mere policy disagreements, presidents may, under certain circumstances, declare that they will not enforce certain laws as written by drawing on their special position of institutional expertise on a given subject.[65] The Supreme Court, for its part, has, on occasion, deferred to the

---

[63] See MARK TUSHNET, TAKING THE CONSTITUTION AWAY FROM THE COURTS, 123 (1999). Larry D. Kramer, *Marbury and the Retreat from Judicial Supremacy*, 20 CONST. COMMENT. 205 (2003).

[64] *See, e.g.,* Trevor W. Morrison, *Suspension and the Extrajudicial Constitution*, 107 COLUM. L. REV. 1533, at n. 235 (2007).

[65] For different variations, see, e.g., David Barron, *Constitutionalism in the Shadow of Doctrine: The President's Non-Enforcement Power*, 63 LAW & CONTEMP. PROBS. 61 (2000); Dawn E. Johnsen, *Presidential Non-Enforcement of Constitutionally Objectionable Statutes*, 63 LAW & CONTEMP. PROBS. 7 (2000). *See also* Johnsen, *supra* at note 12–13 ("Presidential non-enforcement policy should respect judicial precedent and Congress's considered judgments about the meaning of the Constitution, but afford greater weight to the President's views when the President possesses special institutional expertise of relevance.").

president, as, for example, in matters of foreign affairs, given its relative lack of institutional capacity to assess the consequences of the actions in question. Similarly, built into the Court's basic doctrines checking the enumeration of powers is an interinstitutional accommodation based in part on a calculus of expertise, as in the numerous doctrines of deference to Congress's assessment of constitutional facts, such as the need for a particular piece of legislation under the commerce clause and the necessary and proper clause.[66]

Turning to Europe again, we see that here, too, claims of expertise have featured prominently in managing pluralism, that is, in managing the unsettled nature of hierarchy within the European enterprise of governance. Arguments of relative expertise featured strongly in the justification of the European Union from the very beginnings of the Community in Jean Monnet's dirigiste vision of an expert body of supranational administration operating far above politics. Indeed, traces of this expertise-based understanding of the legitimacy of the European Union can still be found in the language currently used to describe the powers of the European Union. The French constitution, for example, denotes the Community's powers by using the technical sounding word *compétences* (which is how the French constitution also terms the powers of adjudication as well as those of local governments) while reserving the more broadly political-sounding term *pouvoirs* to denote the powers of the French president and parliament.[67] Indeed, the pervasive European usage of the word *competence* to describe what Americans would term the *powers* of the European Union may well reflect a latent, expertise-based understanding of European integration even today. This language of expertise serves not only to lay out a vision for what the European bureaucracy might do well but also to overcome the obvious weakness of the Community's argument for legitimacy based on voice.

Despite the European Union's progression from bureaucracy to body politic, the idea of expertise and the instrumental values of bureaucracy and efficiency have retained a significant place in the institutional accommodation of conflicts of hierarchy within the system. Because the conflict of hierarchy in the European Union is a conflict among competing levels of governance, the expertise-based argument taps into principles of federalism and subsidiarity much as the voice-based argument did. Indeed, expertise and instrumental rationality figure prominently in the treaty itself in the

---

[66] More generally, Jeff Powell speaks of the Court examining constitutional meaning through "screens of deference." H. Jefferson Powell, *The Province and Duty of the Political Departments*, 65 U. Chi. L. Rev. 365 (1998).

[67] *Compare, e.g.*, Constitution du 4 octobre 1958, arts. 88–1 & 2 *with* arts. 7 & 25.

formulation of subsidiarity as a crosscutting principle to moderate European involvement in the governance of the system. According to Article 5 EC, the Community may exercise its concurrent powers only to the extent that a given goal cannot be properly achieved by member state action alone. The question at issue in Article 5 EC, then, is not one of voice but one of instrumental rationality, that is, the relative institutional capacities for achieving a particular desired result.[68]

At the political level, the expertise-based accommodation of constitutional pluralism can be found, for example, in the subsidiarity protocol, a procedure that institutionalizes contestation of the instrumental rationality of Community action.[69] Notice that this contest is not simply one of voice, that is, of voting down a community proposal – although it is that, too. Moving away from voice, the protocol expressly demands engagement among the various levels of governance on the issue of expertise. Member state parliaments may challenge the necessity for Community action and force a reevaluation of the instrumental justification for Community action at the Community level. Although the procedure, from the perspective of Community law, does not formally unsettle the European Commission's prerogative of decision in these matters, it reflects a pragmatic accommodation of the problematic nature of the Community's ultimate claim of primacy within the system. Even apart from the specific protocol, the Community has already responded to member state contestation of the need for Community action by creating a mechanism of review within the European Commission of the necessity of Community action according to the principle of subsidiarity.[70]

The ECJ, too, has tapped into instrumental ideas of subsidiarity in yielding to member state concerns about a runaway European Community. In the judgment regarding the Tobacco Advertising Directive in 2000,[71] the ECJ can be seen as responding to an earlier threat of member state high courts to defect in the event that the Community did not curb its enterprise.[72] The ECJ arguably accommodated this concern when it decided for the first time ever to declare that a Community policy had exceeded the sum total

---

[68] Cf. Halberstam, *Comparative Federalism, supra* note 12, for a discussion of the instrumental nature of subsidiarity in Article 5 EC.

[69] Treaty of Lisbon, Protocol on the Application of the Principles of Subsidiarity and Proportionality, Dec. 17, 2007, 2007 O.J. (C 306) 150.

[70] George A. Bermann, *Taking Subsidiarity Seriously: Federalism in the European Community and the United States*, 94 Colum. L. Rev. 331 (1994).

[71] Case C-376/98, Federal Republic of Germany v. European Parliament and Council of the European Union, 2000 E.C.R. I-08419.

[72] Bruno Simma, J.H.H. Weiler & Markus-Zöckler, Kompetenzen und Grundrechte 68–83, 161 (1999).

of the Community's powers. Asserting the instrumental capacity to reign in
Community powers, the court based its substantive decision on a calculus
of expertise as well, holding that certain parts of the original directive were
simply unnecessary to the functioning of the common market.

C. Rights

In the United States, as elsewhere, rights tend to mean courts. The thought of
individual rights usually conjures up the image of a court declaring that a law,
executive act, or official action has invaded a protected liberty. As a result,
one might think that in the case of protecting rights, the judiciary invariably
has a stronger claim to interpretive primacy with regard to rights.[73] And yet
here, too, the pluralism we find in the United States complicates matters quite
a bit.

Just as the U.S. Constitution does not definitively settle the institutional
hierarchy among the various branches on matters of constitutional interpretation generally, it does not clearly settle who is to protect individual rights. To
be sure, the usual practice of deference to judicial interpretation obtains, but
this practice is subject to disruption here as well. The disruption of the usual
deference to the judiciary can, of course, be based on familiar arguments of
voice and expertise. For example, the argument may be made that the judiciary has no business enforcing what are often vague rights provisions against
the specifically declared will of the majority or that the judiciary is no better
than the political branches at balancing relevant interests or at ascertaining
constitutionally relevant facts.

Interesting for present purposes, however, is not that a court's jurisprudence of rights can be questioned on the basis of countervailing concerns of
voice and expertise but that the usual practice of deference to the judiciary
on individual rights protection may be called into question on the basis of
rights protection itself. Put another way, the interinstitutional accommodation of pluralism in the United States with regard to the protection of rights
at times hinges not on a general argument about voice or expertise or on an
argument about the trade-off between individual rights and other values but
on arguments about which institution will better protect rights.[74]

In the United States, there is good reason to distrust the judiciary's claim
of monopoly – or even preeminence – in the realm of rights protection. As
a textual matter, each of the Civil War amendments, which revolutionized

---

[73] See, e.g., RONALD DWORKIN, A MATTER OF PRINCIPLE (1985).
[74] Compare, e.g., Joseph Raz, Disagreement in Politics, 43 AM. J. JURIS. 25 (1998), with Jeremy
Waldron, The Core of the Case against Judicial Review, 115 YALE L.J. 1346 (2006).

the protection of rights in the United States, ends by granting the Congress the specific power "to enforce" the general rights provisions of each amendment.[75] This textual hook for Congress's claim as authoritative guardian of rights is itself grounded in the historical realization that the antebellum Court, especially in its *Dred Scott* decision, had miserably failed to protect individual rights properly. As if to confirm this suspicion, a backward-looking Reconstruction Court similarly declined to provide much meaningful rights protection when it came to interpreting the Civil War amendments. Instead of putting its weight behind the new rights regime, the Reconstruction Court eviscerated core provisions of the Fourteenth Amendment[76] and declared that the amendments did not support Congress's civil rights agenda.[77] Even when the specific question of protecting African American equality and the African American franchise came before the Court, the judiciary proved useless for decades.[78]

Although the U.S. Supreme Court gradually came to protect individual rights more aggressively, especially after World War II, the federal Congress and the president were frequently by its side. With a series of civil rights acts, most prominently the Civil Rights Act of 1964[79] and the Voting Rights Act of 1965,[80] Congress enlisted the executive branch to become a forceful protector of rights. The rights guaranteed by congressional legislation often exceeded those pronounced by the Court and retained their vitality even after the Supreme Court's own rights activism receded in the late 1970s.

For many years, the Supreme Court expressly recognized the authority of Congress to vindicate a broader vision of constitutionally based rights than that embodied in the Court's own interpretation of the Constitution. For example, even though the Court had found that the Constitution did not automatically prohibit states from requiring voters to pass a literacy test as a condition of voting, Congress could nonetheless protect an individual's constitutional right to vote by prohibiting states from using such literacy tests.[81] In short, for many years the Court's own jurisprudence of rights accommodated the multiplicity of authoritative interpreters of constitutional rights.

75 *See* Akhil Reed Amar, *Intratextualism*, 112 Harv. L. Rev. 747 (1999).
76 *See* Slaughter-House Cases, 83 U.S. 36 (1872).
77 *See* Civil Rights Cases, 109 U.S. 3 (1883).
78 *See* Giles v. Teasley, 193 U.S. 146 (1904); Plessy v. Ferguson, 163 U.S. 537 (1896).
79 Civil Rights Act of 1964, Pub. L. No. 88-352, 78 Stat. 241 (codified in scattered sections of 42 U.S.C.).
80 Voting Rights Act of 1964, Pub. L. No. 89-110, 79 Stat. 437 (codified in scattered sections of 42 U.S.C.).
81 Katzenbach v. Morgan, 384 U.S. 641 (1966).

In recent years, however, the Supreme Court has asserted its monopoly over the interpretation of constitutional rights. In a series of cases, beginning with *City of Boerne v. Flores*,[82] the Court has denied Congress the power to deviate from the precise scope of constitutional rights as declared by the judiciary. For example, given that the Court held that the First Amendment's religion clauses do not protect individuals from neutral government regulation that happens to burden the free exercise of religion, Congress can no longer pass federal legislation insisting that states justify such burdens by a compelling state interest.[83] Put simply, the Court has now arrogated to itself the conclusive power to determine the precise scope of constitutional rights and has severely limited Congress's discretion to vindicate a more expansive vision of rights.

Interesting in this recent development is not that the Court seems to have lost its understanding of pluralism in the interpretation of rights. Instead, the remarkable fact is that even in the midst of the Court's recent arrogation of power, the justices nonetheless seem aware of their own limitations in the American constitutional constellation. The Court has, for instance, not ventured forth to apply its new jurisprudence either to the Voting Rights Act or to the core of the Civil Rights Act of 1964 – Title VII. Indeed, *City of Boerne* specifically noted that the Voting Rights Act would remain untouched under the new approach despite the fact that it strains the Court's new reasoning to do so.[84] And in a recent case that would have had disastrous implications for Title VII, the Court treaded lightly, paying only lip service to its new jurisprudence while allowing the federal Family Medical Leave Act to stand.[85] Thus, even in the midst of the Court's general assault on interpretive pluralism, we see signs of pragmatic accommodation based on a calculus of rights.

If we turn to the European Union, we see that fundamental rights still tend to mean domestic constitutional rights or, perhaps by now, domestic constitutional rights plus the European Convention on Human Rights. In short, the classic locus of fundamental rights protection lies not at the level of the European Union but elsewhere. The traditional story about fundamental rights in the European Union was, indeed, that the Union's own ambitions

[82] City of Boerne v. Flores, 521 U.S. 527 (1997).
[83] *Id.* at 535–536.
[84] *See id.* at 518, 530–32. *See* Ellen D. Katz, *Congressional Power to Extend Preclearance: A Response to Professor Karlan*, 44 Hous. L. Rev. 33, 40 (2007) (discussing application of *Boerne* standard to the Voting Rights Act).
[85] *See* Hibbs v. Department of Human Resources, 538 U.S. 721 (2003). *Cf.* Post and Siegel, *supra* note 28.

had to be tempered to accord with fundamental rights as they were recognized and protected at the member state level.[86]

One element of the constitutional standoff between the Community and member state legal orders famously turned on member state resistance regarding rights protection.[87] Here, the ECJ garnered the deference of member state courts to the ECJ's (and the Community's) claim of superior authority by incorporating central aspects of member state constitutional rights into Community law itself. To take the best-known example, Germany's Constitutional Court declared that it would defer to the ECJ on case-by-case fundamental rights protection while keeping a watchful eye on the ECJ's track record on rights generally.[88] The ECJ, in turn, not only has incorporated general rights protection into its own jurisprudence but also has begun to defer to specific domestic claims of legislative rights protection that exceed a Europe-wide standard, even when those protections run up against free movement claims.[89]

Most interesting for the present discussion is the possible shift in accommodating the respective boundaries of European and member state jurisdiction over rights. According to cases like *Mary Carpenter*,[90] for example, the ECJ could investigate virtually any member state legislative, administrative, or adjudicative act that might negatively affect the exercise of an individual's rights to free movement under the European Community Treaty. As the *Carpenter* case illustrated, jurisdiction under this rubric is potentially vast. It led to ECJ fundamental rights review of Mary Carpenter's residency rights on the reasoning that her residency in the United Kingdom provided (non-pecuniary) support to her husband, who exercised free movement rights by working throughout the European Union. Moreover, with the *Chen* case,[91] the already vast potential of the ECJ's fundamental rights review may have expanded even further, as the ECJ might now intervene to protect all fundamental rights of all EU citizens.[92]

---

[86] N. Lockhart & J.H.H. Weiler, *"Taking Rights Seriously" Seriously: The European Court and Its Fundamental Rights Jurisprudence* (pts. 1 & 2), 32 Common Mkt. L. Rev. 51, 32 Common Mkt. L. Rev. 579 (1995).

[87] *See* 37 BVerfGE 271 (1974) (Solange I); Case 11–70, Internationale Handelsgesellschaft mbH v. Einfuhr- und Vorratsstelle für Getreide und Futtermittel, 1970 E.C.R. 1125.

[88] 73 BVerfGE 339 (1986) (Solange II).

[89] *E.g.*, Case C-36/02, Omega Spielhallen- und Automatenaufstellungs-GmbH v. Oberbürgermeisterin der Bundesstadt Bonn, 2004 E.C.R. I-9609.

[90] *E.g.*, Case C-60/00, Mary Carpenter v. Secretary of State for the Home Department, 2002 E.C.R. I-6279.

[91] *See* Case C-200/02, Chen v. Secretary of State for the Home Department, 2004 ECR I-9923 (finding right of residency for mother of EU citizen).

[92] *But cf.* Case C-212/06, Government of French Community and Walloon Government v. Flemish Government, judgment of 1 April 2008 (not yet reported), at paras. 38–41 (refusing

Whatever the precise limits of the ECJ's jurisdiction over rights, one thing is certain: to date, the ECJ has clearly not exhausted its vast power over fundamental rights protection, almost certainly for reasons of mutual accommodation. An aggressive use of the ECJ's jurisdiction over fundamental rights would invite the member state courts to retaliate in kind, engaging the logic of mutually assured destruction that Joseph Weiler pointed out long ago.[93] More important, though, for present purposes is the nature of the accommodation and the values that lie at the heart of this accommodation – in particular the value of rights protection itself.

As a general matter, member states' fundamental rights records have been passable, at least when coupled with protection through the European Court of Human Rights in Strasbourg. There has been little need for the ECJ to intervene, except to preserve the sphere of Community law where the fundamental right did indeed have a particular connection to free movement.

With the accession of member states with possibly more questionable fundamental rights records, however, the current state of mutual accommodation might be shifting. As an initial matter, the Community's political branches have been placing greater burdens on new member states to demonstrate their bona fides on the protection of fundamental rights.[94] Similarly, the ECJ might begin to review fundamental rights claims – especially those coming from the new member states – more aggressively. The ECJ may be viewed as laying the foundation for such intervention in cases like *Pupino*,[95] in which the court broadly read a European framework directive under the third pillar to protect basic rights of criminal procedure. In that case, the ECJ specifically made reference to the European Court of Human Rights, as if to lend its own institutional support to what is becoming an important (but increasingly overworked) ally in this venture.[96]

The new accommodation on rights, then, may play out something like this: First, the member states will continue to refrain from reviewing fundamental rights violations involving European law as long as the ECJ generally provides an acceptable level of rights protection. Put simply, the *Solange*

---

to review for fundamental rights violation the application of Belgian law to Belgian nationals that have not exercised their freedom of movement).

[93] Robert Stith & J.H.H. Weiler, *Can Treaty Law Be Supreme, Directly Effective, and Autonomous – All at the Same Time? (An Epistolary Exchange)*, 34 N.Y.U. J. INT'L L. & POL. 729 (2002).

[94] Indeed, here the Union often imposes obligations on new member states that exceed what the Union demands of existing members of the club. *See* Christophe Hillion, *Enlargement of the European Union – The Discrepancy between Membership Obligations and Accession Conditions as regards the Protection of Minorities*, 27 FORDHAM INT'L L.J. 715 (2004).

[95] *E.g.*, Case C-105/03 Criminal Proceedings against Maria Pupino 2005 E.C.R. I-5285.

[96] *Id.* at paras. 48–50.

compromise that the German Bundesverfassungsgericht reached with the ECJ will continue unless there is a change in the European Union's track record on rights protection. Although unlikely, such a change is conceivable. For example, if, following the Court of First Instance's suggestion, the ECJ had abdicated responsibility for fundamental rights review in considering the European Union's implementation of UN Security Council sanctions, the member states might well have suspended their current restraint under *Solange II.*[97]

Second, and even more intriguing, the ECJ will refrain from aggressively reviewing all fundamental rights claims within its jurisdiction but only on the analogous terms. That is, the ECJ will not tap into the full potential of its jurisdiction over fundamental rights under *Carpenter* and *Chen*, but it will restrain itself only so long as member states generally maintain a satisfactory level of fundamental rights protection throughout their system. Thus, the ECJ may shoot a warning shot across the bow of potentially rights-infringing member states, just as the member states have done with regard to the ECJ. Such a "reverse-*Solange*" compromise may indeed already be brewing at the court.[98] Just as the member state courts have generally heeded their compromise over the past two decades, the ECJ is also unlikely to become very active in enforcing fundamental rights beyond the traditional scope of core free movement issues.[99] And yet, in the case of new member states with sketchy human rights records, the ECJ might nonetheless reach more broadly than it traditionally has done with regard to the old member states.

IV. Conclusion

The European Union and the United States are both systems marked by what this chapter has called constitutional heterarchy. In both, important issues of final legal authority within the system are fundamentally unsettled. In both, the unsettled nature of authority is not a defect but an essential feature of the system. And in both, the lack of settlement does not result in anarchy within the system or destruction of the system but in productive

---

[97] For an analysis of pluralism with regard to the ECJ's decision in the *Kadi* decision, see Daniel Halberstam and Eric Stein, *The United Nations, The European Union, and the King of Sweden: Economic Sanctions and Individual Rights in a Plural World Order*, 46 COMM. MARKET L. REV. 13 (2009). *Cf.* C-402/05 P, Kadi v. Council (Grand Chamber), Judgment of 3 September 2008, nyr.

[98] *See* Case C-380/05, Centro Europa 7 Srl v. Ministero delle Comunicazioni e Autorità per le garanzie nelle comunicazioni and Direzione generale per le concessioni e le autorizzazioni del Ministero delle Comunicazioni, 2008 E.C.R., paras. 14–20 (Opinion of AG Maduro).

[99] *See* Case C-212/06, *supra* note 92.

conflict. Constitutional heterarchy is therefore not a principle of disorder but a principle of organization. In the United States and in the European Union the institutions and levels of governance ground their conflicting appeals to authority in the values of constitutionalism and reach multiple points of spontaneous mutual accommodation to maintain the productive functioning of the system as a whole.

An examination of this process of constitutional contestation reveals that the conflict in each system surrounds three primary values of constitutionalism. I have called them here the values of voice, expertise, and rights. These values roughly combine the two basic insights from traditional liberal theory – the liberty of the ancients, as participation in governance, and the liberty of the moderns, as the freedom from coercion by the community – with the basic insight from the development of the modern administrative state that (social) legitimacy also depends on bureaucratic capacity, professionalism, and knowledge-based governance.

Constitutional heterarchy means that none of these values is predictably associated with any particular level, unit, or institution of governance. In the United States, for instance, the judiciary may challenge the authority of the political branches by invoking arguments based on voice, just at the political branches may challenge the authority of the judiciary by invoking arguments based on rights. Similarly, each branch of government can draw on arguments of expertise. And, of course, each branch can combine several of these primary values in search of a more persuasive hew of legitimacy. In Europe, the European Union as well as the member states can and do base their competing claims of authority on any combination of these three values.

Constitutional heterarchy means that the organization of this conflict is not grounded in any hierarchy outside the system. It would therefore be mistaken to suggest, as some scholars have,[100] that the pluralism of systems in the European Union is organized under the umbrella of international law. Similarly, one may search in vain for a hierarchical organization of the pluralism of interpretive institutions in the United States within or beyond the U.S. Constitution. Instead, the organization of contestation in each system is the result of concrete actions and interactions of the competing institutions, each drawing on the primary values of constitutionalism to support their stance of authority or deference. In short, as a form of organization, constitutional heterarchy is spontaneous, decentralized, and immanent.

The comparison of constitutional pluralism across these two very different settings – the pluralism of systems, sources, and norms in Europe as

---

[100] *See, e.g.,* NEIL MACCORMICK, QUESTIONING SOVEREIGNTY, *supra* note 7, at 121.

compared to interpretive pluralism in the United States – leads to important insights into the role of constitutionalism in global governance. The examination of these two rather different settings of constitutional conflict reveals the values that lie at the heart of constitutionalism itself. Having identified these values, it seems plain that the traditional state-based setting of constitutional governance is becoming increasingly challenged in promoting them successfully. Whether a result of shifting realities or shifting perceptions, the quest to vindicate the voice of those affected by policy determinations, to develop the instrumental capacity to govern effectively, and to protect the rights of individuals has gained global dimensions in the modern world. At the same time, the institutions and systems of global governance do not fit neatly into a new hierarchy of norms and institutions but are, instead, fragmented along both systemic and interpretive dimensions. Put another way, global governance embodies both a pluralism of systems, sources, and norms, as well as a pluralism of interpretive institutions. As the comparison between the United States and Europe demonstrates, understanding the problem of fragmentation in the register of constitutionalism need not entail a search for an overarching hierarchy of systems or of interpretive authorities. Instead, we can find constitutional order in spontaneous, mutual accommodation that seeks to vindicate the values of voice, expertise, and rights at the level of global governance as well.

12. Courts and Pluralism: Essay on a Theory of Judicial Adjudication in the Context of Legal and Constitutional Pluralism

MIGUEL POIARES MADURO

There is an emerging body of literature that describes a context of constitutional and legal pluralism. Usually constitutional pluralism identifies the phenomenon of a plurality of constitutional sources of authority that create a context for potential constitutional conflicts between different constitutional orders to be solved in a nonhierarchical manner. More broadly, legal pluralism can be used, in this context, to refer both to the multiplication of competing legal sites and jurisdictional orders and to the expansion of relevant legal sources. Such context affects the role of courts and the character of judicial adjudication and interpretation. This chapter aims to review the impact of pluralism in models of interpretation used by courts and in the institutional dimension of judicial adjudication.

I will undertake this analysis by reference to a broad notion of constitutional and legal pluralism that encompasses different dimensions. In this respect, it is necessary to distinguish between internal and external forms of pluralism. Internal pluralism refers to a pluralism that is internal to a particular legal order. In other words, it refers to a legal order where multiple sites of power coexist, are mutually recognized, and may not always be organized in a nonhierarchical relationship. The best-known example of such a legal order is the European Union. We can identify four main sources of internal pluralism in the European Union. First, there is a plurality of constitutional sources (both European and national) that have fed the EU constitutional law and, in particular, its general principles of law. Second, the acceptance

Advocate General, Court of Justice of the European Communities. The views expressed in this article are purely my own. I would like to thank Aude Bouveresse, Félix Ronkes Agerbeek, and Suvi Sankari for their comments and suggestions on an earlier draft. I am also thankful for comments made by the participants in the workshop leading to this book and in seminars at the Helsinki Law School's Centre for Excellence on the Foundations of European Law and at the Universities of Fribourg and Paris II.

of the supremacy of EU rules over national constitutional rules has not been unconditional and has been even, at times, resisted by national constitutional courts. This confers to EU law a kind of contested or negotiated normative authority.[1] Third, the European Union has coincided with the emergence of new forms of power that challenge the traditional constitutional categories. This is the case both at the EU level (with the emergence of institutions whose legitimacy and model of power cannot be traced back to the classic conception of the separation of powers) and at the national level (with state and private entities increasingly assuming legal forms that challenge the traditional private-public distinction and the different mechanisms of accountability associated with them). Such pluralism in the forms of power challenges, in turn, both the traditional legal categories drawn by courts and the existent criteria for the allocation of power. Fourth, the European Union is also dominated by a form of political pluralism that can assume a rather radical form, as conflicting political claims are often supported by corresponding claims of polity authority: a particular political idea is supported also as the expression of the political identity of a particular political community.

External pluralism derives from the increased communication and interdependence among different legal orders, both state and supranational or international legal orders. From this, different relationships emerge. First, increased economic and political integration has led to a multiplication of international legal regimes and jurisdictional fora. This creates risks of fragmentation but also increased appeals for judicial bodies to actively promote integration and coordination between the different legal orders.[2] This could be done either by international judicial bodies integrating, through interpretation, the rules of a particular international legal regime into another

---

[1] This is the core and starting point of traditional constitutional pluralism analysis in the context of the European Union. Miguel Poiares Maduro, *Contrapunctual Law: Europe's Constitutional Pluralism in Action, in* SOVEREIGNTY IN TRANSITION 501 (Neil Walker ed., 2003); Mattias Kumm, *Who Is the Final Arbiter of Constitutionality in Europe? Three Conceptions of the Relationship between the German Federal Constitutional Court and the European Court of Justice,* 36 COMMON MKT. L. REV. 356 (1999); Samantha Besson, *From European Integration to European Integrity: Should European Law Speak with Just One Voice?* 10 EUR. L.J. 257 (2004); Jan Komárek, *European Constitutional Pluralism and the European Arrest Warrant: Contrapunctual Principles in Disharmony* (Jean Monnet Working Paper No. 10/05, 2005). *See also* Neil Walker, *The Idea of Constitutional Pluralism,* 65 MOD. L. REV. 317 (2002), which, however, already presented a broader picture of constitutional pluralism.

[2] *See* Martii Koskenniemi, President of the International Law Commission, *Fragmentation of International Law: Difficulties Arising from the Diversification and Expansion of International Law: Report of the Study Group of the International Law Commission,* U.N. Doc. A/CN.4/L.682 (Apr. 13, 2006), *available at* http://www.un.org/law/ilc/ (follow "Texts and Instruments" hyperlink and then "Sources of Law" at "1.9").

international legal regime,[3] or by domestic courts increasingly relying on international law arguments in deciding domestic disputes. Second, there are increased conflicting jurisdictions among different legal orders (state, supranational, and international). This generates instances of what we could term *interpretative* and *adjudication competition* among courts. Courts sometimes compete on the interpretation of similar legal rules and other times compete on the quality of judicial outputs they provide to similar legal questions (with consequences, for example, on the jurisdictional choices of mobile legal actors). This context also gives rise to possible legal externalities (where the decision taken in a certain jurisdiction has a social and an economic impact, albeit not a formal legal impact, in another jurisdiction).[4] Finally, there is also an increased cross-fertilization of legal concepts. This is so for two reasons: first, the growing transnational character of economic litigation and legal services means that lawyers tend to circulate legal arguments and legal strategies among different legal orders; second, the circulation of legal ideas through networks of academics, lawyers, and judges also entails a mixture of legal cultures.[5] Neil Walker has described this legal openness to external legal arguments as one of sympathetic consideration.[6]

My argument is that such a context of internal and external pluralism affects different dimensions of the role of courts. Such pluralism changes both the nature and scope of the legal issues to be addressed by courts and their communities of discourse. It also affects (and sometimes challenges) the normative authority of their decisions. As a consequence courts have to adapt the nature of their judicial reasoning, the normative preferences that determine their judicial outcomes, and the self-perception of their institutional role.

---

[3] *See, for a discussion,* Ernst-Ulrich Petersmann, *Time for a United Nations 'Global Compact' for Integrating Human Rights into the Law of Worldwide Organizations: Lessons from European Integration,* 13 Eur. J. Int'l L. 621 (2002); Robert Howse, *Human Rights in the WTO: Whose Rights, What Humanity? Comment on Petersmann,* 13 Eur. J. Int'l L. 651 (2002); Philip Alston, *Resisting the Merger and Acquisition of Human Rights by Trade Law: A Reply to Petersmann,* 13 Eur. J. Int'l L. 815 (2002); Ernst-Ulrich Petersmann, *Taking Human Dignity, Poverty and Empowerment of Individuals More Seriously: Rejoinder to Alston,* 13 Eur. J. Int'l L. 845 (2002).

[4] An example is the prohibition in a certain legal order of a merger between companies that also operate in other jurisdictions.

[5] *See* Laurence R. Helfer & Anne-Marie Slaughter, *Toward a Theory of Effective Supranational Adjudication,* 107 Yale L.J. 273 (1997); Anne-Marie Slaughter, *A Brave New Judicial World, in* American Exceptionalism and Human Rights (Michael Ignatieff ed., 2005); Anne-Marie Slaughter, Judicial Globalization, 40 Va. J. Int'l L. 1103 (2000); Courts Crossing Borders: Blurring the Lines of Sovereignty (Mary Volkansek & John F. Stack Jr. eds., 2005).

[6] Neil Walker, *Rethinking Constitutionalism in an Era of Globalization and Privatization* Int'l J. Con. L. (forthcoming).

There is already an important body of literature that has studied some of the consequences for courts of the pluralist context that I have described earlier.[7] Such literature has, however, departed from a more limited conception of such pluralism. The focus has been on the emergence of more or less formal networks of dialogues among courts. The approach has been predominantly descriptive and external to courts. Here, my focus is both internal and predominantly normative. How should courts adapt the nature of their legal reasoning and judicial adjudication to such a pluralist context?

The point of departure has to be the interaction between the context of legal and constitutional pluralism and the models of interpretation to be employed by courts. Interpretation can perhaps be suggestively described as the software of courts. In a narrow sense interpretation can be understood simply by reference to the methodologies to be employed in the interpretation of rules: the types of legal arguments used by courts, their techniques of exegesis of the text, and the rules of logic that make legal reasoning a form of practical reasoning. However, debates about legal interpretation often assume a broader dimension linked to the proper role of courts in a democratic society. In this broadest sense, interpretation is a function of hermeneutics but also of the institutional constraints and normative preferences that determine judicial outcomes in light of an existing body of rules. Interpretation is here at the intersection of the debates not only about different methods of interpretation (or forms of legal reasoning) but also about broader questions on the proper role of courts in a democratic society. The concrete interpretation to be given to legal rules is therefore a product of legal reasoning and of the institutional constraints and normative preferences that determine the role of courts in a given political community.

There is a constant interplay among the three dimensions. The scope of valid legal arguments and the weight to be given to them, for example, depend on the normative preferences of courts and on how they conceive their institutional position in a particular legal system. It should be stated that by normative preferences I am not referring to the subjective value judgments of judges, which, albeit to different degrees, will always be part of judicial decisions. I am referring to a systemic understanding of the legal order that is the product of a normative reconstruction of that legal order on the basis of its overall body of rules and judicial decisions so as to be conceived of as a coherent body of rules anchored in certain fundamental principles.

---

[7] *See supra* notes 2 and 6; THE EUROPEAN COURTS AND NATIONAL COURTS: DOCTRINE AND JURISPRUDENCE – LEGAL CHANGE IN ITS SOCIAL CONTEXT (Anne-Marie Slaughter et al. eds., 1998).

There can certainly be disagreement as to the correct systemic understanding of a particular legal order. To that extent this also involves some degree of subjectivity. But the important thing, in this respect, is the objectivation of legal interpretation that is promoted by the process of systemic reconstruction of the legal order and by the need to remain consistent and coherent with the systemic conception the interpreter attributes to his or her particular legal order. In this way, even if the systemic understanding adopted by a particular interpreter may, in part, be perceived as subjective, the need to articulate it and remain faithful to it puts a constraint on judicial discretion and limits the scope of subjectivity.[8] Furthermore, because agreement is frequently easier at the systemic level, such articulation of the normative preferences of a legal order at the systemic level may be more conducive to agreement. Finally, the necessary link between individual decisions and systemic preferences increases transparency regarding the reasons for disagreement, frequently allowing us to construct it in terms of first order choices.

The institutional dimension of the judicial role is another aspect that is closely dependent on the systemic understanding of the legal order in which courts operate. But, conversely, the institutional constraints of courts and the institutional context in which they operate also determine the systemic preferences they attribute to their particular legal order and the weight they will give to different legal arguments.

The blending of these different dimensions may be presented in the form of a theory of constitutional or judicial adjudication. As stated, the methods of interpretation used by courts as well as their institutional and value choices reflect (or ought to reflect) a certain systemic understanding of the normative preferences and institutional constraints of the legal order in which those courts operate. Only such an approach is capable of securing both the coherence and integrity of that legal order (by fitting individual decisions into a coherent whole) and judicial accountability (by constraining the power of courts in individual decisions and subjecting them to a normative scrutiny with regard to the normative preferences they attribute to their legal order).

---

[8] I am well aware that this view can be criticized as naive if one assumes that the gap between such systemic normative preferences and particular legal rules is such that it can easily be manipulated so as to be conducive to any interpretation. I do not believe that to be the case, and, in event, I believe that is also to be controlled by the other dimensions of interpretation I refer to. Ultimately, I believe that this approach makes judicial deliberation and legal reasoning more transparent and accountable than do theories that dispense such systemic requirement and focus, for example, on formalism or consequentialism. The margin of appreciation (not to say discretion) that is at the core of this debate will always exist in legal interpretation (and, in my view, it will increase with the current pluralist context), and the question turns on how best to objectivize it.

Understood in this way, a theory of judicial adjudication serves not only to objectivize and constrain the subjective preferences of judges but also to define and legitimate the proper role of courts in a given political community.

The issue here is how the current context of legal and constitutional pluralism affects a theory of judicial adjudication. In this contribution I focus on assessing its impact on two of the three dimensions of judicial adjudication while taking into account that they are all closely connected. I start by briefly reviewing the impact of pluralism on the reasoning and methods of interpretation that ought to be employed by courts. In the second part, I focus on the institutional impact. My argument is that the context of legal and constitutional pluralism stresses the importance of institutional choices and institutional awareness on the part of courts, and this, in turn, requires a meta-methodological framework for judicial dialogues.

Reasoning with Pluralism

In my view, legal and constitutional pluralism require an expansion of the scope of legal arguments to be employed by courts and an increased focus on systemic and teleological reasoning. This means that the reasoning of courts has to become more contextual and normatively thick. Some will fear an increase in the scope of judicial subjectivity and activism. I will try to explain why that is not necessarily true.

Courts employ a variety of methods of interpretation: text, legislative history, context, purpose, and telos are among those most used in judicial decisions. Moreover, judicial reasoning is filtered through the canons of practical reasoning, highlighted by the classical recourse to syllogism. It is through this arsenal of professional techniques that judges construct the legal arguments on which they justify their judicial decisions. This is the standard language of the community of judicial discourse, and adhering to it lays the first step in the objectivation of the interpretative process.[9] However, this language can be used to defend rather different legal arguments, depending on how those methods are used, the weight to be given to each of them, and what normative preferences guide their application.[10] There are four ways of dealing with such normative gap.

---

[9] *See* Owen M. Fiss, *Objectivity and Interpretation*, 34 STAN. L. REV. 739 (1982).

[10] That is why I have considered that an articulation of the systemic normative preferences that a particular interpreter attributes to the legal order in which it operates is a necessary condition of the objectivation of the interpretative process. Without it, the gap between the rhetoric of the classic methods of interpretation and the reality of judicial decisions would be a fertile and safe space for unaccountable subjectivity.

First, we can simply assume that such a normative gap, inherent in the process of interpretation, ought to be filled by courts, and, while it may be a purely subjective process, it is fully legitimated by the institutional authority of courts in the legal system. Interpretation is a subjective process that renders law objective by reason of the meaning attributed to particular norms by courts. It is the authority of courts that renders legal interpretation objective and not vice versa. To a certain extent, this is the unarticulated theory of interpretation and constitutional justice that has largely dominated legal practice in Europe, including its reliance on formalism. But it is an assumption that others have made transparent (and, therefore, detached from formalism) as the only viable and honest conception of the process of interpretation.[11] It is an approach that emphasizes the power of courts at the expense of the political process in giving meaning to the law.

Formalism can also be defended, however, with a rather different purpose. A second set of theories argue that the normative gap identified in the process of interpretation ought to be filled by the political process and that the best way for that to happen is to limit courts to a formal interpretation of the law. I call this "formal constructivism." Formal constructivist theories adopt formal methods of interpretation even to artificially govern areas that could be considered of substantive judicial discretion in light of the legal text. The argument is that formalism is what best constrains courts and that, even if it will produce some bad judicial outcomes, it will produce better judicial results overall and leave to the political process the correction of unwanted legal outcomes.[12] These theories require, in practice, an objective meaning of the norm, which is static in time. If the text itself is not clear, then such meaning is to be found in the historical context of its enactment, the intent of the legislator, or any other purportedly objective and formal meaning that allows

---

[11] Michel Troper, *La motivation des décisions constitutionnelles, in* LA MOTIVATION DES DÉCISIONS DE JUSTICE 287, 293–295 (Chaïm Perelman & P. Foriers eds., 1978); *see also* Michel Troper, *Justice constitutionelle et démocratie,* 1 REVUE FRANCAISE DE DROIT CONSTI- TUTIONNEL 31 (1990). Troper departs from the notion of interpretation as an act of will and not knowledge, very similarly to STANLEY FISH, DOING WHAT COMES NATURALLY – CHANGE, RHETORIC, AND THE PRACTICE OF THEORY IN LITERARY AND LEGAL STUDIES (1989). This does not mean that there are no constraints imposed on judges, only that such constraints are external to the process of interpretation.

[12] *See* Antonin Scalia, *Originalism: The Lesser Evil,* 57 U. CIN. L. REV. 849 (1989); MARK TUSHNET, TAKING THE CONSTITUTION AWAY FROM COURTS (1999); ADRIAN VERMEULE, JUDGING UNDER UNCERTAINTY – AN INSTITUTIONAL THEORY OF LEGAL INTERPRETATION (2006). I would also include here judicial minimalism (*see* CASS SUNSTEIN, ONE CASE AT A TIME (1999)). Even if it is not a formalist approach (but the same could be said of originalism), it artificially limits substantive debate on legal interpretation so as to, purportedly, limit the scope of judicial activism.

for a syllogistic reasoning.[13] There are three basic problems with such an approach. First, norms often do reflect multiple meanings, and to artificially limit the burden of justification inherent in the process of interpretation to formal arguments may increase judicial discretion and not to limit it.[14] Second, some of these norms agreed on correspond to universal principles, and it is a matter of debate whether the agreement on those norms centered on the meaning acquired by those principles at that particular historical moment or, instead, on the universal potential of such principles abstracting from their concrete historical meaning. An example: when we enshrine in a constitution the principle of equality, are we adopting it with the content that it has in that particular moment in time or are we adopting it, in light of its universal character, abstracting from that particular meaning in time? Only the latter is fully compatible with a constitution's universal character, which requires a certain "veil of ignorance" regarding the full extent of the commitment it binds us to.[15] Third, the formal constructivist theories of interpretation have to define the criteria for the artificial delimitation of substantive discretion, but such criteria are themselves subjective. Justice Antonin Scalia, for example, recognizes that his own brand of originalism is difficult to apply both in practice (because it requires consideration of a wealth of historical materials) and because it must be so in a moderate manner (so as not to lead to interpretations that, in his own words, would become "a medicine that seems too strong to swallow").[16] But it is obvious that both of these variables are liable to introduce a great degree of discretion back into the process of interpretation.

Most important, however, even if we were to accept the feasibility and objective character of such formal construction of interpretation so as to limit judicial activism, there is an underlying question that needs to be answered: why should the political process always be presumed to be superior to the

[13] "Objective" here implies a meaning external to the interpreter's preferences.

[14] *See, with a similar critique*, DAVID M. BEATTY, THE ULTIMATE RULE OF LAW, 11 (2004).

[15] This may also be presented as an instrument of the commitments inherent in constitutionalism highlighted by Jed Rubenfeld. Such commitment does not simply entail that constitutional norms have a meaning that is not dependent on a changing political will, but that such commitment is not fully, ex ante specified. As stated by Rubenfeld: "This openness in constitutional law is sometimes condemned for imparting too much uncertainty into our basic legal order and for conferring too much discretionary power on the judges who interpret that order. But this openness is part of what it means to live by self-given commitments over time. It is part of the nature of commitment that its full entailments can never be known until they have been lived out, and lived under, for an extended period of time." JED RUBENFELD, FREEDOM AND TIME – A THEORY OF CONSTITUTIONAL SELF-GOVERNMENT 188 (2001).

[16] Scalia, *supra* note 12, at 856–62, 861.

judicial process in giving meaning to substantive areas of discretion of the law? Such theories do not choose formalism because they necessarily believe it to be the best method of ascertaining or giving meaning to the law (in particular constitutions) but because they believe that it is the method that most effectively leaves the meaning of the constitution to be determined by the political process and not courts. But such a general presumption in favor of the political process in "interpreting constitutions" is itself a product of a systemic understanding of the constitution and its legal order;[17] one that must be justified.[18]

The third way to approach the normative gap inherent in the process of interpretation is by making a clear-cut distinction between the validity of judicial decisions and their appropriateness or correctness. The first is an objective process while the latter is largely subjective and has to be legitimated by the adherence of courts to a particular normative theory of the common good (substantive or procedural) or measured by its consequences.[19] To a certain extent, these theories appear to distinguish between the methods of interpretation to be employed by courts (which would determine the extent of indeterminacy of the rule) and the theories of constitutional justice or judicial adjudication that ought to guide them in the areas of judicial discretion ascertained by that indeterminacy. I am much closer to such an approach, but I also argue against a clear distinction between the objective and the subjective elements of interpretation. As stated, the subjective dimension is inherently part of all those methods of interpretation (even the more formal ones), and the best we can hope is for a process whereby the subjective preferences of judges are rendered objective in the interpretative process in two ways. In the first place, they are filtered through a process of justification that, as stated by

[17] Let me note that, paradoxically, departing from such systemic understanding is in contradiction with a formalist conception of interpretation.

[18] Some of these authors (notably Vermeulen) put forward some arguments highlighting what they perceive as the institutional malfunctions of courts, but even if we were to fully accept their portrait of courts, we would need to compare that with the institutional malfunctions of the political process. Neil Komesar has consistently noted this problem of single institutional analysis in legal scholarship. See NEIL KOMESAR, IMPERFECT ALTERNATIVES: CHOOSING INSTITUTIONS IN LAW, ECONOMICS, AND PUBLIC POLICY (1994) and NEIL KOMESAR, LAW'S LIMITS: THE ROLE OF COURTS, THE RULE OF LAW AND THE SUPPLY AND DEMAND OF RIGHTS (2001).

[19] See, e.g. (and ignoring the remarkable differences among them), JOHN HART ELY, DEMOCRACY AND DISTRUST: A THEORY OF JUDICIAL REVIEW (1980); NEIL MACCORMICK, LEGAL REASONING AND LEGAL THEORY (1978), and Neil MacCormick, On Legal Decisions and Their Consequences: From Dewey to Dworkin, 58 N.Y.U. L. REV. 239, 250 (1983); RONALD DWORKIN, TAKING RIGHTS SERIOUSLY (1977) and RONALD DWORKIN, A MATTER OF PRINCIPLE (1985) (which, however, also has elements of the fourth approach); RICHARD POSNER, THE PROBLEMS OF JURISPRUDENCE (1990).

Owen Fiss, "is bounded by the existence of a community that recognises and adheres to the disciplining rule used by the interpreter and that is defined by its recognition of those rules."[20] In reality, the constraints of this community and its language become embedded in the interpretative process, and this corresponds to the idea of interpretation as the cultural software of judges. It is in this way that such constraints are not external but internal to the process of interpretation. Furthermore, objectivity is promoted by the requirement built into the process of justification of fitting individual judicial decisions into a systemic understanding of the legal order. But that systemic understanding is not simply a product of the adoption of a particular normative theory; it is constructed in discourse with other actors and institutions. This is so both because courts internalize the power of those institutions to challenge their decisions and, mostly, because courts want their decisions to be internalized in the behavior of other institutions. Judicial decisions will be appropriated by other institutions that compete in giving meaning to the legal rules, and they will be more effective the more that they are susceptible to institutional internalization by those institutions. Only in this way will judicial decisions change decision-making processes and not only particular outcomes. In developing a systemic understanding of their legal order, judges therefore become bound by the intellectual path that it imposes on future decisions and by the need to be institutionally effective.

In my view, the first three approaches to the normative gap involved in the process of interpretation are increasingly unfit for a context of legal and constitutional pluralism. The first expects too much from courts and ignores the limits of their legitimacy, while the second trusts the political process too much and always perceives courts as subsidiary in shaping the normative preferences of a particular political community. The third approach is still too court centered. It tries to guide courts toward the best normative outcomes without taking into consideration that the latter may have to be the product of a discourse between courts and other actors and institutions. Instead, we need to emphasize methods of interpretation that require courts to articulate the systemic impact of their decisions and that are more apt to engage them in a dialogue with the other institutions that compete in giving meaning to the law. It is this that will be increasingly necessary in a context of legal and constitutional pluralism, as I try to demonstrate next.

One of the consequences of both internal and external legal pluralism is the multiplication of the rules that compete in addressing a particular legal issue and the tendency to produce normative ambiguity in rule making. In other

---

[20] Fiss, *supra* note 9, at 745.

words, courts are increasingly required to arbitrate among normative claims that are equally substantiated in formal terms either by virtue of conflicting rules or by virtue of normative conflicts that are internal to the rules themselves. This may be so because the political community has committed itself to competing legal orders (state, supranational, and international), because within a particular legal order there are different instances of normative production dominated by different interests, or simply because agreement is so difficult to achieve in the process of producing legal rules that they are bound to reflect competing normative claims. The textual ambiguity of rules is, in this instance, a simple reflection of a deeper normative ambiguity. The pluralism of power that I mentioned previously and the particular institutional contexts of rule decision making in the international context, for example, often entail that radically different normative preferences are entrenched in strong bargaining positions, which make it particularly difficult to reach a real normative agreement. As a consequence, such rules can often be characterized as "incompletely theorised agreements,"[21] agreements reached on the basis of different normative assumptions. They are the product of a complex political bargain where, to a certain extent, there was an agreement not to agree. So long as the political process itself is unable to follow on that incomplete agreement, such decisions are bound to lead, intentionally or not, to a delegation to courts of the final decisions on those issues. Often, in this context, courts cannot even defer to the political process, either because they are required to give specific meaning to rules in particular individual disputes where the political process is no longer present or because – as is often the case in international, supranational, and federal systems – they face a conflict between different political processes. This is not necessarily negative: a political community may legitimately decide to exclude certain issues from the passions of the political process and delegate them to more insulated institutions. Similarly, political communities can decide to agree on very broad principles without articulating solutions to the conflicts that will necessarily occur in the practical application of such principles. This may be so to prevent collective action problems. We trust in the long-term advantage of committing to such principles and in its universal potential while reducing the transaction and information costs involved in agreeing rule by rule on each specific question. Political communities also allow agreements on delicate and controversial political questions by politically deferring their practical effects to a legal solution to be derived from a universally agreed-on

---

[21] The expression belongs to SUNSTEIN, *supra* note 12, but it is used here for a rather different purpose.

principle. Furthermore, in light of the increased rigidity of law making, doing so creates the risk of freezing particular legal solutions (and therefore imprisoning current generations to the decisions of the past), and principles have the advantage of being open to the future.[22] They allow for a more dynamic interpretation.

All this creates a paradox. Pluralism leads the political process to increasingly delegate to courts decisions of high political and social sensitivity through the adoption of conflicting norms or very open-ended rules and principles. But this same context of pluralism tends both to increase the contestability of judicial decisions and to make rigid their legal outcomes (because the political process is less capable of overcoming them).

The only way for courts to deal with such paradox is by developing a particular model of interpretation. First, they must be open to arguments that are sensitive to the complex economic, social, and political questions that arc raiscd in such cascs. This is also a consequence of the fact that such decisions of particular social and political visibility will be addressed by a larger community of actors and by the public opinion in general.[23] But, as stated earlier, judges should not simply recognize the limits of formalism and take notice of the economic, social, and political impact of some of their decisions. It is not even enough that they make use of such arguments in light of a particular normative theory.[24] They must do so in a legal manner. The legal manner requires those arguments to be presented through a language familiar to the legal community (the cultural language of law) and fit to a particular systemic understanding of the legal order.[25] It is this process that filters the subjective preferences of judges into an objective process of interpretation of the law, legitimating the use of those arguments. Second, judicial reasoning must not ignore the fact that law is interpreted in competition

---

[22] *Cinquanta anni di attivita della Corte constituzionale – Relazione del Presidente Emerito G. Zagrebelsky*, in OCCASSIONE DELL'INCONTRO DEL (21 aprile 2006) al Palazzo del Quirinale.

[23] See Chaïm Perelman, *La motivation des décisions de justice, essai de synthèse*, in LA MOTIVATION DES DECISIONS DE JUSTICE, 421ff. (Chaïm Perelman & P. Foriers eds., 1978).

[24] Such as utilitarianism, rights based or any other.

[25] Even Stanley Fish recognizes this type of language constraint on the interpretative process: "the constraints will inhere not in the language of the text (statute or poem) or in the context . . . in which it is embedded, but in the cultural assumptions within which both texts and context take shape for situated agents" (STANLEY FISH, DOING WHAT COMES NATURALLY – CHANGE, RHETORIC, AND THE PRACTICE OF THEORY IN LITERARY AND LEGAL STUDIES 300 (1989)). My point is that such cultural assumptions are particular to the law and to the community of judicial discourse. Therefore, my reference to the methods of interpretation as the software of courts uses the expression in a similar sense to that used by Jack M. Balkin (see JACK M. BALKIN, CULTURAL SOFTWARE: A THEORY OF IDEOLOGY (1998)). See also Fiss, *supra* note 9.

and/or cooperation with other institutions (notably, political processes and other jurisdictions). In this way, judicial decisions should take into account this discursive dimension with other institutions. For example, with respect to the political process, it is important for the democratic delegation to courts that I have mentioned not to become so extensive or systematic as to reduce the space for democratic deliberation. The answers to be given by courts, in this context, should be mindful of this concern and, as far as possible, should not preempt future democratic deliberation on those questions but, instead, help to promote and rationalize such deliberation. The same regards the relationship with competing jurisdictions. When courts consider that a proper understanding of their role requires them to engage with other jurisdictions, they must reason so as to present legal arguments that, as far as possible, can be understood beyond their unique context of application on those cases.

The way for courts to answer to the need to contextualize the reasoning that emerges from their broader communities of discourse and the increased normative ambiguity of the legal framework in which they are called on to operate, while remaining faithful to an objective conception of the process of interpretation, is by a reinforced use of teleological reasoning coupled with a clearer articulation of the systemic understanding of the legal order that guides the reconstruction of the telos. We could talk, in this way, of teleological and meta-teleological interpretation.[26] Teleological and meta-teleological interpretation force courts to articulate the normative preferences that they attribute to particular rules and to relate them to the normative preferences of the overall legal order. Discussion of the goals of the rules and of the legal system allows for contextual arguments while also requiring such discussion to take place in legal terms, subject to the mechanisms of objectivation involved in the use of legal methods of interpretation and in the requirement to fit them to an overall normative understanding of the legal order. Judges are constrained precisely through the reasoning necessary to demonstrate what the particular goal of a legal rule is and how it fits with the overall normative systemic preferences of their legal order.[27] In this respect,

---

[26] The latter expression is borrowed from Mitchel Lasser. *See* Mitchel Lasser, Judicial Deliberations: A Comparative Analysis of Judicial Transparency and Legitimacy (2004).

[27] Bengoetxea, MacCormick, and Soriano talk of a teleology that is bounded "by the need to connect the texts to values that belong to the whole constitutional enterprise, not just to a judge's own idiosyncratic world view and personal value system." Joxerramon Bengoetxea, Neil MacCormick & Leonor Moral Soriano, *Integration and Integrity in the Legal Reasoning of the European Court of Justice, in* The European Court of Justice, Academy of European Law European University Institute 45 (Gráinne de Búrca and J. H. H. Weiler eds., 2001).

teleological and meta-teleological reasoning reinforce judicial accountability, as they increase transparency as to its normative choices involved in hard cases. In the context of ambiguous or conflicting norms, telos and systemic arguments impose a greater constraint than pure reference to wording or intent. They bind courts to a consistent normative reading of those provisions.

But such reasoning also promotes the second requirement of judicial reasoning under pluralism. It furthers discursive engagement with other institutions. First, by articulating the normative goals of rules and their connection to the overall value system of their legal order, courts set the stage for a substantive discussion. Instead of presenting interpretation simply as a product of their interpretative authority, they recognize that it involves normative choices that are highlighted in their reasoning, even if they are ultimately attributed to the legal system itself. While teleological reasoning favors a debate among alternative normative preferences in the interpretation of a rule, a simple appeal to text would hide those alternatives and preclude a debate. Teleological reasoning fosters the conditions necessary for such a debate in which the plurality of actors of the community of judicial discourse can participate.

Second, while being constrained by the need to relate particular interpretations to broader systemic preferences, courts also shape the actions of other institutions with which they will engage in such systemic thinking. While formal arguments must accept a lack of coherence in the legal order (because the authority of interpretation derives only from the text of each rule, and, as a consequence, a deeper normative compatibility between rules should not play a role in interpretation), systemic interpretation has built in the requirements of coherence and consistency. It is not enough for a court to be consistent in how interprets a particular legal rule; it is necessary for it to try to make an interpretation of a rule that is consistent with its interpretation of the entire legal system, pursuing the ideal of a coherent legal order. These consistency and coherence requirements can be pursued only by teleological and meta-teleological reasoning, which highlights the underlying values of the rules. This is not to say that a legal order will always be fully coherent. It is, instead, a recognition that the role of courts in political communities that have subscribed to the rule of law is also that of maximizing coherence. And, in this role, they interact with the political process because such systemic interpretation of the law, and its inherent pursuit of legal coherence, impose a similar requirement of political consistency and coherence on the political process, which the latter may ignore but must do so in a transparent and justifiable manner. Such judicial reasoning is therefore conducive to greater transparency and accountability on the part of the political process. This is particularly important in the context of pluralism, where coherence tends to be increasingly challenged.[28]

Third, one of the consequences of legal and constitutional pluralism highlighted here is the increased integration of different courts and jurisdictions and the multijurisdictional application of legal rules. Courts from one jurisdiction increasingly apply law from another jurisdiction or decide cases that will be put into effect in another jurisdiction. Some supranational courts (e.g., the European Court of Justice) have to interpret law that will be applied by courts from very different legal orders. Moreover, in some of these instances there is no clear legal or jurisdictional hierarchy, or, at least, it is a contested one. In such a context, it is only natural for the classic forms of jurisdictional hierarchy to be replaced by more complex forms of interaction in which interpretation plays a mediating role.[29] Teleological interpretation is the methodology of interpretation that most favors communication between those different jurisdictions. It is also the form of interpretation that can best guide courts in a decentralized context involving a plurality of legal orders. First, because it not only provides a specific legal outcome for the case at hand but also offers a broader normative lesson for addressing future cases, it reduces the legal information and transaction costs of courts.[30] Second, because more formal types of arguments (e.g., text) tend to be more dependent on the legal culture and language of a particular legal order, they travel less easily among different legal orders.[31] These difficulties of legal translation are even more manifest where courts have to interpret rules that have been adopted in a plurality of languages, all with equal legal value. It is not

[28] For a discussion of this challenge and a presentation of coherence as one of the ideals of constitutionalism, *see* Julio Baquero Cruz, *The Legacy of the Maastricht-Urteil and the Pluralist Movement*, 14 EUR. L.J. 389 (2008).

[29] *See* Geneviève Giudicelli-Delage, *Les jeux de l'interprétation entre discontinuités et interactions*, *in* LE CHAMP PENAL, MELANGES EN L'HONNEUR DU PROFESSEUR REYNALD OTTENHOF 20 (2006).

[30] This is also why judicial minimalism is difficult to fit with such types of legal orders even if, in some instances, it can be presented as an attempt to preserve courts from the increasingly difficult choices that political pluralism tends to delegate to them. For an introduction to judicial minimalism, *see* SUNSTEIN, *supra* note 12. I believe that, though judicial minimalism might be a necessity (arising out of the particular difficulties of deliberation or of the social context surrounding it), it ought not to be transformed into a normative theory for judicial decision making. Instead, whether a judge should adopt a judicial minimalist approach in the particular circumstances of a case ought to be a function of a different normative theory of judicial adjudication.

[31] Christian Baldus & Friedrike Vogel, *Metodología del derecho privado comunitario: Problemas y perspectivas en cuanto a la interpretación literal e histórica*, 10 ANUARIO DA FACULTADE DE DEREITO DA UNIVERSIDADE DA CORUÑA 77, 84ff. (2006).

uncommon for the same legal rule to be susceptible to rather different textual interpretations depending on the linguistic version one appeals to. Because they all have the same legal value, courts must arbitrate such linguistic disputes under different criteria.[32] In all these instances they must develop a reasoning that looks beyond the form and into the normative values and goals that can be attributed to those rules.

Institutional Choices and Judicial Dialogues

As stated already, judicial adjudication is also a function of institutional constraints and must take into account the interplay between courts and other institutions.[33] This is so both at a pragmatic level and at a normative level. Courts must be aware that they are one among a set of institutional alternatives that compete in giving meaning to the law. Traditionally this competition takes place between courts and the political process within a state. I have argued before that, in this respect, there is nothing fundamentally new about constitutional pluralism: pluralism is inherent in constitutionalism because its ideals authorize, if not promote, equally normatively valid and competing constitutional claims.[34] There can be no monopoly of constitutional claims, and often competing constitutional claims are expressed by different institutions all empowered to give meaning to the constitution. What the current forms of legal and constitutional pluralism have done is multiply these institutions, notably, courts from competing jurisdictions and different sites of power even within a state.

But this entails a normative lesson as well as a pragmatic one. At the normative level, a court should not a priori assume that it is superior or inferior to any other institution in giving meaning to a constitution (and the law). This requires us to move beyond either the traditional American debate of countermajoritarianism (which always assumes a weaker legitimacy of courts) or the recent European Continental tradition of unquestioned judicial supremacy. Courts have a legitimacy different from the legitimacy of the political process. The formal authority of courts with regard to the political process flows from the legal document that attributes them powers of judicial

---

[32] *Id.*   [33] Poiares Maduro, *supra* note 1.

[34] *See* Miguel Poiares Maduro, *Europe and the Constitution: What If This Is As Good As It Gets?* *in* Constitutionalism beyond the State (Marlene Wind & Joseph Weiler eds., 2003); Miguel Poiares Maduro, *From Constitutions to Constitutionalism: A Constitutional Approach for Global Governance, in* 1 Global Governance and the Quest for Justice (Douglas Lewis ed., 2006); Jan Komárek & Matej Avbelj, *Four Visions of Constitutional Pluralism, A Communication between Miguel Poiares Maduro, Neil Walker, Mattias Kumm and Julio Baquero Cruz* (EUI Working Paper forthcoming).

review. When that is the case, it is that legal document (e.g., a constitution) that creates the framework for such institutional competition. If the idea were that courts' legitimacy could never be opposed to that of the democratic legitimacy of the political process, then the idea of judicial review itself would be under attack.[35] Whether courts should defer to the political process therefore has to be a function of a more sophisticated theory of institutional choice that is part of the three dimensions of judicial adjudication that I have mentioned. In this way, the degree and forms of judicial intervention must also be a function of the institutional alternatives to courts. Courts must build in the capacity to make such institutional judgments in light of the body of rules that they are called on to interpret and apply. Part of the process of interpretation involves, therefore, an element of meta-interpretation: which institution is in a better position to give meaning to the values inherent in the relevant legal rules and to arbitrate the competing legal or constitutional claims that they give rise to.[36] Naturally, there is no reason not to extend such reasoning to the increased institutional competition among courts.

This normative conclusion imposes a certain degree of institutional modesty on courts, but this ought not to be confused with a weaker legitimacy or a general preference for judicial self-restraint. On the contrary, my claim is that no such general propositions are useful or correct. Constitutionalism (and pluralism) requires a normative theory guiding institutional choices among courts or between courts and the political process, and does not establish a general, ex ante preference for any of those institutions.

I am particular interested here in the institutional competition among courts that has been generated by the recent forms of pluralism. That is the case with internal forms of pluralism, such those in the EU legal order,

[35] This is not to say that the idea of judicial review is conceivable only where courts are given powers of constitutional review, and much less that the pursuit of constitutional values is primarily a task of the judiciary. There are certainly states that do not have a system of constitutional review and, nevertheless, by reasons, among others, of political and constitutional culture, may be even more effective in protecting those values. The only point made here is that the legitimacy of courts, when given powers of judicial review, and the extent of those powers, is not weaker than the legitimacy of the political process. These differences may explain why the debate in the United States is much stronger and dominated by the countermajoritarian fear. In the United States, judicial review was, to a large extent, a creation of the Supreme Court itself. The American debate is therefore contaminated by a kind of original sin syndrome (Alec Stone Sweet, *Why Europe Rejected American Judicial Review – And Why It May Not Matter*, 101 MICH. L. REV. 2744 (2003)).

[36] Neil Komesar has consistently argued in this sense, a view I have subscribed to. *See* KOMESAR, IMPERFECT ALTERNATIVES, *supra* note 18; KOMESAR, LAW'S LIMITS, *supra* note 18; MIGUEL POIARES MADURO, WE THE COURT – THE EUROPEAN COURT OF JUSTICE AND THE EUROPEAN ECONOMIC CONSTITUTION (1998).

where the supremacy of EU law over national constitutional law is some-times contested by national constitutional courts and where, more generally, the application of EU law ultimately depends on national courts. But it is also visible in forms of external pluralism. The fragmented character of the international legal order increasingly means that different legal regimes and courts may compete in addressing the same issue. Such competition among courts may even take place in interpreting the same body of rules, as some international legal rules are also increasingly invoked and applied across a variety of international jurisdictions. That will be, for example, one of the consequences of applying international human rights rules in the context of the World Trade Organization. The interpretation of such human rights would no longer be exclusive of the bodies that have been specifically created for that purpose (e.g., the UN committees) and would also be taken over by the WTO judicial bodies. Finally, the legal externalities that I described earlier also entail an indirect form of jurisdictional competition.

How should courts deal with this? Should they continue to act purely under the internal logic of their legal order, or should they take into account such competition? One could develop normative arguments to sustain that courts ought, in effect, to shift their allegiance from their own legal order to a broader legal order that would be, for example, a global order composed of all these legal orders. But courts are ultimately bound to the political community to which their legal order is associated, and any such debate would lead us into a very difficult inquiry into what exactly the new political community would be or whether we could abandon such a link between courts and the particular legal order whose integrity they are supposed to protect.[37] My assumption here is much more modest: courts act to maximize the integrity of their legal order, but that does not mean that they should not be aware of the external impact of or on their decisions. This is so for two reasons. First it may be the courts' own legal order to impose openness to the outside. It may require them, for example, to internalize the effects of some of their judicial decisions on external legal orders and outside interests. Or it may impose on them the construction of certain domestic normative values in light of a broader community of values than simply their domestic political community. Second is because courts should act so as to protect the substan-tive and not the formal integrity of their legal order. In other words, they should be more concerned with the promotion of the normative preferences of their legal order than with the protection of its formal and jurisdictional

---

[37] It would, in fact, require us either to abandon the constitutional democratic ideal that all law must ultimately be traced back to the will of the people or to enter into inquiry of what the new people or peoples will be.

purity. In a pluralist context where the effect of their rules and decisions may be influenced by other jurisdictions, this may require a more flexible approach.[38] Certainly, it does require them, as argued herein, to develop forms of institutional choice and institutional dialogue with other courts. Such institutional awareness becomes, in this case, a pragmatic imposition. As to the criteria for institutional choice, it will necessarily depend on the legal order in which those courts operate, but we can highlight the conditions necessary for judicial dialogue and deference.

The first necessary condition for judicial dialogue is some form of common language. We need such language to secure the communication between courts and between legal orders that is necessary to reap the benefits of constitutional and legal pluralism while also preventing and managing potential conflicts.[39] There must be some voluntary agreement on a basic set of meta-methodological rules.[40]

First, courts must recognize such pluralism and the fact that it imposes some form of recognition and adjustment of each legal order to the plurality of equally legitimate claims of authority made by other legal orders. Second, courts' awareness of the constitutional and legal pluralism in which they operate demands that, when deciding in areas of jurisdictional conflicts, they should, as much as possible, try to frame their decisions so as to fit both with their own legal order and with competing legal orders. This is how courts can secure the integrity and coherence of the law, and of their legal order in particular, in a context of competing legal orders and jurisdictions over a particular issue.

One must note, however, that there is an important difference between instances of internal and external pluralism. In the context of pluralism that is internal to a certain legal order supported by its own political community, all competing courts must commit to the integrity and coherence of that legal order. They are, in effect, equally bound by their particular legal orders and by

[38] Robert Ahdieh argues that an exclusive reference to dialogue might be misleading because some of the forms of interaction between courts in the international domain include elements of both horizontal comity and vertical hierarchy (he refers, in these cases, to dialectical review). *See* Robert Ahdieh, *Between Dialogue and Decree: International Review of National Courts,* 79 N.Y.U. L. Rev. 2029 (2004).

[39] I discuss many of the benefits of legal and constitutional pluralism in a variety of texts, notably: on the EU, *see* Poiares Maduro, *Europe and the Constitution, supra* note 34, and Poiares Maduro, *supra* note 1; in the international context, see Poiares Maduro, *From Constitutions to Constitutionalism, supra* note 34. See also Komarek & Avebelj, *supra* note 34.

[40] Klaus Günther talks, more ambitiously, of a universal code of legality (a metalanguage involving substantive values) that "already works in the daily routine of legal communication in spheres of interlegality." *Legal Pluralism or Uniform Concept of Law – Globalisation as a Problem of Legal Theory,* 5 No Foundations 16 (2008).

the broader legal order; the effort required of them is that of trying to reconcile the potentially conflicting claims between the legal orders. Such commitment flows from their own domestic political community commitment to a broader political community. This is the case of the European Union. National courts when acting as EU courts are obliged to reason and justify its decisions in the context of a coherent and integrated European legal order. In fact, the European legal order integrates both the decisions of national and European courts interpreting and applying EU law, and, as such, any judicial body must justify its decisions in a universal manner by reference to the EU context. The decisions of national courts applying EU law must be grounded in an interpretation that could be applied by any other national court in similar situations. This is the core of the CILFIT doctrine.[41] It requires national courts to decide as European courts and to internalize in their decisions the consequences to the European legal order as a whole.[42]

The situation is different with regard to external pluralism, where there is no order of orders supported by a commitment to a new political community. Or, perhaps better, we cannot state that courts have an allegiance to competing legal orders. They cannot be considered as bound by the international and/or foreign legal orders as they are by their internal legal order. As I have already stated, I believe that to defend that would challenge the link between the judiciary and a particular political community. Such a move would require a particularly strong alternative normative justification, which I have yet to find. Moreover, it would affect the separation of powers within the political community to which those courts belong, as they could oppose their respective political process with a legitimacy flowing from a different or broader political community, something that could no longer be arbitrated by the constitution of their own political community. Instead, in the context of external pluralism, courts must take account of their legal order's external commitments and openness and of the need to negotiate their effectiveness with other jurisdictions. In this respect, what we can demand from them is that they interpret the law, as far as possible, in a manner that minimizes potential jurisdictional conflicts.

While in the context of internal pluralism courts are bound by competing legal orders and have a mandate to reconcile them in light of a requirement of "universalizability," in the context of external pluralism, courts are bound by a particular legal order. However, both the external openness of their legal order and the need to negotiate their jurisdictional effectiveness with other

---

[41] Case 283/81, Cilfit e.a., E.C.R. 3415 (1982).
[42] *See* Miguel Poiares Maduro, *Interpreting European Law: Judicial Adjudication in a Context of Constitutional Pluralism*, 1 EUR. J. LEGAL STUD. (2007).

legal orders may require them to, as far as possible, interpret their legal order so as to minimize conflicts with those other legal orders.

These differences between internal and external pluralism are also relevant with regard to the use of foreign legal sources and comparative law. This is a particular useful form of establishing judicial dialogues, but it is not devoid of controversy and difficulties. In the context of internal pluralism, the use of comparative law arguments is both a requirement imposed by the commitment to an order composed of a plurality of orders and a pragmatic necessity generated by the gaps encountered by judges in the bottom-up process of construction of that legal order and by the search for the social acceptance of judicial decisions in such a plurality of legal orders.[43]

In the context of external pluralism, the use of foreign legal sources and comparative law has also emerged, but it is even more contested.[44] I believe that there are three ways one can use and make reference to foreign legal sources and foreign courts in our own legal order. The first is consensual: when a foreign legal source is mostly a matter of fact in the decision of the court. This is the case of private international law, where a court might have to use international legal sources or the rules of another legal system as a matter of fact to reach a decision in a case.

The second model of using foreign legal sources is already more controversial: the use of foreign legal sources (including decisions of other courts) as an argument (but not an argument of authority) in the context of deliberation and/or the justification of a certain judicial decision. There are three possible reasons to use foreign legal sources in this way. The first one is intellectual persuasion, which is the same thing as scholarship. As a judge one may ask

---

[43] On the importance of comparative law in the context of the EU legal order, *see* Pierre Pescatore, *Le recours, dans la jurisprudence de la Cour de justice des Communautés européennes, a des normes déduites de la comparaison des droits des états membres, Conférences et rapports, in* II REVUE INTERNATIONALE DE DROIT COMPARE 337 (1979–1980). *See also* K. Mortelmans, *Les lacunes provisoires en droit communautaire,* CAHIERS DE DROIT EUROPEEN, 410 (1981); Pierre Pescatore, *La carence du législateur communautaire et le devoir du juge, in* RECHTVERGLE-ICHUNG, EUROPARECHT UND STAATENINTEGRATION- GEDÄCHTNISSCHRIFT 559 (G. Lücke, G. Ress, M. R. Will-Carl Heymanns eds., Verlag KG 1983), and Koen Lenaerts, *Interlocking Legal Orders in the European Union and Comparative Law,* 52 INT'L & COMP. L.Q. 873 (2003). For a more in depth discussion, also regarding how comparative law should be used, *see* Poiares Maduro, *supra* note 42.

[44] *See* Konrad Schieman, *A Response to the Judge as Comparatist,* 80 TUL. L. REV. 281 (2005); A. Rosas: *With a Little Help from My Friends: International Case-Law as a Source of Reference for the EU Courts,* 1 THE GLOBAL COMMUNITY: Y.B. INT'L L. & JURIS. 203 (2005). This issue has been particularly discussed in the United States. For a notable example, *see* the debate between Justices Scalia and Breyer: *The Relevance of Foreign Legal Materials in U.S. Constitutional Cases: A Conversation between Justice Antonin Scalia and Justice Stephen Breyer,* 3 INT'L J. CONST. L. 519 (2005).

oneself: has that court solved a legal problem that is similar to the one I face in a manner that is convincing to me? If it has, then I will use it. And maybe the best way to do so is by including in my justification reference to how that other court has decided: it flows from the requirement to fit the justification of the decision with its deliberation process.[45]

The second reason is as a form of communication between legal systems. This is even more controversial, but it is most likely justified when legal systems interpret the same rules or when their legal orders communicate or interlock between themselves. It corresponds to the instances of interpretative competition and legal externalities that I have already identified in the context of external pluralism. To a certain extent, looking at the jurisprudence of another court promotes some form of informal coherence between those legal orders where they jurisdictionally interact: this helps manage the legal externalities of the jurisprudence of one court in another court or in another legal order. A court may want to prevent such legal externalities because it is aware that it is equally subject to the externalities created by the other jurisdiction. By paying attention to the decisions of this jurisdiction, the court invites this jurisdiction to reciprocate and pay equal attention to its decisions. A good example is the mutual attention that the European Court of Justice, the European Court of Human Rights, and the European Free Trade Association court give to one another's case law. Through this communication among legal systems, courts manage legal overlaps.

The third possible reason is what former Chief Justice Aharon Barak of Israel described, in a rather beautiful metaphor, as foreign law being a mirror of oneself. This is the idea that by looking at other courts you can better differentiate yourself or enter into a process akin to judicial introspection, an effort to better understand what you yourself are doing.

These are three reasons to use foreign legal sources as an argument of persuasion in judicial reasoning. Much more controversial and contestable is the use of foreign legal sources as legal authority, so as to argue that judges are, to a certain extent, bound by such foreign legal sources. This depends, in my view, on the instrument that the court is called on to interpret and on the normative preferences of the legal order in which it operates. As I have insisted, the legitimacy of a court comes from a particular political community, and it is based on the values of that polity, values that are expressed in the legal document that the court is supposed to interpret. It is this that guarantees that we are subject to the rules for which we have participated in the process of adoption. Hence, to use a foreign legal source without reference to the

---

[45] *See* MacCormick, Legal Reasoning, *supra* note 19.

domestic political community can be perceived as challenging the very ideal of democracy and the rule of law. At the same time, however, it may be that political community itself that requires courts to recognize a particular legal authority to foreign sources of the law. This might be so if the legal instrument the court is supposed to interpret and the normative preferences of its legal order adhere to a universal construction of their own legal values – in other words, if courts are instructed to interpret the rules of their legal order in light of the rules of another legal order.

There is a final issue that needs to be addressed. The institutional awareness and modesty demanded by legal and constitutional pluralism will necessarily express themselves in forms of jurisdictional deference. Courts must define the conditions under which the protection of the substantive integrity of their legal order might be better achieved by deferring to other jurisdictions. Also in this respect, it is likely that differences will emerge in cases of internal and external pluralism. The internal pluralism commitment to an integrated and coherent legal order of orders can be secured only if there is a systemic compatibility among all the involved legal orders. Different legal orders and institutions can defer to one another and accommodate their jurisdictional claims so long as they are compatible in systemic terms. For example, the supremacy and direct effect of EU law is, de facto, recognized by national constitutional orders because it is assumed, and properly so, that there is a systemic compatibility between the former and the latter; that is, there is an identity as to the essential values of those legal orders.[46] Law of the European Union does not challenge the constitutional identity of national constitutional orders because it is grounded in the same legal values. In the same way, national legal orders can be part of the EU legal order and a vehicle for its implementation because they also respect the same fundamental values.[47] The same approach has, to a certain extent, been adopted by the European Court of Human Rights regarding potential conflicts between European Convention case law and acts of the European Union.[48] These approaches can be seen as a result of the development by the Court of Justice of the basic principles of the European Union's legal order precisely by reference to national constitutional

---

[46] *See* Poires Maduro, *supra* note 1, at 504; THE EUROPEAN COURTS AND NATIONAL COURTS: DOCTRINE AND JURISPRUDENCE – LEGAL CHANGE IN ITS SOCIAL CONTEXT (Anne-Marie Slaughter, Alec Stone Sweet & J. H. H. Weiler eds., 1998); Bruno Witte, *Direct Effect, Supremacy, and the Nature of the Legal Order, in* THE EVOLUTION OF EU LAW 177–213 (Paul Craig & Gráinne de Búrca eds., 1999).

[47] *See* Treaty on European Union, arts. 6 & 46; Case C-380/05, Centro Europa, 7 E.C.R. 0000 (2008), particularly Opinion of Advocate General Maduro.

[48] Bosphorus Hava Yolları Turizm ve Ticaret Anonim Şirketi (Bosphorus Airways) v. Ireland [GC], no. 4036/98 Eur. Ct. H.R. (2005).

orders and to the European Convention of Human Rights and Fundamental Freedoms. This fostered the systemic compatibility necessary to support a fruitful dialogue between courts. Such systemic compatibility allows, in turn, for a systemic and comprehensive jurisdictional deference. Deference, in this case, takes place at the systemic level. It is a deference of systems and not simply of rules. This is clear in the EU context, where national constitutional courts, once having recognized the fundamental identity between the two legal orders, tend to fully defer to the jurisdiction of the EU legal order.

The situation is different in the context of external pluralism, where such general systemic identity cannot normally be established (in particular, as a consequence of the absence of an underlying political community). In this case, what courts might develop are criteria for functional equivalence. In certain areas of the law or with respect to certain rules, courts may have to accept that the protection of the normative preferences of their legal order might be achieved as well or even better by deferring to a foreign or international jurisdiction. For that to be the case, however, a case-by-case assessment of the functional equivalence of that international rule and system is necessary.

Ultimately, however, the objective for courts in all these instances should be the same: not to confuse their jurisdictional authority with the integrity of their legal order. This a good final example of the challenges brought by constitutional and legal pluralism to courts: not to change their constitutional allegiance but to adjust their forms of reasoning and institutional role to their new constitutional context. It is in this way they will be not only subject to legal and constitutional pluralism but also able to shape it.

The Puzzle of Democratic Legitimacy

13. Whose Constitution(s)? International Law, Constitutionalism, and Democracy

SAMANTHA BESSON

Introduction

International constitutionalism is *en vogue* among scholars of general international law. Promoted since the 1930s in Europe[1] and rediscovered in the 1990s,[2] it has meant different things to different people, has been promoted

---

[1] *See, e.g.*, Alfred Verdross, DIE VERFASSUNG DER VÖLKERRECHTSGEMEINSCHAFT (1926); Hermann Mosler, *The International Society as a Legal Community*, 140 RECUEIL DES COURS 1 (1974).

[2] *See, e.g.*, Pierre-Marie Dupuy, *The Constitutional Dimension of the Charter of the United Nations Revisited*, 1 MAX PLANCK Y.B. U.N. L. 1 (1997); Bardo Fassbender, *The United Nations Charter as the Constitution of the International Community*, 36 COLUM. J. TRANSNAT'L L. 529 (1998); Bardo Fassbender, *"We the Peoples of the United Nations"*: *Constituent Power and Constitutional Form in International Law, in* THE PARADOX OF CONSTITUTIONALISM: CONSTITUENT POWER AND CONSTITUTIONAL FORM 269 (Martin Loughlin & Neil Walker eds., 2007); Christian Walter, *Constitutionalising (Inter)national Governance – Possibilities for and Limits to the Development of an International Constitutional Law*, 44 GERMAN Y.B. INT'L L. 192 (2001); Brun-Otto Bryde, *Konstitutionalisierung des Völkerrechts und Internationalisierung des Verfassungsrechts*, 42 DER STAAT 61 (2003); Thomas Franck, *Is the UN Charter a Constitution? in* VERHANDELN FÜR DEN FRIEDEN – NEGOTIATING FOR PEACE, LIBER AMICORUM TONO EITEL 95 (Jochen A. Frowein et al. eds., 2003); Thomas Cottier & Maya Hertig, *The Prospects of 21st Century Constitutionalism*, 7 MAX PLANCK Y.B. U.N. L. 261 (2003); Anne Peters, *Global Constitutionalism Revisited, in* A CENTURY OF INTERNATIONAL LAW – CENTENNIAL ESSAYS (The American Society of International Law, *available at* http://law.ubalt.edu/downloads/law_downloads/ILT_11_2005.pdf (last visited on 22 February 2009)) (2004); Anne Peters, *Compensatory Constitutionalism: The Function and Potential of Fundamental International Norms and Structures*, 19 LEIDEN J. INT'L. L. 579

Professor of Public International Law and European Law, University of Fribourg (Switzerland). This chapter was written within the framework of the SNF Project for a European Philosophy of European Law (PEOPEL). Special thanks are due to the editors Joel Trachtman and Jeff Dunoff and to Vicki Jackson for their detailed and valuable comments, as well as to my assistants Stéphanie Murenzi and Joanna Bourke-Martignoni for their help with the formal layout of the chapter.

for very different reasons, and has also been criticized on many different grounds.[3] For a long time, the idea of constitutionalism worked mostly as a heuristic device of unification or coherence in times of legal fragmentation within international law and of denationalization of constitutional law, but recently it has also become a catalyst of change and a promise of increased legitimacy both of and within international law.

Interestingly, and by contrast to what has been the case in discussions of European constitutionalism in recent years, international lawyers have only reluctantly started grappling with constitutional theory. They usually focus on what they take as material evidence of constitutionalization in international law, or draw, a contrario, compensatory conclusions from the deconstitution-alization of national law[4] or the internationalization of national constitutional law.[5] Thus, the development of relative normativity in general international law (e.g., the emergence of objective standards, the recognition of imperative international norms, the development of *erga omnes* rights and duties) and the emergence of new lawmakers besides states (e.g., the development of mul-tilateral law-making under international organizations' (IOs) auspices and the increasing influence of nongovernmental organizations (NGOs)) have gradually become the bits and pieces of a reconstructed international con-stitutional order,[6] whereas some of them may actually amount to little more

---

(2006); Essays *in* TOWARDS WORLD CONSTITUTIONALISM: ISSUES IN THE LEGAL ORDER-ING OF THE WORLD COMMUNITY (Ronald St.-J. MacDonald & Douglas M. Johnston eds., 2005); Erika De Wet, *The International Constitutional Order*, 55 INT'L & COMP. L.Q. 51 (2006); Armin von Bogdandy, *Constitutionalism in International Law: Comment on a Pro-posal from Germany*, 47 HARV. INT'L L.J. 223 (2006); Stefan Kadelbach & Thomas Kleinlein, *Überstaatliches Verfassungsrecht: Zur Konstitutionalisierung im Völkerrecht*, 44 ARCHIV DES VÖLKERRECHTS 235 (2006).

[3] For a genealogy, *see* Cottier & Hertig, *supra* note 2; Hélène Ruiz Fabri & Constance Grewe, *La constitutionnalisation à l'épreuve du droit international et du droit européen*, *in* LES DYNAMIQUES DU DROIT EUROPÉEN EN DÉBUT DE SIÈCLE, ÉTUDES EN L'HONNEUR DE JEAN-CLAUDE GAUTRON 189 (Loic Gard et al. eds., 2004); Jan Klabbers, *Constitutionalism Lite*, 1 INT'L ORG. L. REV. 31 (2004); von Bogdandy, *supra* note 2; Fassbender, "*We the Peoples of the United Nations*," *supra* note 2, at 270–73.

[4] *See* Jost Delbrück, *Exercising Public Authority beyond the State: Transnational Democracy and/or Alternative Legitimation Strategies?* 10 IND. J. GLOBAL LEGAL STUD. 29 (2003); Peters, *Global Constitutionalism*, *supra* note 2; and Peters, *Compensatory Constitutionalism*, *supra* note 2, at 580.

[5] *See* Cottier & Hertig, *supra* note 2, at 265–75.

[6] *See, e.g.*, de Wet, *supra* note 2, at 57–63; Erika de Wet, *The Emergence of International and Regional Value Systems as a Manifestation of the Emerging International Constitutional Order*, 19 LEIDEN J. INT'L L. 611 (2006); Bardo Fassbender, *Sovereignty and Constitutionalism in International Law*, *in* SOVEREIGNTY IN TRANSITION 115 (Neil Walker ed., 2003); Fassbender, "*We the Peoples of the United Nations*," *supra* note 2, at 276–81.

than disparate signs of deeper legalization, integration, or institutionalization of international law.[7]

When promoters of an international constitutional legal order address issues of constitutional theory, however, recent contributions address them without a definite conception of the complex normative concepts of constitution and constitutionalism. The reason for this reluctance usually lies in the (founded) fear of statism and, more precisely, of direct transposition of national constitutional concepts onto the international legal order, which would turn the latter into a world state constitutional order.[8] Most discussions of international constitutionalism still rely, however, on many a prioris in national constitutional theory without questioning or reinterpreting them. Basic constitutional questions like those of the constituent and constituted power, those of the values and interests it is meant to share in the constitutionalization process, and those of the procedures by which that entity constitutes itself as a polity and decides which values it wants to protect are often settled very intuitively by reference to positive international law or simply assumed to be self-evident. The problem is that they are not, and their reinterpretation in the international context actually lies at the core of any constitutional inquiry.[9]

Another related albeit often-eluded difficulty is that international constitutionalism can be understood fully only if it is apprehended together with national constitutionalism.[10] Traditionally, national constitutionalism entails a claim to unity, centralization, and hierarchy, and that claim has to be fundamentally revised in light of the partial overlap of different constitutional norms in the same legal order. Further, national constitutions in constitutional democracies traditionally constitute political sovereignty, and this self-constitution postulate needs to be revised when many constitutions are said to overlap on the same territory and the same population. What

---

[7] Peters, *Compensatory Constitutionalism*, supra note 2, at 597; Alec Stone, *What Is a Supranational Constitution? An Essay in International Relations Theory*, 56 REV. POL. 441 (1994).

[8] *See, e.g.,* Fassbender, *"We the Peoples of the United Nations," supra* note 2, at 274, 281.

[9] *See, e.g.,* Nicholas Tsagourias, *Introduction – Constitutionalism: A Theoretical Roadmap, in* TRANSNATIONAL CONSTITUTIONALISM, INTERNATIONAL AND EUROPEAN PERSPECTIVES 1 (Nicholas Tsagourias ed., 2007).

[10] *See* Samantha Besson, *The Many European Constitutions and the Future of European Constitutional Theory*, 105 ARCHIV FÜR RECHTS- UND SOZIALPHILOSOPHIE BEIHEFT, STAATS- UND VERFASSUNGSTHEORIE IM SPANNUNGSFELD DER DISZIPLINEN 160 (2006); Samantha Besson, *The Concept of European Constitutionalism: Interpretation in lieu of Translation*, 3 No FOUNDATIONS 49 (2007), *available at at* http: www.helsinki.fi/nofo/ (last visited on 22 February 2009).

makes the issue even more difficult is that international constitutionalism can no longer be conceived of separately from subbrands of constitutionalism in some more developed regional or functional (sectorial) legal orders that overlap in the same territory, such as European constitutionalism in the European Union (EU),[11] or arguably the World Trade Organization's (WTO) constitutionalism.[12]

Understanding the constitutionalization of international law implies, this chapter claims, refocusing the discussion on the legitimacy deficit, and more specifically on the democratic deficit in current global law-making processes, whether national, European, or international. It is common knowledge that European and international legal claims not only to normative authority but also to supremacy in certain areas previously covered only by national law have triggered a need for greater legitimation of international norms on the part of all legal subjects affected, including individuals and international organizations. The constitutionalization of material constraints on international, regional, and national law-making is often put forward as part of their legitimation. In a constitutional democratic framework, however, this is only a first step and formal constitutionalization is also needed to make those material constraints democratically legitimate.

As a result, the ambiguous relationship between constitutionalism and democracy deserves to be unpacked in international law before the promises of constitutionalism can be fully understood in that context. This implies in particular identifying the constituent power(s) in international law. Then only will the relationship among national, regional, and international constitutional norms, but also the relationship among norms, sources, and regimes within the body of international law itself, become clearer.

---

[11] *See, e.g.,* Neil Walker, *The Idea of Constitutional Pluralism,* 65 Mod. L. Rev. 317 (2002); Neil Walker, *Postnational Constitutionalism and the Problem of Translation, in* European Constitutionalism beyond the State 27 (Joseph Weiler & Marlene Wind eds., 2003); Neil Walker, *Post-Constituent Constitutionalism? The Case of the European Union, in* The Paradox of Constitutionalism: Constituent Power and Constitutional Form 247 (Martin Loughlin & Neil Walker eds., 2007); Miguel Poiares Maduro, *Europe and the Constitution: What If This Is as Good as It Gets? in* European Constitutionalism beyond the State 74 (Joseph Weiler & Marlene Wind eds., 2003); Miguel Poiares Maduro, *The Importance of Being Called a Constitution: Constitutional Authority and the Authority of Constitutionalism,* 3 Int'l J. Const. L. 332 (2005); Samantha Besson, *From European Integration to European Integrity: Should European Law Speak with Just One Voice?* 10 Eur. L.J. 257 (2004); Besson, *The Many European Constitutions, supra* note 10. See also Walker and Maduro, Chapters 6 and 12 of this volume.

[12] On the latter, *see, e.g.,* Dunoff and Trachtman, Chapter 1 of this volume.

1. Concepts and Conceptions of Constitution and Constitutionalism

a. Concepts

Constitution and constitutionalism are complex normative concepts.[13] In national constitutional theory, the concept of constitution may be used to refer either to what the constitution should be or to what it is. First of all, the constitution is often referred to as a text. This is the most basic and literal use one may encounter, even though constitutional practice shows that there could be a thick national constitution without a text or based on many different constitutional texts. Second, and most commonly, the constitution is used to refer to a legal norm albeit of a superior rank. A third meaning is that of a process (i.e., the constitution of a political entity). This explains why the concept of constitution is said to be gradual: it is difficult to distinguish a constitutional order from a nonconstitutional order in an all-or-nothing fashion. Fourth, one refers to the constitution to mean the political order that stems from it. That outcome may either be constituted, in which case the constitution is actually constitutive, or be formalized, in which case the constitution has a merely regulatory function. A final dimension of meaning is that of the constitution as source of legitimacy. In this sense, the constitution not only is a norm, a process, and an order but also has the legitimating function of that order.

Within the second and most common dimension of meaning of the concept of constitution qua legal norm, one finds two useful pairs of distinctions: first, the distinction between thin and thick constitutions and, second, the distinction between the procedural and the material elements of the thick constitution.[14]

The first distinction between thin and thick constitutions corresponds roughly to the opposition between a small-*c* constitution and a big-*C* constitution. The thin constitution is an ensemble of secondary rules that organize the law-making institutions and processes in a given legal order. Any autonomous legal order entails a thin constitution. The thick constitution is a thin constitution, but it is one that also has a more elaborate content and

---

[13] For an overview, *see* Dario Castiglione, *The Political Theory of the Constitution*, 44 POL. STUD. 417 (1996); Christoph Möllers, *Pouvoir Constituant – Constitution – Constitutionnalisme*, *in* PRINCIPLES OF EUROPEAN CONSTITUTIONAL LAW 183 (Armin von Bogdandy ed., 2007); Besson, *The Many European Constitutions*, *supra* note 10, at 163–5. The political and normative approach to constitutionalization endorsed in this section differs from the economic and functionalist approach taken by Dunoff & Trachtman, Chapter 1 of this volume.

[14] *See* Joseph Raz, *On the Authority and Interpretation of Constitutions: Some Preliminaries*, *in* CONSTITUTIONALISM 152–3 (Larry Alexander ed., 2001).

that encompasses specific procedural elements, such as revision clauses, and substantive elements, such as fundamental rights and democratic principles. More precisely, a thick constitution is a superior legal norm that is usually but not always laid down in a written document and adopted according to a specific procedure (1) that constitutes and defines the powers of the main organs of the different branches of government (2) and that is in principle protected through specific revision rules against modification by ulterior legislation, over which it therefore has priority (3). The thick constitution constitutes a political and legal order qua sovereign and autonomous legal order.[15]

The second opposition is that between the procedural and the material elements usually present and complementary in a thick constitution. The procedural element in the superiority of the constitution lies, first of all, in its rigidity; it is more difficult to revise a constitution than it is ordinary law. This procedural superiority flows, second, from the constitution's adoption procedure, as it is usually adopted unanimously or by qualified majority by the people as constituent power or at least by an ad hoc constituent assembly. Of course, the procedural superiority of the constitution does not always match its denomination and some fundamental laws are entrenched, while so-called constitutions need not always be. The thick constitution's material content consists of fundamental elements for political life and order, such as the separation of powers, checks and balances, the rule of law, democracy, and fundamental rights. Those elements may vary, and all constitutions do not entail the same ones.

Through its material content, the thick constitution actually guarantees fundamental rights and principles, which constrain the democratic and political order it constitutes. The formal or procedural constitution ensures the stability and resilience of the material political and legal order constituted by vesting its constraints with formal (source-based) and not only material (content-based) superiority by reference to the process by which it was constituted and to the process by which it can be amended. This formal superiority in the legal order implies, however, that the constitution be adopted through a superior constitutive procedure, such as an inclusive constitutional convention.[16] Formal and material elements of the thick constitution are, as a result, not only complementary but also often in a necessary mutual relationship in a constitution that both constrains and constitutes the political and legal order.

---

[15] See Raz, *id.*, at 152–3; Möllers, *supra* note 13, at 184–94; Walker, *Idea of Constitutional Pluralism, supra* note 11.

[16] See Besson, *The Many European Constitutions, supra* note 10, at 165.

The many meanings of the concept of constitution also imply that there are many definitions of constitutionalism. Constitutionalism can mean anything from a theoretical and philosophical political model to a normative theory or to an ideology pertaining to the constitution in its various meanings. Although constitutionalism can take different forms, its main and common claim is that political and legal power should be exercised only within the limits of a constitution, such as the separation of powers, checks and balances, the rule of law, democracy, and fundamental rights.

Importantly, there can be traces of constitutional law in a thin and non-political sense without constitutionalism, although the reverse is not true. This could also be said about the international legal order if the term *constitution* is used in this thin and relatively uncontroversial sense. After all, there are to date obvious secondary rules of organization of general international law-making pertaining to the various legal sources and instruments of international law,[17] but also to the international institutional order.[18] In fact, the terms *constitution* and *constitutional law* are traditionally used in international law to refer to this kind of secondary norms, and for instance to the constitutive charters of international organizations and their various rules of organization,[19] without any further implications in terms of international constitutionalism. One even finds reference in the literature to a codified albeit incomplete version of that ensemble of superior norms qua formalized text: the UN Charter.[20]

In this chapter, however, I will refer to the concept of constitution in a thick sense (with its procedural and material elements), as this is the sense in which promoters of international constitutional law seem to be using it.[21] Further, the thick meaning of constitution is the only meaning of the concept with added value in the current search for greater legitimacy of international law. International constitutional law will hereby be understood as the ensemble of materially and formally superior norms of international law that constitute the background of all other special regimes and norms of international law.[22]

---

[17] *See* Samantha Besson, *Theorizing the Sources of International Law, in* PHILOSOPHY OF INTERNATIONAL LAW (Samantha Besson & John Tasioulas eds., 2009).

[18] *See* José Alvarez, INTERNATIONAL ORGANIZATIONS AS LAW-MAKERS (2006); Jan Klabbers, AN INTRODUCTION TO INTERNATIONAL INSTITUTIONAL LAW (2002).

[19] *See* Wolfgang Friedmann, THE CHANGING STRUCTURE OF INTERNATIONAL LAW (1964); Klabbers, *supra* note 3.

[20] *See, e.g.,* Fassbender, *United Nations Charter, supra* note 2; and Fassbender, *supra* note 6.

[21] *See, e.g.,* de Wet, *supra* note 2, at 51–3; Peters, *Compensatory Constitutionalism, supra* note 2, at 581–4; Fassbender, *supra* note 6, at 130–1.

[22] I will be focusing on general international law in this chapter qua background international law (see the 2006 ILC Report on Fragmentation, *available at* http://untreaty.

b. Conceptions

Whatever comes out of formal constitutional debates in European and international law, the constitutional reality is changing rapidly at the national, regional, and international levels. International human rights norms, for instance, which are often taken as the epitome of international constitutional norms, apply to the same territories and populations as national constitutional rights and usually become an integral part of national legal orders with constitutional rank. It is, as a result, increasingly difficult to draw a line between national and international constitutional law in terms of their objects and subjects.

The difficulty is that the conceptions of constitution and constitutionalism traditionally pertain to a single and unitary norm per legal order and polity. Translating those concepts to fit the multilayered international political structure is therefore necessary, unless what is aimed for is a world state's constitution constituting the world's human community qua single polity. Many attempts at such translations to match the features of international law may be found in the literature.[23] One may doubt, however, whether mere translation of a given concept to transpose it to the fragmented international context is adapted to connect the very concept of constitution, which is traditionally unitary, to the pluralistic international legal order *lato sensu* in which the boundaries among national, European, and international law can no longer be drawn.[24] It seems difficult to refer, in the same legal orders, to a concept of constitution that cannot accommodate conflicting conceptions and uses of the same concept and that needs to be translated into the European or international context every time a constitutional issue arises in the latter, or worse that needs to be translated from one regime of international law to the next.

This could be acceptable if one's conception of international constitutional law referred to the constitution of a society of states completely distinct from the community of individuals. This is clearly not the account most proponents of international constitutional law have in mind, however, as they usually refer to the international community to include not only states

---

un.org/ilc/documentation/english/a_cn4_l682_add1.pdf (last visited on 22 February 2009)), but each international legal regime may have its own constitution if the conditions are fulfilled. *See, e.g.,* de Wet, *supra* note 2, at 53; Fassbender, *supra* note 6, at 130; Peters, *Compensatory Constitutionalism, supra* note 2, at 582.

[23] *See, e.g.,* in the EU context, Walker, *Postnational Constitutionalism, supra* note 11; and in the international context, Fassbender, *United Nations Charter, supra* note 2; Peters, *Compensatory Constitutionalism, supra* note 2, at 597–602.

[24] *See* Besson, *Many European Constitutions, supra* note 10, at 165.

but also individuals and/or international organizations.[25] Translation leaves the preexisting concept untouched, whereas international constitutionalism clearly puts the concept of (national) constitution itself into question.[26] What the coexistence of many constitutions requires, in other words, is not only a translation of the concept of constitution in another legal order but also a reinterpretation of the concept itself within all legal orders at once so as to produce an encompassing constitutional theory that can explain all of those uses together. This implies, first of all, going back to the paradox of constitutional democracy and then revising the concept of constituent power and constitutionalizing processes in light of the requirements of democratic legitimacy in a globalized world.

2. International Constitutionalism and Democracy

The relationship between constitutionalism and democratic sovereignty is a complex one.[27] A constitution constrains the legal order, thus making it (materially) legitimate in a constitutional democracy. But it can do so democratically only if those constitutional constraints also constitute that democratic order. This is the paradox of constitutionalism: that a constitution should work as a constraint on democracy, but also, if those constraints are to be (formally) legitimate, as constitutive of democracy itself. And this in turn requires a self-constitutive process by a democratic constituent power – as democratic as possible given the other paradox inherent in the boundaries of democracy.[28] If this complexity pervades national constitutional theories, this should be even more so at the international level, where different law-making entities are vested with normative authority at the same time.

a. From the Material Constitutions of International Law...

In the context of international law, constitutional discourse is actually used mainly by reference to the material constraints certain international legal

---

[25] *See, e.g.*, Peters, *Compensatory Constitutionalism, supra* note 2, at 592; de Wet, *supra* note 2, at 55 and 75.

[26] *See* Besson, *Concept of European Constitutionalism, supra* note 10, at 52.

[27] On the many paradoxes of constitutional precommitment, *see* Jon Elster, *Introduction to* CONSTITUTIONALISM AND DEMOCRACY (Jon Elster & Rune Slagstad eds., 1988); CARLOS S. NINO, THE CONSTITUTION OF DELIBERATIVE DEMOCRACY (1996); JEREMY WALDRON, LAW AND DISAGREEMENT (1999), at 255 et seq and 282 et seq; Jürgen Habermas, *Constitutional Democracy: A Paradoxical Union of Contradictory Principles?*, 29 POL. THEORY 766 (2001).

[28] *See, e.g.*, Robert Goodin, *Enfranchising All Affected Interests, and Its Alternatives*, 35 PHIL. & PUB. AFF. 40 (2007); Samantha Besson, *Ubi Ius, Ibi Civitas – A Republican Account of the International Community, in* LEGAL REPUBLICANISM, NATIONAL AND INTERNATIONAL PERSPECTIVES (Samantha Besson & José L. Martí eds., 2009).

norms place on national but also on regional and international law-making processes. Rapidly, indeed, constraints on the law-making power of national, regional, and international law-making entities were needed to protect individuals against direct violations by national, regional, and international law, but also to ensure legal coherence overall. Evidence of this is often found in the limitations on individual state consent in new multilateral international law-making processes; the development of relative normativity and in particular of imperative, objective, and *erga omnes* norms; and the consolidation of general international law qua background law.

Those constraining functions of international constitutional law may explain some of the normative hierarchies at work in international law. Those hierarchies are deemed material only, because they are based on content or normative weight, without reference to those norms' formal sources or origins. As a result, those hierarchies are flexible or transitive, both internally and externally. On the one hand, imperative international norms may stem from any source of international law and constrain norms from all other sources and regimes in international law, both special and general. On the other hand, materially weightier norms may constrain national as much as international law-making processes, as exemplified in the recent case law of the Court of First Instance of the European Communities scrutinizing the Security Council's resolutions on the basis of European *jus cogens* norms.[29]

Under those circumstances, international constitutionalism may at first have worked, or still be said to work, exclusively as a legitimating constraint without constituting any kind of international or national polity. To refer to the two components of thick constitutional law alluded to before, international constitutional law may be said to entail the material without the formal dimension of a thick constitution.[30]

This is confirmed by the observation that, whereas there are clearly material hierarchies of norms in international law, there is to date no formal hierarchy of norms; there is no general priority of the norms issued according to one formal source of law over those of another or of those norms stemming from one regime of law over those of another. This may be reckoned, first of all, by reference to current lists of sources such as article 38 of the ICJ Statute, despite its numbering and the reference to subsidiary means for the determination of rules of law. Thus, although *jus cogens* norms are imperative, their revision

[29] *See, e.g.,* CFI, Case T-315/01, Yassin Abdullah Kadi v. Council of the European Union and Commission of European Communities, [2005] ECR II-3649. *See* Samantha Besson, *European Legal Pluralism after* Kadi, 2 EuConst (2009).
[30] On low-intensity constitutionalism in the European Union, see Maduro, *The Importance of Being Called a Constitution, supra* note 11.

process corresponds to the processes of revision applicable to their sources in each case, whether treaty based or customary. Nor is it possible, second, to consider the norms stemming from certain regimes of international law as taking general priority over norms in other regimes merely by reference to their origin in a given regime. Thus, not all norms of general international law necessarily take priority over international trade or environmental legal norms. There is a major exception, of course, and that is the priority given to (all, and not only secondary) UN norms by article 103 of the UN Charter.[31]

Various reasons might be ventured for the hiatus between material and formal hierarchies in international law. A primary reason for the absence of hierarchy of sources of international law pertains to the content of the norms issued according to certain sources. Fundamental rights are usually protected by constitutional law in domestic legal orders; it is their ultimate value that explains the need to make their source hierarchically ultimate as shorthand for their material superiority in case of disagreement. Here again, the fact that international legal norms protecting important values are scattered across different legal sources does not favor their formal prioritization over other international legal norms. In fact, even if they were centralized in one source and not the other, as in the case of human rights treaties, the diversity of lawmakers and the moral and social pluralism that prevail over such fundamental values might explain the fear of formal entrenchment of certain international legal norms over others. Of course that fear is usually counterbalanced by the interest in having clear formal priorities set beyond material disagreement. Even then, however, formal entrenchment of material constitutional constraints requires formal processes of adoption of those constraints that are inclusive, deliberative, and democratic.

As a matter of fact, a second reason to recognize a formal hierarchy of sources would be to acknowledge the superiority of certain law-making processes over others in terms of their legitimacy and in particular of their democratic legitimacy. The democratic superiority of constitutional law over legislation might be explained in terms of the unanimous and self-constituting process and of the inclusion of all subjects in the deliberative process as opposed to a majority-based legislative process. Given the still largely limited democratic dimension of international law-making processes in terms of equality,[32] inclusion, and deliberation, the influence of the traditionally consent-based approach to international law's legitimacy, and the diversity

---

[31] See Fassbender, "We the Peoples of the United Nations," supra note 2; Doyle, Chapter 4 of this volume.

[32] See Eric Stein, International Integration and Democracy: No Love at First Sight, 95 Am. J. Int'l L. 489 (2001).

of the sources of international law, it comes as no surprise that sources of international law have remained equally ranked so far.[33]

b. ... To the Formal Constitutions of International Law

Difficulties arise when international constitutional law is also said to constitute, just as European material constitutional constraints have recently given rise to, a constitutive-constitutional discourse.[34] While this development might not seem irresistible at first, regional legal integration in the European Union has shown that the pressure to constitute has been and is likely to remain very strong.

European and international legal claims to normative authority and even to supremacy in areas previously covered only by national law (e.g., human rights law, environmental law, public procurement law, investment law) have triggered a need for greater legitimation of international norms vis-à-vis their legal subjects.[35] If the constitutionalization of international law is understood as a reaction to the legitimacy deficit in current global law-making processes, whether national, European, or international, developing material constitutional constraints or even procedural or democratic constraints is only half of the story. In a pluralistic and complex international community, where social and moral pluralism are even more pervasive than at national level, procedural legitimacy remains the most obvious and broadly acceptable form of legitimation of international law.[36]

Democratic legitimacy actually requires a self-constituting process when constitutional constraints have started applying and unilaterally constraining law-making processes without giving individuals affected a right to have a direct or indirect input into the identification of those constraints.[37] Granting

[33] *See* Bruno Simma, *Self-Contained Regimes*, 16 Neth. Y.B. Int'l L. 111 (1985); Martti Koskenniemi, *Constitutionalism as Mindset: Reflections on Kantian Theories about International Law and Globalization*, 8 Theoretical Inquiries in Law 8 (2007), at 19.

[34] *See* Maduro, *The Importance of Being Called a Constitution*, *supra* note 11.

[35] *See* Allen Buchanan, Justice, Legitimacy and Self-Determination: Moral Foundations for International Law (2004); Allen Buchanan, *Legitimacy of International Law*, in Philosophy of International Law (Samantha Besson & John Tasioulas eds., 2009); John Tasioulas, *Legitimacy of International Law*, in Philosophy of International Law (Samantha Besson & John Tasioulas eds., 2009); Samantha Besson, *The Authority of International Law – Lifting the State Veil*, 31 (3) Sydney L. Rev. (2009); Besson, *supra* notes 17 and 28.

[36] *See* Besson, *supra* notes 17 and 35; Allen Buchanan & Robert Keohane, *The Legitimacy of Global Governance Institutions*, 20 Ethics & Int'l Aff. 405 (2006).

[37] *See* Jürgen Habermas, *Eine politische Verfassung für die pluralistische Weltgesellschaft?* in Zwischen Naturalismus und Religion 324, at 325 (Jürgen Habermas ed., 2005); Jürgen Habermas, *Kommunikative Rationalität und grenzüberschreitende Politik: eine Replik*, in Anarchie des kommunikativen Freiheit 406 (Peter Niesen & Benjamin Herborth eds.,

international human rights without recognizing the "right of rights" and the possibility for the beneficiaries of human rights to take part in the identification of those rights would be profoundly self-defeating.[38]

3. Constituting the International Constitution(s)

a. The International Community qua Community of Communities

Most accounts of international constitutional law to date refer to the international community as the entity whose constitutional law it is. The whole debate pertaining to the constitutionalization of international law has revolved around the idea that there is or should be an international community with a shared objective and universal interests, on the one hand, and institutions to promote those interests, on the other.[39] Rarely, however, do those accounts actually expand on the exact constituency of that community or on its qualities as constituent power.[40]

2007); Samantha Besson, *Institutionalizing Global Demoi-cracy, in* INTERNATIONAL LAW, JUSTICE AND LEGITIMACY (Lukas Meyer ed., 2009); Besson, *supra* note 28.

[38] *See, e.g.,* Richard Bellamy, *The "Right to Have Rights": Citizenship Practice and the Political Constitution of the EU, in* CITIZENSHIP AND GOVERNANCE IN THE EUROPEAN UNION 41 (Richard Bellamy & Alex Warleigh eds., 2001); Besson, *supra* note 28. See for a similar democracy-based challenge to the idea of international constitutionalism, Koskenniemi, *supra* note 33, at 19: "Constitutionalism responds to the worry about the (unity of international law) by suggesting a hierarchical priority to institutions representing general international law (especially the United Nations Charter). Yet it seems difficult to see how any politically meaningful project for the common good (as distinct from the various notions of particular good) could be articulated around the diplomatic practices of United Nations organs, or notions such as *jus cogens* in the Vienna Convention on the Law of Treaties. Fragmentation is after all the result of a conscious *challenge* to the unacceptable features of that general law and the powers of the institutions that apply it. This is why there will be no hierarchy between the various legal regimes in any near future. The agreement that some norms simply *must* be superior to other norms is not reflected in any consensus in regard to who should have final say on this. The debate on an international constitution will not resemble domestic constitution-making. This is so not only because the international realm lacks a *pouvoir constituant* but because if such presented itself, it would be empire, and the constitution it would enact would not be one of an international but an imperial realm."

[39] *See, e.g.,* Jonathan Charney, *International Law-Making in a Community Context,* 2 INT'L LEGAL THEORY 38 (1996); Christian Tomuschat, *Die internationale Gemeinschaft,* 33 ARCHIV DES VÖLKERRECHTS 1 (1995); Christian Tomuschat, *International Law as the Constitution of Mankind, in* INTERNATIONAL LAW ON THE EVE OF THE TWENTY-FIRST CENTURY: VIEWS FROM THE INTERNATIONAL LAW COMMISSION 37 (1997); Fassbender, *United Nations Charter, supra* note 2, at 561–66; Jürgen Habermas, *Hat die Konstitutionalisierung des Völkerrechts noch eine Chance? in* DER GESPALTENE WESTEN. KLEINE POLITISCHE SCHRIFTEN (Jürgen Habermas ed., 2004); Habermas, *Kommunikative Rationalität, supra* note 37.

[40] *Compare* Fassbender, *"We the Peoples of the United Nations," supra* note 2, 275, *with* 286–90.

Since the 1920s,[41] but even more post-1945 with the adoption of the UN Charter and post-1989 with globalization and the emergence of other subjects of international law besides states, international lawyers and theorists of international law have made a repeated use of general concepts such as international community and international society to refer to some or all subjects of international law and/or their objective interests.[42] International law itself sometimes refers to the notion of international community, especially pertaining to the nature, degree, and scope of normativity of those very international legal norms deemed as material constitutional norms of international law. It is the case, for instance, in the *jus cogens* definition of article 53 of the Vienna Convention on the Law of Treaties, in the reference to international crimes in article 5(1) of the Rome Statute for the International Criminal Court or in the reference to obligations erga omnes or omnium in the law of international state responsibility (art. 48 of the International Law Commission (ILC) Articles on the Responsibility of States for Internationally Wrongful Acts).[43]

Curiously, there are no shared understandings, however, among international lawyers of what this community is or should be.[44] Without a clear conception of the nature, boundaries, and constituency of the community or communities concerned by international law-making and of the ways to link

[41] *See, e.g.,* Verdross, *supra* note 1.

[42] *See, e.g.,* Mosler, *supra* note 1; Hermann Mosler, *International Legal Community*, 74 ENCYCLOPEDIA OF PUBLIC INTERNATIONAL LAW 309 (1984); René-Jean Dupuy, LA COMMUNAUTÉ INTERNATIONALE ENTRE LE MYTHE ET L'HISTOIRE (1986); Jochen A. Frowein, *Das Staatengemeinschaftsinteresse – Probleme bei Formulierung und Durchsetzung, in* FESTSCHRIFT FÜR KARL DOEHRING ZUM 70. GEBURTSTAG 219 (1989); Nicholas Onuf, *The Constitution of International Society*, 5 EUR. J. INT'L L. 1 (1994); Bruno Simma, *From Bilateralism to Community Interest in International Law*, 250 RECUEIL DES COURS 217 (1994); Tomuschat, *Die internationale Gemeinschaft, supra* note 39; Georges Abi-Saab, *Whither the International Community?* 9 EUR. J. INT'L L. 248 (1998); Bruno Simma & Andreas L. Paulus, *The "International Community": Facing the Challenge of Globalization*, 9 EUR. J. INT'L L. 266 (1998); Andreas L. Paulus, DIE INTERNATIONALE GEMEINSCHAFT IM VÖLKERRECHT – EINE UNTERSUCHUNG ZUR ENTWICKLUNG DES VÖLKERRECHTS IM ZEITALTER DER GLOBALISIERUNG (2001); Emmanuelle Jouannet, *L'idée de communauté humaine à la croisée des la communauté des États et de la communauté mondiale*, 47 ARCHIVES DE PHILOSOPHIE DU DROIT 191 (2003); Emmanuelle Jouannet, *La communauté internationale vue par les juristes*, IV ANNUAIRE FRANÇAIS DES RELATIONS INTERNATIONALES 3 (2005); Besson, *supra* note 28.

[43] *See* the ICJ decisions in Barcelona Traction, Light & Power Co., 1970 I.C.J. Rep. 3; and in Legality of the Threat or Use of Nuclear Weapons, 1996 I.C.J. Rep. 226. *See also* the ICJ's opinion in Legal Consequences of the Construction of a Wall in the Occupied Palestinian Territory, 2004 I.C.J. Rep. 131.

[44] *Contrast* Onuf, *supra* note 42; Abi-Saab, *supra* note 42; Simma & Paulus, *supra* note 42; Paulus, *supra* note 42; and Besson, *supra* note 28.

their interests and decisions back to national political communities, how-ever, efforts made to institutionalize global democracy, or at least to develop mechanisms of international accountability, are seriously hindered.

In a nutshell, there are two main prongs in the idea of a political inter-national community:[45] one that favors a society of democratic states[46] and the other that promotes a world state's community of individuals.[47] The society-of-democratic-states approach is limited, however. It does not pay sufficient attention to the interests of individuals and the importance to pro-tect those interests against (normative and practical) domination by those of a majority in the same national polity. This applies whether the latter is democratic or not, because some interests might be minority interests or simply because foreign policy is largely and increasingly deparliamentarized at the national level. Nor does the society-of-states model protect against domination by those of a (potentially smaller, in absolute terms) majority in another national polity in an international system based on sovereign equality (and hence decision making grounded on unanimity or, at least, consensus). The democratic-world-state model falls in the reverse excess, however, by not paying sufficient attention to the interests of national polities themselves, as vested with political interests worth protecting distinctly from those of all individuals constituting them, and to the equal respect of national popular sovereignty in international law-making.[48] Nor does it pay heed to the dis-tinct interest of states and individuals grouped in international organizations, such as those of the European Union, for instance.

As a result, the international community is better understood as both a community of states (and groups of states in IOs) and a community of indi-viduals (and groups of individuals); when seen as a political commu-nity, the international community has both states and individuals as its "citizens."[49] This complex and multilateral international political community

[45] See, e.g., Besson, supra note 28.

[46] For a more detailed discussion, see Thomas Christiano, International Institutions and Democ-racy, in PHILOSOPHY OF INTERNATIONAL LAW (Samantha Besson & John Tasioulas eds., 2009); Philip Pettit, Legitimate International Institutions: A Neo-Republican Perspective, in PHILOSOPHY OF INTERNATIONAL LAW (Samantha Besson & John Tasioulas eds. 2009).

[47] See, e.g., Dupuy, supra note 42; see Paulus, supra note 42, at 45–220, on the details of this opposition.

[48] See Jean Cohen, Whose Sovereignty? Empire versus International Law, 18 ETHICS & INT'L AFF. 1 (2004).

[49] On this dual constituency in international law, see FRANCIS CHENEVAL, LA CITÉ DES PEO-PLES 144–53 (2005); Jouannet, L'idée de communauté humaine, supra note 42, at 220–32; Habermas, Kommunikative Rationalität, supra note 37; Habermas, supra note 39. On the European Union, see Walker, Post-Constituent Constitutionalism? supra note 11, at 264–65 and this volume. The proposed conception of the international community differs from

of communities[50] ought to be conceived and constructed as multilevel, with different overlapping communities deliberating and deciding at different levels of national, transnational, international, and supranational law-making. Most important, the international community is also pluralistic at each level and implies the functional inclusion in deliberation of all those whose fundamental interests are significantly affected by a decision, even when they cannot by physically present or even represented. In short, the international community is not located at one level only, but it internationalizes as it were each political community at all levels of governance including national ones.[51]

b. The International Community qua *Demoi*-cratic Constituent Power

A constituent power is the political community that considers itself as such and therefore constitutes itself by adopting constitutional norms. In the case of the international community, this requires identifying, first, whether it can be regarded as a political community at all and, second, whether it can actually constitute itself as such procedurally.

i. *The International Community as Political Community*

A community can share interests and values without being necessarily regarded as a legal or political community. The international community, however, is clearly an international legal community as opposed to a purely social community.[52]

Even though the international community is legal in the sense that its interests are both gradually being developed by law and constraining the law,[53] it is not yet regarded as a legal entity under international law: it is not, in other words, vested with the quality of subject under international law.[54] This is paradoxical because it is strictly speaking both the right bearer of many duties erga omnes and the duty bearer of duties omnium. In terms of procedures, however, *erga omnes* obligations are due to each state individually, as exemplified by the implementation of article 40 of the ILC Articles in case of violations of *jus cogens* norms. Moreover, when human rights violations

---

a federal state reconstruction; see, e.g., Ingolf Pernice, *Multilevel Constitutionalism and the Treaty of Amsterdam: European Constitution-Making Revisited*, 36 COMMON MKT. L. REV. 703 (1999); Cottier & Hertig, *supra* note 2, at 299–304.

[50] *See* Paulus, *supra* note 42, at 161; JANNA THOMPSON, JUSTICE AND WORLD ORDER: A PHILOSOPHICAL INQUIRY (1992).

[51] *See* Besson, *supra* notes 37 & 28.

[52] *See* Simma & Paulus, *supra* note 42, at 267–9.

[53] *See* Onuf, *supra* note 42, at 7.

[54] *See* James Crawford, *Responsibility to the International Community as a Whole*, 8 IND. J. GLOBAL LEGAL STUD. 303, 307 & 319 (2001).

are at stake, procedures remain eminently bilateral or intersubjective – that is, between two states or between one state and an individual (no *actio popularis*). Further, there is as of yet no directly invocable notion of public interest (that is not reducible to individual state interests) in international law.

The real question, therefore, is whether this legal community is or can be matched by a political community. There is no agreed-on set of criteria as to how to judge what makes a multitude of people a political community. Self-rule or self-legislation that lies at the core of democracy also implies self-constitution; the community, which binds itself by the laws it generates, defines itself at the same time as a democratic subject by drawing its own boundaries. True, these boundaries usually match historical, cultural, or ethnic boundaries.[55] Comparative politics and history have shown, however, that this is not always the case. All it takes often is some kind of "we-feeling," a form of solidarity among different "stakeholders."[56] In fact, solidarity need not necessarily be prepolitical at all; it can be generated by the political exercise itself.[57] There is no reason why solidarity should be confined to state boundaries,[58] as recently exemplified in the European Union. Of course, this raises the well-known question of the boundaries of the democratic polity and the paradox that its boundaries cannot be identified democratically.[59] As I have argued elsewhere, however, that polity should include all those whose fundamental interests are significantly and equally affected by a given decision.[60]

In short, members of a political community are usually thought (1) to share common, interdependent, or reciprocal interests and goals and (2) to organize themselves autonomously to reach those goals.[61] At the moment, the international community's members – states and individuals – clearly have objective interests in common.[62] Examples of the latter abound in international law guarantees, and one may mention collective interests such as peace, environment, self-determination, and common heritage, but also individual interests such as human rights. Moreover, there are substantive guarantees of those common interests and references to their general and objective scope in

---

[55] *See, e.g.,* Margaret Canovan, Nationhood and Political Theory (1996); David Miller, Citizenship and National Identity (2000). *See* Goodin, *supra* note 28.

[56] *See* Daniele Archibugi, *Cosmopolitan Democracy and Its Critics: A Review,* 10 Eur. J. Int'l Rel. 437 (2004).

[57] *See* Habermas, *supra* note 39; Joshua Cohen & Charles Sabel, *Extra-Rempublicam Nulla Justitia?* 34 Phil. & Pub. Aff. 147, 159–64 (2006).

[58] Craig Calhoun, *The Class Consciousness of Frequent Travellers: Towards a Critique of Actually Existing Cosmopolitanism,* in Debating Cosmopolitics 86 (Daniele Archibugi ed., 2003); Cohen & Sabel, *supra* note 57, at 159.

[59] *See* Goodin, *supra* note 28.   [60] *See* Besson, *supra* note 28.

[61] James Bohman, *Republican Cosmopolitanism,* 12 J. Pol. Phil. 336, 340–41 (2004).

[62] Simma, *supra* note 42, at 236–43; Paulus, *supra* note 42, at 250–84.

international law. On the other hand, the international community is already largely institutionalized and international law-making organized according to secondary international legal norms. In this sense, the international community already has a thin constitution. One may even argue that it already shows material dimensions of a thick constitution. The question is whether those material norms can be formalized to constitute formally superior law to ordinary international, regional, and even national law.

ii. The International Community as Self-Constituting Political Community

To be considered a fully fledged political community, the international community also needs to be able to constitute itself as such (i.e., to organize itself autonomously and set up institutional procedures of law-making). This is made particularly difficult in international law by the hybrid and pluralist nature of the international community of communities qua constituent power. On the one hand, it comprises individuals (and groups of individuals) and states (and groups of states), as opposed to federal groups of states only. On the other, it includes as a result national constituent powers in certain areas, thus giving rise to a complex multilayered or *demoi*-cratic constituent power.

At this stage, it is difficult to argue that the international community is organized autonomously. True, as we have just seen, there are various international institutions in place, together with different law-making procedures. However, all international subjects do not seem to be entirely conscious of their common interests and goals, and of the need to defend them collectively.[63] International law-making remains largely state centered despite increasing informal influences by groups of individuals and IOs. While the United Nations is the closest one may get to an inclusive institution,[64] it remains, despite reforms, run for and by states. As a result, there is an international legal order, but the subjects of that legal order, whether states or individuals, do not yet constitute together the political community that can legitimize those legal norms.

Of course, this does not mean that the international community cannot become political or that it should not. On the contrary, first of all, the constitution of such an international political community is a normative requirement based on mutual interests and interdependence. One may even

---

[63] *See* Abi-Saab, *supra* note 42, at 248; Simma & Paulus, *supra* note 42, at 276; Paulus, *supra* note 42, at 285–328; Ruth Grant & Robert Keohane, *Accountability and Abuses of Power in World Politics*, 99 Am. Pol. Science Rev. 29, 33 (2005); Koskenniemi, *supra* note 33, at 30.

[64] *See* Hersch Lauterpacht, International Law: A Treatise: A Revision of Oppenheim (1955), at 420. *See also* Simma & Paulus, *supra* note 42, at 274.

consider it a duty of democratic states to their own citizens, who can claim for as inclusive and democratic political communities within and beyond the state as possible in order to protect their interests and freedom from domination on the part of that state's authorities, other individuals in that state, other states, and IOs. Because democratic rule is one of the values protected by popular sovereignty, the correct exercise of state sovereignty implies looking for the best level of decision to endow those affected by that decision with the most voice, but it also implies listening to them.[65] This could even require the decoupling of popular sovereignty from state sovereignty in certain cases. Often, it might mean giving priority to the level of governance closest to those affected, depending on which community gathers all those significantly affected and with equal stakes in a decision. But one could also imagine cases in which those sharing equal stakes in a given local decision are situated at a regional or global level rather than at the local level. This corresponds to a democratic and transitive reinterpretation of the principle of subsidiarity that need not necessarily favor the local level.[66]

Second, some authors have argued, however, that the international community cannot become a political community because of the lack of plausibility of the political and democratic processes required for it to develop and consolidate. True, aiming only at full and direct democratic participation on the model of what applies in national democracies is implausible for reasons of size and plurality.[67] Democratic representation is a far more realistic and promising model to pursue given the circumstances of size and diversity prevailing at the international level.[68] Moreover, representation actually allows for the reflexive inclusion of all affected albeit nonterritorial interests and for editorial and contestatory democracy-enhancing mechanisms.[69]

4. Internal Implications of International Constitutional Pluralism

International constitutional pluralism of the kind presented so far has internal and external implications. Internal constitutional pluralism amounts to the coexistence within the same legal order (in this case, the international legal order) of many constitutional norms stemming from different sources or

---

[65] *See* Besson, *supra* note 37. For a similar argument, see Halberstam, Chapter 11 of this volume.

[66] *See* Besson, *supra* note 37; Samantha Besson, *Sovereignty in Conflict, in* TOWARDS AN INTERNATIONAL LEGAL COMMUNITY, THE SOVEREIGNTY OF STATES AND THE SOVEREIGNTY OF INTERNATIONAL LAW 131 (Colin Warbrick & Stephen Tierney eds., 2006).

[67] *See, e.g.,* Grant & Keohane, *supra* note 63, at 34.

[68] *See* Besson, *supra* notes 28 & 37; Christiano, *supra* note 46.

[69] *See* Besson, *supra* notes 28 & 37; Philip Pettit, *Democracy, National and International,* 89 MONIST 302 (2006).

regimes. It can be divided between vertical and horizontal forms of pluralism depending on whether it pertains to the relationship between sources of international law within one or among many regimes, on the one hand, or to the relationship between those regimes themselves, on the other.[70]

a. Vertical Internal Constitutional Pluralism

The first question to arise from the constitutionalization of general international law, but also of other regimes of international law, is whether it could and should encompass a formally superior ensemble of norms comprised of the main secondary rules and principles of the legal order and/or regimes. This leads, second, to the question of whether there could and should be a hierarchy of sources within general international law, or within any other regime of international law.

As to the first question, one could easily figure out constitutive procedures that are as inclusive as possible of all members of the international community and as deliberative as possible. It is important that these many constitutionalizing processes include all subjects in the international community and associate, as a consequence, national constituencies to the process both qua states and qua individuals. The recent development of multilateral law-making conferences confirms that this is a plausible way forward in the constitutionalization of international law.[71] Those processes may be plural, however, and take place many times for many different constitutional norms without aiming at issuing a single text or ensemble of norms. Nor need this constitutionalization process aim at entrenching all materially weightier norms if a consensus cannot be found on all them.

A second question would be whether the existence of a formally entrenched constitution might imply the progressive development of a formal hierarchy of sources of international law, just as it would in a national constitutional order. Prima facie, the existence of a formally superior set of constitutional norms need not necessarily require a hierarchy among the other sources of international law that it identifies as such. It would be the case only if it

---

[70] Note that Dunoff & Trachtman, but also Maduro, Chapters 1 and 12 of this volume, use the distinction to refer to the opposition between internal and external constitutional pluralism. Either way, the terms *vertical* and *horizontal* are remnants of a hierarchical approach to the articulation between legal orders, regimes, sources and norms and ought to be used with caution, as they unduly influence the outcome of the argument by suggesting the existence of a hierarchy of norms, sources, regimes or orders, or the absence thereof. The same may be said about the opposition between *internal* and *external* legal pluralism, given the concept of intervalidity and the absence of formal primacy of one legal order over the other.

[71] *See, e.g.,* ALAN BOYLE & CHRISTINE CHINKIN, THE MAKING OF INTERNATIONAL LAW (2007), at ch. 3.

foresaw it expressly.[72] Nor need constitutional norms necessarily stem from the same sources; some might be constitutionalized qua customary norms, while others might be constitutionalized as multilateral treaties.

Of course, a constitutional democratic form would require the democratization of given international law-making processes. Inclusion and deliberative quality might therefore gradually provide the constitutive elements of a hierarchy of sources in general international law, just as they did in national and European law.[73] However, the fact that the lawmakers in those different law-making processes do not necessarily match one another (yet), independently from the quality of the processes themselves, with states being the only ones officially involved in customary law-making by contrast to what applies to multilateral treaty making, threatens the possibility of a general normative ranking of sources according to democratic pedigree.

This leaves as a result issues of rank between constitutional norms, but also between nonconstitutional norms to a case-by-case assessment of those norms' democratic credentials. This could be done by reference to the degree of inclusion of significantly affected interests and of the respect of the principle of political equality among those sharing roughly equal stakes, along the lines set by the democratic reinterpretation of the principle of subsidiarity presented before.

b. Horizontal Internal Constitutional Pluralism

In the absence of general formal priority of general international legal norms over the rest of international law, one may wonder whether the constitutionalization of general international law, but also of other regimes of international law, would affect the current pluralism between different legal regimes.

Given the multilateral and multilevel nature of the international community qua community of communities, and the pluralistic nature of the demoi-cratic constituent power in international law, replacing horizontal constitutional pluralism by a formal hierarchy would be illegitimate. This is because of the lack of perfect overlap between the political communities in question. For the same reasons, even the hierarchy of sources that could potentially develop within general international law could not be said to apply across international legal orders. In the absence of material hierarchies between norms – or in spite of them – conflict resolution could take place only in each concrete case by comparing the democratic quality of law-making processes behind the norms in conflict.

---

[72] *See* Besson, *supra* note 17.   [73] *Id.*

5. External Implications of International Constitutional Pluralism

The pluralist nature of the constitutionalization of international law also has external implications. External constitutional pluralism (i.e., the coexistence of many constitutional norms stemming from different legal orders within one legal order) provides an opportunity to revisit difficult questions pertaining to the relationship between autonomous legal orders once constituted.

a. Validity and External Constitutional Pluralism

Traditionally, the relationship between national and international law was organized either according to the principle of monism (one single order into which all legal orders are integrated and whose norms therefore have immediate validity) or according to the principle of dualism (separate legal orders whose norms have no mutual validity, unless one legal order, usually the national legal order, incorporates or translates norms from another legal order). An alternative developed in recent years has been the principle of pluralism (separate legal orders whose legal norms coexist in the same social sphere and overlap in their claims to validity over the same issues, people, and territory, without constituting a single legal order but without translation or incorporation).

Nowadays, neither monism nor dualism can fully account for the increasing intermingling between national and international legal orders, with certain international legal norms being vested with immediate validity and direct applicability in national law but not others. Nor can they accommodate the fact that, even if a priori formal incorporation in a legal order no longer really matters nowadays for the reception of international law in domestic law,[74] neither national nor international law gets priority in deciding which international legal norms have immediate validity in all cases, thus infirming both monism and dualism qua accounts of validity.[75] As a result, the model of pluralism between legal orders is usually favored as a default account.[76]

---

[74] See, e.g., Paul Craig, Report on the United Kingdom, in THE EUROPEAN COURTS AND NATIONAL COURTS, DOCTRINE AND JURISPRUDENCE 195 (Anne-Marie Slaughter, Alec Stone Sweet & Joseph H. H. Weiler eds., 1998).

[75] See Andreas Paulus, The Emergence of the International Community and the Divide between International and Domestic Law, in NEW PERSPECTIVES ON THE DIVIDE BETWEEN INTERNATIONAL LAW AND NATIONAL LAW 216, 228–34 (André Nollkaemper & Janne Nijman eds., 2007); Giorgio Gaja, Dualism – A Review, id., 52.

[76] See Mattias Kumm, Democratic Constitutionalism Encounters International Law: Terms of Engagement, in THE MIGRATION OF CONSTITUTIONAL IDEAS 256, 257–58 (Sujit Choudhry ed., 2007); Samantha Besson, How International Is the European Legal Order? 5 No FOUNDATIONS (2008), available at at http: www.helsinki.fi/nofo/ (last visited on 22 February 2009); Besson, supra notes 11 & 29.

The constitutional model of general international law propounded here provides elements for a more principled account of the pluralist relationship between national and international law, however. Prima facie, the constitutionalization of international law would be expected to bring about the creation of a clear hierarchy between national and international law, eventually leading to full monism. Once the international constituent power is understood as a complex and interlocking community of communities, however, considerations of democratic self-constitution explain how the respective constituted legal orders can neither be regarded as overlapping completely and hence as constituting a single order, on the one hand, nor be regarded as entirely disconnected orders given their increasing integration and partial overlaps in their constituency, on the other. Of course, the national constitutional order may remain the one allowing incorporation into national law and then regulating potential conflicts and direct effect. This may be explained, however, in terms of the proximity of national law to individuals and of the complete system of national institutions implementing international law.

External constitutional pluralism amounts, in other words, to a democratic requirement in a constitutionalized international legal order. This is even more interesting, as the protection of constitutional democracy against international law was long put forward (albeit for different reasons) by promoters of both dualism and monism. This synchronic validation by an integrated and complex constituent power of a plurality of constitutional norms stemming from different overlapping constitutional orders corresponds to what I have referred to elsewhere as a form of intervalidity.[77]

b. Rank and External Constitutional Pluralism

If the question of the primacy of international law over national law is a difficult question, it becomes even more controversial when international law claims to take priority over national constitutional law. The constitutionalization of general international law therefore provides the opportunity to revise some of the traditional approaches to the rank between (general or special) international law and national (constitutional or ordinary) law.

Traditionally, and despite claims to primacy made on the part of international law on any kind of national law (e.g., art. 26 and 27 of the Vienna Convention on the Law of Treaties), constitutional national law has often been regarded in national constitutional theory as taking priority over international law, typically on democratic grounds. It is one thing to recognize that international constitutional law can be immediately valid within another

---

[77] *See* Besson, *supra* note 76.

autonomous legal order and claim normative authority, for instance, based on its democratic legitimacy, and another thing to claim that that authority preempts that of national law.[78] Given the lack of commensurability of the conflicting claims to authority, but also to primacy, made by both legal orders in democratic terms, the rank of international law over domestic constitutional law remains a heavily contested question in constitutional democracies.

Prima facie, the development of internal formal hierarchies in international law, combined with the strengthening of international legitimation mechanisms, could also lead to the development of hierarchies between national, regional, and international constitutional law. Once international constitutional-type constraints are regarded as democratically constituting the international community qua *demoi*-cratic community of communities, however, a priori hierarchy talk would simply miss the point of constitutionalizing international law. The fact that the constituent powers in those separate legal orders only partly overlap calls for a democratic differentiation of the norms in question according to their inclusive and deliberative quality pertaining to the questions at hand. This would depend in particular on the degree of affectedness of those taking part in the decision-making process at each level and on the equality of stakes of those included at those respective levels of decision making. This approach can privilege the national, regional, or international level depending on where the principles of inclusion and political equality are most respected.

The pluralist approach to rank precludes, therefore, a general a priori judgment of democratic superiority of the norms stemming from one or the other constitutional order. In an era of globalization and growing interdependence, there can no longer be a presumption that national democracy is necessarily the most inclusive and deliberative locus of decision making.[79] Nor can we assume that indirect democratic legitimacy suffices to vest international legal norms with superior legitimacy to national legal norms,[80] given the deparliamentarization of international negotiations and the potential hiatus between

---

[78] *Contra* Kumm, *supra* note 76, at 261–62; Cottier & Hertig, *supra* note 2, at 307–10, who seem to be conflating both. On the distinction, see Besson, *supra* note 35.

[79] *Contra* Cottier & Hertig, *supra* note 2, at 310–3.

[80] This also applies to states where the ratification of international agreements requires a parliamentary approbation, or even an optional or compulsory referendum, like Switzerland. Agreements are not indeed deliberated over democratically and are simply submitted to an internal vote in all-or-nothing fashion. For a discussion of those mechanisms, see Allen Buchanan & Russell Powell, *Constitutional Democracy and the Rule of International Law: are they compatible?*, 16:3 JOURNAL OF POLITICAL PHILOSOPHY 326 (2008).

national external interests and minority or even majority individual interests in a given state.

This conclusion also precludes any purely theoretical assessment of the democratic quality of national or international law.[81] Respecting democratic outcomes implies organizing and trusting the democratic process about difficult substantive issues rather than replacing that very process with a theoretical judgment of what its results should be. Nor can democracy be deemed as one criterion among others in the weighing and balancing of international and national norms in conflict. It ought rather to be the supercriterion: when its conditions are given, it subsumes all others as it were, as it constitutes the most legitimate way of deciding on the others.[82]

Of course, identifying the democratic pedigree of each norm in conflict, whether of international or national law, remains extremely complex. The assessment could be simplified a little, on the one hand, by the gradual development of a formal hierarchy of sources within international law itself as alluded to before. Thus, the rank of an international multilateral treaty might be judged more easily as superior to customary international law in democratic terms. And this in turn might make the ranking of multilateral international norms easier when they conflict with domestic or regional constitutional law. Given what was said before about the thin prospect of developing such formal hierarchies within international law, however, alternative rules of conflict would still need to be used in the meantime. National constitutions, on the other, could themselves foresee blanket or specific rules of priority and identify priority tests in favor of international law. It has been the case in the German Basic Law that specifies the democratic and constitutional conditions under which the primacy of EU law may be recognized (art. 23, para. 1).

It is, of course, always possible to revert to the transitive material hierarchies of norms presented before. Those hierarchies that straddle autonomous legal orders coexist with formal hierarchies. Thus, when the same human rights are guaranteed in international and national constitutional norms, those norms, whether national or international, providing the highest degree of protection should be given priority. In any case, in the absence of formal and material rules of priority, preventive rules of coordination that provide background stability among legal orders may be found, for instance, in judicial dialogue

---

[81] *Contra* Kumm, *supra* note 76, at 261–62 and this volume; Cottier & Hertig, *supra* note 2, at 310–13.

[82] *But see* Halberstam, this volume, who ranks voice equally to his other two criteria of expertise and rights.

or in the principle of legal coherence and the duty of integrity of state officials active in legal orders affecting the same subjects.[83]

6. Conclusion

The postmodern take on the constitutionalization of international law is correct in one main respect: it would be wrong to associate international constitutionalism with unity in international law. But this is not because there can be no constituent power in international law or because, if there were, it could be only an empire. On the contrary, there is a democratic argument for adopting formal constitution(s) of general international law by entrenching various international legal norms in different regimes: international law can only constrain states and individuals materially in a legitimate fashion if it also constitutes them formally as a political community of communities and gives them an input in drafting those constraints. Praising and prioritizing material values is not enough, and material international constitutionalism alone might become the very empire that national constitutional democracies should endeavor not to promote.

Of course, it is correct to say that the constitutionalization of international law would actually entrench the fragmentation of international law in different sources and different regimes. But rather than be a source of concern, this could actually be seen as a consequence of the pluralism inherent to the international constituent power. Indeed, once the multilateral and multilevel international political community is understood as a pluralistic community of communities and as a hybrid community of states and individuals, the equivalence of sources and the plurality of specific regimes within international law becomes a democratic requirement. The same applies to the relationship between the national, regional, and international constitutional orders. The formalization of material constitutional constraints in international law could have complete hierarchical implications within general international law and each international regime only if the lawmakers were identical in each case. The main benefit of international constitutionalization is demoi-cratic legitimacy, that is, an inherently pluralist form of legitimacy that requires developing national as much as regional and international democratic and constitutional requirements.

True, approximating the proposed ideal of constitutionalism might at first sight give rise to more questions than it can resolve. It is difficult, however,

---

[83] See Besson, *supra* notes 11 and 76, in European law; Besson, *supra* note 37, in international law.

to see how the internal and external organization of the international legal order might become more opaque than it already is. All this might have to wait, of course, until the international community is ready to constitute itself. The recent regress in the constitutionalization process in the European Union and the return to an intergovernmental modifying treaty is a blatant demonstration of how comfortable the society-of-democratic-states model has become with its account of indirect constitutional legitimation. There are no clear signs, however, that the EU legitimacy crisis will be put to rest by the mere negation of the constitutional nature of the European legal order *lato sensu*. But getting over that crisis might require first and foremost realizing whose constitution this is: one of individuals, but also one of states.

Index